Counting Sheep

FROM OPEN RANGE TO AGRIBUSINESS
ON THE COLUMBIA PLATEAU

Counting Sheep

FROM OPEN RANGE TO AGRIBUSINESS
ON THE COLUMBIA PLATEAU

Alexander Campbell McGregor

UNIVERSITY OF WASHINGTON PRESS

Seattle and London

Library of Congress Cataloging in Publication Data

McGregor, Alexander Campbell.
   Counting sheep.

   Bibliography: p.
   Includes index.
   1. McGregor Land and Livestock Company—History.
2. Animal industry—Northwestern States—History.
I. Title.
HD9419.M36M36   1982   338.7′63′09797   82–15903
ISBN 0–295–95894–4

This book was published with the assistance of a grant from the Andrew W.
Mellon Foundation.

Acknowledgments

Many people contributed to this ranching and farming history—historians, relatives, friends, neighbors, photographers, artists, farm journal and newspaper editors, farmers, sheepherders, and librarians. Vernon Carstensen offered encouragement, guidance, and provocative criticism and patiently read many drafts of this book. As my major professor in graduate school, Dr. Carstensen helped me understand the McGregors and the interior lands of the Pacific Northwest in the context of national agricultural trends and coaxed and prodded me toward better writing. His wife, Jeanette, reviewed the chapter about the role of women in plateau farm life and it was she who suggested the book's title, *Counting Sheep*. I am grateful to the Carstensens for their friendship, support, and trenchant criticism. Dr. Carstensen encouraged me to do several months of graduate work at the University of Wisconsin where contact with historians Morton Rothstein and Allan Bogue and historical geographer Daniel Gomez-Ibanez inspired fresh perspectives on historical, economic, social, and cultural trends of the American West. Donald W. Meinig of Syracuse University, a Palouse country native whose own work taught me much about the region, read two drafts of this study, responding with encouragement and helpful suggestions. Although I was not his student, Dr. David Stratton of Washington State University took an early interest in my career, offering advice and encouragement along the way. I benefited from his incisive critique of this manuscript. I am also grateful for the friendship and support Robert and Lola Whitner have offered me through undergraduate years at Whitman College and beyond.

Many people provided research material for this book, including B. R. Bertramson, long-time chairman of the WSU Agronomy Department, who gave me access to an "archives" file he gathered during twenty-five years of researching Columbia Plateau agriculture; botanist Richard Mack of WSU, who loaned me his manuscript studies of the advance of "cheatgrass" and other "weeds" onto the rangeland; John Armstrong,

former editor of the *Washington Farmer-Stockman*, who let me borrow
a voluminous collection of early issues of *Ranche and Range*, a Pacific
Northwest livestock and farm journal previously unavailable to historians; Duane Swanson and Lucile Kane of the Minnesota Historical
Society, who helped me find pertinent materials in the massive collection
of Northern Pacific Railroad records at St. Paul; George Rugg, secretary of the Washington Wool Growers Association, who loaned me
boxes of records and correspondence of that sheepmen's organization;
Dr. H. Stanley Coffin III, who made available the records of his family's
sheep business and the manuscript autobiography of his grandfather;
Glenn Mickelson of the firm Lemaster and Daniels, who gave me access
to seventy-five years of tax returns, profit and loss statements, and correspondence of the McGregor companies on file with that accounting
business; Bill Wilmot, editor of the Colfax *Gazette*, who granted me
access to many early issues of his paper; J. H. Walters, wool buyer for
the Pendleton Woolen Mills, who provided statistical information about
wool prices and woolen mill output; and C. J. Storey, McGregor Land
and Livestock accountant, who explained the early bookkeeping methods employed by that corporation and sorted through reams of old
inventory books and tax returns to find pertinent information. I am also
appreciative of the assistance offered by the library staffs at Washington
State University (repository for 150 lineal feet of McGregor Land and
Livestock business records), University of Washington, Whitman College, University of Wisconsin, Washington State Library (Olympia),
University of Wyoming, and the Federal Archives and Records Center
(Seattle).

My research material was enriched by the contributions of many of
my relatives. Mrs. Betty Jean Peatross of Glendale, California, assembled
and organized two hundred pages of letters written by Archie Mc-
Gregor in the 1890's and made available numerous other old letters and
photos. Archie's daughters, the late Marie Boone of Glendale and Jessie
Medby of Pasadena, loaned me early photographs and shared their reminiscences with me. Mark Lemon of Annan, Ontario, generously made
available information about the McGregor family that he had gathered
in courthouses and church archives in Scotland and Ontario. William
McGregor of Owen Sound, Ontario, the long-time owner and operator
of the Canadian farm settled by McGregors in the 1840's; Mr. and Mrs.
Robert Darrah of Calgary, who saved and made available the reminiscences and letters of Euphemia MacGregor; and many other friends and
relatives helped me track down information about the early history of
the McGregor family. The present managers of McGregor Land and
Livestock, my cousins John and William McGregor and my father

Sherman McGregor, allowed me access to all corporate records; they also assisted and encouraged me in every way. All three men explained in detail the intricacies of managing sheep, cattle, and fertilizer operations during a period of rapid agricultural change. My mother, Norma McGregor, provided many incisive suggestions, read several rough drafts, and always remained enthusiastic about my historical studies. My wife, Linda, shared research chores, transcribed taped interviews, and typed the manuscript—all the while offering patience, understanding, and moral support throughout the seemingly endless project.

Becky Steever of Pulman drew the maps and diagrams used in the text. Artist Ruth Burden of Livermore, California, contributed the sketch of shearer Bill Dorman. Clifford Ott of Moscow, Idaho, restored faded old photographs to provide a vivid record of the early days in the Channeled Scablands. Mikki Tague of Colfax spent many months helping me assemble and type an earlier draft of the manuscript.

Over forty people shared their rich and varied experiences with me and helped make vivid this portrait of a century of ranching and farming on the Columbia Plateau. Sheepmen Tom Drumheller, Jr., of Ephrata and Charles Brune of Yakima gave first hand information about the growth and decline of the range sheep business. The late Ralph Snyder often shared with me his colorful recollections of wheat growing and cattle raising in the Palouse and Big Bend. Arthur Buhl, Virgil Bennington, and Lenora Torgenson were among those who offered vivid insights into the early days of wheat farming. From long-time McGregor agronomist Harley Jacquot I learned much about the vast technological and scientific changes that have characterized the last forty years of wheat production. Clemente Barber and other Basques told me of their homeland and of their motives for emigration to the Pacific Northwest interior. The best materials of all and the inspiration for this book were provided by the late Emile Morod. A McGregor sheepman for over fifty years, he was a close personal friend and the man who taught me the trade of sheep herding.

Contents

Illustrations

(*All photographs not otherwise credited in the captions were taken by the author*)

Peter and Mary Campbell
Tramp sheepmen John and Archie McGregor, about 1886
The Channeled Scablands of the lower Palouse River
The Pullman Hardware Company, about 1893
Archie McGregor watching a band of sheep during lambing season
Shearing crew at Archie's Camp
John McGregor, about 1898
Peter McGregor, 1907
Archie McGregor, about 1895
Alex C. McGregor, late 1890's
Fifteen-year-old Emile Morod, 1913
Sheepherders at play

Counting Sheep

FROM OPEN RANGE TO AGRIBUSINESS
ON THE COLUMBIA PLATEAU

Introduction

Agricultural Change in the Bunchgrass Country

"The country around, as far as the eye could reach, seemed to be a perfect desert of yellow, hot sand, with immense masses of broken rock jutting abruptly up here and there over the surface. No trees or shrubs of any kind relieved the monotony of the barren waste. A few patches of tuft-grass, thinly scattered here and there, were the only representatives of vegetation, while animal life seemed to be entirely extinct."

Paul Kane, 1847

" 'Bunch-grass' has become the synonym for things good, strong, rich, and great: the bunch-grass country is the best and finest country on earth; bunch-grass cattle and horses are the sweetest, fleetest, and strongest, in the world; and a bunch-grass man is the most superb being in the universe."

Thomas W. Symons, 1882[1]

This is a study of three generations of a Scottish–Canadian family, who came to an austere and unpromising land in the interior of the Pacific Northwest and created a ranching and farming business that has survived a century of rapid agricultural change. The McGregor Land and Livestock Company (in business for nearly one hundred years) herded sheep, ran cattle, traded land, and sold merchandise, learning by trial and error to adapt to a land long considered fit only for grazing at best. This single-family-owned enterprise participated, and sometimes led, in the transformation of a 22-million-acre region of eastern Washington, northeastern Oregon, and northern Idaho from open range to agribusiness. The hundreds of linear feet of business correspondence, sheep tally books, ledgers, store bills, tax returns, and even love letters kept by the McGregors provide an unusual historical record of management in nineteenth and twentieth century land-extensive agriculture in the Northwest. The experiences of the McGregors and their employees, as well as many other wheat growers, livestock raisers, and merchants of the region, illustrate the processes by which remote, isolated lands of the semiarid West became a vast farmland. These areas came to be part of a complex, capital-intensive agriculture dependent on international markets, on chemicals manufactured from natural gas and petroleum, and on the very expensive machinery that has displaced most of the labor force on American farms.

The Columbia Plateau, a region once dismissed by most observers as an ugly, barren desert, had, by the early twentieth century, replaced California as the primary wheat-producing district of the Pacific Slope and, with the Dakotas and Kansas, become one of the nation's three major wheat belts. Wheat yields of the district were generally the highest in the United States. Yet immigrants from lands east of the Rocky Mountains had to endure a long and painful process of adaptation to the distinctive production and marketing demands of this Pacific Slope region. During the lifetimes of many pioneer farmers, production techniques changed from the walking plow aptly known as a "foot burner," hand broadcasting of seed, and harvesting with cradle and scythe to elaborate horse- and mule-powered machinery guided by large crews of laborers and, finally, to huge diesel-powered tractors and self-propelled combines.[2]

Livestock production in the area has changed from the semi-nomadic style of open range days to a far more intensive business of fenced pastures, feedlots, feedmills, chemical additives, and supplements. The desert lowlands of the region have been converted from sheep pastures of sand and sagebrush into irrigated fields of potatoes, sugar beets, and corn. The businesses that serve farmers and ranchers have changed, as well: The general store and small hardware and implement dealerships have declined and given way to specialists in farm machinery, herbicides, insecticides, and chemical fertilizers.

The McGregor business experienced all these changes, beginning as an open range "tramp" sheepherding venture, expanding to develop large-scale ranching and farming operations on more than 34,000 acres of owned lands, and diversifying into a series of agriculturally oriented enterprises. The McGregors raised sheep, cattle, and hogs; operated feedlots and a packing plant; grew wheat, barley, alfalfa, and apples; organized an irrigation company; made loans; sold general merchandise, insurance, farm machinery, and agricultural chemicals; hired their own agronomists; became land merchants; and even organized a gold mining company—all as an independently financed family corporation headquartered in a small company town. The history of this enterprise illustrates the impact of the application of agricultural science and technology on a specific ranching and farming business during a century of "agricultural revolution." The McGregor business is a study of agricultural history involving several generations of a single family going through a series of "stages," hanging on, making mistakes, having their squabbles, but on the whole responding to the challenge of the environment, the changes in market conditions, the pressures on farming and farm enterprises that capital-intensive methods have brought—and responding well.

Immigrants arriving in the sparsely settled interior region in the late nineteenth century would have had difficulty foreseeing the vast changes that were to occur in sheep, cattle, and wheat raising. The first task of newly arrived settlers was to find some means of gaining a livelihood in a region frequently described by travelers as the "Columbia Desert." Donald Meinig has described the land that the immigrants encountered in the following terms: "In the far Northwest of the United States lies an unusual land. So sharply is it set apart from its surroundings that it can be recognized immediately, at a mere glance. Approached from any direction the visible change at its borders is striking: the forest thins then abruptly ends, the mountains lower then merge into a much smoother surface, and a different kind of country, open and undulating, rolls out before the viewer like a great interior sea."[3] This study describes the fortunes of the McGregors and other ranchers and farmers who sought to adapt their skills to the demands of the new region.

Chapter 1 ⚒

Immigration to the
Grasslands of the Columbia Plateau

"The great body of the country . . . stretching eastward from . . . [the Cascades] to the Rocky Mountains, while it contains many fertile valleys . . . , is yet more especially a grazing country—one which as its population increases, promises, in its cattle, its horses, and, above all its wool, to open a vast field to American enterprise."

Isaac Stevens

"The poor man, desirous of making a home for himself and family, and willing to work, can find no country which offers greater inducements than Washington Territory. . . . The great Columbia Plain, lying between the Cascade Range on the west and the Blue and Bitter Root Ranges of the Rocky Mountains on the east . . . constitutes one immense grazing ground, 150 miles in width and 500 in length. . . . The whole region is . . . covered by a perennial growth of the richest grass in the world."   Washington Immigrant Aid Society, 1879[1]

A peculiar land of striking contrasts and austere beauty confronted those who came to settle on the Columbia Plateau. Surrounded by forested mountains—the Cascades in the west, the Okanogan Highlands in the north, the Bitterroots to the east, and the Blue Mountains in the south—it was a treeless region seared by heat and drought during the long summer months. Only a meager variety of wildlife could be found—coyotes, rattlesnakes, jackrabbits, squirrels, sagehens, burrowing owls, badgers, and (near streams or alkali lakes) kildeer, long-beaked curlew, gaunt giant blue heron, and migratory ducks and geese.

Travelers approaching the plateau on horseback from settled areas to the west could, in a single day's ride, leave snow-capped mountains and humid forests receiving sixty to ninety inches of precipitation and enter desert lowlands of sand, sage, and five-inch annual rainfall. Yet an immense volume of water funneled into this parched low point of the plateau, for it was here that the Columbia, Snake, Yakima, John Day, and other rivers carrying waters from the four mountain ranges joined to flow through a gorge toward the sea. There was no other way for streams to leave the mountain-girdled plateau. Leeward of the Cascades, this land contained a series of low ridges running east to west—Frenchman Hills, Saddle Mountains, Horse Heaven Hills, Yakima Ridge, Snipes Mountain—through which rivers and streams made deep trenches. But the ridges, like the low-lying flats, were parched and barren, supporting only scanty vegetation.

Proceeding eastward, those reconnoitering the region found that the land became more hospitable as they followed the gradual slope that led out of the arid bottomlands. Flats of sagebrush and greasewood gradually merged into broad, undulating prairies of blue-bunch wheatgrass, sheep fescue, and Sandberg bluegrass in a land named after the Big Bend of the Columbia River. As one left the Big Bend and entered the higher, wetter lands of the Palouse and Walla Walla regions, the prairie became an intricate collection of smooth, steep hills covered with a luxuriant cover of stirrup-high, waving bunchgrass and took on the appearance of a rough sea at the height of a storm. Continuing the gradual ascent toward the Idaho border and Kamiak and Steptoe buttes, two sentinels of granitic rock jutting above the grassland sea, the elevation surpassed 2,500 feet, rainfall neared 20 inches, and scattered stands of pine trees intruded from the mountains along protected north slopes of creek and river valleys. To the southeast, in an opening in the mountains of Idaho, lay the Camas Prairie, a land separated from the main portion of the plateau by the canyons of the Clearwater and Snake rivers. Here the traveler encountered a more level land with much shallower soils and scattered rock outcroppings. But this land, isolated by canyons and mountains, received plentiful rainfall and was thickly covered with bunchgrass.[2]

The prairie lands of the Columbia Plateau were in places broken up and divided by another type of country, composed of huge canyons of barren basaltic rock. The Snake River canyon, a mile and a half wide and more than a thousand feet deep, separated the Palouse hills from the grasslands of southeastern Washington. Within the canyon walls was a much warmer, drier land of sandbars and sage. Even more unusual were areas of the Big Bend and Palouse where the thick epidermis of soil had been stripped away and deep, almost vertical canyons had been incised into the underlying basalt. Here, in a land lacking the rainfall to maintain a single permanent stream from its own runoff, were 3,700 square miles of labyrinthine channels, rock basins, widely scattered boulders weighing several tons each, giant ripple marks ten feet high, and huge gravel bars—a single one of which covered twenty-four townships of the Quincy Basin. Toward the western edge of the plateau, in the heart of the Big Bend country, were an odd collection of these bizarre erosional forms. Within a nine-mile area that became known as Drumheller Channels were almost 150 different dry canyons, each one to ten miles in length. Moses Coulee and Grand Coulee were canyons nine hundred to a thousand feet deep. The latter, some fifty miles long and one to five miles wide, contained Steamboat Rock, a square-mile butte six hundred feet high, and Dry Falls, the relic of an immense cataract three hundred feet high and four miles wide. Farther east was the largest tract of broken, scarred land, an area seventy-five miles long and twenty miles wide that separated the Big Bend and Palouse districts.[3] Here, in the center of the plateau, the Palouse River abruptly left its gently sloping valley and plunged through a narrow vertical canyon four hundred feet deep, over three spectacular cataracts, and into the Snake River Valley. This region, generally stripped of all but a thin layer of soil, contained a complex collection of deep, dry coulees, gravel bars, and the Palouse River channel, interspersed with occasional long, narrow "islands" of deep Palouse soils. Pioneers used the graphic names "scabrock" and "scablands" to describe this giant series of wounds on the surface of the plateau.

Man has long resorted to stories of catastrophic events to explain the striking diversity of lands contained within the 250-mile length and 200-mile width of the Columbia Plateau. Indians whose ancestors had lived on the plateau for at least eleven thousand years told legends of huge creatures that had torn apart the country, leaving permanent scars on the land. Several tribes told of a struggle to the death between Wishpoosh, the terrible Big Beaver, and the giant coyote God, Speel-yi, in which channels had been torn through mountains, diverting rivers and lakes and unleashing great floodwaters. Geologists provide an even more cataclysmic account involving the greatest floods of lava and water known to have occurred anywhere in the world. First a series of lava flows, each about a hundred feet thick, issued from giant cracks in the earth. A single one of these flows has been traced over twenty thousand square miles. Between layers, sufficient time sometimes elapsed for soil to form and for forests of giant ginkgo and other varieties of trees to grow. The lava flows finally reached an average depth of more than two thousand feet, covering all but Steptoe Butte, Kamiak Butte, and a few other quartzite mountaintops with deep layers of basalt. The uplifting of surrounding mountain ranges and a gradual sinking and warping of the basalt isolated the plateau from the marine coastal climate and caused it to dip away from the ranges and slope gently to the southwest. Prevailing winds out of the southwest slowly eroded lowland floodplains and dry lakebeds, leaving only sand and thin soils along western lowlands and depositing dunes of loessial soil a hundred feet high on the central and eastern plateau.

During the Pleistocene age the plateau was flooded several times when tongues of glacial ice blocking the Clark Fork Valley in Montana gave way, sending water rushing southward. The last, greatest ice dam, formed some eighteen thousand years ago, reached a height of several thousand feet above the valley floor. The lake formed behind this dam drained completely in less than two weeks, sending an immense volume of water over the plateau at speeds of up to forty-five miles an hour, ripping off the loessial soils, etching deep scabrock channels into the underlying basalt, and reaching a depth of nine hundred feet at the gateway to the Columbia River Gorge. The rush of water onto the plateau was ten times the combined flow of all the rivers in the world.[4]

Early visitors to this country of deserts and grasslands told of a rainless, lifeless, worthless land. Few saw the region during the cool, wet winters when storm fronts bringing rain and sleet to lowlands and heavy snows to lands farther east were followed by warm, westerly, "chinook" winds that quickly moderated the cold. Few saw the land during the rainy spring months, when the verdant perennial grasses provided lush forage for the sleek cayuse and Appaloosa ponies the Indians rode when they hunted deer, elk, or buffalo in distant regions.

Many people did pass through the land in midsummer or fall. David Thompson, traveling along the Palouse River scabrock country on August 9, 1811, gave a typical account: "The land very rocky and full of rocky hills cut Perpend. wherever the rocks show themselves, and exactly of the same kind of rocks as along the Columbia, with much fragments in splinters etc. Very bad for the horses and the soil a sandy fine impassable powder which suffocated us with dust and no water to drink where we camped." Artist Paul Kane traveled through the Palouse and Grand Coulee districts in 1847 and reported "a curious and strange region" that in the canyons assumed "a new aspect of increased wildness and magnificence at every turn." But above the canyons he could find only "a barren, sandy desert." Immigrants moving to the Willamette Valley generally arrived on the plateau during the hottest days of late summer and followed trails through barren lands along the Columbia. Few liked what they saw. They wrote of an ugly, disgusting desert: "Exactly the old scene over again. Sage, sand, weeds—sand, weeds, sage "

James Nesmith found "sand banks not possessing fertility enough to sprout a pea," and concluded that "the whole country looks poverty stricken." Thomas Farnham found "some beauty and sublimity in sight, but no fertility."[5]

Gold, not agriculture, brought the first permanent settlers to the Columbia Plateau at the conclusion of the Indian wars in 1858. Walla Walla, on the southern perimeter, by the mid 1860's had become the largest town in Washington Territory, with a population of about three thousand. Walla Walla had gained its importance by serving as an en-

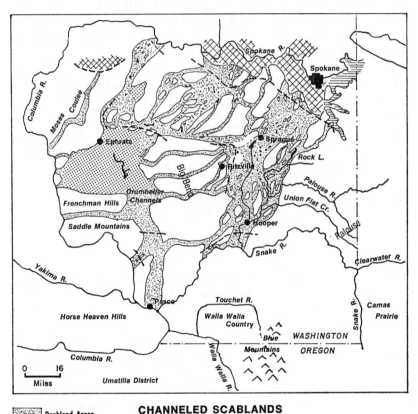

CHANNELED SCABLANDS
OF THE
COLUMBIA PLATEAU

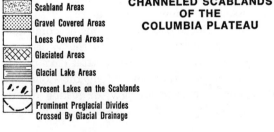

	Scabland Areas
	Gravel Covered Areas
	Loess Covered Areas
	Glaciated Areas
	Glacial Lake Areas
	Present Lakes on the Scablands
	Prominent Preglacial Divides Crossed By Glacial Drainage

trepôt for miners and packers en route to the mountains of Montana, Idaho, and British Columbia. The prairies of the Columbia Plateau were significant only as an access route to other regions. But a halting process of adjustment to the land had begun.

High food prices in the mining districts provided the initial stimulus for agricultural development. The Walla Walla *Statesman* reported in 1868 on the local market for livestock: "There is a brisk demand for cattle in this Valley and speculators are in the market buying up every hoof that offers. . . . One firm alone—the McMorris Brothers—have paid out over $10,000. . . . The cattle in this Valley are in better condition than any where else on the coast, and consequently the brisk demand. The mining districts beyond depend upon us almost exclusively for their supply of fat cattle." Miners and "mule skinners" knew the markets and learned more about the land in their repeated trips to pick up supplies in Walla Walla. They traveled beyond the lifeless deserts of the Columbia and found green valleys and hills thickly covered with bunchgrass. The freighters learned that the land was not "rainless": They not only ate dust in the dry summers, they also mired their teams in mud after heavy spring rains or sudden June cloudbursts and were stranded by blizzards on return trips to winter quarters in Walla Walla. Some of these travelers liked the land enough to stay. George Lucas, an Irish immigrant who came west during the California gold rush and then prospected in Idaho and Montana, decided to settle at a favorable location along Cow Creek near the junction of the Mullan and Colville roads, where he set up a "way station" and raised horses and cattle. Veteran freighters Dan and Jesse Drumheller developed an open-range sheep business in the scabrock of the Big Bend. William Kirkman, an Englishman who followed gold strikes north from California to the Pacific Northwest, decided to stay and run cattle. Another freighter, "Uncle Jim" Kennedy, became a cattleman.[6]

Cattlemen and sheep raisers from the Willamette Valley brought their herds and flocks to the best grasslands of the interior. A. J. Splawn, a pioneer cattleman of the Yakima Valley, claimed that, despite the long hard winter of 1860–61 that killed "about all the cattle" of his district, as a general rule "cattle were fat the year around. . . . Cattle could be seen grazing the white sage in the coldest weather absolutely shaking with fat. . . . The annual drives would start from Yakima in the spring, occupying several months on the journey. Prices ranged at $40 per head in Yakima and from $75 to $100 at the mines. Men did not do business for their health as the risk in driving was considerable from swimming streams and the lurking savage who was ever hovering on the trail." Other districts were equally promising. Alfred Holt, a Willamette livestock raiser who moved into the Palouse in the 1870's, declared: "I think this country is perfection in the stock raising line."[7]

The mining camps also needed flour. "To you of Walla Walla we must look for our flour, bacon, fruit, &c.," a correspondent from the Kootenai district of British Columbia wrote in 1869, "but we can return you gold dust worth $18 per ounce. Treat the boys kindly who visit you and in every grey shirt who comes to your country recognize the bulwark that sustains your greatness." Marcus Whitman had grown wheat at the Wai-ilatpu mission in the Walla Walla Valley more than twenty years earlier, and the new market encouraged a gradual expansion of cultivation along nearby streams and creek beds. Damase Bergevin, Philip Ritz, William Reser, Milton and Newton Aldrich, and other miners and freighters who had come north from the California diggings to the strikes of the Pacific Northwest were among those planting crops. But lingering doubts about the potential of the land had to be overcome: Could crops be grown in a treeless country? Could a region with long summer droughts produce grain? Was productivity limited to the creek bottoms?[8]

Marketing[9] was another problem after the mining rush abated in the early 1870's. Philip Ritz shipped fifty barrels of flour to New York in 1868 in an effort to create a new market for Walla Walla wheat. Liverpool, England, some eighteen thousand miles and five months distant via sailing ships around Cape Horn, emerged as the most important marketplace. By 1879, almost eighty ships per year moved grain from the Pacific Northwest to Liverpool. But hauling wheat to the piers at Portland was a difficult project. Farmers who grew crops in the northern portion of the Walla Walla country had to sack the grain and haul it by team or wagon down the tortuous grade to Snake River or reopen the bags, dump the wheat down 3,200-foot-long wooden pipes, and then resack the grain. The wheat was then stored for subsequent shipment downriver by steamboat to Umatilla, where it was transferred to another boat for shipping to Celilo. There it was unloaded, stored, moved by portage railroad, and transferred to another boat destined for the Upper Cascades landing, where it was unloaded, stored, reloaded for rail portage, only to be reloaded again for water shipment to Portland. Even before the wheat sacks were piled on outgoing vessels, half the value of each bushel had been spent for transportation costs. Yet the Walla Walla area was productive and farmers continued to grow crops. A Washington correspondent to the Sacramento *Daily Union* estimated a crop average of 22½ bushels of spring wheat and 45 bushels of winter wheat to the acre.[9] The fertility of this district was enough to encourage farmers to begin moving to the Palouse and other areas of relatively high rainfall along the eastern uplands of the plateau.

The stage was set in the early 1880's for the first major influx of immigration to the Columbia Plateau. By then most of the promising forests and humid prairies of the American West had been settled, and farmers had begun to move onto lands once thought of as deserts—the semiarid High Plains west of the 98th meridian in the western Dakotas, Nebraska, and Kansas, and the interior of the Pacific Northwest. In the High Plains, a succession of wet years caused farmers to move west "like a plague of locusts" in the futile hope that the climate had permanently changed.[10] On the Columbia Plateau the construction of local railroads after 1880 and the "completion" to salt water of the northern transcontinental line in 1883 was crucial. It ended the isolation of the region, made immigration easier and cheaper, and vastly improved the marketing of the agricultural products grown on the land. To enhance their investment, railroads extensively promoted the region. Immigrants arriving in the area reported that "Washington Territory was the best advertised region on the continent." Prospective settlers were informed of the unsurpassed quality of mutton and beef raised on the bunchgrass and read that the region "is probably destined to become the richest and most productive wheat-growing region in the world." The population of Washington Territory increased almost fivefold in the 1880's, with portions of the Columbia Plateau growing at an even more rapid rate.[11]

Immigrants came to the semiarid prairies from lands west of the Cascades; from Missouri, Kansas, New York, and Pennsylvania; and from Germany, England, and other European countries. Twenty-one-year-old Archie McGregor and his twenty-year-old brother Peter were among the thousands who came from forest lands and humid prairies of the Old Northwest and Ontario. Like many of these immigrants, Peter and Archie McGregor came from a large family whose parents had been pioneers a few decades earlier. (The two brothers and their siblings began abbreviating the family surname, MacGregor.) Their parents, Peter MacGregor and Mary Campbell, were born on the Isle of Mull in western Scotland, where their Highland families had been small farmers and livestock raisers for generations. An austere region of constant poverty, this land had presented many obstacles to those growing crops and raising sheep and cattle: "In almost any month, winds of near hurricane strength can lash the country with torrential rain; and from the coasts they carry over the land salt spray which blasts all plant life and can even kill trees. . . . Few activities are more dispiriting than farming under such conditions."[12]

Political and economic forces threatened to foreclose even this meager existence for hundreds of thousands of Scots. Redistribution by the Crown of the landholdings of the MacGregors and other clans who had fought with Charles Edward Stuart ("Bonnie Prince Charlie") in the disaster at Culloden in 1745 accelerated the breakup of the traditional clan-oriented economic and social structure. By the early nineteenth century, many of the MacGregors had become tenant farmers ("crofters") on the Isle of Mull. Much of the MacGregor land was acquired by their traditional enemies, the Campbells, who had prospered by their support of the English cause. But by the 1840's the Campbells, the MacGregors, and other residents of the Highlands were all suffering from a rapid decline in living conditions. On Mull conditions were particularly bad, and "a state of unexampled destitution" was said to exist. Bad harvests and a potato famine made the 1840's the "hungry forties" and provided a powerful incentive for immigration. In addition, the crofters were victims of the "Highland clearances," a process involving the leveling of farm cottages and whole villages to make way for large sheep raising operations. The British government encouraged the destitute to emigrate by offering free land grants in Ontario and other parts of eastern Canada and by helping to pay ocean passage. A "Guide for the Emigrant to North America" was published in Gaelic in 1841. The Canadian Emigration Association chartered a sailing vessel in 1842 to carry destitute tenants from the isles of Mull and Tyree.[13]

"The Scotch," as the Ontario Scottish-Canadians would call themselves, outnumbered all other settlers in many of the new lands. The MacGregors and the Campbells joined the numerous immigrants traveling to Sydenham Township, a frontier region on the shores of the Georgian Bay of Lake Huron. Archie and Peter McGregor's paternal grandfather, a sixty-six-year-old tenant farmer, sheep raiser, and church elder named Peter MacGregor, left by sailing ship for the new land in 1842 with his wife Janet and their children, Anne, Euphemia, Dougald, Donald, John, and Peter. Three other daughters, Mary, Janet, and Catherine, probably accompanied them also but this cannot be determined with certainty from the extant records. The youngest of the children, fifteen-year-old Peter, would later be the father of the two men who came to the Pacific Northwest. Their maternal grandfather, Archibald Campbell, a widower in his sixties, sold his land on Mull to a large sheep raiser and in 1850, with his four sons and three daughters, took a sailing vessel to Ontario. The six-week period required to cross the Atlantic on the sailing ships was typically a difficult one, with scanty rations, overcrowding, discomfort, and disease. Another period of five to six weeks' overland travel was required before the immigrants reached their destinations in the woods of Ontario.[14]

The land upon which these families settled resembled the rocky terrain of their Scottish homeland, but here the forests grew thick with giant maple, elms, birches, spruce, cedar, and towering hemlocks. To claim their land grants the immigrants had to build log houses, live on the land for three years, and clear at least two acres of forest. Adjusting to the demands of the heavily timbered region required different techniques than those learned in the Highlands of Scotland. Donald MacGregor, Peter's eldest son, acquired his own land and "built his first shelter by striking a pole into the ground between two big trees and then covering the top and banking the lean-to with hemlock boughs." He and a companion "built their enclosure up against a big maple tree. When the hemlock boughs dried out, they would catch fire and the men would hastily drag out into the open their bedding. . . . Then they would go to work again and gather fresh green covering. This went along until one day a neighbor came along and told them to move before the big maple tree toppled over on them. The tree had been burned almost right through by the great fires piled up against the foot." The sons of Peter MacGregor began clearing land by girdling the five-foot-thick elms of Sydenham. But the MacGregors had not yet learned from their neighbors the proper means of felling the giant trees. One of the trees fell without warning on a snowy winter day. John MacGregor "realized it was coming straight for him and there was no escape in the deep snow. By a miracle he was spared between the branches." [15]

Settlers soon learned that some of the obstacles of farm making could be better handled in a community fashion. The spirit of cooperation became a notable feature of pioneer life in Ontario, as elsewhere: "There were hauling bees, ploughing bees, bees at hay cutting and harvest time, [and] bees to build stone or rail fences." "A farmer would cut ten acres in the winter and then in the early spring he would hold a logging bee with ten yoke of oxen, a yoke for every acre. Each acre would be staked off and the men would draw lots for positions. Then they would make of it a grand race with a signal to go, long black whips flashing . . . [and loud calls] to the oxen. In a miraculously short time the big elms would be piled and ready to burn off. . . . Whiskey was served by a 'grog-boss' who passed pail and dipper." Such occasions usually ended with a dance or "hoedown." [16]

Shortly after his father's death in the late 1840's Peter began improving the fifty acres of uncleared forest he inherited from the 160-acre family holdings. His marriage to Mary Campbell in April 1859 brought with it an equal acreage of adjacent Campbell-owned land. The couple first lived with Peter's mother while he built a log cabin, then began felling enough trees to make farming possible. The settlers, like previous generations, were unable to use much of the abundant timber, so the large elms and maples were stacked in piles and burned. Before roads were built, Peter MacGregor and his farm neighbors carried grain on their backs to a grist mill and returned with flour. Later, crude homemade ox-drawn sleighs known as "jumpers" were used. Wheat growers and sheep raisers in Sydenham had to deal with a harsh climate: The long and cold winters meant, for example, that sheep had to be kept in barns and fed hay for at least five months a year. Farmers' wives also faced hard work. Mary Campbell MacGregor spun wool, wove cloth for clothes, milked cows and made butter, boiled maple sap for sugar, and made soap and candles from tallow.

Peter and Mary MacGregor raised nine children in their cabin and gave them the old family names of Dougald, Peter, Archibald, William, John, Alexander, Euphemia, Jessie, and Donald. Mary Campbell was determined that all her children would have several years of school. Her own mother had died when Mary was in her early teens, and she had been forced to leave school to assume family responsibilities. The children learned English at Briar Hill Elementary School and taught the language to their Gaelic-speaking parents. All the children completed primary school and had some exposure to secondary education.[17]

By the early 1880's, several of the children had begun to seek their own careers in Sydenham and other lands adjacent to the shores of Lake Huron. But, although the region had been converted from forests to farms only a few decades earlier, it had now become "overcrowded" in the minds of the settlers. Throughout the province of Ontario, lands desirable for farming were apparently all taken. Those able to acquire land found that the prices of their grains were forced down by increasing importation of wheat from the American West.[18] The nine MacGregor children would either have to find careers outside of farming or emigrate to a new region that offered greater opportunity.

Dougald McGregor, the eldest child and the first to leave, secured a job as a railroad fireman on the Canadian Pacific run from Lake Superior to Winnipeg. He later reluctantly abandoned his desire to go west and returned to manage the family farm. Donald, the youngest, was the only other of the nine children to remain in his native province. He became a Presbyterian minister in London, Ontario. The other seven children came to the American West. Euphemia became a schoolteacher in eastern Washington. Jessie was a nurse, first in Portland, Oregon, then in Spokane. William died a young man after returning from a futile western trip made to improve his health. Alex taught school and worked as a druggist until the late 1880's, when he left for Chicago, a city that young men of Ontario viewed as "the Mecca of their ambition." He later told of arriving in that city with only eighteen cents in his pocket. As he walked down street after street in search of a job, he occasionally noticed signs saying "free lunch" in the windows of taverns. He was incredulous, but hunger finally got the best of him, according to his son Sherman:

> *Dad said he just couldn't believe it. Here were all kinds of beautiful sliced meats, pickles, breads, and other fine foods spread out on a big counter and people were lined up helping themselves, so he stepped up and had a fine meal. When he was through, he thanked the big man in a white jacket back of the counter and started out the door only to be yanked back by the same big man who said 'Come off it, young fellow, that will be fifteen cents.' Of course had Dad known you could eat all day by purchasing a five cent glass of beer, he would have ended the day with thirteen cents instead of three cents.*

Alex stopped at a nearby pharmacy after leaving the tavern and got a job, but he always saved the three big Canadian coppers as a sign of his good fortune.[19]

Archie, Peter, and John McGregor were also among the more than one million Canadians who came to the United States between 1881 and 1891. John Addison, a cousin, emigrated to Dayton, Washington Territory. He sent back reports about the great agricultural possibilities of the Pacific Northwest and the opportunities there for young men. Encouraged by these glowing reports, Peter and Archie left Canada in 1882 for the Pacific Northwest, where "there was a better show for to make a start." John came to Washington to join his brothers four years later. In 1900 Alex left his Chicago drugstore and became the fourth of the McGregor brothers to emigrate to the Columbia Plateau.[20]

Peter and Archie McGregor left Toronto on October 10, 1882, carrying a two-hundred-dollar loan from their father and having promised their mother to be good boys, to "remember thy Creator in the days of thy youth," and not to engage in such vices as card playing on Sunday. Archie was given a tintype album by his Uncle John and a Bible by his mother. The two young men shared an autograph album signed by relatives and friends: Younger brother John reminded them to "love, honor and obey God . . . and your days will be peaceful and happy"; their mother admonished them to "heed the instructions of thy father. . . . And let thine heart keep my commandments through your long life. . . . For they shall be an omen of grace unto thy head, and chains about thy neck. . . . If sinners entice thee, consent them not. . . . Let not mercy and truth forsake thee. . . . Write them upon the table of thine heart." Three decades later Archie described the farewell scene in a letter to his mother: "Little did we think then how it must have rung your and father's hearts to see us go away, without a word, just choking.

Never will I forget that parting and when I went to bid father goodbye he gave me a roll of bills, not a word being spoken on either side, but his actions told it all. I do not remember whether I ever thanked him in later years for that roll or not. It was not as hard on us as it was on you for we were confident that we would come back in three years, but you knew, and so did father. . . . We needed some trials in order to use the resources you gave us. After we broke the home ties we were not ever all at home at the same time again."[21]

The brothers went by train to Chicago, where they boarded an immigrant railroad train bound for San Francisco. Like the other passengers, they slept in their own bedrolls on straw ticks and did their own cooking on a stove in the train. They had armed themselves with ball-and-cap pistols to ward off possible Indian attack. The only Indians they encountered were hunters who met the train at stations to sell buffalo meat to the travelers. From San Francisco, the brothers proceeded by boat to Portland and thence up the Columbia River to Wallula and overland to Dayton. They arrived on October 26, 1882.[22]

The McGregors and many other newcomers first stayed in Dayton or Walla Walla, established towns on the southern rim of the plateau near the forested foothills of the Blue Mountains. Here they began analyzing the opportunities of a treeless, semiarid prairie far different from their previous homes. Archie and Peter McGregor had no specific plan, but they were determined to find economic success so they could encourage their Canadian sweethearts to move west and marry them. They first lived in Dayton with their cousin, John Addison, and worked with him in a flour mill. Then they worked in the Blue Mountains, clearing land for twenty dollars a month. During the winter of 1882–83, they cut ice on the Snake River north of Dayton. Other young, single, male immigrants stayed with relatives, friends, or brought letters of introduction to people acquainted with the region and then took temporary jobs as blacksmiths, clerks, ditch diggers, carpenters, stagecoach drivers, or farm helpers.[23]

The immigrants began an unsettled period of adaptation and experimentation when they started to drift away from the towns into the unsettled bunchgrass country. They were forced to begin the often painful process of adapting their expectations and skills to the soil and climatic conditions of the land. As Ladd Haystead and Herrell DeGraff have written: "Into all parts of the frontier, settlers took the livestock and every crop they had produced in the widely divergent areas whence they came. Then began the great experiment. What part of that varying past experience was good and could be continued? What part had to be discarded because it did not fit the new environment?"[24]

Some settlers tried raising exotic plants and animals—including tobacco, grapes, sorghum, ginseng, sugar beets, and even llamas and camels—but met little success. People from the Midwest quickly learned that the Columbia Plateau was not well suited to corn production. William Snyder, a twenty-three-year-old storekeeper's son from Ohio, sent a sample of an oily film he found on the surface of a spring to the U.S. Department of Agriculture in the futile hope that he had found petroleum. He sought the advice of agricultural scientists again after open-range cattlemen ridiculed his idea of growing wheat on Rattlesnake Flat:

> "*Well, what are you going to do over there?* [*rancher J.F. Coss asked*] "*You can't grow nothing there. Never get any water there.*" "*Well,*" *I says* "*We're going to try. Maybe we can't grow nothing and maybe we'd never get any water but we are going to try.*" *That gave me the incentive to send a sample of that soil back to Washington DC for analysis. That analysis . . . said we have to have alkali in our soil to grow wheat but we had too much and with cultivation and exposure to the elements in time it would make good wheat country. And we had an awful big percentage of phosphorous and other things in there needed to grow wheat. So that's what actually happened. The first years we had little or nothing for crops. After a while why we was able to grow good crops.*[25]

Many immigrants entered the livestock business after pursuing other occupations: Charles Brune ran a ferry, homesteaded, and finally decided to enter the sheep business. Fred Gerling worked in a sawmill and a flour mill; became a placer miner; served as a steamboat deck hand; and raised cattle before acquiring a band of sheep. Ulrich E. Fries, a Danish immigrant, had heard erroneous reports of large logging operations on the Columbia Plateau and, after arriving in the treeless region, worked first as a railroad laborer and then began raising cattle. Philip Cox raised fruit trees for several years before deciding to run sheep. H. Stanley Coffin and his brothers, Lester and Arthur, were merchants who began raising sheep on the grass-covered hills. Max and Hans Harder worked on farms and as railroad laborers before becoming sheepmen and cattle ranchers. William Granger was a miner, freighter, cattleman, and deputy sheriff before entering the sheep business. William Whipple worked in a dairy, ran a hotel, and then purchased a band of sheep. Willis Mercer left his Illinois home to work as a logger in Wisconsin, moved to the eastern slope of the Cascades and failed as a homesteader in the arid Horse Heaven, worked in a Walla Walla dairy, and returned to the Horse Heaven to raise sheep.[26]

The McGregor brothers began their acquaintance with the new region in the spring of 1883, when they decided to go "land looking" in sparsely settled areas north of the Snake River. Much of the land thought to be best suited for wheat production, particularly the eastern portion of the Palouse country and the areas near Dayton and Walla Walla, had already been claimed. The McGregor brothers joined the large number of immigrants exploring drier lands in the Big Bend and western Palouse, areas previously thought inhospitable to farming. Immigration to the Big Bend was said to have reached "land rush" proportions in 1883, with twenty-five wagons of land seekers reported in the town of Sprague in one day. The settlers used homesteads, preemptions, or "timber cultures" to gain possession of lands in the public domain. Many staked out quarter-section homesteads on the prairie grasslands. The homestead law required the building of a home, five years' "continuous" residence, cultivation of a portion of the land, and a modest fifteen-dollar filing fee to perfect title. An alternative was to reside six months, make certain minimal improvements and pay $1.25 an acre under the preemption law. The Timber Culture Act enabled settlers to acquire an additional 160 acres by planting and maintaining ten acres of trees on the tract. Farmlands in the eighty-mile-wide swath of alternate sections granted to the Northern Pacific Railroad were also for sale at from $2.50 to $6 per acre, with liberal credit terms.[27]

Archie and Peter persuaded their father and two cousins, Jack Livingston and Malcolm McCloud, to come to Washington Territory and help them locate and improve a homestead. The elder Peter MacGregor and the cousins went by train to San Francisco and took the ship *Queen of the Pacific* to Portland, where they were met by the two brothers. With two teams of horses and two wagons, the group explored the Big Bend country in search of homesteads. They began their search in the most arid portion of the Columbia Plateau, an area that another immigrant, Ulrich E. Fries, described as "the worst country I had ever seen. There were no settlers and no grass—nothing but sagebrush, howling wind, and drifting sand." The men were unable to find suitable land in the parched and dusty region. At Pasco they saw a prospective townsite, with only the fading sign "Watch Pasco Grow" to distinguish it from the surrounding desert. The elder MacGregor thought this amusing because he could not believe that anything could be grown in this dry, dusty, and treeless country. He had pioneered once and apparently had no desire to do it again. Moreover, when the party arrived in Sprague on a payday for railroad workers, there was such havoc as to convince the father that this was not a desirable region in which to live.[28]

The McGregors and their cousins sold their teams and wagons and returned to Portland, whence they would all depart for Canada. But, according to later accounts by younger brother Alex, Peter and Archie "did some strong pleading with father to permit them to remain with the understanding that they would not let the frontier life influence them too much for the worse or they would return on their own accord." The plea was successful, and the two brothers returned to eastern Washington to continue their search for desirable land. Archie described his efforts to his father in a letter written in Dayton, on May 14, 1883:

> I have the pleasure of writing you a few lines concerning the Big Bend country. . . . We were sorry parting but glad that we were staying in Washington Territory, for we did not want to leave dissatisfied. We returned to Dayton and went to work for awhile when I decided to go see the Big Bend. I got to Sprague, then went on foot with my blankets on my back. Sometimes I slept on the prairie and I found that it was a hard matter to get anything to eat. I walked for miles without anything to eat. The longest walk I had without anything to eat was 60 miles. I always felt happy on the way for I could see the country or hunt. So I did and I took up 160 acres of land and now I have more land than a good many on the Lake Shore. Of course I have not the deed yet but I am a Yankee all the same. The land is rolling prairie, lots of water to be had for the digging from 5 to 16 feet. Lumber is scarce but that's nothing. I think there will be logs afloat down the Columbia and that is about 10 miles from where I took the land. The soil is lighter than around Dayton but it lays nicer by far. If we would have gone out sooner, we would have had our choice of this country but there is not much choice in the land. I spent a month away in my travels and saw that there was a better show for to make a start here than in Canada but to take it as it comes for awhile. The hardships will not be equal to what yours were when you went to the Lake Shore, but they will be hard enough for us. If you will send that money back we will see you the interest paid. We will send you the interest in January and don't you fret about that. All a person wants is a start. If we would have kept our teams we would have made a good thing out of them. The old gray bluff that bought the mares wants $375 for them now without harness. He has also taken a place, and was running down the . . . [region] to you. It was the mares he wanted, but never mind, there is a good time coming. It was very well for you going back, but the others were foolish and they will find out someday, but now keep all things quiet to see how things go. It is their loss, not ours. Don't fret about us for we are happy and everything looks prosperous. I'm not sick of this place yet.[29]

The homestead claim was in the arid, rocky Grand Coulee canyon near Steamboat Rock. A reporter for a Norwegian newspaper noted that this area was "settling fast" and that roads were being built to facilitate the hauling of logs from the Columbia. But the McGregors and the other settlers had chosen a hot, desolate portion of the Columbia Plateau, a land that can look rich and productive in May and utterly barren two months later. Archie became further discouraged when three Indians on horseback robbed him as he walked through the Big Bend. He escaped by hiding in a steep rock outcropping. But the only food he could find during the next two days was a potato that had fallen from an immigrant wagon. Archie and Peter decided to abandon the claim and return to Dayton to wait for news of more promising homestead locations.

In the fall of 1883, the two men decided to investigate the unsettled portions of a more hospitable land, the Palouse country. Archie and Peter left Dayton on foot, with a small pony to carry their baggage, and walked fifty miles north to Alkali Flat Creek (four miles from the present village of Dusty), where each claimed a homestead. They promised a man forty dollars to build two cabins, one on each 160-acre claim. Before construction costs had been paid, a prairie fire destroyed both residences. When they acquired enough money to rebuild, a new cabin, half on Peter's quarter section and half on Archie's, was constructed and a well dug.

The two men earned money by working for a short time on railroad construction crews near the towns of Colfax and Tekoa. The McGregor brothers sought to conserve their resources during this difficult period. At the boardinghouse where they lived during their days of railroad work, Archie developed a habit of filling each cup of coffee almost half full of sugar. The owner took a dim view of such an attempt to gain free food and finally asked them to move out. In later years, Archie claimed that the surest test of wealth was the ability to use unlimited quantities of sugar to sweeten a drink. Archie and Peter also found employment with farmers and livestock raisers in the region, for whom they worked for wages as low as twenty dollars a month. The two men herded sheep during the winter and spring in the rugged Snake River canyon, south of their Alkali Flat headquarters. They worked on ranches about ten miles apart. Archie later recalled that they would get together "for a chat on Sundays by each walking five miles across the hills to meet and talk all day."[30]

The two men considered their future prospects as farmers and decided that the costs of fencing and cultivating the land were prohibitive. Sheep raising, an ancestral occupation in both Scotland and Canada, appeared to offer a more attractive future. The men turned their homestead cabin into a sheep camp and worked "on shares" for Charles Johnson, a sheepman from the nearby village of Almota. Archie and Peter McGregor worked fifty to a hundred miles apart, each with custody of a separate band of sheep. They took only minimal pay and exchanged their herding talents for part ownership of future lamb crops, on the "shares" arrangement popular on the western ranges. The shares system had a great attraction to men short of capital. "The very poorest men," Oregon sheepmen John Minto wrote in 1892, have developed their own sheep businesses, "with their labor only, by undertaking to care for a flock purchased by the capital of others." Many immigrants arriving on the Columbia Plateau during the days of the open range—particularly men from France, Spain, England, Ireland, and Scotland—entered the sheep business in such fashion.

The McGregor brothers had encountered what they later described as a period of "severe privation" in their attempts to adapt to a new environment greatly different from their forested Ontario homeland.[31] After trying to set up farms in the new region and working at various jobs, the men had finally decided to take advantage of a resource unavailable on the shores of Lake Huron—the thick cover of native grasses that was such a major feature of the interior lands of the Pacific Northwest. The youthful immigrants, after some casting about, concluded that sheep raising on open ranges of the Columbia Plateau offered a great opportunity.

Chapter 2

Sheep Raising on the Open Range, 1882-93

"By following the plans adopted by experienced sheepmen and attending strictly to business, by vigilance and employing competent and trustworthy herders and hands, success and profit are certain."

Ezra Carman, H. A. Heath, John Minto, 1892

The shepherd "is never quite sane for any considerable time. Of all Nature's voices, baa is about all he hears." John Muir, 1911[1]

"Cattle owners are running from a pestilence—sheep," a pioneer Yakima cattleman complained in 1880. Sheep "drive us out and ruin our ranges and business." "There should be a United States law," he concluded, "confining them to certain limits, from which they should not encroach upon cattle ranges and take the life out of the enterprise." A writer visiting northeastern Oregon in 1882 told of "many a growl have I listened to from the cattle-men, and most absurd threats as to what they would do to keep back the wooly tide: even to the length of breeding coyotes or prairie-wolves for the special benefit of the mutton." Travelers in the Klickitat Valley observed a series of signs along roadways:

NOTISE

All land in woods past
Draper Springs is for Settlers
cattle. No sheep is allowed.
Sheep men take notise
Comitee

One of these signs was followed by a cryptic note on a dead pine tree:

Turn ye. Turn ye.
For why will ye die.[2]

Similar complaints and dire warnings were heard in many open range areas of the American West in the late nineteenth century. Sheepmen were gaining control of western ranges long used for cattle production. Between 1860 and the mid-1890's, the number of sheep in western states and territories increased from less than 10 percent of the nation's flocks to more than half. By 1890, four times more sheep than cattle were grazed on the Columbia Plateau, and during the next decade sheep numbers in the region would surpass 1.1 million, more than eight times the size of the remaining cattle herds. Similar trends occurred in Montana, Wyoming, Colorado, Utah, and many other grassland areas of the West.

Sheep raising offered young immigrants a promising opportunity for economic advancement. Sheepmen throughout the western range states cited "numerous instances where men are today prosperous and independent, who a few years since were getting their start under the share system." Experienced woolgrowers reported that sheep "can be profitably kept by any man exercising good judgement and attending to his business." John Muir noted that California sheepmen were able to keep large flocks at slight expense and realized "large profits, the money invested doubling, it is claimed, every other year."[3]

Sheep raising was part of a process by which settlers in frontier regions in the United States, Canada, and Australia began "as soon as possible after initial settlement to produce and export cash crops." Pioneers, often equipped with a minimum of capital, were forced to find the farming system that required the smallest capital outlay. The nature of the available resources further limited the choices available to farmers and ranchers. In the prairie peninsula of Iowa and Illinois, as Allan Bogue has shown, livestock production was expensive, and undiversified cash grain farming brought quick returns. The farming potential of the ranges of the American West was uncertain. Cattle required a larger initial investment than sheep and matured more slowly, thus bringing smaller returns during the first few years. Sheep could be raised cheaply on unclaimed range, and settlers short of funds but imbued with what Frederick Jackson Turner described as materialism, optimism, and energy found that sheep production offered a promising avenue to wealth.[4]

The men who decided to tend flocks of sheep found that "to be a sheepman is to be ostracized from society in some places." "Few people," a Montana sheep raiser wrote in 1892, "dare to be so bold as to face the prejudice which is founded on the false idea that the business is debasing." Frederick Coville, a forest inspector visiting the Columbia Plateau sheep ranges in the 1890's, found that "a popular impression seems to prevail that sheep herders in Oregon, as elsewhere, represent a comparatively low class of humanity." But Coville noted that "many bright and reputable young men have undertaken sheep herding in default of opportunities for more desirable work." To many observers, a life of solitude with thousands of bleating sheep had little appeal. Wallis Nash, writing in 1882 of his *Two Years in Oregon*, gave a typical analysis: "Day in, day out, the same deadly sound of monotonous duty, until . . . [a herder] hated the look, the smell, [and] the sound of a sheep. . . . If he would stay, he could have a share in the flock to secure his interest, and he could also take his pay in sheep, which would thus start his own individual flock. The offer was a tempting one; the path was the same that all the successful self-made sheep-men had followed; cold and privation alone had not many terrors to a hardy man."[5]

There was nothing romantic about owning or herding sheep. Satisfaction had to come either from economic gain or from pride in ensuring the safety, health, and nourishment of animals that needed constant human supervision in order to survive. Sheepmen could not compete in popular esteem with cowboys, who were already becoming legendary as rugged, hard-working, hell-raising individuals. Yet by the 1880's, conditions were changing in many western range areas, and cattlemen found themselves retreating before a rapidly expanding sheep business.[6]

The grasslands of the Columbia Plateau were changing in ways that proved detrimental to the cattle raisers. Because the grasses grew in clumps, unlike the sod-forming grasses of the mid-continent, stock disturbed the soil surface more readily than on the Great Plains. The bunchgrass had seldom been grazed by large numbers of animals before the mid-nineteenth century. Bison had been only infrequent visitors to the grasslands of the interior Northwest for the previous 2,500 years. Antelope had not been in evidence. The rapid introduction of millions of head of livestock onto a once sparingly grazed range was certain to bring changes. The native perennial grasses were highly palatable to cattle and were subjected to intensive grazing pressure. The native cover of bunchgrass (blue-bunch wheatgrass), giant wild rye, Idaho fescue, Sandberg bluegrass, and other perennial plants was significantly reduced. This set the stage for the rapid advance of annual "weeds" (forbs) unwittingly introduced from Europe and Asia. Many of these plants, including "Jim Hill" mustard, "China lettuce," alfilaria, yarrow, lamb's-quarters, pigweed, and quack grass, were of only marginal use as cattle feed. Cattlemen found that fewer steers and heifers could be grazed per acre and that their animals failed "to lay on fat as readily as formerly." Sheep, on the other hand, preferred succulent green annual "weeds" to dried grasses and used the latter to supplement their diet during winter months. Sheep could also crop the short grasses left behind by cattle.

Twenty years of heavy cattle grazing had made the plateau grasslands particularly suited to sheep production.[7]

The steady encroachment of farmers onto the open ranges made matters worse for cattlemen. A Klickitat County cattle raiser complained in 1881 that his range was overstocked, "permanently injured by sheep," and broken up by preemption and homestead claims that "will gradually drive all cattle from the country; large bands went out in 1880." Cattle lacked the herd instinct, and several men were needed to move even a hundred head to a new range. With labor scarce and rangeland unowned and unsupervised, cattle raisers preferred to let the animals "drift by their own instinct," leaving them "ranging over the same common territory, as it is impossible to keep different herds of cattle apart." They hired "outfits" of a dozen men or more to scour the range from early May throughout the summer and fall to search for their cows and to brand "whenever and wherever we find calves," including all unclaimed "slick-ears" or "mavericks" whose mothers were not nearby. Some of the cattle owners were poor managers, lured into the trade by promotional literature that portrayed Columbia Plateau cattle raising as an almost effortless enterprise, offering "a life where manly sport is an ever present element." But even the most experienced and able open range operators could do little to improve the care of their stock. One of the few cattlemen to raise hay for winter feed found that "the great difficulty in this sort of provision is the impossibility of getting our stock to the hay when a hard winter does come, owing to deep-crusted snows, which prevent stock from being driven far."[8]

Pioneer settler W. J. Davenport suggested that "cattle industry" was a misnomer during open range days: "The term 'industry' . . . presupposed business methods, proper supervision, and care. . . . During the period mentioned cattle raising was wholly lacking in these essentials. To be a cattle raiser in those days one had only to purchase the stock and turn the same loose to shift as best it might, without food or shelter during the winter months. If the herds managed to survive under these conditions, the owner was counted as a successful cattleman. . . . It took but one hard winter to undo all that had been accomplished." The winter of 1880–81 was one such severe period; it was said to have marked the "passing of the cowman in central Washington. Soon afterward large flocks of sheep began to graze on hills bordering the Columbia River." Several open range cattlemen joined forces in 1882 to stage what was later called "the last big cattle roundup." Five hundred cowboys spent two months separating the widely scattered stock.[9]

The decline of the cattle business was hastened by a catastrophic drop in beef prices. Cattle that had sold for $40 per head on local markets in the 1870's sold for only $10 by the early 1880's. The low prices caused many cattlemen to trail their livestock to more lucrative markets in Rocky Mountain states, where ranges were being more fully stocked. During the year 1880, for example, seventy-two thousand cattle were driven from Washington into Wyoming. The price decline hit other western areas a few years later—cattle that were worth $9.35 per hundredweight in Chicago in 1882 brought $1 in 1887. H. A. Heath of the Bureau of Animal Industry noted in 1889 that "the depression which has befallen the cattle business set men to thinking. . . . There is more profit in sheep than there is in cattle, and . . . one-third the capital required to stock up with cattle is sufficient to start with sheep."[10]

Sheepmen were able to take advantage of the changed circumstances. One sheepman and his dogs could effectively handle as many as three thousand sheep, trailing them quickly to the best pastures or to protected canyons where they could be sheltered from storms. The herder carefully guarded his gregarious, docile flock, moving them long distances to the most hospitable portions of the range. Cattlemen and settlers described the peripatetic herders as "tramps," complaining that they "just drift around in search of good feeding ground and camp wherever such areas are found, regardless of the interests of anyone else. As the sheep are constantly under herd, they stay just as long as there is any grass, and move without trouble whenever the feed is exhausted." In the spring, when the range grasses were succulent and green, sheep could be grazed several days without water, enabling herders to reach rangelands where cattle could not survive. Woolgrowers knew, from the cattlemen's bitter experiences, of the need to keep a supply of emergency feed available in case severe winter weather struck.[11]

The sheep business was well suited to frontier areas far from markets. Wool, one of the most valuable and least perishable agricultural commodities, could be stored indefinitely and shipped to Boston, one of the largest international marketplaces for that product. Sheepmen could receive additional income by selling wethers (castrated rams) to buyers who assembled flocks of five thousand to forty thousand head, hired a few herders, put bells on a few sheep chosen as leaders ("bell wethers"), and trailed the animals slowly to Kansas and Nebraska feedlots. En route the sheep were fattened on surplus feedstuffs and on rich grasslands previously unusable for livestock. These flocks were part of the fifteen million sheep trailed eastward from the Pacific Slope during the last third of the nineteenth century, a movement of livestock five times larger than the fabled "long drives" of cattle north from Texas after the Civil War. But mutton sales were supplementary, for open range operators found they could raise sheep "very cheaply and very profitably just for the wool. There was always an outlet for it and if it took two or three years to get . . . to Boston . . . it really didn't matter. It might have to be sent around the Horn but it was still of value." Wool prices had steadily improved after a slump in the 1870's, and a tariff protected domestic producers from low-cost foreign wools.[12]

Columbia Plateau woolgrowers patterned their yearly operations on the transhumant system: the seasonal migration of men and sheep between mountain and lowland pastures. Similar patterns of movement had been practiced for thousands of years by Celtic shepherds in Scotland and by Basque and Bernais herders in the Pyrenees. The shepherds of the Old Testament likewise trailed their flocks in a cyclical pattern between semiarid lowlands and upland pastures. Transhumance was introduced into the American West in the 1860's by California sheepmen who used the San Joaquin Valley for winter quarters and the Sierra Nevadas for summer grazing lands. The procedure spread rapidly in the next few decades and became common throughout the western range country. The itinerant grazing system proved especially well suited to the rangeland of the Columbia Plateau. Sheep were kept on sheltered lowlands during winter and spring months to take advantage of the ample green feed of early spring and the relatively mild winter weather. As the native bunchgrasses and other perennial plants of these regions ("ice cream plants," as cattlemen called them) were replaced by exotic, early maturing annual forbs ("hard tack"), the lowland ranges produced increased amounts of early green forage and smaller percentages of year-round feed. The ranges became less useful for cattle grazing but better adapted for seasonal sheep feeding.[13]

Lambs were born on the lowland pastures in March and April and remained there with the ewes until June, by which time hot weather had cured and dried the green forage. Herders then began slowly trailing their flocks to higher elevations, stopping frequently en route on any suitable unclaimed grass. Shearing took place at Sprague, Washington; Shaniko, Oregon; and other railroad towns located between lowlands and mountain pastures. Herders and sheep then continued their journey to the cooler, more humid meadows in the mountains that surrounded the plateau. Sheepmen trailed their stock in all directions—the McGregor brothers, for example, herded some sheep east to the forests of Idaho and others north to the Colville area; the Harder brothers and Tom Drumheller used the Chelan and Wenatchee areas of the Cascades; the Coffin brothers and Malcolm McLennan used the Wenas range near Mount Rainier; and R. A. Jackson and Charles Cunningham trailed their sheep south to the Blue Mountains. The mountain forests were strictly seasonal pastures—they provided late-maturing green grasses and shrubs for summer grazing but were snowbound from late fall until spring. Sheepmen left the mountains in October as cold weather and snow began to threaten the welfare of the flocks. Rams were placed in the flocks for the homeward journey, and breeding took place as the sheep were trailed slowly back to the lowlands. Wheat stubble and open range grasses provided forage for the two to five weeks spent trailing back to the low-lying prairies of the Columbia Plateau.[14]

The sheep best suited to the rolling prairies and steep, mountainous summer ranges were the Spanish Merino and a derivative type, the Rambouillet ("French Merino"), a breed originally developed by the French Royal Court in the 1780's. These sheep yielded large fleeces of fine-grade wool that commanded a premium in the marketplace. They were big, hardy animals, able to withstand seasonal drought and scanty food, and possessing a strong flocking instinct that kept them from scattering across the open range. These sheep were bred to the original stock, the so-called "native" Oregon sheep—hardy, lanky mongrels whose ancestors had been trailed from Mexico to California and thence to the Willamette Valley. The sheep were divided into "bands" of 1,500 to 3,500 animals, depending on weather, topography, and other conditions. Each band of sheep was tended by a solitary herder and his two dogs, usually small black and white border collies of Scottish or Australian ancestry. The herder was pivotal to the success of the range sheep business. He had to be dependable, hard working, and willing to endure solitude and discomfort in order to guard his band at all times during all seasons.[15]

Archie and Peter McGregor were among the numerous French, Scotch, Basque, English, Irish, and Canadian immigrants who first became acquainted with the vicissitudes of the open range sheep trade during the early 1880's by herding sheep for men already established in the business. They spent the years 1883–85 tending bands of sheep owned by Charles Johnson, a sheep raiser with headquarters on the lower Snake River. Like many other young herders, the McGregors received minimal pay, only enough for overalls, boots, tobacco, and a few other supplies. Johnson gave them their share of the flock in 1885 and the two men began developing their own business. They purchased an additional 950 sheep from Johnson at two dollars a head, on credit. The two men paid 1½ percent interest per month. The McGregors were able to establish credit, Archie recalled, "by industry, work, character, honesty, and fair dealings." Sheepmen J. P. Stine and J. W. McIntosh sold them an additional 450 head, at two dollars each, in October 1885. Alfred Coolidge, a local sheepman and president of the Second National Bank of Colfax, provided a loan at 1½ percent monthly interest to cover their operating costs. Coolidge and Walla Walla cattleman–banker Levi Ankeny were well known in the area as bankers who made livestock loans to operators of "good character." Veteran cattleman–farmer Ralph Snyder described the two as "those wonderful bankers, men not necessarily in favor of the big fellow. If a man was willing to work and had a half dozen horses and a plow, why Al Coolidge or Ankeny would finance him." The 18 percent interest rate was standard in Montana, Colorado, Wyoming, and several other areas at this time. The high rates reflected the chronic shortage of money and the high risk, as well as the high expectations, of agriculture in newly settled regions.[16]

Bankers had good reason to extend loans to capable young men whose only major capital assets were their sheep: Wool prices were good, flocks were rapidly growing in size, and sheep production was booming in the Far West—with stock numbers up 400 percent in a decade, to more than 18 million head. The outlook was encouraging, and Archie and Peter McGregor urged their younger brother, John, to come to eastern Washington and help them tend the sheep during the 1886 lambing season. John arrived in the spring of that year and joined the partnership of "McGregor Brothers, sheepmen." The three men concentrated almost exclusively on wool sales in an effort to expand their holdings as fast as possible. They sold only "gummers" or "broken-mouths," old sheep unlikely to survive winter weather, and spent some of the earnings from wool sales to purchase more sheep. Barring severe weather, scanty grass, or insufficient winter feed, the McGregors and other Columbia Plateau sheepmen could expect the annual lamb crop to bring an additional increase of 80 percent in the size of their herds. During one especially favorable year, the McGregors reported a percentage of 135 percent lambs born to ewes bred, a remarkably favorable figure for an open range operation, and one that required exceptional care, a mild winter, and a good grass crop. The number of lambs surviving after a few months on the range would have been below 100 percent, but the results were excellent nonetheless.[17]

Some of the transhumant sheepmen were able to increase the size of their business spectacularly within a decade. The McGregor brothers expanded from less than a thousand to twenty-two thousand sheep from 1885 to 1890. Phil Cox entered the sheep business in 1882 with a small band of sheep and, by 1885, was said to have almost twenty-five thousand sheep in his operation. Many sheepmen claimed that the value of their investment doubled every year. Some of the figures flowed from overly optimistic bookkeeping, but the returns were sufficient to enable sheep raisers to enlarge their operations within a short period of time. The records of a Umatilla, Oregon, sheep business of the preceding decade,

1870–80, provided an example of rapid growth: Beginning with a small band of 1,512 sheep in July 1870, the firm had 20,000 head a decade later. Clarence Gordon, a U.S. Census Bureau employee, visited the unnamed firm in 1880 and summarized its business records in his report:

July 1870—we had 1,512 head—Sold during summer 460 head, raised 700 lambs, and sold wool in the following amounts:

1870	$ 663.00	1876	$ 5,287.50
1871	1,393.25	1877	9,309.44
1872	2,583.05	1878	13,626.00
1873	2,911.36	1879	18,600.00
1874	3,653.28	1880	27,395.00
1875	4,754.75		$90,146.93

During 10 years sold 8,500 sheep at from $1.50 to $2.50.[18]

Sheepmen had to be on the alert constantly for suitable grazing grounds for their ever-increasing flocks. Competition for the range was becoming more intensive every year as sheepmen, cattlemen, horse raisers, and farmers worked to extract profit from a land that seemed to have "hills that reached from hell to heaven, with bunchgrass from top to bottom." By the mid-1880's, plows had turned over substantial areas of the 250 by 200 mile prairie. More than a million sheep needed sustenance. Large, open range cattle herds were on the decline, but in their stead were the half dozen or more cattle that most homesteaders kept on land adjacent to their farms.

Some sheepmen became known as "coyotes" for their cunning adaptations to the changed circumstances. Doug McAllister, an old Scotch sheepman, was said to have instructed his herders that "there was no such things as fences": "Homesteaders in the Simcoe Mountains and wheat ranchers in open country found his philosophy had been put in practice when they gazed upon grain fields, fenced pastures, and gardens, after his flocks had trampled them. When they pursued him angrily he placated them by stating that his sheep were hungry and beyond control. . . . If he thought a homesteader was unreasonable, he would dismiss the matter with a wave of his arm as he said: 'Aye mon, I'll go to the courts with ye.' " McAllister once found that six thousand of his sheep had trampled a large garden. He immediately went over the hill to see the homesteader, offered him twenty dollars so his packers could take a few vegetables, and had the man sign a bill of sale: "I hereby sell one garden to Douglas McAllister." When the homesteader found his ruined garden he pursued the sheepman, only to be told, "Hoot mon, ye gave me a perfectly good bill of sale. . . ." Mc Allister was said to have stopped the argument by commenting: "Aye, mon, we will let a jury of 12 good men . . . decide that."[19]

Few sheepmen deliberately provoked trouble by such surreptitious grazing programs. But misunderstandings were hard to avoid on ranges of unappropriated, unregulated government land available to whomever "got there first with the most." The McGregor brothers, Preston brothers, William Ensley, T. R. Troub, Sweeny and Montgomery, Baxter Renshaw, Phil Cox, and numerous other sheepmen used the central portion of Whitman County, between the towns of Endicott and Penawawa, as a favorite location for winter operations. Sheepmen wintered more than eighty thousand sheep in the Endicott area and shipped four hundred thousand pounds of wool from that location in 1885. Land to the south along the Snake River and near the hamlet of Penawawa was grazed by some fifty thousand sheep during the same season.[20]

Relations between sheepmen and cattle-raising homesteaders in these areas became strained during the fall of 1885 and the spring of 1886. Settlers claimed that the transient sheepmen were grazing unowned portions of land near their homesteads, thus "stealing" range they wanted for their cattle and horses. There was some sporadic opposition. In November 1885, the Colfax *Palouse Gazette* mentioned the case of Territory vs. John Smith. Smith, "charged with setting fire to Sweeny and Montgomery's sheep camp below Endicott," was held in jail on eight hundred dollars bond to await trial by jury. The following spring, the Whitman County Wool Growers Association took up a subscription "for Mr. Cox to aid in the prosecuting of the party who fired his herder's tent some time ago." During March 1886, "a dastardly attempt was made to poison Poe Brothers sheep at the 'Cross Hollows' near Taxsas [Riparia]. . . . The poison used was saltpetre. It was unsuccessful." The "Cattleman's and Horseman's Association of Southwest Whitman County" and similar groups met in Pampa, Lone Pine, Pleasant Valley, and other small towns in unsuccessful efforts to devise "some means by which to keep the sheep men from bringing sheep in and eating the grass from our stock." The sheep raisers held a meeting and determined to take steps to defend their property. A correspondent writing to the *Palouse Gazette* from Sutton, a station south of Endicott, commented in March 1886: "It looks bad to see so many traveling the roads to and from their sheep camps, carrying arms as in time of war."

Discouraged by the hostile spirit developing in the Endicott area, Archie, John, and Peter McGregor decided to move their winter range further west to the protected valleys of the lower Palouse and Snake rivers. The area, long recognized as an attractive livestock range and sometimes described as a "stock raiser's paradise," was sparsely populated, for the land was thought to be inhospitable to farming.[21] The McGregors chose an area with a thick cover of grass, several sheltered canyons, numerous potholes and lakes, sufficient rainfall (a fourteen-inch average, far more than adjacent areas to the west and south), and three streams—Cow Creek and the Palouse and Snake rivers. They had chosen one of the best available areas for open range sheep production—a locality situated between the extensively farmed lands to the east and the hotter and more arid lands of central Washington. Here glacial floodwaters had overflowed existing stream channels, creating an elaborate series of angular buttes and cliffs, rock basins, gravel bars, deep circular depressions, and a rugged canyon that diverted the Palouse River over steep cataracts to its confluence with the Snake. East of the scabland were the intricate, dune-shaped hills of the Palouse country. To the west were drier, more level lands of the Big Bend. This transitional zone would become permanent headquarters for the McGregor sheep operations. For almost a century, flocks owned by the McGregor family have been grazed in this district.

Peter, John, and Archie came to the valley of the lower Palouse to winter their sheep, "thinking that the season would be mild and the flock would need relatively little feed." Natives of a land where livestock had to be fed hay several months a year, they knew the value of a temperate winter climate. Several other sheepmen and cattle raisers had found that the area "had a mild winter, good strong grass, and running water." Sheepmen D. S. Bowman; Albert J. Hooper; Jacob, Hans, and Max Harder; and Philip Cox, and cattlemen "Uncle Jim" Kennedy and Joseph Milam were among those taking advantage of the forage available on nearby hill country in the 1880's. A few homesteaders were beginning to test the theory that the region could never produce wheat. The only village of any consequence within forty miles was tiny Pampa, which, according to an early resident, had a general store, "a shed housing lumber and machinery, a blacksmith shop, two or three pioneer homes nearby, a one-room school house with thus far few pupils, and a pigeon hole postoffice in one corner of the store, whose proprietor was postmaster."

Competition for the range was much less severe in this remote district. Pioneer settler Virgil Bennington recalled that "the bunchgrass was tall and just marvelous. It grew up eighteen to twenty inches high and would just wave like golden grain." But there were signs of future trouble. In 1886, Northern Pacific Railroad officials tried to restrict access to an eighty-mile-wide swath of alternate sections in the new wintering location by issuing an "order requesting sheep owners to remove their bands from company lands." Henry Copley and Alfred Coolidge of the local woolgrowers association complained bitterly, and plans to evict the sheepmen were postponed. A territorial law passed in 1888 "to prevent trespassing by sheep" upon all lands, enclosed or unenclosed, belonging to "any person other than the owner of such sheep," seemed ominous. But the law, passed in response to complaints by Palouse country farmers about transhumant sheepmen, was not enforced for several years.[22]

The search for adequate winter range was but one of the problems demanding attention. Sheepmen had to protect their flocks from inclement weather, predators, poison weeds, and a series of diseases. "Scab," a particularly harmful form of animal itch, ravaged central Washington flocks and was dreaded by sheepmen everywhere. Scabies, tiny mites that dug into the skin and reproduced rapidly, caused large patches of wool to fall from the sheep, exposing bleeding sores and bare, inflamed flesh. Pioneer Klickitat County sheepman George W. Smith was given the nickname "Scabby George" because it was said that his flocks were usually infected with the parasite. Newcomers to the central Washington sheep ranges sometimes found that the flocks they purchased were covered with the microscopic pest. County and state quarantine laws restricted the spread of this infectious condition, but sheepmen throughout the plateau protected their bands by dipping the sheep in a solution of hot water, sulfur, and Black Leaf (a nicotine compound squeezed from boiled tobacco leaves).

Sheepmen also worried about operating costs, marketing, and credit. H. R. Roub of Penawawa claimed that a twenty-five-dollar "inspection tax" levied on flocks grazing on summer pastures in the Moscow Mountains was used to outfit each county official with "fine Havanas, a plug hat, and a gold top cane." Sheepmen learned to circumvent the inspection fee by keeping their flocks in remote locations far from county seats. Roub complained about other expenses: "Herder's wages are entirely too high at $30 per month . . . [and merchandise] costs are entirely too high yet. The average merchant of this section has more cheek than a brass monkey and one does well to let them alone when it is possible to do so."[23]

Woolgrowers worked to keep to a minimum the expenses of shearing, shipping, and marketing their clips. Members of the Whitman County Wool Growers Association agreed in 1885 to pay shearers no more than six cents a head for their services. Wool shipment to the Boston market by Columbia and Snake River steamboats and oceangoing vessels was, sheepmen complained, "as slow as molasses in January." The wool producers reached an agreement with the Northern Pacific Railroad for uniform shipping rates from a railhead on the main line at Sprague. The railroad company constructed corrals there, and the McGregor brothers and other Whitman County sheep raisers herded their sheep from winter ranges to Sprague, where shearing took place. The sheep were then trailed to summer grazing grounds in nearby mountains. But Columbia Plateau woolgrowers joined other western farmers and ranchers in criticizing the arbitrary, expensive, shipping procedures of the rail line. While trying to limit labor, merchandise, and shipping expenses, sheepmen also had to face the vagaries of credit and international wool markets.

Eastern commission companies sent representatives to the Columbia Plateau to inspect and buy the wool clips. Some of the buyers were shrewd operators who brought with them "a quart or two of low grade whiskey" and offered generous cash advances, but "invariably . . . swindled" the woolgrowers. Well-established Boston and Philadelphia firms gave fewer promises and no spot cash, but their agents were generally honest and reliable. The McGregors sold their clips to the E. A. Pierce Company of Boston and to R. L. Rutter, the local representative for Justice, Bateman of Philadelphia and had few troubles. The Whitman County Wool Growers Association warned its members to be wary of the practices of some buyers: "In cases where pressure of debts compels the acceptance of advances on wool it would be better to borrow money at 1 ½ per cent per month or even 2 per cent than to take the advance of 7–8 per cent per annum of the commission merchants."[24]

The difficulties with the wool buyers reflect the chronic shortage of working capital and the unstable credit situation on western ranges and farms. Sheepmen paid interest rates of 15 to 25 percent or more for their money. But even worse was the short time allowed for repayment, often six months or less. In June 1889, the McGregor brothers entered such a short-term arrangement with Charles Johnson, the man for whom Archie and Peter once herded sheep. The McGregors borrowed $2,000 on a mortgage and assigned as collateral a band of 2,700 sheep (1,700 ewes and 1,000 lambs) that was being grazed on summer range in the Moscow Mountains, eight miles east of Viola, Idaho. John, Peter, and Archie agreed to pay the debt, plus 1 ¼ percent monthly interest, within one year or at any earlier date if demanded by Johnson. Good wool prices and favorable operating conditions enabled the men to repay the loan. But the mortgage could have forced liquidation at any time. Such financing agreements were readily renewable when the markets were strong. But, should a downturn occur, a livestock raiser might face a situation where loans were falling due and renewals refused, making it necessary to sacrifice his stock at a loss.[25]

The hazards of raising livestock on the Columbia Plateau increased in the late 1880's. Several years of severe winter weather left a path of destruction across much of the West. Cattlemen, horse raisers, and those sheepmen who gambled on a mild season and failed to purchase hay for the winter of 1886–87 lost a sizable portion of their stock. Woolgrowers who had hay for their stock were not seriously hurt. The McGregor brothers wisely chose to buy hay from F. W. Young, Absalom Taylor, and William Thomas, homesteaders near their wintering grounds on the lower Palouse. When the snow crusted over and the sheep were unable to break the surface and reach grass, the McGregors purchased additional wheat hay from Taylor. In the range country to the east many of the large cattle corporations, unable or unwilling to feed their stock, were forced into bankruptcy. Blizzard conditions from Dakota to Texas left a grisly sight: "Carcass piled upon carcass in every ravine, gaunt skeletons staggering about on frozen feet, heaps of dead bodies along the fences, trees stripped bare of their bark."[26]

Columbia Plateau livestock raisers learned from bitter first-hand experience during the winter of 1889–90. Two years of abnormally light rainfall meant that the range was poor and hay expensive and in short supply. A correspondent from Hooper, a new village near the Mc-Gregor winter range, described the outlook in mid-December 1889: "Scarcely enough hay was raised to satisfy the local demand. . . . The grass on the range is very short and nearly all of it is young and tender. As a consequence stock, except sheep, are poor and weak before the worst of winter and are likely to die when the weather becomes severe."

Snow began falling on December 15, and heavy snowfall and cold weather continued for more than a month. The ground was covered with more than two feet of snow. A "chinook" wind, rain, and warm weather then melted some of the snow. The weather again turned cold, a heavy crust of ice formed, and the cold weather held for another month. On February 25, the temperature dropped to 21 degrees below zero. The extreme weather finally abated, and by the second week in March the crisis was over.[27]

There were reports of large livestock losses from many portions of the Columbia Plateau. From the Big Bend country of central Washington, word was received that "80 per cent is a very low estimate of the loss . . . of range cattle and horses." The Franklin County assessor estimated that in his area "75 per cent of the cattle died during the winter." Some cattlemen reported losses of 60 percent to 90 percent or even more. The first reports exaggerated the losses, but the range cattle industry of the region was "almost crushed." William S. Lewis later claimed that in the spring of 1890: "The range was piled five and six deep with dead stock. When the first ones died the others climbed on top of them to get out of the snow and died. Others did the same, so they were in heaps. They ate the hair off the dead ones, so that they were almost bare."

Sheepmen who had purchased large stocks of hay during the previous fall could herd their flocks into protected valleys and minimize losses. But in some areas, especially where inadequate steps had been taken to secure hay, "whole flocks were wiped out." H. Stanley Coffin traveled through eastern Oregon buying thousands of sheep pelts and claimed that "all the sheepmen in the interior of Oregon went broke and lost practically all their sheep. Some had owned as many as 5000–6000 and lost every one of them." [28]

Sheepmen who tried to purchase feed after winter's first onslaught found local supplies exhausted and many roads and rail lines blocked with snow. Even if the feed arrived, the sheep might not survive. Charles Cunningham shipped two cars of corn and prairie hay from Kansas to his winter range near Prosser, but "he was [headquartered] 15 miles from the railroad. . . . and by the time the feed arrived the sheep were too weak to trail out." F. A. Phillips recalled that "he gave me $40 per ton and furnished two men with shovels to help me haul the feed. . . . The snow drifted so deep it took two days to make the 15 miles on the first trip with the feed." Only four hundred sheep of the several thousand owned by Cunningham survived. A man named Hewitt wintered his flocks near the range used by the McGregor brothers, but "didn't put up much hay for sheep. They had big drags and they'd put on about 12 head of horses on a big wooden drag, and they'd drag the snow off. If there wasn't snow, why they'd just winter out. Well there come the bad winter and boy the snow covered everything. They couldn't get it off. They had a railroad into Pampa then and Hewitt went down to [banker Levi] Ankeny and borrowed $5000 [to purchase] and ship in barley to Pampa. This fellow took his wagons and hauled it from Pampa and the sheep died anyway. You can't put sheep on grain right off from nothin'." [29]

Even sheepmen who had acquired feed well in advance ran precariously short of hay for their livestock. Archie McGregor summarized the McGregor brothers' fortunate experience during that terrible winter: "We fed from the 16th of December until January 25th. The snow all went and it turned real warm. Then on February 5th it snowed without freezing and turned real cold and continued until the 10th of March. Sheep had to be fed until the 12th when a real chinook hit and the grass was fine, having shot up under the snow. Hay sold at 2¢ per pound and we had three bales left."

The McGregors and other raisers of sheep, cattle, and horses who had managed to avoid catastrophic losses were able to keep their open range businesses intact. But the future of such enterprises was increasingly clouded. Farmers plowed up ever-increasing portions of the grasslands, and unclaimed forage became more and more scarce. In Whitman County, unimproved rangeland decreased from 1,300,000 acres in 1879 to 380,000 twenty years later. The reduction of acreage available for grazing led to overuse of the remaining grasslands. A representative of the Bureau of Animal Industry observed in 1892: "As the [Columbia Plateau] country fills up with settlers . . . , the freedom and advantages of grazing on the public domain are diminished and the trouble and expense of keeping sheep in this manner increase from year to year."[30]

The two eldest McGregor brothers, discouraged by the outlook, decided to sell their sheep. In 1891, Archie and Peter sold their livestock to Peck and Rice, a firm from Montana, a state where the sheep business was rapidly expanding onto millions of acres of open range. Indeed, several of the Columbia Plateau sheepmen moved their flocks eastward to the vast unbroken grasslands of Montana during the next decade. After paying all their debts, Archie and Peter each had nine thousand dollars—enough money, they figured, to last them the rest of their lives. The men first planned to travel for a few years, hoping to visit their family in Ontario and attend the 1893 World's Fair in Chicago, where their brother Alex was a pharmacist. But the McGregors, like many other young men in the West, remained alert to new opportunities to exercise their entrepreneurial skills. When Archie and Peter were told of the organization of a new hardware firm in the town of Pullman, they decided to invest their funds in the project. Archie soon tired of "city life" and rejoined brother John on the open range. He described life in Pullman in a March 1892 letter: "It is quite evident to me that I will not stay in Pullman. Living in town is not what country people think it is. The worst feature about it is that a person cannot go and come as he wants to. This is what I call settling down without feeling settled either. I would sooner eat sour dough bread in a sheep camp, potatoes in a frying pan, etc. than live in a hotel."[31]

Archie returned to "the rocks" (his term for the Channeled Scablands) later that spring and began helping John with the remaining bands of sheep. While tending their sheep on this winter range, John and Archie boarded, when possible, with nearby homesteaders. Archie lived with the William Thomas family; John lived nearby at the Ab Taylor residence. Both later married daughters of these homesteaders: Archie married Nellie Thomas and John married Minnie Taylor. Peter married Minnie's sister, Maude, and took her to Pullman where his hardware store was located.

Many other homesteading families followed the Taylors and Thomases onto the lower Palouse, scabland, and Big Bend sheep ranges during the early 1890's. Archie and John McGregor and other tramp sheepmen found more neighbors every time they trailed their flocks back to these winter pastures. The homesteaders lived in plain houses made of rough lumber, fueled their kitchen stoves with cow chips and sagebrush, grew vegetable gardens and small acreages of wheat, and raised milk cows. Making a living on the interior prairie required the concerted efforts of all members of a homesteading family. Ralph Snyder described the efforts of his father and grandparents to gain some income from their quarter section on nearby Rattlesnake Flat:

> *I remember when they had this homestead going my father was able to get five head of cows from a fella that was driving a bunch of steers through from Yakima to the mines at Kellogg. Grandmother [then was able] . . . to make butter all summer. There was lots of bunchgrass around there and they'd bring the cows in and milk them and she made butter; saved the cream and worked that butter down and then she kept that butter . . . in gerkins . . . and it was fresh all summer. In the fall it was shipped over to Tacoma to sell to the sailing ships over there. That was the only source of income they had. They raised a little wheat but they harvested with a scythe and threshed it out with horses walking on it. But she was the only one who got cash in for that family.*[32]

Virgil Bennington lived with his parents, grandparents, and younger brother in a shack in Adams County. At the age of seven he was given charge of the fifteen milk cows that "were our livelihood. My mother and grandmother made butter and we . . . traded it for groceries and clothing." He had to watch the cows closely. "If I didn't stay right with them, they'd take off and go four or five miles a day . . . and it'd be difficult to get them in at night." He watched for coyotes "lookin' for cripples or something they might devour" and for wild stallions that always "seemed to enjoy chasin' the cattle. . . . Oh it was a great experience. Always rode bareback, never had a saddle till I was about 13 or 14. Always had a good lunch. Couple of slices of bread with plenty of butter and sugar on it." In the fall he helped his father corral and break wild horses. His father worked with the horses all day, "tryin' to break 'em to lead and work 'em."

> *At night, oh about 10 o'clock, we'd turn 'em out on the bunchgrass. 'Course they were all hungry and they'd feed till just about daylight. Then they'd start heading east toward Cow Creek. My job was to herd 'em and bring 'em back. . . . I'd hobble my horse during the night and*

then at daylight I'd try to go out and get the wild horses and bring 'em in. In the winter time it'd get pretty cold but it was warmer out on bareback than in the saddle. The horses would grow long hair in the winter . . . but right where I'd sit and where my legs were that hair would all be worn off. . . . My father would wrap my feet and legs up in gunny sacks and tie strings around them. You'd be surprised how that helped keep you warm.

The homesteaders made the best of the circumstances. When provisions ran low, barley was ground and used as a substitute for coffee, and the crushed and strained centers of watermelon were used as "sweetening." Window decorations were made by emptying and stringing magpie eggs. A social occasion for many of the women was a twice-yearly trip to Hooper Lake, where they made large fires to heat the water and spent the day doing their laundry. Dances, literary society meetings, cayuse horse races, community dinners, horse rides to Palouse Falls or two smaller waterfalls on the Palouse River, and, in season, sleigh rides and ice skating were major leisure activities.[33]

The McGregors and other tramp sheepmen participated in many of the social activities organized by their more sedentary neighbors. They also bought hay from the newcomers and stayed with them when the flock was nearby. But the farmsteads scattered across winter and summer ranges made sheep pastures scarce and increased the difficulties of sheepmen and the herders and camptenders in their employ. The herder and his dogs kept year-round watch on a band of a few thousand ewes and lambs. Good herders adjusted their techniques to a system called "loose herding." When using this procedure, the herder "let his flock feed over fresh ground every day in the most leisurely manner consistent with preventing any from getting permanently separated from the main flock and so lost." While moving the sheep he would walk ahead of them, holding back those most anxious, then working around the sides of the band to prevent straying, and returning to the rear to bring up stragglers. Meanwhile, the sheep were permitted to spread out and graze.

Where feed was plentiful, the band soon settled down to regular grazing habits. William McGregor, a visitor at his brothers' sheep camps on the summer range in 1892, described the jobs of herders at such times as "easy . . . for they go out about sunrise and then about ten o'clock the sheep will bed down and won't start to eat again until three o'clock when it gets a little cooler." The sheep were then grazed toward camp, where they arrived about sundown. "The herder then commences preparations for his supper, doing all he can toward his breakfast and lunch next day, not forgetting his friend and helper, the dog. In the morning he is up with the dawn. He makes his coffee and fries his meat, and generally has finished his breakfast, fed his dog, and put up his lunch when the sun strikes his sheep and they begin to repeat the process of the day before." [34]

For every two or three bands of sheep, a camptender (also known as a camp rustler, packer, or roustabout) was required. This man "goes ahead of the sheep, picks out a camping place, keeps the camp stocked with food and supplies, leaving the herder free to look after his sheep." On the scabrock winter range, McGregor camptenders used wagons to haul supplies and move herders' camps. Transporting provisions to the mountainous Idaho summer range required a three-day journey, with a wagon, over rough roads to Moscow, Idaho. When a herder was camped in an area inaccessible to wagons, the camptender had to transfer the supplies to a pack horse and transport them through the woods. William McGregor, a camptender for his brothers in 1892, described his new employment: "The camptender is kept far busier than the man who herds. I like it better for I don't find the time so long. . . . I have to move two herders while . . . [Archie] is away. I don't mind moving when I can move everything with a wagon, but when it comes to packing a horse it is not very nice, and I have to move one that way." [35]

While their employees watched the flock and hauled provisions, the sheep owners searched for good rangeland, bought winter hay, bargained with wool and mutton buyers, and performed many other managerial duties. The sheepmen became experts at determining the quality of feed. When sheep first reached summer pastures, they could be grazed on "light" feed, which allowed for rapid weight gain but produced a "soft" fat easily lost if the sheep had to be trailed long distances. Late in the summer the sheep were pastured on "strong" feed, which brought slower gains but produced a "hard" fat, which enabled sheep to be trailed to winter pastures without serious weight loss. The sheepmen often joined the herders and camptenders at the "sheep camps," sheltered locations near the flocks where tents were set up, horses fed, and the evening meal prepared. The camps generally were supplied with bacon, beans, potatoes, butter, dried fruit, syrup and molasses, huckleberry preserves, and flour. Olive oil provided the main cooking grease. Many herders proclaimed themselves capable of making "the best sour dough biscuits in the country," a specialty of the sheep camps. The food was cooked in a Dutch oven, a cast-iron pot five inches deep and twelve to eighteen inches wide, around which hot coals from the campfire were spread. [36]

Archie and William McGregor described life on the sheep ranges in a series of letters written in 1892 and 1893. Letters by open range sheepmen are very rare. Accordingly, the two letters from William to his brother and sister and the 34 letters, totaling more than 200 pages, from Archie to his future wife Nellie Thomas, provide unusual first-hand information about the day-to-day lives of tramp sheepmen.

William McGregor left the family farm in Canada in 1892 to visit his brothers, hoping that the invigorating climate of the Pacific Northwest would help him recover from bad health. He described his arrival and meeting with Archie on the Idaho summer range in a July 21, 1892, letter to his sister Jessie:

> I got up about five o'clock and started out to meet Archie and the sheep. After walking about ¾ of a mile, I could hear the sheep bleat. Then in a short time I could see Archie and his two herders at their breakfast alongside the road. I took my grip and went walking past them to see if Archie would know me. Archie looks at me and calls out "Will, hallo!" I came over and shook hands with them all and had breakfast with them. They were surprised for me to find them out in the bush the way I did. . . . Well, we kept right on moving towards the mountains and in two days John came out to meet Archie. He is a fine looking fellow and he has got a good deal stouter but his features have not changed any. He has been healthy ever since he came out. I have not seen Peter yet. He is in the store at Pullman. He keeps the books there and gets $75 a month. He is president of the board of managers. Archie likes to be with the sheep better than to be in the store. They have three bands of sheep all back here. It takes about $25 a day to run them and still they expect to clear over $3000 this year on them. . . . They have $17,000 in sheep. . . .

William mentioned his first impressions of the sheep business:

> It is very lonely out here with the sheep. I felt the first days as long as weeks at home but it is healthy out here.
> I have done no herding yet as Archie has a man herding that owes him about $100 and he says he can't get it out of him any other way so he will keep him about two weeks more and then I will take hold. I think I can manage all right. I am helping them move along just now. Excuse my writing as my desk is an old box and it shakes.

After spending a month helping Archie and John "move from one place to another" and substituting for herders who "would want to go away for a day," William wrote his brother Dougald. Although he described the summer range as "a poor farming country," he told his brother that many new settlers had moved into the district. "[Archie and John] . . . have to go fifty miles further back [into the mountains] than when they first came here. It is pretty nearly all Swedes that settled here and they are pretty cranky when they see sheep coming into the mountains. They want to keep all the grass for their cattle." The search for range became increasingly difficult in late summer. Much of the grass dried up in the hot weather and sheep feed became scarce. Archie commented in August 1892: "We were looking for Peter and his folks up here and I was in hopes that my Nellie would get to come along with them. Yet I did not think she should. We would get lots of camping out, then fish, eat, and sleep. It is real nice up here for a while, but it is getting too late for John and I to have much of a time. It is so hot and dry. I wonder if it is hot in the rocks? [i.e., the winter range.]" Some forage could be found in the midst of the settled areas. William Mc-Gregor learned that "every few miles there are sections of 640 acres left for school purposes so whenever we would strike one of these we would stay a few days and rest the sheep. Sometimes we would not drive them over a mile a day if there was good feed. There is no hurry, you know, in getting out of here. The idea is to get good feed for all summer and if we get it on the way out it does just as well. But these people who live near these school sections kick. They want that for their own stock and have no more right to it than anyone else."

Scattered school sections provided only temporary sustenance for the three bands of sheep, and on August 16 William told of herding into an area where:

> *The timber is so thick you can hardly see a few yards ahead of you. This is where the sheep like to be in hot weather. The kind of grass here is pine grass and is a kind of dry grass the sheep don't eat. They just eat the brush and leaves . . .*
>
> *[John and Archie] have to hunt up range now here for it is not the way it was when they first came. First they could find range anywhere but now there are so many settlers got in here and they are all along the water so it makes it pretty hard to find range. Archie and John were away for two days looking for range and they struck a pretty good place at the head of the river where any body else don't know. They had to go in through a thick bush leading their horses and after travelling about two miles in from the road they struck a large meadow about 3 miles long and lots of water. John and I were moving a band up yesterday, that will last this band till the 1st of October and then they will be going back to the stubble fields and their winter range.*

The month of September was even more hectic for the tramp sheepmen. "Next month Archie says makes it busier for the herders and for them too for the feed begins to get pretty dry and they run more and split up sometimes and very often lose a bunch and then they have to pull out to find them and they may be several days away before they find them." The McGregors also had to purchase winter feed: "Archie is away down to Pampa and will be away for two weeks. He is looking after hay for the winter."[37]

By early October, frost had nipped the leaves of the underbrush in the mountain forests and the sheepmen became fearful of an early snowfall. They began to move to lower altitudes, grazing the sheep slowly toward winter rangeland in "the rocks." Archie wrote Nellie Thomas in October 1892: "I cannot be down there much before Xmas. . . . If you do not go to school all winter we will have a fine time. That is if I do not have to feed sheep every day. I guess I can get to see you anyway as I will probably board at your place if I can board as cheap as what I have done last spring and that is not all of it. You know." Archie supervised trailing the sheep out of the mountains but ran into trouble when a herder forgot to feed his team at night. A horse turned up missing and Archie feared that the delay would force him to miss his brother's marriage ceremony: "I hope that we will get to Peter and Maude's wedding. Peter should have known that we could not get off very well this month. . . . They may be married before we get out of these woods."

Archie reached the scabrock winter range in December and began boarding with the William Thomas family. But Nellie Thomas was in school in Sprague and the letters continued. Archie wrote about life on the winter range and told Nellie of the unusual precautions he and John were taking to protect the stock, including liberal use of hay and construction of a stable for the team and a lean-to for the sheep.

> [*December 2, 1892:*] *I intended to write last night but as soon as your Ma got the dishes washed we all had to play cards and it is that way every night. I have not had time to write in the day as we are hauling wood and one thing another preparing for winter. It is raining this morning but I have to go to Pampa for lumber to build a Stable to put our team in. . . . I will try to get up there Xmas if I possibly can. No dances yet but I think I will go to one on the 9th at Pampa.*

> [*December 4–8, 1892:*] *Would I could be with you tonight but I cannot. I am hauling wood now until I go over there. I hope that it will not storm so I will have to stay here and feed sheep or do anything with them. We have sold 800 head more. Took 418 here at your corall [sic] and he wants the rest about holidays. Must I help cut them out? I am afraid of it. John is well and told me to remember him to you whenever I wrote. He is a fine fellow.*

> [*December 8, 1892:*] *I am just longing to go out there. I am hauling wood yet and even if I am busy I long and I sigh as I go along the road thinking all the time of my girl. . . . There is a dance up Willow Creek tonight. We intended going but came to the conclusion to have a little dance of our own in the School House tomorrow evening.*

[*December 11, 1892:*] *I have got all my wood hauled. Have to build a Shed Yet and haul some hay, look after the sheep some, and then go to Sprague. Just think of it and smile. . . . We have great times here Joicing one another at cards. Your Pa and I beat the Teacher and Jim.*

[*December 13, 1892:*] *If you come home for Christmas when do you want to start or would it be proper for me to come home with you on the train? It is very cold and about two inches now of Snow. Whoop La. Love you only. May soon have to feed sheep.*

Nellie came home for Christmas, but by early January she was back at school in Sprague and Archie was again writing lengthy letters. John was boarding at the home of his future in-laws, the Ab Taylor family, about a mile from where Archie was staying. Archie told of the long hours the two spent herding sheep, moving camps, feeding the flocks, and protecting their sheep from deep snow and cold weather. He wrote, too, of the time they found for ice skating, card playing, dancing, and other leisure activities. The two men were also busy selling sheep. In earlier years they had concentrated almost exclusively on wool sales in order to increase the size of their flocks. But the declining areas of winter and summer range made the men decide to keep only a few thousand sheep. Archie told of one sheep sale and of a French sheepman who was encroaching on their winter range in a letter written in February 1893: "We sold 400 sheep the other day for $1750 to be taken before the 1st of May. We will not have over 3450 to shear this year. . . . Wish I could go up to see you but do not know yet Nell when I can go. If it was not for this French man I could go up in about two weeks but we will have to fight him, so I may not get to see you soon."

Lambing became the major concern in March and April. Sheepmen were too busy caring for the welfare of their flocks at this critical time to dicker with sheep buyers or worry about other livestock raisers. Archie described this hectic period in several letters to his fiancee.

[*March 5, 1893:*] *We are beginning to move part of our corall* [sic] *and camps into the rocks preparing for lambing. Just about three weeks more.*

[*March 12, 1893:*] *Peter asked me what I was going to do this summer. I told him I was going to run sheep. He says would you take Nell into a camp. I said I believe if I asked her she would go and the probability is if we get married in the early part of summer we will go to the mountains unless we go home* [to visit the family farm in Ontario]. *Maude would go with Sheep now but not in this country but in Montana for people would laugh at her here. She knows Peter cannot go to Montana.*

. . . If it had not been for you I would probably be chewing tobacco yet. . . . A man will sacrifice anything for one he loves.

[March 15, 1893:] I must say we have been courting under disadvantages since we left with the sheep for the mountains last spring.

I would like ever so well to go out to see you now but I cannot as John and I are very busy preparing for our harvest. We expect a few lambs by the 20 or 21st inst.

[March 22, 1893:] Fred is herding for us now. I think he is going to make a splendid hand. He is not a bit lazy. . . . I wanted to go down and stay at the sheep camp since you were not here . . . and John could do the running around . . . but he said he would rather go down to camp. . . . I am going down on the 24th or 25th to stay about three weeks.

[March 25, 1893:] I was at camp to-day hauling supplies. I am going down tomorrow to stay about three weeks. We have 30 lambs now and we will be busy now until we get to go to the mountains again.

Parkie is herding. He lost most of his band. They must have been out 3 or 4 nights. Found all but 7 today. Coyotes must have killed them. Expensive herding. Do not know as we will keep him any longer for we cannot stand such rackets as that.

I do not expect that I will have much time to write until after lambing. The grass has not grown much here yet but soon will grow now. The French man is camped at Hooper Lake. He herded up to Mr. Town's house yesterday and Mr. Town fired him off. He told him that he owned that section east of him. Great times in the rocks. Nellie as I read your loving words I feel guilty. I have taken a few chaws of tobacco this spring. . . .

[April 9, 1893, Green Lake Sheep Camp:] We have had Splendid luck until the rain of the 5 and 6 struck the rocks. We lost 50 or 60 in the storm. I have been so tired at nights that I could hardly eat Supper but the worst is over now. We have about a thousand lambs. We expect 6 or 7 hundred yet So will be busy about two weeks more. I wish you were at home to night then I would go up to see you. It is such a long time since I saw you. 2½ months. Wouldn't we have a fine chat. My feet are so sore now I limp but will Soon get all right again. . . . Jim, Fred, Parkie, and Harris are helping us lamb . . . I have not had time to go to John's Camp yet to night.

And Mr. Crowell is going to Start a gambling and dance hall and you hope I will never go into such a business. Nellie I will have to change wonderfully if I ever make an attempt. I . . . would have more respect for myself and friends than to throw myself away for the sake of a few dollars.

[April 14, 1893:] It rained and snowed here all day on the 10th. We lost several lambs and it is still blowing and cold but I must go to Pampa.

So William and Mable are engaged. Minn is the only girl left now. I suspect [John and Minnie] will get married next fall or winter....I was talking to John and he said he thought it best for me to go home [to Ontario] first and then he would go in the fall and stay all winter. ...We aim to go back one at a time for we cannot get anyone to take care of the sheep.

Do not be angry with me because I did not write sooner. We were so busy and it was cold and disagreeable.

[May 14, 1893:] So you will be down in two weeks.... The chances are I will be at the shearing corall (sic) [at the Northern Pacific Railroad siding at Sprague]. Our luck, when you come I go, I come you go.[38]

The letters and the two-year courtship ended in July with the marriage of 32-year-old Archie McGregor and seventeen-year-old Nellie Thomas. Archie convinced his family that "there was just as sweet and lovely women in the U.S. as there is in Canada" and that "what little I possess was not the means of winning her affection." The tramp sheepman fixed up a small house near the Thomas residence for his wife. Nellie and Archie were married in a ceremony at the local schoolhouse. The occasion featured a dance in the school, followed by a supper served "under a spacious tent, [where] tables laden with the products of city and farm and decorated with roses and pinks, whetted the most sluggish appetites."

By the summer of 1893, John and Archie McGregor had become experienced and successful open range sheepmen. They had been hard workers and good managers of a transhumant sheep business well adapted to the sparsely settled open ranges of the Columbia Plateau. They had followed practices long recommended for successful sheep production. During the Civil War, Texas open range sheepman George W. Kendall had learned to watch the flocks closely, provide emergency fodder, safeguard the welfare of young lambs, and build special shelters for the weak and ailing. The McGregor brothers had used similar procedures to adapt their open range sheep operations to the interior lands of the Pacific Northwest. But after a decade as tramp sheepmen, the McGregors found themselves in a business with an uncertain future.[39]

The days of the open range were reaching an end, and a more intensive pattern of land use was coming to the interior of the Pacific Northwest. Millions of acres of the best bunchgrass had been settled, forcing sheepmen to crowd into the scabrock canyons, lowland deserts, and other portions of the Columbia Plateau that were apparently unsuitable for farming. The seasonal patterns of grazing practiced by the sheepmen had allowed them to prosper for many years after the decline of open range cattle raising. But by 1893, tramp sheep raising had also become a marginal enterprise.

The McGregor brothers had advanced from herders to owners of a profitable livestock business well adapted to the broad, open prairies of the plateau. But the unclaimed pastures upon which they had depended were becoming a thing of the past. In 1892 William McGregor was convinced that his brothers would abandon sheep raising. "They don't aim to run [the sheep] any more out here. Next spring they will sell all after shearing and go home."[40] But John and Archie did not make plans to return to Canada. They decided instead to remain in the sheep business. The rapid settlement of the Columbia Plateau made it apparent that the next few years would be difficult ones. To this picture was added an unforseen crisis: the Panic of 1893.

Chapter 3

"These Hard Times"

THE PANIC OF 1893 AND THE DECLINE
OF THE NOMADIC SHEEPMEN, 1893-96

"[Wool prices] can't go any too high for the sheepmen who for three years preceding '97 felt like committing suicide and were only deterred by the thought of the funeral expenses that would be entailed on an estate that was too weak to give evidence of existence anywhere but on the assessment list."   *Ranche and Range*, 1898

"Defendants forthwith . . . [must] remove . . . all sheep which they, their agents, servants, or employees are tending, herding, and pasturing on said land."   Circuit Judge C. H. Hanford, 1896

"The natural result of [excluding livestock from the Cascade forest reserves] . . . will be the wholesale emigration of the flocks and droves to other parts. British Columbia will welcome most of them to her verdant hillsides, for her statesmen have not yet reserved them as a playground for the gilded sports and scions of degenerate aristocracy. . . . The army of herders, packers, shearers, drivers and other employees who now throw their money so freely upon our counters of trade will be only a memory. In short, the whole thing will settle as a blight on every class."
Ranche and Range, 1897[1]

The Columbia Plateau had been through a decade of "rapid growth" and "wonderful development" by 1893. The wheat harvests were among the best in the nation. The sheep flocks produced larger wool clips and bigger lamb crops than those of any other western range area. By 1890, more than two million acres of the plateau had become "improved" farmland. Despite the huge livestock losses of the previous winter and the incomplete tabulation of open range stock, enumerators found more than 825,000 sheep and 189,000 cattle on the plateau. Settlers optimistically claimed that the land offered agricultural opportunities "unexcelled anywhere in the world." Editor W. W. Corbett of *The Ranch*, a local trade journal, described the effect of the land on ranchers and farmers: "Men seem to renew their youth remarkably in this young and vigorous country. . . . It is in the soil and the air, in the blood and the spirit, to push things, to build up and develop."[2]

But a period of bewildering change was beginning. Cattlemen of the Columbia Plateau were the first to feel the impact of the new circumstances. Under the pressure of competition from sheepmen and farmers, the range cattle industry was, "like the savage Indian, dying out." A. J. Splawn, a pioneer cattleman, asserted that the cattle raisers could not compete with sheep businesses organized by a "hardy race of Scotchmen." Splawn advised the cowboy to "sell his schapps and rope, take hold of the plow handle with both hands and go at it, for his day has gone."[3]

Sheepmen, as well, faced a critical situation. Unoccupied grasslands were increasingly hard to find. Moreover, no organized pattern of range use had been developed. Hence, each tramp sheepman sought to use all the grass he could when he found ungrazed range. One observer declared that "the only way to prevent another outfit from obtaining a given range was to strip it utterly naked" (a practice that became known as "sheeping off" a range). The frontier emphasis on individualism and the rapid exploitation of unregulated natural resources left the western rangeland in a chaotic state: "No matter what class of stock was grazed, whether sheep, cattle, or horses, the owners 'gave no heed for the morrow'. . . . Nobody dared save an acre for future uses." There were other difficulties. The 1890's saw the creation of national forest reserves from which sheep were excluded or their grazing regulated. *Ranche and Range* described this issue as "one of the gravest questions that has ever confronted the people of Eastern Washington" and noted that "the prosperity of the country largely depends on our live-stock interests." Moreover, during the same period the Northern Pacific Railroad took steps to assert its ownership over its land grant lands, threatening to bar sheepmen from their winter range. Added to all these difficulties was the Panic of 1893.[4]

The national depression of 1893 magnified the problems faced by the sheepmen and cattle raisers and brought to a halt the rapid economic growth of the Columbia Plateau. Banks and stores throughout the region closed their doors. By 1894, western wheat, wool, and mutton prices had dropped to their lowest point since the Civil War. Local wheat producers suffered from a period of three years "when the farmer either lost his crop of wheat or could not sell it for what it had cost him." The drastic decline in national and international agricultural prices caused particular hardship in the Columbia Plateau and other western areas that had been developed as "colonial" economies, producing raw materials for distant markets.[5] The optimism of many settlers quickly turned to bitterness. Some found themselves in agreement with Populist charges about the conspiracy of the "privileged few" that had turned the "great plain people" into "helpless servants of a poorly concealed plutocracy."[6] The early boom years had ended. Settlers on the Columbia Plateau were entering a critical period of readjustment and accommodation.

Archie, Peter, and John McGregor had been among the "industrious and ingenious persons who succeeded on the frontier with very little capital." But the bunchgrass country was no longer a frontier, and prospects for tramp sheepmen were limited. The McGregors would either have to make drastic changes in their ranching operations or find new employment. The two eldest brothers, Archie and Peter, began a search for profitable new activities. Only John remained committed to the sheep business.

Archie and Peter began to speculate in urban real estate at scattered locations in Washington, Idaho, and Oregon. The construction of a railroad through Latah, Idaho (renamed Kendrick, in honor of the chief engineer of the Northern Pacific), a town near the McGregor brothers' summer sheep range, encouraged a fever of speculative land buying. On one afternoon in May 1890, $5,200 worth of city lots in Kendrick were sold in three hours' time. Archie was attracted by the town's promise, and in June and July 1890 he purchased two lots for $316 and, with Abraham Ensely of Colfax, acquired another location for $450. In December of the same year, he bought Ensely's interest in the latter site for $400 and acquired ownership of another lot from Ensely for $650. Archie kept his lots for two years and prospects for sale remained good. In a letter from a nearby sheep range, William McGregor reported that "a man from the east bought a farm near Kendrick the other day and in a weeks time sold it and made $1100 on the bargain." John Addison, the cousin who had encouraged Peter and Archie to come west, was also involved in speculation in Kendrick. But, William noted, "I don't think Addison did as well as he might there for he would not sell at first reasonable. They started the town a little way down from where he owned so he is on the suburbs." The McGregors bought several other pieces of real estate. Peter, for example, bought lots in Pullman, Olympia, Portland, and Kendrick.[7] The Pacific Northwest was rapidly growing in population, land values were increasing, and speculation in urban real estate seemed to offer a promise of good profit.

But the McGregors and their cousin guessed wrong. Kendrick, for example, remained a small town in spite of promoters' optimistic predictions. The four lots for which Archie had paid $1,591 in 1890 were sold twenty-six years later for $52. The men knew little about the individual properties, had no experience in dealing with urban real estate, and were unable to extract profit from the new endeavor.

Peter and Archie McGregor had joined the many young men of the inland region seeking respectable livelihoods as merchants in 1891. H. Stanley Coffin, another Columbia Plateau sheepman, had a similar goal: As he later recalled, it was his "ambition to be a merchant prince, that is, to have a general store and sell goods." The McGregors came from a region in which a mercantile career had been viewed as an indication of high status. Sherman McGregor commented: "In the old country people have always had the idea that to be a merchant meant that you were a gentleman and that you were influential in the community. Pete and Archie felt that they had made enough in ten years to enable them to go to Pullman and become pillars of the community."

The mercantile business appeared to offer good prospects. The big wheat crops and good prices that had prevailed in Whitman County for several years had created a market for agricultural equipment. Peter and Archie and three other men organized the Pullman Hardware Company in 1891. Archie and Peter invested most of the $18,000 from the sale of their sheep in the $40,000 capital stock of the hardware store.[8]

The store enjoyed a promising beginning. Archie worked blackening stoves for $75 a month, then drove dray and served as a delivery boy. In February 1892 he was in charge of farm machinery: "At present the implements are consigned to my care. Farmers are coming in inquiring for ploughs, harrows, seeders, etc. and we must try and accommodate them for it is on them we rely for a living." Peter began as a stove blackener, then was elected president of the company's board of managers. He kept the books, for which he received $75 per month. D. C. Monroe, another officer of the company, went to the East Coast, where he purchased "the finest available machinery and hardware." Specialties of the store included "Clarks Celebrated Buggies, surries, jumpseat carriages, spring wagons . . . McCormick Twine Binders, and Cumming's Improved Header." *Northwest* magazine wrote in 1892 of the Pullman Hardware Company: "The company owns two stores. One, 40 x 80 feet, is occupied by a full and well-selected line of hardware, tinware, stoves, etc. The other, 30 x 80 feet, is occupied by a stock of farm implements, machinery, buggies, wagons, etc. They do a business of $150,000 annually and enjoy a reputation unexcelled for uprightness and honorable dealing."[9]

Archie soon tired of the sedentary business life. He felt "lonesome when Peter is gone" and too shy "to get acquainted in town." Although Pullman was a "bachelor's delight, with some kind of amusement very near every night," Archie was tired of being a bachelor and returned to the McGregor range near the residence of his sweetheart, Nellie Thomas. To finance his return to the sheep business, Archie sold three Kendrick city lots to John for $1,500.

Peter McGregor stayed in Pullman and was hailed as one of the town's most promising young merchants. He married Maude Taylor, the girl he had met several years before while sheep herding in "the rocks," and settled down to the life of a businessman. Peter and Maude bought a house that, Archie commented, they had "fixed up nicely [with] . . . a fine piano and sewing machine." Maude enjoyed the town's social life, and went "out on a great deal of calling and receiving callers." Her sister Minnie had helped her keep house, but Maude "did not know what she would do after Minn left for it would take all her time to make calls and take music lessons." Archie was disdainful of such a life: "Who would want such a woman fashion?" Archie also disagreed with Peter's plan to spend money to build a new home instead of visiting Ontario, and gave him "a reprimanding" for failing to ask their brother William "to go up to Pullman to live with them last winter when he was sick." The idea had not occurred to Peter, who was devoting all his attention to being "so steady at the store." An admirer wrote in 1893 that Peter McGregor, now thirty years of age, had come "to Washington practically without a dollar . . . [and] by the exercise of sound natural judgment and great foresight in matters of business and indomitable energy, accumulated in a very short space of time a fair competence."[10] The judgment was premature.

Peter and Archie McGregor lost their "fair competence" in the Panic of 1893. When his brothers ran short of capital, John helped them finance the purchase of land and the construction of buildings by guaranteeing one loan and paying an overdue $2,000 mortgage for Peter in exchange for a half interest in a Pullman city lot. But the two men continued to have difficulties, as a letter written by Archie, dated March 5, 1893, indicates:

My mission to Moscow was to pay our taxes. Our [city lot] property in Idaho was sold for taxes and I went up to redeem it. . . . The Pullman Hardware Company . . . [is] going to have a meeting. Our investment there has not yielded us any return last year. If we don't [make money] this year we will sell out. Peter and Maude see that we have made some in sheep so that is the reason they want to keep sheep but not until they found out we were going to keep them. Peter asked me if we could run some for him. Saying he would rather run them himself than [have us] give them up. I told him he could get out [and herd] then. I will not do it if we get married and there is not apt to be anything come between us now...Peter is my brother and I love him dearly but he should not expect me to run sheep for him under the circumstances.

The difficulties mounted for the Pullman Hardware Company. Corporation officials followed the general practice of selling implements to farmers and allowing them credit until after harvest. The price of wheat on local markets dropped from more than seventy cents a bushel to thirty cents in 1893 and eighteen cents in 1894. Farmers purchased no new machinery and had difficulty paying off existing debts. The 1893 harvest was largely ruined. J. B. West, an early Palouse country settler, described the harvest season: "It rained for three weeks. By that time the fields were so muddy nothing could be hauled across them. The wheat sprouted in the heads and began growing. The standing wheat became green again and the shocks became green mounds. The wheat sprouted in the sacks but some of it was saved for feed. There was no fall seeding."[11]

The collapse of wheat prices, coupled with crop failure, was catastrophic for farmers and their creditors. A group of local merchants attempted to form "a protective association against bad debts." But the firms that had granted extensive credit were forced out of business. The dimension of the disaster that befell the Pullman Hardware Company is reflected in fragments of evidence that remain. In 1893, the company officials obtained $1,850 on two promissory notes, due in six months. Two years later, the men had been able to repay $526 of the $850 note and $1,023 on the $1000 note. An additional $927 was due on the first note and $60 remained unpaid on the second. The owners of the store simply could not collect money owed them or obtain additional funds.

The company's only remaining assets in 1895 were twenty-five promissory notes signed two years earlier by farmers, varying from ten to more than three hundred dollars each and totaling almost two thousand dollars. The company was forced to go through bankruptcy proceedings, and the twenty-five notes were sold at a sheriff's sale for ten to fifteen cents each and a total price of $2.55. Peter McGregor decided that "he did not believe he could stand to work in the store always," and Archie had earlier returned to tramp sheep raising. The Panic of 1893 left the two with little choice but to abandon storekeeping and return to the open range.[12]

Merchants in towns throughout the Columbia Plateau were hard pressed. Only the most clever entrepreneurs could prosper during the depressed times. Although H. Stanley, Arthur, and Lester Coffin of Yakima found that "times were very hard" and local stores "were all going broke," they nonetheless devised means of profiting from their sheep and mercantile businesses. When the price of wool dropped, they had the clip made into Indian blankets, which were sold on reservations throughout the West. H. Stanley Coffin recalled that the blankets, valued at $1.90 each, were sold "as high as $12.50, making the price according to the pattern and not the quality of the robe. . . . The Indians would readily give $12.50 for the patterns they liked best." When other stores went bankrupt, Coffins bought them out "for from 25¢ to 40¢ on the dollar. We would go up into their buildings to put on a sale taking the full bolts of gingham, calico, etc. . . . and overalls and other articles down to our store, and bring some of our pointed toe shoes and stuff that we wanted to get rid of and put on a big sale with a big advertisement. . . . We had a white mule and a great big dog and used to have young Charlie Bartholet ride the mule around with a big banner that read, 'Everything is cheap at Coffin Brothers.' "[13]

H. Stanley Coffin remembered that "we were rustlers in those days and worked from six o'clock in the morning till eleven or twelve at night. . . . So we were bound to make a success, and did so and made lots of money." The Coffins were shrewd businessmen: "Business was run rather loosely and it was a survival of the fittest. I remember we would get Lyons' and Arbuckles coffee, sell it in packages at 25¢ a package and dump it into bins and sell it for 35¢ a pound, equivalent to a package . . . [After butter] started to smell badly and became unfit for sale . . . [a woman developed] the scheme of working it over as fresh milk and then bringing it back to us in very good shape, that is, quite salable and all right. The hotels used to buy large quantities of this butter from us."

The Coffins enjoyed their greatest success as Indian traders and opened their stores on Sundays, when Indians received their pay for working in the hop fields:

> *We would paint our faces and put on red or calico shirts, big cowboy hats, wear blankets and shawls and go at them in true Indian style. . . . We would accumulate a great big pile of perhaps half a carload of watermelons in front of the store, and with every purchase of $1 that the Indians made they would get a ticket entitling them to a watermelon. If trade got a little dull my brother Lester would jump on a horse bareback, ride up the Avenue in front of . . . the other stores and holler "Conie was tillicums owis cais slowitz, kie tom umwaetz, Coffin Broth-*

ers' store." Which was all meant to call their attention to Coffin Broth-
ers' store, where everything was cheap.[14]

By developing a specialized market for their wool and store goods,
the Coffin brothers were able to survive when others failed in a collapsing national economy. Other merchants were unable to escape their dependence on trade with farmers and livestock raisers, whose grain, mutton, beef, and wool sold for a loss in national and international markets.

Although Archie and Peter McGregor left merchandising to return
to the sheep trade, that business was also in trouble. Wool, unlike other
agricultural products, had traditionally been extended the protection of
a tariff. The passage of a "free wool" bill in 1893, during the Democratic
administration of Grover Cleveland, coincided with a drastic drop in the
value of western fleece. The McGregor brothers and other woolgrowers blamed the Democrats for their troubles, and "for many years after
Cleveland. . . . nearly all sheepmen were Republicans." But the Panic of
1893 was the major reason for the market collapse, and the role of "free
wool" in the price drop remains uncertain. Whatever the cause, the
depressed market conditions were readily evident.

When the wool prices fell, Miller Freeman of *The Ranch*, a local
trade journal, contended that Columbia Plateau sheepmen had been
"spoiled" by several years of large profits. He told them they would not
succeed as long as they watched "the tariffs on wool at Washington,
rather than keeping the burrs out of it at home." Freeman chided them
for "cussing 'Old Cleveland' and the democratic administration for the
depression" and claimed that the sheep raiser "refuses to take his medicine like a man." Free wool, argued Freeman, "is no bugbear to any
producer who is free from the influence of politicians." "Isn't there something supremely ridiculous in the idea of men who pasture their flocks
upon the public domain, beseeching congress to add to this pasturage
donation a tariff protection which results in a direct and heavy tax upon
the rest of their fellow citizens?" "There is a glorious possibility," a
writer for *The Ranch* claimed, "of making a handsome profit from
raising sheep even now."[15] But the optimistic predictions did little to
dispel the immediate gloom.

George McCredy, a Klickitat County woolgrower, described the
panic as a time when "a sheepman went to bed not knowing if he would
wake up a sheepman or sheepherder." Peter McGregor remembered that
"sheepmen were going broke all over the country." A Texas sheep raiser
later recalled that the panic had caused his partner to commit suicide:
"Wealth had been within his grasp after he'd waited for it to come to
him all his life; now he was faced with failure again, and poverty, and
the long trail back to success." One writer claimed that on the Columbia

Plateau "flocks of sheep wandered without a shepherd or anyone to claim ownership." Sheepmen near Hay Creek, Oregon, demonstrated their frustration about the poor markets by using wool to repair roads. Palouse country sheep raiser Phil Cox had a land contract on which he had already paid nine thousand dollars declared forfeited when he fell behind on payments. Cox recalled the difficult period: "The price of sheep and wool declined until there was no market for either. Land values started on a downward slide and continued until equities became liabilities." Sheepmen throughout the West found that "money was hard to get and banks were calling in their notes." William McGregor recalled a story that western sheepmen first began telling during the panic years: "A fellow sent his wool to Boston during the depression. When it arrived, it wasn't worth enough to pay the freight. His broker in Boston wired him and told him that he owed $150 to pay the freight. . . . [The sheepman] wired back and said 'I do not have $150. Am sending more wool.' " [16]

The McGregor Brothers partnership struggled to remain solvent. John McGregor had retained two bands of sheep after his brothers had sold out, and these were to serve as "the beginner of the industry" for the men. Archie and Peter began herding for other woolgrowers and then tended John's sheep, using their pay to regain an interest in the business. One-third of the livestock of the original tramp enterprise had to support the brothers at a time when markets were steadily growing worse. In 1892, John and Archie sold their wool "in the grease" (uncleaned) at from 12 to 15 cents, their ewes and lambs for $2.25 a head, and their fat wethers for $3.50, prices at which "a reasonable profit" could be made. Two years later the price of grease wool was 5 to 7 cents, lambs and ewes were almost unsalable, and wethers brought $1.25 to $1.50. Transportation alone absorbed more than 40 percent of the value of the clip. Sheepmen operated at a loss. The McGregor brothers dropped the wages of their herders from $40 to $25 per month and then were "forced to let out most" and do the herding themselves. [17]

Many woolgrowers, discouraged by heavy indebtedness and "free wool," sold their flocks at a sacrifice to outside buyers. Almost one hundred thousand sheep were shipped by rail or trailed eastward from the Umatilla area alone in 1893 and 1894. After reaching midwestern stockyards, many of these sheep "were slaughtered by droves and fed to hogs as the best way of realizing anything from them." The men who decided "that it is good policy to 'stay in' sheep" needed maximum lamb crops, heavy fleeces, and low death losses to have any hope of survival. They battled ticks, lice, maggots, internal parasites, scabies, and other diseases by treating sheep with turpentine, snuff, salt, or sulfur, or by burning corral fences "and everything [else] that has come in contact with the scabby sheep." But few could afford much winter feed. J. H. Smithson, a Kittitas County woolgrower, described the outlook in the fall of 1893:

> Speaking of my own case, and every sheepman's experience has been the same, last year I sold my clip for $3,600 without any trouble. This year the clip from the same band netted $1,260. Besides this the price of mutton is extremely low now; in fact it can scarcely be sold at any price. Contrast the price of wool last year, 15 cents, with the present price of 5 cents, and you can easily see the sheepmen cannot afford to feed, because, cheap as feed is, it does not take a sheep long to eat its head off. The sheepmen will naturally take chances and turn the animals into the hills. If the snow is not too deep, they will come out all right; but a deep, lasting snow will practically wipe them out.[18]

The winter of 1893–94 was described as "exceptionally favorable" for "the vast herds of wool bearers on the Washington and Oregon hills." Lamb crops were large, and sheepmen reported that ample spring forage meant "the bleaters will go upon the [summer] ranges this year in shape to do their best." The McGregor brothers, Duncan McAllister, William Peatross, and other sheepmen supplemented their meager income from the good wool clips by selling some of their wethers for mutton. Conditions were far worse in Texas and the Midwest, where drought left ewes weak and undernourished: "Instead of raising lambs, we had to kill them as they came, in order to save their mothers. . . . The acres about us were a stretch of dry dust, parched vegetation, and dead sheep."[19]

Both wool and mutton prices were at their lowest points in the history of the western range livestock industry, and the sheep businesses of the Columbia Plateau were in a precarious condition. Archie, Peter, and John McGregor had released the last of their crew by the fall of 1894. All three men herded. John also tended camp and Archie handled most of the cooking chores. By the end of September, they had moved the sheep out of the mountains and had set up their tents near Pullman. Archie wrote his wife, Nellie, urging her to be "contented and happy" and telling her "I feel at home herding again." He described his sheep tending work in two subsequent letters from the Pullman area.

> [October 14, 1894:] I am still at the old trade. Got 16 days in already. Wish I could buy some sheep but it takes money. Never mind, Nell, just so we are happy. We will work together and come out all right yet. I got a new pair of shoes and a pair of gum boots. Shoes $2. Gum boots

$4.50. . . . I have one pair of Drawyers [sic] full of holes I am going to use for rags to go around my feet when it gets wet.

It may be a month before we go below. The weather is fine here. I often wonder what you are doing and if you feel disheartened. You must feel cheery. . . . The happier a person is the healthier they are. I wish Nell you would read Fowler's works. . . . You could get an insite [sic] into a great many things of great importance. One of our sheep died, since I came up, that is $2. We will get squared up yet. . . . Very near all the farmers up here are worse off than nothing. The once rich men are the worst off. The rocks are the best yet.

[October 30, 1894:] It is not pleasant to live apart this way . . . [but] circumstances shapes things as they are and we must be contented, which is practically better than wealth. If we were wealthy and contented it would be better still. It would not be any use of us Saying that it would not be our luck and give up and not try. [We will not] let everything come and go as easy as Chas. Town and that outfit does. You must not think . . . that you are a burden to me Nellie . . . I love to work for you. What enjoyment would it be for me to work and not [have] one to enjoy it with me afterwards. . . . I do not aspire to be rich but to enjoy life as well as we conveniently can. I know you dearly love me and you help me a great deal more than you probably imagine. Encouragement from wives all over this country during these hard times is about all that stimulates men to work.

I do not know when we will start below. In about three days more we will move about four miles nearer. Then we will be about five miles north of Pullman. Three weeks may bring us to Rock Flat if there is grass there. It is no use going down until the grass grows. . . . I have only one dirty undershirt for you to wash yet. . . . Just changed on the 28th inst. Next time I expect will be at home . . . then I will have a bath also.

Nellie had suggested that her husband purchase or rent a farm. But Archie preferred to remain in the sheep business: "A person can get . . . [farms] up here easy enough and they are Sure of crops but there is not any money in it. There would not be anything in it down there unless we had a band of sheep and use[d] what we would raise for hay . . . [Furthermore] I do not know anything about farming. I do not think I can go through Colfax to see about renting a farm. We will have to keep moving with the sheep when we start. At the present prospects for wheat there would not be any money in it. . . . The Capitalists have a contraction of the Currency. . . ."

Archie's October 30, 1894, letter included a listing of credits and debits that indicate the marginal nature of the McGregor Brothers enterprise:

My bill since I came here is:

Taxes at Kendrick	$23.25	
Paid on lot at Portland	40.00	
Paid old bill at Moscow	71.35	
	$134.60	
My ⅓ — — — — — — — — — — —	44.87	$44.87
[Additional expenses included:]		
2 bucks [i.e. rams]		16.00
John running sheep to Nov. 1		50.00
Gum boots		4.50
1½ Suits Under wear		4.50
1 pair mitts		1.25
Stamps		.50
Medicine for cold		.50
Tobacco		.90
OverShoes		1.50
		$124.52
1 pair boots		4.00
Quite a Bill		$128.52

Here is what is paid on that bill:

Worked 15 days in Spring	$20.00
Cash to John	18.10
Pd. Geo Getty [herder]	7.50
Cash from wool and hides	18.80
1 months herding [for John]	40.00
	$104.40

$128.52
−104.40
Owe John— 24.12 *—yet*

If I do not draw any more next month we will Stand as follows:

[balance now due John]	$24.12
Payment on lot	6.66
running Sheep	10.00
Stubble	10.00
	$50.78
Months herding [for John]	40.00

Will owe John $10.78 by Dec. 1st. Will do well to be even with him by 1st Jan.

Will have about $200 worth of wool in spring and $1.50 for [each of the] ... *150 lambs* ... *I may sell 100 sheep if I can buy ewes with the money. I am going to Moscow to-day. See if I can sell 100 mutton at $2 each. Peter and John are out herding and it is raining. Hope you have lots of rain down there [i.e. on the winter range].*[20]

Archie hoped that his frugality would enable him to continue his $6.66 monthly payment on a lot in Kendrick, yet save enough money to repay a $24 debt to his brother in two months. But it was not enough to cut costs; credit was desperately needed. McGregor Brothers needed money to cover operating expenses. John, Peter, and Archie also needed more sheep, for earnings from the few thousand head they owned could hardly support them all, even during good times.

Peter McGregor remembered that the McGregors and other sheepmen who weathered the panic "were carried by the banks." The McGregor brothers were fortunate in having two men willing to finance their business. Archie visited his friend, Alfred Coolidge, a sheep raiser who headed the Second National Bank of Colfax, and was able to convince him to advance enough money to permit purchase of two additional bands of sheep. Ewes of excellent quality were for sale at depressed prices, and Coolidge and Archie were optimistic that market conditions would improve enough to allow the loan to be repaid. The McGregors used the capital to buy 4,600 sheep from a Craigmont, Idaho, woolgrower for two dollars a head. After paying back part of the loan, they signed a chattel mortgage for $5,480 to guarantee the balance. The McGregor brothers were also able to obtain loans to cover operating costs from Simon Dreifus, a Colfax merchant and vice president of a local bank. Dreifus, an acquaintance of the McGregors, admired Peter and Archie's efforts to repay the obligations of the ill-fated Pullman Hardware Company. In making his loan, Dreifus stipulated that Archie and Peter stay in the sheep business and abandon their efforts to become merchants. Dreifus also provided them with a team of horses, a wagon, and other necessities for the sheep business. Such arrangements were not unusual during the panic years. Credit was scarce, and when available, was provided by solvent bankers who knew the borrowers personally and "relied on the character and ability of their clients."[21]

Although the McGregors could obtain credit, they still needed to find rangeland for their sheep. Several factors contributed to a shortage of forage on the Columbia Plateau in the 1890's. During the 1880's, the inland region had become one of the nation's important wheat-producing areas, and much of the best grazing land had been taken over by wheat farmers. The acreage devoted to wheat increased sixfold between 1880 and 1890, and doubled again by the end of the century. Moreover, while wheat farmers claimed more and more of the land, several years of below-average precipitation reduced the productivity of the remaining range. The numbers of livestock using the open range increased. These circumstances caused a decline in the quality and quantity of lands suitable for livestock.[22]

In these circumstances, everyone wanted to place the blame elsewhere. Open range cattlemen and homesteaders who kept cattle complained loudly that sheep had "destroyed" the rangeland, that cattle did not like the "smell" of lands once occupied by sheep and would refuse to graze such areas, and that waterholes were "poisoned" by sheep. Cattleman A. J. Splawn blamed sheep for the introduction of alien "weeds," and claimed that heavy sheep grazing had ruined the native grasses. Sheepmen blamed cattle and wild cayuse horses for the damage done to the rangeland. Most of the arguments were either misleading or inaccurate. Perhaps H. L. Davis, in his novel *Honey in the Horn*, placed the blame as accurately as anyone. Davis blamed hogs for the damage: "Two legged ones who judging that somebody else would get the grass if they didn't, hustled in every class of stock they could lay hands on to eat it clean. . . . "

Many observers claimed that the Columbia Plateau rangeland had been permanently injured by "overgrazing." But reports of sere, desiccated grassland told more about the effects of summer heat and low rainfall than about range use. Federal botanist E. V. Wilcox described the difficulties of evaluating range conditions: "The effects observed as the result of overgrazing of one season may be only of a temporary nature, and . . . while the range may appear to have been left in a barren condition after the stock is removed, these same conditions may nevertheless have prevailed essentially unchanged ever since an accurate knowledge of western grazing land was obtained. The failure to recognize the great natural powers of recuperation of the arid range country has led to many unjustifiable assertions regarding the destruction of the range grasses."[23]

The disagreements among livestock raisers and the damage caused by indiscriminate grazing resulted in belated attempts to conserve and manage western grazing grounds and forest ranges. Congress enacted a law that set aside millions of acres of land as "forest reserves" (later known as "national forests") in 1891, and restrictions on the use of timber and grass followed. The Cascade Mountains reserves in Washington and Oregon were declared off limits to sheep in 1894. Many sheepmen defied the ban and continued to use their accustomed summer pastures. But in the summer of 1896, federal marshals, "acting under special instructions from the Attorney General of the United States," arrested and jailed sheepherders and sheep owners who defied the restrictions. Restraining orders were issued to enjoin several other wool-growers from using these mountainous grazing grounds. The injunctions were discontinued several months later, and government scientists were sent to evaluate the condition of the forest ranges. But it was apparent that sheepmen would no longer be allowed unregulated access to Pacific Northwest forest reserves. Residents of Klickitat County in south central Washington complained to the state legislature that sheepmen with winter headquarters in Oregon and summer grazing grounds in Washington "have been known to utterly ignore the rights of farmers to sufficient range for a few milch cows" and to "tramp out the grass and spoil the range for home stock." The legislature passed a "quarantine" law effectively designed to prevent eighty thousand sheep from crossing the state boundary into Klickitat County.[24]

Some sheepmen took ingenious steps to avoid the new restrictions. Malcolm McLennan, after wintering ten thousand sheep in eastern Oregon, took advantage of a loophole in the quarantine law and "chartered a special steamer to transport his sheep down the Columbia into Skamania county" where the quarantine was not legally binding. McLennan then trailed his sheep to the Klickitat summer range. *Ranche and Range* editor Miller Freeman commented that McLennan's plan "proves him a true son of his strategical Scottish highland ancestors." Another Columbia Plateau sheepman, Alex McAllister, visited an island in the Bering Sea in the futile hope of finding suitable rangeland. In central Washington, sheriff's officials reported that "the sheepmen usually try to evade the officer and sometimes by stealth and in the night drives have been known to get by certain stations of lookout." Yet despite the attempts to find new rangeland and to avoid local regulations, the sheepmen found their migratory travels increasingly restricted. Columbia Plateau sheep raiser Thomas Drumheller, Jr., noted that cattlemen were less troubled by grazing restrictions: "The cattlemen never had to lease range like the sheepman. [The sheep raiser] . . . had a herder out there that the sheriff could come out to and take into jail. It's pretty hard to drag one of those steers into jail."

Cattlemen and farmers had also agitated successfully for special state laws to limit the sheepmen's access to the grasslands. The Idaho legislature twice tried to limit sheep grazing, first with a statute limiting importation of sheep into this state; later with a law that prohibited sheep pasturing within two miles of a residence. But a law that had been on the statute books of Washington for several years was to cause more trouble: Sheepmen who pastured their stock on unfenced private lands without permission were guilty of trespassing. Federal Judge C. H. Hanford explained the reasons for the special statute: "Whether founded in truth or not, the belief is prevalent in this state that, wherever flocks of sheep are herded, the land is injured for grazing purposes, and the interests of cattlemen and other farmers have prevailed with the legislature."[25]

In 1895, Northern Pacific Railroad officials learned of "the peculiar trespassing law that was in effect in the state of Washington." Railroad Land Agent E. F. Benson recalled that the corporation alertly took advantage of a law "designed to prevent the sheep from trespassing on unfenced land of homestead claimants," using it to restrict grazing on five million acres of unclaimed railroad land in Washington. The railroad was particularly interested in controlling grazing on two million acres of alternate sections in the Palouse, Scablands, Big Bend, and Yakima areas; hundreds of thousands of sheep were trailed to these important winter ranges every year. The Northern Pacific developed a grazing lease program for the Columbia Plateau. This system would have an effect later on open range livestock raisers in many western areas, for it served as a model for similar leases of railroad lands in other states, a leasing program for forest reserves, and a proposed leasing arrangement for all rangeland remaining in the public domain.[26]

Northern Pacific Land Department officials in Tacoma and St. Paul heard of the bitter competition for railroad range in 1893, when complaints were received from the Channeled Scablands, winter headquarters for the McGregor brothers and several other sheepmen. Settlers in the area blamed the sheepmen for decimating the range and asked the railroad to evict them, claiming that "if something was not done to improve their condition they would be obliged to give up their places and go elsewhere to live." The area, once primarily devoted to open range sheep production, had been rapidly settled by homesteaders, many of whom were small-scale cattle raisers. These new residents complained bitterly about the destruction of the range. Newspaper articles written by correspondents from the area complained that "the sheep threaten to eat up every spear of grass in sight" and that sheepmen had taken "absolute possession" of the range. Cattlemen in the early 1890's formed an organization that declared the area off limits to sheep. An imaginative correspondent later claimed that "some sheep camps were burned and gun plays were quite frequently indulged in, although no one was seriously hurt, and the stockmen carried the day and enforced their notice." The report was inaccurate, for it was the McGregors, Joseph Escallier, Phil Cox, and other sheepmen who remained in control of the bunchgrass hills. Yet the influx of additional stock made the sheepmen's search for rangeland more difficult. In 1893, Archie McGregor sardonically described the competition for grass as "great times in the rocks." In the same year, when a horse raiser named Moore ran his stock through a band of sheep owned by Hewitt and killed 200 of them, a Northern Pacific official called a meeting and successfully worked out a compromise.[27]

Disputes continued to flare up sporadically in 1895 and 1896. Cattlemen complained that the presence of sheep bands on the ranges again had "the customary result that not a vestige of grass is being left on the range for cattle." Once again reports were received that cattlemen had formed an organization to drive off their opponents, and it was also said that the sheep raisers would retaliate. "Several efforts have been made to force the sheepmen to vacate," a local resident claimed, "but they have successfully resisted all efforts in this line and still hold the fort." Reports were circulated that more than a thousand tons of hay had been burned and that confrontations were "of daily or nightly occurrence." The reports were exaggerated. Phil Cox acknowledged that three of his haystacks, totaling thirty tons, had been burned, but denied that there "is any serious difference between the stockmen and the sheepmen as classes." Another sheepman, Sam Blue, admitted that his cabin had been burned, but described as preposterous "the statement that it was with difficulty that he saved a band of 1000 sheep from cremation." A *Spokesman-Review* correspondent investigated the rumors of "an extensive and deadly war . . . between sheepmen and cattlemen," and found that the destruction of the haystacks and cabin had been the result of "a family row" that "arose over a practical joke two of the Cox boys attempted to play" on a neighbor woman.

The skirmishes for "the rocks" grasslands, like most of the western range "wars," had involved dire threats, scattered property damage, and little actual violence. Cattlemen had marked out "deadlines" across which sheep were forbidden to pass, in the scabrock and Klickitat regions and on the Blue Mountain summer ranges. Farmers who sold hay to sheepmen sometimes received threatening letters, with matches enclosed as a warning of incendiary reprisal. Over the next several years, there were scattered sheep camp burnings and a few bands of sheep were shot, clubbed, poisoned, or driven over precipices. In 1896, the Seattle *Times* carried a sensational report about a desperate range battle in eastern Oregon in which three sheepmen and two cattlemen were killed. But the report was probably inaccurate and certainly atypical.[28]

The increasingly bitter struggle for the winter ranges of the Channeled Scablands prompted John McGregor to purchase 120 acres of land on Rattlesnake Flat, several miles north of the main McGregor winter range, in May 1895. The land was acquired from Alfred Coolidge, a Colfax banker, for the large price of one thousand dollars—more than eight dollars an acre. Colfax merchant-banker Simon Dreifus loaned enough money to enable McGregor Brothers to fence the new location. The area, unlike the lands to the south, was not well suited to sheep production, but John's 120-acre purchase included one of the few water holes. Should the McGregors be unable to acquire sufficient pasturage in the contested lands to the south, the new area might provide an emergency location for their flocks. But even this precautionary action did little to ease the crisis caused by the decision of the Northern Pacific Railroad to prosecute the sheepmen for trespassing on alternate sections of railroad-owned land.

After receiving reports in 1895 that "bad blood exists" between the sheepmen and cattle-raising settlers and that "its lands in that section are being denuded of verdure," railroad officials sought "to put a stop to the depredations of the sheepmen." Northern Pacific Land Commissioner William Phipps instructed Western Land Agent Thomas Cooper to "prepare a good case, putting in the field if necessary, some reliable person or persons to obtain evidence of the trespass by sheep owners on our lands, then bring action under the [trespass] statute and see if we cannot collect damages or compel purchase of some of our lands."[29]

But Phipps soon realized that "the present conditions of the markets for wool and mutton" had left most sheepmen financially unable to purchase land. Railroad officials decided to adopt a leasing system for grazing lands. Phipps, Cooper, and local agent E. F. Benson cited three reasons for adopting the new policy: the desire to prevent the destruction of the forage, "the direct effect of which . . . was the reduction of railway traffic"; the need to secure revenue to pay taxes on the unsold lands; and most important, the wish "to demonstrate the increased value of the land when under individual control and thereby stimulate its purchase by the lessees or others."[30] The new policy was of crucial importance to the McGregor brothers and other livestock raisers of the Columbia Plateau.

As a first step in implementing the new system, railroad attorneys applied to Judge Cornelius H. Hanford of the U.S. Circuit Court in April 1896 for a temporary restraining order enjoining Joseph Escallier; Leon Jaussaud; John, Peter, and Archie McGregor; J. B. Poe; and thirteen other of "the most prominent sheep owners" of Adams, Whitman, Franklin, Columbia, Garfield, and Walla Walla counties from grazing their sheep upon railroad lands. Although Land Commissioner Phipps stated a year later that wild cayuse horses had been the "curse of Eastern Washington" and that the intensive, unregulated grazing practices of all livestock owners had caused damage to the most convenient ranges, the complaint filed by railroad attorneys could have been written by the most irate cattleman. The defendants, the complaint alleged,

*wrongfully and unlawfully drove upon said lands . . . great numbers of
sheep in roaming flocks . . . [thus causing] great and irreparable injury
and damage. . . . The bands of sheep which the defendants are herding
and pasturing upon said lands in ranging and roaming from place to
place thereon and eating and trampling the grass therefrom, destroy
completely the already scanty growths of grass. . . . The sheep in feeding pull and tear out much of said grass by the roots and poison and
kill what they do not eat. . . . Said lands are left and remain stripped
and bare of grass and utterly ruined and valueless. . . . Wherever sheep
browse the lands are rendered worthless for cattle grazing or other
purposes.*

The defendants could not be sued for damages, the complaint stated,
because they "are financially insolvent, irresponsible, and unable to
respond for the injury done by said use. . . . The migratory character of
defendants renders it impracticable to pursue . . . with suits of damages
in various counties of the State over which they roam, even were they
able to respond in damages, which your orator believes they are not."
Northern Pacific attorneys sought, and were granted, an order enjoining
the defendants "from feeding, herding, pasturing, or keeping any sheep"
on the railroad lands. U.S. Marshall James Baker and his deputy Frank
Parker spent a week in April delivering the temporary restraining order
and a summons to the sheepmen. On April 16th, John, Archie, and Peter
McGregor received copies of the documents "at their sheep camp on
Snake River in Whitman County."[31]

The seriousness of the order was obvious to the recipients. The railroad lands comprised alternate sections of an eighty-mile-wide strip
through the Columbia Plateau that included most of the favorable wintering locations used by the transhumant sheepmen. To be barred from
the railroad sections meant that they were also excluded from the in-
tervening sections in the public domain. Sheep owners cried prejudice,
claiming they had as much right to the land as did the cattlemen. But
cattle raisers had successfully pushed for a trespass statute directed against
sheep, and the state law did not include restrictions on the grazing of
livestock other than sheep. The sheep owners contended that the Northern Pacific action was instituted because they had "been shipping all their
sheep to eastern markets over the OR & N."

Upon receipt of their summons, the sheepmen, by mutual agreement,
"went to Walla Walla and employed as their attorney the attorney of
the Union Pacific Railroad Company, Mr. [Lester S.] Wilson, who had
received instructions from the headquarters of the Union Pacific freight
department to look after the interests of the sheep men, as also being

the interests of the company, as concerning wool shipments." The sheep-men appeared in court on May 6, 1896, to contest the order restraining them from grazing on Northern Pacific lands. A demurrer to the rail-road complaint filed by attorney Wilson was rejected. Archie Mc-Gregor remembered that the railroad officials had packed the courtroom with cattlemen prepared to testify about the destruction of the range caused by sheep grazing. A correspondent reported that "the sheep men offered evidence to show that it would be impossible for them to vacate the lands before June 15, which time the attorney agreed to leave them unmolested. This will give them time to shear and get the herds to the summer mountain ranges." The case was continued until the fall session of the court, and the restraining order was to remain in force until then. Although some of the sheepmen claimed that their talk about instituting a boycott of shipping via the Northern Pacific "had an effect on bring-ing the attorney to make the terms he did," the railroad had planned to delay action on the case in order to develop and implement a leasing system.[32]

The victory apparently belonged to the cattlemen, for action had finally been taken to restrict the migratory herding practices of the tramp sheepmen. Local railroad land agent E. F. Benson met in Sprague with members of the "Stock Grazing and Protective Association" to discuss the "depredations" of the sheep raisers. He recommended that the cattlemen combat the nomadic sheep operators "by fair means, in conjunction with efforts of the railroad company, rather than by putting yourselves in the attitude of lawbreakers." The cattlemen and the rail-road agreed to give the sheep raisers a driveway to the Northern Pacific siding at Sprague, in conjunction with the plan to use that location for shearing corrals and a major wool shipping center. They also agreed to post the following note:

PUBLIC NOTICE!

To All Owners and Herders of Sheep
You are hereby notified not to herd or graze your
sheep north of a line running west from the head
of Walled Lake to Cow Creek, and east from the
head of Walled Lake to Rock Creek.

By order of the Stock Grazing and Protective Association.

Although the Northern Pacific had given nominal support to the edict, the sheepmen paid little heed to this attempt by the cattle raisers to limit their domain.

The trespass case was a more serious matter, and the sheepmen returned to Walla Walla to attend a conference, where railroad officials explained the policy of the company and the details of the proposed leasing system. John McGregor told those attending that the restraining order would force him to go out of business. E. F. Benson explained that the railroad had no desire to evict the sheepmen—it merely wished them to agree to lease the lands being occupied. John McGregor considered the scheme and on July 1, 1896, agreed to sign Northern Pacific Grazing Lease #1, an agreement covering 22,359 acres. The lease was to run ten years. McGregor was to pay $200 the first year and $400 annually thereafter. The agreement covered grazing lands along the Snake and lower Palouse rivers and gave the McGregor Brothers the legal right to continue using the winter range upon which they had run sheep for several years. Certain clauses required the lessee to ship wool and mutton over Northern Pacific rail lines, stipulated that "he will not at any time overgraze said land," and permitted him to fence the leasehold. In October of the same year, John agreed to purchase from the railroad an additional 2,755 acres of land for seventy-five cents an acre.[33] The land purchased included four strategic sections of land in which were located the five best watering places and two of the most favorable sites for lambing camps in the entire area.

Other sheepmen with winter quarters in the six counties covered by the restraining order began taking steps to acquire leaseholds: Phil Cox of Hay leased 9 sections; H. F. Troub of Colfax acquired 10; Leon Jaussaud of Walla Walla, 13; Alex Smith and J. W. Barr of Hay, 24; Jacob and Hans Harder of Washtucna, 12; Joseph Escallier, Lacrosse, 8; J. T. Person and J. B. Poe of Endicott, 12; and Duncan McGillivray and Thomas Durry of Ritzville, 15. Within 8 months, 110 agreements were signed, covering over 300,000 acres. Adrien Magallon of Walla Walla refused to make a lease agreement, and railroad lawyers sought—and received—a restraining order against him in May 1897. Thomas Cooper, Western Land Agent, reported to Northern Pacific Land Commissioner William Phipps in September on the dispute with Magallon and the progress of the leasing system:

> *This lease is in final outcome of a quarrel that we have had with Magallon extending over a year. Magallon is a Frenchman and has about fifteen thousand sheep and to a certain extent is recognized as a leader of the sheepmen of that nationality. He preemptorily refused to make a lease with us and we commenced legal proceedings against him and secured an injunction. He finally, at the suggestion of Levi Ankeny, a banker in Walla Walla, came here to see me and as a result of the talk we had entered into the enclosed lease. We will now drop the legal proceedings,*

and we have about cleared up all our grazing land in the district between the . . . [railroad] and the southern boundary of the grant. What little we have left is gradually being picked up a piece at a time. . . . We have a large number of sheepmen yet waiting for us to find ranges for them, so that really our difficulty now in the districts in which we operated [the leasing system] is to find sufficient range for all the sheepmen.[34]

In 1897, the railroad land agents began to expand their grazing lease program to other railroad-owned lands on the Columbia Plateau. Northern Pacific land agent E. F. Benson mailed notices in July 1897 to sheepmen of Yakima, Kittitas, and Klickitat counties in central Washington, informing them that he was planning to parcel out rangeland in that area. The Washington Wool Growers' Association called a meeting in North Yakima and signed an agreement to "stand together and refuse to accept the company's proposition." Benson recalled that "the sheepmen had their session all day and resolved their momentous resolution, pledging the officials of the organization their financial support to fight this proposition. They declared that they would not lease any lands from the railroad unless the railroad would agree to keep off their land horses, cattle, or other trespassing livestock. It was really a most humorous resolution and when I was called to talk upon it, I made nothing but the pleasantest references to the people." But Benson also informed the woolgrowers "that if they would not accept the land alloted the company would allow the land to go to outside sheepmen. . . . The meeting broke up about 10 o'clock that night, and before midnight I had . . . received checks for down payments for three of the most important ranges in the Rattle Snake hills."[35]

Within the next few years, the railroad leasing system was expanded to include more than 1.5 million acres of winter rangeland on the Columbia Plateau. Additional lands were purchased on long-term contracts. Many sheepmen alertly acquired large leaseholds: W. H. Peatross of North Yakima leased 31 sections of land; Alex McAllister, from the same area, leased 24; Charles McAllister, 21; Coffin Brothers, 23; George Prior, 34; George Drumheller of Ephrata, 84; Antone Vey and Smythe Brothers, both of Pendleton, Oregon, leased 19 and 58 respectively; Cunningham Sheep Company of Pilot Rock, Oregon, 26; and Frank Rothrock of Spokane, 14. Malcolm McLennan, who had evaded the Klickitat County quarantine law earlier, agreed to lease 12 sections but was found to be occupying an additional 51 and was charged back rent. There is no record of any Columbia Plateau range sheep operation that remained in business for more than a few years without acquiring winter grazing grounds from the railroad.

Many of the 777 leasing agreements entered into by the railroad were with small farmers and ranchers and covered only a section or two. But seldom did open range cattlemen lease large acreages. Many cattle raisers had already gone out of business by the time the railroad plan was implemented. Others doubted the effectiveness of the Northern Pacific plan or expected it to limit sheep grazing, yet continue to give cattle raisers free access to the unenclosed range. James M. ("Uncle Jim") Kennedy of Hooper, the Wenas Cattle Association of North Yakima, and T. S. ("Lord") Blyth of Coulee City were among the few cattle raisers to acquire leaseholds. Blyth, who claimed to be the son of an English aristocrat and was said to receive a stipend from his father, signed the only extensive cattle leases—in 1896 he agreed to lease 29 sections, and he entered short-term agreements later to lease 32 and 41 sections. Much of Blyth's land was later to become part of the 110,000-acre Drumheller sheep ranch (and Kennedy's land was purchased by sheepman "Jimmy" Richardson).

The trespass law designed to restrict the tramp sheepmen had forced many woolgrowers to acquire land through lease or purchase. Veteran Columbia Plateau wool buyer Charles Brune of Yakima commented on the results of the restrictions placed on the sheepmen:

> *Ninety percent, at least ninety percent, of the rangeland in eastern Oregon and Washington was put together by sheepmen not cattlemen. The cattlemen, when they had to start buying land, well, by then the sheepmen seemed to outbid 'em or get the land in their possession first. There were sheep ranches from the Cascade Mountains along the Columbia and along every river. Along the Deschutes River in Oregon, the John Day River, the Snake River, and well, all the rivers in [eastern] Washington. I can remember the time when there were no real cattle ranches in the State of Washington.*[36]

By the end of the decade, sheep outnumbered cattle on the Columbia Plateau ranges by almost a million head. Cattle had a much higher value per animal, however, and the remaining 137,000 head were an important source of income for many settlers. The combination of financial panic, depleted rangeland, and the implementation of the leasing system had forced the large range operators out of business. Ben Snipes, once the owner of tens of thousands of cattle, saw his last 1,500 head sold at a bankruptcy sale, and by 1897 was preparing to be "one of the 'boys' in the Klondike rush next spring." When Snipes' former partner, H. H. Allen, sold his last 500 cattle, *Ranche and Range* reported that "the last band [i.e., herd of cattle] of any importance in Central Washington" was gone and that the largest remaining herd was one of 300 head. "Year by year," a *Rural Northwest* correspondent reported in 1898, "the lines are closing in upon the range cattlemen." The range cattle business "may come again, but barbed wire and sheep will have made such inroads that the area of free range will be but a shadow of its former self."[37]

By leasing and purchasing large amounts of land, many sheepmen were able to continue their operations on the scale of former years. The sheep trespass law and the railroad injunction had forced them to abandon their "tramp" open range practices. The woolgrowers who decided to lease railroad lands not only gained control of large acreages for small rental fees, they also gained de facto control of alternate sections of public domain. In effect they doubled their range. The Public Lands Commission later reported that the Northern Pacific leasing program had replaced "a disorderly, gregarious, wasteful, and costly system of harvesting the natural grass products of the region by an orderly, safe, economical, and productive system." The days of unregulated livestock grazing were rapidly nearing an end. "The stock raiser with vision" leased railroad land or purchased "waste stretches" of government land to provide for his animals. "Those who have been too slow to realize the changed conditions have found themselves without range land, and for the most part the men have been compelled to go out of stock raising as a business."[38]

But even those sheepmen who had taken steps to purchase or lease land had a tenuous hold, at best, on their sheep pastures. Tramp sheepmen, accustomed to operating with few expenses, large numbers of sheep, and only meager additional assets, entered a period in which vastly increased capital outlay was to become necessary for grazing lands, fencing, improved stock, and better supervision and care of the flocks. The Panic of 1893 had brought three years of critically low wool and mutton prices and had forced the sheep raisers to struggle for survival. Sheepmen were in a poor position to make the transition from tramp operations to a system in which they leased or owned their rangeland.

John McGregor had gained temporary control of more than 25,000 acres of rangeland that could serve as the nucleus for a large McGregor Brothers sheep ranching operation. Only 120 acres had been paid for, however, by the fall of 1896. John had been able to raise $200 to pay the first installment of the grazing lease; but the fee was to double in 1897. In October of that year, he signed a long-term contract to purchase four sections of land crucial to the control of the best portion of the winter range. But he could not meet the $407 obligation. His brothers, Archie and Peter, could provide little financial assistance, for both had lost money in town lot speculation and had invested heavily in the bankrupt Pullman Hardware Company. In fact, the two men were unable to pay a $28 tax bill on some of the property they had purchased earlier in Pullman.[39] A chattel mortgage for $5,480 on 4,600 McGregor sheep was due on demand of Alfred Coolidge and the Second National Bank of Colfax. Peter and Archie owed additional money to Simon Dreifus. The next few years would be critical to the survival of McGregor Brothers and other Columbia Plateau sheep businesses.

Chapter 4

"The Changed Times Call for Changed Methods"

MCGREGORS AS LAND BROKERS

AND

"THE SHEEP KINGS OF THE PALOUSE COUNTRY"

"Stockmen who continually proclaim that there is no longer any profit in their business, should sell out and give place to men who know that such enterprise, properly followed, is as profitable as ever, only that the changed times call for changed methods." *Ranche and Range*, 1897

"Every season sees many old-time flock owners on the range quit the business. . . . Not that the old plan was unprofitable or unpopular, but . . . the changing conditions have made it no longer possible. . . . What the future of the range industry will bring is an open question."

American Sheep Breeder, 1903

"The new method of handling sheep is entitled to be called the new sheep industry."   *Rural Northwest*, 1898[1]

The McGregor Brothers partnership, crippled by the decline of the open range and by the Panic of 1893, began the 1896–1905 period with very little capital, a few bands of sheep, and some newly acquired railroad grazing leases. Forced into a hectic struggle for available rangeland, and evicted from winter pastures by court order, John McGregor had boldly entered into several agreements to lease and purchase land. But loans were falling due, land contracts remained unpaid, and Archie and Peter had only recently completed bankruptcy proceedings. Yet a striking change occurred in the nature of the McGregor operations within the next decade. The McGregor Brothers, a partnership of four after the arrival of younger brother Alex in 1900, purchased and fenced more than thirty thousand acres of the best winter rangeland on the Columbia Plateau and leased an even larger area of summer pasture in the northern Idaho mountains. The partnership took steps to improve the care of their 15,000–20,000 sheep by acquiring a capable crew of employees, adopting systematic patterns of rangeland use, and raising more than a thousand acres of wheat for use as winter feed.

The dramatic growth of the McGregor sheep business occurred during a period of transformation for Columbia Plateau agriculture. The region was rapidly being developed and settled and land prices rose sharply, trebling and quadrupling in a decade in many of the 22 counties of the inland area. The Panic of 1893 had temporarily slowed the pace of settlement, but by the late nineties farmers were again moving westward, reaching the arid lowlands of the Big Bend and Umatilla, where the annual rainfall was ten inches or less. By 1905, the last few open range livestock raisers were gone. Federal botanist W. C. Barnes noted that these nomads "had used the public domain so many years without oversight or supervision that they could not grasp the fact that a new era in the western grazing ranges had come about." Even the sheepmen who leased or purchased land had difficulties, for they found that under the existing methods of operation, the earning capacity of rangeland was too small to make such investment profitable. To be successful, the new landowner would need to build fences, improve his breeds of stock, market better grades of wool and mutton, and refine procedures for efficient livestock handling. The changed conditions forced many livestock owners out of business. D. W. Meinig comments that the eastern Washington stockmen of the 1890's, "his ranks reduced and squeezed upon a dwindling portion of his old rangelands, knew that he had to look back to view his expansive years."[2]

But those who looked forward and adapted to the new circumstances could begin building stable livestock enterprises. A few of the most successful sheepmen were able to build livestock businesses far more extensive in scale than their open range operations of previous years. Several sheep raisers who had acquired railroad land were able to continue tending large flocks during this period, among them Max, Jacob, and Hans Harder of Kahlotus; George and Jesse Drumheller of Ephrata; Robert A. Jackson of Dayton; Arthur, Lester, and Stanley Coffin of Yakima; and the McGregor brothers of Hooper. The McGregor Brothers sheep business, a small, marginal enterprise in 1896, provided dramatic evidence of the expansion possible during this period of change.

John McGregor, the only one of the McGregors to remain in the sheep business during the 1890's depression, realized that the most important immediate task was the acquisition of land. In 1895 he bought the first grazing land for the partnership, paying eight times the prevailing rate of a dollar an acre for a 120-acre tract in Adams County. The land was wisely chosen and well worth the high cost, for it surrounded the largest of the only two waterholes on the southern portion of Rattlesnake Flat. Although this area was less suited to sheep production than the well-watered canyons of the Channeled Scabland range already used by the McGregors, when fenced it provided an assured source of water and feed. But a year later, the McGregors and other tramp sheepmen were enjoined from trespassing on all Northern Pacific lands in eight eastern Washington counties. To make use of acquisitions, such as the Rattlesnake Flat tract, that were surrounded by checkerboard sections of railroad land, some method of access had to be established. The McGregors had to lease land or move their winter quarters to the arid Big Bend, where the leasing system had not yet been enforced. Although he and his brothers were operating with mortgaged sheep and very limited capital, John McGregor acted quickly in order to get his choice of the railroad land. He agreed to pay $200 the first year and $400 for the remainder of the ten-year lease for more than 22,000 acres of winter range already occupied by McGregor sheep. Because the leased land enclosed and prevented access to alternate sections of public domain, the McGregors had gained de facto control of almost 45,000 acres. The range was worth the gamble, for it continued to offer the advantages that had attracted the McGregors to the area in the 1880's—good "strong" grass cover, generally mild winters, numerous sources of water, and sheltered valleys and canyons.[3]

Northern Pacific officials were eager to sell (or, if necessary, lease) additional Pacific Northwest grazing lands whenever possible. The railroad needed operating capital: The corporation had been placed in receivership in 1896, and the U.S. Supreme Court had ruled that unimproved railroad land was subject to taxation. President Mellen and Land Commissioner Phipps regarded much of the Columbia Plateau range as "wild lands, utterly unprofitable," and decided "the sooner we can dispose of them for grazing or other purposes the better." By selling quickly and at low prices, the land could be taken off the tax rolls and increased railroad traffic could be generated. John McGregor took advantage of the opportunity and entered into several additional contracts for railroad land. In the fall of 1896, he agreed to pay seventy-five cents an acre for 2,755 acres of land adjacent to the northern portion of the grazing lease. The new agreement covered strategic sections of land that contained five important lakes and several sheltered locations ideally suited for wintering sites and lambing camps. During the following year, John agreed to purchase 5,440 acres of land on Rattlesnake Flat, adjacent to the land he had acquired in 1895. The new contract included another waterhole and gave McGregor Brothers ownership of the two major water sources in the southern portion of that Adams County prairie. During the next few years, John signed Northern Pacific grazing leases 192, 290, and 297, each requiring a twenty- to twenty-five-dollar annual payment for sections of land situated along the periphery of the McGregor range at locations where outside access to areas of federal domain could be eliminated.[4]

The ambitious series of land contracts gave John McGregor and his brothers nominal control of an area of range twenty-one miles long and seventeen miles wide. But the leases and purchases were of little value until the McGregors made improvements on the land. The newly acquired property needed to be fenced in order to protect it from roving bands of cattle, sheep, and horses. Several thousand dollars' worth of barbed wire and other fencing material would be necessary for such a project, and the McGregor brothers were unable to consider such expenditures until their financial resources improved. Living up to the obligations of the lease and purchase agreements was in itself a difficult task. John McGregor had been able to delay making the initial payment on grazing lease #1—the contract that covered the 23,000-acre nucleus of the winter range—by agreeing to ship wool and mutton on the Northern Pacific rail lines. Although finally able to make the first payment of $200, he and his brothers had difficulty raising the $400 second-year fee. By April 1897, John had convinced Land Commissioner William Phipps and Western Land Agent Thomas Cooper to lower that year's rental by $100. The first payment on John's contract to purchase 2,755 acres adjoining the leasehold—$344 principal and $103 interest—was due in October 1896. But despite letters requesting payment in October and April of the following year, John and his brothers were unable to pay. Railroad officials agreed to wait until June 15, when income received from the wool clip would become available.[5]

Even more dangerous than the financial crisis was the threat that local railroad agents might sell the lower Palouse River lands covered in the original grazing lease. The terms of the lease did not specifically preclude the sale of the land to other parties, and the railroad company sent a "waterhole appraiser" to the area to determine the value of the rangeland. An effort was made to convince John, Archie, and Peter to purchase the land at fifty cents per acre. Although willing to make such a purchase, the three brothers could not obtain funds for the down payment. Other offers were solicited, the highest of which was ten cents an acre by a man from the nearby town of Riparia. The McGregor brothers had herded sheep on the land for several years and realized what the railroad's appraiser did not—that several lakes were included within the leasehold. They knew, therefore, that the land was worth far more than the asking price and were determined to retain control somehow. The three finally proposed to pay two and a half times the original asking price of fifty cents after five more years of leasing. Archie McGregor remembered that "the deal was closed with a handshake as the only contract."[6] By stretching their meager assets as far as possible and by postponing payment of land contracts, the McGregor Brothers business was able to remain in operation temporarily. But the McGregors had staked their business survival on the prospect of a good year in 1897.

Sheepmen throughout the Columbia Plateau—both those who continued to employ "coyote" open range practices and, more particularly, those who had begun to invest in winter rangeland—desperately needed good lamb crops, large wool clips, and a reversal of the disastrous commodity prices of the previous four years. Reports from lambing camps in March and April were encouraging. E. F. Benson, a Northern Pacific land agent, visited the McGregor Brothers' and several other woolgrowers' sheep ranges and reported that the sheepmen "have had remarkable success during the lambing season this spring," with lamb crops equal to 103–115 percent of ewes. Benson also noted that sheepmen were able to sell their mutton at prices "higher than for many years past." In the Yakima Valley, crops of 90–105 percent caused sheep raisers of that section, as well, to rejoice "over uniformly good returns." The wool clip—still the most important source of income for the sheepmen—was reported to have "turned out unusually large this year." Nelson Mars, in charge of a crew of sixteen shearers operating on the Columbia Plateau, reported in May that he "has more shearing in sight than ever before." Mars' busy crew was said to have broken the state shearing record twice within a week, first by shearing 2,200 head in one day, then by clipping 1,578 sheep in only half a day. The large wool harvest sold well, with prices as high as twelve and a half cents, more than double 1896 prices. A tariff bill, designed to protect sheepmen from competition with inexpensive Australian wool through an eleven-cents-per-pound duty on raw foreign fleece, was before Congress in 1897. Public knowledge of this pending legislation, according to President E. Y. Judd of the Pendleton Woolen Mills, resulted in a "buying wave [which] swept over the country based purely on the prospects for the tariff."[7]

Columbia Plateau sheepmen were enthusiastic about the improved financial conditions and became convinced that their business was "destined to make great strides." In July 1897, *Ranche and Range* reported that "the tariff bill has been signed by the president and is now a law and the sheepmen of the Northwest confidently expect a return of the old time 50 percent dividends." Yakima sheepman Hugh Gray explained his financial position to the editor of the same paper with "a sly wink, a droll smile, and a merry jingling of the yellow gold in his jeans." The *Rural Northwest* in 1897 carried a report claiming that sheepmen "can live off the 'fat of the land' if they want to." Miller Freeman of *Ranche and Range* described the new circumstances facing sheepmen: "The funds realized from this year's yield will enable them to pay off all back debts and leave them on Easy Street, with every indication of remaining in that delightful thoroughfare for some time to come."[8]

The general market conditions for agricultural products, both nationally and locally, were indeed improving. Freeman reported that Columbia Plateau farmers found "wheat jumping up a cent a day and the grain buyers falling all over each other to make offers." W. J. Spillman of Washington Agricultural College claimed that, because of "phenomenal" wheat yields and improving prices, "the Palouse Country is again like a mining camp, full of excitement, trade heavy, no idle men except from choice, and all the talk is wheat, wheat, wheat." Cattle prices had also advanced. But the heady optimism of the farm journals was more reflective of the changing mood than of the actual situation faced by sheepmen. The value of sheep and wool had returned to about the levels of 1893, thus providing badly needed income for woolgrowers who had suffered from four years of unfavorable business conditions. Despite the improved prices, sheep raisers faced a difficult period as they sought to adapt their operations to the changing circumstances on Columbia Plateau ranges.

Many coyote sheepmen repaid mortgages incurred during the panic, only to be forced to liquidate their holdings because "the large influx of settlers has caused so much of the vacant land of the country to be taken" that it was no longer feasible to own large bands of sheep. Men who had agreed to lease or purchase range had land contracts and mortgages to pay. The McGregors were overdue on land payments in the fall of 1896 and had their flocks pledged for mortgages "due on demand." Only the friendship and confidence of creditors Alfred Coolidge and Simon Dreifus and the sufferance of railroad officials enabled them to remain in business. The improved wool and mutton prices of 1897 came at a critical time, enabling the McGregors to fulfill their immediate contractual obligations and begin paying off their creditors.[9]

The McGregor brothers began taking steps to solidify their control of the newly acquired rangeland. Like other Columbia Plateau sheepmen, they were becoming aware that a more orderly pattern of range use was necessary. At the "First Convention of Sheepmen of the Pacific Northwest States," held in The Dalles in 1898, it was the consensus of Oregon,

Washington, Idaho, and Montana sheepmen that the availability of forage plants had become the "paramount question." The second annual meeting of the Pacific Northwest Wool Growers, held the following year in Pendleton, featured an address by James Withycombe of the Oregon Experiment Station. Withycombe told the sheepmen that "indiscriminate pasturing is destroying the grass" in many areas and advocated leasing, fencing, and other steps to restore the value of the winter range. John McGregor and several other sheepmen and cattlemen formed another group, the Northwest Livestock Association, in 1898. This organization's first meeting featured a keynote address by William J. Spillman, an enthusiastic, dynamic young lecturer from Washington Agricultural College, who discussed "range grasses" and efforts being made to develop new, hardy forage plants. Spillman and officials of the U.S. Department of Agriculture offered possible future improvements in range management.[10]

Before such experiments could be of use to them, the McGregor brothers had to stop other cattle and sheepmen from grazing on their winter range. First they fenced in the major watering holes. Landless cattlemen, deprived of watering places for their stock, reacted angrily. Fences were cut, and gates were torn out and thrown into the Snake River. But the fences were rebuilt and remained standing. The grasslands in such areas, depleted by the haphazard grazing practices of open range days, began to recuperate. The leasehold on Rattlesnake Flat in Adams County was unfenced and the land was barren, having been grazed to the ground by free-running livestock. Because they could not afford fencing costs, McGregor Brothers had to pay one man to take his horses away from their land and graze them elsewhere. The conflicts were less serious than those faced by "coyote" sheepmen of Morrow and Umatilla counties, who, cattlemen claimed, were continuing to "crowd out" cattle from the remaining unclaimed winter ranges. In 1897, for example, the Morrow County Wool Growers Association "made up a fund of $1000 for the purpose of sending detectives . . . to ferret out and prosecute the persons who have been shooting sheep." The following year the same group offered $500 "for the arrest and conviction of the person or persons who killed A. B. Thomson's sheep" and $100 "for the arrest and conviction of any person robbing and burning sheep camps."[11]

Sheepmen also had some difficulties in acquiring summer rangeland for their flocks. Conditions were particularly unsettled in the Cascade Mountains forest reserves. Uncertainty, confusion, and distrust had surrounded the federal forest grazing program since the enforcement of a ban on sheep grazing in the Cascades in 1896. A General Land Office ruling in 1897 allowed sheepmen to use the Oregon and Washington reserves but banned sheep grazing on all other forest reservations. But this was a temporary policy, and the grazing question remained unsettled. The first lengthy debate about grazing on federal forests occurred in the late 1890's and centered on whether sheep should be allowed on forest reserves in the Pacific Northwest mountains. Naturalist John Muir, members of the Oregon Alpine Club, and other conservationists claimed that sheep grazing retarded reforestation and denuded watersheds. Angered by the excesses of some of the "tramp" operators, they wanted sheep kept out of the Cascades permanently and unconditionally. They were opposed by Oregon sheepman John Minto, an articulate spokesman for the woolgrowers who grazed two million sheep on these ranges. An ardent polemicist who was said to believe "that Oregon hung suspended from the universe by a hank of wool," Minto gathered scientific evidence favorable to grazing. Sheepmen sent a lobbyist to Washington, D.C., and promoted their cause to Oregon Senator John H. Mitchell and a sympathetic fellow Oregonian, Binger Hermann, Commissioner of the General Land Office. Joining in the effort to exclude sheep were city officials from Willamette Valley towns whose water supply came from streams originating in the Cascades, recreational users of the forests, and cattlemen. Two U.S. Department of Agriculture specialists, F. V. Coville (head of the Department of Botany) and Gifford Pinchot (chief of the Bureau of Forestry) inspected the Cascades ranges and decided on a compromise plan that allowed restricted grazing. Coville discounted claims that the sheepmen were disreputable foreigners, dismissed the "popular but erroneous idea that the responsibility for the present system of grazing in eastern Oregon rests with the sheepowners," and concluded that the effect of moderate grazing "is the same as the effect of the judicious removal of a grass crop from a fenced pasture . . . ; a forage crop is secured without material detriment to the land and the herbaceous vegetation it bears." Permits were issued allotting specific areas for each flock. Muir's biographer, L. M. Wolfe, noted that the decision opened a rift "between the two schools of conservationists—the strictly utilitarian, commercial groups who followed Pinchot, and the aesthetic—utilitarian group who followed Muir." The continuing dispute caused grazing policy to remain unsettled. In September 1899, for example, the U.S. Department of the Interior abruptly cancelled the permits of 68 sheepmen who had flocks grazing on the Rainier Reserve in the Washington Cascades and ordered the woolgrowers to remove their 200,000 sheep from that district immediately. In October, the Department reversed itself and regulated grazing was allowed once more.[12]

The McGregor brothers and other sheepmen who trailed their sheep eastward to the Moscow Mountains of Latah County, Idaho, were able to avoid most of these problems. The northern Idaho rangeland was not included in the federal forest reserve system. Although the arrival of sheep continued to engender the ill feeling and hostility of local settlers, the McGregors were able to find sufficient forage for their stock. But maintaining sheep on the unregulated summer pasture had become an arduous task. Archie McGregor, in a letter he wrote to his wife in the late fall of 1896 or 1897, discussed a problem—evidently a serious storm— that forced the men to haul hay for their sheep and delayed trailing the sheep across the stubble fields and back to the winter range.

I cannot say when I will get to go home. . . . We have got to make a determined effort to hold our own and that calls on us to Stay here. I was So Sure of going back that I did not even buy me a Shirt and Peter did not take in anything. We will have to get gum boots and wearing apparel. We aim to Stay with it now. We will get down when we get out of Stubble. Anyway for a few days This Sheep business is a Terror . . . Peter and I are well. We felt awful last night when we came in but we are reconciled. Orun and Jansen [McGregor herders] have done all right. The misfortune might have happened to anybody. The Sheep look very well. John will be mad when he hears about us having to stay up here as well as we were but we have resolved to Stay with it and feel contented.[13]

Continued improvement of business conditions enabled John, Archie, and Peter McGregor to go on with the expensive, demanding job of transforming their open range sheep business into a durable ranching operation. The value of mutton and wool continued to increase in 1898 and for several years thereafter. A *Ranch and Range* correspondent claimed in 1898 that "if you want to hear good, rich, hearty laughter just offer a sheepman last year's price for wool—and last years wasn't so bad either." The promising outlook prompted the men to encourage their younger brother, Alex, to come west and join their partnership. By 1895, Alex had managed to purchase the drugstore in which he had worked since his arrival in Chicago eight years earlier. He carried a wide variety of products in his Chicago pharmacy. One of his journal books included a list of ingredients for the following:

corn remover	poison for bedbugs	telegraph oil
battery fluid	removal of freckles	goose grease
cold cure	chocolate syrup	sherbet
asthma cure	solution strychnine	browning gun barrels
genuine brickdust	piano polish	cough mixture
furniture polish	plant food	good cough mixture
	curry powder	

After corresponding with and visiting Alex, the three older brothers convinced him that "he could make dollars in Washington where he had made pennies in Chicago." Alex visited the Columbia Plateau in 1898 and came west to stay two years later. While working in Chicago, Alex had boarded with the family of C. Z. Sherman, a tool and dye maker for a steel mill, and had met Sherman's young daughter, Jennie. After she married Alex in 1903, Jennie also moved to eastern Washington.[14]

The headquarters for the McGregor families and the center of operations for their sheep business was a location six miles south of the village of Hooper, in a draw between rolling Palouse country hills. To the north were the Palouse River and the Channeled Scablands; to the south were the rugged "breaks" of the Snake River. The area, located on an alternate section in the middle of the leased winter range, later became the headquarters for their farming business. Archie, Peter, and John all purchased quarter sections and had houses built on the locations for their families. Alex later acquired an adjacent 160 acres, where his family home was constructed. Barns, harness shops, a bunkhouse, and other facilities were built nearby.

Hiring a crew of capable employees was an important step in the McGregor brothers' efforts to develop a well-organized and efficient sheep business. The McGregors were fortunate to secure the services of John D. ("Jock") Macrae, a colorful young Scotchman who began tending McGregor flocks in 1898 and soon became sheep foreman, a position he held until his death in 1945. Macrae, a hard-working and dedicated sheepman, proved a good flock master. Employees were quick to carry out his orders, and, as sheep shearer Bill Dorman remembered, "When Mac told 'em to jump, all they asked was 'How high?' " McGregor Brothers hired Maurice Morod (Morreau), Camille Myer, Maurice Vasher, and several other Frenchmen who began long careers as McGregor employees. By earning the loyalty of these men, the McGregors helped to assure themselves of a competent crew for future years. Several of these herders told friends and relatives of the work opportunities, and some of them came later to join the business. An outstanding example was Maurice Morod's brother, Emile, who arrived in 1913 to begin a 55-year career as herder, camptender, and finally sheep foreman. James Hunter, James Campbell, Robert Clyde, and other sheepherders of different nationalities also entered the McGregor business during these years.[15]

The herder, often the sole guardian of a band of sheep worth ten thousand dollars or more, was vitally important. In 1897, Miller Freeman of *Ranche and Range* described the duties of these men: "Good sheepherders have always commanded good pay, for a good herder is not met with every day. There are lots of men who think they can herd sheep. A week of it convinces them and their employers they are not adapted to the work. A good sheepherder has to be a man of some judgment and lots of patience. While his labors are not the hardest from the standpoint of manual work, he has to exercise more or less judgment in the selection of feeding places for his flock and care against bad weather." Sheepmen of the Columbia Plateau, as well as woolgrowers in other western range areas, frequently complained about the shortage of good herders. Sloppy herding could be costly. In 1898, for example, W. H. Vessey of Prosser lost 117 sheep when they were not moved in time to avoid an approaching train. Because sheep had been bred to have a "flocking instinct" (a necessity for a business based on movement between seasonal pastures), if one sheep bolted the rest would follow. Maurice Turner, a Kittitas County sheepman, experienced a serious loss one evening when 600 of his sheep "ran into a log, piling up all of them, and killing more than two-thirds of the bunch." *Ranche and Range* described the unfortunate experience of one new herder:

> J. H. Smithson, of Ellensburg, met with a severe loss last Saturday. He had employed a man by the name of Bryon Turner, late of California, to take charge of a band of sheep. . . . In some way the sheep ran off a cliff about 35 feet high, and Mr. Kimball [the foreman] says from the looks he should judge that fully 400 sheep were killed by the fall. At first he thought Turner was under the sheep, supposing that he had tried to keep them from going over the bluff, and in so doing had been crowded off himself; but Monday morning Kimball became convinced that Turner had left for a climate more congenial to his health.[16]

To justify the expense of hiring a large crew and acquiring rangeland, McGregor Brothers worked to increase the efficiency and productivity of their business. They improved lambing facilities; took steps to cut sheep losses to a minimum; grew wheat to provide hay for the sheep; developed a flock of hardy, good wool-producing Rambouillets; organized what E. N. Wentworth described as "extremely economical methods" of wether production; and acquired additional lands desirable for sheep raising.

The McGregors and other sheepmen who were beginning to provide more intensive care for their sheep found that "with regard to the flock, eternal vigilance is the price of safety." Herders and sheep owners had to be alert at all times for various diseases that could infect their sheep. Sheep with infected eyes could become blind. Scabies, ticks, and other parasites could "sap the life out of and torture your sheep and lambs." Another disease, "grub in the head," if unattended, caused the sheep's head to swell "to twice its natural size" and brought first blindness, then death. Sheep troubled with worms were treated with a mixture of linseed oil, pine tar, and turpentine. *Ranche and Range* offered its own cure for another difficulty, "running at the nose": "Blow tobacco smoke in the nose, through a long clay pipe, and then give a good pinch of fine Scotch snuff blown into the nose as far up as possible through a tube of any kind."[17] McGregor herders were expected to be good sheep nurses when occasion demanded.

The McGregor Brothers and their employees spread their winter sheep operations over six townships located on the western edge of Whitman County. The Adams County leasehold, several miles to the north, could also be used if necessary. To allow their grasslands to improve, efforts were made to graze rangeland uniformly, periodically shifting from one area to another to avoid damaging the bunchgrass of any one portion. Four cabins, complete with stoves and provisions, were built for herders on the rolling hills between the Palouse and Snake rivers. Tents were also purchased for the use of herders tending sheep on other portions of the winter range and on summer pastures. "Camp buildings" were built at Clear Lake, Round Lake, and Canyon Lake. Watering troughs and other equipment were also installed.

The men began to experiment with new ways to produce supplemental winter feed. Sporadic attempts were made to raise rye, corn, and barley. Efforts to raise wheat for hay, begun after the turn of the century, were far more successful. The main leasehold contained the best potential areas for cultivation, but the railroad required these lands to be used "solely and exclusively for the purpose of grazing." After taking an option to purchase the lands in 1901, the McGregors began to "break" large areas of their Palouse hills. By 1905, McGregor Brothers had 1,096 acres in wheat, 435 in summerfallow, and 369 acres of newly broken "sod," for a total of more than 1,900 acres of cultivated land. Their "wheat ranch" had a large crew of employees and a variety of implements, including four-horse cultivators, gang and walking plows, harrows, rod weeders, drills, hay rakes, mowers and binders, wagons and sleighs, and a chop mill and fanning mill. Wheat was cut while green, chopped, and left in haystacks scattered through the area. When needed, this livestock forage (known as "wheat-hay") was then hauled to feeding racks located near the bands of sheep. Although sheepmen in more arid regions to the west generally had to ship hay from other areas, a few other woolgrowers were fortunate enough to have land suited for raising supplemental feed. Perhaps the most exotic winter forage was produced by J. E. Smith and Sons, who began growing mangel-wurzels (a variety of beets) and carrots for their sheep.[18]

The decision to raise hay enabled the McGregors to prepare adequately for winter storms. Jacob and Hans Harder, J. P. Poe, and other Franklin

County sheepmen ran out of feed during the winter of 1900–01, at a time when two and a half feet of snow was said to be on the ground. The Harders lost a third of their three thousand sheep; Poe, almost half of his flocks. H. Stanley Coffin described his difficulties during a serious blizzard that winter:

> It snowed and blew and got colder until such a fierce blizzard came on that I could hardly see the horses' heads at times. . . . We froze our noses, ears, and fingers pinning blankets with nails on my horses . . . [Herder Hugh Sheppard] and I rubbed each other with snow and thawed out. [The wind blew so hard we could not keep a fire going]. . . . Well we walked back and forth in the Tent wagon until three in the next morning when it quit blowing and snowing and turned zero weather. . . . [After the storm] We hunted sheep for about five or six days and got most of them gathered together. Some had smothered in snow drifts; others were killed by coyotes. . . . We even found sheep stuck in drifts with their heads partly eaten off by coyotes. The wind [had been] so bad that it actually blew snow and sand right into the sheep's wool so that it stuck there in big blocks for several weeks before finally melting and working off. . . . The old ewes . . . had gotten so weak during the storm and being old and heavy with lambs they just kept dying.

A less severe blizzard caused serious losses in scattered portions of central Washington two years later. But these storms were atypical, and McGregor Brothers and other sheepmen generally described winters of this period in such terms as "splendid," "mild," "exceptionally favorable," and "excellent."[19] Both winter and spring climatic conditions proved to aid the sheepmen's efforts to produce large wool clips and good lamb crops. Sheep raisers could no longer afford to gamble on mild weather, however, and the wise policy was to minimize the risks involved by providing large amounts of winter feed and gaining control of sheltered lowland valleys.

The most critical period for sheepmen came in mid-March, when lambs were born. Because lambing time is "the sheepman's anxious period," when careless herders or unexpected storms may cause him to lose an entire year's profits, the availability of good lambing grounds has always been one of the major requirements for a successful sheep business. A few good sites for lambing camps had been included in the original grazing leases, and John McGregor bought additional sections of land with sheltered valleys and sources of water, the two major necessities for suitable lambing quarters. The McGregor Brothers gradually began to intensify their lamb-producing methods and abandoned the "broadcast" system of former years in favor of new procedures. The old system, based on a minimum of labor and little supplemental feed, had provided no protective quarters for ewes and their newborn offspring. The expectant ewes (the "drop band") had been herded over the range, and as each ewe yeaned (gave birth to) her lamb she was left behind, while the band drifted away. After ewes and lambs had been "broadcast" across a valley in this fashion, a herder then "worked" the sheep together and bedded them down for the night.

Although the old system was inexpensive, it had several drawbacks: The sheep had little protection from sudden storms; lambing took place relatively late in the spring when the weather was milder, thus depriving lambs of the good green feed of early spring; and ewes dependent on the natural forage might not be able to produce enough milk to support twin lambs. To improve lambing the McGregors built corrals, sheds, and lean-tos, and put up tents to provide artificial protection for their ewes and lambs. Additional laborers were hired, and the amount of hay fed to the sheep was increased. The more intensive procedures made the flocks less vulnerable to inclement weather and predator damage and helped ensure larger lamb crops. John Cleman of Yakima, Charles Cunningham of Pendleton, and a few other sheepmen had refined the old methods even further by adopting "shed lambing," a procedure later adopted by McGregor Brothers.[20]

Lambing took place at three main camps (one run by Archie, one by John, and one by Peter) and at several other sites in the scablands and along the Palouse River. Experienced herders working at these locations kept a constant watch on the bands of expectant ewes. The old procedure of broadcasting ewes and their lambs over wide areas and leaving them unattended after dark was abandoned. The drop band was corralled at night and watched, and lanterns were put up to ward off coyotes. A "night picker" patrolling the corral throughout the night was responsible for separating newborn lambs and their mothers from the rest of the sheep and placing them in separate pens. During the day, lambing took place upon nearby pastures where the drop band was grazed. Lambs and their mothers were separated into groups, first of five or six and gradually of increasing numbers. After the lambs were a week old or more, buck lambs were castrated and lambs of both sexes were docked (i.e., had their tails removed).

Harry Windus, a McGregor employee from 1903 to 1905, spent two lambing seasons at Archie's camp. He recalled that Archie and his wife, Nellie, would move from ranch headquarters to the camp during lambing—Nellie to cook, and Archie to supervise the employees. In the evenings after dinner, the crew would gather at the night picker's house to sing and pass the time. Archie often joined the men, and after reading a few chapters of the Bible, he would chat and chew Star Plug tobacco with them.[21]

The increased expenses of wintering, lambing, and acquiring range forced Columbia Plateau sheepmen to discontinue the practice of keeping their stock for "as long as they could walk around and shear a fleece." The old policy of concentrating on wool sales and selling only the oldest sheep as mutton was no longer feasible. The old method of selling mutton had involved trailing bands of as many as forty thousand sheep from the Columbia Plateau to the stubble fields of the Dakotas or the corn-raising region of Nebraska. As settlement increased in the western range country, this inexpensive method of fattening and marketing sheep became impractical, and the sheep movement began to go east by rail. Sheepmen were often unhappy about the dependence on the railroads: *Ranche and Range* complained in 1897 about the "prohibitive" rail rates being charged to "a large class of stockmen who had suffered for years to the very verge of ruin and who now, just as they begin to see their way out of the financial woods, have new forces to meet, scarcely less exacting, merciless, and destructive than the professional tariff reformers of '93."[22]

But the increased railroad shipments made possible a change in the methods of marketing western sheep. Fat, young sheep could quickly reach markets where they were slaughtered as premium quality meat. Chicago sheep buyers C. H. Shurte and "Big Jim" Harris came west in 1893 to meet "a party of railroad men" at Portland and to organize a coordinated "effort to get sheepmen in Idaho, Washington, and Oregon to bill stuff to Chicago." Kauffman Brothers of North Yakima, William Wyman and Malcolm McLennan of Ellensburg, George Smythe of Arlington, Oregon, and a few other Columbia Plateau sheepmen shipped "fat western lambs from succulent mountain pastures to the market." Shurte recalled that although "western stock was a novelty at Chicago," the young sheep sold at top market prices, "and the Eastern mutton eater was put in possession of an article that soon forced itself into popularity." These first shipments "demonstrated the possibility of a great traffic" in young western mutton that expanded rapidly in the late 1890's and would soon be "measured annually by the million head." In 1898, *Ranch and Range* editor Miller Freeman commented on the changing market conditions: "An entire revolution has taken place in the business. The demand for the young mutton is steadily growing until it tops the market."[23]

There was a brisk demand for lambs six to nine months of age, and the presence of Chicago commission agents on the summer ranges indicated to *Ranche and Range* "that the banks will be kept busy paying out the coin to the flock and herd owners." But the raising of young market sheep marked a radical change, and failing to gauge the condition of the lambs or the vicissitudes of the market could be costly. The Chicago *Gazette* reported in June 1897 that "James Wright of Yakima, Wash. had 600 spring lambs here Tuesday. The lambs were shipped entirely too early and being too young to eat arrived in a rather famished condition. The experiment was a costly one, and, it is claimed, will lose the owner $1 per head."

McGregor Brothers found that improving their methods of raising wethers brought them more favorable results than switching to lamb production. Wethers (castrated male sheep) were excellent wool producers, with fleeces generally weighing two pounds more than ewes'. By selling them as two-year-olds, rather than as lambs, the men were able to receive a year's wool crop from these sheep and still sell them at a good market price. Although their value as mutton was slightly lower than that of lambs, the wool proceeds more than made up the difference.[24] In later years, as the price differential between lambs and wethers increased, the McGregors followed the examples of other Columbia Plateau sheepmen and switched to lamb production.

The McGregors kept close watch on the wethers and gave them the best of everything—feed, water, and care—to ensure a good wool clip and fat mutton. A band of wethers was run near Starbuck—across the Snake River, several miles to the south of the main McGregor winter range. The man who ran the wethers was, Harry Windus later recalled, "an excellent herder and a fine man but an alcoholic." Like many of those employed in the lonely profession of sheepherding, he drank freely when alcohol was available. One time when the herder was close to the village of Riparia, he went to the tavern and got drunk. Archie took Harry Windus down to gather up the sheep and herd them for awhile. When the wethers were moved north to Sprague for shipment to the stockyards, "Archie had to take charge of the herder to get him through towns." Archie often did some of the winter herding and lived in a sheep camp equipped with a tent, stove, and bed. Nellie hauled supplies and arrived back at camp in the evenings in time to share a meal of sourdough and mutton with her husband.

In addition to the wethers, McGregor Brothers ran five to seven bands of ewes at scattered locations on the main winter range. The ewes were the most important part of the business. By careful management of these sheep in the winter and spring, a large increase in the size of the flock and a good wool clip were ensured. After the lambs were born, the herders and their dogs trailed the ewes and their offspring to areas of the rangeland with ample amounts of green forage. The herders led an isolated life, and they were sometimes alone with the sheep several days or even weeks. Harry Windus recalled that he and the other herders enjoyed the times when they were able to trail the sheep to the north end of the range overlooking the Palouse Valley because they could watch the passenger train (nicknamed the "Sagehen") go by once in awhile. When herders had the opportunity to leave their sheep, they sometimes rode to Palouse Falls, a 198-foot waterfall on the western portion of the range, to have lunch and drink beer. Harry Windus, a friend of Archie and Peter when they had the hardware store in Pullman, was also able to corral his sheep a few times at night and go to their houses for dinner. Harry recalled that table tennis was the "great rage in those days," and that after dinner with Maude and Peter he was invited to play against Peter, "who considered himself quite a shark." Harry was victorious and remembered that Peter "was a fine man but not a good loser." He was never invited to the house again because, according to Peter, "he shouldn't leave the sheep so long."[25]

Ewes, wethers, and the few rams kept as breeding stock were shorn in late April or early May. Because one of the provisions of the Northern Pacific land purchases and leases had called for shipping wool via that rail line, before 1900 the McGregors had trailed their sheep eighty miles to the Northern Pacific siding at Sprague, where shearing took place. Buyers for eastern wool commission houses were on hand and purchased the McGregor wool and shipped it by rail to their headquarters. The provision was not enforced after 1900, and the McGregors began shearing on the winter range in the shed located at Archie's camp. The clip was then sent east over the nearby Oregon Railroad and Navigation (OR & N) rail line. The location was an excellent shearing quarters—a protected valley with four lakes—and has served as the McGregors' shearing camp for more than 75 years. The men adopted a technique of bringing the sheep in to the area and holding them on the hills south of camp, a procedure that McGregor sheepmen continue to use today.[26]

The shearing crews were usually composed of migratory laborers who worked for sheepmen throughout the western range states. Many of the most skilled shearers were union members. In 1903, several small unions ("sheds") joined forces to form the Sheep Shearers Union of North America, the first stable union of American agricultural workers. The union was generally successful in establishing and maintaining a uniform price per head of sheep shorn for this tough, highly skilled work. Sheepmen complained and sometimes tried to hire less expensive non-union crews, but they generally found that the inexperience of these local laborers made them far less useful than the seasoned migratory crews.[27]

After shearing, the McGregor herders trailed their sheep to the summer range in northern Idaho. A leasing agreement with the Potlatch

Lumber Company and contracts with several other landowners were made after the turn of the century. These agreements gave the Mc-Gregors uncontested control of more than thirty thousand acres of summer range near Vassar Meadows, an area they were to use for seasonal grazing for the next sixty years.

The McGregor brothers came to this mountainous range every summer and supervised the operations. Archie did much of the sheep tending himself for, as his daughter Marie recalled, he "was more content doing the herding than any of the others." Nellie frequently accompanied Archie when he took the sheep to the mountains. In 1897 Nellie, her year-old daughter Marie, and her sister Ellen took a wagon loaded with supplies and "went up there and camped out," living in tents all summer. Marie was placed on a blanket, while her mother and aunt "picked huckleberries which they canned while we camped." But, according to Marie, Archie "feared that a cougar or bear would attack me so that practice was eliminated."

Summer herders had to watch for coyotes, cougars, eagles, bears, and other predators that endangered the flocks. Even magpies could cause losses, for they sometimes pecked the eyes out of lambs and dug meat from open sores on a sheep. Bears were dangerous predators. George Aeschenbrenner, a herder working for sheepman William Patterson on another northern Idaho range, was described by the Colfax *Gazette* as a "gallant gentleman in defense of the ewe lambs" when he successfully routed four bears that had invaded his flock. But when one of Jacob Harder's herders, working on their summer range near Wenatchee, tried to stop a bear from carrying off one of the sheep, the bear attacked. Mrs. Harder recalled that the herder "had his face all torn to pieces" before his dogs "came to his rescue and chased the bear off." After spending summer months warding off predators and protecting their flocks, in November the herders began the long, slow process of trailing their sheep back to the winter ranges.[28]

The success of McGregor Brothers in developing a transhumant sheep business suited to the changed circumstances is evidenced by reports from their winter quarters during the first three years of the new century. The McGregors, Phil Cox, Cyrus Neal, John Miller, and other sheepmen who had been able to acquire land on the excellent sheep ranges of western Whitman County reported mild winter weather and large lamb and wool crops. Sheepmen herding their flocks through the town of Colfax in May 1900 claimed that conditions had been "especially favorable for sheep":

> *A heavy crop of wool has been taken from them this spring and the crop of lambs is the best ever known. . . . The young lambs are strong and*

*healthy and the ewes are in unusually good condition. The yield of wool
was considerably above the average of past years. . . .*

*Some idea of the profits of the sheep business can be gained from
the experience of McGregor Bros., who have about 16,000 head. They
have sold, since January 1, $31,000 worth of sheep and wool and yet
have 1000 more sheep than at the beginning of the year.*

In one band of old ewes owned by the McGregors in 1900, an increase
of 137 percent was reported; in others, 125–130 percent, and the overall
average was 122 percent. Two other local sheepmen (Phil Cox, who ran
7,600 head, and John Miller, who had 3,000) reported 120 percent increases, thus making "the present season one of the most profitable sheep
men have ever known."[29]

The favorable conditions continued during the fall of 1900 and the
following spring, with a good crop of native grasses, mild weather, and
a 112 percent lamb crop reported. The improved outlook for their sheep
business enabled John, Alex, Archie, and Peter to spend more time away
from their headquarters on business trips and family vacations. The
change in the fortunes of Peter and Archie, bankrupt only four years
before, had been remarkable. Archie and Nellie's "anticipation concerning a piano and a nice home some time" had seemed impossible in 1894.
But by 1900 they lived with their daughters, Jessie and Marie, in a large,
comfortable house at ranch headquarters. And a Lacrosse correspondent
reported in April of that year that "a fine organ was received at this
point for Archie McGregor." Peter's outlook had changed greatly, as
well, and he had begun laying the groundwork for a career in politics.
The Colfax *Gazette* reported Peter's visit to Lacrosse in May 1900:
"Peter McGregor, of McGregor Bros., the successful sheepmen of the
Hooper neighborhood, stopped here on his way to Colfax. Peter's face is
always beaming with a smile, and as he has a pleasant word for everyone,
we are always glad to welcome him."[30]

The sheep business continued to bring favorable returns for the next
few years. The McGregors, like other sheepmen who had established
their winter operations on the protected ranges of the lower Palouse,
avoided the serious losses reported in 1900–01 by the Coffins, Harders,
and other woolgrowers of the Big Bend region. The success of Mc-
Gregor Brothers as wether and wool producers is evidenced by reports
made during the 1901 season. Stock buyers were reported to be riding
"over the country buying every head of stock offered for sale at prices
that make stock growing a profitable industry." The McGregors sold
7,000 head of wethers for $4 a head after they were shorn. In May, the
brothers loaded and shipped four carloads of wool. Despite the large sale
of wethers, the firm was said to have more than 20,000 sheep still on

their ranch. The following year McGregor Brothers, now referred to as "the sheep kings of Whitman" County, had 15,000 sheep and announced plans to purchase a herd of cattle to augment their livestock interests. Their 150,000-pound clip was sold to an eastern buyer for 9-¾ cents per pound, bringing an income of almost $15,000.[31]

The increased income from wool and mutton gave sheepmen the opportunity to purchase and fence their grazing leases. John McGregor completed payment on his first railroad land purchase in 1900, and by 1901 he was able to make plans to purchase the lands in the original grazing lease. The willingness of railroad officials to reduce the grazing fee $100 in 1897 and $50 in 1898 (the latter in return for a bridge McGregor Brothers had built on the leasehold), and their allowance of an eight-month extension of the 1896 land purchase agreement had enabled McGregor Brothers to hold on to the land. By 1902 the McGregor brothers were able to announce plans to enclose the entire leasehold, a project that required an additional 100 miles of fencing and was expected to cost $6,000. Northern Pacific Land Commissioner William Phipps gave the following recommendation to Western Land Agent Thomas Cooper on a proposal submitted by John McGregor: "I am in receipt of your letter . . . regarding grazing lease Nos. 1 and 192 now held by John McGregor. I note Mr. McGregor's proposition to fence the land, providing the company will give him an option for one year for all the lands included in the two leases at price of $1.25 per acre on the ten year plan, the acceptance of which I recommend. I am inclined to the belief that the proposition is a very good one for the company and authority is hereby given for you to carry it out. . . ."[32]

Sheepmen who held on to their leaseholds and later purchased and fenced them reaped immediate benefits: They were able to improve forage output from the range, and they acquired title to land at a time when it was becoming increasingly expensive and scarce. U.S. Department of Agriculture botanist David Griffiths in 1903 found that "there was a very evident difference between the open-range and the fenced areas" along Cow Creek, near the McGregor ranch. The change to fenced pastures, Griffiths found, "has yielded results far beyond the expectations of the ranchers." Some ranchers reported as much as a fifty percent increase in grazing capacity within two years. "The open range question," Griffiths concluded, "is here practically a thing of the past." A correspondent to the *American Sheep Breeder* noted the difficulties faced by those depending on unfenced western land: "Conditions have about reached a crisis. It is no longer sheep against cattle, but flock is fighting flock for a chance to get at the available grass." "Nomadic sheep and shepherds," that publication concluded in 1905, "have had their day."

Men who waited too long to begin leasing and purchasing land found that acquiring a ranch had become a difficult matter. Miller Freeman of *The Ranch* reported in 1902 on the problem faced by many Columbia Plateau ranchers: "Distinctly audible just now is the wail of the man who intended to buy a farm during the recent period of depression, but neglected to carry out the intention until the rise came and prices soared. Too late he realizes that he has permitted a golden opportunity to slip by."[33]

The outlook was encouraging for those who had acquired ranches. *American Sheep Breeder* described 1904 as "a red letter year for the sheepmen," a year that the woolgrower would remember "as one of the best, if not the best, in his recollection." The following year that publication asked its readers, "When were times better, profits greater, or prospects brighter for sheepmen than now?" The McGregor livestock operations had become well established during this prosperous period. During the winter of 1904–05, seven bands of sheep (15,738 total) were run by the men, a figure that had remained relatively constant during the preceding four or five years. In 1905, 145 cattle were run along the Snake River, and an additional 352 at Wood Gulch, near the main ranch.[34] With control of winter and summer ranges, good wool and mutton prices, and a well-organized operation, the McGregor sheep business of 1905 bore little resemblance to the "tramp" days of a decade earlier.

Shrewd land dealings had played a vital part in the transformation of the McGregor business. Archie, John, Peter, and Alex McGregor were able to buy and sell land in a way that enabled them to consolidate control of their winter and summer ranges and gain income from sale of lands peripheral to their main ranching area. Northern Pacific officials unwittingly provided the opportunity for the McGregors to profit from land sales when they forced sheepmen to pay for grazing their flocks on an apparently unproductive, barren land. Railroad president Howard Elliot reflected on the marketing of Northern Pacific lands in a 1910 letter to Thomas Cooper, the man who engineered the grazing lease system and later became railroad land commissioner: "In considering . . . land values, I am more and more impressed with the fact that our own people, including you and myself, having lived in an atmosphere of low prices, have not had sufficient imagination to judge of prices as accurately as we should . . . I fear we have not obtained as much as we have been fairly entitled to for some of the things we have been selling and renting."[35]

To railroad land agents and many early settlers, the hills of the western Palouse and the flatlands of the Big Bend seemed suitable only for livestock grazing. Jock Macrae described the prevailing attitude he encountered upon his arrival in the region in 1898: "There were very few old men in the country at that time—the general attitude was one of optimism as regards the future, though they didn't look for this land to become an extensive farming country. They didn't think they could raise enough feed here to feed their chickens." But wheat farming expanded rapidly in the late 1890's, and by the end of the century the Columbia Plateau had replaced California as the most important wheat-producing area of the Pacific Slope.[36] The western Palouse country rangeland occupied by the McGregor brothers had a lighter colored soil and received less rainfall than the Palouse hill country near the Idaho border; thus, it was viewed as less desirable for wheat production than the lands further to the east. The improving outlook during the decade after the panic brought a new wave of settlement, and farmers began to move onto grasslands near the McGregor ranch and other areas long thought suited only for sheep and cattle production. Land values escalated rapidly, reflecting the growing competition for farms and ranches. Open range operation became impossible, and land was expensive and hard to acquire. One sheepman claimed that his most persistent enemy was "the farmer and his shotgun." But McGregor Brothers, Coffin Brothers, and other sheepmen who acquired land before it became valuable were able to resell portions of their ranches at inflated prices, thus benefitting at the expense of the wheat raisers.[37]

The farmers who began "breaking" the bunchgrass hills of the western Palouse recorded good yields. The wheat crops of 1898–1901 were not only adequate, they were said to be larger than the rest of the Palouse country. In 1901, Henry Williamson, a custom threshing machine operator, told the Colfax *Gazette* that: "the finest wheat I ever saw is on the new wheat lands of western Whitman county. . . . Throughout all this region is the finest wheat that ever delighted the eye of grower or threshing machine operator. Last year was a good crop—in fact, excellent. But 1901 knocks the blossom from 1900." P. N. McKenzie, a stockman on lower Willow Creek, a half dozen miles from the McGregor Brothers ranch, reported threshing 800 acres of spring wheat that averaged more than 25 bushels an acre. Because of the encouraging results, *The Ranch* claimed, "plows are running all over the western Palouse country." A correspondent from Pampa reported on the encouraging outlook: "The Pampa country has more than doubled in population and real estate more than trebled in value in the past three years. And why not? The bountiful crops, fat stock and health of this part of the country is inducement enough to settle it to its fullest capacity."[38]

Settlers who began farming operations on the western edge of Whitman County found (according to Sadie Hunter, the daughter of a farmer from Riparia) that "for miles and miles the land was owned by the McGregor Brothers." J. M. Brown, a farmer who arrived at the town of Hay in the early 1900's, remembered that the McGregors were "a very strong force in this region and had acquired title to most of the land around here as well as leased much of the other, such as the school, government, and railroad land. They sold or leased this land to many of the early comers but in all their transactions have maintained a very friendly relationship with those they had or have dealings with. . . ." The lands owned by McGregor Brothers increased rapidly in value. A *Spokesman-Review* reporter described the McGregor land business in 1901: Their "land was bought at about 65 cents per acre and is now worth $6 per acre, making a snug fortune the McGregor brothers have made in the increase in the value of their land, aside from that made in raising sheep." The McGregors began selling lands on the edges of their sheep ranges. The *Spokesman-Review* reported in 1902 on the progress of the land sales: "McGregor Bros. . . . have made a fortune in raising sheep, but have made more money from the increase in value of the land they were compelled to buy for pasture than from their flocks. They recently sold 640 acres for $5,500 cash for which they paid a few years ago less than $1 an acre."[39]

The McGregor landholdings on Rattlesnake Flat in Adams County were isolated from the main winter range and were only marginally useful for sheep raising. When John McGregor entered the agreement to purchase the eight and a half sections of land in 1897, a few farmers in the area had begun experimenting with wheat production, with only indifferent results. The prevailing theory was that the land was fit only for grazing. But farmers reported excellent crops in 1897 and 1898 and thereafter the wheat fields pushed "the range back into the coulee regions . . . with great rapidity." The Washington State Bureau of Statistics claimed in 1903 that nearby Ritzville had become "the largest initial wheat shipping point in the United States." The Northern Pacific formally deeded the 5,389-acre tract of land to John McGregor in November 1901 for the price agreed upon five years earlier—one dollar per acre. During the next month, four of the sections were sold to farmers for a total of $19,640. The remaining lands, plus the adjacent 120 acres acquired from the Second National Bank of Colfax in 1895, were sold during the next two years. John McGregor received a total of $31,127 for property that had cost him $6,389. The McGregor brothers used the proceeds of these sales to purchase additional fencing needed for their main ranch in Whitman County and to enlarge and improve their sheep-raising business.[40]

While selling peripheral lands, such as the Rattlesnake Flat tract, the McGregor brothers worked to strengthen control of their major sheep ranges. Title to sections of land containing important waterholes, such as Wildcat Lake and Hooper Lake, was obtained. Green Lake Sheep Camp and several other important locations used by the McGregors during their "tramp" days were purchased. The four men also bought lands near the ranch headquarters that appeared to offer potential for raising wheat. In 1902, they exercised their option to purchase the 22,359-acre original railroad lease, signing a contract that pledged payment of almost $28,000 on a ten-year plan with a 10 percent down payment. A contemporary account described the "gigantic land sale":

> McGregor Bros., the sheep kings of the Palouse country, purchased 23,000 acres of NP railroad lands, in odd sections. . . . The McGregors already owned a large acreage in that vicinity, and the big deal gives them proprietary control of 30,000 acres of fine grazing land, though not fit for agricultural purposes. The tract is grass land and not sage brush and is an excellent stock range. . . . This holding will make one of the most magnificent stock ranches in the state . . . being an especially good winter range. McGregor Bros. occupies the land under a lease which still had five years of life, but they preferred to buy while the opportunity offered.[41]

The Northern Pacific grazing land policies gave Columbia Plateau sheepmen and cattle raisers an opportunity to use legal means to acquire large areas of the semiarid rangeland. Livestock raisers in western range districts not containing railroad lands had difficulty obtaining title to their grazing grounds. A few hundred acres of public domain could be acquired by fulfilling the requirements of the homestead law and other federal land legislation. But even an entire 640-acre section of land, as John Wesley Powell had recognized in his famous critique of public land policies, was a woefully inadequate unit of production in the western range states. Livestock raisers seeking to gain control of their ranges used a wide variety of methods to secure the lands. Wyoming cattleman John Clay once commented: "There is scarce a ranchman in the West who has not transgressed the land laws of the country."[42]

Livestock raisers who purchased railroad lands were able to build the nucleus of a ranch without having to evade federal land policies or devise other techniques of land acquisition. But the purchase of checkerboard sections of railroad land solved only half the problem. Woolgrowers somehow needed to gain control of the alternate sections of land not included in the railroad properties. McGregor Brothers and other ranchers had been able for several years to exert de facto control of these lands by controlling adjacent railroad acreage. The influx of homesteaders and the increasing competition for the land meant that the sheepmen could no longer rely on uncontested use of the alternate sections of public domain.

Columbia Plateau sheepmen used several methods to consolidate their ranch holdings. The failure of the public land policies to provide legitimate means by which livestock ranchers could acquire large acreages of federal grazing lands invited abuse of the provisions by sheepmen and cattlemen. In a 1907 article in *World's Work*, Arthur W. Page launched a scathing attack against western livestock men "who have driven out honest settlers," illustrating his case with the following hypothetical conversation between a lawyer and a rancher: " 'How can I keep the land along the X creek,' he asked. 'Homestead, desert claim, scrip, 'most any way,' was the answer. 'Yes, but how about the law, and the affidavits?' 'Well, I'll tell you,' said the lawyer. 'Those laws were passed for the East. . . . They don't fit out here. But the government wants to get rid of the land. Don't you suppose the local land office knows its business?' " [43]

Some of the Columbia Plateau livestock raisers who flagrantly abused the land laws found themselves forced to defend their actions in federal court. Crook County sheepman (and Congressman) John Williamson and his partner, Van Gesner, were convicted for inducing 100 fraudulent entrymen to claim 16,000 strategic acres of their summer range under the Timber and Stone Act of 1878 (an act lobbied through Congress by lumber interests that enabled any citizen to purchase a quarter-section of government timberland). The bogus entrymen were to acquire title and then transfer the tracts to the sheepmen. S. A. D. Puter, the self-styled "King of the Oregon land fraud ring," in his contemporary work, *Looters of the Public Domain*, details further efforts by land speculators, stockmen, and lumbermen to manipulate federal lands in the Blue Mountains. Congressman Williamson, Oregon Senator John H. Mitchell, and General Land Office Commissioner Binger Hermann were among those indicted in the eastern Oregon land fraud schemes. In 1904, *The Ranch* detailed another unsuccessful effort to acquire land:

> A case of great interest was that of the government against the Oregon sheep king, Charles Cunningham, and some of his associates. They were under indictment for attempting to defraud the government out of public lands. . . . When arraigned Cunningham and his friends, with one exception, plead guilty and the judge imposed a fine of $1,000 on the leader and $100 each on four of his fellow conspirators. . . . Cunningham had furnished the money to secure the government land and those who were

indicted with him made proofs upon the land selected but which they never saw. Cunningham is one of the largest owners of sheep in eastern Oregon. . . ."[44]

The McGregor brothers cautiously avoided such flagrant abuses of federal land laws. The four men frequently circumvented the avowed goals of public land policies in their efforts to strengthen their hold on the rangeland. But they generally adhered to the letter of the law, while manipulating it for their own purposes. The McGregors and many other western livestock men were able to use "land paper" to claim strategic portions of federal lands. Under certain conditions, individuals and corporations could exchange tracts of land for scrip entitling them to choose an equal acreage of federal property elsewhere. Dealers willing to sell such scrip to ranchers and farmers were located in almost every land office town in the West. The following 1882 advertisement in the Colfax *Palouse Gazette* was typical: "If you want any kind of land scrip, with which to prove up your preemption or your homestead, or with which to locate on any of the vacant tracts in this vicinity or elsewhere, without living on them, call on H. M. Chace."[45]

John, Peter, Archie, and Alex McGregor found scrip obtained under the provisions of the Forest Lieu Land Act of 1897 useful in obtaining key tracts of land. By using the scrip to claim lands surrounding waterholes or cutting off access to other public domain, the McGregors were able to ensure that adjacent federal lands could not be used by anyone else. Alex McGregor commented: "We were able to obtain valuable water sights by means of the script [sic] land privileges, and by so doing it made it easier to acquire the adjoining lands for grazing purposes."

The Forest Lieu Land Act provided that any person or corporation with land in an area scheduled to become a federal forest reserve could relinquish the claim and receive land scrip entitling him to an equal acreage of public land elsewhere. Designed ostensibly for the benefit of settlers who found themselves isolated within federal forests, the statute was often used as a vehicle for fraud. A Senate investigation disclosed that the act had been "taken advantage of in a speculative way by buyers of land from states whose lands had little or no value for timber or grazing . . . relinquishing these in exchange for valuable land outside the forests which could not be bought."[46]

McGregor Brothers made 16 purchases of the scrip during a two-year period, 1903–05. Much of the land paper was acquired from Edward B. Perrin, J. L. Washburn, Aztec Land and Cattle Company, and the Santa Barbara Water Company, all of whom were notorious because of their abuse of the principles of the Forest Lieu Land Act. Perrin obtained 176,000 acres of Atlantic and Pacific Railroad land in Arizona for 70 cents an acre. When the land was subsequently included within a forest reserve, Perrin was able to sell land scrip throughout the western states for several times the original purchase price. Aztec Land and Cattle sold its rights to 132,000 acres in a similar fashion. The Santa Barbara Water Company and Jed Washburn successfully agitated to have lands they owned included in a forest reserve. Thus, they were able to acquire valuable scrip in exchange for property a federal investigator later described as "brush land country of small value." Scrip land dealers gave power of attorney rights to Alex and Peter McGregor; E. T. Coman, an officer of a banking firm with whom McGregors dealt; T. W. Murphy, their Spokane lawyer; William Harvey, a man who bought land from the McGregors; and Jock Macrae and other sheepmen employed by McGregor Brothers. The McGregors generally purchased the scrip for five dollars an acre and used it to claim strategic tracts of land scattered throughout their winter range. The lands were chosen to connect disparate sections of McGregor land, enclose important portions of rangeland, or give the men exclusive control of adjoining federal lands.[47]

John McGregor also entered into a series of agreements to purchase land scrip from the Northern Pacific Railway. Railroad Land Commissioner William Phipps seldom became directly involved in land sales to individual western ranchers. But John McGregor's proposal of a series of Forest Lieu Land Act transactions was unusual enough to cause Northern Pacific's western land agents in Tacoma to write to St. Paul for Phipps' advice. Phipps feared restrictive action by the General Land Office to limit the railroad to "exchanging forest reserve rights for other lands . . . of like character and value." To avoid this risk, he warned regional land agents to allow John McGregor to choose only "lands upon which there is no present claim or settlement." During the year 1902 alone, John McGregor entered four agreements to purchase railroad lands enclosed within the Priest River Forest Reserve in Northern Idaho. In some cases, the railroad transferred title of the forest lands directly to John McGregor, enabling him to exchange the areas for land scrip. In other instances, the railroad officials received the scrip in the name of the railroad, applied it to lands on the McGregor winter range, and then sold the lands to John McGregor. The key tracts acquired from the railroad enabled McGregor Brothers to gain control of surrounding areas and proved well worth the $5–5.50 per acre asking price.[48]

The McGregors acquired additional lands from homesteaders who had claimed quarter sections of winter range. Only a few hardy locust trees and the bleached wood structures of abandoned frame houses remain as evidence of settlers who learned, from bleak experience, that 160 acres of a land with less than fourteen inches of rain could not sustain a family.

Some of the settlers never did plan to till the soil, taking up residence near waterholes to force livestock men to pay a high price for their land. In 1899 and 1900, John McGregor bought numerous quarter sections near McGregor Brothers ranch headquarters from homesteaders for $2–5 an acre. The following year he acquired a piece of land that bisected government property. The strip of land purchased was a sheltered valley containing Winn Lake—an ideal watering place for livestock. The homesteader at that location, after financial reverses forced him to sell his horses to John, sold the 160-acre tract at a price of $1.25 an acre. Some land purchased at a similarly low price was good grazing ground along the Palouse River Valley or surrounding waterholes. Other land, seemingly of less desirable nature, sometimes commanded a higher sum. The determining factor was often the financial position of the seller. If the seller was a man in debt to McGregor Brothers or to loan companies, the men could purchase his land at a more modest sum than might be possible with an individual of better economic standing.

McGregor Brothers also purchased land from banks, real estate mortgagees, the federal government, insurance companies, and other parties. In 1900, John McGregor acquired three tracts of excellent grazing land from the Phoenix Mutual Life Insurance Company, one from Walla Walla merchant Abraham Schwabacher, and another from Alfred Coolidge of the Second National Bank of Colfax. Archie bought two quarter sections that had once been homesteads but were now in the hands of a mortgage company. Some federal land was purchased outright—Peter received two U.S. "patents" for land at a price of $1.25 per acre, and Alex and John each acquired one such government tract. Other federal land was gained through the homestead law, one of the homesteaders being Euphemia MacGregor, a sister who spelled her last name in the traditional Scottish manner. "Of course, I did not mean to stay there so I sold it to the MacGregors."[49]

The McGregor brothers and other western stockmen further consolidated their rangeland holdings by leasing state lands. Washington and several other western states had been awarded two sections of every township by the federal government for support of public schools. Sheepmen and cattle raisers were able to lease such school lands at a low price per acre. The states were given the right to select additional lands under certain grants. Northern Pacific land agent G. H. Plummer noted that the State of Washington was "induced to select large areas [of such lands] in various localities where it appeared possible to create a valuable range." Sheepmen and cattlemen, unable to purchase or lease sections of public domain, found such state selections, Plummer recalled, to be "of very great value as they enable the stockmen to gain entire control of their range." Livestock raisers could purchase such lands, but they generally preferred to pay two to ten cents per acre per annum to lease the properties. Peter McGregor, who began a career in the state legislature in 1904 and two years later was selected as a member of the Senate standing committee on State Granted and School Lands, joined other legislators from eastern Washington in working hard to encourage the selection of lands located on sheep and cattle ranges. The state chose thirteen full or partial sections of such lands in the Whitman County holdings of the McGregor Brothers. The McGregors followed the usual procedure and leased most of these lands from the state.[50] In later years, when rents were raised and the lands were no longer open for purchase, stockmen were to regret their decision to lease instead of buying the tracts.

By purchasing land scrip, buying out homesteaders, acquiring land from mortgage companies and other sources, and leasing state land, McGregor Brothers was able to form the basis for a ranching business. Successful acquisition of large acreages enabled the men to take advantage of rising land values by selling scattered outlying acreage at a profit. The assets of the partnership increased dramatically. In 1905, McGregor Brothers owned 30,218 acres of deeded land, all purchased within the previous five years at a cost of $56,329—$1.86 per acre. The four men during that year estimated the current value of the property to be $194,988, more than $6.45 per acre and almost three and a half times the purchase price. The McGregors had also benefitted from much higher wool and mutton prices, reflecting a general improvement in agricultural commodity prices in the aftermath of the panic. In 1896, woolen mills paid an average of 36 cents per pound for clean ("scoured") wool. They paid 70 cents in 1905. The "grease" price paid Columbia Plateau woolgrowers climbed from 7 to 18 cents. Young wethers sold for $1.50 in 1896 and $4.75 in 1905. The editor of *American Sheep Breeder* visited the region in the spring of 1905 and found that "the whole northwestern range country is aglow with enthusiasm over the wool and mutton situation."[51]

The McGregors used money obtained from real estate sales and from wool and mutton to purchase more land, augment the bands of sheep and herds of cattle, to fence, dig wells, build lambing camps, and hire a competent crew. In their effort to provide consistent, economical, and nutritious supplemental feed for their sheep the four brothers began producing wheat hay, thus setting the stage for a future expansion into commercial wheat raising. The men also purchased a general store in the nearby village of Hooper in 1903. A local resident claimed the store was "the best one between Colfax and Dayton." First acquired as a commissary for McGregor employees, the store was soon expanded to provide a wide variety of supplies for neighboring farmers. With the purchase of the store and other nearby facilities and the acquisition of all the lands surrounding Hooper, McGregor Brothers gradually developed a company town to provide services for their ranching and farming business.[52] Archie, Alex, Peter, and John McGregor did not fall prey to the temptation to sell every piece of real estate upon which a profit could be made. Many of the Columbia Plateau livestock men fortunate enough to have title to land attractive to wheat raisers abandoned their sheep and cattle and devoted all their energies to land speculation.[53] The McGregor brothers did not do this: They sold peripheral lands and reinvested the profit in an expanding livestock business. By thus judiciously selling, buying, and improving land, the four men established an extensive ranch for their sheep.

Each brother had a different assignment in the management of the ranch during this period. During lambing and other crucial times, the brothers would superintend the several thousand sheep at each of the camps. John served as the general manager, purchased and sold land, and supervised the employees. Fellow sheepmen F. M. Rothrock noted that "in the early days of the district's development," John McGregor "labored hard to bring the land and stock of the family business to a high state of efficiency." Archie, an efficient "office man," did much of the bookkeeping and supervised some of the day-to-day activities. Alex also did some of the office work and managed the general merchandise store. The improved financial conditions enabled Peter to retire from active work in the partnership and move with his wife (Maude) and sons (Maurice and Alex T.) to Colfax, where he began a career in politics. Colfax, the Whitman County seat, was the center of local political activities. Peter told the Colfax *Gazette* that he and Maude were also attracted by "city life" because their children could receive a better education in Colfax than in rural schools. Peter was elected to the State Legislature in 1904 and served two terms, one in the House and one in the Senate, before returning to active participation in the McGregor business. Though not active in the daily business affairs of the McGregor operation, he nevertheless played an important part in dealing with bankers, livestock buyers, and government officials.[54]

A Republican, like most of the sheepmen who blamed their troubles during the panic on "free wool" and the Democratic party, Peter entered public life at a time when local politics was in a state of ferment. The Populist party had won most local offices during the election of 1896. William Jennings Bryan, a staunch Democrat and "the great orator of the day," gave speech in Colfax in 1900. Eugene V. Debs delivered an address two years later on the courthouse steps on "The Ethics of Socialism." During the summer of 1902, a thousand local residents were reported to have attended a conference in Colfax, where James J. Hill of the Great Northern and presidents Mellen and Mohler of the Northern Pacific and Oregon Railroad and Navigation rail lines spoke to the assembly. As a result of the widely felt dissatisfaction expressed about grain shipment rates, the three railroad officials were said to have agreed to lower the charges by 10 percent.[55]

Peter McGregor proclaimed himself a member of the "boxer," or Progressive, wing of his party and was elected at a time when Republicans won an overwhelming victory locally and across the state. He claimed to be "an advocate of the direct primary law" and pledged "to use all honorable means in my power to bring about the enactment" of such legislation. But he took a more active interest in issues that promised more immediate benefits to McGregor Brothers and other eastern Washington ranchers and farmers. Peter McGregor joined other local Republicans in registering "our emphatic protest against the degrading influence of the railway lobby over the Republican party of this State" and voted for the establishment of a state railroad commission to regulate transportation rates.[56] He served as chairman of the standing committee on the agricultural college and was a member of the appropriations, and dairy and livestock committees during his first term in office. The bills he introduced during this session were all related to the livestock industry (for example, a bill to place a bounty on coyote scalps and a bill to prohibit the importation of horses, cattle, and swine into the state without a certificate of health). In a campaign speech in Colfax, U.S. Senator (and fellow Republican) Samuel H. Piles reported on some of Peter McGregor's activities during the first term:

> *I was told by Peter McGregor and other members of the legislature from eastern Washington that I could not secure their support unless my delegation from King county would support them in their effort to secure the passage of a railway commission bill satisfactory to the people of eastern Washington and unless I would support the president in his effort to confer upon the interstate commerce commission the power to fix railway rates . . . I know that Peter McGregor was unwilling to support me unless I made the promise. . . . He subsequently came to me and said there was a matter in which he was personally interested for the benefit of the students of what was then known as the Washington Agricultural College and School of Science, located at Pullman, in this county, and that was that he wished to secure the support of the King county delegation to have the name of the college at Pullman changed to the Washington State College. I promised him that I would support that change . . . I know Mr. McGregor was honest and sincere in bringing about the results I have before mentioned. . . . Furthermore,*

I know that Mr. McGregor is in a position to accomplish much good for this county. I know that there is not a man who will represent King county in the next legislature who will not extend a friendly hand to Peter McGregor for the great kindness which he rendered the people of my county in electing me to the United States Senate. . . .[57]

By advocating a new name for the college at Pullman, Peter McGregor backed the viewpoint of E. A. Bryan, president of the school, in a long-standing debate that had been carried on in regional agricultural trade journals. Bryan had argued that the school should teach a wide range of subjects and that the field of "agriculture" should be defined broadly. The editor of *Rural Northwest* attacked Bryan's claim that the "agricultural college" designation was misleading: "If it is misleading it is unfortunate for the people of Washington that such is the case. . . . The more true to name the agricultural colleges of Washington and Oregon are made the more useful they will be to the states in which they are located." "Hayseed," a correspondent to *The Ranch*, alleged in 1900 that the school was "deviating from agricultural instruction and really becoming a second state university." The debate continued over the next three years, with some farmers arguing that the school should confine itself to "more practical" research and others claiming that "the legislature did not intend to narrow the course of instruction to a single department." By working to gain legislative approval to change the name of the Pullman school to Washington State College, McGregor helped Bryan carry the day and also laid the framework for his subsequent nomination as a member of the Board of Regents of that institution.[58]

The Pullman *Tribune*, a Democratic paper, in an editorial entitled "What McGregor's Election Means," criticized Peter McGregor on a different issue. McGregor strongly defended himself in a letter to the Colfax *Gazette* against the *Tribune*'s claim that he would oust the incumbent state grain inspector in favor of a man of his own choosing and ignore the interests of Whitman County farmers. The *Gazette* painted a glowing picture of the efforts of all local Republicans and described McGregor's first term in the following manner:

> A vote for Peter McGregor is a vote for a farmer. The only argument advanced by his enemies is that he is the largest landholder and heaviest taxpayer in Whitman county. Besides handling many sheep and cattle, McGregor Bros. are extensive cultivators of the soil. . . . Mr. McGregor is a living example of one who avails himself of opportunities presented. His foresight was good. The farmers' interests need foresight in the legislature. He is a man to be trusted and the farmers of Whitman county know it. His record in the last legislature is an open book.[59]

Ralph Snyder, a neighbor and friend of the four McGregor brothers, attributed their success to their willingness "to work like hell with the sheep" and to their ability to avoid personal disputes that could dissolve their business partnership. Snyder also described his recollections about each of the brothers:

> Pete was a politician. The McGregor boys was just like the rest of 'em, they had to get along with their neighbors . . . and Pete . . . his neighbors never liked Pete. He was a little [too] aggressive. But John— They was fortunate in having John. John was the operator and handled the men. He had that smooth ability to make friends. By God, he could really treat with his neighbors and get their range and buy their stuff and he'd make a sharp deal, and be easy in settlement, and they'd like it. But old Pete was pretty tough and he was a little hardened.

Archie, Snyder recalled, was a "good worker" who "looked after the business" but who "just followed along" with the others and "wasn't aggressive at all." Alex, the newest member of the partnership, was an office worker and "a good storekeeper" who helped his older brothers resolve differences of opinion and reach a consensus.

The Northern Pacific Railroad had forced the four Scotch–Canadians to build the foundation for a prosperous ranching business by evicting them from railroad-owned winter range. Faced with abandoning the sheep business or moving to overcrowded open ranges outside the railroad land grant, the McGregor brothers decided to stay and lease the tens of thousands of acres of grazing land that provided the framework for their ranching business. Fortuitous increases in mutton, wool, and land values made possible a striking improvement in their enterprise. Their ability to hold, use, consolidate, and manage the rangeland and water sources of the Channeled Scablands enabled the men to take full advantage of their enforced departure from the tramp sheep business.

The McGregors began the years 1896–1905 with few sheep, numerous debts, and a bankrupt store, but they possessed toughness of character and the shrewd ability to exploit the changing conditions. Theirs was a congenial and cohesive family unit able to exploit individual talents to serve common goals. They combined the thrift, determination, and "pure love" of money that John Kenneth Galbraith finds typical of the Scotch with the ability to innovate successfully in a new and rapidly changing style of agriculture.[60] As the Columbia Plateau developed from open range to complex ranching and farming, the McGregors outgrew the limitations of a simple partnership, and in July 1905, combined their assets in the $200,000 capital stock of the McGregor Land and Livestock Company.

Chapter 5

Boom Days in the Sheep Business, 1905-20

"Never were prospects brighter for sheepmen than now. Wool and mutton are high and it looks as if the day of free wool and poverty-stricken flockmasters is gone for good."   "Shepherd Boy," 1907

"If I ever get these old buzzard baits sheared and turned off to ship, I'll kill the next man that says 'sheep' to me. . . . There ain't a jury in the land that would cinch me for it, the provocation I've had."

H. L. Davis[1]

At the first meeting of the McGregor Land and Livestock Company (held in Hooper on July 18, 1905), Archie, Peter, John, and Alex McGregor decided that their corporation would "buy, sell, hold, pasture, and cultivate real estate." The men also included in their corporate charter provisions enabling them "to buy and sell cattle, sheep, horses, hogs, grain, farm implements and machinery and to buy and sell goods, wares, and merchandise of every kind and character whatsoever necessary and incident to conducting a general merchandise business." The four men sold more than 32,000 acres of land, 15,000 sheep, 500 cattle, 50 horses, and miscellaneous farm equipment to the new corporation. Peter McGregor was selected as company president at this session, Alex was named vice president, Archie was chosen as secretary, and John became manager. John was given the task of running the daily business affairs and was "authorized to employ the necessary help to run the business and to pay the same," to buy and sell livestock, and "to borrow sufficient money" if needed for the operations. The manager was to be subject to the rules and plans adopted by the board of directors, a body that included all four brothers. One-third of the net earnings was to be declared as a dividend each year. The corporation was to be private—no sale or transfer of capital stock would be valid unless the other members of the company were first given the preference right to purchase.[2]

The McGregor brothers had decided to switch from a partnership, a popular form for western livestock organizations of the 1890's, to a corporate form that, they felt, would provide increased business stability and "a more convenient ownership arrangement than a four-way partnership." Partnerships lacked the cohesiveness of a corporation: Disputes among members could spell the end of the business, or the death of one individual might cause a division into small holdings owned by several heirs. The corporate arrangement, with detailed by-laws and divisions of authority, promised a better organized operation that could deal more efficiently with banks, sheep buyers, and other business associates. Other Columbia Plateau livestock raisers made similar modifications in their businesses. F. M. Rothrock incorporated his holdings as Rothrock Land and Livestock Company. Rothrock had run a meat market in the 1890's and acquired enough money to enter the livestock business when a rich body of ore was found in the Hercules mine in which he had invested a portion of his earnings. Coffin Brothers, ingenious Indian traders and merchants of previous decades, organized the Coffin Sheep Company. Prineville Land and Livestock Company, Cunningham Sheep Company, Camas Prairie Land and Livestock, Hooper Land and Livestock, and several other sheep and cattle corporations were also formed.[3]

The formation of the livestock companies indicated that major changes had occurred in Columbia Plateau agriculture. Settled patterns of ranching and farming had been imposed on the 22-million-acre inland region. By 1905, the hectic competition for control of the sheep pastures and wheat fields was over, and little land remained unclaimed. Most of the prairie lands with soil deep enough to plow had been broken, and the remaining canyons and sandy flatlands had been claimed by sheepmen. The days of informally organized, low-cost, and marginally productive livestock operations were at an end, and those who remained in business had made more or less successful adjustments to the changed circumstances. The drastic fluctuations in market prices of the previous decades were replaced by slowly rising commodity values, and a period later described as "the golden age" of American agriculture had begun. Agriculture "had emerged finally as a comparatively stable business, with gradually advancing land values, an improving physical plant, fairly tolerable conditions of tenure and debt, and a strengthened voice in national affairs."[4]

The McGregor Land and Livestock Company became involved in a wide range of activities during this generally prosperous period. Although John McGregor's favorite term of contempt was "Ya farmer," he and his brothers, recognizing the promise of a new business, plowed up several thousand acres of prairie bunchgrass and became commercial wheat raisers. The productivity of the newly cultivated land and the improving market for grain led them to expand a farming operation begun initially to produce wheat-hay for their sheep. Their wheat business, both on tenant farms and on the McGregor-operated cropland, expanded by 1917 into an operation with a gross annual income of more than $85,000. A merchandise and hardware enterprise, begun as a commissary for McGregor employees, did more than $200,000 worth of business annually by 1920. The sale of lands external to the main sheep and wheat-producing areas also provided an important source of income.[5] The corporation made loans to farmers and ranchers; sold them machinery, implements, buggies, autos, and dry goods; and purchased their crops of sheep, cattle, wheat, and apples. In turn, the McGregors bought property that suited their needs: a hotel to feed and house their employees, a blacksmith shop, lumberyards, and various other facilities in the town of Hooper. The four brothers also invested in mining, irrigation, and cattle-raising enterprises that were organized outside the corporate structure of the McGregor Land and Livestock Company.

Despite the expansion and diversification of their business interests, it was sheep—sometimes described by Emile Morod as "them God damned sheep"—that remained the mainstay of the McGregor brothers' enterprises. The sheep business of the Columbia Plateau had been through a rapid process of change. Unlike other western range areas, where "coyote" sheepmen were still competing for unclaimed forage, the open range sheepmen of the Pacific Northwest interior were out of business. In fact, in 1907 Peter McGregor, chairman of the state Senate livestock committee, recommended passage of a bill that he and his brothers would have opposed strongly a few years before. Thomas J. Drumheller, himself a sheepman, explained to the *National Wool Grower* the result of House Bill 187 "relative to the trespass of sheepmen on certain lands and providing a punishment therefore": "A state law requiring the owner of a flock to control lands on which to run it has put the coyote sheepman out of business. Like the coyote he was a vagrant and his extinction will not be regretted. Eventually he had to go and the industry will hereafter be on a permanent basis. . . . Keeping in the sheep business . . . has been no easy stunt, but the man who has succeeded in controlling his range is in good shape for all time." The new statute revised and tightened the 1889 trespass law that the Northern Pacific Railroad had used to evict tramp sheepmen from railroad grazing lands. Both laws enabled owners of unfenced range to sue intruding sheepmen for trespass damages.[6] Such restrictions did not yet apply to most western range areas: As late as the 1930's, some sheepmen wandered from California through eastern Oregon and into Idaho, with not an acre of land under their control. The statutes anticipated the Taylor Grazing Act of 1934, a law that divided millions of acres of public domain into grazing districts, available for lease only to livestock owners who owned a "home ranch." The Taylor Act did not apply to the Columbia Plateau, where livestock raisers had long since acquired most of the lowland ranges and where open range production had been gone for thirty years.

The sheepmen of the Columbia Plateau continued the process, begun shortly before the turn of the century, of modifying and intensifying their production techniques to bring income commensurate with the costs of land ownership. Yakima sheepmen V. C. Pauhlman noted in 1918 that woolgrowers of the inland region had become "better acquainted with the benefits of good breeding stock, better equipage, and the best of care." New procedures for lambing, shearing, feeding, and marketing were introduced. But many of the old hazards of the business remained—the dangers of losses from predator attack, inclement weather, poison weeds, and the herd instinct of sheep. The sheep losses of open range days could not be tolerated by sheepmen with expensive lambing camps, high feed bills, costly breeds of stock, and thousands of acres of owned land.

Proper supervision of the sheep required conscientious foremen and attentive herders, lambers, camptenders, and other employees. There were many horror stories about careless sheep crews. Western sheepmen told the apocryphal story of a man "who was sent out to herd sheep and a few days later . . . [was] found sitting in his tent in the middle of the day. To the question as to why he was not out with his sheep he replied that he would have to . . . [be given] more sheep, as he had lost the last of his band the day before." Washington sheepman Gus Harras employed a new herder in 1906 and sent him to tend a flock in stubble next to a field of standing wheat.

The sheep herder was particularly instructed not to let the sheep get into the wheat and for several days he followed instructions. One day, when the foreman . . . visited the field, he found the herder in a straw stack peacefully sleeping off a jag and the field dotted with dead and dying sheep. The foreman, on counting the sheep, found that nearly 300 were dead and since then the number has increased to 500. . . . Dry wheat eaten in large quantities causes a fermentation that results in the sheep swelling to huge proportions. Many of the dead sheep had actually "exploded."

But sheepmen also told of men "who are faithful even to the risk of their own lives, diligent to the limit, and who conscientiously watch their employer's interests as they would their own."[7]

McGregor Land and Livestock Company required a large crew to tend from 12,000 to 15,000 sheep. The sheep were run in bands of 2,000 to 2,500, each band requiring a herder. A camptender hauled supplies to two or three herders. Teamsters hauled hay to the flocks during winter. "Drop pickers," "night men," "lambers," "bunch herders," and several additional employees were used during lambing. Almost sixty men were on the sheep payroll in lambing and shearing seasons, and from fifteen to forty men were employed during the rest of the year. The two employees most responsible for the success of the sheep business were John D. ("Jock") Macrae and Emile Morod. Macrae, a Scotch immigrant, worked in the McGregor sheep enterprise 47 years; Morod, a Frenchman, was employed 56 years by the corporation. "Jock" began working for the McGregors in 1898 and was sheep foreman from 1905 until his death in 1945. Emile was hired in 1913 and became Macrae's assistant before succeeding him as foreman.

Jock was a colorful individual who recited "Bobbie" Burns, talked Gaelic, drank great amounts of Scotch, and had sweethearts, even when in his eighties, at each of the areas through which McGregor sheep passed. Justice William O. Douglas tells a typical Jock Macrae story heard from another Scotch sheepman, Billy McGuffie:

> *One summer nicht John Duncan McRae, a freen o' mine, and I went into Spokane, dirty and thirsty, from a weary job a'loading sheep. We went into a pub and had a drink. As we came oot we met up with a Salvation Army street corner meetin'. As we paused there a moment, a Salvation Army lassie with a tamboreen walked up to Jock for a donation. "What dae ye want, lassie?" Jock asked. "Some money for the Lord," she replied. With a twinkle in his eyes, Jock countered, "How old are ye, lassie?" "Eighteen," was her answer. Jock said, "Well, I am eighty-seven and will be seein' the lord lang afore ye and I'll just gie him the penney mysel'". There was a pause and then Jock said, "It all goes to show that the Scotchman isn't stingy; he's just cautious."[8]*

Macrae had been a restless youth who resisted relatives' efforts to make him settle down. His cousin gave up on him: "All he cares for is to roam over the face of the earth with his bottle of whiskey with him." Jock came to the United States in the 1880's after working in a law office in his native Inverness, Scotland. He arrived in Denver, where he worked as a contractor's assistant for a few years. In 1889, Macrae left Denver for work in a rock quarry near Salt Lake City and then lived in

Fiji and the Samoan Islands, prospected in Australia, visited New Zealand, and went to Chicago—but "didn't like the East," so he "came out to Cheyenne, Wyoming and remained on a sheep ranch there several years." Then he "went to Victoria and Vancouver but didn't like it there," traveled to Calgary where conditions "didn't look so good," and then came to the Pacific Northwest. He spent a few months in jail in 1896 for selling whiskey to a woman on the Yakima Indian Reservation and then worked on his cousin's farm in Pomeroy, Washington. Uneasy after two years on the farm, he went to Spokane. "I had $250 when I came to Spokane," he recalled, "but lost all but $10 playing Fargo." He then intended to go back to sheepherding in Cheyenne but stopped in Lacrosse, Washington, "slept in a bunch of corn stalks," and inquired about jobs in the sheep business. Jock heard that the McGregors ran sheep and walked the fifteen miles to the McGregor ranch. Arriving in the morning, he stayed out of sight by sleeping in a haystack until afternoon, thinking that if no work was available he would at least be given a place to spend the night. Jock met Peter McGregor and asked for a job, only to be turned down. Allowed to sleep in the barn, the next morning he asked Archie for employment and was hired. Thus began his fifty-year association with McGregors.[9]

The roving life of a sheepman proved suited to Macrae's disposition and he became a capable, dedicated flockmaster. When Macrae temporarily left the McGregors in 1906, to search for fortune in South America, Peter McGregor described him as "our manager for 15,000 head of sheep" and "one of the most faithful men we have ever had. While we regret very much his decision to leave this country, and we thusly lose his services, we know that he who is fortunate enough to procure them will profit by it." Macrae remained in South America only briefly and visited Georgetown, British Guiana, but "didn't like the country—the people had to use too much quinine." He then "went to Buenos Aires but had a hunger to come back to the State of Washington again. Went back to Georgetown and found a letter from John McGregor and was glad to hear from him." Macrae wrote back and promised to be "in Spokane on Sept. 14th [1907] to buy the stubble fields for the sheep." He "got a little elevated" and missed his ship, but he still found time to visit Scotland before returning to Washington. He worked for McGregor Land and Livestock the rest of his life, claiming he found "more pleasure among the rocks and the sage brush" than in all his travels.[10]

John McGregor found Macrae "a very useful man" and a foreman of unusual calibre. Yet John, a strict Presbyterian opposed to heavy drinking, became alarmed in 1915 about reports that Jock "was drunk for over a week in Spokane." After receiving a letter demanding an explanation, Jock wrote John:

> *I paid off the man Maurice [Morod] had and I sent that Dutchman that I spoke about for chores by the train. As I told you he is a first class man for that work and I am fully satisfied he will make a first class herder altho' . . . he "won't set the Spokane River afire." . . . I am still on Rock Creek. Got both bands here with feed good for one week yet. . . . Now John when I seperate [sic] I am going to cut all 2 and 3 year olds out for Pete's Camp and I think I can fix them so I won't have to seperate them in the fall next year.*
>
> *Well maybe I won't be there as from the letter I got from you yesterday I guess I had better quit. . . .*
>
> *I admit I got full in Spokane. John I had three bands of sheep to feed and you know what that is. I had to do it. Well, John you know me well enough that when things beat me, I fly to drink. Maybe for a day. Then next day there seems to be something that puts everything right. It made me so sore that them farmers would burn that stubble them knowing I was on the road with the sheep. Well, John to shorten the story. As you said in your letter the first one you tore up and the second you said you couldn't write. Now, John, I am going to take the sheep home and seperate them. . . . I'll put all the sheep and the camps together and stay a month longer at my own expense. Then John I am going away for good. . . . But in case you might want me a week or so longer, I'll do it. . . . I want you to understand that I'll draw no wages from the time I cross the bridge at Hooper. . . . John don't you think for one moment that I'll neglect my business. I've taken care of it ever since you entrusted it to me. I don't say that I'm an angel. If I was I wouldn't be here. I'd be above along with the rest of them. . . . Don't get sore at what I say in this letter. . . . But John I'm telling just as I think. I swear I am not drinking. And you can depend on the sheep being cared for until I get through with them.[11]*

Jock Macrae and John McGregor reached an understanding, and McGregor Land and Livestock Company continued to rely on Macrae's assistance in tending its flocks.

Emile Morod entered the sheep business in a different fashion. In 1913 his brother Maurice, a McGregor herder, sent Emile one hundred dollars, enabling him to purchase a ticket for a boat trip to New York. Both of Emile's parents had died when he was thirteen, and Emile had then spent some time doing odd jobs on a neighboring farm. The job was a satisfactory one until the farmer's son came home from the army and began to criticize Emile's performance and "cussed him out." Emile decided to quit the job as soon as possible. As an orphan, he had also acquired a reputation as somewhat a juvenile delinquent and feared being sent to a reformatory. Like many other French youths who came west to herd sheep, Emile was certain that he "didn't want to serve in the French Army." The combination of circumstances provided sufficient incentive for Emile to come to the Pacific Northwest.

Emile took a train to Le Havre and there boarded a ship for New York. Seasick the first two days, he was too shy to grab a helping of food at the smorgasbord meals and finally, in desperation, went to the kitchen where he was able to get food from the sympathetic cook. Government officials at Ellis Island detained Emile because he had only two dollars, eighteen less than was required for incoming immigrants. Emile slept in a hammock provided by the authorities for a week, until his brother Maurice sent additional money from Hooper. After boarding a train heading west, Emile found that all the overnight quarters were taken. He had to sit on his suitcase in the aisle all night. In the cold draft he caught the flu, and he was groggy and dizzy when he got off the train in Chicago. Unable to speak any English, Morod obtained information during his layover in Chicago by putting his ticket in his hatband and pointing at it for directions. When he reached Pendleton, Oregon, and pointed at the ticket a conductor motioned north. Emile walked a long distance down the track before realizing he could not get to Walla Walla without another train ride. When he finally arrived in Walla Walla, he was to meet his brother in a saloon run by a Frenchman. First Emile entered the wrong saloon and was forcefully evicted. The fifteen-year-old immigrant tried again, until he found his brother and the considerable comfort of a warm welcome enhanced by drinking and talking with other Frenchmen.[12]

"The McGregor Brothers," an observer noted in 1913, "prefer and usually secure French herders, of whom there is quite a colony in the vicinity of Walla Walla." The demand by Columbia Plateau sheepmen for capable herders had prompted many French immigrants to come to the region, and a district in Walla Walla served these men as a convenient base of operations. Adrien Magallon and several other Frenchmen who began as herders had organized their own sheep businesses by the time Emile Morod arrived. After exploring job opportunities in conversations with these men, Emile considered his brother's favorable experiences with the McGregors, and decided to begin work in Hooper. Emile's first job with the McGregor brothers in 1913 included work in the apple orchard and the milking sheds with a German who had little regard for a "dirty little Frenchman." The following year, Emile's situation improved when he became a camptender and sheepherder. His career as a herder began in an unfortunate manner when he filled his camp stove with pine needles and the resulting explosive fire burned down his tent. Because it rained steadily during the week, he had to take his only change of clothes off and leave them by the stove to dry while he was herding. He survived these early trials, and Emile went on to become one of the most important McGregor sheepmen within a few years' time.[13]

Jock Macrae and Emile Morod were only two members of a large group of men who had important jobs in the McGregor sheep operations. John Belliour, Maurice Vasher (Vasser), Ernest Biques, the Morod brothers, and several other herders came from Haute-Alpes, a province in eastern France where sheep raising was a common occupation. Belliour, unlike the men who came to eastern Washington to avoid three years' service in the French Army, returned to his native land and was killed in action during World War I. Lee Burden, a McGregor herder and camptender from 1915 until his death in 1948, had been a logger near the northern Idaho summer range before entering the sheep business. William James, an assistant to Jock Macrae for several years, followed a pattern of life common to many western sheepmen—six to eight months on the range and then a drunk of several weeks to two months in a city. Robert Clyde and Bunyan C. Lee were two other employees who had positions of authority for several years. John McGregor, in a 1918 letter to the chairman of the district draft exemption board, listed men of eighteen to forty-five years of age "who have had years of experience and are essential to the continuance of our business on a productive and efficient basis": [14]

Emile Morod	In charge of 2–12 men
Maurice Vasher	"
Maurice Morod	"
Thomas McCammon	In charge of 1–2 men
E. D. Starr	"
Lee Burden	Herder and substitute foreman
Sidney Lenthal	"

The sheep crew was paid monthly wages and board. When possible during winter months, these employees ate at the McGregor-owned Hotel Glenmore (now Hooper Hotel), where cooks served three meals a day for twenty to thirty-five patrons. But most of the crew's food was cooked over open fires on the rangeland near the bands of sheep. Charles H. Brune, a veteran Oregon and Washington sheepman, remembered the food served at sheep camps:

John McGregor
To M dse

Item	Amt	Item	Amt
Gard seed &c		4 Cas Corn	10 20
1 x Rad Gloo	100	2 Bbl Flour	9.75
Lamp	50	2 Sk Graham	1.00
3 Pkg Tooth Pk	75	2 Cas Coal Oil	6.30
1 Pr Shoes	3.50	3 Pkg Currents	.45
1 "	3.60	3 Pkg Raising	60
3 Sk R. Oats	1.05	8 ℔ Raisins	1.00
75 ℔ Peach	8.62	Gem Pans	25
100 Apples	5.75	47 ℔ Bro. Bean	2.55
1 Gal M.L.	50	46 ℔ Wh. "	2.55
3 Gal Red	1.35	6 Bk Red Bell	3.00
2 Cas Tom.	5.00	6 Cans Maple S.	9.00
3 Pr Overall	1.85	1 Sk Sugar	6.25
1 Bucket	45	Coffee	1.00
2 Sk g Pickle	230	Rice	2.00
1 Bucket K	60	Mace	50
2 Cof. Pot	1.30	3 Br Crackers	2.25
4 Blew Ket.	2.25	2 Gal Vineg	.80
2 Set K & F	1.30	16 Towels	2.80
2 Set Tea S.	90	Bro Sugar	1.50
3 Dippers	.75	3 Cas Eggs	11.25
4 Gal Oil Cl.	1.20	10 ℔ Butter	2.00
6 Pkg Corn S.	60	2 Drip pan	.50
Wallnuts	25	4 Fry Pans	1.50
After	25	2 Hats	.30
2 Gran Pans	40	3 Pr Overalls	1.80
2 Lamps	20	2 Hats	30
Whet Rock	20		5 40
2 Buckets	1.50		
2 Wash Bas.	75		
	45.67		

Provisions for a lambing camp: John McGregor account at Gordon Brothers store in Pampa (from store ledger books of Ethel Gordon Metzger)

The fruit was all dried—dried raisins, dried apples, dried peaches. We had very little beef in the camps, it was mostly mutton. But we put up our own pork for ham and bacon. Butter and eggs came from the ranch. Coffee came in sixty pound wooden drums and was ground by the cook with a hand grinder. Only three canned goods—canned Carnation milk, tomatoes, and corn. And you didn't have a can opener. You'd open the cans crosswise with a butcher knife. . . . Most of the bread was made right in the top of the flour sack. You'd take a fifty pound sack of flour out to a camp and you'd tap a little hole in the top . . . and add a cup of water plus a little salt and a teaspoon of Shilling's baking powder . . . and you stirred up your dough right in the flour sack . . . and no one ever had a bread pan. . . . The dough would run quite a little and you'd have to hold the sack just right . . . Then you'd flip it and go clear around and get that bread stiffened up on the outside. . . . We had three frying pans all fit together and the biggest one was used to make bread. First you greased the pan and made a little hole in the middle of the loaf with your finger. You put the pan on top of the fire and looked at the hole to tell when it was time to flip it. It was quite an art making that bread.[15]

Big Bend sheepman Thomas J. Drumheller, Jr., remembered the crews and provisions of the Drumheller sheep business:

We had a lot of Frenchmen work for us in those days because we had two French foremen, Victor Robbin and John Fore, and they used to spend what little vacation they took down in Walla Walla. . . . Fella named Jean Burnett was one of the best camp cooks, he was just neat and clean as a pin. By gosh those fellas were bread makers. . . . They'd take the fifty pound sack of flour I'd bring up, roll the top down and scoop it out and use it as a large mixing bowl. . . . They'd use a Dutch oven—put the coals in and their dough in there—and they made the lightest bread. . . . Those fellas . . . kept their camps up. . . . You enjoyed going into a camp in those days. By golly you had the best mutton stews and things like that. We used to always take sacks of onions, cabbage, lettuce, and beans, and things like that up to 'em. In the early days I can remember when they started ordering store boughten bread and I thought, "My God, what's this world coming to?"

Drumheller remembered one of his crew, "Old Frenchie, we called him":

You'd swear he couldn't walk the next five miles because he kind of walked on his heels but that old fella was tough as nails and he hiked all over these mountains when he was up in his seventies. He was really powerful. He couldn't speak French and he couldn't speak English. He'd nod and smile. I think he knew what you were talking about all the time. I remember I counted his sheep up on top of the hills and then a month later I counted again and by golly, he was only out one sheep. I said "One, Frenchie, you lost one." And he said, "We eat 'em." He was quite an old boy.[16]

The herders were well paid for their strenuous, lonely work. In 1913, for example, McGregor herders were paid an average of $42 per month and board, 25 percent more than the statewide average farm wage. During World War I, increased profits from sheep raising, a serious labor shortage, and an inflationary trend in general combined to cause a dramatic increase in pay for herders, camptenders, and other employees. Archie McGregor, at a 1917 meeting of county commissioners, urged a raise in taxes so county officials could receive better pay, stating that:

He paid uneducated men as sheep herders from $60 to $100 a month and board, which was a better wage than many college graduates could command. At this point a former county commissioner interrupted to ask . . . the wealthy sheepman of Hooper . . . if he could get a position at such a price. "Yes sir," replied McGregor, "I'll give you a job tomorrow at $60 a month and board, and when you make good, I'll raise your wages and return your train fare in coming to the ranch."[17]

To earn these wages, the herders had to live according to a pattern of seasonal migration practiced more than forty years before by the first sheepmen to arrive on the Columbia Plateau. The lowland winter ranges were now in rocky canyons or desert ranges where wheat farming was impractical. The steeply walled scablands of the lower Palouse and Snake rivers were owned by the McGregors, Phil Cox, Leon Jaussaud, and other sheepmen. The arid sagebrush flats of the Umatilla were winter quarters for Cunningham Sheep Company, Rugg brothers, Baldwin Sheep and Land Company, and many other eastern Oregon sheep raisers. The Coffin brothers, Charles Brune, Archie Prior, and W. H. Peatross used the sandy, windswept Rattlesnake Hills ranges. Thomas Drumheller and former "cattle king" T. S. Blyth had winter sheep quarters on the rocky flat lands of the Big Bend. Sheep outfits were scattered through the sagebrush deserts along the Columbia River, near the townsites of Vantage, Hanford, and White Bluffs. Herders remained at these locations with their sheep from October or November until May, when hot, dry weather had dried out the green rangeland forage.

On the McGregor ranch, the herders' winter quarters consisted of tents, sheep wagons, or small wooden cabins equipped with stoves, beds, tables, tin dishes, and utensils. The shacks, each adjacent to a large corral, were located at various sheltered areas on the range, such as Winn Lake, Palouse Falls, Pete's Camp, Hooper Lake, Wildcat Lake, John's Camp, and

Green Lake. Tents were used in other areas where the terrain was too rugged to permit a camptender to haul the ponderous steel-wheeled wagons to the herders. The sheep wagons, first developed in Wyoming in the 1890's, were similar in appearance to the old Conestoga wagons, but shortened and widened, with two layers of canvas pulled taut over the top, a small window in the back, and a door at the front with two independently swinging halves. A stove was located near the front of the wagon, and a stovepipe was stuck up through the canvas. The divided door permitted the herder to ventilate the wagon without cooling off the stove. It served other purposes as well: "You may want to keep the dog in or out without keeping the door shut, so you close the lower half. Also, if you open the full door, the effect is somewhat like opening the entire side of a house. But by keeping the bottom half closed you prevent floor drafts, while the top half, being fastened with a chain, may be kept open at any angle desired, thus affording a perfect means of ventilation." The wagons also contained a dish cupboard, two long benches (with a trapdoor in the middle of each leading to the "grub" boxes), a bed, and a hinged table. The McGregors were able to stop using tents altogether when Dan Kuster and Emile Morod designed and built a lighter, rubber-tired wagon that could be transported throughout the winter rangeland.[18]

Jock Macrae hauled supplies to the men every few weeks in a long, narrow-boxed wagon that was filled with sacks of food and a variety of other provisions ordered by the herders. A typical page of one of his early "workmen's time books" listed some of the wide variety of materials requested by herders:

Pete's Camp	*For Emile*	*Lee Batrick*
$1 tobacco	2 lanterns	one doz. socks
butter, coffee, ginger	10 panels	overalls
needle & thread	tent & corral	shaving soap
sack twine	lantern globes	50¢ velvet tobacco
lamp black	grub	2 corncob pipes
wrench & water buckets	apples	

The sheep dog was an indispensable ally on the rangeland. Without a capable dog, the herder had to be on the run at all times to control the two thousand or more sheep in his custody. As one western sheepherder has written: "A dog is the one thing of which sheep are afraid. They move merely enough to keep out of a herder's way, and they care nothing about a horse, in case the herder happens to be riding. ... There is, however, a great difference in the way sheep react to different dogs. . . . From a fast-working dog they run in terror, while for a slow dog . . . they move with corresponding leisure. The ideal dog is one that works slowly but steadily, looking back frequently for further directions from the herder." [19]

Sheepmen and herders had personal preferences for the type of dog best suited to the trade, although most sheep dogs were descendants of the collie breeds used in open range days. The McGregor sheepmen bred and trained dogs that were crosses between collies and Australian wolfhounds. They trained the dogs by the "apprentice" method. A herder took a puppy a few months old to his sheep camp and allowed him to work with two experienced dogs for a season. The young dog learned from his companions to respond to the hand signals and the English, French, or Spanish commands of the herder. These lessons were supplemented by the herder with long hours of individualized training. A properly trained dog knew how to encircle a scattered flock quickly or slowly trail a band through scabrock, forests, or stubble. The dog learned to nip the legs of errant sheep gently and to follow on the heels of sheep located on the flanks of the band to change the direction of the flock without causing alarm. Felix Zozaya, a McGregor herder of recent years, taught his dog to herd thousands of sheep through a gate without assistance, to separate a particular sheep from the band on command, to catch and pin a young lamb for inspection, and even to "sing," "whistle," and jump through a flaming hoop. The devotion of sheep dogs to their herders is legendary. One McGregor herder and his loyal dog spent a frantic week trailing a band of sheep over mountainous country away from a rapidly advancing forest fire. Peter McGregor told of a herder's astonishment when a dog, missing for a week, returned with an errant sheep he had been following. One McGregor herder, disconsolate when his best dog failed to return to camp, committed suicide.[20]

Another form of canine, the coyote, was the herder's constant enemy, following the sheep from wintering grounds to summer pasture. Coyotes had been shot, poisoned, and hunted with hounds for thirty years. But despite the attempts to eradicate these dangerous predators, coyotes increased in numbers as the western ranges were settled and developed. Usually operating at night or in the twilight period just before sunrise, coyotes worked with deadly precision in isolating and killing their ovine prey. Novelist H. L. Davis describes a favorite method used by coyotes in attacking the bands of sheep run by the McGregors and other western woolgrowers:

> *The sheep were jammed together on account of the chill. . . . The strays bored their way into the herd, which settled into drowsiness, with only one old ewe left moving around them at a worried sort of amble.*

*She raised her gait to a jog, glanced down at her side, and then put on
still more speed, like an old lady being pursued by a cheap pitchman in
the street. As she circled the herd she drew farther away from it. . . .
An old he-coyote was trotting beside her, his shoulder pressed against
hers, holding a little back so she would keep trying to get ahead and
rubbing her close so her shrinking from him would carry her out of
range of the herd that she was working her best lick to get back to.
He made no effort to hurry or hurt her; she was still so close to [the] . . .
guard-fire that he didn't dare to. If she had blated or turned on him and
started a rumpus, she would have been saved. But she was too scared to do
anything but avoid him and try to outrun him. She trotted faster, and he
let out another hitch of speed and rubbed her as if to remind her that
he was still there. When they rounded the herd a second time, he had
worked her a quarter of a mile away from it. . . . The sheep and the
coyote trotted their round solemnly, pressed close like a pair of small
town lovers on Sunday afternoon. . . . [The ewe finally stopped]
and stood with her legs spraddled and her head dropped so it almost
touched the ground, and the coyote stood watching her and waiting
for her to look up . . . as ceremonious as the preparation had been, the
slaughter happened with no ceremony at all. The sheep lifted her head
and the coyote trotted close and cut her throat with one swift open-
fanged swipe.*

Coyotes sometimes traveled in packs and worked in unison killing
sheep. A favorite tactic was for a few of the predators to go to the far
side of the band, attracting the attention of herder and dogs with their
distinctive howl—a series of sharp, high-pitched barks followed by a long
and mournful wail. Meanwhile, the remainder of the pack cut in from
the other side and silently made the kill. The herder would find a few
dead sheep and several crippled ewes and lambs when he inspected his
flock the following morning. Further losses on the winter range were
caused by bobcats and domestic dogs. Settlers' dogs were known to chase
and kill dozens of unattended sheep in a single evening. To minimize the
danger of serious loss from these adversaries, McGregor sheepmen built
dozens of corrals, each located near a winter campground. The herder
(sleeping in a nearby wagon or shack) and his dogs could detect restless
activity among the enclosed sheep and put a stop to the predators'
schemes. But if a herder was inattentive and lost sheep or left them out
overnight, Emile Morod recalled, "You figure next morning there would
be half a dozen tore up." Emile remembered one occasion when a coyote was audacious enough to strike in broad daylight: "I was out herding
by Donald's Well and had a big band, 2400 and some. When I went
around 'em here was a God damned coyote had one of 'em tore up and
was eating its belly out. . . . You know, out on the range where I was,

they was bad them days. . . . But we was out with the sheep all the time and never gave 'em too much chance." Because newborn lambs were particularly vulnerable to coyote attack, the sheepmen took precautions after lambing time: "We had scarecrows. We'd pack three or four scarecrows and a lantern and before we'd leave them that night we lit up the lanterns and put the scarecrows up so the coyotes wouldn't get 'em that night." [21]

A sheep raiser always faced the dangers of bad weather. The Columbia Plateau lowland ranges had cold winters but seldom had deep snow cover for prolonged periods. Pioneer sheepman Phil Cox tried to eliminate the long migrations of his flocks between seasonal ranges in 1906 by wintering 12,000 sheep near their Montana summer pastures, instead of trailing back to eastern Washington. Cox's experiment failed, for the Montana winter was "unusually severe" and he lost nearly half his flock. Sheepmen who continued to use the canyons and arid hills of eastern Oregon and Washington reported far better results. A correspondent commented on the condition of a band of McGregor sheep the following spring: "A band of 2500 sheep belonging to State Senator Peter Mc-Gregor . . . passed through Palouse en route from the Senator's land on the Snake River to St. Maries [Idaho] where they will be pastured during the summer. The sheep give evidence of having wintered well and the lambs are in especially good condition."

The winter of 1907–08 was an unusually good one for many sheepmen. "Peter McGregor, senator from this district, who is a member of the firm of McGregor Brothers, sheep and land kings" described the season on January 6, 1908: "This has been an ideal winter for stock. Cattle, horses, and sheep are in prime condition, and owners have not had to feed a day yet. There is plenty of feed, and the season is so far advanced that it is certain we will not have a long, hard winter. Prospects never looked brighter for stockmen than at present." The following winter was similarly mild, for a report from the McGregor ranch stated that "sheep have come through the winter better this year than for many years." But to count on such mild weather was to invite disaster. Sheepmen who had not prepared adequately for the winter of 1915–16 encountered severe losses. K. O. Kohler of Ellensburg reported to the *National Wool Grower* that the season was the "hardest . . . on stock in the Northwest that I have seen in 28 years," with a blanket of two feet of snow covering the Columbia Plateau for an extended period.[22]

"The old way" of providing winter feed, sheepman Charles Brune recalled, "was to do it cheap. It'd break a man's heart to have to haul a load of hay out to his sheep." But Columbia Plateau sheepmen now had an investment of twenty thousand dollars or more in winter rangeland alone, with large and expensive crews, increasing costs, and valuable sheep. They could no longer tolerate the possibility of high losses from exposure, disease, and even starvation that sometimes resulted from insufficient winter feed. The McGregors hired teamsters who used long, canvas-covered vehicles known as "gut wagons" to haul wheat-, rye-, and alfalfa-hay; cottonseed cake; and pea silage to their flocks. By feeding 694 tons of wheat- and rye-hay grown on the ranch to their 13,416 sheep during the winter of 1905–06, the McGregors were able to record the exceptionally low winter loss rate of 1.45 percent. But providing just enough hay to ensure survival of the flocks was no longer sufficient—for gaunt, skinny ewes produced poor wool clips, small lamb crops, and insufficient milk for lambs. McGregor Land and Livestock Company gradually expanded its supplemental feeding program from 78 pounds of hay per sheep in 1906 to more than 188 pounds a decade later. The large crops of wheat-hay grown on the ranch helped provide much of the increased supply. But as the McGregors became more concerned with commercial wheat production, they phased out wheat-hay and began to grow alfalfa, a more nutritious livestock feed. Wells were dug, and in 1911 a crew of Italian railroad workers was hired to haul rocks from a few hundred acres of the Palouse River Valley in order to prepare the land for irrigated alfalfa-hay production. Additional feeds were purchased. In 1918, for example, McGregor Land and Livestock bought 250 tons of hay from a Walla Walla farmer, 180 tons of clipped oats from a local grain merchant, and 33 tons of cottonseed "cake" from a Utah corporation. Some of the extra feed was used as a supplement for rams just before breeding time. Grain and the cottonseed product were used as a protein source for pregnant ewes. William McGregor detailed the reasons for feeding ewes extra nutrients:

> *We fed before lambing really as a supplement not because the sheep needed it in the sense they were starving to death. When a big ewe is very pregnant, particularly with twins, the lambs take up so much space inside her that she hasn't got much room in her stomach and has trouble getting enough to eat. That's a period when the energy demands on the sheep are very high . . . so we fed . . . not because there wasn't enough grass to see them through but simply to get a better lambing percentage, easier lambing, and better milk.*[23]

The invasion of the Columbia Plateau by "cheatgrass" (bromus tectorum), an aggressive "weed," had a marked effect on the amounts of supplementary feed required. Botanists had gathered a few samples of the European annual grass on their travels through the plateau in the 1890's. These scattered samples of the grass probably came from contaminated wheat seed shipped into the region. Scientists at Washington Agricultural College, in their search for new grasses for depleted range, grew a stand of cheatgrass at Pullman in 1897 from seed imported by the USDA. Cheatgrass began to spread widely after 1905, and by World War I it had become the most abundant weed on much of the plateau. Botanist Richard Mack says of the cheatgrass invasion: "Seldom in the recent transformation of the earth's vegetation by mobile Occidental man and his plants has the vegetation of such a large area been transformed so swiftly and (apparently) permanently." Cheatgrass became the most ubiquitous plant species on the Columbia Plateau, particularly in areas where the native bunchgrass had been closely grazed. A shallow-rooted plant, cheatgrass dried out in early summer and turned the rangeland a dark red color. Ranchers disliked the mature plant—for the thick stands were highly flammable and were filled with spiked seeds that sometimes became imbedded in the wool, hide, and even the flesh of stock. Farmers had little regard for the hardy weed that invaded wheat fields and "cheated" them out of the opportunity for a good yield. But cheatgrass provided lush, rank early spring forage at a time of the year when ranchers had once been forced to feed hay to their stock. After the arrival of the new grass, sheepmen were able to concentrate more on specialized protein supplements and less on substituting hay for depleted range forage.[24]

As the winter season came to a close and a new crop of grasses appeared on the rangeland, the sheep became difficult to control. Sheep, used to dry feed, would scatter over wide areas of green forage. Herders somtimes found the pastoral life less than idyllic: "The truth is that, after you have turned the sheep back for the sixth or seventh consecutive time and they start off in a new direction with undiminished enthusiasm, there arises something within you that demands expression, just like the hot lava welling up in the bosom of an overdue volcano. The output is somewhat similar also." Sheepmen frequently found cause to agree with John Muir's contention that "sheep brain must surely be poor stuff." The flocking instinct of sheep continued to cause losses after the end of the open range. Jacob Harder told of losing a band of sheep when the flock "for some reason became excited and a few of the leaders jumped over a cliff" on his scabland range near Kahlotus Lake. The herder, Pierre Rambeau, "tried to stop the sheep from following the leaders, but before he could succeed over 2,000 sheep had jumped" to their deaths over the hundred-foot embankment. The intelligence of sheep was questioned most frequently during lambing season, a period of several weeks beginning between March 10 and 20. McGregor sheepmen had to tend 8,300 to 11,000 newborn lambs every year. Lambing

crews throughout the West put in their own sort of eight-hour day—
"eight hours before dinner and eight hours after. . . . This has one single
advantage. It gives the herder time mentally to reshape his future life,
so that he will never again under any circumstances herd through another spring." [25]

Ewes are a rarity among mammals in their frequent indifference, and
occasional active hostility, toward their offspring. Besides not knowing
her lamb from the others by sight, the ewe initially does not recognize
the noisy bleating of her offspring. Able to distinguish the lamb only
by smell, a ewe separated from her lamb will search for it by smelling
every lamb she sees until she gets tired of looking. Unless an alert drop
picker, herder, or night picker quickly reconciled the two, the lamb
would die. The crew had to remain vigilant at all times during a lambing
season full of worry and toil. As one observer remarked: "One of the
peculiar things about sheep is the extraordinary facility with which they
take leave of life, and the great variety of ways in which they make their
exit. You might almost accuse them of having a morbid strain." [26]

McGregor herders, drop pickers, teamsters, camptenders, night pickers, and bunch herders were scattered over 25,000 acres of scabrock
range during lambing season. Three main lambing camps, Archie's Camp,
John's Camp, and Pete's Camp, served as the headquarters for the sixty-
man crews. Each camp had a cook, an individual who was responsible for
slaughtering and butchering the livestock to be eaten, and for preparing
the food for the large crews of men. The regular crew was supplemented
by two dozen extra helpers. Lambing help was generally in short supply
on the western ranges, and men possessing the specialized skills necessary at this critical period could command good wages. A correspondent
to *The Shepherd's Criterion* complained in 1908: "Plenty of men are
willing to undertake the job, but they are a lot of dubs and know nothing about the business, so that the masters are put to the usual annual
inconvenience of suffering great loss." McGregor Land and Livestock
Company was able to secure a competent, but unusual, group of transient laborers. One man, a teamster about five feet, three inches tall, would
find the meanest horses on the range and conquer them for his team. An
eccentric character and a heavy drug user, this individual was nevertheless a competent man for hauling hay to the various lambing camps.
Another helper, "Shorty" Ritter (a short, fat man who wore perfume,
rouge, and women's underwear), was accepted by the crew because of
his abilities as a teamster. Ritter and another man, Bill Swanson, almost
died several years later during a beer drinking session at one of the
bunkhouses. The two mistook strychnine for salt, added it to their

beers, and shot windows out of the store and bunkhouse before they passed out. But they recovered and rejoined the lambing crew.[27]

Columbia Plateau sheepmen had begun improving upon the old open range methods of lambing after 1900 by building corrals to protect lambs born at night. Arthur and Phil Cox, pioneer Palouse country sheepmen, devised a makeshift system to protect the "night drop": "In our early days in the sheep business in lambing season we had no corrals. Lambed out on the open range. In later years we used the coralls [sic] [but left] what we called the day drop on the range. We made small pens out of wire with sticks about four feet apart . . . large enough to hold 30 ewes and their lambs. [The corrals] had to be moved every day and the mode of moving them on those Snake River hills was to roll them up and put them on your back and take them to the new location." The McGregors improved the corral system they had developed a few years earlier. They built a series of permanent structures that were functional rather than substantial: Lambing camps were fenced and divided into dozens of small enclosed areas surrounded by wooden panels everywhere patched and tied together with baling wire; small, unpainted sheds were built of rough, low-grade lumber that became warped and weatherbeaten with age. The sheds faced into the wind and were open on the protected east side. Emile Morod recalled bringing the sheep "in at nights, around the sheds. . . . Just the overnight drop. . . . The day drop, they stayed outside. . . . But at night the drop band was kept all around there, in a fence." Herders gradually improved these lambing camps by reinforcing sagging panels, putting up additional fencing, and building new sheds whenever they had slack time.[28]

But the most important modification in corral lambing after 1905 involved the development of elaborate patterns of trailing ewes and lambs across the scabrock so as to take maximum advantage of available water and forage, sheltered canyons, and improved lambing quarters. The activities of the sheepmen headquartered at Archie's Camp, the largest lambing location, were typical of these procedures. "About a week before lambing, when there wasn't much to do," Emile Morod recalled, "we'd go out, three or four men, with shovels and fill up all the badger holes. Lotta God damned badgers in those days. Lambs would walk around, fall in the badger holes. You could lose a lot of 'em that way." The day before lambing, herders plowed the various corrals to be used by the drop band with a team to cover up manure and provide a sanitary location for the lambs. The entire drop band, totaling as many as five thousand sheep, was kept overnight at a large corral in the deep sheltered canyon at Wildcat Lake. "At daylight we'd go out there and pick the ewes and the lambs, straighten them out, not too many [were born that night] maybe twenty to fifty." These sheep were kept in the sheltered location and fed hay. The remaining expectant ewes were then trailed slowly in a semicircular fashion toward the lambing sheds at Archie's Camp. Each ewe that "dropped" a lamb was quietly left behind as the band drifted away. Drop pickers were responsible for watching all these sheep closely and working them slowly into small groups of fifteen to twenty at scattered sheltered locations, where scarecrows and lanterns were put up and the sheep were bedded down for the night. The remain-

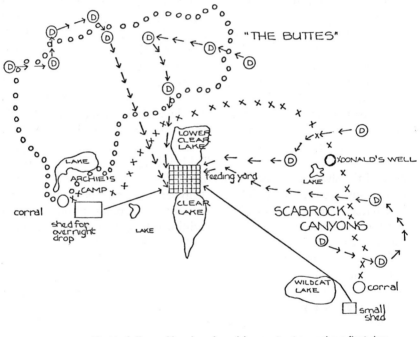

x x x x x	Route followed by drop band (expectant ewes) on first day
o o o o o o	Route followed by drop band on second day
Ⓓ	Small groups of ewes and lambs born during daylight hours
→ → → →	"Day drop" (lambs born during day) en route to Clear Lake
———————→	"Night drop" en route to Clear Lake feeding yards

The first two days of "corral" lambing at Archie's Camp. On the third day, the band might be grazed in a circular pattern north of Archie's Camp; on the fourth, perhaps a similar cycle to the east would be used. The purpose of these cyclical routes is clear—to spread operations over the maximum possible area of rangeland and thus take advantage of large areas of range forage.

der of the band stopped for water at Donald's Well and was herded into the large corrals adjacent to Archie's Camp, arriving there at dusk. The night picker then began his job of sorting out lambs and ewes and placing them in "jugs," small pens just large enough for the newborn lambs and their mothers. The following day, the remainder of the drop band was trailed slowly to the south in a circular pattern, thus providing fresh forage for the drop band and for the new bunches of lambs and ewes left behind in the scabrock. At night, the ewes yet to produce lambs were again corralled at Archie's Camp. The pattern was repeated throughout the lambing period until the last ewes had finally given birth.

As the drop band continued its cyclical grazing pattern around Archie's Camp, a herder and two drop pickers slowly gathered the small groups of sheep from the previous "day drop" and trailed them to a feeding yard that had been built at Clear Lake. Moving the small groups was a major problem: Some ewes went too fast and had to be headed back into the bunch; some lambs were weak and were always lying down behind rocks or clumps of sagebrush. Lambs left behind would die of starvation or be killed by coyotes. Additional employees moved the "night drop" from the sheds and trailed them to the pens at Clear Lake. Maurice Vasher (the foreman of the feeding operations) and his several employees separated the sheep into a large series of enclosures and fed the sheep hay for about two weeks. The lambs and ewes were gradually put into larger and larger groups until they were ready to be sent out in bodies of a hundred or more onto the rangeland, where they were in the custody of a "bunch herder." After a week or so of close care on the range, the ewes could usually recognize the bleating of their offspring and the sheep could be placed safely into bands of two thousand or more. A similar procedure was used at John's Camp, Winn Lake, and the other lambing headquarters.[29]

This pattern of lambing offered distinct advantages over the old open range "broadcast" system. The lambs born at night were closely supervised and sheltered against predator attack and severe weather. The increased use of supplemental feed ensured healthier lambs that fattened more quickly, as well as better milk-producing ewes. McGregor Land and Livestock was able to save about 12 percent more lambs annually, according to sheep tally books kept by John and Archie McGregor, Jock Macrae, and other men. But this system continued to have a drawback: The "day drop" was left out on the range overnight, with lanterns and scarecrows their only defense against predation, and canyons and rock outcroppings their only protection against sudden storms.

Columbia Plateau sheep raisers began to experiment with "shed" ("hothouse") lambing, a new procedure that, *American Shepherd's Bulletin* claimed in 1907, offered a "source of great profit to those engaged therein." Shed lambing required large amounts of fairly inexpensive winter feed, relatively mild winters, and an early supply of green grass—conditions that made it better suited to the lowland pastures of the interior Pacific Northwest than to any other western range area. Sheepmen using the new system could abandon the old procedure of trailing the drop band across wide areas of winter range. Long rows of covered lambing pens, sufficient to accommodate all newborn lambs and their mothers, had to be constructed. McGregor Land and Livestock Company began to build such pens and sheds in 1910. Seven years later Archie McGregor supervised construction of the "big shed," a sturdy structure 150 feet long and 192 feet wide, with a roof 17 feet high at the eaves rising to 28 feet at its peak. This building could house the entire band of expectant ewes. The new shed at Archie's Camp was to serve as the main lambing location for fifty years, and it is still the headquarters for shearing operations. After the McGregors switched to shed lambing, the day drop was no longer left unattended in "the rocks." Employees using horse-drawn "drop wagons" quickly sorted out the ewes and lambs and hauled them to the sheds, where they were placed in small enclosures. Large amounts of alfalfa-hay and grain were fed to them, both before and after the birth of the new lamb crop.[30]

By providing feed and shelter, sheepmen were able to commence lambing much earlier, generally in the last week of February. The lambs matured sooner and made better use of the early spring range crops of cheatgrass, june grass, and bunchgrass. Columbia Plateau sheep raisers, therefore, were able to sell their sheep earlier in the year, when fewer lambs were on hand at the Chicago and St. Paul stockyards. Thomas Drumheller, Jr., explained the main reason for his family's switch to the more expensive shed system. "In 1912 we built our present lambing camp. . . . We started what we called hothouse lambing right off the bat. We built a big shed. The drop band usually consisted of 2,000 to 3,000 sheep and they could all go under shed at night. . . . We hauled a good portion of hay up for lambing time. It was an expensive way to operate but it was about the only way to get lambs off to markets early when the price was good." Herman Oliver, an eastern Oregon sheepman, built sheds to keep his sheep out of the freezing wind and "never had heavy losses again. We got on early markets, had bigger lambs. . . . The early lambing paid off at 3–5¢ a pound more at selling time, and we got many more pounds of lamb from each ewe."

By employing what sheep buyer E. N. Wentworth described as "intelligent use of shed lambing," the McGregors were able to increase the profits of their business. The more intensive care brought a gradual increase in the size of the lamb crop. Even "bummers," lambs whose mothers had died or could not produce milk, could be saved—something nearly impossible on the open range or even with corral lambing. The Mc-Gregors and other shed lambing outfits sorted out these sheep and gave them to ewes whose lambs had died. The ewe would not accept a strange lamb, so the hide of the dead lamb was removed and tied to the one to be adopted. "Getting a whiff of familiar hide smell usually works," two observers reported, "if not, some of her own milk is squirted on the lamb, whereupon the ewe thinks the stranger is her very own." The results of the lambing season varied somewhat according to weather, availability of hay and range grasses, and ability of employees. William James, in charge of a band of McGregor sheep in 1912, reported a 136 percent increase in the sheep over which he had custody. "I had a good crew of men this year," said Mr. James, "men who were interested in working for the interest of the Company, otherwise the high percent increase would have been impossible." The lamb crop percentages gradually increased, from 98 to 104 percent (at docking time) during the first five years of shed lambing to a later average of 115 percent or higher.[31]

The rapid spread of the shed system, particularly in the Yakima, Snake, and Palouse valleys and the Big Bend region, made the Columbia Plateau one of the most efficient lamb-producing areas in the western range states. In most areas, 90 percent lamb crops were regarded as "very successful," and reports of 100 percent increases were generally "considered as an exaggeration." But Columbia Plateau sheepmen regularly recorded 110 to 125 percent averages for their flocks. Even in the spring of 1916, after the worst winter weather in twenty years, a survey of members of the Washington Wool Growers Association indicated an overall average of 92 percent, a figure local sheepmen regarded as extremely low. Two government investigators found that "probably some of the heaviest lambs produced on the ranges in the West come from the Washington flocks." The procedures used in the Pacific Northwest interior were in marked contrast to "broadcast" methods employed in Rocky Mountain states and other areas unsuited to production of early lambs. In such areas, range lambing crews often killed one of a pair of twin lambs, for the mother would be unable to find enough forage to produce milk for both.[32] Under the shed lambing system, twin lambs were welcomed, for the heavy feeding at lambing time and the availability of early spring forage provided the ewe with more than adequate nourishment to support two offspring.

The growing expenses of feeding and caring for ewes and lambs meant that sheepmen had to maximize returns by paying closer attention to the demands of midwestern markets. The McGregors improved the mutton quality of their yearling wethers by crossbreeding their fine-wool Rambouillet ewes with Shropshire, Hampshire, Oxford, Lincoln, and other "mutton" breed rams. These sheep were shipped to Chicago in June and July to take advantage of favorable markets. F. M. Rothrock and several other Columbia Plateau sheepmen sold their crossbred wethers during the same period. *The Shepherd's Criterion* reported in 1907 on the success of these men in satisfying the market demand:

> Eastern butchers await with ill-concealed impatience initial arrivals from Washington and Idaho which usually reach Chicago early in July. Feedlots having been practically exhausted meanwhile mutton soars to a high level, this year's altitude eclipsing all previous market performances. This is known in the trade as "the gap." Early arrivals from the Pacific Northwest yearlings and dry ewes usually fetch stiff prices. . . . Ten years ago most of the western . . . [sheep] reaching Chicago were wrinkly little Merinos that made mutton that people swore at. Since then the coarse-wooled ram has effected the transformation and converted American mutton into a much prized article.[33]

By carefully improving the quality of their yearling wethers and selling at an optimum time, the McGregors, E. N. Wentworth noted, "bridged the interval when most sheepmen were switching from older wethers to lambs." But the *National Wool Grower* took notice in 1916 of "the passing of the wether," remarking that "the public has been educated to lamb—this is the lamb age." McGregor Land and Livestock followed the trend and began marketing fat lambs in 1912 in order to take advantage of a 20 percent premium that Chicago packers offered for these young sheep. Black-faced Hampshire rams were crossbred with white-faced Rambouillet ewes in order to "get the big, fat lamb." The progeny of this cross fattened rapidly on summer pastures and were ideally suited for early marketing. But the wool was coarse and inferior. All these lambs went to market. The other half of the ewe flock was bred to registered Rambouillet rams, a hardy breed that produced excellent clips of fine wool. White-faced wether lambs were sold, and the purebred Rambouillet ewes were kept as breeding stock. This breeding program allowed the McGregors to maintain the quality of their wool clip and to produce lambs preferred by packers. Shropshire rams were sometimes used in place of the Hampshires, and these too sired lambs that were easily fattened and early maturing. The crossbreeding of "mutton" and "fine wool" varieties of sheep became popular throughout the Columbia Plateau range districts as a way of producing satisfactory lamb and maintaining good-quality fleece.[34]

When the progeny of the breeding stock were a week or two old, the herders faced the job of docking the tails and castrating ("marking") the buck lambs. Marking was gruesome work. Two herders held each buck lamb in a seated position on a board several feet above the corral. A third herder then used his knife, his fingers, and his teeth to castrate the lamb in a procedure long used by western range sheep operators. The grisly ritual attracted onlookers who came to the ranch every year to observe marking and to dine on Rocky Mountain oysters. Sherman McGregor recalled that "a group of Spokane businessmen came to the ranch every spring. They'd have dinner out at the corral and they'd always fix up big helpings of lamb-fries. Then they'd go to Hooper and set up card tables all through the store. They all drank and played poker until God knows when."[35]

The arrival of another group of annual visitors, the migratory sheep shearers, in late April or early May marked the beginning of another busy period for the woolgrowers. A crew of twelve to eighteen men spent about three weeks shearing 100,000 to 123,000 pounds of wool from 11,000 or more McGregor sheep. Either hand clippers ("blades") or machine shears could be used for this arduous work. The McGregor brothers and many other Columbia Plateau sheepmen preferred to use "the blades," the traditional method. They hired unionized hand-shearing crews who had begun their work in January in the Southwest and traveled to sheep ranges in California, Oregon, Washington, Idaho, Nevada, Wyoming, and Montana as the year progressed. One highly skilled blade shearing crew, composed of Mexican laborers and headed by Joe Lopez of San Francisco, handled the McGregor clip for more than twenty years. Machine shearing, a somewhat faster and less physically exhausting process, was handled by several crews based on the Columbia Plateau or in nearby range states. Some of these crews were unionized; others were composed of independent "greenhorn" operators attracted to the trade by reports of the good pay earned by shearers. Both machine and blade shearers worked fast—they were paid according to the number of sheep shorn, not the total days worked. The Sheep Shearers Union established a price of nine cents per head in 1905 and later devised a sliding scale of pay that varied with the price of wool. A peak of fifteen cents was reached during World War I. A competent man using blades could shear about 150 sheep per day, although an average per man was usually about 120. Machine shearers could handle up to 175 and averaged about 140 per day. The machine shears were powered by a gasoline engine. The rest of the shearing process was essentially the same for all crews.[36]

When the professional shearers increased their charges during years of high wool prices, sheepmen complained that the crews were searching "at will through the change-pockets of their short-term employers" and advancing "roughshod over the bleeding and helpless financial forms of the stockmen." Some woolgrowers talked of hiring untrained laborers or graduates of a one-semester shearing course offered at Washington State College. But the sheepmen still made a profit, and the shearing crews needed good pay to compensate for a seasonal job requiring extensive travel and long hours of back-breaking work. The shearer had to grab a ewe, flip her into a sitting position, and quickly but carefully begin clipping her in long, sweeping motions from head to tail, working to remove the fleece in one piece. Sheepmen could not afford to hire inexperienced shearers who cut the fleece into ragged patches of uneven length, for woolen mills paid premium prices for uniform grades of wool. Good shearers were able to grab, shear, and release a ewe and drag another into position every four minutes. Few Washington State College graduates were eager to spend long days wrestling 150-pound sheep into place so they could stoop over them and clip their fleece. Emile Morod remembered that the veteran McGregor shearers were capable men, both when clipping fleece and when playing cards with sheepherders. One of the shearers, Gileroy, was "a nice fellow to talk to. . . . A gambler . . . crook, oh boy, he's a crook gambler." But neither shearer nor herder had much spare time during shearing season.

As the shearers worked, McGregor employees were kept busy herding sheep from nearby pastures to the shearing pens, located in the main lambing shed at Archie's Camp. When the sheep entered the shed, ewes and their lambs were separated, the former to be shorn, the latter to await the return of their mothers. Herders moved the ewes down an alley into a series of small pens, one of which was located near each shearer. These pens had a gate at the entrance, panels on two sides, and an exit, facing the shearer and covered only by a burlap "gunny sack." As the shearer finished clipping one sheep, he reached under the burlap, grabbed another by the leg, and dragged it out to be shorn. After each sheep had been shorn, it was headed into a runway to rejoin the lambs. As the ewes and lambs left the shed they were run through a long alley, where they were "paint branded" with a special compound that could be removed when the wool was shorn and scoured a year later. Meanwhile, a "tier" picked up each fleece as it came from the shearer, tied it with string, and tossed it onto a platform. Here a "wool stamper" put fleeces into a long, free-swinging sack and stamped them down. When filled, the sacks (weighing up to four hundred pounds) were closed, sewn, pushed off a platform, rolled to a ramp, shoved onto a wagon, and transported to the warehouse at Hooper.[37]

Sheepmen and shearers engaged in spirited debates on the virtues of shearing with blades and machines. *The Shepherd's Criterion* came out in favor of the machines, claiming that "the shearing machine is as important to the flockmaster as the mowing machine is to the farmer." *National Wool Grower* reported that "there is no doubt that it is desirable to use machine shears whenever the climate will permit it." Machine shearing saved more wool, caused fewer cuts, and left a smoother looking animal. The McGregor brothers decided to give the machines a try in the 1911 season. A visitor reported on the "modern methods employed by [the] enterprising wool growers of [the] Palouse district":

> *Eleven thousand sheep are now being sheared at the ranch of the Mc-Gregor Land and Livestock Company by power, a horse clipper operated by a three horsepowered gasoline engine being used. . . . Shearing by this method is far more humane, and better returns are obtained, as the sheep are sheared more closely. . . . The man who owns the gasoline engine and machinery, H. Hill of Klickitat, Wash., gets 12 cents a head and the men who run the clippers get 9 cents per head. . . . 1000 head for six men is counted a good day's work. Every one has own position to fill. There are no idlers. . . . John McGregor, who is a practical sheepman, spends most of his time with his foreman, Robert Clyde, and a large crew. This is the busy season with them, for not only have the sheep to be sheared, but the wool has to be taken care of, sacked and marketed. Mutton sheep have to be gotten out of the way before the ewes and lambs leave for the mountain ranges or summer pasture.*[38]

Despite the machines' advantages, sheepmen worried that the closely shorn sheep "are apt to be lost if caught in cold storms immediately after shearing." The fears seemed justified to the McGregors in 1915, when cold weather threatened their machine-shorn sheep. The McGregors put up big circus tents and, in the words of Emile Morod, "Everybody in town went with teams and wagons . . . bringing them and puttin' them in the tents, and they all die." Four hundred ewes were killed by the cold. The McGregors rehired their old crew of Mexican shearers the following season and continued with "the blades" for another decade. But even hand-shorn sheep could die if cold, rainy weather occurred immediately after shearing. Emile Morod recalled his efforts to save a band of sheep during the first year after machines were abandoned: "I started off for the woods with them sheep, one band, the rest wasn't sheared yet. . . . And I got up to Nigger Lake and them God damned sheep were just a bunch of ducks. East cold wind, raining. . . . And I took 'em down there around that Nigger Lake. They had an old house and a big barn there. . . . God damned sheep got in the barn and the cellar and everyplace. . . . We had a hell of a time, all night holding 'em under the bluffs." Emile Morod, Peter Lloyd, and another herder carried the sickest sheep to shelter in wagons and stayed up until six in the morning working to save them. Because of their efforts, losses were less than twenty sheep. The work was enough to make one lose affection for ovines: "I wish I never saw another sheep that day." The storm abated, and during the next day Morod continued to trail the sheep northward to their summer range. He soon encountered Peter McGregor and his son, Alex T. McGregor, who "had been looking for me . . . way up ten miles the other side of the lake. . . . 'What're you doin' way back here' . . . [Peter asked.]I said, 'Mister, if I'd a been up there, you wouldn't have no sheep today. If they'd a got away from that Nigger Lake, wouldn't have been no protection . . . just all them flats. We'd have lost everything . . . pretty near all them God damned sheep.' "

Western sheepmen sardonically described such weather conditions as the "annual sheep shearing rains." [39] The vulnerability of freshly shorn flocks to a combination of cold weather, wind, and rain, and the desperate efforts required to save sheep under such circumstances were not easily forgotten. But such weather conditions were unusual. And the

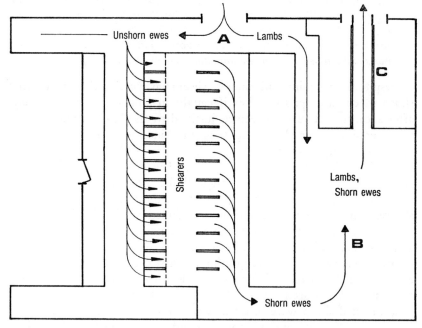

Procedure used during shearing time at Archie's Camp
A. Incoming ewes and lambs separated, ewes moved into holding pens awaiting shearing, lambs moved to large pen to await return of their mothers
B. Shorn ewes rejoin lambs
C. Shorn ewes and their lambs "branded" with special paint as they leave shed

McGregors, Drumhellers, and other sheepmen with large shearing sheds could usually put their sheep under cover when inclement weather threatened. Only when the weather changed suddenly and the newly shorn sheep were distant from shelter were serious losses likely to occur.

These were boom days in the sheep business, and from 1905 until the end of World War I Columbia Plateau woolgrowers were generally satisfied with the condition of the fleece and the value of the clips. "Some of the largest fleeces ever produced come from the state of Washington," the *Shepherd's Journal* reported in 1913. A typical description of the wool clips was provided by a 1906 correspondent to *American Shepherd's Bulletin*: "Reports from North Yakima state that sheep shearing is in full blast in the valley and that the clip is heavy and the price good. The sheep men have no cause for complaint this year." Some sheepmen sold their clips locally to the Pendleton Woolen Mills or sent them to that company's scouring mills to be cleaned before shipment to Boston. The large wool clips kept the Pendleton mills busy during shearing season. In 1907, for example, *The Shepherd's Criterion* reported that the scouring plant was "being operated night and day with full crews and about seven million pounds of wool will be handled during the run." Wool buyers from the Pendleton, Oregon, firm and from Justice, Bateman and Company; Crimmins and Pierce; and other Boston and Philadelphia woolen mills came to the McGregor shearing shed every year to inspect the newly shorn fleece and bid on the clip. They picked up handfuls of the wool and looked at the length, uniformity, and texture; pulled it to test resiliency; and checked for burrs, cheatgrass, and other impurities. The wool buyers offered Columbia Plateau sheepmen 10 to 12 cents in 1905. Wool prices gradually advanced and reached 20 cents in 1910, slipped to 14 cents in 1912, and then rebounded and climbed to 24 cents in 1916. "The high prices paid for wool," a Washington State Department of Agriculture study concluded in 1916, "have made sheep growing an unusually profitable industry."

When the United States entered World War I in 1917, wool was needed for military uniforms and blankets, and the price moved upward rapidly. The McGregor clip, worth an average of $16,965 annually during the years 1910–16, was valued at $50,161 per year during the period 1917–20. William Hislop, president of Hislop Sheep Company and former professor of animal husbandry at Washington State College, commented on the sale of the 1919 McGregor clip:

> *At the highest price on record in eastern Washington . . . the McGregor Land and Livestock Company of Hooper sold its 1919 wool clip to Crimmins and Pierce, wool merchants of Boston. The price is 4 cents higher than any other range clip bought this year and is 3 cents higher*

than any other clip of any kind. The McGregor clip is the biggest in the state . . . and represents 10,200 fleeces, which will average about 11½ pounds of wool. At 44 cents, the sale represents approximately $50,000. . . . There was keen competition for the wool, which is one of two clips in the state that will classify as original wool bag clip [i.e. wool of a uniform grade]. . . . It is estimated to be 68 percent shrinkage wool and is fine, long staple wool from Rambouillet sheep. The wool is all hand shorn. . . .[40]

The lowland winter ranges became less desirable for sheep production after shearing as warm weather dried and cured the green forage crops of early spring. During the month of May, herders began trailing their bands of sheep to mountain ranges surrounding the Columbia Plateau. R. A. Jackson, Cunningham Sheep Company, and other woolgrowers moved their sheep south to the Blue Mountains of Oregon and Washington. The Coffin brothers, Harder brothers, and several others trailed westward into various portions of the Cascade Mountains. McGregor Land and Livestock herders were among those moving sheep north to the Spokane Indian Reservation and east into the foothills of the Bitterroot Mountains in Idaho. The McGregors sent three to four bands (6,000–8,000 ewes and lambs) to the reservation and to adjacent lands near Deer Park and Loon Lake that had been leased from private landholders. Black-faced "market" lambs and their mothers were sent to these northern ranges, where a good crop of green summer forage enabled lambs to fatten quickly for fall shipment to Chicago. An equal number of purebred Rambouillet lambs and ewes were trailed to leased lands in the Moscow Mountains of Idaho, a rough country in the foothills of the Bitterroots, where adequate early summer pastures and excellent fall forage were available. Wether Rambouillet lambs and all the young black faces were shipped directly from the summer ranges to Chicago. The rest of the sheep returned to the winter range as breeding stock.[41]

The sheep were trailed along back roads, through fields of summer fallow, and across unfenced rangeland. Emile Morod remembered some areas near Sprague where "You could run sheep any damned place . . . herd all over that country up there . . . free, just open range." When trailing to the summer range, the sheep generally traveled about eight miles a day and reached their destinations in ten days to two weeks. A watering place near Pampa was purchased for use as the first stopping point en route to the Idaho range. But most of the stopovers had to be arranged by making agreements with farmers along the route. Such understandings were particularly necessary on the return trip, for the sheep were then moved slowly, arriving back on the winter rangeland only when cold weather threatened the upland areas. Green weeds and stubble provided inexpensive, nutritious forage for the homeward-bound flocks. Sheep foreman Jock Macrae worked hard to find suitable pasturage, and his letters to the McGregor brothers typically contained information similar to the following: "I'm going towards McElroy to look for feed as Gene told me there was lots of green volunteer [wheat] and from what he says I can get a weeks feed without water. . . . I am still on Rock Creek. Got both bands here and Maurice's is on the other side of the Road. Feed good for one week yet."[42] Emile Morod described the availability of forage for the bands of sheep en route between winter and summer pastures: "In those days there was lots of summerfallow, late

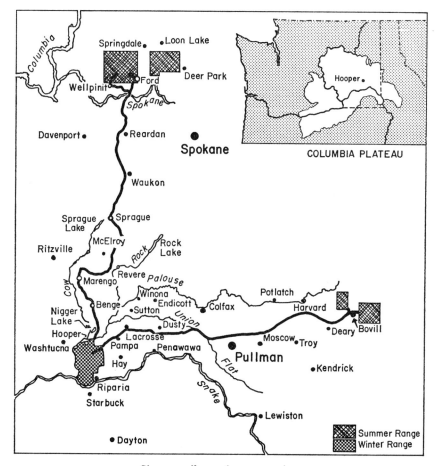

Sheep trails to the mountains

plowing. . . . And old Jock knew all them farmers on the road. Hell, you could stay there a long time if you wanted. You could feed all that Jim Hill mustard in the summerfallow. There was a lot of feed in them days."

Some farmers felt that having sheep on their lands served the useful purpose of converting excess stubble into manure to fertilize the next crop. Less enthusiastic farmers could sometimes be convinced by adding a fifth of whiskey and a side of mutton to the standard payment of five dollars for allowing a band to graze one day. A 1913 letter from one landowner to Macrae indicated a favorable response to a gift of mutton: "When I cam' home th' other day, For quite a bit I'd been away, The guidwife met me at the door. . . . Says she t' me 'Ye'll never ken Just whit I hae that's cookin been.' Wi nose in air I gave a sniff. Says I, 'I'll tell ye sine enough. Youre a roastin' I shid say Which must hae' cam' frae Jock Macrae.' Maister Jock ye're unco' kind Tae keep us thusly in ye're mind." [43]

Sheepmen herding their flocks to and from the summer ranges had to be alert constantly for poisonous weeds. Other noxious substances could kill sheep: Woolgrowers of the Butter Creek district, near Umatilla, Oregon, reported losing hundreds of sheep that "were undoubtedly poisoned from licking a certain mineral substance which appears on some of the rocks throughout the country when the hot sun comes out just after a heavy rain." But the most serious losses in the western range country were caused by a number of weeds fatal to sheep—lupine, death camas, chokecherry, goldenrod, greasewood, sneezeweed, loco-weed, and several others. On the Columbia Plateau, the most frequently encountered noxious plant was lupine, which caused some death losses during early summer but was even more dangerous in October, when the highly toxic seed pods ("beans") ripened. John McGregor described the difficulties caused by lupine in a 1918 letter:

> *We run during the summer months seven bands of sheep ranging from 2200 to 2800 head per band. From May to December it takes two ex-perienced men with each. In trailing from our winter to summer range we pass through a country infested with poisonous weeds on which there has been as many as 900 head lost out of one band in two hours time. . . . For twenty years I have been breaking these men in so that they now know the country and the poisonous areas. . . . Until a man knows these areas he is practically useless to us.*

The best way to avoid lupine poisoning was to provide sheep with sufficient feed before they entered the dangerous areas. When this was impossible and a band encountered a lupine patch, alcohol could some-times save the poisoned sheep. In June 1910, *The Shepherd's Journal,* a Chicago paper, described the "discovery" of the occasionally successful antidote:

> James Campbell, pioneer sheepman of the McGregor Land and Livestock Company of Hooper, declares the district between Sprague and Deer Park, which has been dreaded by sheepmen compelled to take that route with their flocks to the mountains in the spring and return every fall because of poisonous weeds, has no more fear for sheepmen. His foreman, John McCrea, [sic] has accidentally fallen upon a cure for sheep poisoned by eating the noxious weeds. Two fat sheep were taken ill and began frothing at the mouth. McCrea had a bottle of whisky in his pocket and by way of experiment gave the two sheep a small dose of the liquor. Mr. McGregor laughed at the man's action and told the herder to drive on. When the band was taken five miles from where the two stricken sheep were left McGregor's attention was called to the bleatings of the two sheep which were given the whisky, running to join the herd, cured. For years the department of agriculture at Washington, D. C. and the Washington State college have been at a loss to know what to do in the matter. To keep herders from drinking the liquor Mr. Campbell says that a small portion of ammonia mixed with the liquor will have the same effect on the poisoned sheep.[44]

Despite Macrae's "cure," lupine continued to be a danger for herders trailing to the Washington summer range. Emile Morod recalled three occasions when sheep he was trailing died from eating the plants. Once, near Rock Creek, "I camped on the bunchgrass, and there was beans. . . . The next day them God damned sheep die like flies." Another time, en route to the Indian reservation, he stopped south of Sprague and found a band of "Bar U" sheep (part of the flocks of the McGregor-owned Taylor Land and Livestock Company) camped nearby.

> *And I says, "I'll fix 'em tomorrow morning." . . . We got up way before daylight. . . . I took them sheep through the streets and hell, we got away to the other side of Sprague. There was two roads the other side of Sprague, and one road, down that road was all good grass. . . . The other road wasn't quite as good. I wanted to take that first road and God damn, we made it through Sprague and they never even had a fire up yet . . . they was still all in bed when we got by with the sheep. When we got up there just before the forks of the road, here come Alec [Peter's son, Alex T.]. . . . He said, "The boss says for you to take the right road." He meant Pete. I didn't want to take the right road, but what the hell you going to do. . . . That's what put us fellows off, and we had to go 22 miles . . . from Sprague to Waukon, that's a hell of a drive . . . and that night the sheep eat that poison.*

"The sheep," Emile remembered, "was all right that night."

Then we get up next morning and there was dead sheep all over the place. . . . I saw some summerfallow . . . and I walked down to that farmer and I says, "By God, we're up against it, we got a lot of sick sheep . . . we can't go any further. . . . Let us fellows in your field . . . and we'd appreciate it. . . . We'd pay you for it." . . . I turned 'em in . . . let 'em loose in there . . . them God damned sheep, lotta them is crazy over that poison. They take off and we chase 'em down . . . tie 'em to the fence or some damned thing. . . . They all die. Every single one. . . . We didn't have enough whiskey. . . . We lost about 25 to 30 head.

Far more serious losses were encountered one October, when sheep were being trailed from the reservation back to the winter range. Morod recalled:

I was comin' back from Ford with a band of sheep one fall. We got below Ford and the lupine . . . the beans was all there . . . there was nothin much else to eat. . . . And I got 'em down there and camped that night. . . . And the next morning I seen two or three sick ones . . . and we made a big mistake. We had had the sheep without any water and we took 'em down a steep son of a gun hill down to the [Spokane] river. . . . When the sheep come out of that doggone water, they go crazy, some of them. Run against a tree, under the wagon, and die right away. That poison was in 'em and the water made it worse. . . . We lost seven or eight that day. . . . And we got over to where we camped that night [and] next morning there were eight or ten dead on the bedding ground. Walter Ross was tending camp and he went down to the draws below the camp and there was all kinds of sheep dead. I lost about 35 head. And that was nothin'. Another band came behind us through Ford and they go across the river and they lost 300 in the one band. . . . And old Jock had a crew from Reardan that he sent to skin them sheep. They had a crew skinnin' sheep and a crew buryin' 'em. God, it was a mess . . . I didn't give a damn if I ever see a sheep again.

The two summer ranges, generally totaling 75,000 to 100,000 acres or more, provided ample feed for the several bands of sheep. Emile Morod described the northeastern Washington rangeland: "There was a lot of feed in them days on the Reservation. A lot of buckbrush. They done good. The sheep would just spread out in that buckbrush."[45] R. Kent Beattie, head botanist at Washington State College, spent the 1911 and 1912 seasons with the McGregor sheep in Idaho and found that the region "furnished an abundance" of buckbrush, huckleberry, and several other species of shrubs "which the sheep consumed with relish." The main Idaho leasehold, two miles wide and twenty-two miles long, was situated between Hatter Creek, a tributary of the Palouse River, and Shay Meadows, four miles west of the town of Bovill. Beattie concluded that the two bands he observed, each composed of three thousand ewes and their offspring, were "well managed," and that the McGregor sheep had done absolutely no damage to the mountain range. His detailed study included an analysis of the system of managing sheep on the mountain pastures:

The sheep reached the summer range at the west end [of the leasehold] and moved slowly eastward throughout the summer, reaching the Shay meadows at the eastern end about October 1. Here they were finally counted and sorted in the permanent corrals kept at this place. . . . In three days they were driven back to the western end of the leased land, feeding on selected grazing grounds which had been saved during the eastward trip. They were then moved into the wheat stubble fields north and west of Potlatch, Idaho, through which they gradually moved south-westward during the month of October and the first half of November. They then returned to their winter range near Hooper. . . .

With the two bands of sheep were four men, a boss, a helper, and two herders. The herders camped with the sheep. The boss and the helper lived at the horse camp . . . or headquarters camp . . ., moved the herders' camps when necessary, purchased and hauled supplies, hauled drinking water for the camp and salt for the sheep, looked up stubble field range for the autumn feeding, repaired the roads, and in general looked after the welfare of the sheep and of the herders who could not leave them. The boss, Mr. Robert Clyde of Potlatch, Idaho, has lived in the region for twenty-five years, is thoroughly familiar with every foot of its intricate geography, and has worked for McGregor Brothers for a long time. The other three men are natives of Hautes-Alpes, a province of eastern France, come from a race of sheepherders, and have had several years of experience with sheep in this country. . . . The typical method of herding . . . was as follows: The herder established his camp on the edge of a meadow, near a piece of level bottom land, or on the edge of a clearing on a hill. Here was the bedding ground of the sheep. . . . To this same ground the sheep returned every night til they had grazed over all the ground available from this point. They were then moved on to the next bedding ground. . . .

In the main they are started out on the side of the range opposite the ground they covered the day before. They are guided and held from too great scattering by careful quiet circling movements of the herder, who, after an early breakfast which he cooks and eats at his tent, puts in the most of the forenoon in handling the sheep. It is his effort to get the sheep out about a mile from the camp in the forenoon and to spread them out in small groups so that all will have an opportunity to feed. Although the herder usually has a couple of dogs with him he uses these but little in the woods except in an emergency. Dogs are used more when the sheep are traveling along a public road. . . . By ten-thirty or eleven o'clock when the heat of the day has arrived, the sheep find their way into the deep shade and lie down quietly for a noon siesta.

When the sheep settle down at noon, the herder goes to camp and cooks his dinner. About two or two-thirty o'clock or even later on hot days, the sheep rouse themselves and begin to graze back toward the bedding ground. The herder guides them back on the side of the grazing ground next to yesterday's path, hoping thus to pick up any stragglers which may have been lost the day before. . . .

By five-thirty or six o'clock the sheep have reached camp. The herder scatters small piles of crushed rock salt over the bedding ground and calls his sheep. They rush out of the woods, lick up the salt and gather closely together for the night. For an hour or two a period of adjustment occurs. During the day, lambs and their mothers have become separated. They now call each other and get together. The shepherd has in his flock a small number of sheep wearing bells and a small number of black sheep. . . . Each night he counts his bells and his black sheep. If one of these is missing he scours the feeding ground for lost sheep. . . .

On moving day, the herder starts the sheep out in the morning and moves them during the day toward the new bedding ground, endeavoring to get them there rather early in the day so that he may have plenty of time to make camp and pick up stragglers. Meanwhile the boss or his helper has come with a wagon and loaded the herder's camp outfit, his tent, his stove, his bedding, and his grub box and moved them around by convenient roads to the new camp site. Here he pitches the tent and sets up the camp and if necessary helps the herder to gather in the stragglers. From this new bedding ground the feeding system is repeated. . . .

While the herders thus remain inseparable from their sheep, the two camp-tenders, the boss and his helper, are headquartered at what is called the 'horse camp'. . . . Here they pasture their saddle horses and draft mules and keep extra dogs for the herders. Here also they pitch their tent and eat and sleep. During the day they are busy. . . caring for the wants of the herders and the sheep.[46]

Trailing sheep back to camp every night was thought to be the best way to graze forest land. Yet within a few years, government botanists were suggesting a new system, known as "bedding out." The new method provided a more uniform utilization of rangeland and avoided the heavy grazing of areas adjacent to the campgrounds. McGregor herders adopted the procedure and kept their flocks away from camp, remaining with the sheep until late at night, when they would return to their tents for a short sleep. The herders were back with the sheep before daylight, and were thus on hand during the early morning hours when coyotes sometimes attacked. "That was the best way. You'd take the lanterns and scarecrows out there. You'd stay with the sheep most of the

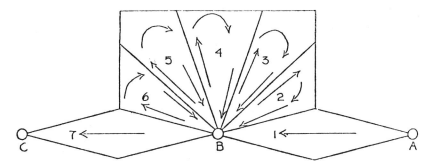

Diagram of the herding system used by McGregor Land and Livestock Company on the Idaho summer range during 1911. Numbers represent days; arrows indicate movement of sheep; letters signify campgrounds. (From Beattie, "Plants Used for Food by Sheep")

time. Always lookin' to see how they was doin'. Sheep could be on fresh feed all night and they would be full next morning. They'd move earlier in the day. If you bring 'em around the camp, they'd stay there and not leave till 9 o'clock." The new system fattened sheep more rapidly and allowed herders to remain in one general area for up to two weeks, instead of five or six days under the old method of operation.

Coyotes were a persistent enemy on the summer ranges. But when the Spokane Indian Reservation was first opened for sheep grazing, Emile Morod remembered, "They didn't bother us too much at first because they wasn't used to it. If a sheep die, I hang him up in a tree with a rope, way up. . . . The coyotes never got a chance to get a taste of fresh sheep. I never lost any sheep because of them . . . that first season." Morod compared the serious losses caused by coyotes since World War II with earlier methods of operation:

> Now days, lucky if you don't lose 80 or 100. They [the herders] don't stay with the sheep now, just leave 'em. Them God damned guys should stay with them sheep. Hell, in the fall and summer, I'd take my lunch and eat near the sheep. I just as soon be sleepin' right out there at noon as be in camp. Flies was around camp more. . . . And it was just better that way. With the dogs right there, they could smell a coyote coming around. But the way they do it now, damn, no wonder they lose a lot of sheep.[47]

The forests sometimes became tinder dry during the long, rainless periods of late summer and herders, camptenders, and sheep owners began to fear fire. In late August 1905, Perry Waldrip, a camptender in the Crooked Fork country of the Blue Mountains, encountered a lightning-caused fire whipped by a hard wind and feeding on tall, dry bunchgrass. It was impossible to get two bands of sheep out of the way, and several thousand head of Pomeroy Livestock Company sheep were burned to death. Waldrip and a herder saved the saddle and pack stock by driving them into some rimrocks and starting a back fire. They were able to slow the progress of the fire enough so that several other bands of sheep could be driven out of the area. Several years later, lightning caused another fire along the Tucannon River in the Blues, and a band of sheep owned by a man named Foredyce were threatened. The herder abandoned his flock when he saw the fire approaching, and the sheep split up into several bunches, some of which were surrounded by fire. A six-man Forest Service crew saved the entire band of scorched-wooled sheep and convinced the herder to return to his flock.

The men in charge of the bands of sheep on the summer ranges usually proved capable and level-headed, although there were some notable exceptions. One McGregor herder insisted on coming to lunch at camp, even though coyotes were killing sheep while he was away from the flock. The herder refused to heed the warnings of fellow employees and was finally fired. Sometimes herders became belligerent after drinking. One drunken herder threatened his camptender, sixteen-year-old Emile Morod, with a knife because he disliked the way the potatoes and mutton had been cooked. Other disagreements sometimes arose— for example, two herders' dogs started fighting, and while one man tried to break up the warring canines the other slugged him in the face.[48]

While the herders were tending their bands on the summer pasture, foreman Jock Macrae and the McGregor brothers were kept busy with the overall supervision of the sheep business. A good sampling of the difficulties encountered on the summer range can be gained from Macrae's 1918 and 1919 correspondence with his employers in Hooper. The following were a few of the problems encountered:

Incompetent herders: "the other fellow was no good and I had to get a new man for Carleton"; "I am going to let Hackenstaff go just as soon as I get a man and maybe Shickler if he don't do better. Just got a letter from Springdale . . . that Crawford wants to quit. Its one D—— thing after another. If any herders comes along that way to Hooper . . . get me word"; "I got that D—— Crawford to stay. He is doing alright. Hackenstaff is the one I have to look after the most. I told Emile to write to Walla Walla to see if there was a good herder down there."

Lack of water: "If it doesn't rain soon, God knows what the stock will do for water . . . everything is almost dried up. . . . There will be no water anywhere."

Poison weeds: "I just got down from Bamise's camp. . . . Well he got a bad dose of poison and lost about 15. . . . There is about 30 out yet that he does not know of but I think they are sick in the brush and I have them all hunting for them."

Insects: "The bugs, a kind of caterpiller, have eaten off nearly all the country. They stripped the buckbrush section by section. They generally do that once in 7 or 8 years but this year is the worst I ever saw."

The need for more leased land: "I'm trying to get Upchurch [the agent at the Spokane Indian Reservation] to promise me the whole Reservation and to get this other sheepman off."

Sheep sales: "I talked with Hislop last Monday. He don't want the ewes before we ship the dry sheep."

Despite these and other difficulties, Macrae generally was optimistic about the condition of the flocks. In a typical letter he commented: "I have had a sweet time ever since I came to the mountains this year. Everything is all OK or just as good as can be looked for." A newspaper correspondent interviewed Macrae in August 1918 and reported:

> "Sheep are doing fine in the mountains," John D. Macrae said last night at the Coeur d 'Alene [hotel]. "The recent rains have freshened things up and the range is good. The lambs are in good condition where they are ranging in Stevens county. We shall begin to ship out lambs the latter part of this month." Mr. Macrae is handling the flocks of the McGregor interests of Hooper, Wash. They range in Stevens county every season. A. C. [Alex] McGregor has been with the flock the past week and is stopping at the Coeur d'Alene.[49]

The leasing and purchasing of summer grazing lands, an important matter during a period when many sheepmen were unable to find sufficient mountain pastures for their sheep, was handled by John McGregor with assistance from brothers Archie and Alex. Jock Macrae searched for stubble to be used for overnight pasturage; the three brothers worked to secure grazing grounds that could be used all summer. Grazing sites in the Idaho forests were leased from the Potlatch Lumber Company, the Potlatch Timber Protective Association (an organization formed by several private landowners), the U.S. Forest Service, numerous small landholders (including historian William J. Trimble), and the State of Idaho. Several thousand acres of Idaho range were purchased from various parties. When the State of Idaho refused to lease state lands to nonresidents Alex C. and John McGregor, an official of the Potlatch Timber Protective Association wrote Idaho Land Commissioner L. A. Smoot that the McGregors were "a splendid outfit—responsible in every way— and I am sure you will never have any trouble with them." Continued intransigence by the state prompted the McGregors to talk of taking the land commissioner to court to force approval of the leases. They finally decided to adopt the less expensive approach of using an Idaho middle-man to acquire the leaseholds. The Washington rangeland was secured by deals with real estate corporations, lumber companies, brick companies, farmers, the State of Washington, and the Spokane Indian Reservation. The brothers were able to dispel doubts of Indian agents "as to whether the consideration is entirely adequate in view of the high prices received for wool." Occasionally, the costs of summer ranges would rise slightly when Jock Macrae and other employees picked up gallon jugs of whiskey and charged them to McGregor Land and Livestock as "grazing fees." But for relatively small leasing charges, generally totaling less than three thousand dollars, the McGregors were able to acquire extensive summer ranges for their sheep.[50]

Western sheepmen using summer pastures in areas designated as forest reserves (known as national forests after 1907) continued to have considerably more difficulty securing mountain grazing lands. President Theodore Roosevelt had tripled the 63 million acres already set aside for reserves in 1905, and supervision of these lands was transferred from the U.S. Department of the Interior to the U.S. Forest Service, a branch of the U.S. Department of Agriculture. Sheepmen depending on these newly created reserves were suspicious. An industry observer at a February 1907 meeting thought Gifford Pinchot, head of the Forest Service, had "the air of an honest man. He is clean cut and absolutely devoted to his hobby of preserving the public domain." But a month later, sheepmen learned of limitations on the numbers of sheep to be allowed on the ranges, claiming that Pinchot had "Czar-like power over a vast domain" and that "the Pinchot policy appears to be one of rule or ruin and the people of the West must pay the freight." Federal policies were more settled in the Pacific Northwest, where a system of regulated grazing had been in effect since 1900. Forest Service administrators inspected the ranges, recommended new grazing practices, marked off areas where they found poisonous weeds, and used funds collected from grazing fees to reseed pastures and to construct driveways, sheep trails, bridges, stock watering tanks, and other improvements. Thomas J. Drumheller, Jr., and many other Columbia Plateau sheepmen found that the Forest Service "generally did as good a job as could be done." But reductions were made in the number of sheep allowed on some depleted ranges, and the restrictions hurt some sheepmen. Limitations on sheep grazing in the Blue Mountains were said, in 1908, to have led to the sale of one hundred thousand sheep once trailed to that region. The Baldwin Sheep and Land Company of Hay Creek, Oregon (a company with more than thirty thousand acres of deeded land and financial support from eastern bankers, doctors, and lawyers), sold out in 1910 because of increased expenses and a reduction in the size of its Forest Service grazing permit.[51]

As the summer months drew to a close, the shipping of lambs and nonproductive ("dry") ewes to market and the breeding of the remaining ewes became the sheepmen's major concerns. The McGregors bred their black-faced "mutton" ewes on the northeastern Washington pastures but delayed breeding the fine-wooled "replacement" ewes until they were returned from Idaho to the winter range. Each ram serviced about fifty ewes per day during the month-long breeding season. Rams were generally shipped to the Washington summer range by rail, but sometimes one herder, with a team and a hay rack, trailed them north from Hooper. The rams were fed hay and grain every night and kept in corrals. Emile Morod recalled one year when the rams found their way out of a corral ahead of schedule: "We shipped the bucks on the train to Springdale and unloaded 'em there and fed 'em one night at the back of the livery stable. Next morning I went to the corral and there was no bucks there . . . I had to track 'em. We had a band of sheep near Long Lake in those days . . . I got way over the hills and them sons of bitches was going straight for where them sheep was. They got under the fences through a fellow's field. . . . I caught 'em just at the foot of the hill below the sheep and turned 'em back."

McGregor herders trailed their flocks out of the forests in August and moved them to railroad sidings at the nearby villages of Springdale, Washington, and Bovill, Idaho. Here the sheep were corralled, and fat lambs were loaded in double-decked livestock cars for shipment to Chicago. The timing of the shipment was important, because Pacific Northwest sheepmen tried to have their sheep on the market before the Chicago stockyards were glutted with lambs from other range areas. Sheep delayed in transit would lose weight quickly on the rations of hay provided at railroad corrals. Sheepmen, the foremen they sent to ride the sheep trains, and the commission companies hired to sell the lambs all complained bitterly about intransigent, callous railroad officials. In 1907, the Coffin brothers were delayed six weeks in their shipment of twenty cars of lambs when the railroad cars were not shipped to a spur near their summer range. Their summer grazing lease expired before the cars arrived, forcing them to feed more than three thousand dollars' worth of hay to the lambs. *The Shepherd's Criterion* concluded in January 1907 that "never before has the sheepman suffered so severely at the hands of the railroad interest. Livestock values figuring into the millions vanished through the slats in the cars. . . . Cars ordered weeks ahead were frequently not delivered a month after the date set." John McGregor, seriously ill during the influenza epidemic of 1918, wrote a series of letters from his bed to the Knollin Sheep Commission Company, the

Kirkland (Illinois) Stockyards, railroad officials, and other parties in an unsuccessful effort to find an explanation for a long delay between the shipment of a carload of McGregor sheep and their arrival in Chicago.[52]

When the lambs finally reached the markets, they generally brought favorable returns, particularly during World War I. The gross receipts from McGregor lamb and mutton sales climbed rapidly, advancing from an average value of $22,788 annually during the period 1910–16 to $55,652 during the next four years. In 1916, the *Spokesman-Review* described a shipment of 30 cars of McGregor lambs and 18 cars by F. M. Rothrock as "the largest exclusive sheep train ever to pass out of the Northwest." A correspondent presented a somewhat imaginative description of the magnitude of the sale: "[The shipment of] 48 cars in all, and approx. 21,600 animals, will go through Spokane today on their way to the Chicago markets. These will probably constitute the record shipments for one day. . . . Estimating an average weight of 75 pounds to an animal, and an average price of 11¢ per pound . . . the [sheep] should bring close to $180,000. Archie McGregor of McGregor Bros., farmers near Hooper, will ship . . . 30 cars of lambs. . . . McGregor Bros. are among the largest sheepmen in the Northwest, having 20,000 head." Two weeks later, the same paper reported that "Peter McGregor, stockman of Hooper, in the city yesterday to attend the fair and the annual stockman's banquet, received a wire reporting the sale by his brother in Chicago of their sheep loaded in Bovill, Idaho two weeks ago. . . . Mr. McGregor reports that the lambs brought $10.85 a hundred and the sheep $9.50. The shipment consisted of about 14,000 animals, about half of them lambs, which brought nearly $75,000 and the sheep about $65,000." [53]

Rapid increases in the value of the lambs and wool crops convinced Columbia Plateau sheepmen that an era of prosperity was at hand. During the years 1905 to 1913, sheep raisers found their business "in a very prosperous condition with a good outlook." Optimistic woolgrowers claimed market prices were "the best ever," gleefully noting that "it does beat all how the cowmen are going into the sheep business." Peter McGregor feared that the removal of the tariff on wool in 1913 would "put us into direct competition with the peon labor of Argentine [sic]," and thus cause a market collapse similar to that of 1893. But increased demand for wool and lamb during wartime caused prices to soar. Columbia Plateau ranchers found that the market prices for wool, mutton, and lamb had more than doubled during the years 1910–18. Thomas J. Drumheller, Sr., noted that "ever since free trade became effective, the price of wool has been working higher. The stereotyped 'bear' argument has been discarded." For the McGregor Land and Livestock Company, the good prices meant that within eight years net profit increased seven-fold, and gross income from wool and lamb quadrupled.[54]

Western sheep enterprises were operated at full capacity during the wartime period. Washington Governor Ernest Lister announced a "great agricultural preparedness campaign," and meetings were held in every county in the state to encourage "the fullest possible food production." The Washington State Department of Agriculture commented in 1918 that "the war needs for wool and the appeals of the Government for greater production have started a campaign for increasing the sheep in every part of this nation." The McGregor Land and Livestock Company, wishing "to help the Government in carrying out its war program," announced that it was "our earnest desire to keep production up to the maximum until the present emergency has passed." In addition to patriotic zeal, the increase in price was a powerful motivation. Reporters spoke of the "almost incredible profits that are being made from sheep."[55] Large profits and easily available credit prompted many sheepmen to go deeply in debt to buy more sheep and more land, hire more employees, and build expensive new facilities. Most sheep raisers discounted the possibility of a postwar recession. Thomas J. Drumheller, Sr., commented in 1916: "Put me down at the head of the list of optimists . . . I cannot see anything ahead but good prices for wool and mutton. We hear a lot of dire predictions as to what is likely to happen after the war, but I am confident that markets will continue in healthy condition." Three years later, Spokane sheepman Julius Fisk noted that "the outlook for mutton and wool . . . is certainly promising. I believe both products will continue to receive fair prices for a long time to come."[56] The many sheepmen who decided to embark on rapid expansion programs during the wartime years were gambling that prices would not drop.

But signs of impending trouble were evident as the war drew to a close. Wool prices began to falter. The federal government had stockpiled wool for three years during the war, and there was talk of releasing the product onto the open market. W. J. Spillman, former member of the state agricultural experiment station and a member of the farm management team of the U.S. Department of Agriculture, warned in 1919 of an imminent collapse in farm commodity prices. Peter McGregor, a long-time acquaintance of Spillman, feared depressed wool prices and made two trips to Washington, D.C., to lobby for the passage of a new tariff bill. Peter responded to an offer by F. R. Marshall, secretary of the National Wool Growers' Association, to reimburse his travel expenses:

"The trip was undertaken voluntarily for the good of the industry. The reimbursement was unexpected but appreciated. I was certainly pleased at the results arrived at in Washington." But no immediate action on tariff legislation was forthcoming. McGregor lambs had sold for the exceptionally high price of $17.75 per head in the summer of 1918, but within a few months John was receiving apologies from a commission agent: "I want to say, Mr. McGregor, that this was certainly a bad market . . . it is nearly impossible to get anything like what looks like a good price when we consider the prices that we were getting a short time ago."[57]

The many sheepmen who had borrowed heavily to expand their operations would face liquidation and foreclosure if wool and lamb prices fell. The McGregor brothers had taken their big chance in 1896, when they had gone deeply into debt to purchase land and expand their sheep operations. The McGregors, Drumhellers, Coffins, and other Columbia Plateau sheepmen who had already purchased ranches and large numbers of sheep and who avoided headlong expansion had a good chance to survive the national postwar depression.

But even established outfits found their costs inflated and their markets uncertain in 1919 and 1920. Shed lambing, better breeds of sheep, more intensive supplemental feed programs, large and costly labor forces, and other new costs indicated to sheepmen that "the haphazard methods of times gone by are at their vanishing point." They also indicated that the days of inexpensive sheep raising had ended. Costs of running the McGregor Land and Livestock sheep business tripled during the years 1910–18. The Coffin brothers estimated that their expenses had risen even faster—from $2.50 per head in 1915 to $8.50 in 1920. T. J. Drumheller, Sr., described the changed conditions to the *National Wool Grower*: "We need good prices owing to an increasing expense bill. Running a band of sheep cheaply is now impossible. . . . To us, it was a matter of buying [land] or going out of the sheep business, and we accepted the former alternative. Now we must earn interest on land capitalization and pay taxes also."[58]

At this critical time, the McGregor Land and Livestock Company was jolted by the death of John McGregor, the brother who had managed the sheep operation for more than 25 years. John had continued in the sheep business while Archie and Peter were attempting to become merchants and Alex was working as a druggist. John had been the first of the four to recognize the necessity of purchasing and leasing rangeland, and he had arranged most of the property transactions. John had supervised the herders and other employees and made most of the policy decisions concerning the sheep business. Sick with influenza in December

1918, he had directed the sheep operations from his bed. After his condition seemed to improve, he suffered from pneumonia and died suddenly on December 28 at the age of 51, a victim of the great flu epidemic. His brothers received letters from throughout the West praising his hard work, fine abilities, and integrity. Associates in Northwest livestock organizations said he had "inherited the Scotch love for sheep." Peter, Alex, and Archie included in the company minutes a resolution praising their brother's "untiring zeal and energy" and stating that: "The foundation of the company, whose policy was chiefly directed during the past years by him as manager, was laid on the basis of honor and integrity, with a kind and neighborly feeling toward all, and the success he achieved is evidenced by the esteem and respect in which he was held by his neighbors and business associates." After John's death, the direction of the corporation remained unsettled as the brothers tried to decide who should become the new manager. An acrimonious dispute between Peter and Archie over this issue clouded the future of the corporation.[59]

But management problems, fluctuating markets, and gloomy predictions did not dispel the optimism that two decades of prosperity had brought to the sheep ranges of the Columbia Plateau. The McGregors and other livestock raisers who had been "enthusiastic in their faith for a bright future" in 1905 had seen a period of agricultural promise that must have approached their most sanguine expectations. Raising sheep in "the rocks" of the lower Palouse had proven to be a profitable endeavor for the McGregors and seemed to be an occupation with a promising future.

Chapter 6

Sheepmen Take to the Plow

WHEAT RAISING ON THE HILLS
OF THE COLUMBIA PLATEAU, 1905-20

"Late in June the vast northwestern desert of wheat began to take on a tinge of gold, lending an austere beauty to that endless, rolling, smooth world of treeless hills. . . . A thousand hills lay bare to the sky, and half of every hill was wheat and half was fallow ground; and all of them, with the shallow valleys between, seemed big and strange and isolated. . . . A lonely, hard, heroic country."   Zane Grey, 1919

"We were at it thirteen hours a day, sometimes far out among the wheat-covered hills that were so steep that they seemed to lean over from the top; again at the big threshing machine, whose howling cylinder and rumbling wilderness of mechanism seemed to be yelling 'wheat, wheat, wheat, more wheat' all the time."   Joe Ashlock, 1919

"The Palouse country is known throughout the entire world as the most wonderful country . . . for the raising of immense yields of superior wheat."   J. M. Risely, 1907[1]

"Almost the whole territory west of the 100th meridian to the coast lands of the Pacific is a sheep pasture, which can never be furrowed by the plow," Henry Stewart, author of *The Shepherds Manual*, asserted in 1882. But the book was out of date; already large portions of western rangeland had been converted to wheat production. By the time the 1907 edition of the book appeared, the expansion of wheat raising had deprived livestock raisers of millions of acres of pasturelands.[2]

Wheat—not wool, mutton, or beef—had become the most important agricultural product of the Columbia Plateau by 1905. Wheat raisers

154

had advanced, hesitantly at first, then with increasing speed, in the face of predictions that the interior "desert" could never produce crops. The region received little, if any, precipitation during the summer months and thus lacked what was thought to be an essential requirement for successful wheat production. But the land proved surprisingly fertile. So great was the interest in this "unique" phenomenon that the U.S. Senate voted to finance an investigation of "the rainless regions of Oregon and Washington" in the hope that the unexpected productivity could be explained.[3] Beginning in the Walla Walla area in the 1860's, farmers had expanded their operations in a northeasterly direction—to the Dayton area in the 1870's and to the eastern Palouse country near the Idaho border during the subsequent decade. After these areas were settled, farmers moved into the more arid lands further west—the Big Bend, Horse Heaven, and western Palouse regions of Washington, and the Umatilla country of eastern Oregon.

The semiarid hills, warmer and much drier than the uplands already in crop, seemed to present numerous obstacles to successful farming. Only seven to fifteen inches of precipitation was recorded annually— an insufficient amount, it was thought, to support a wheat crop. The soils were lighter in color and different in texture than those encountered previously. Some claimed that sagebrush was the only plant hardy enough to prosper in the light, dry soil. For many years bankers refused to lend money to farmers seeking to raise crops in the lowland areas. Railroad circulars predictably discounted the pessimistic reports. In *The Northwest Coast*, a pamphlet promoting the Northern Pacific line, the Rev. G. H. Atkinson assured prospective settlers of the arid Columbia Basin that "the plow proves to be the cooler" and that, once furrowed, the soil would attract an "invisible cloud of vapor constantly borne inland from the Pacific." The inland areas of Washington and Oregon were touted as "the only regions on earth where three or four crops of wheat are sometimes grown from one sowing." In 1901 Edwin S. Holmes, a U.S. Department of Agriculture scientist, made the equally implausible claim that Wasco County, Oregon, farmers raised "heavy crops without a drop of rain from seedtime to harvest."[4]

The McGregor brothers and other sheepmen were skeptical about the agricultural possibilities of their lowland ranges. They watched immigrants experiment with raising corn, flax, and other crops and saw the indifferent results. A few farmers planted wheat near the McGregor winter range during the 1880's. William Snyder, a farmer on Rattlesnake Flat, remembered watching hot, early spring weather ruin the 1886 crop. "You couldn't see the wheat in a coulee near Snake River on account of the steam from wheat a cookin'. The whole country smelled like a new mown hay crop. . . . The days was raring hot and the nights were freezing cold. A quick change and they'd had a wet spring. The wheat was awful tender. Father had ten acres and he mowed it down to the ground. Thought he'd save it for hay but he couldn't pick it up with a pitch fork. It was just like saw dust." Prairie fires and invasions by squirrels plagued early wheat raisers of western Whitman and Adams counties: "The squirrels stole the wheat seed almost as soon as it came out of the ground. If the wheat gained a height beyond the squirrel's reach, he would either straddle the stalk to bring it down or simply chew it through near the base." Sarah Snyder (not a relative of William, but also an Adams County farm resident) noted in a June 1889 letter: "The squirrels have injured the wheat crop very much. They have been a real pest this year. Our boys have got about 8 dollars worth of tails. They are paid two cents a tail bounty."[5]

The skills and techniques required for successful wheat raising were far different from the style of agriculture that the McGregors and other settlers had known in their eastern homes. Everything related to farming, from the sowing of seed to the harvesting of grain, had to be done differently in this semiarid land. Frank Andrews of the U.S. Department of Agriculture concluded in 1911 that "the production and marketing of grain on the Pacific coast constitutes a distinct chapter in the economic history of the United States." The varieties of wheat, production techniques, scale of operation, and other facets of Columbia Plateau wheat raising were similar to those used in earlier decades by farmers in the Sacramento Valley, another region that possessed the unusual "summer-dry" climatic conditions. But they bore little resemblance to wheat culture east of the Rocky Mountains. Instead of shipping their crops to Chicago and other midwestern markets, for example, Columbia Plateau farmers sold most of their wheat overseas, first to Liverpool, England, and later to the Orient, requiring an extensive ocean transport.[6]

Two decades of experimentation were necessary before the western Palouse ranges became a part of this international grain trade. William Snyder recalled that the first crops were seeded "by hand broadcasting . . . with a wheat sack over your shoulder. We threshed our first wheat by taking eight or ten horses and tying them to each others tails and running them around in a circle in the barn yard. Turned the straw and took a fork and fanned the wheat out in the wind." Snyder hired a newly arrived Russian–German immigrant and learned from him the proper procedure for preparing a seedbed.

> He went down there and seeded by hand and I paid him a dollar and
> a half a day and he said that wasn't enough. 'Well,' I said, 'I could have
> gotten any of my neighbors to have done this for a dollar a day but I

*felt sorry for you'. . . . He raised up his hand toward the sky and said
'You will find that whatever that hand soweth God Almighty will bless
a thousand fold!' Incidentally that was a twenty bushel crop and my
neighbors had five. The neighbors broke that brush and stuff in dry weather and it never rotted. This fella that broke this land for me he turned
it nicely and that was all. I supposed that I was beat on that deal. Just
wasn't deep enough. But in harrowing that left all the rough stuff on
top and made a nicer seedbed for the wheat. My neighbors were farmers
that come over here from Dayton and they plowed deep. In harvest
why you'd go up to your shoe tops in dust. You couldn't expect anything to grow.*

Several successful crops were raised in the late 1890's, and it became
evident that many of the winter sheep ranges could be converted into
farms. In 1905, a writer for the *Pacific Monthly* discussed "The Triumph
of the Palouse": "Each year lighter and lighter land is sown and no
failures of crops have been known. Experience has not marked the limit
beyond which it will be useless to plant. The superstition that the
Palouse country was going to 'pan out' proved unfounded." Reports
that wheat crops were "yielding well" and promising "some big profits"
induced a few sheepmen to begin their own farming operations. Jacob
Harder raised wheat on Eureka Flat, south of the "breaks" of the Snake
River. George Drumheller developed a large farming operation near
Walla Walla. Phil Cox and P. N. Mackenzie plowed under some of their
western Palouse ranges.

Surveyor Thomas W. Symons had claimed in 1882 that the entire
"Bunch-Grass Country" of the Columbia Plateau, a vast rangeland of
22,000 square miles, "as large as Massachusetts, New Hampshire, Con-
necticut, and Rhode Island together" would one day become "a waving
field of grain." By 1905, Symons' prediction had come close to being
realized. The Columbia Plateau had replaced California as the most important grain-producing area on the Pacific Slope. Washington farmers
had raised less than 6 million bushels of wheat in 1896, far less than the
31 million bushels produced in California. By 1905, Washington wheat
growers, most of whom were located on the Columbia Plateau, raised
more than 25 million bushels, while California production declined to
less than 11 million. Several million additional bushels were grown by
farmers on the Oregon and Idaho portions of the plateau.[7]

John, Peter, Archie, and Alex McGregor slowly and cautiously acquainted themselves with the wheat business. For twenty years they had
watched Dallas Carter, Lee Shropshire, George and Andrew Getty,
Charles Towne, and other nearby homesteaders "break" the range with
"foot burner" walking plows. But most of the adjacent area remained

in bunchgrass until the first years of the twentieth century, when a large number of farmers arrived to claim homesteads on quarter sections of federal land. Lenora Torgeson remembered that when her family arrived in 1901 to homestead land adjacent to the McGregor range, "there were hills and more hills . . . [with] wonderful grass as far as one could see."

The McGregor brothers hired crews to plow up four sections of bunchgrass during the years 1901–05. About 1,100 acres were in crop each year; the remainder were summer fallowed. But the land was used to raise wheat-hay, not to produce grain commercially. Only a fifth of the more than ten thousand acres of McGregor range suited for wheat growing had been cultivated by 1905. The large profits claimed by many Columbia Plateau wheat farmers interested the McGregors. Their experiments with irrigated alfalfa in the Palouse River valley near Hooper promised to provide a more nutritious and economical source of sheep feed than wheat-hay. In 1905, the four men decided to expand their acreage of wheat land and become commercial grain raisers. During the next decade, McGregor Land and Livestock converted about eight thousand acres of its Palouse country hills to wheat production. The total cultivated acreage reached a peak of between ten and eleven thousand acres during World War I. Twenty-five thousand acres of shallow-soiled, rocky scablands to the north and west remained as sheep pastures.[8]

The McGregor brothers were troubled by the management problems involved in transforming thousands of acres of sheep range into commercial wheat production. Farming several thousand acres of land would require that they obtain a considerable amount of machinery, hire large seasonal labor forces, and employ experienced foremen. The McGregors had been sheepmen and storekeepers, and they had no background in commercial farming. Their only experiences with farming in previous years had been bitter—the competition with cattle-raising farmers during the declining days of the open range; the failure of the farm implement business run by Archie and Peter McGregor. If the profits of operating a large wheat farm offered considerable promise, the hazards of making a large capital outlay in a new business were equally evident. The McGregors decided that dividing the land into parcels and obtaining good tenants was the most prudent way to enter the wheat business. Archie, Peter, Alex, and John McGregor began making preparations in 1905 for "a part of their grazing land to be divided into ten distinct farms to be rented for cultivation." A tenantry system said to be similar to that employed in Scotland was to be adopted. Hugh C. Todd reported on their operations in his 1906 Washington State College undergraduate thesis:

An increase in tenants is really a good condition of affairs. The Mc-
Gregor Bros. own thousands of acres in the western part of the County.
They farm most of it themselves, using it for wheat raising and for
grazing purposes. Peter McGregor . . . stated that they were preparing
to divide a portion of their land into ten farms and rent them all. Here
no decrease in owners would follow, but the result will be an increase
of ten tenants. . . . In this instance McGregor Brothers will no doubt
receive a rental as large as the income which they formerly enjoyed
from the land, and at the same time ten wage earners will be elevated
to the position of cash or share tenants.[9]

The McGregors rented portions of their land to tenants for more than
twenty years, until the postwar depression of 1920–23 and the near crop
failure of 1924 forced an end to tenant farming. But John, Peter, Archie,
and Alex McGregor took direct supervision of some of the cropland.
They received management help from their eldest brother, Dougald
McGregor, who leased out the family farm in Ontario in 1908 and spent
a decade working as a McGregor Land and Livestock Company foreman. "Johnnie" Knox and "Andy" Mays sometimes worked as a tenant
partnership on a 3,400-acre McGregor wheat "ranch," and at other
times served as foremen and operated their farm without a contract.
Some of the other "ranches" were farmed by McGregor employees,
particularly when a tenant quit and no capable replacement was available. Perhaps two-fifths to three-quarters of the farmland was generally
under tenant control.

The McGregor leasing agreements called for payment of a third
of the hay, wheat, and livestock raised on the premises and contained several clauses designed to ensure proper supervision of the lands. Tenants
were obligated to "plow, summerfallow, and harrow" the lands not in
crop "in a first class manner." Should either tenant or landowner wish
to terminate the lease, the McGregors were to pay "two dollars per
acre for summer fallow plowing . . . where done in first class shape and
harrowed once." The McGregor brothers were to furnish sacks, fenceposts, wire, and other necessary materials. Houses, implement sheds,
barns, windmills, cisterns, bunkhouses, hog houses, and various other
facilities were constructed on the properties by McGregor employees.
The new structures not only benefitted the tenants, they made the land
more valuable either for sale or for later use by the McGregor Land and
Livestock Company.

The rental agreements were advantageous to the tenant in that he
could commence farming without the capital outlay necessary to acquire
and improve real property. However, if the owners were not satisfied

or decided to sell the land, the agreement could be terminated in short
order. Dissatisfied with the way in which a section of grassland had
been "broken" and plowed, Peter and Archie McGregor sent the following notice on October 23, 1907:

> To J. E. Clemens, Tenant in Possession:
> You are hereby notified that on the first day of November, 1907, your
> lease or tenancy for the premises you hold possession of . . . will termi-
> nate and you are requested and required to quit said premises and deliver
> possession to the McGregor Land and Livestock Company, a corpora-
> tion, the owner thereof, on said first day of November, 1907.[10]

Many of the renters, however, remained on the McGregor farms for
a decade or more. John Banks, Roy and E. L. Jeremiah, "Billy" and O. L.
Harvey, Roy Weeks, Walter Lloyd, Charles and "Andy" Mays, "Johnnie" Knox, Harvey Barr, and other tenants leased land for several years.
Lenora Torgeson, a woman who grew up on one of the wheat "ranches"
and who was related to the Jeremiah, Harvey, and Barr families, recalled
that the McGregors made a policy of "always being real good to their
renters." The welfare of the renters and landowners was closely related.
Most of the tenants' business dealings were with the McGregor Land
and Livestock Company.

The McGregors provided their tenants with a variety of services—for
a fee—including threshing, hauling, storing, insuring, marketing, financing and bookkeeping. The corporation frequently purchased the renters'
wheat crops directly or sold the grain on their behalf. McGregor officials also operated local wheat warehouses owned by Balfour, Guthrie,
and Company, a San Francisco-based organization formed by Scotch entrepreneurs that exported a large portion of the grain raised in the
Pacific coast states. Several renters raised from a few hundred to a
thousand hogs on their farms. The McGregors purchased the farmers'
two-thirds interest in these animals and shipped them by the carload
to urban markets. The company had dealership agreements with Ad-
vance-Rumely Thresher Company, John Deere Plow Company, and
other farm machinery producers. Some tenants purchased harvest equipment from the corporation. In other cases, McGregor crews harvested
the grain. Commissioned to act for two insurance companies, the Mc-
Gregor Land and Livestock men sometimes sold policies to the renters.
Long-term loans, sometimes for amounts in excess of ten thousand dollars, were also available. Storekeeper Alex C. McGregor called on renters
to give them advance notice of special grocery and merchandise sales.
McGregor tenants purchased apples, cabbage, potatoes, and carrots and
stored them in pits for winter and spring use. Chickens, turkeys, hogs,

and dairy cattle were raised to supplement the food supply. Lenora Torgeson recalled that her family also ate rabbits, "prairie chickens," and wild birds and animals; cut "Jim Hill" mustard for use in salads; and planted onions, radishes, spinach, and watermelons on their dryland farm.[11]

Business records for the renters were kept by McGregor secretary H. R. Rudd. In an effort to solve a dispute between two tenants, the McGregors explained the relationship to their lawyers: "Barr and McKenzie rents a large wheat ranch from us, as does Mr. Knox, and all their business and records as pertains to farming operations are kept on our books in our office in Hooper." The McGregor brothers also handled legal matters for some tenants and endeavored to explain to creditors why certain bills owed by the renters could not yet be paid, or, if necessary, made part of the payment themselves. The McGregors came to be on particularly close terms with some of the tenants and helped them when possible. When J. L. Knox left the McGregors to buy a cattle ranch in Oregon, a letter on his behalf was written to the Portland Cattle Loan Company: "Mr. Knox has dealt with our firm for many years, his business dealings with us having been very considerable, and we have always found him to be upright and honorable in all deals he made with or through us and strictly a man of his word." Mr. and Mrs. John Banks, other tenants, were regarded as "very good people, oldtime friends of ours," and legal action was undertaken to help them avoid what was thought to be an unfair bill.[12]

The renters generally received stable incomes from their farming operations during the years before World War I. Wartime inflation meant a rapid increase in prices received for wheat crops. One tenant netted $13,000–15,000 annually from wheat raising during the years 1915 to 1918. But the wartime period also caused difficulties for both renters and landowners. A decision by the federal government to take control of the nation's 1918 wheat crop restricted the grain-buying activities of the McGregor Land and Livestock Company. Archie McGregor received a letter from an official of the U.S. Food Administration, stating that "It would not be permitted for you to buy wheat outright from your tenants and then ship direct or consign to some grain corporation or to the Food Administration Grain Corporation without a license." After the notice, most of the wheat was acquired indirectly, to pay harvest and store bills or repay loans. The increased costs of wheat raising that accompanied the wartime inflation caused problems for the farmers during the years 1919 and 1920. Renters were charged $332 per day for harvest operations, and some ran up bills of almost $5,000 for threshing expenses alone. In August 1920, the McGregors discussed the sale of

75,000 bushels of grain stored in their elevators: "We own practically every bushel of this wheat, as one third of nearly all of it belongs to us for rent and the other two thirds will be ours on account of the farmer's store bill and harvest expense. It would take a price of $2.50 per bushel for the renter down here to make any money this year. The threshing expense has been the highest ever known." [13]

The McGregor brothers acquired much of their knowledge of farming techniques from members of the Washington state agricultural experiment station. John and Peter McGregor became acquainted with agricultural college officials during regional livestock producers' conventions. "Farming demonstration trains" stopped at Hooper, Lacrosse, Hay, and other local points, and "farmers' institute" meetings were held at Colfax. The McGregors and other local residents attending these meetings heard talks by William J. Spillman, E. E. Elliott, and other officials of the state agricultural experiment station, as well as by "dry farming" enthusiast Hardy W. Campbell and other visiting lecturers. Peter McGregor was appointed a regent of Washington State College, served for a decade as member (and later president) of the state agricultural experiment station "board of control," and was a member of the state House and Senate standing committees on agriculture. He was an acquaintance of W. J. Spillman, who served as an experiment station official and later organized and headed the federal Office of Farm Management. A 1906 meeting that Peter McGregor and Spillman had with officials of the U.S. Department of Agriculture was indicative of the McGregor brothers' increasing interest in wheat farming: "The Hon. Peter McGregor, who is in Washington, D.C. representing the Northwest at the national livestock convention . . . [has visited] Sec'y Wilson, head of the U.S. Dept. of Agriculture. In company with Prof. Spillman he extended to Sec'y Wilson an invitation to be present at the great farmers' meeting to be held in Pullman next June. . . . The meeting . . . will be attended by farmers from all parts of the state who will come 1000 strong to visit the college and experiment station." The McGregors' ties with agricultural scientists helped to provide them with easy access to most current information on successful wheat farming techniques. While Peter McGregor was promoting agriculture at conventions and in the state legislature, his brothers were learning to manage the rapidly expanding company farm and increasing their control of the local grain trade. A correspondent commented in 1911 on the expansion of the McGregor wheat business:

A venturesome settler broke up some of this "semi-arid" land and planted it to wheat. He got a good yield. Others followed and soon wheat raising became the leading industry of this section and the pasture lands became wheat fields, yielding millions of bushels of the finest milling wheat produced in the west. Land values began advancing. The profits made from the sheep industry, which had been considered large, dwindled into insignificance compared with the profits made from the wheat crops. Much of this land produced yields of 20 to 40 bushels an acre and the quality of the grain being high always brought better prices than that grown in heavier soils. McGregor Brothers became known as the 'wheat kings' for their crop in a single year has run well over 100,000 bushels."[14]

The task of turning sheep range into wheat fields was slow and laborious. The native grasses were usually burned to make the initial turning of the "sod" less difficult. Sagebrush was too sparse to burn readily and it could not be plowed under easily. The William A. ("Billy") Harvey family cut, stacked, and burned sagebrush in preparation for plowing. Louis Banks, son of one of the early farming families, recalled that another technique was to hook a chain to the plow drag in order to push sagebrush forward, and follow with a harrow to put the plant under the soil. Sometimes troublesome clumps of sagebrush were also hooked to a chain and dragged out by a team of horses. Once the land was reasonably clear of vegetation, plowing began. Fred W. Clemens, son of a farmer who broke land near the McGregor ranch and brother of an early McGregor tenant, described the walking plow—often described as a "foot burner":

> [The] first plow to break that native sod was a single furrow one pulled by two horses (sometimes three). It was known as a one-bottom and consisted of three major parts: A heavy, curved iron plate some 10 by 16 inches in dimensions and called the moldboard; a pointed steel share bolted to the lower end of the moldboard in such shape and position that it cut through the sod roots four or five inches below the surface of the ground and the width of a 10-, or 12-inch furrow; and a wooden or steel beam four or five feet long to which moldboard and share were rigidly bolted at one curved end and to which the horses were hitched at the other end.
>
> As the team moved forward the share cut the sod and the moldboard turned it over. The plowman walked behind in the newly made furrow, driving the team and steadying the plow with a pair of handles that extended backward. With the sod thus plowed . . . it lay in parallel strips. . . . The uprooted grass lay underneath; the root-bound sod on top.

Double-furrow, "two bottom" plows drawn by six-horse teams and triple-bottomed, eight-horse plows later came into use for "breaking" the steeply rolling hills of the McGregor range. Such implements could break twice or three times the ground of the one-bottom plow in a day. Four-bottom plows pulled by sixteen-horse teams were used on some relatively level farms in Adams County. Farmers on Eureka Flat, in Walla Walla County, and Rattlesnake Flat, in Adams County, experimented with steam-powered tractors and sixteen-bottom plows for the first plowing. The cumbersome tractors, twelve feet high and weighing from fifteen to twenty-five tons, were popular in some "bonanza" farming districts in the Dakotas and California. But these machines, hard to operate even on level ground, were poorly suited to the topography of the Columbia Plateau and never gained wide acceptance.[15]

Farmers in the interior wheat country of the Pacific Northwest had to become expert teamsters, for horses or mules were required for every aspect of wheat production, from plowing and seeding to harvest. The first teams used in a newly cultivated area were often small. But multiple hitchings of large teams soon became a striking feature of this agricultural region, to a degree uncommon in most wheat-producing areas. Farmers worked to combine several operations into one, enabling a single teamster to plow or harrow as much land as possible with as many animals as he could control. Labor was more expensive in the grain-producing districts of the Pacific Slope than elsewhere. Farms of several hundred acres or more were common in the eastern Palouse, Big Bend, Umatilla, and other districts. Barley and oats were grown as alternate crops in some of the higher rainfall upland areas, but most of the Columbia Plateau was a wheat monoculture, unsuited to other crops because of climate and distance to market. From the time the land was first broken, the trend was toward limiting human labor while using large horse- and mule-powered machines to cover extensive areas of land. The same scale of operation had been common in the Sacramento and San Joaquin valleys in the 1870's and 1880's, but irrigation, fruit-growing, and diversification caused these California wheat districts to decline in importance after the turn of the century.

Both horse and mule teams were common on Columbia Plateau farms. Horses (generally medium-sized animals with Thoroughbred, Clydesdale, and Indian pony ancestry) were well suited to smaller operations where they could be given individual attention. Carl Penner, a Ritzville and Eureka Flat farmer, recalled: "Horses were used throughout the country. But on the large farms mules were used because they stood the heat better. A horse would come in and drink too much water and founder and be no good the next day and maybe a whole week." Clarence Braden, a Franklin County farmer, remembered that "mules knew how to take care of themselves." They ate and drank sparingly on hot days. "Hot weather, any other bad weather, they'd never overwork to the point where it would be damaging to the animal. I've seen horses drop dead on the way in. With mules it would never happen." Horses moved somewhat faster, but at a less regular pace, making them more difficult to control in large teams. Mules tired more easily and were at a disadvantage when pulling machinery through soft dirt. Both mules and horses were used on the McGregor ranch. Smaller teams, particularly on tenant farms, often were composed of horses. Mules were preferred for larger scale operations. Columbia Plateau farmers used several different techniques to get maximum performance from their work animals. Walla Walla farmer Ernest McCaw "applied the whip to make the lazy mules get up and to teach 'em." Virgil Bennington, a Rattlesnake Flat farmer, "learned to have patience. I learned never to lose my temper 'cause if you lost your temper the mules knew it right away. They'd be afraid of you and someday you'd be in a place where it'd hurt you." Carl Penner claimed "you couldn't beat the meanness out of 'em. It just don't work. But if you'd treat 'em halfway right and try to pet him a little bit and curry him nice and give him plenty to eat and a little bedding they soon learned who was boss." Bennington advised that "when you start 'em going never, never talk to your team. Fellas get in the habit of talking to 'em. They sing themselves to sleep and their team to sleep. They don't pay any attention to him." But Walla Walla County farmer Bill Drumheller, Sr., claimed that

> . . . mules could understand at least a certain kind of talk. This was born out by an episode of my adjoining neighbor to the north, Craig Fulfs. One spring Craig had a minister working for him who had trouble getting his mules to move along as they should. Finally Craig told him that the mules just understood one language and that if he would listen to the other mule skinners and use the same language they did, his mules might step out a little faster. Next morning Craig saw the preacher's mules really travelin'. And he also heard some words that even he had not heard before. That noon at dinner the minister said, "Now I want all of you to know that I was not takin' the Lord's name in vain. I was just talkin' mule talk."[16]

The first job for the teamsters and their animals after breaking the bunchgrass was preparing a seedbed. Fred Clemens remembered that the upturned roots of the native soil "had to be broken up, torn to pieces, and somewhat pulverized." This was done with horse-drawn wood or iron-framed harrows ("drags") equipped with four- to six-inch steel teeth. The first harrows were rather crude, homemade implements. Virgil Bennington described the first harrow he built for his Rattlesnake Flat farm: "You'd cut thin pieces of railroad ties. Drive nails in 'em. Cut the heads off and sand 'em back. Then the next thing was to take two by fours and drive long spikes down through them. Then put three or four of those two by fours together. Then nail a one by two on top so the spikes wouldn't come back up. Fasten all that together and bend the spikes back a little ways and you've got a good wood harrow. It did a pretty good job." The McGregors, their tenants, and other farmers in the semiarid region sometimes planted their first year's crop by hand-broadcasting seed along the newly plowed furrows. "Billy" Harvey seeded his first wheat by standing in the rear of a wagon and casting the seed. His daughter Lenora, too young to attend school, was given the job of driving the wagon. She recalled that the combination of an inexperienced driver and a stubborn team hampered the seeding operations. The land was harrowed after hand-seeding to cover the broadcast wheat seed. Hand-sowing was soon replaced by "what we called a shotgun seeder, a power wheel that was fastened to the back end of the wagon." By 1907, the McGregors had begun to use horse-drawn mechanical seeders, devices that dropped seed uniformly over an eight- to nine-foot swath, on their newly broken lands. These were superseded by drills, horse-drawn machines that dug small furrows and dropped the seed. The eight-horse or -mule teams that pulled the drills covered almost three times the number of acres that could be hand-sown in a day.[17]

The wheat was planted in the fall or spring, depending on the vagaries of weather. Winter wheat, generally sown in September after the first heavy fall rains, usually outyielded spring grains by five bushels per acre or more. With favorable weather conditions, the wheat plant began growing in the fall, was protected from cold winds by winter snowfall, and resumed growth as the snow cover melted and spring rains fell. But adequate fall rains and winter snowfall were essential. John McGregor once commented: "The only trouble with this country is that the fall rains come too damn late." Sometimes farmers "dusted in" (i.e., planted in nearly dry soil) the seed, anticipating the rain, and the wheat germinated and died from lack of moisture before the heavy rainfall began. When freezing winds hit unprotected green wheat, the fall planting could be winterkilled. The McGregors and their renters generally received enough rainfall by late September to begin planting. Like other farmers of the intermediate and higher rainfall areas of the plateau, they usually had adequate snowfall to protect the green wheat. Occasionally, they had to go to the time and expense of replanting in the spring when the winter wheat was killed. Fall rains and winter snows were less dependable in the arid Big Bend country further west, and spring wheats were commonly raised in that district. But spring wheats matured later and were sometimes "burned" ruinously by hot, dry winds during the

heading and blossoming periods. Arthur Buhl, a Rattlesnake Flat farmhand, recalled that spring wheat "wouldn't get ripe quick enough. Hot
weather'd hit it. It would be green yet and we'd get them old dust
storms that would cook it."[18]

Farmers experimented with a wide variety of wheat seeds—searching
for an ideal type that was high yielding, disease resistant, winter hardy,
early maturing, and easy to harvest. In 1908, for example, the McGregor
brothers reported to the state experiment station that their stands of
Turkey Red and Jones Fife had averaged 20 to 25 bushels per acre.
Turkey Red, similar in nature to a wheat first introduced into Kansas
by Mennonite immigrants, was a hard winter wheat that, according to
agronomist Byron Hunter, "probably stands the winters the best of any
wheat grown in the Columbia Basin." But it was a bearded variety, and
Hunter reported that "men do not like to work in it." Work horses and
mules "are usually fed on headed wheat and the beards make their
mouths sore." When raised in the Pacific Northwest it tended to become starchy and low in protein, making it poorly suited for flour. Jones
Fife, for several years the most common winter wheat on the plateau,
was hardy and drought resistant but it shattered easily, and much of the
wheat fell to the ground during harvest. The McGregors also seeded
Bluestem, a variety introduced into the Sacramento Valley from Australia in the 1850's, and Early Baart, an Australian spring wheat introduced in 1900 by the U.S. Department of Agriculture. But these wheats
all had some unsatisfactory qualities—as did Fortyfold, Red Russian,
Salt Lake Club, Mediterranean Red, Jenkins, Crooked-Neck Club, and
several other types brought to the Columbia Plateau.[19]

W. J. Spillman and other agricultural scientists at Washington State
College began crossbreeding wheats and promised farmers that a new
variety "exactly suited to the Palouse country" would be developed.
The McGregors and other farmers had fair success with some of the hybrid strains, but no single wheat proved ideal. Many Columbia Plateau
farmers were enthusiastic about the experiments of the agricultural
scientists. Palouse country farmer Girard Clark commented in 1909
that "in the work of cereal improvement there is no limit to the possibilities, hence no stopping place." The most promising varieties of wheat
were "soft white" types, with soft kernels high in starch and low in
protein. These varieties had two advantages: They were well suited to
the climatic conditions, and they commanded good prices on foreign
markets, where they were found to be well suited for use in pastry,
macaroni, and breakfast cereals. Instead of trying to prevent hard wheats
from taking on high-starch, low-protein qualities (traits that led to

overly viscous bread flour), scientists began to concentrate on the soft "pastry" varieties. The Columbia Plateau became the leading district in the nation in the production of these starchy wheats.[20]

Most farmers seeded only half their cropland every season. Attempts to make the prairie produce wheat every year had been successful on only the most humid uplands. Summerfallowing, an ancient farming procedure, had become standard practice in the Pacific Northwest interior by the time the McGregors and their renters began raising wheat. Farmers gave three reasons for adopting the summerfallow system: to conserve moisture, to eradicate weeds, and to get the soil in satisfactory condition for crop production. But no one was certain why leaving the land idle every other year helped maintain good yields. Byron Hunter, head agronomist at Washington State College, suggested in 1907 that "while land is being fallowed certain changes take place within the soil that give it renewed fertility. As to just what these changes are and how they take place, there is much to learn."

Wheat growers received advice from many quarters about the best ways to care for these idle lands and prepare them for future crops. The "Campbell system of soil culture" (a method of "dry farming" first used in semiarid areas of the Northern Great Plains) was promoted extensively by local journals, Northern Pacific Railroad officials, and a national "Dry Farming Congress" held in Spokane in 1910. Hardy W. Campbell, the foremost promoter of this style of farming, advocated the use of the subsurface packer and other specialized implements. Byron Hunter claimed the machines could improve wheat yields materially on the semiarid farmlands of the Pacific Northwest. But fellow experiment station scientist R. W. Thatcher, traveling on a farming demonstration train that stopped in Hooper in 1910, expressed doubts about the usefulness of the equipment. The McGregors purchased four $150 packers several years later to break a "crust" that had formed on their fall wheat. They found the implements unsuited for both cropland and summerfallow and spent several years trying to sell them. "They did not do the job," the McGregors wrote to a farm machinery company in 1926, "and after running them a few days we put them back in the shed. We do not see that we will have any more use for them." But most Columbia Plateau wheat raisers and agricultural scientists were quick to agree with the central concept of "dry farming"—the idea that the soil needed to be cultivated intensively to create a "dust mulch" that would preserve a maximum amount of soil moisture. Byron Hunter surveyed farmers in 1907 and found that most were "ready to concede that the more cultivation the better." He told of wheat growers who had tilled their fallow land six, eight, and ten times in a single year, and he concluded that "there is much to commend this method." Only Professor R. W. Thatcher had serious reservations. Thatcher suggested that farmers "leave the ground rough," avoid burning stubble, and take steps to protect the soil humus. "Conserving moisture," Thatcher warned farmers in 1912, "is not enough." His warnings went unheeded, and by the outset of World War I "the dust mulch theory of dry farming was reaching full vogue and the best farmer in each community was the one who could attain the honor . . . of the dustiest, smoothest, cleanest, least lumpy, and least trashy field surface. Soil pulverization became a main objective, and new ways of improving the dust mulch were sought."[21]

Summerfallow work began in the fall, after the fields had been harvested. Because teams of horses had difficulty pulling plows through heavy stubble and weed growth, Columbia Plateau farmers had adopted the practice of burning off their fields after harvest. William McGregor recalled that "They'd burn the stubble every fall with a fire harrow. You'd drag a harrow around, get it full of straw and get it burning and then the team would drag it around to keep the fire going. . . . They'd burn the field until it was slick." Plowing, harrowing, and weeding the fallow land was difficult, time-consuming work and kept a large labor force busy for several months. Practices varied greatly. Plowing sometimes began in the fall after harvest and crews occasionally worked through most of the winter, walking their teams and machinery through areas not covered by snow. The major cultivation work began early in the spring, and farmers hired large crews to complete their tillage operations as rapidly as possible. Alex McGregor's March 1907 payroll book lists seventeen men, earning wages of $1.25 to $1.75 per day, employed in summerfallowing operations. Each man stood or sat atop harrows, slickers, blade weeders, or two- or three-bottom "gang" plows and used a few sets of reins to control the six to twelve horses or mules that pulled the machinery. After some of the teamsters guided their plow teams across the stubble fields, others followed with harrows and weeders and worked frantically to turn the dry, cloddy soil into a powdery seedbed. The plows "ran" well into the summer months before the last of the previous year's cropland was furrowed. Plowing was particularly slow in spring wheat areas, where teamsters had to hitch their animals to seed drills for a few weeks before resuming cultivation. Arthur Buhl recalled that in the Rattlesnake Flat district "we had mostly spring wheat. Well, by the time you got through with your seeding and started plowing the weeds had just about sapped all the moisture out of the ground. You'd just plow that old dead soil. You didn't conserve any moisture at all, because it was all gone." But William McGregor noted that even in winter wheat areas, "with horses it took so darned long to get the job done that they would end up plowing into July. By that time the ground was hard as a brick and all dried out and the weeds and volunteer wheat were knee high."

The methods used for harrowing and plowing were also less than ideal. William McGregor commented that farmers generally "mulched the soil up fine and harrowed it to death and let it blow awhile." Many early weeders had blades fastened at an angle to cut the roots underground. But the blades were spaced too closely, and they plugged up continuously. "Dump slickers" represented a slight improvement, but Carl Penner recalled that "You'd jump onto this thing and go maybe twenty feet and you'd have to jump off into knee-high dust and dump the weeds off." The McGregors and other farmers tried stationary rod weeders, machines built by fastening pipes to a sled-type frame. These pulled hard, dragged the ground up badly, and had to be cleaned frequently.[22]

The intensive cultivation practices, already difficult because of cumbersome machinery and slow-moving teams, were complicated further by the rapid spread of alien weeds unwittingly introduced into the region. Russian thistle, a spiny, cylindrically shaped weed that broke loose and tumbled in the wind when mature, was observed at a few scattered locations in eastern Washington in 1897. In July 1898 Professor C. V. Piper of Washington Agricultural College was "thoroughly convinced that with the sum of $1,000 annually placed at our disposal," the weed could be eliminated. "The plan," he announced, "is simply to have all lines of railway in Eastern Washington carefully inspected by special agents on horseback, who shall destroy any chance specimens of Russian thistle found." Piper soon instituted a more modest program, sending "W. M. Duncan, a student of the college, on an 800 mile trip on foot. Mr. Duncan's work is to walk along the railroads and destroy all Russian thistles that he finds. . . ." But the weed continued to spread rapidly, for *The Ranch* noted in 1904 that "the whole Russian army . . . if it were here engaged in destroying this thistle, could hardly exterminate it."[23]

"Jim Hill" mustard (another plant that tumbled in the wind), tarweed, Canadian thistle, morning glory, wild oats, "China lettuce," and other weeds also prospered in the wheat fields. Washington State College botanist R. Kent Beattie reported in 1906 that "Jim Hill" mustard "now occurs very abundantly all over the Big Bend and down into the Palouse Country." Beattie claimed that in some areas "hand pulling alone can save this year's crop. If the weed is too abundant to make this feasible, the crop should be mowed and put up to hay before the mustard seeds ripen. Or if it is impossible to do anything with the crop it should be mowed and burned." State Senator Peter McGregor worked closely with

Beattie in 1907 to secure passage of a law requiring eradication of noxious weeds. Beattie was made ex-officio State Botanist and was given the
power to declare "that a certain plant is a noxious weed and is likely to
become detrimental to the agricultural interests of the state and that
therefore it should be destroyed." Landowners who knowingly allowed
such weeds to grow would be given misdemeanor fines. County road
supervisors were given "the sheriff's duty in the matter." Whitman
County officials vowed that the law would be strictly enforced in the
Palouse.[24]

The weed control programs all were dismal failures. Farmers further
increased their tillage operations, grazed sheep on summerfallow infested
with alien plants, and altered seeding times to combat the pests. The
McGregors and other farmers sometimes tried to keep winter-germinat-
ing annual weeds in check by planting spring wheat. But the invading
weeds continued to take valuable moisture and nutrients from the soil.
Scientists from the USDA introduced hairy vetch, a creeping legume,
to replenish nitrogen-deficient soils. Vetch, a forage crop, was said to
be of "great value" because of its drought resistance and winter hardi-
ness. But vetch spread rapidly, defying all efforts to eradicate it and
promising "to become a serious pest in grain fields. Its seeds are the same
size as wheat grains and cannot be perfectly separated from wheat."
Commercial fertilizers, including "blood, bone, and tankage" available
from meat-packing houses, were advertised in regional farm journals.
The *Washington Farmer* noted in 1919 that nitrate, "originally produced
to help in blowing the German armies off the map," would be available
for "the more peaceful work of increasing the fertility of American
farming soil." But few farmers were willing to purchase the expensive
fertilizers. The decline in soil fertility was gradual and the wheat crops
grown on the plateau continued to be better than those of any other
region.[25]

The dust mulching practice also left the croplands vulnerable to wind
and water erosion. The results of destructive farming practices first
became evident in the shallow, sandy soils of the Big Bend. In 1909, one
newspaper recorded the all too typical observation of conditions in that
region: "For several days the wind has been blowing a gale and people
traveling from the Mesa country say seed wheat has been blown clear
out of the ground." Peter McGregor and other state college regents organized the dry land division of the experiment station in 1914 after
meeting with "a group of gentlemen living in Eastern Washington
[who urged] . . . that greater attention be given to the agricultural and
economical problems of the district. . . . These gentlemen pointed to
the fact that farmers had settled in this district, raised large crops with

little effort on the virgin soil, became over-confident, increased their holdings and exploited the soil until it became deficient in humus and infected with weeds, thus resulting in agricultural disaster. . . ."

Peter Jacquot (father of Harley Jacquot, who later served almost thirty years as a McGregor Land and Livestock agronomist) and other staff members of the "Dryland Demonstration Department" concluded in their first annual report, issued in 1915, that "a great deal of the farm-land of the Washington dry belt has thus far been exploited rather than farmed." A "Country Life Commission," appointed several years earlier by President Theodore Roosevelt, concluded that farmers had engaged in wholesale soil "mining" and thus caused a marked decrease in soil fer-tility "in every section of the United States, even in the richest lands of the prairies. It marks the pioneer stage of land usage. It has now become an acute national danger. . . ."[26]

Despite the dust storms and "blown out" areas on the western fringe of the plateau, few farmers in the more fertile Palouse and Walla Walla regions saw signs of catastrophic damage. Water erosion left rills in hillsides that had been in crop several years, but much of the farmland had soils forty to a hundred feet in depth and few farmers were alarmed. Some scientists claimed that the soil had been formed by decomposition of the massive underlying layers of basalt.

Miller Freeman of *The Ranch* in 1903 interviewed USDA agrostologist W. J. Spillman, formerly of the experiment station in Pullman, and re-ported that the Palouse country soils had been formed from "overflow lava beds." "No soil, it is said, exceeds in fertility disintegrated lava, and there is practically no bottom to this soil. In one place the Snake river has cut through this lava 2,000 feet, forming a gorge hardly second to the grand canyon of the Colorado." Erosion was not a major concern if the dark, black rock visible throughout the scablands and river can-yons was available as a source of future topsoil. But further study would soon suggest that windblown volcanic dust, not lava beds, had produced the fertile soils of the plateau. By World War I, some scientists began to fear that farmers would one day reach the bottom of their productive soil. Stubble burning and other farming practices that accelerated erosion were criticized, but agricultural experts admitted that yields remained excellent. On the McGregor ranch and in other newly cultivated areas the soils retained a high amount of organic matter, and evidence of water erosion was hard to find.[27]

There were scattered reports of gullies and ditches in older farming districts. In 1916, a warm chinook wind and a cloudburst after a heavy snowfall caused severe erosion in some areas south of the Snake River. Carl Penner recalled that "it washed canyons that you could throw boxcars into. A lot of farmers never did fill the ditches." But Penner and several of his neighbors put up closely wired fences and built a series of dams of baled straw to catch future runoff. The dams "would catch everything," and Penner claimed that "in three or four years it was full up." Walla Walla country farmer Ernest McCaw later claimed that poor farming practices had ruined some of his land:

> They all thought in those days the best farmer was the one who could plow ground quickest in the spring and work it the most times during the summer. I don't know where they got the idea . . . I think extension service. Well Dad thought so too and he harrowed that whole place fifteen times one year. And he ruined that land. Made such a fine mulch, packed right down, but when it rained it run off. Just ruined the structure of the soil. Too much workin' ruins the soil.

Some efforts were made to modify tillage practices and to stabilize the soil. Major changes in cultivation practices did not occur until the 1930's, when erosion damage became severe and the federal government began offering subsidies for conserving the soil.

While they cultivated the summerfallowed lands, farmers watched the wheat closely, taking care to prevent invasions by squirrels. These rodents could eat fifteen-foot swaths through the growing grain. Lenora Torgeson supervised a crew of eight children who carried a tub of strychnine-coated grain through the fields and scattered it on squirrel hills. Fred Clemens remembered that the treatment was effective, "but no sooner did we get our crop land fairly free of the pests than other thousands marched in from the bunchgrass." Farmers in the Big Bend encountered a different foe in the form of "coulee crickets." Virgil Bennington described them as "big, hideous things that came up from The Dalles and along the Columbia River. We only had 'em about two years." The Washington State Department of Agriculture reported on the efforts to keep crickets out of wheat lands: "During the two months of April and May [1917] a hundred people were used, averaging a force of 16 persons continuously for sixty days. During this time six distinct armies of crickets were encountered, moving as persistently in their different directions as an army of soldiers. These were all successfully conquered. It is reported that one army made six successive charges against different portions of a four mile defense line."[28]

The wheat crops were harvested during the months of July, August, and September. Although the first crops raised on the Columbia Plateau had been harvested with scythes and cradles, by 1905 headers, binders, and "combined" harvesters ("combines") were used. The first two methods were used to cut the standing grain. The wheat then had to be hauled to a "separator" ("threshing machine"), which was belt-driven by a self-propelled steam engine. Combines performed both cutting and threshing in one operation. Climatic conditions, the size of the farm, and the lay of the land had much to do with the way in which a crop was harvested. Binders, horse-drawn implements that cut six- to eight-foot swaths of grain and bound the wheat into bundles for later threshing, moved more slowly than headers. An observer reported in 1909 that these machines were "used exclusively" on small farms in the most humid upland areas of the Palouse country. The grain ripened late in the summer in these districts, increasing the danger of fall rains damaging the wheat. Here the slow-moving binder had several advantages. It was somewhat cheaper—McCormick binders, for example, were retailed to Columbia Plateau farmers in 1908 for $109, $70 less than a header. Wheat had to be fully ripe before it could be cut with a header and stacked in the field. Farmers using binders could cut the wheat early and leave it in the field to cure. The bundles could then be arranged in stacks and threshed by custom crews. In 1898, *Rural Northwest* compared binders with headers and concluded that "no one can deny that harvesting can be done more expeditiously with a header than a binder. . . . The binder is essentially a poor man's machine, for any ordinary farmer can, with one hired hand and his usual number of horses, cut and stack a quarter section of grain."

The header was standard equipment for many years in the semiarid districts of the Columbia Plateau wheat country. Crops matured earlier and fall rains came later at these lower elevations. Farms were perhaps twice as large as in the uplands. Here the speed and smaller labor requirements made headers more useful than binders. Observers in these districts reported that "the long sweep of the headers tell of strenuous times among the hills and vales," and noted that "threshing engines are heard whistling early and late."[29]

Combines offered further savings in time and labor. By combining heading (or binding) and threshing into one operation, these machines promised to eliminate up to 80 percent of the harvest labor force. Combines with twenty- to thirty-foot cutter bars had been used on the flatland "bonanza" farms of central California in the 1880's, and in 1891 the Holt Company of Stockton designed a "sidehill" machine with a leveling device especially designed for the Columbia Plateau. But the combines were cumbersome and expensive and were a rarity in the region until about 1906. They then began to displace headers, first on Rattlesnake Flat and other level lands of the Big Bend, and later on rolling farmland further east. The combines were a spectacular sight. A favorite picture postcard widely circulated throughout the region before World

War I showed five ponderous Holt "Oregon Specials" pulled by 165 horses, attacking a waving field of grain on the George Drumheller farm in Walla Walla County. Combines were widely used on most portions of the plateau by 1920.[30]

The McGregor brothers and their renters tried all three methods of harvesting. John McGregor purchased a binder in 1906, and several tenants later acquired these implements. Binders were used to cut swaths along the fencerows and across the fields, enabling harvest hands and machinery to move freely across the hilly land. The bound grain was stacked and used as feed for mules and horses. Reports that the Haines-Houser Combined Harvester was "a grand success" and saved time and labor prompted McGregor Land and Livestock Company to spend $1,785 for one of the machines in 1907. But the machines, produced by a Stockton, California firm, had two drawbacks. The harvesting and threshing equipment was propelled by a large, ground-powered "bull wheel" driven by teams of thirty-three horses or mules that pulled the combine over the rolling hills of grain. Arthur Buhl recalled watching the early ground-powered machines on the steep, soft sidehills of the western Palouse: "They were awfully heavy machines. You get a bunch of horses out in the heat and dust on those steep hills and it was tough to maintain a uniform speed so that everything would work properly. It was soft ground and the bull wheel kept digging in and pushing dirt out in front of it." Howard Burgess worked on a bull-wheel combine during the summer of 1914. He remembered one day when

> We were just going over a hill, a steep pitch, and the back doubletree broke square in two. Sounded like a rifle shot. That meant all 33 horses lunged ahead. Lurched the driver out of the seat and damned near broke his shoulder and the machine immediately started to weave back and forth downhill. The separator man knew enough to put his brake on and slow it down. The rest of the crew jumped off because we didn't want to capsize. We ran over the hill to where that team had piled up. They had ... gotten tangled up in the doubletrees and all that rigging ... and some of 'em were choking. It was an awful mess. The boss said "Get out your jacknives, boys, and cut hame strings and nose bands." That's what we did. ... Got 'em all up ... one horse had broken a leg.

Added to the difficulties of running the ground-powered machines was another serious shortcoming: The combine scattered straw that could be saved when headers were used. The McGregors depended on the straw stacks as a source of feed and bedding for their livestock. They used the Haines-Houser machine on level areas of the farm, particularly in areas too full of weeds to be cut with a header. No more combines were purchased until World War I, when a labor shortage and the availability of more versatile models (equipped with gasoline engines instead of bull wheels) prompted the McGregors and some of their renters to add a few of the machines to their harvest equipment.[31] But the McGregors used headers more than any other harvesting machinery.

The harvest work begun with the headers was completed by a "threshing outfit," consisting of a separator powered by a steam engine fueled with coal, wood, kerosene, or straw. The engine was supplied with water by horse-drawn 400- to 500-gallon wooden tanks ("water wagons"). The threshing machinery was owned either by the farmer or by a traveling custom operator who owned the machinery and hired a threshing crew. Another variation, common in the Midwest, was the "threshing ring," a system whereby ten to twenty farmers joined to provide the labor for the threshing operations. But these "rings" were uncommon on the Columbia Plateau. The McGregors, their tenants, and other wheat raisers either purchased machinery and harvested their own fields (and perhaps those of neighboring farmers) or hired custom crews from other areas. A good threshing outfit usually cost about four thousand dollars. Most farmers were reluctant to purchase such expensive machinery for only two months of work each year. Accordingly, the custom threshers emerged. The period between the turn of the century and World War I marked the boom years of custom-operated steam threshing outfits. By 1903, western custom operators had an estimated $225 million worth of equipment.

Most Columbia Plateau farmers cut and stacked the grain themselves and left it in stacks for the custom operator to thresh whenever he happened to arrive. But if the traveling crews arrived late, fall rains could seriously damage the cut grain. The *Spokesman-Review* reported on October 9, 1905, that "the almost continuous rainfall during the past 10 days is resulting in serious damage to unthreshed wheat. The machines are unable to hold their crews together, and are pulling in, making it a doubtful matter if all grain will be threshed. The threshed grain in the fields is sprouting." Another report gave evidence of the difficulties encountered by farmers in areas near the McGregor ranch: "There are 15 days threshing to be done in the vicinity of Lacrosse, Pampa, and Washtucna. . . . There was an unusually large acreage, a big yield, and fewer machines than ordinary in that section. Heretofore threshers came up from the country south of the Snake River and helped to thresh the grain of Whitman County after the grain south of the river had been threshed. This year the machines did not come. . . . Many farmers will lose practically all their crop." The threshing machinery was again in short suppy in 1913, for the *Thresherman's Review* received reports that crews in the Pacific Northwest had been at work all winter until they were stopped by heavy snows in February.[32]

The McGregors and their renters minimized the danger of such losses by purchasing their own steam engines and threshing equipment. Acquisition of the machines enabled the McGregor farmers to control the time of their threshing. Moreover, the McGregors also developed a system of cutting the grain with headers and then threshing it immediately. Two tenant-operated threshing machines, one run by "Billy" Harvey and one by E. L. Jeremiah and H. S. Barr, handled the 1905 McGregor harvest without serious loss. Three more threshing outfits were purchased before World War I. At least two of the outfits were acquired through the McGregor implement dealership and financed by McGregor Land and Livestock. The renters supplemented their farming incomes by using the machinery to thresh the crops of neighboring farmers after the completion of the McGregor harvest. Bitter competition sometimes emerged for the local work. Billy Harvey purchased H. S. Barr's half interest in the Jeremiah threshing outfit in 1908 on the understanding that Barr was abandoning custom work. Barr then purchased a new outfit, undercut Harvey and Jeremiah in price, and obtained most of the local business. Angered by the competition, Harvey and Jeremiah refused to speak to Barr for several years thereafter. But by moving their equipment further east to the Palouse uplands near Colfax, the renters were able to remain busy threshing during most of the fall.

A large crew of men, horses, and mules was required for the grueling work of the harvest season. Veteran McGregor employee Ernest Osmond estimated that the three separate heading and threshing operations and an additional crew employed to move sacked wheat from the field to the warehouse required a total labor force of 118–121 men and about 320 mules and horses. The McGregors worked to streamline the harvest crews, and before 1920 steam-powered pistons and fans and other innovations had displaced some crewmen. The hot, dry summer days, with temperatures frequently over one hundred degrees, took a toll on both men and work animals. In August 1904, for example, the Colfax *Gazette* reported that "horses are dying in the harvest fields in the western part of the county from the intense heat." Joe Ashlock, writing in 1919 of his experiences as a "green harvest hand," described his first impressions of the work: "A threshing machine, a hot sun that boils the sweat from you in trickling rivulets, seven bathless, shaveless, soapless days with no clean clothing and your blanket roll getting filthier every day."[33]

The men performed best, Alex McGregor remembered, when they

were divided into distinct outfits, each of which was responsible for a certain portion of the cropland. Dividing the crews into separate working units encouraged the spirit of competition that was a common feature of the wheat harvests of the American West. McGregor heading and threshing crews shared the attitude Stewart Holbrook finds typical of western custom threshers: "Like a regiment, every threshing crew believed firmly that it was the all-mightiest crew on earth, and bragged accordingly. . . . It worked harder, faster, longer, better than any other gang. It piled more straw and bagged more grain. . . . In it were the champion feeders, pitchers, hoe-downs, sack sewers, forkers, the incomparable waterbucks, firemen, and engineers."[34]

Each harvest outfit began the assault on the uncut grain with three headers, machines that cut the heads and the top ten inches of stalk from a twelve-foot-wide swath of grain. All three machines were kept busy supplying wheat for the steam-powered threshing equipment. Unlike most farm machinery, the header was pushed, not pulled, through the fields. The cutting bar was positioned ahead of the eight-horse team to avoid wasting uncut grain. Fred W. Clemens, a brother of one of the McGregor tenants, described the appearance of a header: "It was a three-wheeled implement—a large, heavily cleated wheel at the left which, by ground traction as it moved forward, powered the reel, the cutter bar, and the grain-carrying drapers; a smaller wheel at the right whose primary purpose was to carry that end of the platform; and a rudder wheel at the rear for steering purposes and to carry the end of a long steel beam to which the horses were hitched. . . ."

The driver, or "header puncher," stood at the rear of the machine between the horses and above a board extending from a rod connected to the rudder wheel. The header puncher had three duties. He guided the team and watched them closely for signs of fatigue. He used a lever to regulate the level of the cutting bar. Because threshing machinery had difficulty handling large amounts of straw, he tried to leave a maximum amount of stubble while keeping the cutter bar low enough to cut all the grain heads. Between his knees was the steering board. By twisting his legs against the right or left portion of the bar, the header puncher directed the motion of the machine so that a full swath of grain would be cut. When fields were heavily infested with weeds a second employee, the mustard puncher, stood near the front of the header and used a pole to push weeds out of the cutting mechanism. Mustard was a particular nuisance, for it was so bulky that it clogged the equipment and forced grain off the platform and back into the stubble.

The heads of grain were carried from the sickle bar on a moving canvas, up an elevator to a wagon driven alongside and to the right of the harvesting machine. These wagons, known as "header boxes," were about twelve feet long and nine feet wide. Because the header box was built to fit under the elevator, it had a rather cockeyed look—the left side, away from the header, was almost five feet high and the right side was only about one and one-half feet high. The header box driver stood in the front of the wagon, close to the four-horse team that drew it. Lenora Torgeson, a driver for her father during two harvest seasons, remembered that the job was especially hard on steep sidehills, for the team tended to drift downhill while the wagon hugged the slope. An inattentive driver could tip the wagon and the box could catch the elevator and upset the header. Former Supreme Court Justice William O. Douglas recalled driving a header box on Ralph Snyder's farm near Hooper, hitting a rock and jumping free as the wagon and team tumbled over and over down a ravine.[35]

While the box driver carefully directed the team, a man known as the loader stood in the wagon and used a pitchfork to distribute the cut grain ("headings") evenly. When a box was completely filled, the header stopped and the loader jumped onto the top of its elevator. The filled wagon was hauled away, and a second header box was driven under the spout. The loader got into the empty wagon and the header was again put in motion. Ernest McCaw, a Walla Walla County harvest hand, remembered that the loader had "one of the toughest jobs. Just the strain of [using] a pitchfork pullin' those heavy headings around. Standin' on a slick canvas movin' around . . . on a hillside with the wheat rollin' in. It would just tear you to pieces. I'd rather do anything else than load header box."

Four header boxes were usually required to haul grain from each header to a stack located near the center of the field. When the header box reached the stack, the driver and another man, the "spike pitcher," began the grueling job of pitching the wheat onto the pile. They were assisted by a third man, the "stacker," who positioned the "headings" atop the stack. When four stacks, each ten to twelve feet high and thirty to fifty feet long, were completed, the spike pitcher, the stacker, and the driver began unloading at a new location.

The four completed stacks were then ready to thresh. A "derrick table," a large platform set on a heavy-duty wagon, was placed between the stacks. Three tall poles were positioned teepee style over the platform and secured into place to form the "derrick." A large cable ran through a pulley atop the derrick and another pulley staked to the ground. The cable was connected at the lower end to a team of eight horses. At the other end was a Jackson fork, a six-pronged, heavy steel, drag-dumping device. The "forker" jabbed the Jackson fork into one of the wheat stacks and yelled when it was set. The "derrick team driver" then moved his horses forward, transporting the load onto the table where it was dumped with a trip rope. After the wheat was unloaded, the forker had to pull the Jackson fork back into position by hand.[36]

The process of moving wheat from header box to the stack and then to the platform was not only exhausting work—it could also be dangerous. The derrick cable used by the H. S. Barr harvesting crew broke when a load of wheat was in midair, sending the prongs of the Jackson fork completely through the body of forker Bruce Barr. Barr miraculously survived the accident and resumed work a week later.

The McGregors and several other Columbia Plateau farmers simplified the unloading process about 1914 by adopting a system used on some bonanza wheat farms in California. The header boxes were lined with canvas nets ("slings"). The driver took the loaded wagon directly to the derrick and hooked a cable to the sides of the net. A team of horses then pulled the load over the platform, and the box driver pulled the trip rope. The Jackson fork was no longer needed, and the spike pitcher and stacker were eliminated from the labor force. The McGregors made another modification after World War I. The derrick team driver and his work animals were replaced by a drum mechanism, powered by the separator that pulled the cable that moved the "sling" from the header box to the platform.

When the wheat hit the derrick table two more men, known as "hoe-downs," went to work. These two employees stood on the edges of the platform and used hoe-shaped forks to pull the grain smoothly onto a canvas feeder (the "long feed") leading from the derrick table to the wide mouth and howling mechanisms of the thresher (generally known as the "separator"). Virgil Bennington remembered working as a hoe-down for a Rattlesnake Flat outfit: "You had to be very careful. You'd take the fork and tie it to you. If the fork got hooked on the slats in the carrier it would get pulled into the machinery and you'd tear up things in the cylinders. Nothing worse than a pitchfork going through the cylinder. So you had to tie 'em on to you with a leather strap." The hoe-down had to rake a steady flow of headings onto the carrier. Novelist H. L. Davis noted that inattentive hoe-downs "would overfeed and clog the separator so that, when it did start, it would boil straw from both ends and not get the wheat out of any of it; sometimes they wouldn't feed it at all, and the great scarlet rig would run wild, clanking and jangling and trembling as if it was about to belch all its iron loose into the sky and give up." The job was a grueling one and required the services of four men. Two hoe-downs worked frantically for thirty minutes keeping the separator filled with grain while two other men rested.

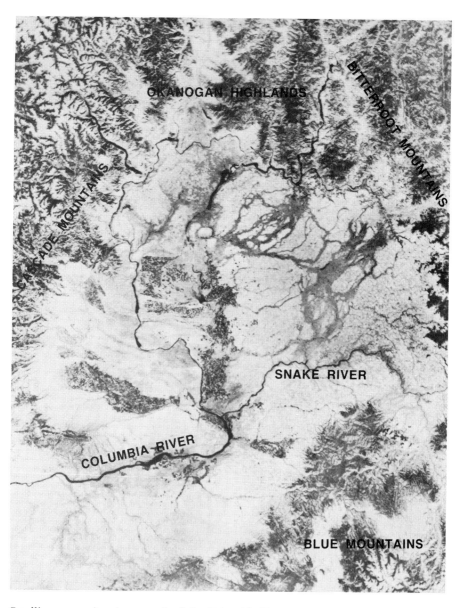

Satellite composite photograph of the Columbia Plateau, 1972. Dark "braided" areas to the right of the center are the Channeled Scablands. The checkered lands to the right of the Scablands are the farms of the Palouse country. The McGregor ranch is at the lower edge of the easternmost scabrock formation and extends into the Palouse farmlands. Dark areas along the Columbia are irrigated lands. (*Courtesy of Larry Dodd and Larry Painter, Whitman College*)

(*Left:*) Peter and Mary MacGregor, Owe
Sound, Ontario, late 1880's. (*Courtesy of Mar
Darrah*) (*Bottom left:*) Tramp sheepmen Joh
and Archie McGregor at Colfax photograph
studio, about 1886. (*Bottom right:*) Archie an
Nellie McGregor, photo taken in Colfax, abou
1895. (*Both photos courtesy of Marie Boone*)

The Channeled Scablands of the lower Palouse River, near Palouse Falls—
McGregor sheep range for ninety-seven years. The rolling hills at the right
mark the edge of the Scablands and the beginning of the plateau wheat lands.
(*Courtesy of Andrew McGregor*)

The Pullman Hardware Company, about 1893. (*Courtesy of William and
Nancy McGregor*)

Archie McGregor watching a band of sheep during lambing season, 1897. (*Courtesy of Jessie Medby*)

Shearing crew at Archie's Camp on the McGregor ranch, about 1900. Archie McGregor is at far left. Shearing with the hand-held "blades" required a great deal of skill and a strong back. (*Courtesy of Marie Boone*)

n McGregor, photo taken in Portland, about 8. (*Courtesy of Mr. and Mrs. Joe Crowther*)

Peter McGregor, 1907, shortly before his election as state senator. The same photo appeared in *Ryan's Legislative Manual, 1907.*

hie McGregor, photo taken in Colfax, about ;. (*Courtesy of Betty Jean Peatross*)

Alex C. McGregor, photo taken in Chicago in the late 1890's. (*Courtesy of Sherman McGregor Collection*)

Fifteen-year-old Emile Morod in Walla Walla in 1913. (*Courtesy of Emile Morod Collection*)

Sheepherders at play, about 1925. Left to right: Maurice Morod, Patty O'Brien, Emile Morod, E. E. Page. (*Courtesy of Emile Morod Collection*)

Sheep near the Palouse River, about 1910. (*Jennie McGregor photo*)

Sheepherder's wagon on the winter range. This wagon was in use for more than forty years. (*From old files of McGregor Land and Livestock, Hooper*)

McGregor sheepmen preparing to haul a load of wool from shearing quarters at Archie's Camp to warehouses in Hooper. (*From February 23, 1919,* Spokesman-Review *article, "Successful Career of McGregor Brothers Typical of Northwest"*)

Six thousand sheep at Archie's Camp during shearing season, 1903. Each 400-pound wool sack was worth about $64. Note living accommodations at right. (*Courtesy of Jennie McGregor*)

Range lambs for sale in Chicago stockyards, about 1925. (*From files of McGregor Land and Livestock, Hooper*)

Sheep foreman Jock Macrae at a herder's camp on the Spokane Indian Reservation summer range, leased by McGregors for almost seventy years. Photo taken about 1918. (*From Macrae's photo album, which he titled "The Life and Loves of John D. Macrae"*)

(*Above:*) Plowing. Five mule teams pulling "footburner" plows through stubble in the fall of 1910. In the wagon at right is ranch foreman Andy Mays. (*Courtesy of Mr. and Mrs. Joe Crowther*) (*Below:*) Oregon Railroad and Navigation Company farming demonstration train at Hooper in 1910. (*Courtesy of Sherman McGregor Collection*)

Steam engine, water wagon, and separator at work on McGregor ranch, ca. 1907. (*Courtesy of Jessie Medby*)

The Jeremiah threshing crew, ca. 1907. The steam engine is a Case 15–45. Partially obscured behind the men are a derrick table and a water wagon. (*Courtesy of Lenora Torgeson*)

Horse-drawn combine at work on the McGregor ranch, ca. 1915–20. Note man at center of combine operating a leveling device. (*McGregor Land and Livestock*)

Looking west toward Hooper, 1913. Note irrigation canal and orchards in distance. At left is Hotel Glenmore (Hooper Hotel). (*Courtesy of Sherman McGregor*)

(*Above:*) Sherman McGregor selling hats in the Hooper general store, about 1925. (*Below:*) The Hooper store in 1954. The same brick structure would continue to be used as a general store until 1978. (*McGregor Land and Livestock*)

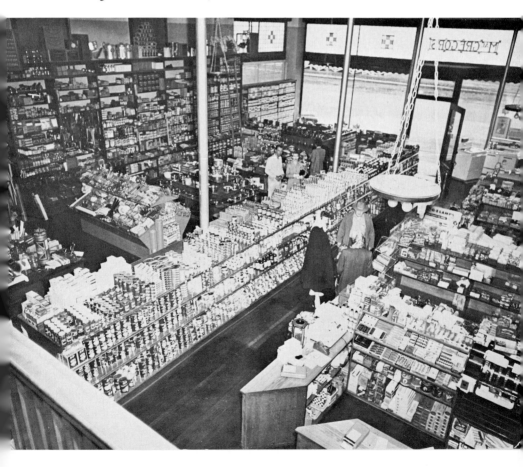

(*Above:*) Branding at the Bar U Ranch, about 1920. Billy Lloyd is at right; the other two cowboys are unidentified. (*Courtesy of William and Nancy Mc-Gregor*) (*Left:*) "The miracle of irrigation." Two McGregor employees stand behind first artesian well in the Palouse River Valley, near Hooper, about 1908. (*Courtesy of Marie Boone*)

(*Above:*) Minnie McGregor driving her new car. Mollie McClure, her seamstress, is beside her and Esther McGregor, her daughter, is in back seat. About 1917. (*Courtesy of Marie Boone*) (*Below:*) Mary Campbell MacGregor with her grandchildren, Christmas, 1916. Left to right: Mary Skene (daughter of Jessie McGregor Skene); Helen McGregor (daughter of Jennie and Alex McGregor); Mary Campbell MacGregor; Elizabeth McGregor (daughter of Dougald and Elizabeth); Sherman McGregor (son of Jennie and Alex). Seated in front: Mary and Marjorie McGregor (daughters of Alex and Jennie). (*Courtesy of Betty Jean Peatross*)

The Clan MacGregor vacationing at Spirit Lake, Idaho, near the summer sheep ranges, 1909. (*Courtesy of Sherman McGregor*)

Archie and Nellie McGregor's home at wheat ranch headquarters, constructed in 1901 (a second home was built in Hooper several years later). This home later served as a dining hall for harvest crews and was occupied by the foreman of the wheat ranch. (*Courtesy of Marie Boone*)

McGregor harvest outfit at work near "Tower Ridge" in 1925. Maurice McGregor and Oscar Shearer built the long feed racks from old tenant-owned header boxes. The gas-powered tractor at right moved the belt that powered the separator. The header boxes were unloaded by a pulley device powered by the tractor. (*Photo by Donald McGregor, courtesy of Dallas Hooper*)

Headers, header boxes, and crew near stacks of unthreshed wheat, ca. 1906. When the stacks were completed, the threshing equipment was moved into place nearby. (*Courtesy of Marie Boone*)

Donald McGregor photo of harvesters at lunch at the cookhouse, 1925. One crew-man, unwilling to wait for the picture to be taken, is already eating. (*Courtesy of Dallas Hooper, the harvest hand at far right in front row*)

McGregors sell their horses and begin tractor farming. Sale of horses, 1929. Left to right: ranch foreman Warren Booth, auctioneer, Jock Macrae, Maurice Mc-Gregor. (*McGregor Land and Livestock*)

Maurice McGregor (left) and A. B. Nielson, Soil Conservation Service official, 1941, "in a field which has had all the crop residue utilized and left near the surface for the past three wheat crops, and has not shown any appreciable decrease in wheat yields, as compared with adjoining fields which were clean-tilled." (*Photo and commentary by H. H. Harris of U. S. Department of Agriculture. McGregor Land and Livestock photo*)

Harvest on the McGregor ranch, 1946. Tractors replaced teams of twenty-four to thirty-two horses that had once been used to pull each combine. Lloyd Bowlin, the combine operator pictured here, and two other combine drivers, Hans Kahler and Charles Tobin, were each employed by the Hooper firm for more than thirty years. (*McGregor Land and Livestock*)

The 1973 McGregor ranch harvest crew standing in front of one of the three air-conditioned, self-propelled combines. Left to right: combine drivers Joe Okzresa and Charles Tobin, "bankout wagon" operator Leland Branum, combine driver Lloyd Bowlin, truck drivers Andrew McGregor, Howard Maier, and John Robert McGregor. (*Courtesy of Andrew McGregor*)

Sherman McGregor testing an early anhydrous ammonia applicator on the McGregor ranch, about 1956. This 27-foot machine was later superseded by much wider application units, with hydraulic devices that enabled the tractor driver to raise and lower shanks and to fold up the machine by pulling levers in the tractor cab. (*McGregor Company*)

Aerial view of the McGregor Feedlot, near the Columbia River and south of Pasco, 1982. With 42,000–52,000 head on feed throughout the year, the McGregor Feedlot is the largest in the Pacific Northwest. Water visible in foreground is an evaporative lagoon containing runoff from adjacent lots. Offices, feedmills, and elevators are visible near the lot. The edge of the packing plant where the stock will be slaughtered is visible on the right-hand side of the photo. (*Courtesy of John McGregor*)

"Cowboys" Norm Miller, Clemente Barber, and Modesto Samper herding cows and calves from pastures to corrals near Hooper. Branding time, fall 1976.

(*Above:*) Palouse Falls, a 198-foot waterfall on the western edge of the McGregor sheep pastures, 1976. (*Courtesy of Andrew McGregor*) (*Below:*) The same waterfall two years later, after a cloudburst.

Modesto Samper in the "drop wagon" with ewes and their newborn lambs, February 1976.

Lorenzo Zozaya feeding orphaned "bummer" lambs, February 1976.

McGregor sheep foreman Clemente Barber moving freshly shorn sheep, Archie's Camp, May 1976.

The last truckload of wool from the 1976 clip, at the wool warehouse in Hooper.

The men then exchanged roles, each team spending half the day resting and half raking. A mechanical feeding device known as an "automatic hoe-down" came into use after World War I and replaced these four crewmen.[37]

The separator was driven by a self-propelled power plant located well off to one side so sparks would not get into the threshed straw. The steam traction engines were huge machines, ten to twelve feet high and twenty feet in length, that moved slowly, even on level land. The ponderous engines could not propel themselves over hills and had to be pulled by teams of horses or mules. But once in place and hooked to a drivebelt, they had the power to drive a separator through huge stacks of grain. The McGregors tried both straw- and wood-powered engines. Their tenants, Billy Harvey, E. L. Jeremiah, and J. A. Mays had straw-fueled Case steam engines. The Jeremiah steam engine of 1907 was a Case 15–45 (fifteen horsepower on drawbar, forty-five on drivebelt). The Mays engine, purchased during World War I, was a more powerful Case 36–58. The straw burners were preferred by the McGregors and many Columbia Plateau farmers, for they used an inexpensive and readily available source of fuel on the treeless prairies. The engine was connected to the separator by a sixty- to eighty-foot drivebelt, crossed in the middle so it would not jump the wheel. The fireman was responsible for running the steam engine. He began work at four in the morning by cleaning the machine's flues and kindling a fire in the engine. Arthur Buhl, a fireman for a Rattlesnake Flat outfit, recalled that once he had built up a bed of red-hot coals in the firebox, he filled it with wet straw to generate heat and pressure for the boiler. "Some guys used to take a sack of wheat and throw it in there. But farmers didn't like that. Wet straw would do it." When the engine had sufficient steam, the fireman blew a steam whistle and woke up the rest of the crew. H. L. Davis described the fireman's work as "the meanest and dirtiest job in the field": "His job was stoking the firebox of the engine with straw. The ordinary temperature of the field was 120 degrees, and, by the time work stopped in the evening, he would have sweated clear through his bullhide shoes and have a drip coming from the brim of his hat." Firing with straw required "constant attention." The 1910 *Thresher's Guide* described the fireman's responsibilities:

> The straw chute should be kept packed with straw at all times to prevent cold air from passing into the flues. . . . Straw forms a great amount of loose ash that must be raked out of the ash pit at frequent intervals or the draft will be poor. It also forms considerable hard clinker . . . [that] must be cleaned out at frequent intervals. . . . There is also trouble from the ends of the flues in the firebox end of direct flue boilers being

capped with soot. . . . When a fireman attends to all these things and keeps steam up and at the same time attends to the pump or injector, he is kept pretty busy.[38]

The head man of the steamer was the engineer. Engineers took pride in their ability to have the harvest machinery into position in record time. Arthur Buhl remembered that these men "would claim that they could move from one setting [i.e., one series of grain stacks] to another in fifteen minutes. They claimed the cylinder would still be revolving. When they got ready to move two guys standing by the engine would stop the sixty foot belt and would run with that belt to the new location." Another man would run with a team of horses, hook them to the derrick table, and pull it to the new stacks. The engineer would run and hook teams to the steam engine, and by the time he arrived at the new stacks everything was in place. Once the machine was in position, the engineer got up steam pressure, shook down the ashes, cleaned off the dust and dirt, and oiled the machine, using the top grade of sperm oil for bearings and pure beef tallow for the valves.

These men were exposed to constant danger, for the steam boiler was under tremendous pressure. The *Thresher's Guide* described steam power as "a good servant or a merciless destroyer, depending upon how it is handled." In a five-year period one Midwest newspaper mentioned thirty deaths caused by injuries from threshing accidents in surrounding communities. Another danger arose from the drive belt, for men caught by it were run through the drive wheel and "pounded almost to a pulp." Men employed around the steam engine were in a great demand, and they usually received wages several times higher than unskilled harvest hands.

The steam power plant engaged the rubber drive belt that powered the separator. The separator consisted of a rapidly revolving cylinder with several rows of steel teeth that meshed with similar teeth on four stationary iron "concaves." Unthreshed wheat moved down the canvas feeder into these teeth where grain, chaff, and straw were separated and dropped into a series of vibrating sieves. The grain fell through the sieves and was carried out of the machine by a rotating auger. A belt-driven fan below the sieves blew chaff and straw out of the thresher. Two men then pitched the straw into a stack several feet away. These men, the "straw pitchers," were eliminated after 1910 by a more powerful fan ("wind stacker"), which blew the straw and chaff twenty feet away from the thresher into the straw stack.[39]

Six men worked near the threshing machine. The "separator man" checked the cylinder for loose teeth, set the sieves, tightened the belts, and performed other tasks. An "oiler" assisted in the maintenance of the machine. Arthur Buhl remembered helping to care for the separator one day when the oiler went to town.

> *We couldn't kill any time. So we hurried up. Mustard got jammed up in what they called the short piece, near the cylinder. There were beaters— sharp rods—in there and you can't imagine how sharp they got. I jumped in there to clear it out. It was full of wheat and I happened to kick into one of those rods. After I got everything cleaned out and gave the en- gineer the go ahead I jumped on the ground and I felt something in my shoe. It was blood. My leg was cut clear down to the bone. We was about fifteen miles out of town and the roustabout had gone to town for supplies. So the fireman says, "I got some turpentine." I said "Well, that will hurt, won't it?" He said "No, if you do it right now it won't hurt." And it didn't. Put that turpentine in there and they had a dirty old shirt and he slapped that around there and you know that never did get sore.*

While the separator man and the oiler kept the thresher running smoothly, a "straw buck" pitched straw from the pile to a location near the steam engine so the fireman would have access to a ready supply of fuel. Three men were kept busy sacking the wheat, which was augered out of the grain spout. The "jig" put an empty burlap bag ("gunny sack") on the spout and jiggled it to fill it with as much grain as pos- sible. "That's hard on the hands," Carl Penner remembered. "The first three or four days the blood would just run out of your fingers where you grabbed the sacks." Two sack sewers each sat on full sacks of wheat and worked rapidly with needle and thread. Fred Clemens described the duties of the sack sewer and remembered one unusually busy day spent at the trade:

> *The sewer's implement was a partially flat spring steel needle. . . . With double twine he threw two half-hitch loops around the left corner of the sack to form an "ear" and then, as deftly as his skill permitted, closed the sack with nine stitches, completing the job with another pair of half-hitches to form another "ear." Quickly rethreading the needle . . . preparatory to the next full sack, he picked up the one just finished . . . [which] weighed from 135 to 140 pounds . . . carried it to a pile some 15 feet from the thresher and hurried back to receive the next from the sack jig. . . .*
>
> *I well remember a certain day when I, just turning 16 years, was one of the two sack sewers. . . . We threshed that day a few more than 1800 sacks. Their overall weight was over 120 tons. Each sewer sewed about 900 sacks, throwing about 3600 half-hitch "ear" loops, making well over 8000 stitches, and picking up and carrying to the sack pile over 60 tons of wheat. Without doubt that was the hardest physical day's work I ever performed, before or since. . . .[40]*

The harvest hands working near the thresher dreaded what they called a "tail-wind." Joe Ashlock explained to the *Washington Farmer* in 1919 that "such a wind comes over the back end of the separator . . . whence emerge the clouds of suffocating dust and pulverized straw and smut. . . . This dense cloud of dust which sets fire to the skin and smarts nostrils and lungs and fills the eyes, is whipped back over the top of the separator down on the men working about the machine." Howard Burgess remembered that when he was eleven years old, working in his first harvest as a straw buck, "I learned about horses there and I learned about tarweed. I remember we used to sit by Coppei Creek at night and wash and the tarweed burned so."

When the dust settled and the separator and steam engine moved to a new location, a crew of several men picked up the sacks and transported them to the warehouse. The McGregor crews used horse-drawn wagons for this work until World War I, when a few trucks were purchased to haul the sacks to Hooper.

Two "water bucks," a "roustabout," a "flunky," a "straw boss," and two cooks completed the harvest crew. The water bucks used cigar-shaped, 400-gallon wooden tanks to haul water to the horses and to the steam engine. The water was pumped by hand into the troughs and the engine. Because an empty boiler could explode at any moment, the job of the water buck was an important one. Ernest McCaw remembered hauling water several miles from the Touchet River to a Walla Walla County threshing outfit: "I'd often leave at nine o'clock at night for a tank of water. I'd get back at twelve and get up at four and start all over again." The trouble and expense of hauling water forced many Columbia Plateau farmers to abandon what Carl Penner described as "the best and smoothest power we ever had"—the steam engine. Penner traded his engine for a horse-drawn combine. By 1920 H. S. Barr, a McGregor renter, was operating a kerosene-powered Advance-Rumley. McGregor Land and Livestock had purchased a 30–60 Rumley Oil Pull tractor to power a separator, and the internal combustion engine had begun to replace steam power on many farms in the semiarid region. The new machines eliminated the need for water haulers and straw bucks. Both steam and gasoline engines required a flunky to haul supplies and move the cookhouse. A roustabout was needed to handle miscellaneous "odd jobs" for the heading and threshing outfits. General supervision of the harvest proceedings was handled by the straw boss. These men marked out the land to be harvested, decided upon the proper procedure for the cutting, and performed other supervisory tasks.[41]

The two cooks spent long days preparing food for a large crew of hungry workers. Lenora Torgeson remembered cooking sixteen hours

a day for sixty-four straight days during one harvest season. A local resident, Harry Fennimore, hauled wagonloads of fresh meat to the threshing outfits on the McGregor ranch. The meat was stored in the shade of
the cookhouse until needed. Potatoes were kept in a trapdoor compart-
ment in the middle of the mobile cook wagon. As many as forty men
took a break after two hours of threshing and sat in the tiny cook
wagon, where they were served six o'clock breakfasts of bread, fried
potatoes and gravy, and meat. The steam engine whistle announced two
fifteen-minute lunch breaks at 10 a.m. and 2 p.m. The crew either came
to the cook wagon or waited as cooks rushed out to meet them with
washtubs full of sandwiches, cookies, cakes, and pies. After the cooks
rested two or three hours, they began making preparations for a large
supper, generally eaten in the cookhouses after 8 p.m.[42]

The harvest crews were made up of local farmhands, schoolboys, and
migratory workers known as "bindle stiffs" who carried extra clothing,
a little food, and their bedrolls ("bindles") on their backs as they followed heading and threshing operations from state to state. An 1898
report in *Ranch and Range* provided a typical description of the traveling workers: "Laborers are pouring into the fields of eastern Washington
by the thousands to harvest the mammoth crops. They make an army
by themselves and have come in afoot and by brakebeam. A representative riding from Portland to Walla Walla last week noted the trucks
of the coaches covered with grimy fellows with blankets strapped to
their backs. The patrol of the train hands was of no effect, and no sooner
were they driven off than they swing under again as the train moves
on." During the fall of 1909, more than a thousand of these nomadic
harvesters left Minneapolis within a 24-hour period, all of them destined
for the wheat fields of the Columbia Plateau. Max Torrance, a harvest
hand employed on the McGregor ranch and many other farms in Washington, Idaho, Montana, and the Canadian prairies, recalled that as many
as 1,500 to 2,000 laborers would arrive in Colfax before harvest and begin
searching for employment. Some of the men had worked their way
north from Texas or California; others had followed the harvests through
the Dakotas and Montana.

Ralph Snyder described some of the additional crewmen:

*A lot of miners came down from the mines [of northern Idaho]. . . .
They'd work there all winter and then they wanted to come out and get
some sunshine. And then there was longshoremen. In the wintertime,
they'd hang out in Seattle and Tacoma and Portland. Then there was a
certain number of young fellas that came from Missouri. You'd be surprised at how many Canadians came down. See the Canadian crop was
later. They were farmers up there and they came down and made a*

*few dollars, maybe 40, 50, 100 dollars. That helped 'em to beat hell . . .
[I learned that you] never wanted to tell a man your troubles, because
he wants to work for a winning outfit. I always said, "Well, we're gettin'
things done, gettin' more acres. . . ." That's the spirit of work and they
liked it.*

These men generally arrived in Hooper by "riding the rails." McGregor
Land and Livestock hired many of them through grimy Spokane bars
that doubled as employment agencies. The labor force also included
many local residents. Some, like twelve-year-old Dallas Hooper, were
so young they "could hardly see over the header box." Others were
middle-aged veterans of the harvest fields. Some Columbia Plateau harvesters were immigrants who did seasonal work as they looked for a
place to settle. Howard Burgess described his family: "We weren't mi-
grants. We were explorers looking for a place to light." The Burgess
family spent several years traveling across the Pacific Northwest by
horse-drawn covered wagon after the turn of the century, moving from
harvest work at Pendleton, to dairy farms in western Oregon, to the
Yakima Valley where there were "apples to pick and prunes and onions
to weed," and then to the wheat fields of Walla Walla County, where
the wife and infant children stayed in tents or vacant houses while the
father and young sons worked for threshing crews.[43]

The harvesters were paid room and board. They ate big meals: Arthur
Buhl claimed, "You'd eat a million hotcakes pretty easily." But the quality of food varied from farm to farm. Franz Wood, a harvester in the
Midwest, recalled that a cook "quite thoroughly discouraged his appe-
tite. He had just sat down with the crew to do justice to a whopping
meal, when he noticed that the woman was feeding cow chips into the
stove, and resumed patting butter into place on a serving dish, not
troubling to wash her hands." Board consisted of the straw pile or other
locations in the field. Ernest Osmond recalled that he and other Mc-
Gregor crewmen usually preferred spreading their bedrolls under header
boxes or other harvest machinery. Cooks slept in tents with straw
floors near the cook wagons. The sleeping quarters provided little protection against lightning-caused fires, rattlesnakes, or runaway horses.
Tom Darr, a member of the Harvey threshing crew, surprised his associates every year by sneaking out of the haystack late at night, shaking
a singletree, and hollering "My God, the horses are stampeding." The
ploy generally succeeded in routing a large number of laborers from their
bedrolls. Ernest McCaw recalled that the same trick was popular in
Walla Walla County. "The crew went to town on Saturday night and
got drunk. When the boys came in . . . along about twelve or one o'clock
they'd watch some of the tenderfeet. . . . Some fella would grab an old . . .

harness, with chains on it. He'd start running over their beds and the fella behind would holler 'Whoa! whoa!' and the tenderfeet would come out of those bags and take off in their B.V.D.'s running all over the area." Howard Burgess remembered harvesting on the Snake River "breaks" when seven rattlesnakes were run through the threshing machine in an afternoon. "By golly they were thick. Of course the old timers had us all scared to death. They'd tell ya . . . [rattlesnakes] would crawl in bed with you at night. 'Ya gotta get your bed up.' So I slept on the wagon or in the sack pile. But that's just part of threshing." The McGregor crews slept in beds only on the rare occasions when harvest operations happened to take place near one of the bunkhouses.[44]

Working hours were interminably long, commencing with the fireman heating up the steam engine before four a.m. The rest of the men curried the horses and mules and were in the field by five. Harvest usually lasted until eight or later each evening. The wages were more than twice as high as those for most farm labor, but they were hardly generous for the backbreaking, filthy work. Some compensations existed: the camaraderie, the storytelling and social atmosphere, the opportunity to meet people with widely divergent backgrounds. Howard Burgess remembered one summer when he worked as a sack sewer: "The boy right with me was one of those sailors. He had been shanghaied as a kid out of Old Ireland. The stories he could tell around the straw stack."

Harvest helpers were proud of their work. When a local citizen secured a harvest job on the McGregor ranch, the occasion would sometimes be noted by the Hooper correspondent to the Lacrosse *Clipper*. In 1916, for example, the correspondent commented that "Herman Langley, our champion lightweight, is handling wheat for Walter Lloyd [one of the McGregor tenants]." Notice was also taken that "Wayne Sperry is hauling wheat for McGregor Brothers." Rube Sutherland, a McGregor harvest hand, stated on October 13 that "after a fifty day run of threshing and hauling wheat he is entitled to wear good clothes and strut around for a week."[45]

The McGregor crews generally worked from early July until October or November. In 1907, for example, Archie McGregor began paying harvest wages to McGregor Land and Livestock Company employees on July 6 for heading and stacking. Jacob Hughes, in charge of the recently purchased Haines-Houser combine, began a thirty-four-day "run" on July 24. Threshing and separating commenced on July 24 and continued until September 19. Wheat hauling was completed on November 6. In subsequent years, when the cultivated lands had been expanded to ten thousand acres, the threshing equipment began operations earlier in July and continued work well into November. The wage scale in 1907 ranged from $2 per day for the cooks and for men employed putting straw under wheat sacks to $8 for E. L. Hughes, the separator man. Most of the crew received $3, but when rainy days or machine breakdowns stopped harvest work, their pay was lowered by fifty cents for seeding, wheat hauling, and other tasks. A labor scarcity and wartime inflation caused a rapid increase in wages during the years 1915–19. By 1919, the McGregors paid engineers $10, separator men $10, derrick drivers $7, sack sewers $6.10, hoe-downs $5, forkers $6, and water bucks $4.[46]

In addition to all the dangers involved in the complex threshing operation, men and machines were endangered by smut. A fungus, it probably appeared first in eastern Washington before 1890, but it did not become serious until several years later. A crop infested with smut resulted in a lower grade of wheat and a lower price for the farmer. Of even more concern, however, was the explosive quality of the smut dust. In 1901, the Colfax *Gazette* reported: "This has been a fatal year for threshing machinery in the Palouse and tributary regions, no less than a dozen separators having blown up and burned, from what is generally considered smut dust, ignited by hot boxes and cylinder tooth sparks." During the following season, *The Ranch* reported that "over in eastern Washington towns the question when farmers meet is: 'Has your threshing machine exploded yet?'" In 1909 "smut explosions and fires" near Colfax were reported to "have destroyed a number of machines." A group of farmers formed the "Anti-Smut Club of the Inland Empire" to seek ways to eliminate the fungus, and regional experimental stations worked on the problem. But little headway was made. The problem became severe for the McGregors, their renters, and neighboring farmers during World War I. On August 13, 1915, for example, the Lacrosse *Clipper* reported: "The machine belonging to Jeremiah Bros. while threshing for H. S. Barr on his farm near Canyon [south of Hooper] caught fire Wednesday afternoon as the result of a smut explosion. The separator and derrick were totally destroyed as also was the grain in the setting and that that had been threshed. Two additional settings of unthreshed grain were also burned before the fire could be controlled. It is estimated that the total loss in wheat will be around 2,500 sacks. The wheat was insured but the machine which was a total loss was not." The following summer a thresher used by four McGregor renters caught fire on two consecutive days, although no serious damage was reported. The next week the machine used by Knox and Barr had "a lively fire."[47]

Harvest fires, a scarcity of laborers, fights among crew members, and disputes between workers and farmers became common during World War I and its aftermath. The "bindle stiffs" had been discontented before—in 1901, for example, a "Harvest Hands Union" was formed to demand that the existing wage scale of $1 to $2.50 per day be doubled. When 492 harvesters signed the pledge in one day, the Colfax *Gazette* reported that "the move is unprecedented and is causing alarm." Five hundred harvesters in the Walla Walla area also vowed to hold out for the higher wage. This action was apparently successful, for the *Gazette* noted on July 26 that harvest hands were being paid $2–5 per day. By 1909, some harvest hands had joined the Industrial Workers of the World ("Wobblies"), an organization that sought to combine all members of the working class into one big trade union. The Wobblies defied a Spokane city ordinance against street corner meetings, and they were arrested en masse as they spoke of the evils of capitalism and the poor working conditions in Pacific Northwest harvest fields and lumber camps. The ordinance was rescinded, but the Wobblies won few friends. In November 1909, Spokane Chief of Police Sullivan told a correspondent that "bread and water with a dessert of fresh air will be the menu for Thanksgiving dinner of the members of the I.W.W. who are being held in custody." An attempt to unionize harvest hands in Pullman in 1909 failed when farmers refused to limit work hours or increase pay from $2 to $3 per day. During the next summer, migrant laborers who refused to leave Spokane for the harvest fields until pay was raised to $3 were told to leave town or be arrested on vagrancy charges. In 1911, IWW organizers "decorated almost every building" in Lacrosse with red stickers announcing: "I won't work more than eight hours after May 1, 1912. How about you? Join the union of your class!" Harvest crews in the Rosalia area went on strike for a $3 wage in 1913. But most farmers reportedly went to town and hired new crews rather than give in to the demand. The bindle stiffs were too unstable and farmers too hostile for the IWW to be successful.[48]

When the United States entered World War I in 1917, farmers feared a shortage of able-bodied workers and began taking the Wobblies more seriously. Some saw IWW members as "outlaws who sympathize with the Kaiser." The State Defense Council in Washington and Idaho sought to remove "Industrial Workers of the World and undesirable aliens from the grain fields." Joe Hill's poem, "Ta-Ra-Ra-Boom-De-Ay" in the IWW's *Little Red Songbook*, described the destruction of harvest equipment, and some farmers began to fear that threshing fires were caused not by smut but by matches thrown into separators by Wobblies. Unsatisfactory, thieving crewmen were thought to be IWW members. Earl and Ralph Snyder remembered that Zane Grey had stayed several weeks in the Hooper Hotel in 1918 while writing *The Desert of Wheat*, a novel that portrayed the Wobblies as a sinister group engaged in systematic burning of farmhouses, barns, and standing grain. Nothing like this happened. Apparently a few members of the Agricultural Workers Organization branch of the IWW did wreck harvest machinery in Iowa and Kansas.[49] But there is no evidence of any organized plan to burn threshers on the McGregor ranch or in other Columbia Plateau wheat fields. The IWW did call a general strike of harvest workers in eastern Washington on August 20, 1917, but the strike failed miserably. Max Torrance, a traveling harvest hand during this period of unrest, recalled that most of the bindle stiffs who joined the organization had pathetically small demands: better pay, the elimination of bedbugs from "fleatrap" bunkhouses, protection from smut fires, shorter working hours, and no work on Sundays.

Ralph Snyder remembered a fight he had during this hectic period and the assistance he received from Joe Frost, a crewman belonging to the IWW:

I was driving header box and there was a fella that was a big Missourian kid, a great big kid. And his brother was foreman of the outfit. And this kid was drivin' water wagon, which was a favorable job. You had you own eight horses and you'd haul water for the outfit. There was just room enough for the crew to eat at the table at the cook shack. And it was a helluva rush. You came in at noon and you had to dig holes for your header boxes, then you had to drive in 'em and the box had to drop in those holes . . . so the horses could eat over the side. . . . It was quite a job [and] . . . I was just about 17 years old. . . . That noon I went out and dug my holes in the hard ground . . . I missed those holes and had to drive around again . . . And I was late gettin' up to dinner . . . everybody'd already washed in the big tub. . . . So, hell, I hurried up, because I was hungry. . . . But this God damned big kid, he was going to take my place. So I followed him right on in and when he got there I just pushed him to one side and sat down . . . and he went on out . . . So afterwards, why there was a fight, he was gonna lick me. And I could box a little but he didn't want to box . . . I hit him two or three times but I couldn't stop him. . . . He finally grabbed me by the overalls . . . and threw me over his shoulder. And I lit on my belly and he sat on my back, pounding me on the head. This all leads up to this old Joe Frost, who was pickin' sacks. A big heavy Frenchman. I kinda liked him, he and I kinda hit it off. . . . He'd tell me all the old stories about the places he'd been . . . and all the women. So I was taking quite a beating and he squatted down and said to me "Bite him, kid, bite him." I'd never had a fight like that before. It was roughhouse. I'd been to college and we stood up and fought. I reached over and I bit him . . . and God damn it he got out of there in a helluva hurry. He hollered you know, and God, you'd think he'd been killed. He climbed off me and as he got up this fellow handed me a singletree, hard wood, with a chain on it. God I made a pass at him and chased him clear down the road. [After] we went back to work . . . he started to get in my header box once when I was unloading. I had a scoop I'd been cleaning out the box with and I walked over and crowned him. That ended that fight.

The bindle stiffs living in "hobo jungles" along railroad tracks in small eastern Washington towns sometimes forced farmers to increase pay by refusing to work or threatening to quit once harvest was under way. Snyder recalled that when he acquired his first farmland, his friendship with Joe Frost again came in handy.

It was the first year I farmed and I needed a crew. And I went to Washtucna and the IWW was runnin' things . . . Even though you had local friends who would help in harvest, you needed outside help. So I knew old Joe, he was the boss. . . . He was swaggerin' down there . . . in charge of the whole damned place. . . . And he says, "Well, kid, do you need a crew?" He says, "How soon you goin' home?" I said "Well, I've got a few groceries to get, be an hour . . ." "Well", he says, "I'll have a crew for you when you get ready . . ." When I got ready to go, there was five fellas sittin' in the back of the hack. So old Joe says to 'em "You finish this boy's harvest before you come back to town." I went through harvest just sailin' away and other fellas were having a hell of a time. [The IWW's] would sit on the sidewalk and say, "How's your land? Rolling? Well, roll 'er in here and let me take a look at 'er." They was gettin' pretty cocky. . . . They took Ralph Burkhart's machine and . . . threw a handful of matches in that damned thing. That happened quite often. Some fellows lost quite a bit of property.

The McGregors twice faced the threat of harvest strikes in World War I. Wages had already trebled, and the McGregor brothers were not sympathetic to demands for further increases. Sherman McGregor recalled that his uncle "Peter got upset when some of the crewmen talked of striking. He got stiff necked and refused to budge." A few harvesters quit but no strike occurred. The McGregors and their renters were able to put together crews of local farmhands, schoolboys, farm women, and traveling laborers. Many Columbia Plateau farmers bought labor-saving machinery because of the shortage of harvest help and the problems with the traveling bindle stiffs. Arthur Buhl remembered that Big Bend wheat growers "started buying those little Deering combines and cut down their labor problems right away."[50]

The feelings of unrest and dissatisfaction among the harvest crews were in marked contrast to the optimism and exuberance common among Columbia Plateau farmers. The years before 1920 were a period of rising wheat prices, rapidly advancing land values, and large crops, and they constituted what some would later describe as the "golden era" of

American agriculture. Undercurrents of discontent were occasionally visible. Phil W. Cox, a pioneer Palouse country sheepman who had begun raising wheat after the turn of the century, was chosen by a statewide conference as delegate to the national convention of the Farmers Educational and Cooperative Union of America in 1909. A sympathetic Colfax *Commoner* writer noted that the two hundred farmers at the state meeting "took Spokane by storm" and constituted "an earnest body of men." The Spokane conference resolved to unite farmers "morally, socially, and fraternally in a brotherhood so strong that the combined forces of capitalistic greed and mammon cannot dissever the bonds." In the Pacific Northwest, the group concluded, "the farmer has been grossly wronged and the speculator [has] fattened on the producer's toil." The organization sought ways "to handle grain cheaper," thus becoming engaged in what constituted "the greatest struggle of mankind, in the greatest battle ever fought on this continent, in the battle of the producers of wealth seeking to hold up the markets of their products, and build up the home life, and thus elevate and enoble mankind." [51]

Most farmers worried more about weather conditions, crop yields, and wheat prices than the struggle against the "forces of capitalistic greed and mammon." "The condition of the golden grain harvest" of 1904 had indicated to *The Ranch* that "an enormous amount of money and big profits will be made." Wheat raisers were confident that prosperity would continue and the "inexhaustible" soil would remain forever fertile. The McGregors and most Columbia Plateau wheat growers recorded "fairly satisfactory" yields of twenty to thirty bushels in 1905 and 1906. Farmers in the western Palouse were "jubilant" the next year: The price of wheat had risen to seventy-eight cents (twenty cents above 1905), and although "extra trains are run every day," the warehouses at Hooper were filled beyond capacity. A 1907 issue of *The Coast* magazine carried a picture of the "Wheat Blockade at Hooper, Washington," showing teams and wagons backed up waiting to unload grain. Some of the wheat headed and threshed near Hooper yielded forty-five bushels, and Peter McGregor noted that "this year's crops have more than paid for some of the land which has lately been bought."

The 1908 season began with the McGregor brothers more optimistic than ever about their future as farmers. Peter McGregor remained enthusiastic about the prospects for the local wheat crops.

> "Winter wheat never looked better, and the acreage is the largest in the history of western Whitman county," said Peter McGregor, Senator from this district, who is a member of the firm of McGregor Brothers, sheep and land kings of that section. Continuing, Senator McGregor said,

"The only thing we have to fear is a blizzard striking the wheat while it is not covered with snow. Should we escape this, the prospects are that an enormous crop will be harvested in that section this year. . . . Prospects never looked brighter . . . and everything . . . looks excellent."

A month later, Peter remained hopeful. "Lacrosse—Peter McGregor of Hooper was in town today and is very sanguine as to the price of wheat. He said: 'Just as soon as the embargo is lifted in Portland, the price of wheat will advance. Our firm, McGregor Brothers, has still on hand 85,000 bushels, harvested last fall, which we are holding for 80 cents.' Mr. McGregor says winter wheat is looking good around Hooper and there is an increased acreage sown in the spring over last year."[52] The predicted price rise did not occur, and wheat stored in the McGregor-operated Balfour, Guthrie, and Company warehouse was shipped for export in February at 67 cents. Further complications occurred in May, when "cut worms and wireworms in vast number . . . [did] great damage to the wheat fields." Often the wheat blades were "eaten off at a height of eight inches." But despite the difficulties, results of the 1908 harvest bore out Peter McGregor's expectations. The first shipment brought favorable results: "McGregor Brothers of Hooper yesterday sold 12,000 bushels of bluestem wheat at Hooper and Lacrosse, receiving 82 cents per bushel, the record price for this season. The fall wheat on the McGregor Brothers ranch is running about 25 bushels to the acre, and they estimate the returns will equal, if not exceed, those of last year." The rest of the crop averaged 20 to 25 bushels, and prices remained favorable. Columbia Plateau farms produced even better crops the following year and the price of wheat had advanced to $1, a figure that was said to be the "highest ever." Almost eleven million dollars' worth of grain was harvested in Whitman County in 1909, and it was declared to be the richest county per capita in the United States.[53]

The 1910 season appeared to be one in which average yields could be expected. In July, Archie McGregor sold bluestem wheat for 80 cents. During the same month, "State Senator Peter McGregor . . . said that his company, McGregor Land and Livestock, had 1200 acres in wheat this year and that 3000 acres rented to tenants will average 20 bushels for fall wheat and 18 bushels for spring grain." A correspondent wrote of "Senator McGregor's Big Crop" and noted that Peter McGregor "had just finished harvesting his crop of 100,000 bushels of wheat." But when the final results from the harvest came in, the McGregor brothers were taken aback. Hot summer weather had seriously damaged the wheat and caused "one of the poorest crop years this country has known." McGregor Land and Livestock declared a loss of $17,000 in capital assets, and Archie sent the Internal Revenue Service a letter lacking the usual McGregor optimism: "Gents: The depreciation in value comes from wheat we inventoried at $1 per bushel Dec. 31, 1909 and sold this year as low as 57¢ per bushel and also sod we had plowed at $2 per acre and our light crops this season left us without any revenue." The McGregors declared a depreciation in the value of wheat inventory in their 1910 statement, their second annual tax return since the corporate income tax was instituted a year earlier. This was disallowed by the District Director because the loss would be reflected when the wheat was actually sold. Had the deduction been allowed, the "loss" would have been reported twice.[54]

The poor returns of the 1910 season prompted many Columbia Plateau wheat raisers to return to spring seeding. Reports from the Hooper area stated that "this is strictly a spring wheat country." But farmers quickly regained their hopes after the disappointment of the previous year. By April, "many of the old timers" declared the crop prospects to be the best ever and anticipated "a heavy yield." The *Commercial Review*, a grain trade publication, described the Palouse country as "the Eden of the Northwest." In June, farmers were so certain of "one of the heaviest yields in history" that they began ordering new combines and other harvest machinery. Wheat growers on Rattlesnake Flat closely watched an experiment designed to minimize the labor force and bring an end to the age of animal-powered farming. The *Commercial Review* reported: "During the past season a 45 horsepower Caterpillar engine was put to practical use ... for the first time. The experiment proved so satisfactory that several others have followed the lead this spring, and have traded their 24 and 32 horse teams for Caterpillars." The next few years were characterized by good prices and crops in excess of twenty bushels, and farmers continued to predict a favorable future for their trade. A study by the Washington State Department of Agriculture concluded in 1914: "Wheat growing has proven one of the most staple [sic] and profitable of all the industries of Washington."[55]

The outbreak of World War I brought a rise in wheat prices sufficient to satisfy the farmers' dreams of a prosperous future. The 1914 crop had been below average on the McGregor ranch, but the McGregor brothers held their wheat and sold it for an excellent price in the fall. The *Spokesman-Review* described the outlook for wheat growers in October 1914: "Fall seeding is in full progress in the Palouse country. The high price of wheat and hopes of continued high prices, due to the European war, are the incentives backing the planting of a large acreage of grain." The following season brought excellent prices, a good yield, and a fine profit margin. A correspondent described the condition of the western Palouse crops in March: "The fall grain is looking fine. I never saw a better stand and I never saw it more even. Every foot is covered with a good stand." The average crop in the Hooper district was about 35 bushels. Some areas were even better: "Andy Mays [the McGregor ranch foreman] has just finished threshing a field of 40 acres that averaged 54 bushels of wheat to the acre. How is this for wheat?" The McGregor Land and Livestock Company ledger books began reflecting the wartime prosperity: The McGregor-operated wheat lands netted $14,819 or 76 percent of gross sales, and the tenant farms netted $11,005 or 59 percent of sales. The McGregor brothers calculated their net earnings simply by subtracting direct annual expenses from gross sales. Like most farmers, the McGregors did not make allowances in their annual statements for interest on their land and company capital.[56]

The Columbia Plateau wheat crops were shipped to England, Italy, the Azores, South America, China, Japan, the Philippines, and several other countries where they sold for high prices. Peter McGregor sold 10,000 bushels of the McGregor wheat at $1.10 in mid-August 1916. By the end of August, the price had improved further: "Wheat sold at Hooper for $1.20 Monday. We'll eat corn bread this winter." Farmers were confident that the 1916 yields would be as spectacular as the price per bushel. George Drumheller, a member of a pioneer family of Columbia Plateau sheepmen and said to be "the largest wheat grower in eastern Washington" with six thousand acres in production, predicted a "big crop." But later in the spring, farmers told of wheat seed rotting in the ground. The *Commercial Review* feared that inclement weather meant the inland region would produce a crop only 55 percent of normal. "Crop prospects," the publication concluded in May, "are the poorest in 35 years." Cold, cloudy May weather had given the wheat the appearance "of having been grown in a cellar." Sunny days dispelled the worries of the wheat growers, and Palouse country croplands yielded an estimated 35-bushel average. By August, more than twenty teams were hauling grain to the Hooper warehouse and large shipments were being made to coastal ports. Two months later, the local storage facilities remained "filled to the limit and hauling has been stopped until some shipments are made."[57]

The price of wheat, already at an "all time" high, doubled the following year. The *Commercial Review* ecstatically announced "record prices for wheat in the history of the North Pacific grain trade." The journal of wheat exporters claimed that "never since the Civil War have these prices been paid." Columbia Plateau farmers were extracting spectacular profits from their desert of wheat. McGregors sold more than $20,000 worth of grain from their "wheat ranch" in 1918, and the cost of sales and operating expenses were less than $7,300, a 64 percent return on sales. The tenant farms brought an even better return of 81 percent, with

sales of almost $20,000 and expenses of $3,800. A correspondent enthusiastically described the sale of some of the McGregor wheat:

> The record Spokane price for wheat, $2.40 a bushel, was paid yesterday
> by the Balfour-Guthrie Company of Spokane for 12,000 bushels of turkey
> red from the McGregor Land and Live Stock Company of Hooper.
> Archie McGregor completed the deal for the company and the check
> was handled through the Exchange National Bank for $28,000. The
> wheat was the remainder of the 1916 crop which the McGregor inter-
> ests had held in the event that spring seeding became necessary. The grain
> was not needed for reseeding. The price was $2.40 f.o.b. Hooper, for
> immediate delivery.[58]

Wheat production helped bring a tremendous increase in the fortunes
of the McGregor brothers. The croplands operated by the McGregor
corporation had improved from sporadic earlier perfomances to register
substantial profits from 1915 to 1918. The landlord–tenant relationship
had enabled the men to realize large returns from additional cultivated
lands. Sales of groceries, farm equipment, hardware, insurance, and numerous other items to the renters contributed to the success of the mercantile division headed by Alex McGregor. Loans to renters and other
local residents had, by 1918, grown to such an extent that the Exchange
National Bank announced that "it is our intention to par all checks for
you as a banking institution, your company being regarded as such." By
1917, overall corporate sales had reached $350,000 and were more than
double those of prewar years. E. E. Flood of the Exchange bank con-
fided to McGregor secretary H. R. Rudd: "I could see your 'finger-
prints' on the statement you sent us and signed by Archie. Confidentially
this is some statement and I believe represents about 25% of their actual
worth." Flood concluded that "the statement of the McGregor Land
and Livestock Company is one of the best, if not the best and strongest statement we have ever had come into the Exchange National Bank."
Rudd contended that the spectacular returns came not from wartime
conditions but from the abilities of Archie, John, and Alex McGregor:
"all three of whom have, since the organization of the company, given
their constant personal attention and labor to the welfare of the company
and to no other interests whatever. These men are recognized as very
exceptional businessmen and it is wholly through their attention to business that this company has made such a wonderful showing."[59]

The wheat business had such a promising future that the McGregor
brothers decided to acquire new combines and build an elevator equipped
for the purchase, storage, and sale of grains raised in the Hooper area.
The new elevator included five large bulk grain tanks purchased from

a company that refused "to guarantee these tanks to stand." Columbia Plateau farmers, for a variety of reasons, had continued to store their wheat in sacks while other western areas had switched to bulk handling, a process that saved labor, time, and expense. Sacks were costly and in short supply during the war, and the McGregors decided to switch to the bulk process. Although admitting that "we are not old hands at the game," the corporation was handling 150,000 bushels annually in its bulk tanks by 1920. The Balfour, Guthrie and Company warehouse was also purchased to store sacked grain. Wheat raised by seventeen nearby farmers, plus grain produced by McGregors and their renters, was stored in the two facilities. As the company expanded its storage and marketing of grain, it also provided a variety of other services for most of the farmers from adjacent areas. Credit was extended liberally, and by 1920 local residents had more than $155,000 in accounts receivable with the McGregor Land and Livestock Company.[60] The McGregor brothers had become deeply committed to the success of commercial wheat production in the western Palouse.

Gross incomes of farmers continued to advance in 1919. McGregor wheat sold for $2.21 a bushel, $2.59, and finally reached $3.15. Columbia Plateau farmers eagerly expanded their operations and responded to the call, "Raise more wheat and win the war." A correspondent to the *Washington Farmer* noted: "We will probably never again see $2 wheat so we are going to try to raise every bushel possible." Many farmers mortgaged their holdings to acquire more land, both as a means of increasing wheat output and for speculation. The value of farm property, both regionally and nationally, had escalated rapidly. Farmland in Whitman County, worth an average of $12.67 in 1900 and $46.45 per acre a decade later, was valued at $91.47 by 1920. Surely the trend would continue. Farmers borrowed heavily to purchase new equipment. A three-day "Farm Power Demonstration" held in Walla Walla in 1919 was said to have been attended by 41,000 farmers, who watched "tractors, big and little, plow acre after acre." Wheat growers were assured by bankers that "every bank welcomes loans" to provide tractors for farmers. Farm mortgage indebtedness had doubled in five eastern Washington counties during the decade 1910–20. "For the first time the increasing wealth of farmers opened up for them new possibilities in a way and to an extent quite beyond any earlier expectations. They were getting rich, why not get richer? They began buying more land. . . . They expanded their equipment. . . . Rich men should live in a manner becoming the rich, and thus they indulged new and expensive habits of life. . . ." Washington farmers were raising the largest crops of winter wheat in the nation—averaging 23.6 bushels during the years 1917–21—and the tremendous productivity seemed to guarantee a secure future for the wheat growers.[61]

But the prosperity had an insecure foundation. W. J. Spillman offered a warning to Columbia Plateau farmers in 1919: "Now ask yourself what we are going to do with the 20,000,000 tons of foodstuffs next year or the year after when we produce it and Europe does not need it. . . . You may sell your wheat for 40 cents a bushel. . . . The farmers of this country are up against some very serious problems of the immediate future." The values of wheat and farmland plummeted rapidly during the fall of 1920. Palouse country farmers who had cultivated and seeded their 1920 crops on the basis of $2 wheat were forced to thresh and sell for $1.25 or less. Prices continued to fall. G. F. Warren of the U.S. Department of Agriculture analyzed the situation a year later: "The Nation is not only confronted with the most violent drop in prices that it has ever experienced, but agricultural prices have dropped so much more than other prices that we have a severe agricultural panic on top of a severe general depression." McGregor Land and Livestock sold wheat and collected back accounts in desperation. Tenants found themselves in trouble, and agreements similar to the following became common: "I hereby sell my entire stock of farm machinery and implements, horses, mules, and all livestock, including hogs, all wheat, and feed—everything now on the ranch—to the McGregor Land and Livestock Company."[62] Migratory farm laborers found that mechanization had eliminated many job opportunities, and the farm crisis had caused a rapid decline in wages. A giddy period of agricultural prosperity had come to a rapid end. By plowing up bunchgrass and sagebrush, the McGregor brothers had expanded both the profits and the potential risks from their Palouse country hills.

Chapter 7

"A Remarkable Region"

EXPLORING NEW BUSINESS OPPORTUNITIES
AND LIFE IN A COMPANY TOWN, 1905-20

"The land, by some mysterious impulse . . . was going to raise ton lots of everything—cattle, hogs, sheep, chickens, turkeys, geese, silver foxes, strawberries, gooseberries, apples, peaches, plums, garden-truck, flax, cut flowers. The climate would cure asthma, tuberculosis, rickets, melancholia, goiter. It was going to be a remarkable region."   H. L. Davis

"Hooper, Washington has advanced . . . from a mere flag station on the O. R. & N. . . . to the dignity of a rural metropolis. . . . The town is in a picturesque valley of the Palouse river . . . and tributary to it is a region rich in agricultural and stock grazing land. . . . Here one finds immense stock ranches. . . . The farms near Hooper this year produced 200,000 bushels of grain. Hooper has made a beginning in the fruit industry . . . and already has taken prizes for its exceptional apples and pears. . . . The new town already has the largest machine shops south of Spokane—a significant fact in connection with railroad activity. Hooper occupies a strategic point . . . on the water grade from Spokane to tide water. . . . The local residents are all enthusiastic in their faith for Hooper's bright future."   Peter McGregor, 1907

"There is one brilliant page in Inland Empire livestock history that is invested with the glamour of romance. It is a typical Western story of the surmounting of obstacles by sheer grit, will power, and determination to make good, of obscure beginnings, of early embarrassments, and of final achievement. It is the story a small boy of today might read with interest and be stimulated to go out and do likewise. In short, it is the story of the McGregor Brothers of Hooper."

Spokesman-Review, 1919[1]

The development of productive sheep ranches and wheat farms on the rocky scablands and rolling prairies of the Columbia Plateau convinced settlers that the region had a remarkably prosperous future. In less than three decades, a thinly populated and seemingly marginally productive land had been converted into fields and farms. Livestock and wheat had commanded good market prices for several years. Prospects appeared to be unlimited. John, Archie, Alex, and Peter McGregor sought to increase their profits by expanding their mercantile businesses, buying and selling farm real estate, and gaining control of various enterprises in the town of Hooper. The men also invested in enterprises organized outside the corporate structure of McGregor Land and Livestock Company: An ambitious irrigation project, with a twenty-mile wooden flume and ten thousand acres of Palouse River Valley land was purchased from a Dutch corporation; stock in oil companies and gold, silver, and copper mines was acquired; two of the brothers bought the controlling interest in what was said to be "the largest cattle ranch in Washington"; and three brothers organized a Nevada silver mining company, with headquarters in the Hooper store. At this time, many Columbia Plateau ranchers and farmers sought ways to increase their wealth by expanding their agricultural operations and exploring new areas of investment for their capital. A high value was placed on individualism and personal achievement, and large landholdings and financial success helped guarantee social prestige, political power, and high community standing.

Increasing prosperity also made more time available for social activities and travel. The McGregors built new homes, and they hired maids and "sewing-ladies" to do work formerly done by their wives. Released from many of the housekeeping tasks, the women devoted more time to community clubs and other activities. But few chances to exert

PETER MCGREGOR, PRESIDENT   ALEXANDER MCGREGOR, VICE PRESIDENT   ARCHIBALD MCGREGOR, SECRETARY   JOHN MCGREGOR, MANAGER

McGregor Land & Live Stock Co.

LOANS
CHOPPED HAY
WOOD
FENCE POSTS
LUMBER
BARB WIRE
PUMPS AND WINDMILLS

DEALERS IN

General Merchandise

GRAIN, CATTLE
SHEEP & LAND

INSURANCE
GROCERIES
DRY GOODS
CLOTHING
FURNISHINGS
FARM MACHINERY
WAGONS, BUGGIES
HARDWARE, ETC.

McGregor letterhead, ca. 1906

leadership were available to them—in Hooper and other rural communities, men still led and women followed. As one observer noted, "clearly the Columbia Plateau is a man's country."[2]

Men who had successfully exploited the agricultural potential of the region became convinced that the resources of their properties had been tapped only barely. Oil found in springs suggested to some settlers that "the Palouse country has a gas belt rivalling in extent and power the natural gas fields of Pennsylvania, Ohio, and Indiana." Wells dug by promoter A. J. Smith promised to make him "the oil king of the Palouse." Representatives of a Scotch syndicate were said to be contemplating the construction of a sugar beet factory. James Stewart of Glasgow, Scotland, arrived in Spokane with assurances that he represented "people who mean business and have millions of capital behind them."

The town of Hooper, nothing but a post office and railroad sign for many years, expanded rapidly during this prosperous period of burgeoning expectations. A branch line of the Oregon Railroad and Navigation Company (O. R. & N.) had reached the town in the 1880's. The construction of "main line" O. R. & N. and Spokane, Portland, and Seattle railroad routes and the proposed building of two additional lines helped spur the rapid growth of the tiny village. Hooper boasted (if only temporarily) a hotel, two restaurants, a general store, a men's clothing store, a blacksmith, two contractors, and six saloons. Many of the businesses were across the river from McGregor headquarters on a section of government land known as "North Hooper." North Hooper contained a series of shanties that provided beer, food, clothing, and women for railroad construction crews. If many of the businesses were of an ephemeral nature, the region held the promise of a far more substantial future. Land near Hooper was reported to be excellent for growing potatoes, peaches, kaffir corn, tobacco, melons, grapes, peanuts, sweet potatoes, walnuts, apricots, hops, strawberries, and alfalfa. An influx of eighty thousand people was imminent, and population in Whitman County could and would reach five hundred thousand. Fraudulent speculators took advantage of the boom period to sell lots in "Cascade City," an unbroken sagebrush prairie in Adams County without access to water. The site was portrayed to gullible Chicago residents as having colleges, parks, thousands of residents, and even steamboat landings.[3]

Men working to build substantial agricultural operations needed to adopt more stable methods of land purchase and sale. A quadrupling of land values during the years 1905–20 increased both the potential profits and the risks of such transactions. The advance of farming into the western Palouse helped to bring a spectacular increase in the values of properties in that portion of the Columbia Plateau. The McGregor brothers had purchased 30,218 acres of land for their "main ranch" during the years 1900–02 at a cost of $56,329 or about $1.86 an acre. Four years later, these properties had a value of almost $195,000, or approximately $6.45 per acre. Such change promised a handsome source of profit. But land transactions had to be managed closely and carefully. The McGregors had to determine how much land could be sold without jeopardizing the efficiency of their ranching and farming operations. Decisions about further land purchases were also becoming complex. Did the increased competition for the land necessitate the purchase of additional wheat- and sheep-raising properties? If so, how much land could one afford to purchase without weakening the financial structure of a farming and ranching business?

Land purchases were attended to in the same orderly fashion that had characterized the real property acquisitions of the McGregor Brothers partnership during the years 1896–1905. The means were similar to those used in the earlier period: Scrip was bought and used to acquire government land; additional railroad lands were purchased; and property was obtained from neighboring ranchers who were willing or forced to sell, and from insurance and mortgage companies who wanted to sell land they had acquired in the course of their business. Other tracts were acquired through purchase of "isolated tracts" of "rough or mountainous" federally owned lands, from sales by an irrigation company, and by leasing state-owned properties. The McGregors' primary consideration in purchasing land was the development of an efficient sheep- and wheat-raising operation. In 1908, the corporation decided "to bid on any lands, school or otherwise, adjacent to its holdings and to buy, providing the price did not go above $20 per acre." Especially desirable were properties that surrounded water holes or cut off access to federal and state lands for other parties. The minutes of the May 1908 meeting of the McGregor Land and Livestock officers describe another purpose for which scrip was used: "The Board of Trustees [favorably] considered the proposition . . . to script [sic] such lands as they deemed necessary to save fencing and have pass ways from one section to another."[4]

The McGregor brothers continued their practice of employing federal and state land laws to advantage. Archie McGregor successfully filed for the purchase of a few isolated forty-acre tracts of federal rangeland but found that the limit per person was 160 acres. Accordingly, Donald McGregor (John's son), H. R. Rudd (the McGregor secretary), and McGregor tenant farmers and sheepherders purchased the additional desired tracts at a cost of four dollars per acre. The land was then resold at a slightly higher price to the McGregor company. Because the State of Washington stipulated that an individual could lease no more than

640 acres, McGregors used the names of relatives, judges, lawyers, sheep-herders, and others to obtain leases of these lands. Archie McGregor, in charge of the leasing of state lands for many years, exercised care in his bidding to ensure that other interested parties would not outbid the McGregors. After his retirement from active participation in the corporation in 1919, Archie McGregor was asked by his successor, H. R. Rudd, to provide recommendations for leasing procedures. Parts of three of his letters, written from his winter home in southern California, suggest the careful attention to detail that characterized so much of the McGregor land operations:

January 10, 1920
name of lessor

John D. Macrae	*I think this should be raised to 12½ to 15 cents per acre. Fence all on west line is ours.*
Mrs. Archie McGregor	*ditto—rate higher. Sheep cabin if not on this is on vacant 40. Close call.*
Alex C. McGregor	*ditto—rate higher. Nothing on land.*
A. McGregor	*rate 20 cts. per acre. Some one trying to hold same and have fighting chance to buy or lease. Cook house $250. 2 cabins $200.*

Your risk at 10 cents per acre is too great. Better meet and talk it over. 15 cents is cheap even without water. 20 cents with water. I hardly think you will have competitors but land has been appraised and it looks good with grass on it.... Geo. Gildersleeve may bid on some sections, especially Macrae's Sec. 8.

Jan. 13, 1920

Evelyn Maude McGregor	*May have opposition. One mile fence west line, ½ mile E. line. Value $300. I do not know the easiest half to keep up but it may be best to keep the part on the SE⁴ to head Brown's horses off....*
Peter McGregor	*15 cts. rate. Lambing sheds on SE⁴ of NE⁴SW⁴. Maybe a cabin also. Macrae or Peter should know.*
H. R. Rudd	*Rate 15. No improvements.*

I think it would pay to go to Olympia to get these tracts.

Jan. 16, 1920

Euphemia McGregor	*15 cts. about right.... Improvements—breaking 320 acres, fencing ½ mile west line.*

W. C. Fudge   *10 cents about right.*
Chas. Scriber   *Rate 15. Lose this section would spoil the*
                                     Stewart Canyon range.[5]

The failure of some homesteaders did not slow the influx of settlers onto the former sheep ranges. But the lust for free land was no substitute for competence and skill in farming. Many of the new arrivals came poorly equipped to meet the demands of the semiarid region. H. L. Davis details some of the more pathetic attempts to adapt to the Columbia Plateau: "Building corncribs on land that wouldn't raise a tassel; ash-hoppers and smoke-houses in a country where the only fuel is juniper . . . cordeling farm-machinery up to the top of a mountain, where there wasn't enough earth to bury a dog." Sheepherder Archer Gilfillan describes the difficulties encountered by homesteaders in semiarid areas: "The whole cycle of homesteading would last little more than three years. First there would be raw prairie. . . . then almost overnight there would be a tar-papered shack . . . on every arable quarter section. . . . Then a year or two later, there would be open cellars where the board shanties had stood, . . . and fields growing up to weeds and grass again." The homesteader's failure worked to the advantage of established ranchers and farmers. After the settler failed, his land—no longer part of the public domain—could be bought for very little. The enactment of the Stock Raising and Enlarged Homestead Act of 1916, legislation that allowed settlers to claim 640 acres of public domain, caused great alarm among sheepmen. But the woolgrowers soon found the acts a "blessing in disguise." Idaho sheepman A. J. Knollin commented: "The 640 acre homestead plan will work to the advantage of the livestock grower ultimately. It is impossible for a man with a family to make a living raising sheep on any 640 acres available in Idaho. . . . After the 640 acre man has done his stint and proved up, the sheepman will be able to buy him out."[6]

While taking full advantage of all opportunities to improve their control of the Palouse country hills, the McGregor brothers also continued their policy of selling selected lands peripheral to the main ranching operations. Most of the properties sold were on the southern extremity of the ranch, along the rugged "breaks" of the Snake River, where topography and distance made the lands expendable. By 1905, the McGregor Land and Livestock Company had developed a systematic land business, designed to provide a valuable supplement to income from sheep, merchandise, and wheat sales. By that time the McGregor brothers needed more money to break new lands for farming. More capital was also necessary to enable the company store to expand and serve a wider community. So they decided to sell some of their land. Between October and December 1905, corporation officials agreed to sell six

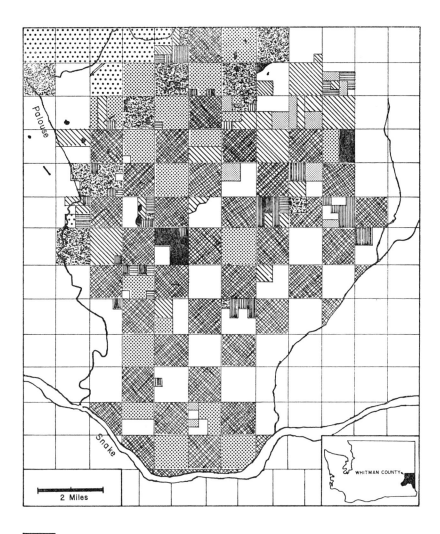

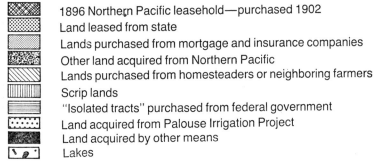

1896 Northern Pacific leasehold—purchased 1902
Land leased from state
Lands purchased from mortgage and insurance companies
Other land acquired from Northern Pacific
Lands purchased from homesteaders or neighboring farmers
Scrip lands
"Isolated tracts" purchased from federal government
Land acquired from Palouse Irrigation Project
Land acquired by other means
Lakes

Methods of land acquisition—McGregor Brothers, 1896–1920 (includes Starbuck Quadrangle only)

parcels of land, totaling about 3,000 acres, for $34,300—lands they had acquired a few months earlier at a cost of $3,339. The high asking price was somewhat mitigated by the low 6 percent interest rate, easily available loans from the McGregor corporation, and the ten-year period allowed for full payment. Not all who wanted to acquire McGregor land had to buy; some started as tenants and later entered into land sales contracts to purchase their farms.

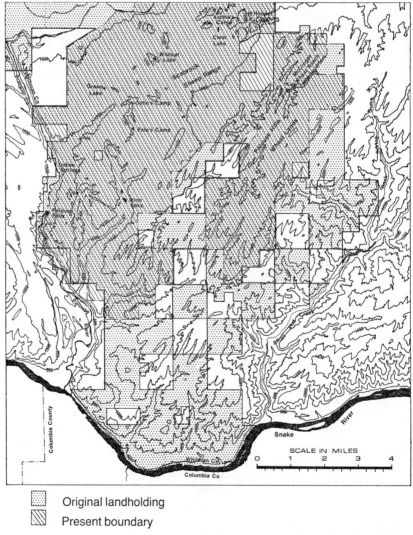

▒ Original landholding

▨ Present boundary

Topographical illustration of landholdings

The number of land sales decreased after 1905. But when financial setbacks hit their farming and ranching businesses, the McGregors improved their incomes by selling additional peripheral properties. In 1910, for example, poor crops and a forty-cent drop in wheat prices resulted in "wheat ranch" expenses of $21,308 and receipts of only $7,454. An increase in land sales in 1911 more than offset the imbalance. During that year, land receipts accounted for $69,119, with expenses of only $5,379. A *Spokesman-Review* correspondent described some of the 1911 sales with more enthusiasm than accuracy:

> McGregor brothers, the "sheep kings," have sold more than 7000 acres in the last few months. . . . The McGregor lands have been sold in tracts from 160 acres to 640 acres at $27 to $40 per acre. It is all agricultural land and a large per cent of it is in cultivation. . . . Most of this land produced 25 bushels of wheat an acre last year, one of the poorest crop years this country has known. . . . The firm has sold more than $200,000 worth of land in the last few months, and still owns enough to make a fair sized kingdom in one of the European countries."[7]

After 1911 land sales continued, but at a slower pace. The highest price the McGregors received for land before 1920 was for 74 acres along the Snake River, which were sold to the Portland and Seattle Railway Company for $12,000—$162.16 per acre. The transaction was an excellent one for the McGregor corporation: The lands sold were on the driest and poorest portions of the forage lands in a canyon more than seven hundred feet below the rest of the range. The topography of the region forced the railroad officials to construct the line through the McGregor lands, and the Scotchmen took full advantage of the situation. A more typical price was received for 3,447 acres near Snake River, sold to Barr and McKenzie at $10.00 an acre.[8]

The McGregor brothers, forgetting their earlier experiences, decided to invest in urban real estate. Three sections of rangeland were traded in 1910 for 16 residences and lots in the city of Spokane. The Spokane transaction seemed to offer promising possibilities. The McGregors entrusted the firm of Wallace and Wallace of Spokane with the job of repairing, renting, and selling the houses. But the project lost small sums of money every year. The managers went bankrupt after falling $6,784 in debt to the McGregors. Three letters written during the years 1918–20 illustrate the difficulties encountered:

> [*Wallace and Wallace to Archie McGregor, December 29, 1918:*] *Mr. McGregor, really and truly I do not know just what is the best to do with these houses, as of late it has been impossible to keep them rented,*

and of course the longer they are idle, the more undesirable they become as the authorities do not seem to be able to cope with the destructive boys.

[Pacific Mortgage Co. to Peter McGregor, November 19, 1919:] I have a party who is in the market for any number of old run down and battered residences that he can buy cheap. . . . Your houses qualify.

[Department of Health, City of Spokane, to Rudd and McGregor, March 23, 1920:] Your attention is called to the expiration of the time limit for the abatement of the nuisance in the shape of unsanitary, dilapidated buildings.

The houses, in which the McGregors invested more than $16,000, were sold in 1920 for $4,000. Shrewd in their transactions involving farmland and sheep pastures, the men failed dismally in their speculation in urban properties. No more city lots were bought, although in 1922 Peter McGregor became enthusiastic about a proposal to trade 7,300 acres of grazing and irrigated lands for a Chicago apartment house complex. But better business sense prevailed, and the project was abandoned.[9]

In 1903, the McGregor brothers purchased a general store in Hooper. This was the first of several services the men offered to the community. Peter and Archie McGregor had gone bankrupt a decade earlier as inexperienced hardware merchants in the town of Pullman. But what became the mercantile division of the McGregor Land and Livestock Company proved to be a reliable and important source of income for the corporation. By 1920, the volume of business at the Hooper store had grown to more than $200,000 annually, and the net profits averaged more than 10 percent of sales, second only to those of the sheep operations. Head storekeeper Alex McGregor had learned the mercantile trade a decade earlier while working as a pharmacist in a Chicago drugstore. The McGregors were well acquainted with the Hooper area and with their customers, many of whom were ranch employees or tenant farmers. Financial conditions were far better than during the 1890's. Seasoned businessmen by this time and settled in their own community, the McGregors were able to prosper there as merchants. Other sheepmen developed successful stores as adjuncts to their ranching businesses during the prosperous period. Phil Cox owned a general store in the tiny Palouse country town of Hay. Coffin Brothers operated a large wholesale grocery in the Yakima Valley. The Coffin enterprise, although more aggressive, had results similar to those of the McGregor store business. H. Stanley Coffin recalled: "We made splendid profits, everything went along fine, and we had no competition." Coffin Brothers, shrewd Indian traders of previous decades, expanded their business in 1906 to the Nez

Perce Indian Reservation, after learning that the tribe was to be paid a million dollars for lands ceded to the federal government:

We put up a tent on the outskirts of . . . [Lewiston], where the Indians would have to pass as they came into the valley. We put up a large cir-¬ cus tent, and as a circus is one of the things of which an Indian is most fond, it proved to be a big drawing card. . . . We fitted up very cheaply. . . . [We purchased] a merry-go-round . . . with a monkey organ grinder and all the fixings . . . [and] a steam calliope. . . . With every $1 purchase we gave the Indians a ticket to ride on the merry-go-round. . . . [We] had banners and would parade the streets . . . and in every way worked up the enthusiasm of the Indians to trade with us. The first three days we entirely cleaned out our shawls, beads, hacks, buggies, harnesses, and saddles. In fact, we practically cleaned out the store.

H. Stanley Coffin even claimed that after all the buggies had been sold he and his brothers purchased a horse-drawn hearse and sold it to an Indian chief.[10]

The McGregor brothers developed their mercantile business cautiously and gradually began to build up a stock of groceries, hardware, and clothing to supply their large crews. As the men consolidated their control of the lands around Hooper, they also purchased a hotel, a hardware store, and two blacksmith shops; opened an automobile dealership; and acquired other facilities in the town. The store and hotel had been acquired originally to supply and house McGregor employees. Alex McGregor later described how the businesses began to change: "The store was purchased primarily as a commissary but we began to supply the families around [here] until today it does a very fine business for this community. We have also acquired the other buildings and sites around here; the hotel is above average and does a thriving business most of the time." Regional newspapers reminded visitors to Hooper of the McGregor mercantile and lodging facilities. In 1915, for example, the Lacrosse *Clipper* commented: "When in Hooper, be sure and visit the Glenmore [the McGregor hotel]." Two years later, McGregor secretary H. R. Rudd described the hotel and the town: "Hooper is a village of about 100 population. . . . The town is practically owned by the company, as is most of the land within 10 miles. The hotel is primarily a boarding house for employees of the company. . . . There is no competition. The hotel handles the laundry, bread, and meat for the whole territory. Average business will run around 20 boarders the year around, sometimes as high as 40."[11]

Residents of the western Palouse country had claimed for many years that "Hooper is on the verge of a substantial boom." But the boom period was short-lived. Railroad construction crews, ranging in size from a few hundred to a thousand men, were occasionally stationed near Hooper during the years 1907–12. Owners of restaurants, taverns, and other facilities that served the railroad workers were able to charge merchandise at the McGregor store, so long as they remained good credit risks. One restaurant owner fell deeply into debt to the McGregors and received notice that "Joe, you will have to pay cash here now, A. McGregor." The man hurriedly left town and wrote John McGregor from Seattle:

> No doubt you were surprised at my leaving the way I did but I was so discouraged I could not help it. Archie refused to give me any more credit and nearly all the money I had on hand I had to pay out to my cook who got drunk and the other two men who quit me just as my big rush was starting. I had no coal and could not get enough bread to feed the men. . . . I left nearly everything I had, bed, suitcase, and clothes. . . . I never had any idea of cheating you . . . but did not have the courage to stop and face the matter. . . . Think as kindly of me as you can. Your friend, J. L. Atkinson.[12]

After the departure of the transient railroad population, the mercantile business changed somewhat as the McGregors increased their trade with nearby farmers and ranchers. But it continued to prosper. In January 1915, a party of townspeople returning from an evening of ice skating at Clear Lake, on the McGregor sheep ranch, found the store ablaze. There was no way to save it. Fire destroyed the store and all the merchandise, including thousands of goods recently acquired "for the spring trade." Although the McGregors were at first "undecided as to whether they will rebuild and again engage in the mercantile business," in April they announced "it is in the best interest of the company to build a new store building and engage in the sale of goods, wares, and merchandise." A correspondent wrote: "That the McGregors believe in the future of the Hooper country will be noted by the fact that they are spending their money there for the purpose of substantial improvements. The latest improvement is the erection of a store building with few equals in the county. The building is to be a one story brick, 46 × 90 with full basement, pressed brick front with terra cotta trimmings and will be equipped with thoroughly modern conveniences."

The structure was also to house the company offices and a post office, and was to have a full basement and a large balcony to "give added floor space and afford more room for the large stock of general merchandise the firm expects to carry." William Swain of Pullman was chosen as architect, and Easum Brothers of Colfax contracted to build the structure for $9,250. Laborers on the project received thirty cents per hour, and final building costs totaled slightly more than $16,000.

By June 1916, the store was reported to be "receiving the finishing

touches in preparation for the ball to be held on the evening of the 16th."
A correspondent described the formal opening of the McGregor Land
and Livestock store:

> Friday, June 16th, was a red letter day for Hooper, being the date set
> for the dedication of the McGregor Brothers new brick store. Early in
> the evening autos and other means of conveyances began bringing in
> parties from all the surrounding country until at least 400 visitors were
> in attendance. Lacrosse, Winona, Endicott, Colfax, Riparia, Washtucna,
> and Kahlotus were well represented. McGregor Brothers spared neither
> time nor expense in interior decorations and in providing for the comfort
> of their guests. The Winona orchestra furnished excellent music. W. A.
> Blundell and Dad Thomas presided over the ice cream and cold drinks,
> while Mr. and Mrs. Nelson Ross furnished an excellent supper in the
> basement. H. R. Rudd and L. W. Wann, promoters of the ball, an-
> nounced on behalf of the McGregor Brothers that no charge would be
> made for dancing and that all that they asked their guests was that they
> might have an enjoyable evening and that they visit Hooper often in the
> future. The small hours of the morning broke ere the last of the merry
> dancers left for their homes, voting Hooper a live burg and the Mc-
> Gregor Brothers royal entertainers.[13]

The McGregors employed three to five men to operate their new mercantile enterprise. Dougald McGregor's son, William, recalled his experiences working in the store: "I worked for Uncle Alex in the store
for awhile, and I often look back on that experience as one of the great
events of my early life. He was a great example to try to follow. It was
my duty to go to the store in the morning and have the sweeping and
dusting done before opening time. One morning I had fooled around too
much and did not have all the dusting done when Uncle Alex walked
in. He did not say a word, but just walked down the store and ran his
finger all along the show case which I had not dusted. I never forgot
that silent lesson." The McGregor store carried a large assortment of
goods. Men's suits were purchased from M. Born and Co. of Chicago,
"The Oldest and Largest Wholesale Tailors in the World," and from
stores in Minneapolis, Tacoma, and Seattle. Hats were purchased from
a St. Paul corporation, gloves from Tacoma, swimwear from Portland,
typewriters from Seattle, saddles and chaps from Pendleton, watches
from Ingersolls of San Francisco, fenceposts from Bovill (Idaho), potatoes from Toppenish (Washington), plows through a Portland company, and silk hose from Spokane. Alex McGregor and his friend and
fellow merchant, William Snyder of Washtucna, saved money on orders
of salt, corn, flour, oats, and other commodities by buying railroad carloads of each item and dividing the loads between their stores.

The McGregor mercantile division also had dealerships for combines, tractors, threshing machines, pumps, barbed wire, insurance, wagons and buggies, Hudson and Essex automobiles, and several other products. William McGregor explained one of the reasons for the diversified mercantile operations: "The idea was to become a dealer in everything and supply yourself wholesale." The numerous sidelines helped to increase further the volume of business done by the corporation. By 1917, the McGregor Land and Livestock Company had purchased most of the adjacent land and acquired ownership of all the businesses and most of the residences of Hooper. Local residents either traded with the Mc-Gregors or traveled to other towns where competing facilities were available. William McGregor noticed the same type of merchandising in other areas of the West and on the livestock ranges of Australia: "In Australia the stock and station agent supplies you with everything, finances you, and buys all your grain and livestock. A lot of early western stores also once operated in that way: they'd be grain brokers as well as having groceries, horse collars, farm equipment and everything else a farmer or rancher would need."[14]

Patrons of the McGregor store were allowed long-term credit on their purchases. Families who needed capital could also enter loan and mortgage agreements with the McGregor corporation. By 1920, McGregor Land and Livestock Company had $266,064 in accounts receivable, including $155,833 for notes and mortgages, and 126 merchandise accounts totaling $47,574. Times had been prosperous and most of the debts were repaid. The corporation was lenient on small overdue accounts. Between 1907 and 1914, 29 notes totaling less than $5,000 were "written off" as uncollectible. McGregor secretary H. R. Rudd analyzed a $15 note signed in 1914: "This note has never been taken into account. Its value is doubtful and anyway, it represents nothing much except blue sky. So it doesn't matter." After one family had spent a decade making payments on a $500 loan, McGregors decided to forego interest charges and the small remaining debt. The debtors wrote the corporation that "words cannot express the gratitude we feel."

The corporation was less sympathetic when large amounts of money were owed. Notes were turned over to McGregor lawyers or to collection agencies, such as the Spokane Claims Brokers (whose slogan was, "An honest man has nothing to fear, but a dishonest man must pay the penalty for his perfidy"). The agencies sometimes had difficulty locating recalcitrant debtors. In 1917, for example, the Inland Merchants Association reported to the McGregors: "We are sorry to report that Thomas McVenes skipped for parts unknown several months ago. . . .

If we had had these notes about two years ago we probably could have made some compromise settlement."

The postwar agricultural depression that began in late 1920 caused a spirit of urgency to enter the McGregor loan business. The McGregor Land and Livestock Company needed the funds invested in the loans to provide operating capital for a badly crippled agricultural operation. The company's letters to its lawyers reflect the pressing need for the money. "Look him up, see what he has, and get his money . . . by any means in your power. You have our consent to garnishee, attach, sue or do anything that might get a dollar out of him legally. He is an old friend of the McGregors, was very hard up at the time the note was given, they helped him out and now he won't even answer their letters. So now you may use him rough as you please. Get the money. We think he owns his own home." [15]

Persistent efforts by the McGregors and their lawyers resulted in payment of most of the overdue accounts. Debtors whom corporation officials regarded as honest and hard-working were allowed additional time. When economic conditions improved, these men were reminded of the many services available in Hooper. H. R. Rudd wrote the following letter to a farmer from Washtucna:

> I don't know who has been writing your growing grain insurance in the past but I want to get it from you this year. . . . We would also like some of your grocery and hardware business this harvest.
>
> Now, Mr. Blankenship, help us out with some business if you can for we have patiently carried quite a load for you through pretty dull times and now that things are looking much better for the farmer, we should like to share in the trade of those we have helped in the past. Anything you can do will be appreciated. We have good stocks of most everything, including lumber, hardware and groceries and will endeavor to give you good service if you let us have the chance.

Loans, mortgages, land sales, and the diverse mercantile business helped make the McGregor Land and Livestock Company and its stockholders increasingly prosperous during the years before the 1920 crash. Financial statements issued by the company, despite the admitted policy of making them "appear about as bad as we could," reflected the growth: Total gross sales more than trebled in a decade, and net profits increased two and a half times. By 1917, the four stockholders shared more than $100,000 annually in McGregor Land and Livestock dividends. [16] Confident of their abilities as businessmen, the McGregor brothers decided to spend some of their personal funds outside the structure of their family corporation.

In 1908, Peter McGregor purchased the "Bar U" cattle ranch, four miles north of Hooper, from his political associate, U.S. Senator Levi Ankeny. Peter, John McGregor, and Eugene Taylor organized a corporation, Taylor Land and Livestock Company, to operate the property. Eugene Taylor, a brother-in-law of both Peter and John McGregor, became manager of the cattle business. But John had little desire to become a cattleman, and he soon sold his interest to the other two stockholders. The Taylor company seemed certain to be a success nonetheless: The rangeland was well watered and had a good grass cover, the property included more than a thousand acres of good farmland, and the best breeds of cattle were purchased to stock the range. Nine full-time cowboys were employed to herd the cattle, and extra crews of thirty or more men were used during haying and calving. The corporation also derived substantial income from land sales. The Lacrosse *Clipper* of January 27, 1911, for example, mentioned that "the Taylor Land and Livestock Company of Hooper has disposed of more than 800 acres of land near Hooper to Spokane parties, who paid $20,000." The future of the Bar U looked promising.

But the McGregors were poor cattlemen. The McGregor Land and Livestock Company had experimented with a herd of three to five hundred cattle and lost money in six of twelve years (1909–20). The Taylor corporation, with more than three thousand head, had serious troubles from the outset. Shortly after the organization of the company, Peter McGregor arranged to lease thousands of acres of adjacent rangeland from the heirs of Albert J. Hooper. The combined ranges gave the cattlemen fifty sections of land for their stock. The arrangement was complicated, because Peter McGregor was serving as an executor of the Hooper estate at the time of the transaction. Hooper's heirs alleged fraud and successfully argued in superior court for a termination of the lease agreement. Peter McGregor appealed the case to the Washington State Supreme Court, where he was vindicated.[17]

Almost from the outset, the corporation had trouble finding a good manager. Eugene Taylor, the only experienced cattleman in the management, became sick with tuberculosis and spent most of his time recuperating in California and Arizona after 1910. He died in 1917 at the age of 37. Peter McGregor decided that his son, Alex Taylor McGregor, should become manager of the cattle ranch. Records were kept in a haphazard fashion, and several disputes arose that required court arbitration. Instead of receiving a salary, Alex T. simply "went to the office and got whatever he wanted to take." Frequent notices similar to the following cause one to suspect that cattle were not always watched with the utmost care: "For several days we have had missing from our ranch in Whitman and Adams counties (near Hooper) thirty cattle, most of which we think are yearlings." Drinking sessions were a frequent feature of life on the Bar U Ranch. One such session ended when two bootleggers shot and killed Art Johnson, the foreman.

Ralph Snyder remembered that his close friend Alex T. McGregor was an interesting man: "I was always fond of Alec . . . Alec was quite proud. . . . He was his father's son—he took after Pete an awful lot. He had Pete's disposition, except that he never had that training of havin' to take care of himself. Alec was good company, a good businessman, and he could handle men well and make quick decisions. But Alec got to drinkin' too much. . . ." Snyder recalled that Peter McGregor once sent Alex T. to Chicago with a load of livestock:

> He sold 'em and he was supposed to bring the money back home. But he met some guys back there and he ended up in San Francisco with gold miners. They had a sure proposition, Alec said. . . . They needed about $150,000 for the machinery . . . to open up this big gold mine. And all they needed was some money to give 'em a down payment on it. . . . So Alec gave 'em all he had, about $30,000. They no more than ordered the stuff up before they wanted him to finance the rest of the deal. But he didn't have any more money. I don't know how Alec got in such a God damned deal. . . . He'd probably been drinkin' with 'em and they was pretty sharp traders. So Alec didn't come home for about six weeks and he finally come home pretty sad lookin', all drug out and looked like he'd been worried quite a bit. I said "By God, I didn't think you was comin' home anymore. Thought you was gonna be a gold miner." "Ralph," he said "I run outa beans."[18]

The dedication and able management that characterized McGregor sheep raising was conspicuously absent from the cattle business. Alex T. McGregor, his cousin Donald (the only son of John and Minnie, and a McGregor Land and Livestock cattleman during World War I), and the other members of the Taylor and McGregor cattle crews played the part of rugged, hard-drinking, boisterous, fun-loving "cowboys." Impressed with their position as cattle herders, the men once tried to recreate a "Wild West" cattle drive and were so slow in rounding up the stock that Peter McGregor and a few other men brought the cattle in themselves, Peter wearing a derby hat to show his disdain for the "cowboys." Ralph Snyder remembered Billy Lloyd, one of the Taylor cattle drovers:

> Billy used to carry a big six-shooter. He was a little man but he wanted to be tough, that's why he carried the gun. I remember when Alec and Billy started to move a bull out there. And this bull shook his head at 'em a little bit and Billy took out his six-shooter and shot 'em in the nose. Alec said "By God, those bulls learned not to monkey around with Billy."

That was really a hell of a silly thing to do. . . . This bull was pretty tough and old Billy was gonna prove how to handle him. I looked at Alec then and thought "My God, why shoot a damned bull just because he was on the prod. Just get around and let him go."

The cattle ranges of the Bar U were converted to sheep production during World War I. Peter McGregor, the largest active stockholder in McGregor Land and Livestock by 1919, sought ways to help his son develop a profitable ranch. The McGregor corporation was induced to sell Taylor Land and Livestock a band of sheep and extensive amounts of fencing at less than cost. The Taylor outfit was loaned $35,000 to help them make the conversion to sheep production.[19] With the assistance of the parent company, the Taylor operation was able to survive and make modest profits. But the experience of the McGregors as cattlemen had not met Peter McGregor's optimistic expectations, and the Taylor company remained in business only by becoming a wholly dependent subsidiary of the McGregor sheep enterprise. Taylor Land and Livestock remained in business, with marginal success, until the death of Alex T. McGregor in 1945, when it was sold.

The McGregors, like many other prosperous Columbia Plateau ranchers and farmers, used some of their personal funds to speculate in a variety of stock ventures. Men needing financing for mining projects learned of the agricultural prosperity of the region and traveled through the area selling stock. Ralph Snyder remembered: "We could have papered the store with the mining stock my dad bought. Men were always coming through, peddling mining stuff." The farmers and livestock men had little background for appraising the new ventures, but the possibility of making a quick profit was compelling. H. Stanley Coffin wrote in his 1912 daybook of the purchase of stock in a Hawaiian sugar company: "We bought $3,000 worth of stock in the Kerr Sugar Co., at par, of McChesney and Sons, who are agents for same. There is big excitement in this sugar stock and big money can be made. We heard of some as high as 700% . . . [and] 750% on the original investment. . . . We did not have time to investigate it, but we think we made a good buy."

The eagerness and haste to participate in new enterprises left the novice investors vulnerable to shrewd salesmen. In 1910 Arthur, Lester, and H. Stanley Coffin joined sheepmen and cattlemen from Montana in investing in the Rosario Mining Company, a Mexican mining concern promoted by one J. L. Davis. Discouraged by the failure of the company to produce any income, one of the Montana stockholders investigated the Mexican operations several years later and wrote Lester Coffin: "After spending some $13,000 on the property, Davis absconded, drawing some

$7,000 in cash from the bank here in Mexico. He is now mayor of Oakland, and we are unable to get redress, for the crime was committed in Mexico." Ralph Snyder remembered his father's investment in the John Day mine of Chewelah, Washington:

> My father was payin' $300 a month assessment and that was quite a thing for a little storekeeper. So he said, "Well, why don't you go up there and see what's goin' on?" ... It was 1910 and I was just 17 ... I got off the train and asked "how do you get to the John Day mine from here?" He said "Well right down there is a fellow playin' pool. He's the foreman. Chances are you'll go out there for dinner." I found the guy shootin' pool and we got in his buggy and went out there. And they had a great big dinner. There was about 20 miners there and they all stowed away a lot of meat 'n potatoes and gravy. ... So after dinner the fellows went back in the shaft. They had a little railroad track running out there and they were taking this ore out and just dumpin' it over the side. ... Dad was the only one payin' his $300 to keep 'em going. But they were just dumping this ore and God I couldn't see any future in that thing. Of course I wasn't a geologist but I could see that they were all just living on his support. And just as soon as Dad quit payin' 'em that damned mine flooded.[20]

John, Peter, Archie, and Alex McGregor invested personal funds in more than a dozen mining concerns based in Wyoming, Idaho, and Nevada; purchased interests in Wyoming and California oil companies; and even bought stock in a New Jersey coal-producing corporation. Superior Court Judge J. N. Pickrell of Colfax and two of his associates, W. P. Edris of Spokane and J. E. Quinlan of Luning, Nevada, had organized several mining projects with minimal amounts of capital outlay. Pickrell convinced the McGregors to invest in some of these concerns—Butte and Coeur d'Alene Mining Company of Idaho, Shipper-Copper Mining Company of Nevada, Butte Mining Company of Washington, and other gold, silver, and copper corporations. Peter McGregor was informed of the promising future of the Butte and Coeur d'Alene project in 1917: "When you consider that the property consists of eight claims which are patented and equipped with good machinery ... [and] with the present high price for silver and copper ... you must feel you are a stockholder of a good property. The stock of the Butte and Coeur d'Alene is closely held, and if each stockholder protects his investment, it will not be hard to make this stock worth a very attractive price in the near future."

Archie, John, and Alex McGregor, in conjunction with Pickrell, Edris, and Quinlan, formed the Alameda Mines Company in June 1915. The corporation, headquartered in the Hooper store, developed a mine in the Silver Star Mining District of Mineral County, Nevada. Alameda

Mines Company was to have 750,000 shares, valued at one dollar each, and the company by-laws listed two major corporate goals: the acquisition and development of mines, water rights, and real estate, and the construction of railroads and smelters for transportation and concentration of ores. The $750,000 capital stock listed in the articles of incorporation was an imaginative figure that bore little relation to the sums of money actually involved. The three McGregors, owners of almost 200,000 shares, invested some cash, but probably not more than a few thousand dollars. The other stockholders invested no money at all, merely trading their mining claims in Mineral County for shares of stock.[21]

The company hired eight men, including hoist engineers, miners, and machinists, and began digging for ore-producing veins. Bills were received for camp equipment, mining supplies, hoist engines, and other machinery. Costs for the fall of 1915, according to receipts kept by the company, totaled about $3,800. The Alameda records reveal no indication of income from the enterprise. Quinlan withdrew from the company, and Pickrell and Edris fell behind on their assessments. G. A. Raymer, Quinlan's successor as manager, wrote Archie McGregor seeking funds:

> *Mr. Harris and self have for some time contemplated going to work again on the Alameda property. Only yesterday we had a gentleman ask us what we would take for the property and we decided to write to you immediately. Last fall we run the tunnell as far as we had money to work with but did not cut the vein at the top of the shaft. . . . In order to continue the work it will be necessary for us to levy an assessment . . . as follows:*

W. E. Harris	*115,380 shares*	*$346.15*
G. A. Raymer	*48,077 shares*	*192.31*
McGregor Bros.	*192,308 shares*	*576.95*
W. P. Edris	*48,077 shares*	*192.31*
Judge Pickrell	*48,077 shares*	*192.31*

> *If all the money was paid we could go ahead and develop the property. . . . With the above assessment, [even] without Edris and Pickrell we can prove it out. We will gamble with you this one more assessment. At the present moment mining conditions are good in this state. There are many Eastern men looking for prospects that have some merit, this is the reason we would like to cut the ore body before placing the Alameda for sale.*

The idea of further assessments was not entertained, and Archie McGregor wrote the Internal Revenue Service, in May 1918, that "Alameda is now defunct." Results of the other stock purchases were similar. The $15,000–20,000 spent on mining stock during the decade 1910–20 brought the McGregor brothers nothing but assessment notices.

Archie McGregor, the brother most deeply involved in the speculation, lost many thousand dollars in the Orogrande mine of northern Idaho and received dismal results from the purchase of four sections of Nevada mineral lands, despite the assurances of his agent that interested miners were making "quite a rush in from California into this valley." Archie complained about the investments in 1938, two decades after the failure of the Alameda project: "I got mining literature from South Dakota today. Can you beat the way they follow a sucker around?" The net result of the mining investments, according to Emile Morod, fifty-five years a McGregor sheepman, was a loss of funds that should have been used for the sheep business: "Pete told me one time . . . 'It all come out of those sheep.'" In a 1921 letter to the Internal Revenue Service, the McGregors sought an answer to a hypothetical question about mining investments: "Will you please advise us on the law as it pertains to the taking of losses. For instance: A man during the year 1917 purchases a certain mining stock which is highly speculative. . . . The mine has turned out to be a failure and the stock is not worth anything. Can such a loss be taken against individual income?"[22]

The McGregor brothers as individuals also used money earned from their sheep, wheat, and mercantile businesses to invest in Columbia Plateau irrigation projects. Plans to irrigate the arid lands of the American West had been promoted with crusading zeal in the 1890's and culminated in the Newlands Act of 1902, a congressional enactment providing for the use of funds from public land sales for the financing of reclamation projects. The most arid lands of Washington and Oregon, once viewed as sandy, barren deserts, held the promise of amazing productivity. William E. Smythe, one of the leading proponents of irrigation, wrote in 1899 of "the blessing of aridity": "The land which the casual traveller, speaking out of the splendid depths of his ignorance and prejudice, condemns as 'worthless' and fit only 'to hold the earth together' is in reality rich and durable beyond the most favorable districts in the humid regions."

The sagebrush lands of the West could become fertile through "the miracle of irrigation." Real estate speculation was a primary concern for privately financed projects begun before passage of the reclamation act: Many promoters hoped irrigation would transform sagebrush deserts they had acquired for a dollar an acre into lands that could be resold for forty to fifty times the initial price. Several efforts were made in the 1890's to unleash the tremendous productivity of the Columbia Plateau: An irrigation project was organized in the Yakima Valley in 1891, only to be ruined two years later by the panic; N. G. Blalock of Walla Walla and other promoters made surveys in 1892 for a ditch to carry water eighty miles from northern Idaho lakes to the lowlands of the Big Bend in the futile hope of enlisting investors in the venture; and during the next decade efforts were made to irrigate lands near Wenatchee, Chelan, and Pasco.[23] One of the most ambitious projects was initiated in 1892, when three Tacoma businessmen and "some eastern capitalists" formed the Palouse Irrigation Ditch Company, a corporation with $500,000 capital stock and a plan to use Palouse River water to irrigate 400,000 acres of Big Bend country from Hooper to Pasco. The original plan called for a wooden flume sixty miles in length and thirty to fifty feet in width. The promoters had seen the Palouse River during the period of spring runoff, for during the summer months the entire flow of the river would not have filled the ditch. Twelve miles of a much smaller ditch were built before the Panic of 1893 brought a halt to the enterprise. The Palouse project was reorganized in 1897 with the assistance of three eastern financiers: Joshua Harris, president of the Philadelphia and Reading Railroad, president Samuel Shipley of Provident Life and Trust, and George Burnham of Baldwin Locomotive Works. An elaborate series of reservoirs was planned to store Palouse River floodwaters for irrigation purposes. William E. Smythe noted in 1899 that " 'the Palouse River project' is the principal [irrigation] project now under way in Washington."[24]

But work advanced slowly on the Palouse project. The corporation organized in 1897 survived three years of heavy construction costs before it was abandoned. Two additional firms also failed to make progress. After the Newlands Act was passed, hopes ran high for federal acquisition of the Palouse project. In the summer and fall of 1904, T. A. Noble, the district engineer for the Reclamation Service, and forty fellow engineers undertook a reconnaissance survey to determine the feasibility of damming the Palouse River near Hooper, diverting water into reservoirs, and using it to irrigate 100,000 acres in Franklin County from Eltopia to Pasco. The Secretary of the Interior seemed ready to approve the Palouse project until F. H. Newell, chief of the Reclamation Service, reported that it would be too expensive. The engineers then turned their attention to the Yakima Valley and organized a 450,000-acre project that was to become one of the largest and most successful Bureau of Reclamation developments. Pasco residents complained of the "fraud and larceny of the Palouse Project" and talked of "high handed treachery" and "senile acquiescence by officials."[25]

A private irrigation project, on a much reduced scale, was developed. The Seattle-based Palouse Irrigation and Power Company rebuilt existing flumes and ditches in 1907 and brought a steady supply of water to ten miles of valley lands between Hooper and Washtucna. Tracts of land were sold to several hundred people, many of whom were from Seattle and Spokane, but some of whom resided in New York, Florida, Texas, Illinois, Wisconsin, Minnesota, Pennsylvania, and other distant points. Ralph Snyder remembered: "I stood on a bluff there in Washtucna and counted two hundred farmers out there in the fields, raisin' onions and spuds and puttin' in orchards between Washtucna and Hooper. All on ten acre plots, that was the limit. They didn't have a chance to make it, but they didn't know any better."

The McGregor Land and Livestock Company, the only large land-holder and the owner of the most fertile lands in the valley, began clearing rocks from several hundred acres of irrigable lowlands in 1905. Orchards were planted and Golden Delicious, Winesap, Winter Banana, and Stark-ing apples; Elberta and Hale peaches; Stella and Supert apricots; and varieties of plums, cherries, and pears were raised on the land. Additional irrigated lands were used to produce alfalfa for sheep hay. A crew of nineteen men was employed to care for the irrigated lands. Emile Morod's first job in 1913 was in the orchards, spraying trees with a horse-drawn cart. Fifteen-year-old Emile worked with an older man: "I was just a kid, the other fellow was my boss. I'd pump and he'd spray the trees." The corporation expanded its apple production and by 1912 was marketing almost ten thousand boxes of apples annually. McGregors began pur-chasing most of the apples raised in the valley, hired an apple sorting crew, and sold their own brand, Glen'een, with a picture of a Scotchman in kilts on each box. Apples were sold through agencies in Minnesota, Iowa, and Wisconsin with generally favorable results. In 1921, for ex-ample, agent O. J. Judd of Fort Dodge, Iowa, wrote the McGregors about their shipment of twenty-one railroad cars of apples: "Am well pleased with the goods and every customer praises them highly and we certainly want to arrange to handle your entire crop next year."[26]

The "miracle" of irrigation had transformed the scabrock canyon of the Palouse River into productive orchards and alfalfa fields. But the company that supplied the water was in serious financial trouble by 1911. The expensive, antiquated wooden flume fell into disrepair and could last only a few more seasons. Alex and Archie McGregor lent the Palouse Irrigation and Power Company a few thousand dollars to assist with maintenance costs. Two Dutch corporations provided money, one of them raising 525,000 guilders ($225,000) and promoting a plan to bring residents of Holland to farm the Channeled Scablands. But the Palouse Irrigation and Power Company defaulted on the debts and was placed in receivership. The storage reservoir at Rock Lake, a major water supply source for the system, was shut down by a State Supreme Court decision restricting the impounding of spring runoff. Supplying customers with water became increasingly difficult. Manager Roy Zahren provided the receiver with dismal reports during the 1913 season. In April, floodwaters topped the banks of the canal and "lacked about an inch of going over the top of the wastegate, and that inch was what saved us. . . . We worked up there [at the dam] 20 hours at one stretch, and it was work too. Old hardened men like Kolberg had all the skin removed from the palm of their hands." Later in the spring the canal became clogged with weeds and mud, and portions of the flume broke. By August, "the whole flume need[ed] repairing," and the wooden structure sagged dangerously on the steep canyon walls: "It is practically impossible to raise [these portions] . . . with the water in the flume. The weight is something like 10,000 pounds . . . and with only screw jacks and soft footings it is very hard to make a raise without dropping the whole thing. We were raising . . . [one section] the other day, when the jacks kicked out, and 6 by 8s and jackscrews flew in all directions. Fortunately no one was hurt, nor did the flume come down, but it was very dangerous." On August 16, the flume silted up and ceased to deliver water until Zahren removed "six slugs from the pipe. They were composed of mud, a few weeds, sticks, cats, fish, bacon, rabbits, and in fact everything found in a first class sewer." Zahren wrote that "no one ever looked twenty minutes ahead on this project": "The one thing that is wrong with this whole system is that we have no factor of safety. When everything is going all right we are just able to deliver the goods, when anything goes wrong we are not." [27]

The McGregor Land and Livestock Company began digging a series of wells on its own property in 1908 to provide a more dependable source of water for their orchards and hay fields. The wells produced ample amounts of artesian water and were said to be the most successful in the state. Eugene Taylor wrote John McGregor about the new project: "You were very lucky . . . [with] the flowing wells in Hooper and you sure showed nerve to imagine you could ever get wells like you have. . . . It certainly is a boost to that valley [and] it will make a great change in the looks of that country." As the McGregors developed an independent water supply, they became difficult customers for the Palouse Irrigation and Power Company. Manager Roy Zahren made three attempts to collect the June 1912 water maintenance fee and reported on the delays of the McGregors in making their payment:

> *June 5: I had a casual talk with the McGregors today regarding their water rent. They told me . . . that they guessed they would shut it off, and then, in case they wanted it again, would pay up. There is something behind that talk . . . They either think you do not dare shut it off, on account of that note of theirs, or they figure the act of shutting it off invalidates their contract.*

June 12: I phoned to the McGregors. . . . They tried to tell me that the water would be good for any land they had down there. (They own all the rest of the land around there).

June 22: I have seen the McGregors. . . . They have been buying an auto and were unable to do business until they had worn the new off it.[28]

Although the McGregors finally paid their water rent, the success of their artesian wells enabled them to develop an ensured source of water independent of the Palouse River flume.

Repeated success with artesian wells near Hooper made Archie, Alex, and John McGregor confident and willing to invest $70,000 for the purchase of the entire Palouse Irrigation and Power project, including fifteen miles of wooden flume and almost eight thousand acres of grazing and irrigated lands. Judge Pickrell, the man who had urged the McGregors to speculate in mining stock, promoted and arranged the transaction and the three brothers formally incorporated the new holding as the Hooper Realty Company. At the first meeting of the new corporation in July 1917, Alex McGregor was chosen president, John became vice-president, and Archie was selected as secretary–treasurer. The Palouse project had had a disastrous history of bankruptcies and large expenses. And despite the more than $250,000 that had been spent on the ditches, flumes, and wooden dams, the entire operation was in a horrible state of repair. But the McGregor brothers had dug successful wells only three miles upstream from the Palouse project, and earlier studies by federal hydrologists seemed to indicate that artesian water might be found throughout the Palouse River Valley. The McGregor brothers liked the modest purchase price, and they hurriedly bought the property in the hope of using artesian water and abandoning the old flume.

The Hooper Realty Company had major difficulties from the start. The corporation financed the digging of five wells—some to the depth of a thousand feet. McGregor Land and Livestock financed the digging of additional wells on its own property adjacent to the irrigation project. Unlike the experience at Hooper, no artesian water was found in the new locations. The inability to strike extensive artesian flows meant that Archie, John, and Alex McGregor had to depend on the leaky, costly wooden flume to serve those people with whom they had water contracts. Because the irrigation flume was a public service, under state law the men were forced to keep it in operation. During the first four years of business, the Hooper Realty Company spent $28,160 on the irrigation system. Receipts from water users totaled $5,102. Archie McGregor estimated in July 1920 that $99,000 would be required, "in the near future" in order to ensure further water supply.[29]

Even with the expensive maintenance, the Hooper company was unable to supply enough water to satisfy people who had bought tracts from predecessor companies. Individuals who had never seen their lots and who hoped to sell them to Hooper Realty received reports similar to the following letters to a Tacoma banker, a Seattle printer, and an army corporal from Saskatchewan:

> *You have so much hard-pan on your [property] that we would not care to make an offer.*

> *Your price is too high. You are evidently not very familiar with the particular block in which your lot is located as the whole block and one or two others near it are not worth over $10. It is nothing but a rocky alkali bed and will not even make good pasture.*

> *We have investigated this matter for you and to express our candid opinion the property is worthless.*

Those people who had located on good orchard lands complained to the Public Service Commission about mismanagement and insufficient water supply. Hooper Realty officials responded to the complaint by detailing the extensive repairs and meager receipts. A Department of Public Works study, "Investigation of Financial Records of the Hooper Realty Company," substantiated the losses encountered by the company.[30]

Archie, Alex, and John McGregor had planned to use the eight thousand acres included in the irrigation project to raise alfalfa-hay and graze sheep. The McGregors knew these enterprises well, and in 1917 and 1918 revenue from sheep and hay more than offset the losses encountered in the operation of the flume. In 1919, Archie McGregor sought to defray additional irrigation repair costs by purchasing (for the Hooper Realty Company) 3,300 lambs for up to $10.25 per hundred pounds. But in 1920 the already weakened financial structure of the corporation was devastated by a drop in lamb prices from $10.30 to $5.30. Archie McGregor described the desperate status of the Hooper Realty Company in a 1920 letter to the Public Service Commissioner:

> *None of the stock of this company has ever been sold or transferred. No one wants it. The owners have given a great deal of their time to the welfare of the company but have never drawn one cent for their services. They have used their personal credit . . . to obtain funds . . . and it is a serious question with them how much longer they can stand up under the load. We have a losing proposition and a big one, and we know it. . . . No financial institution will even consider loaning us money. . . . The Commission may wonder why we, as businessmen who have lived here for thirty years, should ever obligate ourselves as we have done in this case. At Hooper, where the bulk of our private*

holdings is located we had discovered an abundance of artesian water. The ditch property was up for immediate sale and we purchased it fig- uring very strongly on striking artesian water in Palouse Falls [the irrigation townsite]. If we had obtained water we planned to discontinue the dam and all the expensive flume. . . .[31]

The Public Service Commission finally allowed the transfer of owner- ship of the irrigation ditch from Hooper Realty Company to the water users. Divested of the antiquated flume, the corporation retained control of good grazing and farm land. But additional funds were badly needed. McGregor Land and Livestock had loaned $35,000 to the Hooper company over a period of several years. But Peter McGregor, the man- ager of the parent corporation after 1919, preferred to finance his son's Bar U ranch instead of providing further assistance to the Hooper Realty Company. Archie and Alex McGregor sold their irrigation properties to the parent company for $35,010—$6 per acre and only $10 more than the outstanding mortgage. McGregor secretary H. R. Rudd described the property in glowing terms to a prospective buyer in September 1922:

There really isn't any better hay land anywhere. . . . The grazing land . . . can be easily fed off with sheep. . . . There are ample improvements such as houses, barns, shops, implement sheds. . . . The irrigation system is in use today . . . and is in fair condition throughout. . . . There are so many good things to say about this property that I could write for hours on the subject. . . . The people who are selling . . . can use the cash today, besides, they are getting old and have too much to handle. . . . The best feature of all . . . is the wonderful speculative value involved. . . .

Two months earlier, in a letter to the Internal Revenue Service, Rudd had described the project about which he "could write for hours" in somewhat different terms: "In 1917 three McGregor brothers purchased a certain irrigation system and organized a corporation called the Hooper Realty Company to operate the property. The project was a loser from the start. They tried sheep and hay but neither would pay. Finally, after a few years, the company was about $35,000 in debt . . . [and] the property was sold for just enough to satisfy the mortgage."[32]

Alex McGregor lost several thousand dollars of his own money when the Hooper Realty lands were sold to McGregor Land and Livestock. But Archie McGregor, the brother who had promoted, organized, and managed the irrigation project, was the biggest loser. His losses on the 1922 land sale alone amounted to almost $23,000. Archie claimed bitterly that his brother Peter had initially agreed to become a member of the irrigation company, only to withdraw after the other three men had committed themselves. Peter then refused to agree to lend additional funds that might have enabled the Hooper Realty Company to survive. Ralph Snyder took another view: "It was supposed to be Archie's baby when they bought that Palouse Irrigation business, but Archie wasn't tough enough to run it." Whatever the truth of the matter, the members of the Hooper Realty Company had gambled with their personal assets— first by purchasing an unprofitable public utility on the untested assumption that artesian water would be found, and then in an attempt to counterbalance their risk, compounding the problem, by buying a band of sheep during a period of extreme wartime inflation.[33]

By 1920, the McGregor brothers had learned some of the limitations of their business expertise. John, Archie, Peter, and Alex McGregor had almost forty years' experience as sheepmen and had developed one of the largest and most successful woolgrowing operations on the Columbia Plateau. Their cautious expansion into wheat growing had proved remunerative and promised to be an important source of future profit. They had developed a diverse and successful mercantile business in the company town of Hooper. Wheat, sheep, and merchandise proceeds had for the first time provided the McGregors with substantial profits. The marked success of the McGregor Land and Livestock Company encouraged the men to organize new corporations and test their skills as cattlemen, mining entrepreneurs, and irrigation ditch proprietors. The new projects, however, bore little resemblance to the initial business and were highly speculative, poorly organized, and loosely managed. In later years, the McGregors were considerably more reluctant to invest in enterprises for which they had no background. Maurice McGregor, the eldest son of Peter and Maude, commented in 1935 on an opportunity for the McGregor Land and Livestock Company to acquire timberland: "We have been farming and raising sheep for a long time and seem to be able to get along but every time we have stepped outside into something we didn't know very well we have always wished we hadn't. We do know something about sheep but we don't know enough about timber to make any venture in it."[34]

The McGregor brothers, like many other Columbia Plateau ranchers and farmers, had trouble learning how to use their new prosperity to advantage. Ralph Snyder, a neighbor of the McGregors and a veteran wheat raiser and cattleman, recalled that "a lot of people had worked all their lives in order to create a fortune and finally created their fortune and then didn't know how to spend it." Some held on tightly to their new assets: "They wouldn't have enjoyed spending that money. They'd saved all their life creating something and they wanted to preserve it." Others speculated with their new funds in the hope of adding quickly to their wealth. Many of the ranchers that had survived the Panic of 1893 and the settlement of the ranges fell victim to inefficient and unwise management during the prosperous years of the early twentieth century. Ralph Snyder described the 1909 breakup of the sheep and cattle ranch of Albert J. Hooper:

> *Al Hooper was a wonderful man. He had three sons and they should have controlled the whole region. They had been one of the first families here. They built a big ranch. But when Al started to spread out, why the boys lacked that ability to manage and they thought they were pretty well established. Al bought a ranch for his son Ernie. . . . In his second year on the place Ernie took a whole trainload of steers to Seattle. . . . Seattle in those times was quite a boomin' town. . . . Grand Opera came out from New York and spent a lot of time there. . . . A lot was goin' on and young Ernie just fell right into that; he didn't come back till spring. When he came back he went up to see Al Coolidge, the banker up there at Colfax. An old time banker. And he was strong for the Hoopers. They were a fine family. Ernie said, "Well Mr. Coolidge, I need a little money to do my work with. . . ." Coolidge said, "What'd you do with that trainload of steers you took over to Seattle? We was kind of countin' on that to come in on your account." "Well," he said, "That . . . a . . . kinda got away from me." . . . So Al said, "You know, we don't finance those kind of people." And Ernie lost that ranch.*[35]

The McGregors had built a solid and profitable ranching operation in a decade, and their rapid success convinced them of their entrepreneurial abilities. Although results of new investments fell far short of their optimistic expectations, profits from sheep, merchandise, and wheat enabled them to view the future with confidence.

The increased agricultural prosperity provided greater opportunity for leisure time and an increased opportunity for social activities for farm families. The festivities of the early years of settlement—all-night dancing parties, chautauquas, trout fishing on the Palouse River, ice skating, Fourth of July speeches, and horse races—were continued, and "literary and debating societies" still argued such questions as "Resolved, that modern inventions are detrimental to the laboring class of men" and "Resolved, that the South had a right to secede." Marie Boone, the eldest daughter of Archie and Nellie McGregor, described some of the recreational activities:

> *Dancing and cards were recreation for young and old. During the winter months also sleigh riding and skating parties ending up at someones house for a taffy pull and refreshments. The dances were held in the school or someone's home and lasted until daybreak when the farmers had to get home to milk the cows. In the summer months, although busy,*

*the young and old would gather for picnics at which everyone in the area
was invited. Each family contributed food—everything from fried chick-
en to the best of cakes and pies. These picnics were usually held ... [at
homes] located on the Palouse River. The women spent days in cooking
and baking for the occasion. Very often platforms were constructed ...
for dancing and music was provided by a fiddler, pianist, and perhaps a
drummer. Everyone came on horseback or buggy or wagon or just
plain walked. Fifteen miles was no barrier whatever the means of transportation.*[36]

Families who had small farms and ranches distant from villages still
led isolated lives similar to those of the early settlers of the Columbia
Plateau. Women milked cows, herded sheep, helped in harvest, raised
gardens, and made many of the management decisions for the family
farm operation. Hooper residents tell of Mrs. George Milam, the wife
of an early cattleman, who agreed that railroad crews could use the
family spring if they would then give Milams the pump when they left.
Forgetting their verbal promise, the workers finished their tasks and attempted to remove the pump along with the rest of their equipment.
They were confronted by Mrs. Milam, who arrived at the spring smok-
ing her corncob pipe and armed with a shotgun. Ralph Snyder remembered Mrs. Milam: "She was a wonderful woman. As long as she was
alive, she ran that family. She was very dogmatic and she knew who
she was gonna support. . . . Quite often, you'd find a woman that was
the head of a family that way. She'd be the strongest and have the most
judgment. The woman kept things going." The families rarely traveled
to towns or cities and, when they did, often felt out of place. In 1901,
the Colfax *Gazette* detailed an attempt to accommodate the visitors:
"Ladies of Colfax are sympathetic. They have observed the discomforts
of country folks visiting town, and finally have perfected a plan to help
them out by furnishing a resting place for the tired women and
children."[37]

But important changes were occurring in farm life. The land suited
to wheat production had been broken and put into crop; the rangeland
had been converted into successful ranches. The period of vigorous
growth and rapid change was over, and the families who remained had
more or less successfully adapted to the region. Those who survived
found themselves with more money and more leisure time than ever
before. The most successful ranchers and farmers traveled widely and
sometimes ostentatiously—in 1914, for example, the H. Stanley Coffin
family of Yakima visited Japan, China, Manchuria, New Zealand, Australia, Cuba, Portugal, and Austria. The three Coffin families also found
time to leave their sheep and merchandise businesses to vacation at their

Puget Sound summer homes. The McGregors returned several times to the McGregor farm in Owen Sound, Ontario; traveled to New York, San Francisco, Los Angeles, and Denver; and vacationed together on the Washington coast and at Spirit Lake, Idaho, near one of their summer sheep ranges. More than thirty McGregor men, women, and children spent the summer of 1909 at Spirit Lake—the men visited their herders on the mountain ranges while the women attended "ladies aid socials," assisted the hired cook, and tended to the daily chores. The widowed mother of the McGregor brothers, Mrs. Mary MacGregor, came west with daughters Euphemia and Jessie to join the family and was the matriarch at such occasions. Mary MacGregor became a strong unifying force for the McGregor families. In 1918, Archie McGregor was asked on short notice to preach to the Hooper congregation meeting in the schoolhouse:

> On Sabbath morning . . . I did not spend the usual time on my Sunday School lesson but began thinking, and what do you suppose I thought of first? It was this, "My son, heed the instruction of thy father, and forsake not the law of thy mother." I suppose you will remember when you gave me that text almost 36 years ago and it has been a rock in my defense ever since. . . . It seems as though you were inspired to build character in your boys and girls in order that they might have a heritage which would never die. . . . Dear Mother; it matters not what your boys may do for you or what they may tell you for they can never express to you in words what they think of you; you will have to get that by intuition.[38]

The McGregor family worked to turn the company town of Hooper into a respectable community. By 1945 Alex C. McGregor was certain of their success: "I am sure . . . that the Hooper community is a more advanced and a happier community to live in because it was founded and fed and nourished by a bunch of MacGregors who were honest, industrious, and God fearing pioneers." The McGregors organized a Presbyterian congregation that met at infrequent intervals for sermons and baptismal rites. Traveling ministers were encouraged to stop in Hooper and deliver orations at the schoolhouse church meetings. The McGregors prided themselves on having brought religion and righteousness to the Channeled Scablands. W. P. Telford, writing in 1919 for the Owen Sound, Ontario, *Sun-Times* in "Appreciation of McGregor Family's Success in the West," described the "good, sound, liberal Presbyterian principles" that he claimed the Scotch-Canadians possessed:

> When the . . . [McGregor brothers] left the Lake Shore Line, Sydenham, to find a home in the State of Washington, in 1882, some of their friends

thought they were pitching their tents towards Sodom; that intercourse with the infidels, atheists, and men of the Buffalo Bill stamp of that region would extinguish their aspirations after higher things than this world offers, and that although they might succeed financially, such success would be purchased at too high a price to compensate them for the moral and spiritual loss they were likely to sustain in a community where the Divine Law was ignored and out of date, but we entirely underestimated the far reaching and permanent effects and influence of being brought up and trained in a Christian home. . . . Neither has financial success made them worshippers of Mammon. . . . In the course of time they were able to more than hold their own with their infidel neighbors . . . [and avoid being] submerged by their pagan environment. . . . In place of being submerged in a Godless community, the McGregor family have made their influence for good felt in many directions, John especially having taken a very active part in organizing a Christian congregation in Hooper, being one of three who guaranteed the minister's salary, his brothers and their wives, and his sisters . . . joining heartily in this missionary enterprise. . . .[39]

The McGregor families displayed their new prosperity by building imposing new homes in the town of Hooper. Marie Boone, the daughter of Nellie and Archie, recalled that the McGregors were able to move from the wheat ranch headquarters, seven miles south of Hooper, "because the women were not needed to cook on the ranch. They could afford to have someone cook for them." Alex C. and Jennie McGregor were the first to leave for town. They lived on the second floor of the original McGregor store for three years until 1905, when a four-room house was built for them. A decade later, the structure was expanded to ten rooms to accommodate their four children and to provide guest quarters. McGregor Land and Livestock Company also financed the construction of large homes for John and Minnie, Archie and Nellie, and Dougald and Elizabeth McGregor and their families during the years before World War I. Peter and Maude McGregor, residents of Spokane, Colfax, and Olympia during the prewar years, occupied a somewhat smaller residence when they stayed in Hooper.

The town bore the name given it by the Oregon, Washington Railroad and Navigation Company when a railroad siding was laid at the site in 1887. But Albert J. Hooper, a pioneer rancher who lived five miles further east, never owned land in the town named in his honor. The McGregors owned most of the land by 1905 and decided to have a plat map made of the town. The *Plat Book of Whitman County*, published by a Seattle map company in 1910, showed Hooper as having five roads that ran parallel with the Palouse River—Front Street and Main, Pacific, College, and Palouse avenues. These were intersected by four roads running north to south—Sherman (named after the parents of Jennie McGregor), Brown (named for the first postmaster), Roosevelt, and McGregor. But the plat was never officially filed, and only half the streets were constructed. By 1912, the McGregors had abandoned plans to sell lots and had begun purchasing all the buildings and homes not yet owned by the McGregor Land and Livestock Company. Within a few years Hooper was owned and operated by the company. The McGregors worked to improve the town's appearance by planting trees and grass along the roads and near the company-owned houses. In 1915, John McGregor objected to a railroad plan to build a stockyard adjacent to its tracks through town: "We have been improving this place extensively, and expect to continue to do so as rapidly as possible by removing all unsightly and objectionable buildings, pig pens, etc. We are, therefore, going to presume unless advised by you to the contrary, that the stockyards will be erected on either side of town, instead of directly opposite our homes." [40]

Married McGregor employees lived in the fourteen houses owned by the company. Single crew members were housed and fed in the hotel and in four bunkhouses—two of which were in town, another on the sheep range, and a fourth at the "wheat ranch" headquarters. A maintenance crew was employed to keep the facilities in proper order and the town clean and tidy. McGregor sheepmen brought sides of mutton to families of employees every few months. A twenty-thousand-dollar brick school was built in 1917, with two rooms for the eight primary grades and a single room for high school students. Alex McGregor remembered the school as "one of the centralizing forces in the community and all enjoyed participating in the plays, debates, and other events. . . . As late as 1926 Hooper boasted of a play company that presented its productions in . . . Ritzville, Washtucna, and other towns in this area." McGregor Land and Livestock Company booked dance bands for the school, rented movies from Paramount Pictures for the entertainment of the townspeople, and even considered publishing its own newspaper, the "Hooper Herald," to announce community events.

The little town had many strengths. Town residents, for example, knew and were close friends with many different types of people—farmers, ranchers, railroad workers, sheepherders, schoolteachers, cooks, storekeepers, and the other employees of a diverse farm corporation. Pioneer farmer and wheat hauler Dave Carter, sheepman Emile Morod, cattleman and farmer Ralph Snyder, store clerk and postmaster Ruby Burden Morod, veteran wheat raiser and farm foreman Hans Kahler, and other early Hooper settlers placed a high value on work and provided the youths of the village with strong models to emulate.[41]

There was a cordial relationship between the McGregors and their employees, tenants, and neighbors. The McGregors invited all the townspeople and farmers to their picnics and community activities. They advanced money to those in need of funds. Townspeople and neighbors remembered that the McGregors made a conscious effort to treat them as equals. But in the isolated, provincial village of the early twentieth century the difference in social standing between the McGregors and the rest of the community was obvious, if unspoken. The McGregors traveled extensively, while others seldom had the opportunity to leave the western Palouse. McGregor children went to the local grade school but were then sent to high school in Spokane, private schools in California, or to military school in Portland, opportunities not available to the other children in town. McGregor women had "sewing ladies," maids, and cooks to help them with the daily work. Some residents remembered feelings of bitterness that offset the positive features of life in a company town. Willard Burden, the son of a McGregor sheepman whose family lived in one of the two homes not owned by the corporation—a tiny converted chicken coop with only a stove for heating— remembered waking up to find snow blowing through cracks in the door and walls. He sometimes felt a sense of injustice when he walked down the street past the expansive house and well-kept yard of his neighbors, Alex and Jennie McGregor.

There were feelings of affection and genuine fondness among the McGregor families. Elizabeth McGregor, Dougald's wife, wrote Nellie's daughter Genevieve in 1948: "It is almost 40 years, 39 to be exact, this month since I went out to Hooper as a happy bride and met such a wonderful galaxy of lovely sisters-in-law. It was a marvelous family circle and Nell was one of the brightest and most generous." But there were occasional undercurrents of resentment even among the McGregors, frequently because of minor matters—the unwillingness of one of the brothers to attend church, or the failure of a hostess to invite all of the families to a dinner party.[42]

The McGregor women had once been an important part of the farm labor force. Nellie McGregor, for example, had cooked for the lambing, shearing, and harvest laborers. Her daughter Marie recalled that when she was five years old she accompanied her mother and father to the shearing camp. "There was a small wooden building consisting of one bedroom and a combination kitchen and dining room where Nellie cooked. The food was plain but lots of it and everything was cooked from scratch—had to bake bread, biscuits, pies, cakes, cook bacon, eggs, potatoes, pancakes. And no running water in the house. For recreation Nellie would take a doll blanket, sit near a squirrel hole very quietly and when he poked his head out, I would quickly grab him and place him in a screened box, later to be released."[43]

The responsibilities of women decreased with the growing prosperity of the family ranching business. Women's activities became restricted to the home. Long hours were spent washing, ironing, and starching children's clothes; cooking; supervising maids; caring for children; and maintaining immaculate households. As washing machines and other conveniences and hired help began to limit even their household duties, the women had to find fruitful and rewarding ways of spending a leisure time that the Old Testament had never prepared them to use. A high value was placed on graciousness and dignity. There was, as Wallace Stegner noted in his history of a small Montana farming town, "the most slavish respect for borrowed elegances." Minnie McGregor, John's wife, purchased fine China ornaments in San Francisco, hired a chauffeur for her new Cadillac, and sent her children to California boarding schools. Jennie McGregor began cooking, washing, and scrubbing at 4:30 each morning so that she could change into her best clothes and begin receiving social callers in the early afternoon.

Some of the women were apparently happy to be relieved of some of the drudgery of farm and household work and enjoyed the teas, "reception lines," and formal dinner parties. But Mary McGregor Hazeltine, the daughter of Jennie and Alex McGregor, remembered that women had to act within narrowly defined limits and had few opportunities to make creative use of their time. It was no longer "proper" for a woman to help on the farm or work in the store. Deprived of many of their earlier duties, some of the women could not find rewarding activities in the company town. Jennie McGregor, a talented artist as a girl in Chicago, abandoned painting because of the demands of raising a family and the fear that such an occupation was not socially acceptable. She pursued photography for a few years before abandoning that hobby as well. Women who moved from outside the Columbia Plateau to join their husbands at Hooper had some difficulty adjusting to the cultural standards of the rural community. An outsider much younger than the other McGregor wives, Jennie McGregor learned from the older women and from her own mistakes that one did not throw out vats of liquid stored in the cool root cellar—the cloudy liquid was precious gooseberry juice stored for use in making jelly; bread was never set to rise on Sunday morning because baking was not a suitable activity for the Sabbath; and bacon grease should never be used on a bread loaf—the resulting speckled bread was "uncivilized." Desperate for something to do when her husband left for the summer sheep ranges shortly after their marriage, Jennie completed cleaning the house and then passed her time sowing grass seed outside her small home and later clipping the lawn with scissors. Women with narrowly defined duties and few social outlets had mixed feelings about life in an isolated town in the scabrock canyons. Elgin McGregor, wife of Maurice, later wrote: "Maude [wife of Peter] . . . and I knew that there is something in that country which doesn't like us! It will purr and relax in the sun of spring and Indian summer so long as you let it alone, but it will turn malicious and malignant if you try to make it serve you, and in the long run it will probably destroy us all. Maude was horribly oppressed by it and John M. [Maurice] and I were both aware of it. He said it wanted to be given back to the Indians and I'm sure he often wished it could."[44]

Women's social groups, formal teas, and parties for children were among the social activities for the ranchers' wives. Typical events were those described in the "Hooper Happenings" column of two issues of the 1915 Lacrosse *Clipper*:

> The Christian Endeavor gave a lawn social at the house of John McGregor, the young folks went for a hay ride, after returning light refreshments were served and a delightful evening was spent. . . .

> Mrs. A. C. McGregor gave a birthday party in honor of her son, Sherman. He entertained about twenty of his young friends at games after which light refreshments were served. . . .

> Mrs. John McGregor gave an afternoon tea in honor of Miss Campbell, who leaves soon for her home in Owen Sound, Canada. . . . A dainty lunch was served by the hostess. There were about twenty guests and a fine time is reported by all. . . .

> The Washtucna tennis players came over and played Hooper last Friday. The score being six to one in favor of Hooper. After the game was over, the Mrs. McGregors served watermelon to the crowd.

Other women in the community attended "medicine shows" and similar festivities at the Hooper school: "Miss Marguerite Wann received the silverware, she being the most popular young lady in the voting contest at the medicine show which has been holding forth here. . . . Mrs. Eccles won the sugar bowl in the nail driving contest at the show." Women played an active part in Red Cross and Liberty Bond fund-raising drives during World War I. In the fall of 1917, Hooper ladies organized dances and "box socials," knowing "that every dollar . . . [raised] was going to help a worthy cause and possibly [to] save the life of a young soldier boy lying wounded on the field of battle." In October, "the Red Cross dance held . . . at the warehouse was attended by one of the largest crowds ever at a dance in Hooper." The community enthusiastically contributed to the Liberty Bond program. McGregor secretary H. R. Rudd described the Hooper fund drive in the fall of 1918:

> *The quota for Hooper has been more than doubled, and as not many towns have doubled up this time we thought you might have it mentioned in the [Spokane] paper what the little place has done. We would prefer that the town receive the credits and honors, reserving only a minor part of glory for the McGregors even though they do take most all the quota. . . . The people of Hooper have helped us to raise and double our quota, inasmuch as they were able, and they have done well, and we are sincere in asking that any mention of Hooper's performance in the paper will give the people the credit and not ourselves.*[45]

The sense of community spirit was less evident in peacetime. Women joined neighborhood clubs organized to promote conviviality and friendship. Many Palouse country villages had such organizations—Mockonema had the "Don't Worry Club"; Clinton, the "Stitch and Chatter Club"; Hooper the "Get-Together Club" and later the "Community Cheer Club" (the "C. C. Club"). The groups had noble aims—the Get-Together Club, for example, was organized "to promote community spirit by seeing, talking, and doing good, and overcoming evil with good." Women met to have teas, play cards, make quilts, perform skits, and raise money for various community purposes. But in postwar years, the C. C. Club was nicknamed by men "the Cat and Cougar Club" for the heated disputes that occurred over trivial issues (for example, whether it was proper to hold dances in the schoolhouse). Norma McGregor, the daughter-in-law of Alex C. and Jennie, described the club of later years as "dreary and artificial," and the meetings as "extreme boredom and mental strangulation."

The stress on elegance and grace that accompanied the agricultural prosperity in many ways robbed the women and the towns themselves of much of their vitality. Minnie and Maude McGregor, daughters of a pioneering family and the wives of John and Peter, were remembered by contemporaries as "ladylike" and "nice," with "motherly charm" and "kindly graces." Jennie McGregor tried hard to conform, channeling her energies into keeping an elegant household. Members of the extended family, visitors, and friends were always welcome at her table. She made hand-dipped chocolates and five-inch sugar cookies and dispensed these good things with a generous hand. Many friends and neighbors still think first of the cookies, chocolates, and cinnamon rolls when they talk of Jennie McGregor. But the price Jennie paid for this way of life was to surrender the development of a considerable talent in painting. Nellie McGregor, who spent summers in Hooper after her family was grown and her husband had retired from active management, developed a skill well suited to the region: she loved to fish and was better at the pursuit than most of the men of Hooper. In two letters to her children in 1928 she commented: "Alex and Sherman and I went up to the dam and fished a while this eve. I caught three catfish. Sherman and Alex did not have much luck. We have all the trout we wanted and gave some away. When we need meat I go out and get . . . [more fish]. . . . I feel a little guilty for not writing oftener but now . . . the fish wont bite anymore . . . so I will try to do more writing." But for some of the newly prosperous women, life in a small town, despite its many strengths, had elements of what H. L. Davis described as the pathetic desperation of a people who, "having whipped a wild corner of the earth into a gentility pleasing to their hearts," find that the process has stripped the region of much of its vigor. Davis described the pettiness that he claimed characterized early twentieth century Columbia Plateau town life: "Civilization came to eastern Oregon, not by farms, but by the institution of the town. . . . [The history of each town] has been one long war for righteousness and in that war the winning of a victory has meant only the opening of an offensive against something else. Just now, the fight is against allowing youths under twenty-one to play pool."[46]

By World War I, the McGregor brothers had gained control of the town of Hooper, had achieved wide regional recognition for the large scale of their businesses, and were recording profits four times greater than ever before from their family corporation. But in 1918 and 1919, in the midst of the wartime prosperity, the working arrangement among John, Archie, Alex, and Peter McGregor was shattered. Beginning as an informal partnership of two in 1882 and increasing to three in 1886 and four in 1900, the men had worked together for up to 37 years. An extraordinary change occurred within a period of a few months. John and Archie McGregor, the two men most responsible for the success of the group effort for more than thirty years, were no longer part of the McGregor Land and Livestock Company. Peter McGregor, the brother who had spent the longest time away from the sheep business in the 1890's, had been active only occasionally in the management of the McGregor Land and Livestock Company since its organization in 1905. In June 1918, McGregor secretary H. R. Rudd noted that Peter McGregor "does not draw a salary as he devotes his time to other interests." Yet by 1919, Peter had emerged as the largest stockholder in the family corporation.

Peter McGregor had led an active political career while his brothers were tending to the company business in Hooper. He was elected to the state senate in 1906 upon the completion of a term in the house.

Elected as a "Progressive" Republican and proclaiming himself an advocate of the direct primary, Peter McGregor had a change of thinking as the session progressed. His votes against the direct election of U.S. senators and for the elimination of state supreme court judges from the direct primary law won the bitter opposition of the Washington State Grange and the local Democratic paper, the Colfax *Commoner*. C. M. Kegley, master of the state grange, in 1909 sent state newspapers "An Open Letter: Addressed to the Voters of the State of Washington," in which he censured McGregor and the other senators who "voted against restoring to the people the nomination of judges to the supreme court": "What induced these senators, who are public servants, to repeal a vital and most important part of the direct primary law which took away from the people the supreme court nominations and placed the same in the hands of conventions where they can easily be controlled by special interests? Will you quietly submit to such an outrage of your political rights?" The president of the state direct primary league commented: "Shall we have a political oligarchy as dictator? [Peter McGregor and those who voted with him] have insulted every intelligent voter in the state of Washington. . . . Let us see that no man is elected again to any office in this state who refuses to assist in restoring the nominations of the supreme court judges to the people." McGregor's other votes were less controversial, although it was claimed that he switched his stands on many issues. The Colfax *Commoner* claimed that the "standpat" Republicans were guilty of "reckless extravagance" and "rank mismanagement of the state's affairs": "How much longer will the voters continue in power a party which, when they ask for bread, gives them a stone. . . . The Republican Party has ruthlessly broken the promises which it made to the voters."[47]

The political future did not look promising to Peter McGregor in 1910. U.S. Senator Levi Ankeny and several of Peter's other friends had been voted out of office. None of the bills McGregor had introduced in the 1909 session passed, although his proposal to authorize the state college experiment station to lease land for agricultural research had strong support. A modified version introduced in the house had been enacted. He had voted with the "insurgent" or "Progressive" wing of his party on some issues, in particular voting for the eight-hour day for women and for an investigation of alleged improprieties in the state insurance office and other state agencies. But in joining the "standpatters" on several issues, he was voting against a reform movement that had strong popular support. He decided not to run for reelection. The Colfax *Commoner* described the returns from the 1910 voting: "Their Waterloo: Standpat Republican Organization Overwhelmed. Progressives

Sweep State."[48] Peter McGregor continued in politics and public life after 1910 and was appointed by Washington governors to serve on the first State Tax Commission, the Western States Reclamation Association, and the first Columbia Basin Commission, a group that studied the possibilities of irrigating central Washington lowlands. During World War I, Peter McGregor also began sixteen years' service as a director of the Spokane branch of the Federal Reserve Bank of San Francisco. Ralph Snyder claimed that Peter had become a close associate of several Washington governors: "Pete was quite a politician. After he was elected to the senate, why he got in with the governors pretty well. There was a little group over there—Hartley and McGregor and, oh, there was four or five from eastern Washington. They really had more to say than those fellows they supported. This fellow from Everett, Hartley, and they run the state. By God, they were kind of an inner circle. And they had a lot to do."[49]

John McGregor's death during the nationwide flu epidemic of the winter of 1918 prompted the company shakeup and the return of Peter McGregor to active management. Alex, Peter, and Archie McGregor had to decide on a new manager for the McGregor Land and Livestock Company. Alex McGregor, the youngest of the three, had eighteen years' less experience in the family business than his brothers and did not compete actively for the post. But Archie and Peter McGregor became engaged in a bitter contest for the position of manager. The two men had been close friends during the open range days. But after the formation of the McGregor Land and Livestock Company in 1905, the relationship became strained. As Peter gained political success he became increasingly shrewd and aggressive. Archie, more emotional and less hardened, disliked his brother's prolonged absences from corporate affairs, disagreed with Peter over outside investments, and felt his brother neglected spiritual affairs and family gatherings. Archie claimed that the brothers had an understanding that he would be John's successor. To ensure his election to the post, Archie attempted to secure the support of Minnie McGregor, John's widow. But Minnie and Peter's wife Maude were sisters, and Archie claimed that Minnie was persuaded to change her mind at the last minute and vote for her brother-in-law. The dispute was resolved in 1919 by the choice of Peter as manager, Alex as vice-president, and Archie as president. Archie retired from active management after the selection, and he and Nellie spent much of their time in California. The decision to foreclose on the Hooper Realty Company mortgage saddled Archie with a large personal debt and caused a further deterioration of the relationship. Two years later, Archie was said to have confronted his brother with a choice of "I buy you out or you buy me out." Peter McGregor chose the latter alternative. In a letter describing the sale, McGregor secretary H. R. Rudd concluded: "The two brothers do not hitch very well in all business matters and neither would be willing to give the other an advantage if he could help it."

Only much later, when Archie and Peter were old men, did the friction between the two subside. In 1941, shortly after Peter's death and a few months before his own, Archie discussed their relationship:

> *Peter had softened wonderfully toward me in the last 6 or 7 years. We would talk . . . [about] life in the dear log cabin . . . [and] about our early days and how dependent we were on each other and how determined we were to make homes for the sweethearts we left in Canada. . . . Those old times were a soothing syrup to us in his last days. . . . I had lots of chats with him which did us both good. . . . He had his burden and I tried to tell him to forget all material things. He would get all he wanted while here. . . . Well, he said, maybe you will not. I told him I was happy and did not worry about that or anything else. . . . When I went to bid him farewell just before we left he said you can't wait for this and as we clasped hands he not only cried but sobbed. . . . Then I told him that he was going to get over his spell . . . that I heard mother say that people that cried did not die. . . . The word mother cheered him so that I could plainly see it. . . . Peter would have been 79 in May. I am 80 in March. It is useless. . . . Rest and comfort awaits us where there is no parting. . . .* [50]

The dispute between Archie and Peter and the death of John McGregor also indicated a serious weakness in the structure of McGregor Land and Livestock Company: The four successful businessmen did not have sons capable or interested in carrying on their ranching enterprise. The McGregor brothers were middle-aged men at the time of the management change in 1919: Archie was 58, Peter 57, and Alex C. 50. John had been 51 at the time of his death during the previous winter. Archie and Nellie had three daughters, Marie, Jessie, and Genevieve, and no sons. Alex C. and Jennie had three daughters, Mary, Helen, and Marjorie, and one son, thirteen-year-old Sherman. Peter and Maude's eldest son, twenty-five-year-old Maurice, planned to attend New York University after his discharge from the Marines. Their other child, twenty-two-year-old Alex T., had not shown the potential of becoming a successful ranch manager. John and Minnie had a daughter, Esther, and a twenty-one-year-old son, Donald, who had not distinguished himself while working in the store and herding cattle.

The four brothers had built a corporation that brought excellent profits for the stockholders during its first fifteen years of business. McGregor Land and Livestock Company had expanded its operations with great success and had consolidated control of extensive sheep ranges, wheat-producing areas, and even of a company town. The agricultural wealth left the Scotch–Canadians with the delightful task of using their new funds to advantage. But unforeseen problems were encountered: Speculation with personal assets hardly proved remunerative, the "respectability" that came with the wealth was a mixed blessing, and the successes exacerbated personal differences among the McGregor brothers. These problems, however, did not impair the economic structure of the McGregor ranching business, which was stronger than at any previous time in almost four decades of operation. The realigned company composed of Alex, Peter, and after 1923, Peter's son, Maurice, was to face far more serious obstacles during the next twenty years. The three men had to cope with two depressions that threatened the survival of the McGregor Land and Livestock Company and crippled agriculture throughout the West.

Chapter 8

Crisis and Change in Agriculture, 1920-40

"We have had . . . over a year now of the severest kind of deflation. In June 1920, wool was 50¢ against 15¢ now, wheat sold for $2.50 against 80¢ today, sheep brought 15¢ against 5¢ this fall, and cattle were 10¢ against 5¢ at the present time." H. R. Rudd, 1921

"I think a man is just as well off to be on one acre as ten thousand these times. The more acres, the more loss on everything." Maurice McGregor, 1931

"We are still operating but we haven't made a dollar for so long we don't know what one would look like. I still have a yen to . . . [travel] but if I went now I'd have to travel like the bonus marchers and live off the country when I got there. . . . Yes, the sun is going to shine again some day and I hope it isn't on an entirely new set of faces." Maurice McGregor, 1932 [1]

In August 1920, McGregor Land and Livestock Company herders coaxed, pushed, and shoved 9,600 fat lambs into more than fifty railroad cars at Springdale, a shipping point on the Washington summer range. Jock Macrae, traveling with the first of the two trainloads of lambs, wrote Peter McGregor from Minot, where the train stopped overnight and the sheep were fed: "Got here Friday—had a fine time and found the feed wonderful. . . . We took the Judge (an old Scotch-Canadian), the editor, and some more of the Big Guns of Minot out to the stock-yards to see the lambs and then to the coach where we spent a few hours of *real* time." The sheep arrived in good condition at Chicago, where Kay Wood (head of Wood Brothers, a livestock commission agency) spent several days arranging their sale. But the Chicago stockyards were overcrowded with sheep, and the market value of lamb had collapsed.

On August 14, H. R. Rudd described the results of the sale: "Sheep are not worth half what they were on March 1. We are making our usual shipments to Chicago this summer and during the past two weeks we have sustained a depreciation, due to a drop in the market, of over $30,000."

McGregor Land and Livestock also "took a licking" on its wool clip. Representatives from E. J. Burke and Company, Pendleton Woolen Mills, and other firms had gone to the McGregor shearing shed in the spring to inspect the quality of the 110,000-pound wool clip. Mel Fell, the Pendleton representative, was sent with instructions to buy the McGregor wool. But Fell, a novice in the business and cautious, decided he could not meet the price asked by the McGregors. His supervisors were irate, for they regarded the McGregor fleece as the best in the region, and Fell remembered that when he returned to Pendleton without the wool he found his job in jeopardy. The McGregor brothers were dissatisfied with all the bids and decided to hold the clip in hopes of higher prices. But the market collapsed, and in the fall of 1920 McGregors sold their wool for a loss. Mel Fell received a thousand-dollar, year-end bonus from his employers with a note attached: "For not buying the McGregor clip." Conditions did not improve during the winter of 1920–21. In January, F. J. Hagenbarth, president of the National Wool Growers Association, claimed that as a result of drought, severe winter storms, expensive feed, and an 80 percent drop in the value of wool, "every sheep in the West is mortgaged."[2]

The deflation of lamb and wool prices was followed by disastrous declines in the value of other farm products. McGregors described the results of their 1920 wheat harvest: "We were hit very hard at Hooper this year. . . . The crop all went to smut and on top of that the price dropped a dollar a bushel." H. R. Rudd wrote a letter pleading for railroad cars so the apple crop could be shipped east: "We are very hard up financially, our present crop of apples are still in the warehouse and we cannot get cars, this causing the apples to spoil on our hands." With "our business losing money every day," the McGregors urged those whose loans and grocery, hardware, farm machinery, clothing, automobile, and seed wheat bills had been carried on the company books to make payments: "We, like many other firms, are having a pretty hard time to make a go of it these days and we must ask those whom we helped in other days to aid us now." Many of the debtors were also in trouble: "I have been trying to get the money but there seems to be no demand for anything I have for sale." McGregor officials wrote creditors that "we simply haven't the money and can't get it." "If we ever needed money in our history," H. R. Rudd concluded, "it is today."[3]

A sudden and severe farm crisis had begun in the wake of the profitable wartime years of peak agricultural production. Wheat raisers and livestock producers had been urged to expand their businesses in order to supply food and clothing for a war-ravaged Europe. President Woodrow Wilson had even ordered a small flock of sheep grazed on the White House lawn to demonstrate the need for maximum production of wool and meat to supply the war effort. But the enormous foreign demand subsided when a peace agreement was concluded in 1919. Many European nations put up tariff barriers in order to spur the recovery of their own agricultural production. In November 1920, market prices for farm commodities "were 33 percent lower than the level of the previous year and by July, 1921 they were down 85 percent." Sheepmen were especially hard hit when huge quantities of wool, stockpiled by the government during the war, were released onto the market. Farm prosperity had suddenly been replaced by a period in which serious indebtedness, bankruptcy, foreclosures, and forced sales for delinquent taxes became common features of American agriculture. Henry C. Wallace, the U.S. Secretary of Agriculture, commented on the crisis in 1924: "The depression which began in 1920 was not merely a stretch of lean years. . . . It was a financial catastrophe. . . . So extreme and one-sided was the drop in prices that the farmers were unable to believe it could last. This mistake . . . aggravated the trouble. Farmers held on and in many cases borrowed money to pay interest and taxes and to meet current expenses. As the depression continued the load of debt increased. Many farmers became discouraged and turned over their property to creditors."[4]

The lowered prices and decreased purchasing power of agricultural products were symptomatic of fundamental changes in farming and ranching. James H. Shideler has described the market collapse of 1920 as a "turning point in the great economic, political, and social trends of agriculture": "It was a gulf between two worlds of American agriculture, an old world of soaring ambition resting upon expansion and land-value increment, and a new world of uncertainty distinguished by diversity, inequality, and contraction." Economist Earl Heady concluded that in 1920 "the basic woes of American agriculture had begun." Livestock and grain production had advanced more rapidly than domestic consumer demand, and glutted markets and huge stockpiles were to become typical features of the next two decades. Farmers and ranchers, long fearful of government intervention in production and marketing, by the early 1930's eagerly sought federal aid for the "farm problem." As individual farmers and ranchers tried to increase production in order to cut losses caused by lower prices, soil erosion and rangeland depletion joined farm surpluses as pressing problems. The interwar years were also a time of fundamental agricultural transformation, as industrial technology came to the farm and mechanical power replaced horse- and mule-powered grain production.[5] Economic survival during this period of depression and change would be a difficult matter.

Before the McGregor Land and Livestock Company management could worry about soil depletion, mechanization, and other long-range problems, they had to weather a sudden and precipitous decline in sales. The company had three active officials after Archie McGregor sold his stock in 1921—manager Peter McGregor, president Alex C. McGregor, and secretary H. R. Rudd, a former railroad engineer and long-time McGregor office manager. Their first goal was to revitalize the sheep business, the backbone of the corporate financial structure and an operation that had never failed to produce a profit. Severe economy measures were taken to minimize losses. Peter McGregor and other Washington Wool Growers Association directors advised sheepmen to make a concerted stand to reduce herders' wages from one hundred to seventy-five dollars per month. As the financial crisis worsened, the McGregors and other sheepmen made an additional reduction to fifty dollars. Wool Growers Association secretary J. F. Sears reported to Peter McGregor in 1921 that "we have had advice from several [sheepmen] that they made wage cut announcement to their men and that no opposition has resulted."

Sixty-five-year-old sheep foreman Jock Macrae and his younger assistant, Lee Burden, drove cars, teams, and walked from band to band inspecting the progress of the sheep and checking to see that all herders kept expenses to an absolute minimum. In small things as well as large, herders were expected to be careful and frugal. Emile Morod remembered that herders were required to sweep up traces of salt spilled from salt licks. Broken fences and gates were tied together with baling wire—their replacement postponed until economic conditions improved. The health of the ewes and lambs in each band was watched closely, and losses of lambs and ewes through inattention or indifference were not tolerated. One herder was getting only a 70 percent return of lambs per ewe because, it was said, he was lazy and paid little attention to his band. When he was replaced by Emile Morod, the determined Frenchman was able to almost double the percentage. Most herders understood quite well why they were being asked to work harder for less pay—they read the trade journals and knew that a drop in wool price from forty-two to thirteen cents in a single year threatened the entire industry. Macrae often wrote the McGregors from the summer range to describe the accomplishments of the herders during this critical time: "Brown and Daniels certainly deserve credit for their sheep. . . . They are certainly looking fine. I think there will be nothing can beat that bunch." The McGregor families became close friends with Morod and other sheep employees whose competence and hard work were crucial to the survival of their business. When Scotch herder John Hood left for his native land a few years later, he wrote the Hooper office: "Never in my life will I forget your kindness, all of you. The way you MacGregors opened your doors, received me into your families as if I had been a life long friend instead of a paid worker was wonderful. I earnestly hope some day—if not in this country, it will be in my own—I will be able to return just a little."[6]

While the herders tended the flocks, corporation officials watched national and international wool and lamb markets. The Babson Statistical Organization of Massachusetts and other economic specialists were asked about "the probability of the wool market going up in the next six months." Peter McGregor traveled to Washington, D.C., to testify before government committees about "the financial indigestion the wool market is suffering." Veterinarians and agricultural experiment station researchers were consulted if lambs became diseased or failed to gain weight fast enough. Wool buyers were reminded of the "strong, healthy staple" produced by McGregor sheep, a value-worthy produce even during "the great stagnation through which the wool market is passing." The longevity and stability of the McGregor sheep business worked to the advantage of the corporation during the depression of the early 1920's and subsequent years. "This outfit," wrote Peter McGregor in 1928, "has been improving its breeding herd for forty years and very few ewes in the Northwest are as good." The McGregors had built a reputation over many years for good-quality lamb and wool, and this helped ease the crisis of the early twenties. In August 1920, for example, one Chicago commission merchant wrote: "When we quote ewes and wethers at these prices, you can always figure yours will bring 50¢ to $1 cwt. more, as they always have, and I guess they always will, as they are worth more than the others that come here." But no matter how much the McGregors promoted the quality of their sheep, drastic measures were necessary at a time when industry spokesmen found prices "so low that the entire industry will be and is badly crippled." The McGregors' gross receipts from lamb and wool sales declined from $138,000 in 1919 to $108,000 in 1920 and $62,000 a year later. By cutting operating costs to an absolute minimum, the McGregors and their foremen were able to reduce expenditures accordingly—from $91,000 to $76,000, and then $49,000. When the McGregors added taxes and general ranch expenses to the operating statements of the sheep division, the return was modest—$14,000 in 1921 and less than $7,000 in 1922. But the corporation made money at a time when bankruptcies and forced sales brought an end to many sheep businesses and caused a marked decline in national wool and lamb output.[7]

Aggressive and assertive Peter McGregor, the largest stockholder in the corporation after his dispute with elder brother Archie, was one of the most persistent Washington sheepmen in the struggle to cut operating costs and in the fight for tariff protection for wool, a commodity that had been on the "free list" since 1913. By 1922, lower national wool and lamb protection put the McGregors and other surviving producers in a position for rapid recovery. Sheepmen also credited the Fordney Emergency Tariff Bill of 1921, which placed a 15 cent per pound ("grease" weight) duty on foreign wool, with helping spur the recovery. By the spring of 1922, Peter McGregor, chairman of the Taxation Committee of the Washington Wool Growers Association, and his associates were urging sheepmen to keep quiet about improving market conditions:

> The press is always anxious for news and is willing to give prominence to the come-back of any market. We are afraid too much publicity is going to the public regarding the sheep and wool market, especially in view of the fact that your Taxation Committee and officers are doing all they can to lower taxes, freight rates, shearing and labor expenses, and charges on leased lands. It is only proper that the sheepmen be thoroughly familiar with the values but usually the public exaggerates these things and in view of all the circumstances, probably the best thing we can do now is to keep quiet about prices, work hard and reduce expenses to the lowest possible point and endeavor to recover some of the losses of the past two years.[8]

As they struggled to keep their sheep business solvent, Alex and Peter McGregor and H. R. Rudd had to improve and strengthen the other operations of the diverse farm corporation. The McGregors and other Columbia Plateau wheat raisers faced what an observer described as "a stiff struggle against overwhelming odds." W. E. Leonard studied wheat farming in southeastern Washington and found that, during the early 1920's, "only one principle seemed to hold with regularity—prices were low when the major part of the growers' wheat had to be marketed." The average per bushel price received by Washington farmers dropped from $2.60 in June 1920 to $1.35 in December, and a yearly per bushel average of $.92 in 1921, $.96 in 1922, and $.85 in 1923. The McGregors bought no new machinery or work animals, and the policy of making extensive improvements on the farmland every year was quickly abandoned. Wages were cut. Favorable weather eliminated expensive reseeding costs. Credit, once easily available to tenants for merchandise, insurance, farm machinery, and other commodities, was severely restricted. H. R. Rudd explained the reason for refusing to finance the widow of long-time tenant E. L. Jeremiah in a letter to one of her creditors: "From time to time we have advanced money to Mrs. Jeremiah to help her with outside bills but there was no surplus after her wheat was sold this year and we could not help her any more under existing financial conditions."[9] During 1921, the worst year of the crisis, McGregors cut their expenses on tenant farms by 43 percent and on their own wheat "ranch" by 54 percent.

Faced with declining foreign demand for grain and oversupplied national wheat markets, the McGregor corporation devised new ways to maximize returns. Much of the wheat raised on the McGregor ranch was fed to hogs. A complex formula was used to compute returns on the investment, based on the idea that four and a half pounds of wheat would produce one pound of pork. The experiment was marred at the outset, when sixty-three hogs died from cholera despite the efforts of Washington State College veterinarians. But after this initial difficulty, the McGregors found that feeding wheat to pigs could bring greater returns than selling the grain for human consumption.

The McGregor management sought to gain further income by becoming involved in grain merchandising. H. R. Rudd admitted that "we are greenhorns at the cash grain business and about all we know is to take it in and load it out again." But the corporation rapidly took control of the local grain trade, purchasing most of the wheat grown within a radius of ten miles of Hooper and selling the grain in bulk carload shipments to exporting firms. More than two hundred thousand bushels of grain were handled during the 1920 season alone. By shrewdly watching foreign and domestic wheat prices and contracting several months in advance, the McGregors twice were able to make a profit while the purchasing corporations, Pacific Grain Company and Interior Warehouse Company, a division of Balfour, Guthrie of San Francisco, bore the brunt of a rapidly declining wheat market. By trading grain, feeding hogs, and keeping expenditures to an absolute minimum, the McGregors were able to make money in the wheat business in 1921. But the future of raising wheat was not promising.[10]

Profitable cash grain sales became increasingly difficult to conclude in subsequent years, as high production costs and continued low wheat prices made farmers desperate and exporters wary. The tenant farms were proving unprofitable to both landlord and lessee by 1922. By cutting down maintenance and repairs and restricting credit, McGregor Land and Livestock had recorded a ten-thousand-dollar operating profit from rented farmland the previous year. But the tenants became desperate, and cash outlays were necessary to keep the farmland in production. An eight-thousand-dollar loss on the rented land in 1922 wiped out the modest gains the McGregors had made on their own wheat operations. Added evidence of continuing troubles for the McGregors, their renters, and other Columbia Plateau wheat growers were the increasing number of farm foreclosures. In Whitman and Walla Walla counties alone, fifteen farmers lost their properties in 1921, more than twenty in 1922, and forty-five a year later. The McGregors would have to make major changes in their wheat-raising operation in the near future.

While the livestock and grain trades suffered from oversupplied markets and declining commodity prices, the McGregor store, headed by Alex C. McGregor, took up much of the slack. In 1920, merchandise sales surpassed $200,000 and accounted for more than half the volume of business done by the corporation. Sales declined in the next few years, but net income increased and reached almost $30,000 in 1924. Between 1920 and 1924 the store earned $100,000, almost two-thirds of the earnings of the entire corporation. In 1922, store earnings of $26,000 offset an $8,500 loss from the other branches of the McGregor Land and Livestock Company. But much of the business had been done on credit, and the large number of outstanding merchandise accounts threatened the survival of the entire McGregor corporation. Recognizing that many of the accounts "will have to be collected by fragments," the McGregors accepted payments as small as five dollars from farmers, ranchers, laborers, doctors, state legislators, and other eastern Washington residents with outstanding store bills. But those who were unable or unwilling to make even small payments or who moved without leaving forwarding addresses were pursued by McGregor lawyers and taken to court. Mortgages were foreclosed and wages were garnisheed. By 1923 most of the back accounts had been repaid.[11]

The McGregor Land and Livestock Company had varying degrees of success with their assorted other businesses. The Fireman's Fund Insurance Company of San Francisco commented in 1920 on the new policies sold by the Hooper corporation: "We are delighted to know that the McGregor Land and Livestock Company have such a fine lot of grain policies this season." The McGregor company was also able to receive incidental additional income by operating the Hooper post office, selling railroad tickets, and miscellaneous other activities. The "West End," the division of the company that raised apples, grew hay for the company livestock, and handled town maintenance, was a perennial loser. In 1920 Peter McGregor gave John McGregor's young son, Donald, the unenviable task of supervising an operation that had been saddled traditionally with all miscellaneous upkeep and repair for the corporation. A year later, when no progress had been made, Peter leased the alfalfa fields, orchards, and gardens to Donald and his wife Ruth and promised to provide teams of workhorses and wood for irrigation flumes. McGregor Land and Livestock agreed to purchase hay at the going price and pay Donald a two-thousand-dollar annual bonus for operating the irrigated ground. Town maintenance would be handled by a separate crew. An exceptionally able operator might have revamped the West End and made it a going concern. But Donald, an alcoholic and a poor manager, lasted only a year before leaving the corporation to become a movie producer and photographer.

The West End was again under direct company control after Donald's departure, and closer supervision minimized the losses. But this division continued to have some problems. When the apple orchards became infested with "aphis wooley," red spider, scale, and other pests, the McGregors consulted the State Department of Agriculture for advice and paid the head of the state college horticulture department to make an inspection. The horticulturalist advised use of a simple (but ineffective) insecticide for the spiders: "Throw ice water on the apples." A few years later, apples treated against disease "showed too much arsenic to be reassuring." "I think, however," wrote H. R. Rudd, "that if the sorters wipe every apple with their gloves they will get by" state inspection. Despite the occasional problems with the apple crops, the West End was able to perform successfully its most important task— the production of large hay crops for the McGregor sheep.[12]

While collecting back accounts and employing more efficient methods of management, the McGregors delayed payment of their own debts as long as possible. H. R. Rudd explained the situation to creditors in 1921: "We are loathe to disappoint you at such a time . . . but . . . we have borrowed up to our legal limit at the bank and besides the bank has entire supervision and absolutely refuses to put up any money except for the immediate necessities of the operation of our business." Land purchase agreements with the Northern Pacific Railway fell into arrears, and H. R. Rudd wrote Western Land Agent G. H. Plummer in 1921 that "we are not going to be able to make the payments this fall and must ask that you cancel our contract." Plummer, a man involved in sales of 27,000 acres to the corporation in earlier years, expressed confidence in the durability of the McGregor company: "We realize the condition of the livestock industry—that all funds are needed to carry on the business, and we want to help." Plummer agreed to continue the contract without interest.

But even the emergency economy measures employed by Peter and Alex McGregor and H. R. Rudd would have been insufficient without the active assistance and cooperation of the Exchange National Bank of

Spokane. Bank president E. T. Coman and vice-president E. E. Flood had handled the McGregor business for a decade, and by 1918 they had recognized it as "one of the best, if not the best and strongest" accounts the bank had ever had. The bankers became close friends of the McGregors and visited the ranch for a "Rocky Mountain oyster fry" every spring. The relationship was also advantageous to the bankers, for Alex and Peter McGregor were stockholders in the Spokane bank, and Peter was a director of the branch of the Federal Reserve Bank that served the Columbia Plateau. The McGregors had been cautious during the wartime prosperity and thus avoided the problems of sheepmen who had borrowed heavily, only to have worried bankers call in the loans after the market collapse.[13]

During the spring of 1920, before the drastic deflation of livestock and grain values, McGregors could count on letters similar to the following receiving a sympathetic response from bank officials: "In a very short time we expect to have sufficient funds to cover the overdraft which must now appear on our account on your books, and unless you advise us differently we shall let the matter rest until we can send you the deposit [of the proceeds] from our wool." But the increased financial needs of the McGregor corporation and the low prices of lamb, wool, wheat, and beef soon made the bankers more cautious about the Mc-Gregor account. Bank president E. T. Coman described a meeting with one of the McGregors in January 1921:

> *I had a talk with Mr. Peter McGregor with reference to the average balance of McGregor Land and Livestock. It is our customary requirement . . . to require a 20% balance. . . . We compromised on 15%. We are hopeful that the profits of McGregor Land and Livestock will be of such a substantial character that they will accede . . . [to our wishes]. I am glad to know of the reelection of the old officers of the company, which is an assurance that the management will rest in the same conservative hands.*

A week after the meeting with Peter McGregor, a bank official wrote H. R. Rudd: "According to our records, a line of $100,000 was granted to you a short time ago. The $30,000 notes bring the amount of your obligations up to $105,000." McGregors were able to gain further concessions from the Exchange Bank, for on January 22 they were told, "$120,000 is the limit. . . . If your requirements go beyond this we would ask that you give us a note of one of the other companies [i.e., Hooper Realty or Taylor Land and Livestock]." By March 1921, the wool and lamb markets had improved somewhat, and the McGregors expressed appreciation for the "help of the Exchange Bank in the crucial period just passed."[14]

If signs of life were visible in the sheep markets of 1921, two years later it was apparent, in the words of Maurice McGregor, that "all sheep products [had] staged a spectacular and sustained recovery." Mills processed their stockpiles of wool, lamb was again in demand, and prospects were "very bright for good, strong markets." Maurice, the eldest son of Peter and Maude McGregor, had returned to Hooper in 1923 to assist his father and uncle Alex after doing graduate work in finance at New York University. Writing several years later, he remembered that since "the first return of national prosperity and increased buying power" after the postwar slump, "the public taste for lamb has seemed to increase resulting in continuously good demand and comparatively high prices so that until . . . 1929 the industry as a whole was prosperous." As the market strengthened, the sheep business began a decade of expansion. Many western cattlemen, discouraged by continued sluggish beef markets, decided to become woolgrowers. As the national cattle population decreased, the number of sheep in the United States climbed from 35 million to 52 million in less than ten years. Although the McGregors had once had what was said to be the ninth largest cattle herd in the state—about five hundred head—the men had not distinguished themselves as cattle raisers. After losing money on cattle for nine out of seventeen years, by 1924 the McGregors had liquidated all their cattle and devoted the use of their rangeland exclusively to sheep.[15]

McGregor Land and Livestock officials took maximum advantage of the improving sheep markets by following the procedure Peter McGregor and other directors of the Washington Wool Growers Association had recommended: "Keep quiet about prices, work hard, and reduce expenses to the lowest possible level." In 1926, the men participated in a successful effort to secure rebates on railroad shipping charges to Chicago markets. Two years later, when the Interstate Commerce Commission (ICC) held hearings on railroad requests for a 40 percent advance in livestock shipping rates, Peter McGregor asked the president of the American Farm Bureau to investigate, warning him that "this advance if granted would ruin the livestock industry of the western states." Peter McGregor, C. L. Mackenzie, J. F. Sears, and other Washington sheepmen traveled east and explained the hazards of the sheep business to the committee:

> The sheep business is a hazardous occupation. Throughout the twelve month period a careful sheep operator frequently has a five percent loss. . . . A few years ago one of our range sheepmen put 1500 yearling ewes

on his summer range in the Colville country. During the summer they came in contact with a field of poison weeds and within a period of 24 hours 1200 head of them died. Many sheepmen have had experiences similar to this but perhaps in a much lesser degree. It is not an infrequent occurrence for a man with a band of 1200 ewes to lose 100 or 200 of them from coming in contact with poison weeds during the summer or fall months, or from a cold rain immediately following shearing, or a heavy snow storm with a severe wind driving the sheep to what we call a "pile up." Now these are things that happen to experienced operators with experienced help and proper equipment. Scab, foot rot, compaction, and many other things cause losses for those who are inexperienced and also sometimes for those who are experienced. Under these conditions it can readily be understood that the sheep business is a much more hazardous undertaking than any other line of endeavor in the livestock industry. . . . Let the price of lambs drop to a point where they net the grower less than ten cents per pound at shipping point and let wool drop to a point where it nets less than thirty cents at shipping point and there is not one sheep outfit in 20 in the state of Washington that can make any money and 20 percent of them will go out of business.

Peter McGregor presented a detailed summary of the 1921–27 earnings of McGregor Land and Livestock to the ICC on the theory that "the very modest return on investment (5½ percent) that is made by one of the oldest and best outfits in the country would be pretty good evidence that sheepmen have not been going through any period of wild prosperity since the deflation of 1920." In evaluating their earnings in this successful attempt to prevent railroad rate increases, the McGregors added taxes, managerial pay, and other general expenses to their usual departmental earnings figures, which were based merely on gross receipts less operating expense, payroll, leases, and supplies. The annual return of less than 6 percent on the value of tens of thousands of acres of grazing land (see Appendix 3) was not spectacular, particularly when compared with the prosperous years of World War I.[16] But farming and ranching seldom brought huge returns on the value of land and equipment, and the numbers indicated that the sheep business had once again become a steady, dependable source of income.

Close supervision and a crew of able employees had made it possible to rebuild the McGregor sheep business. Peter McGregor had not exaggerated when he told the ICC that sheep raising was a hazardous enterprise. McGregor sheepman Emile Morod remembered that "them God damned sheep find a thousand ways to die." Herman Oliver, an Oregon sheep raiser who decided to abandon the trade, explained the problems he had encountered: "Eventually foot rot took us out of the sheep business. We could control the flukes and all the other diseases, but foot rot beat us. So wildcats, coyotes, dogs, cold rains, poison weeds, liver flukes, and the herd instinct of sheep all combined to give us trouble. Cattle aren't quite so likely to die from either disease or herd disasters but . . . fluctuating prices can change a man from rich to poor almost overnight."

Sheep raising, more than any other ranching or farming business, required trained, hard-working crews. Sheepmen who were able to hire and keep competent foremen, herders, camptenders, night men, and other employees were able to avoid many of the trade's hazards. Thomas J. Drumheller, Jr., a member of a Big Bend sheep-raising family with nine bands and 110,000 acres of range, found a capable crew the most important element of success during the interwar years:

> It takes experience around sheep, that's for sure. . . . I've gone clear to Spokane and taken herders from there up into the High Cascades and some of them pretty nearly beat me back to town. I've come back out and had them right behind me. I don't know how sheepmen avoided committing some kind of crime on those fellows. . . .
>
> But in earlier days we had a crew that took pride in their work. Our losses in the summer would be anywhere from 20 to maybe up to 35 in a band. The fella that had 34 was really apologetic about it and felt pretty bad. But in later years if I could keep it under 100 I was really happy. . . . It wasn't so much that the fellas didn't try but they just didn't know sheep. . . . In earlier days in the mountains the camptender would go out and cut the trail to the next camp. First thing he'd do when you move the sheep would be to go back and see if any sheep had gone back to the last bedgrounds. Most of the fellows were awfully good about looking for the sheep. That's why the losses weren't there. When you hunt sheep all your life you learn there's certain things they are liable to do. They don't always do it—you find 'em everyplace. But most of them will go to the top of a ridge unless they've been out quite awhile or they'll try to get where they are somewhat protected from varmits and coyotes. But I've also seen little bunches that go right down to water near where they've been unloaded . . . clear back to the ferry boat if you'd let 'em. The trick was finding 'em before they were out too long.

The well-managed Drumheller sheep operation was able to prosper despite sheep losses from scours (acute diarrhea), "stiff lambs," mastitis, botulism, and other problems.[17]

McGregor Land and Livestock Company officials constantly sought ways to upgrade their sheep production techniques. A botanist from Washington State College spent a month in 1926 analyzing the McGregor winter range and making recommendations about proper grazing methods. A veterinarian hired for the 1927 lambing season gave herders instructions on how to treat ewes that had difficulty giving birth:

Inject sterile camphorated oil—2cc. under skin . . . as stimulant

Lubricant—made with: carbolic acid—one ounce

                            oil eucalyptus—one ounce

                            light mineral—one gallon

                            rub on hands while pulling lambs

Burn carcasses—if not burned cover 10 carcasses with 4 pounds chloride
of lime

To return womb—dissolve level teaspoon chloral hydrate in 4 oz. water
and give as an injection. . . . Wait half hour . . . return
womb. Take a couple of stitches. Keep [sheep] with
head down.

For maggots—2 oz. Lysol

                       14 oz. coal oil

                       Shake well and apply to [affected] parts once daily.

C. M. Hubbard, an extension specialist in livestock from the state agri-cultural experiment station, assisted in culling McGregor sheep to in-crease the size of the wool clip. The herders were culled as well: The annual sheep tally books kept by Emile Morod included an analysis of the abilities of each member in the thirty- to forty-man crew—e.g., "good," "no good—quit," "too old," "very good."[18]

The herder's job remained a lonely, demanding one, both on the scab-land winter range and on the rough, mountainous summer pastures. Jock Macrae, Lee Burden, and Macrae's newest assistant, Emile Morod, visited the herders and, when on the summer range, wrote the Hooper office to keep the McGregors informed of their activities. Macrae wrote in 1929 of herder Bunyan C. Lee, who had had a heart attack when running up a hill after stray sheep: "Well, by the time you get this B. C. Lee will be under the sod. . . . Dr. Thompson said he was as good as dead when he arrived. . . . Selected a lot as near as I could to [the grave of veteran herder] Anton Roble so they could have company at the midnight hours. . . . Too bad I couldn't be at the funeral but I can't get away as I am having all I can attend to."

Herders frequently wrote directly to the company office to explain their problems. The following are samples of letters from herders Sidney Lenthal, W. A. Crawford, Claude Carleton, L. C. Bigelow, E. E. Page, and others:

Princeton, Idaho, May 31: *I got here with my band of sheep and will stay 8–10 days on 18 pieces of 40 acres [each], plenty water and feed to rest up lambs before I go on range toward Bovill. We made the trip all right, only was awfully hot and hard on sheep, too many bands was ahead of me. Now, please, I like to have my wages up to 1st of May. Dan S. Mann.*

Avon [Idaho] July 19: *I have a lot of stiff lambs. I had them in a farmers pasture but the pasture has gave out. I wonder if you could send the truck up to get them as it is impossible to herd them in the band without losing them. There is 13 head . . . can haul them in the small truck. P. S. everything else is setting purty. Claude Carleton.*

Springdale, Wash., Aug. 8: *We have 25 or 30 lambs in our herd, blind from gnats and they follow the herd only by sound. . . . The blind ones would follow up better if we had more bells. . . . Will you send us some. . . . We need a pair of old sheep shears too. C. A. Jensen.*

Bovill, Idaho, Aug. 22: *The sheep are fine and dandy except a few stiff lambs. . . . The [fat] lambs [were] loaded out yesterday . . . shipped 1500 lambs and no ewes. . . . We are at the separating corrells [sic] as yet will start to Moose Creek tomorrow morning. . . . We have 1548 left in the band yet. Bill and Sidney.*

Loon Lake, Wash., 8/29: *Moved the sheep over to Pend Orielle [sic] county Sec. 22T31N where there is plenty of water and feed. . . . We have been feeding this range for a number of years but this year we found another band of sheep on the same section owned by Mr. Omen of Chewelah. E. E. Page.*

Camped on Smith Medows [sic], Avon [Idaho] Sept. 2: *I miss informed [sic] you about the sheep as the lambs are picking up some and the ewes are looking fine. . . . I counted them and that gave me a good chance to look them over. . . . We are out 8 or 10 can't count for but coyotes are pretty bad tho' we can hold out for some time yet. Have been out all afternoon looking for water and feed . . . found plenty. . . . Everything is satisfactory. H. A. Crawford.*

Usk [Washington] Sept. 7: *I am on the way out with the sheep and am badly in need of funds. L. C. Bigelow.*

Garfield [Washington] Oct. 11: *I stopped on Mr. Millers place—100 acre peas, 80 a. wheat stubble and Palouse River running through place—sure is a good place for every fall . . . if you can get me a letter to Garfield [include] a check for $100. Crawford.*[19]

The herders lost sheep to some of the dangers that had always beset the trade: A sudden storm after shearing killed 274 ewes in 1924; two years later, 125 head were killed when they "piled up" against a log while fleeing in panic from lightning during an evening rainstorm on the Spokane Indian Reservation; and a forty-thousand-acre forest fire resulted in some death losses during another season. But despite the peculiar nature of sheep and the vagaries of weather, the flocks generally remained in good condition. In March 1927, for example, the McGregors reported: "Lambing is going very well. Ewes in good condition and lots of grass and water will make a good percentage this year." Maurice McGregor wrote his uncle Archie two months later: "Shearing is finished. The clip was unusually good both for staple and shrinkage and the average weight, a little over twelve pounds, was satisfactory." During the 1920's, McGregor Land and Livestock was able to register slow but significant improvements in fleece size, lambing percentage, and number of "fat" lambs ready for slaughter.[20]

By 1925, Maurice McGregor had begun taking over many of the management duties of the sheep business that were once handled by his father and uncles. Fellow rancher Ralph Snyder remembered Maurice as an enthusiastic worker, eager to learn about innovative methods of ranching and farming but also cautious and careful in directing his family's business. Maurice gave the company the badly needed stability that the other young second-generation McGregors, Alex T. and Donald, lacked. One of Maurice's first responsibilities was to purchase good breeding stock. He bought high-quality Rambouillet and Hampshire bucks from the Idaho Agricultural Experiment Station and other breeders of registered sheep. He also strengthened the company's ties with wool and lamb buyers and took over the job of leasing the hundred thousand acres of summer range used by the McGregor flocks every year. Maurice and Jock Macrae maintained a close working relationship with Indian reservation and U.S. Department of the Interior officials, one of whom wrote the McGregors that "your company has proven an entirely satisfactory tenant." To secure an additional strategic tract of land, Maurice promised a friend: "If you can talk those people into letting me have that pasture for $100, I'll buy you the best suit of clothes Archie McLeod has in his shop." Maurice took over from his predecessors what he called the "monkey business" of evading the 640-acre limit on state land leases by signing up Spokane tailor Archie McLeod, doctors, dentists, sheepherders, family friends, and anyone else willing to sign grazing leases on behalf of McGregor Land and Livestock Company. His father Peter, meanwhile, chaired a Washington Wool Growers committee that protested the decision to close Idaho national forests to sheep and successfully "took up with the Forest Department at Washington the question of the damage to timber from grazing with the hope that the ruling of the Department may be rescinded."[21]

After lambs had been fattened on the summer ranges, one of the McGregors—Peter, Alex C., Maurice, or Sherman (Alex's young son, who worked summers in Hooper while studying for a journalism degree at Washington State College) rode with the sheep on the train to Chicago. Notes for four days from Maurice's log of one such trip in 1923 illustrate some of the problems faced en route.

> *Aug. 4—finished loading 8:02. Left Springdale 8:30. At Deer Park stopping 20 min. find two car ends slightly jammed [with sheep]. Mac [Jock Macrae] broke seal, went in and straightened them. . . . Mac bawls out engineer for slamming cars. . . . Mac and I make bunks in caboose. Drunk.*

> *Aug. 5—Arr. 7:00 Whitefish [Montana] . . . unloaded . . . one dead . . . on lower deck and smelling high . . . baled hay and alfalfa good . . . scattered out in small bunches . . . clean out rotten water 4:30 PM start loading. Leave Whitefish 9:00. Have our own caboose.*

> *Aug. 7—Arr. 3:30 New Brighton. Water troughs too high and too old. [Railroad] crew upon being requested to change—insolent— tell us to look after it ourselves. Start loading 2:30 PM. Arr. Minneapolis 6:00. . . . Cars were not sealed at New B. Negligence of agent.*

Herder John Hood described arriving in Chicago on one of the sheep trains: "I think Sherman and I passed O.K. in the Union Stock Yards as big sheepmen from the Northwest. At least we did our best."

Jock Macrae was the most effective drover on the McGregor sheep trains. He often represented himself as the owner of the sheep, not the foreman, and insisted that his train of lambs be given the utmost attention. Newspaper columnists interviewed the veteran sheepmen about "his" ranching operations at the various stations where the sheep were unloaded and fed. Macrae issued orders to section hands, stockyard operators, and anyone else responsible for the welfare of the sheep. Once when the railroad crew refused to provide him a new caboose or suitable sheep feed, he wired the president of the Great Northern and threatened never to ship his vast herds on that line again unless the problems were remedied within 24 hours. Eight hours later he found a brand new drovers coach and an excellent stock of hay waiting for him at the next stockyards. The McGregors wisely allowed Macrae to portray himself as the big ranch owner from the Northwest, for the close attention he gave to the trains ensured that the stock would arrive in Chicago in excellent shape.[22]

The "big sheepmen from the Northwest" were met at the stockyards by representatives of Wood Brothers, the commission firm with which the McGregors had dealt for many years. Kay Wood and Ed Spain assured the Hooper sheepmen that they would give the trainloads of sheep "the most intensive attention" and would act "as we would do if we owned the lambs." Good market demand, the favorable quality of the McGregor sheep, and a harmonious working arrangement with the commission firm helped ensure excellent returns from the Chicago sales. In August 1926, for example, Wood Brothers described the sale of one train of McGregor sheep in the *Livestock Market Digest*: "We sold for the McGregor Land and Livestock Company of Washington this week range lambs from $14.10 to $14.45, which is the extreme top of the market on killing lambs." During the following August, Kay Wood wrote Peter McGregor about a newly arrived load of McGregor sheep: "We are all on tiptoes about these lambs as from the reports I hear of them they are about as good as any that will come out of Washington this season." The lambs were sold two days later, and Ed Spain informed McGregors of the results: "Your sale at $14.50 represents the extreme top of the market. . . . This is undoubtedly one of the finest strings of lambs shipped to Chicago this year and we are exceedingly happy to have them strike such a good market. . . . The packers tried hard to get us to sort some of the heavies off, but we fought such a move to such an extent that we were able to get around it." Kay Wood wrote the McGregor Land and Livestock Company about the sale:

> *Your telegram received this morning was very much an inspiration to our organization. Your sale was not only 15 cents above everything else on the market . . . and we had around 55 cars of Western lambs on the market the day before yesterday and about as many yesterday . . . but it was also the highest price obtained for any lambs since July.*
>
> *But the thing which gratified me the most was the fact that our success in handling your business makes even more possible the lovely relationship which has maintained with your family and myself now for a term of years, which I know would be somewhat marred should the ability to handle your business right not be in evidence.*[23]

With steadily improving commodity prices, capable employees, and experienced managers, the McGregor sheep operation was again sound and profitable. Wheat farming, on the other hand, was in poor health in the wake of the postwar agricultural depression. Foreign and domestic grain markets were glutted with wheat, farm labor was expensive, crops were heavily damaged by disease, and soils were becoming seriously depleted. F. J. Sievers and H. F. Holtz of the Washington Agricultural Experiment Station studied wheat raising on the Columbia Plateau in 1922 and found that "the evidence is conclusive that the present system of agriculture does not make for permanency." McGregor Land and Livestock had made a big investment in the continued success of grain farming. Almost 11,000 acres of McGregor sheep range had been converted into wheat fields by 1922. A 6,400-acre wheat farm, twenty miles south of the main ranch, across the Snake River in Columbia County, was acquired a year later. About 1,200 acres of the Bar U Ranch, eight miles north of Hooper, was planted in wheat every year. The stopgap measures employed during the crisis of 1920 and 1921 had merely postponed the need for a major reorganization of the McGregor wheat business.

Tenant farmers on the McGregor ranch, and elsewhere on the plateau, were in desperate trouble by 1923. Farmers with owned land could weather a few bad years, but tenants had less risk-carrying ability and quickly ran short of operating capital. Banks were reluctant to extend credit to the operators of rented property, and the McGregor corporation agreed to make advances to cover farming costs in exchange for crop mortgages and other securities. G. R. Hendrickson, a tenant described by the McGregors as "a good farmer . . . [who] has produced good crops on his small place," used first his farm livestock, then his crop, machinery, and finally one milk cow for security on loans from the corporation. The McGregors assisted renter John Banks by providing loans and improving the cropland and house on his farm. But Banks had lost money since 1921, and the efforts of the corporation did little to improve the outlook for his farming business. H. R. Rudd presented an unsympathetic description of Banks's plight: "John Banks is discouraged, as well as several other ranchers down this way . . . his morale is all shot to the devil and we will have to humor him. . . . Why in order to keep his wife and himself in fairly good humor we spent nearly $2000 remodeling and renovating the place where they now live but if there is any gratitude shown for our efforts I have failed to notice same."[24]

By 1923, two of the tenants owed almost $20,000 each to McGregor Land and Livestock, another owed $15,000, and the rest had similar obligations with no relief in sight. Two years later, the last tenant was gone from the McGregor ranch. Some had declared bankruptcy. Others sold all their farm equipment and personal properties to McGregor Land and Livestock to cover debts incurred through loans, store bills, and harvest expenses. The corporation terminated the leases of the few remaining renters and foreclosed mortgages on their crops, livestock, and farm equipment. Tenants left without money or property. The McGregor company was able to recoup some of its losses through foreclosures and complicated court proceedings. But several unpaid bills, one for $19,000, remained as evidence of the difficulties of small acreage farming during a period of depressed markets and high operating costs.[25]

The McGregor farming business was beset by other troubles, as well.

Speculation in the wheat "futures" market in 1924 and 1925 brought indifferent returns and a change in management. H. R. Rudd, the McGregor secretary for a decade, invested personally in the grain trade and also handled corporate expenditures on the Seattle and Portland wheat markets. But fellow officers Alex C. and Peter McGregor found that successful transactions were credited to Rudd's personal account, while losing ventures were charged to the McGregor Land and Livestock Company. Rudd was asked to look for another job, and in 1926 thirty-two-year-old Maurice McGregor replaced him as company secretary. Further losses were encountered on farmlands acquired in exchange for the properties of the Hooper Realty Company, the irrigation firm organized in 1917 by three McGregor brothers. Alex and Archie McGregor had already lost tens of thousands of dollars in personal funds by the McGregor Land and Livestock foreclosure on a mortgage that covered the ditch properties.

The corporation had similar difficulties after acquiring the land from the defunct Hooper Realty Company. Despite repeated attempts to sell the property, few buyers were willing to make solid offers during a period of deflated agricultural prices. When Theodore Grote, a farmer from the Columbia County town of Starbuck, offered to exchange 6,400 acres of excellent wheat land (subject to a $110,000 mortgage) for the old irrigation property, H. R. Rudd and Peter McGregor eagerly arranged the trade. Grote also purchased the "Wood Gulch ranch," a section and a half of wheat land regarded by the company as "rough and inaccessible." Conscious of "the apparent low state of Mr. Grote's finances," the corporation directed its lawyers to secure the transactions with mortgages "good and binding in every respect."[26] A year later Grote was bankrupt, the company again owned the Wood Gulch property, mortgage payments were due on the Starbuck ranch, and H. R. Rudd claimed "we are out $70,000 in cash . . . trying to make a go of that [Starbuck] place." No buyers were willing to pay the McGregors the $350,000 asking price for the ranch acquired from Grote. After turning down offers to exchange the farm for timberland or an eighty-apartment complex next to the Olympic Hotel in Seattle, the McGregors finally sold the property for $240,000 and an irrigated farm near Yakima. Maurice McGregor described the transactions as "another hangover of the Hooper Realty, which we some day hope, God willing, to clean up and forget." But Maurice wrote Archie McGregor in 1928: "We had just finished trading the Starbuck place for a Yakima irrigated ranch and cash when the frost knocked the tar out of Yakima land values." The corporation finally was able to sell the property a few months later after a series of court cases, the result of which McGregor lawyer H. W. Canfield described as "the Clan MacGregor . . . taking a good handful of hair out of . . . [the buyer's] scalp."[27]

Poorly managed grain speculation, the problems with the heavily mortgaged Starbuck farm, and the failure of the tenants all indicated the need for efficient management of the wheat farming operations. The McGregors sought the help of the agricultural experiment station at Pullman in fighting crop diseases. They learned, for example, that smut damage could be lessened by planting certain smut-resistant varieties of wheat and by using a copper carbonate seed treatment. They tried to cut costs and improve operating efficiency. They hired Oscar Shearer, an experienced farmhand with horse- and mule-powered equipment, to help manage the farmlands under direct company control. The cost and labor expense of handling wheat in sacks was cut when the Mc-Gregors purchased movable grain tanks and modified the separators to handle bulked grain. Wheat was augured from the separator into a storage tank, and then hauled to the elevator in wagons and trucks equipped to handle grain in bulk. Sack sewers and jigs were eliminated from the threshing crews. But the McGregors also used a combine and these machines, when equipped with bulk grain tanks, were poorly suited to the steep terrain of the Palouse. The wheat sacks were expensive. Furthermore, although the McGregors were dealers for a regional grain bag distributor (the Ames, Harris, Neville Company of Portland), they sometimes had difficulty obtaining a sufficient supply of the foreign-made burlap bags. In 1922, for example, Ames, Harris notified the Mc-Gregors: "We have received information that our material is being held up at Calcutta because of a strike at Hong Kong." The McGregors further cut back their use of sacks. Wheat threshed by the combine was hauled to the elevator in sacks. The twine was cut and the sack dumped and reused. Some of the expense, if not the inconvenience, of handling sacked grain was thus eliminated.[28]

The McGregors also worked to keep harvest expenses to a minimum. In the summer of 1923, two 23-man threshing crews, an eight-man combine crew, and a few cooks, roustabouts, wheat haulers, and other laborers made up the harvest work force. The pay scale ranged from three dollars per day for the header box drivers to twelve dollars for the separator men. A few men known as "bankers" followed the combine outfit, picked up scattered 140-pound wheat sacks, and hauled them to easily accessible locations, where they were unloaded and propped ("banked") against each other and left for a separate crew to haul to the elevator at Hooper. The "bankers," unlike the rest of the crew, were paid a variable wage—two cents for every sack they loaded and moved. One of these men, eager to make a good wage, in one day loaded and "banked" a thousand sacks. Pay at two cents per sack came to twenty dollars. Twenty-nine-year-old Maurice McGregor, in his first year with the company, decided this was too much pay and cut the wage in half. The energetic "banker" got mad and quit. Dallas Hooper, the grandson of pioneer rancher A. J. Hooper, recalled another labor problem of the 1923 season. One Saturday morning Hooper and the eleven other header box drivers in one outfit, all young high school students, walked off the job demanding three dollars and fifty cents per day, a fifty-cent increase. Hooper remembered that they had been urged on by veteran header box loader Fritz Reiman who, it turned out, wanted to quit work early on Saturday. The boys went to the Palouse River and spent the day swimming. When they returned on Monday, the McGregors had twelve new men from Spokane on the job in their places. Hooper and another boy went to Walla Walla to look for work, but harvesting was already finished in that area. Dallas Hooper returned to the ranch and went to work for the other threshing outfit—at the old wage. He remembered that the timing of the strike had been poor. Had they walked off the job in midweek, they might have held up harvest operations long enough to force the McGregors to raise the pay.[29]

Farmers might save money on grain sacks and harvest wages, but they had no control over the biggest variable in wheat production on the semiarid plateau: weather. The 1923 crop had been raised under excellent conditions—a moist spring; a sunny, but temperate, growing season; June rains—and the McGregors and their remaining tenants raised a crop of more than 25 bushels an acre. The state department of agriculture estimated the total Washington crop at 61 million bushels, or about 25.3 bushels per acre, the best in 45 years of grain production on the Columbia Plateau. Hot, dry weather the following year brought disaster. The state wheat output decreased to 27 million bushels, an average of fourteen bushels per acre, and the Columbia Plateau had what still remains its worst crop of the twentieth century. Wheat growers in upland areas of the eastern Palouse had disappointing yields. But in Adams, Franklin, Columbia, and western Whitman counties conditions were far worse. Much of the crop was too poor to harvest. By June, after watching the eight thousand acres in crop on the "home ranch" and the adjacent "Wood Gulch" farm shrivel in the heat and dust, the McGregors announced that they probably "would not harvest an acre." If they get some rain, a correspondent reported, "they will get some [horse] feed out of it, if not, they will hog it off." The last of the McGregor tenants and many other farmers in the area, already hurt by several years of low wheat prices, were forced to declare bankruptcy. Alex C. McGregor described the 1924 crop: "Our harvests have been very good as a whole; the nearest to a failure was in 1924 because of an extreme drought. Our returns that year were but about ten bushels per acre from one third of the best and the remainder we hogged because of its being so light."

The McGregors purchased 1,500 hogs for the main ranch, fed them on the uncut grain, and later received almost $20,000 from their sale, thus gaining badly needed income from portions of a crop too poor to pay the costs of harvesting. The wheat ranch still lost money in 1924. But the hog-raising operations begun during the crop failure would help produce almost $60,000 of operating income for the West End division during the years 1924–25. Wheat raising had provided a very modest return for McGregor Land and Livestock from 1920 to 1924—an aggregate of $25,000 net operating income from the main ranch and the tenant farms. This was substantially less than the $100,000 income from the store and the $90,000 from the sheep business earned during the same period. But with low market prices, inefficient tenant operations, some management problems, and a crop failure the McGregors had done well to break even on their wheat-raising operations. A remarkable change occurred between 1925 and 1930: The wheat ranch became the largest income-producing enterprise for the company. In 1926 alone, the McGregors recorded more than $100,000 of operating income from wheat raising and grain trading.[30]

During the 1925 crop year, the McGregor Land and Livestock Company planted 6,950 acres of grain on their Palouse hills. An additional 5,000 acres of cultivated land were in summerfallow, storing up moisture and nutrients to be used in the 1926 crop year. Few Columbia Plateau wheat farms were this large—the average wheat farmer in Whitman County, for example, had about 414 acres in cultivation in 1925. For the first time, McGregor Land and Livestock had direct control of the entire acreage and Maurice, Peter, and Alex McGregor worked to develop methods of operation suitable for such a large farm. Oscar Shearer and Maurice fixed dilapidated old machinery left by tenants and built large mobile feed racks and new header boxes. A combine, 9 headers, 28 header-boxes, 4 separators, 4 steam and gasoline engines, 54 wagons, and 334 horses and mules were used during the 1925 harvest. But during the next five years, the McGregors worked to take advantage of the scale of their operations by purchasing several combines, machines that saved labor and covered large acreages with great speed and efficiency.

McGregor Land and Livestock had experimented with combines for almost twenty years, since purchasing a ground-powered Haines-Houser in 1907. Two combines purchased during World War I were far more maneuverable and had threshing equipment that was powered with gasoline engines instead of the cumbersome "bull wheels." But during the early 1920's, long after many Columbia Plateau farmers had switched to combines, headers and separators had continued to do most of the harvest work on the McGregor ranch. Tenants had been responsible for their own harvest expenses and few could afford to purchase new machinery. The straw stacks saved by harvesting with headers had made useful sheep and horse feed. But combines covered 30 percent more acreage in a day with less than a third of the labor force required. McGregors sold their old combines and in 1925 purchased a new Holt for use on the main ranch and the Bar U and began phasing out the old system of harvesting. By 1930 three combines did all the harvest work once performed by headers, separators, and steam engines.[31]

The new Holt and Harris combines were far more versatile and mobile than their predecessors. But the motive power remained the same: teams of twenty-seven to forty-four horses or mules hitched to the machine and guided by a skilled driver perched on a seat high above the animals, equipped with two reins and a bucket of rocks to throw at unruly horses or mules. Primitive by later standards, the new combines nevertheless brought savings in time, labor, and dependence on outside help. Only four men were needed to assist the combine driver—the header tender (separator man), who regulated the height of the sickle bar; the mechanic, who kept the machine greased and in working order; and two other crewmen—the sack-sewer and the jig—who worked on a platform with a makeshift canvas roof (the "doghouse"). An extra man, the roustabout, sometimes rode a saddle horse alongside the combine and helped handle problems with the team.

The animals were hooked to Schandoney or Harrington hitches, specially made to ensure that every horse or mule had to pull an equal share of the load. The driver whistled or cracked a bullwhip loaded with shot and then hollered at the animals to get the combine under way. Walla Walla County farmer Carl Penner recalled one man who claimed to be an expert combine driver: "He said to the team, 'proceed.' The team didn't know what to do but the boss knew what to do. He just told him to get off the seat. He'd never drove combine. I suppose he came from college. Didn't they have them words in college? We didn't have them on the farm." The driver had to be highly skilled, particularly when turning a corner with his big team. "The right way," Virgil Bennington recalled, "is to pull your machine out just past the line of the [uncut] grain. Then stop your team. Dead still. Then start turning and turn your end team sharply to the right . . . till you get half way around. Then straighten up with the hitch. Slowly. . . . Then stop again and then turn 'em sharply and come right around to the grain. That way they're not pullin' [against each other] when they turn around the corner and they're not . . . stepping on each other's feet." After working six days, from four-thirty in the morning until eight in the evening, the combine crews went to a river or creek on Sundays to bathe, clean their clothes, and gather sacks of egg-sized rocks for the driver to use the next week. Some men eliminated this work by purchasing air guns to use on lazy mules, but Carl Penner remembered that "the humane society got after 'em." [32]

As the McGregors purchased new combines, they also began an even more important change in their farming operations: They began to use gasoline, instead of hay, as the source of energy for plowing, harrowing, hauling, and harvesting. Conditions in the semiarid interior of the Pacific Northwest and throughout the nation were favorable in the late 1920's for the replacement of animal power with internal combustion farm machinery: Farm income was improving, horse feed and labor were expensive, and improved gasoline tractors were available. During the five-year period in which the McGregors mechanized their farm work, the number of tractors in use on farms almost doubled, both regionally and nationally. Many more Columbia Plateau farmers acquired gasoline tractors during the Great Depression. Clarence Braden, a salesman for Best and its successor, Caterpillar Tractor Company, estimated that during the years 1931–37 he accepted ten thousand horses and mules in trade for tractors in the Walla Walla area and adjacent regions. He sold the animals to loggers and buyers from the south. Another Caterpillar salesman traded for thousands of work animals in the Lewiston area. Braden recalled: "With the horses and mules and the hay it was fairly close to an even trade. . . . It didn't cost farmers a lot of money 'cause they had some awfully nice stock in this country. Most of the horses you'd buy . . . for 30, 40, 50 dollars apiece but if you got hold of some real first class three or four year old mules, you'd go clear to $175. . . . [But] I found lots of 'em you didn't want at all. Take 'em for $5 and kill 'em for meat." The successful application of industrial technology to farm operations made possible major improvements in productivity and output. A U.S. Department of Agriculture study concluded in 1940: "The tractor, more than any other force, has brought an industrial revolution to our farms."

In 1935, E. F. Landerholm of the Washington Agricultural Experiment Station asked eighty-nine Columbia Plateau tractor-owning farmers what they considered the chief advantages of the new machinery. Four of the most frequent comments were: "makes it possible to get work done on time," "is faster than horses," "eliminates hired labor," and "no care necessary when not in operation." Speed and efficiency of operation were of crucial economic importance on the semiarid Columbia Plateau, where wheat farming was conducted with from eight to twenty inches of rain, far less than the precipitation received in most grain-producing areas. With severe limitations on the amount of rainfall available, farmers needed to take full advantage of all the moisture on hand. Summer-fallow, for example, had to be worked quickly after each rainfall to preserve the tilth of the soil, store precipitation, and prevent the growth of moisture-robbing weeds. By the time horse teams finished summer-fallow work on the McGregor ranch, weeds were knee-high, the top-soil was caked, and most of the moisture from spring rains was gone.[33]

Tractors made a great increase in speed possible: A twenty-horsepower tractor could harrow ninety acres in a ten-hour day, three times the amount horses could cover; a tractor could plow twenty-eight acres, a five-horse team only four. Winter-seeded wheat generally produced better crops than spring wheat on the Columbia Plateau. But by the time September or October rains had provided sufficient moisture for planting, horse-drawn teams seldom had time to finish the work before the arrival of winter. Tractors could cover almost three times the acreage in a day and, if necessary, a second shift could move the seed drills over an equal amount of land at night. McGregor Land and Livestock agronomist Harley Jacquot later estimated that the first decade of tractor use on the McGregor ranch brought an improvement of five to ten bushels per acre in the annual crop yield.

Despite the numerous advantages offered by tractors, the switch from animal to machine power was a difficult process. E. F. Landerholm wrote: "The early tractor farming history of the Palouse and Big Bend regions is strewn with disaster and failure." Farmers who sold all their horses and mules during the boom years of World War I found the tractors expensive, unwieldly, and difficult to operate. The flywheel alone on one such machine weighed over a ton. Discontented operators reported leaving the giants running all night because they were so hard to start. The McGregors purchased a huge cast iron 30–60 Rumely Oil Pull tractor during World War I. But they did not use the ungainly tractor to try to pull farm machinery over the thirty- to forty-degree slopes of the Palouse. The Rumely had excellent belt power, and the McGregors used it solely to operate separators for the heading and threshing outfits.[34]

The McGregor Land and Livestock Company made its first serious venture into mechanized farming in 1925, when three Holt '75' tractors were purchased, one for the Starbuck farm and two for the "home place."

These machines, like the Rumely, were purchased primarily to power drive belts for separating machines. They were big and cumbersome and lacked the power to pull combines. McGregor employees were able to do some plowing, discing, and harrowing with the '75's. A "half-track" machine with two steel-tracked wheels in the rear and a third wheel (used for steering the ponderous implement) in front, the Holt '75' had the disconcerting habit of tilting into the air on steep hills, thus making navigation impossible. The machines were started by placing a crowbar in the flywheel, pulling, and standing aside as the bar flew into the summerfallow. When one of the tractors quit during the night shift, work was often delayed while the driver searched the field for the starting mechanism. Adams County farmer Levi Sutton complained that the Holt '75's offered the operator his choice of two speeds: "slow and damn slow."

The three-wheeled Holt tractor, with all its limitations, represented a major change in farming practices. Donald Meinig comments that the introduction of the improved internal combustion tractor meant that "the day of small investment and small acreage wheat farming was doomed." The capital outlay required for wheat production had changed greatly since 1905, when the McGregor brothers incorporated their ranching business. The "wheat ranch" implements owned by the McGregor Land and Livestock Company during its first year of operation included 2 4-horse cultivators, 4 gang plows, 2 walking plows, 3 harrows, 2 drills, 2 discs, 7 sleighs, a grinder, a sewing machine, a chop mill, and a fanning mill. The total value of implements during that season was $1,599. Two decades later, the investment had climbed to $102,371. The 1926 ranch inventory illustrates an intermixing of the old systems with the newer technological refinements. Retained were 3 separators, 2 Case steam engines, 24 header boxes, 24 header-box wagons, and 189 mules and horses: evidence that the old methods of wheat raising had not been totally discarded. New equipment included combines, the Holt '75's, and a few trucks. The transformation was almost complete by 1930. Four 60-horsepower Holt tractors, lighter and more versatile than their predecessors, had been purchased for $5,000 each. The separators and steam engines were gone and the tractors pulled three new combines, one Holt and two Harrises, over the steep hills of wheat. New trucks were purchased and a contractor, veteran farmer Dave Carter, supplied additional vehicles to haul the newly cut grain to the McGregor elevators. The hundreds of draft animals used a few years before were nearly all gone, and only 28 mules and horses remained on the McGregor ranch.[35]

The technological improvements brought a rapid transformation in farming methods. Expensive machinery required larger than average farms for effective use. Small farmers were under severe pressure as agriculture became mechanized. Veteran wheat raiser Ralph Snyder recalled: "The machinery business broke more farmers than any other thing. It wasn't that they didn't work, but the farmers didn't have the volume to support the machinery." Mechanization tended to bring increased production, which meant further trouble for those farmers unable to keep up with the pace of change. The trend toward large-scale farming was reflected by a drop of 42 percent in the rural population of Adams County and 24 percent in Whitman County during the 1920's.

Even large farms had major management difficulties during these years of rapid technological change. Portions of Maurice McGregor's 1928 daybook illustrate some of the problems encountered in supervising a crew of more than fifty full-time employees and operating a large and complex farming and ranching business.

Feb. 21: *Sheriff Shaeffer & Deputy arrest [ranch employee] Mickey Martin—forgery.*

March 6: *Oliver Plow man calls. Tells us we made a big mistake . . . over tractors. The ranch expense is excessive. I'm afraid this is going to be a bad year . . . Dr. Baker says U sheep have foot canker. Says our [McGregor Land and Livestock] ewes and lambs look much better than year ago. Advises mixture sugar, lime & sulphur.*

March 8: *There are too many of our men standing around on the ranch. Wheat on Sec. 36 looks good. It all looks like a good stand.*

March 10: *Lambs coming. Over 200 a day.*

March 12: *Tractor starting plowing in sec. 19 draw.*

March 13: *Plow hit rock on hill, broke share. [Foreman] Art [Bowman] says Case plows tilt downward throwing rocks too high—must get John Deere.*

March 28: *Wood Gulch—tractors finished plowing last night. Moved over in night and started on Taylor in afternoon.*

April 18: *About 30 shifts [plowing] on Taylor place since moving from Wood Gulch 3/28—about 350–400 acres. 3.5 gal [gasoline] per acre & 30 acres per day. Something wrong here. Shearing starts. Wool very clean. Peaches, apples, cherries, apricots, prunes to be picked.*

April 19: *Stanfield sees wool. Is pleased—offers 33½¢.*

April 20: *first 2500 sheep–25,000 wool. Tractor laid off at midnight last night until noon today.*

April 23: *Emile's camp–6112 ewes, 7990 lambs, 130+%*

April 30: *shipped 2 cars wool from Hooper. Not shearing a/c rain. Finished with Cat [tractor] on Taylor.*

June 5: *Fall wheat is filling 2 kernels to mesh. Is in bad condition, thick with milk, to be hit by hot wind . . . 85,000 bu. looks like maximum. All expenses must be cut to bone.*

June 9: *Barometer fairly high with east wind. Looks very bad.*

July 10: *Ranch plans to start harvest Saturday–both stationary & combine.*

July 13: *The blower works well at U [for handling wheat in bulk] moving about 12 bu. minute.*

July 14: *combine started today–home ranch.*

July 16: *combine cut 1077 sacks today–est. 2300 bu.*

Aug. 1: *high wind this morning. Stationary shut down. This will shatter grain.*

Aug 6: *fire on 31 covering 15–20 acres. Start just after stationary left field.*

Aug. 10: *think average of 25 bu. will hold.*

Aug. 13: *Ranch wheat est. 65,000 bu. Triplett @ 84¢, 23,500 Turkey Red @ 85¢, 9,000 bu. Ridit @ 87¢, 9,000 Early Baart @ $1.10, 14,500 bu. Federation @ 95¢, total 121,000 bu.*

Aug. 15: *Fire on 31 burns straw stack P.M.*

Aug. 18: *fire started about 3 on S.W. side of sec. 36–apparently along road. Burns whole section.*

Oct. 9: *hogs put in [on burned wheat]. Hog days to Oct. 9–6914–9464# grain, per day 1.39.*

Oct. 10: *bot [sic] about 3200 head pigs.*

Oct. 29: *bot [sic] 2 ton Cat [tractor], standard with drive pulley.*

Nov. 1: *127 hogs fed 4160# burned wheat–gain per day 2.18. Turned [hogs] in to apple orchard at beginning of this six day period. It seems that change to apples had no detrimental effect on rate of gain.*

Nov. 5: *saw light in office 2:10 A.M. Macrae, Vickery, and Page waiting for coroner & sheriff.* [*Herder*] *Anton Robb put rifle in his mouth and shot himself. Page heard muffled shot & later a gasp or two.*

Nov. 9: *4 cars* [*Wine*]*saps & 4 cars Newton* [*apples*] *shipped.*

Nov. 23: *hay chopping starts at shearing corral.*[36]

Despite the two harvest fires and unfavorable weather late in the growing season, for the third straight year McGregor Land and Livestock raised more than 120,000 bushels of wheat and averaged more than 23 bushels per acre—excellent results for such a large acreage of cropland. Harvest hand Dallas Hooper recalled that after the 1928 harvest was completed, "boy, oh boy how it rained. So the next year there was a whopping big crop and a long harvest." He remembered that the 1929 "harvest was almost over—down to the last setting—when it started raining. It rained and rained and one outfit was hauled to the ranch and the men left. But the other crew stayed through the rains—more than six weeks—and played poker. When the rains finally quit one man, Brown, had won all the money earned by the whole crew." Big Bend farmhand Arthur Buhl claimed that "there was guys that made a living gambling off those crews. They was tickled to death with rain." The 1929 crop year was the last time the McGregors would use large crews of traveling harvest hands. The sailors, miners, Canadian farmers, "hoboes," "card sharks," and various other trained horse and mule skinners were no longer necessary. A much smaller number of year-round tractor-drivers ("Cat skinners") and ranch hands, assisted by local high school boys, would handle the harvest. As early as 1928, Maurice McGregor noted that "the use of tractors is eliminating men."

At a time when the labor requirements of sheep production and other McGregor operations remained relatively static, tractors and combines operated by a few men were able to handle farm work that had once required far larger crews. The 1927 to 1930 payroll books illustrate the manpower changes caused by the phasing out of mules, horses, header boxes, and separators.

WHEAT RANCH

Number of men employed each month

	Jan.	Feb.	March	April	May	June	July	Aug.	Sept.	Oct.	Nov.	Dec.	Total
1927	3	50	46	41	36	55	164	118	124	57	32	11	737
1928	8	32	47	44	34	32	109	48	25	33	20	6	438
1929	10	18	29	34	22	15	96	46	0	21	0	0	291
1930	8	12	22	17	15	15	29	35	19	22	9	5	208

SHEEP RANCH

Number of men employed each month

	Jan.	Feb.	March	April	May	June	July	Aug.	Sept.	Oct.	Nov.	Dec.	Total
1927	8	17	47	66	27	18	18	14	13	15	12	11	266
1928	13	20	57	70	38	25	15	17	14	15	13	10	307
1929	11	26	60	67	36	24	16	20	13	15	14	11	313
1930	11	21	50	65	30	14	16	16	14	14	11	12	274

By the late 1930's, most Columbia Plateau farmers had made similar reductions in their farm labor forces. The large traveling harvest crews no longer came to the region. Some farmers who still had horses and mules during the Depression blamed New Deal employment programs for the lack of experienced workers. "That W.P.A. ruined this area for good help," a Walla Walla farmer claimed. But the continuing mechanization of Columbia Plateau wheat farms had made the long journey to the Pacific Northwest wheat country impractical. Plenty of men eager for work were available, but few had the necessary experience and training in handling work animals. Some farmers were reluctant to give up the old farming methods. "You hated to quit the mules," Walla Walla County farmer Carl Penner remembered. "They was just some life. You know you get attached to a mule the same as you do people. . . . But you couldn't get anybody to drive the mules. . . . The Caterpillar came along and you bought a Caterpillar."[37]

The hazards of employment changed greatly with the new technology. Accident reports from the horse and mule farm operations on the McGregor ranch were similar to the following:

> *One of our ranch hands, Mickey Donahue, was kicked in the right hand by a mule yesterday. . . . His leg seems to be bruised and the knee may be strained.*

> *Chick Swanson injured his hip when he fell in a badger hole while fighting fire.*

> *Howard Russell was watering a mule when his glove caught in halter chain. The mule ran off and dragged him.*

Combines and tractors brought new dangers. Max Van Pelt was hurt "when combine motor which he was cranking kicked back and injured right arm." Ranch foreman Warren Booth was talking to a tractor driver when "the driver accidentally touched clutch bar, causing tractor to run over Booth's foot." "Ted Carmen had his arm broken and suffered burns about the face and hands last night in a jump for his life from a tractor. Gasoline being poured into the tractor ignited when it came into contact with the hot pipes on the machine." [38]

The McGregors worked quickly to adapt their operations to the new technology. They sought talented mechanics and an assistant for foreman Warren Booth. When one of the new '60' Caterpillars broke down, Maurice McGregor sought a trained mechanic and heard about Henry Lee, a man who worked in a machine shop and drove tractor on a Columbia County farm owned by Carl Penner. Penner remembered that "Henry was a machine man if there ever was one. He had quite a talent with the new machinery. He was working in a garage and they got him to come and fix a Caterpillar. He was one of the only fellas that really knew a Caterpillar and boy he could take one apart and put it together and it would just purr from then on. And the first thing I knew he was workin' for McGregors instead of me. There was just somethin' about him. He could get a crew to work harder than anybody you ever seen. He was always laughin' and joking and teasing the men but they liked him and respected him."

Working with Booth and Lee, Maurice McGregor began making changes in methods of soil management. Horse-drawn teams had difficulty making sharp turns and farmers generally plowed, harrowed, and seeded in a direct line up and down steep hillsides, a practice that caused serious water erosion. Because mules and horses lacked the power to plow through heavy stands of straw, standard practice on the McGregor ranch and elsewhere on the plateau was to burn the stubble. But experiment station scientists had warned farmers for many years that burning crop residues accentuated the already serious depletion of soil humus and plant nutrients and caused serious wind and water erosion. The power and maneuverability of tractors enabled the McGregors to begin contour plowing, a practice that restricted water erosion on steep hillsides. They also decided to retain the stubble instead of burning it. The decision was unpopular with some employees, for even with tractors, cultivating the thick straw in draws was a difficult task. To combat the persistent practice of burning stubble in draws, William McGregor recalled that his father, Maurice, "finally put out an order that anybody that burned anything was going to get fired, so the boys told me that they used to have to wait until after dark to go out and burn." McGregor Land and Livestock did not have a well-developed soil conservation program by 1930. But the new farm machinery at least enabled them to eliminate some of the most destructive cropping practices.

The switch from draft animals to internal combustion engines also helped improve the grazing capacity of the winter range, for the sheep pastures no longer had to satisfy the voracious appetites of three hundred draft animals. The McGregors sought the advice of E. G. Schafer, head of the Washington State College agronomy department, rangeland specialist A. L. Hafenrichter, and other college scientists in efforts to make further improvements. When a new weed was noticed on the McGregor range, Schafer visited Hooper and reported: "The light colored weed . . . on your rangelands is plantago aristata—bracted plantain. I was indeed happy to have the opportunity of spending . . . an afternoon with you . . . and learning of your grazing practices. You have apparently been more successful than many others in maintaining a satisfactory range condition." [39]

Labor-saving equipment, several large wheat crops, and slowly improving commodity prices had enabled the McGregors to develop a successful large-scale wheat farm by 1929. The other branches of the diversified corporation had also recovered from the postwar agricultural depression. Sheep raising, for forty-seven years the mainstay of the family ranching business, appeared to face a profitable future. The returns from the Hooper store decreased as farm mechanization brought a decline in the number of employees living in the company town, but the merchandise trade continued to be profitable. McGregor Land and Livestock was again a strong and profitable agricultural business. The stockholders of the company—Peter McGregor and his sons, Alex C. McGregor, and John McGregor's widow Minnie—shared annual dividends of forty to fifty thousand dollars.

The Exchange National Bank of Spokane and several other banking institutions with whom the McGregors did business sent frequent notices congratulating the Hooper firm for its large volume of sales. A 1928 letter from E. E. Flood of the Exchange Bank was typical: "In going through the annual statements . . . my attention was attracted to that of the McGregor Land and Livestock Company, which has, indeed, made a remarkable showing. When you realize McGregors have faced unusual conditions in the particular industry in which they are operating for a period of nearly ten years, and those engaged in like employment have been having difficulties, it is quite remarkable and I think it highly appropos that we should take notice of this." Credit was again readily available. When the McGregors wrote S. A. Kimbrough of the Exchange Bank to request additional operating credit, a loan was quickly arranged: "We have a surplus of funds at this time and you have been paying us too rapidly and we are really glad to get the loan."

The stability and prosperity of the McGregor ranch enabled the McGregor families to pursue a variety of personal interests. Maurice McGregor, for example, interviewed pioneer settlers and transcribed Indian legends told by Sam Fisher, the last non-reservation Palouse Indian. The McGregors provided legal assistance in Fisher's continuing effort to retain control of a remnant of the ancient tribal fishing grounds, a struggle begun in 1886 when the Northern Pacific Railroad had laid claim to the land. Peter McGregor successfully testified on Fisher's behalf before a U.S. Department of the Interior hearing in 1927, when a cattleman who had already incorporated the homestead claims of three other Palouse Indians fenced and claimed the Fisher land.[40] The McGregor families found time to travel—to Canada, Mexico, the eastern United States, and elsewhere. They participated in numerous social activities in Spokane. In 1924, for example, the McGregor families attended a dinner at the Spokane Hotel "in Honor of Heilan Laird Pater MacGregor" (in honor of Highland Lord Peter McGregor). The program featured a talk by Peter McGregor on "The Shortcomings of Jock Macrae," a rendition of Tam O'Shanter by "Jock Macrae, a Lowland Gillie," and two discussions of "Scotch Virtues" by Tacoma and Seattle judges. A few of the Gaelic foods served are listed below:

"Fair fa' your sonsie face,

Great Chieftan o' the Sheepherders' race

Some o' the Things We'll Hae

Sheep's Heid Kail	Cockie-Leekie	Hen Bree, an' a Dram
Cauld Salmon	Troots	Tawties an' Herrin'
Haggies, wi' a' the honours		
Sautit soo's leg biled	Gigots o' Mutton, Roasted	
	Bashed Neeps	Anither dram
Tawties, biled and chappit		
Roastit Bubblyjocks, stuffed	Roastit ducks	Doo pie
Trumlin' Tam Heck	Anither toastin	
Grozet Tairt Saps	Shortbread, wi,	
Kebbucks, Green and Mitey	Raisins on't	

Wine list a la Volsteadt—tea, coffee, charged water.

The McGregor women were kept busy cooking, washing, ironing damask table cloths and napkins, caring for their families, supervising their help, and entertaining visitors. The letters of Jennie McGregor and her daughters to friends and relatives describe some of the activities: "I have to entertain the club next week. Wish you were going to be here to assist me in the receiving line. Think I'll either serve Yankee plum pudding or hot rolls and salad"; "we washed today and the pups had a good time spilling the clothes pin basket"; "we had a terrific job of washing and ironing today." But Hooper offered few career opportunities for young women, and the three daughters of Jennie and Alex McGregor would soon leave the company town. Mary, the eldest, by 1930 was preparing for a career as a professional pianist with graduate study at the Curtis Institute in Philadelphia and the Juilliard School of Music in New York. After completing their education at Washington State College, Helen and Marjorie would also leave the Palouse—Helen to work as a radio announcer in Honolulu, Marjorie to become an actress in New York City.[41]

Economic conditions had improved greatly for the McGregors since the postwar depression. But some indications of trouble remained: Many fellow wheat raisers had already been forced out of business, low prices had left others with precarious finances, and continued national grain surpluses were a sign of danger. The McGregors and many other Pacific Northwest farmers saw the McNary–Haugen bill as a way to stabilize wheat prices and dispose of surplus grain. The measure called for the establishment of a federal corporation to purchase excess wheat and other farm products for resale abroad at world prices. The disposal of surplus grain and tariff protection against cheap imports were supposed to allow farm prices to reach a "fair exchange value" ("parity"). But the bill was vetoed twice by President Coolidge, in 1927 and 1928, because of its supposedly socialistic nature. Peter McGregor, the only delegate from Whitman County at the 1928 Republican convention in Kansas City, felt the measure was vital to the future of eastern Washington wheat farmers. Despite the opposition of Coolidge and his successor, Herbert Hoover, strong midwestern support for the McNary–Haugen proposal convinced observers that the agricultural platforms "will be the storm center of the Republican National Convention." The resolutions committee of the convention, reporters claimed, was "overwhelmed . . . by an inrush of men and women bearing the familiar yellow agricultural badges." McGregor refused to follow the decision of the Washington delegation to support Coolidge and Hoover on the issue and voted in favor of a platform sponsored by dissident midwestern delegates. The *Spokesman-Review* reported that "MacGregor Staged Bolt":

> Although the Washington delegation stands solid for Hoover and has been one of his loyal supporters for months, one of the 17 delegates, Peter MacGregor, this afternoon in convention broke away and cast his vote for adoption of the McNary-Haugen substitute plank, which had

been offered by the corn belt as a substitute . . . [for the agricultural platform] reported by the resolutions committee. While there have been several members of the Washington delegation sympathetic with the . . . [McNary-Haugen] cause from the beginning, they have been bound by institutions to stay with the majority as to candidate. At least on the matter of platform, MacGregor believed he was at liberty to break away and accordingly cast his vote with the hopeless minority that sought adoption of a plank that would have been entirely inconsistent with the record and views of Herbert Hoover and of President Coolidge, the two being in entire accord on agricultural relief.

Peter McGregor was "incensed" about the report, claiming he had voted according to his conscience and the wishes of his region on a matter critical to the future of wheat farmers.[42]

The huge farm surpluses had not been reduced when the gradual economic improvement ended with the stock market crash of 1929 and the onset of the Great Depression. While millions in urban areas went hungry, farmers and ranchers suffered from what Vernon Carstensen calls "the tragedy of abundance." Statistical surveys indicated the critical condition of American agriculture. Income received by American farmers declined almost 60 percent, from $6,741 million to $2,285 million, between 1929 and 1932. Farmers in the Pacific Slope states of Washington, Oregon, and California received an average income of $2,031 in 1929 and $661 three years later. National cash income from sheep and lambs fell from $224 million to $93 million, and wool receipts dropped from $99 million to $30 million during the same period.

Ranchers and farmers, regardless of the size of their operations, faced a difficult struggle for survival. Small farmers were the first to feel the impact of the catastrophic decline in agricultural prices. But even the Wheat Farming Corporation, a company with a mechanized farm that included 65,000 acres of Kansas cropland, failed to survive the tumultuous period. Economist Philip Raup contends that the Great Depression caused the collapse of most large-scale corporate farms. Columbia Plateau farmers had sold much of their wheat to England or the Orient. But the world grain trade collapsed as the Depression spread from America to Europe. The Federal Farm Board, organized in 1929 to encourage cooperative agricultural marketing associations, held millions of bushels of surplus grain but did nothing to stabilize prices. A proposal by Secretary of Agriculture Arthur M. Hyde for a "national campaign to encourage greater consumption of wheat flour and food products made of wheat" did not inspire confidence in his ability to alleviate the plight of wheat growers.[43]

Farmers met in Colfax, Walla Walla, and other towns in hopes of finding solutions to the crisis. In September 1931, for example, the *Commercial Review*, a journal of Pacific Northwest wheat dealers, noted: "A meeting of grain growers, businessmen, and bankers was held at Walla Walla last week to attempt to find a way out for farmers." Two years later the newly formed "Whitman County Farmers' Protective Organization" resolved that "farmers should not be required to pledge that part of their labor and commodities necessary to their families support and that the practice of mortgage creditors in demanding the entire assets of farm debtors is unjust and indefensible."

The McGregor Land and Livestock Company had remained in good economic health until 1930 when, as Maurice McGregor noted, "the hard times hit and put us all in the hole." By 1932 the corporation was in desperate trouble: "I want you to realize that we are not making any money," Maurice wrote a creditor, "that we are selling all of our products at less than costs of production and that we need every dollar we can get... just to hold on ... in the hope that conditions will eventually turn." Alex C. McGregor discussed the outlook in a 1932 letter to his daughter Mary:

> *The wild and wooly West ... [is] not so wild and wooly this year.... [We] are more like lambs that have been sheared and are just taking stock of ourselves as we feel the coolness of the financial temperature. We have just finished shearing a very fine clip but so far buyers don't seem particularly interested.... We are still able however to eat three good meals a day although maybe not so well able to don such fine spring togs but still optimistic as to the future.... Wool and wheat prices are not going to be good but expenses have been coming down too. Let us hope they will balance some day.*[44]

The sheep business, the mainstay of the corporation, was badly hurt by the economic collapse. Maurice McGregor explained the difficulties in 1931 correspondence with the financial experts of the Bradstreet Company:

> *A very large crop ... of lambs ... has had to be put upon a market where the buying power was greatly weakened by the current depression and very low prices have resulted. Prices for wool and lambs are very much under the cost of production and currently the sheep industry is operating at a large loss. Although drastic economies have been introduced into the operation of all sheep outfits it is impossible with the present level of prices for the industry as a whole to show any profit. Should present prices continue for another year or two, most of the sheep raisers would be forced out of business. Although the present picture is very dark, there are good reasons for viewing the future optimistically and anticipating the necessary rise in prices.*

The situation was bleak. The average price of Washington lamb fell from $10.80 per hundredweight in 1929 to $3.90 in 1932. Wool declined from 28¢ to 8¢ per pound. Wheat sold for $1.13 per bushel in 1929 and only 38¢ in 1932. On many local markets the price fell below 30¢. During the worst of the Depression, wheat literally could not be sold for no one was willing to put out cash for it. Agronomist Oliver E. Baker, in his 1933 study of the agricultural regions of North America, told of the "extraordinarily fertile" wheat lands of the Pacific Northwest interior, which generally recorded "the highest [per] acre yields in any non-irrigated wheat region in the United States." Yet he was convinced that poor market prices and soil erosion would force an end to wheat raising in this productive district: "Wheat farming on the Columbia Plateau, despite soil originally as fertile as any in the Nation, if not in the world, appears to be going the way of wheat farming in Wisconsin and California, where, after 30 to 60 years of cultivation, yields became unprofitable and wheat production gave place largely to dairying . . . and to more general systems of farming."[45]

The McGregors entered the Depression with a strong, stable family corporation begun as a partnership almost fifty years before. Two of the four brothers who founded McGregor Land and Livestock, sixty-eight-year-old Peter and sixty-one-year-old Alex C., remained active in the business and provided experienced leadership. The longevity of the corporation and the large scale of the farming and ranching business meant that the McGregors were well known by many bankers, meat packers, and wool and wheat buyers. The McGregor brothers had been dismal failures in urban real estate, mining speculation, irrigation companies and other enterprises. Yet after learning the limits of their business expertise, they had the sense to concentrate on those businesses that had built their corporation and established their reputations—sheep raising, wheat production, and merchandising. Many corporate farms organized to take advantage of the increased scale of operations possible with tractors, combines, and other farm machinery had not developed experienced management and stable labor forces before the Depression. The size of such firms proved a liability: They had huge capital requirements and large payroll expenses but lacked a proven management record. McGregor Land and Livestock, on the other hand, was able to combine the close supervision and experience of a family farm with some of the advantages of large-scale operation. The corporation also was fortunate to have Maurice McGregor, a young, innovative manager educated in economics and business finance, to take charge of the daily business affairs.

But McGregor Land and Livestock still lost money on its store, sheep, and wheat. For the first time the corporation registered deficit annual net incomes. Losses totaled $48,000 in 1930, $14,000 in 1931, and $28,000 in 1932. Emile Morod recalled the desperate status of the business: "When we sold them lambs for 6½ ¢ in St. Paul, God, they couldn't even buy a load of coal here. McGregors couldn't pay for it. Everybody went to work herding sheep that fall . . . Pete says 'Everybody got to go herd sheep.' Nobody loafin' around town here . . . there was no money, McGregors couldn't do it, couldn't pay their bills. But they came out."

The experience and reputation of the corporation helped the men achieve top market prices and minimize losses. But without adequate credit the business could not have survived. Stockholders, directors, and long-time patrons of the Spokane and Eastern Trust Company (successor to the Exchange National Bank), the McGregors were able to acquire $175,000 in loans from that firm after a collapse in wheat and sheep markets in 1930. The funds lasted less than a year, and the McGregor ranch was on the brink of failure when government programs enabled the men to obtain hundreds of thousands of dollars of additional funds in exchange for real estate, crop, and livestock mortgages. Even the town of Hooper was mortgaged. Maurice McGregor described one of the mortgage agreements to his uncle Alex: "I would suggest that you sign this form without reading it, as it seems to hold all signers as personal guarantors from now until death do us part. It seems almost similar to marriage to be dissolved only by death or other grave causes. However, we've all signed our names to so many thousand dollars of obligations I'm sure there is no point in backing away from this one."[46]

Smaller farms had far greater difficulties obtaining capital. Wheat raiser Ralph Snyder described the problems he encountered when his banker refused to provide loans and tried to foreclose on a $5,000 mortgage:

> [Wheat] prices went down from a dollar and a half to a dollar and then to eighty cents and six bits and finally in '32 the banker, Pierce, called me up. There was three of us, we was the biggest growers in the Washtucna area, Paul Helm and Johnny Burns and I. And he called us up and said "I want you to sell that wheat." . . . I said "Pierce, if you force this wheat sale now, it'll break your God damned bank and it'll break us too." "Well," he says, "I can't help it. . . . My orders are to get the money." So Paul Helm got 28¢ for his white wheat and Johnny Burns and I got 32¢. But that night, I don't know why I did it, but I drove my pickup out in the Sand Hills and I sat all night in that pickup, wonderin' what I was gonna do. . . . The next year, my cousin, a 16 year old kid, and I harvested that wheat with a combine and piled it up in the field

*and put straw over it. And I went to butcherin' hogs, sold enough to pay
my labor. . . . We was trappin' coyotes to beat hell [to collect bounties].
. . . The banks wasn't puttin' out a dime. . . . I owed the insurance, and
the merchant, and the blacksmith shop, and the doctor, and anybody
else that would trust me with anything. But I saw Pierce in town one
day and he said "What did you do with your wheat this year? Where's
the tickets for it?" . . . He said, "I can get the sheriff to force you to
bring it in." I said, "I know it Mr. Pierce, you could if you wanted to.
. . . It's yours." He couldn't raise that wheat as cheap as I could and he
knew it. So he turned around and walked off and he never said another
word to me. Well the next spring wheat went up to 58¢ and a broker
in Walla Walla called me and bought two carloads. . . . So I loaded those
two railroad cars myself. I don't know how in the hell I did that. Dug
'em out of the straw pile, hauled 'em in and loaded 'em.[47]*

The first sign of serious trouble for the McGregor Land and Livestock
Company came in the spring of 1930. Maurice McGregor described conditions at Hooper in a letter to "Aunt Minn" (John McGregor's widow,
Minnie): "Everyone is well and we are having wonderful weather following a splendid rain. . . . The country is lovely now and we're forgetting the winter. Prices on sheep, lambs, and wool however are very much
depressed and it looks as if it would be almost impossible to make any
profit in the sheep business this year." The good weather helped the corporation record "an exceptionally good lambing," with "the largest
lamb crop we have ever had." Despite hot and dry June weather the
wheat averaged about twenty bushels, a "fair" crop. Wheat crops further west were much worse. Adams County farmers averaged seven
bushels to the acre. Arthur Buhl recalled that in an area west of Ritzville,
"there just weren't any crops. Not enough wheat for farmers to winter
their horses. You had to haul straw in for the animals. It got to be a dust
bowl. Farmers harrowed to get rid of thistles and stirred it up. We had a
few days of northeast wind and the dust started moving. Then the wind
turned right around and picked that sand right back up again. Got so a
five mile wind would stir up the dust. Once you get that sand moving
you can't stop it."

Although weather in the Palouse country was more favorable, the
market outlook was dismal. The McGregors found that wheat prices
had fallen "to almost unheard of levels." Wood Brothers, the Chicago
commission firm, sold a shipment of McGregor lambs at a price higher
than that received by any other range sheep business. But the receipts
failed to cover production costs. The McGregors first tried to deal with
the crisis by opening an account with the eastern brokerage firm of
Logan and Bryan and by contracting their products for future delivery.[48]

As the futures market fell, the McGregors searched hard for a new source of income.

McGregor officials analyzed the "bearish" farm prices and decided that wheat would bring better returns when fed to livestock than when sold for foodstuffs. Maurice McGregor commented: "Feeding livestock is the only way out on this sixty cent wheat." Thirty-five hundred lambs were kept off the crowded August sheep markets of Chicago for sale at a more advantageous time: "We have to either shove them onto this sick market or feed out and with plenty of cheap grain it seems to me that feeding for the December–January market is the only thing indicated." The McGregors had fed grain successfully to thousands of hogs during earlier years. The procedure again appeared logical in 1930: "We believe that hogs ready for shipment next March will return a great deal more per bushel than present wheat prices." Results were favorable: When wheat was worth 45¢, for example, hog feeding resulted in net receipts of 70.3¢ per bushel on one shipment and 90¢ on another.

Maurice McGregor checked with hog raisers throughout the West in a search for skinny young pigs that could fatten rapidly on wheat. Trainloads of pigs were shipped to Hooper from North Dakota, Minnesota, and Montana. Regional agricultural specialists took an interest in the results of the fattening of midwestern hogs, claiming that the McGregors were the first Pacific Northwest farmers to implement such a scheme. The 3,300 hogs kept during the winter of 1930 were fed carefully regulated diets of hay, wheat, apples from the McGregor orchards, slaughtered workhorses, and tankage. Additional revenue was received by selling skinny midwestern hogs to neighboring farmers and purchasing the fat livestock for shipment to distant markets. Adams County farmer Ralph Snyder commented on his hog business:

> The way I got by then [i.e., during the Depression] was with hogs. McGregors was buyin' and sellin' hogs and they would ship carloads at a time. So I would raise hogs and haul 'em over there to McGregors. . . . Then hogs got pretty cheap so I decided to butcher them myself and I butchered 75 head one winter. Cut 'em up down in the basement. . . . Hogs that would have brought me about $10 a head brought me $25–$30. . . . And I'm not particularly proud of it now, but horses were pretty cheap. Well, a hog needs protein besides wheat. . . . I'd take an old horse and shoot him out there in the corral and open him up. Then those hogs would eat that thing right out from the inside, bones and all. People would buy my sausage and come by and see those hogs eatin' that damned thing and some of 'em got kinda squeamish. But it was fine protein for them and cheap as hell. Oh we used to buy a little stuff from the packing house at $30–$40 a ton. But I could get a horse for a dollar a ton, with no freight bill to pay.[49]

McGregors developed a farrowing operation near Hooper and contructed hog houses. William McGregor described his father Maurice's efforts in the pig business: "There was a good demand for meat [unlike grain crops] so at least you could get cash for it. . . . Dad always brought the books home and all Sunday afternoon he'd be sitting in there working the books. . . . When he had a payday and he was trying to figure out what he could sell to meet the payroll, frequently the answer was a load of hogs." The Spokane and Eastern Trust had advanced the funds necessary to purchase the thousands of hogs, a new combine, a tractor, and other equipment. The McGregors' decision to hold most of their livestock and grain off the market in 1930 brought further increases in their needs for capital. But by December 1930, the McGregors were over their $175,000 credit limit and the Spokane and Eastern bank was becoming increasingly hard pressed. Bank vice-president Sam Kimbrough wrote Maurice McGregor: "It is our understanding that from the sale of wheat, lambs, and hogs you would be able to finance yourself without calling upon us for additional money." Although the bank continued to provide operating capital, requests for funds in excess of the credit limit would no longer be routinely accepted. The decision to grain-feed livestock helped ease the money shortage. The McGregors staggered their feeding program so that shipments would be ready at periodic intervals, thus providing a better distribution of yearly income and allowing some cash inflow during usually slack periods. The procedure enabled the corporation to meet immediate obligations without having to wait for April wool sales or August wheat and lamb sales.[50]

The initial sales of the wheat-filled livestock were disappointing. After receiving the results of a January lamb sale, Peter McGregor wrote Ed Spain of the Wood Brothers commission firm:

> *Your Tuesday wire left us shocked, surprised, and disgusted. This was our first venture into feeding lambs and the performance of the lambs in the feedlots was very pleasing. They gained consistently and well on our cheap hay and wheat ration and when we cut our nine cars for shipment they averaged 98 pounds on the day they left and they were good. . . . We thought we were sitting pretty. Imagine our astonishment. We arrive in Chicago with a lot of half fed lambs and heavy feeders. Something happened to these lambs, where or how we don't know, but . . . we want to find out where the responsibility lies. . . . This, our first experience in this game, is going to make us very careful in the future.*

The McGregors found the railroad to be the culpable party and received reimbursement after threatening a lawsuit. Ed Spain reported on the sale of the remaining portion of the McGregor shipment: "Today's wire will go far towards re-establishing your faith not only in the sheep market but in myself which I believed might have been shaken after the sale on your first 3 cars." A February hog shipment topped the market, but the McGregors received apologies from the commission firm at the Portland, Oregon, stockyards: "We are sorry that you struck such a poor market here this week. I think it was the worst to sell on that we have had this year." Later in the spring the McGregors were more fortunate on the "dangerous" and "treacherous" hog and lamb markets, and shipments of both varieties of livestock were sold shortly before calamitous market declines of a dollar or more.[51]

By the summer of 1931, the McGregors had begun to attract regional attention for their efficient methods of management. In June, the U.S. Department of Agriculture and Washington State College sponsored a field tour for those attending a conference of the Western Farm Economics Association in Pullman. The group made the 120-mile round trip to the McGregor Land and Livestock ranch at Hooper for a "Large Scale Farming Demonstration," including a display of tractors, combines, and other farm machinery and tours of the sheep ranges, wheat fields, hog barns, orchards, and various other facilities near the company town. The McGregors described some of the economy measures being employed. "Sheep expenses," corporation officials explained, "have been cut by cutting wages, lowered cost of materials, by elimination of luxuries in camps, and by reduced numbers of men." In a business prospectus compiled earlier in the year, the men noted that "the possibility of earning profits depends on management which can cut expenses without decreasing production by the process of doing without and getting along with a minimum of all labor and materials." Herders' wages were dropped 50 percent, combine crews' by 40 percent or more, and Peter, Alex, Maurice, and Sherman McGregor cut their own pay by half. Sherman, the son of Alex C., had assisted in the store since his graduation from Washington State College in 1929. When further cuts in wages were made in 1932, he left Hooper to search for work in San Francisco. The McGregors figured that with the economy measures and favorable weather the wheat ranch might lose only $3,500 while sheep could earn them $11,000, hogs $10,000, and merchandise sales $2,000.

The predictions proved far too optimistic. Weather during the spring of 1931 posed the first threat: "We have had every other kind of weather, heat, wind, dust, and frost, but no rain." Maurice McGregor described the outlook in June: "Business conditions do not improve but are getting a little worse if anything. The hot, dry weather of the last month has hurt our wheat and has taken the prospects of a bumper crop out of the picture. . . . Prices continue low and prospects for lamb prices are poor. Lamb conditions are good and everything is running along in good shape.

The distressing thing is that in spite of production which will be above normal and with costs much below normal these low prices give no promise of any profit." [52] Rainfall later in the month improved the condition of the wheat, and 25- to 35-bushel yields were registered on various portions of the McGregor cropland. Again there were reports of drought and dust storms in the drier districts further west. Maurice McGregor reported that the 120,000-bushel crop raised on the ranch "in ordinary years would mean a nice income but at present wheat prices is insignificant. I have consigned three cars of wheat but the amount that can be drawn on them is so small that it can hardly be shipped fast enough to meet current expenses." Wheat was sold at 33¢ a bushel and lambs at $4.50 a head: "a big cut from our ideas of $6 for lambs and 50¢ [for wheat] which we thought conservative this spring."

Harvest fires caused further losses on the McGregor ranch and elsewhere on the Columbia Plateau during the dry summer months of 1931. Thousands of acres of standing grain burned in the Walla Walla, Prescott, and Waitsburg areas. With a breeze and a spark from a truck or combine, the tinder-dry fields would erupt into flames and a wall of fire sometimes ten to twenty feet high would race along the steep hills of wheat. McGregor Land and Livestock lost hundreds of acres of grain in two fires. Harvest hand Dallas Hooper remembered that the worst fire began southwest of the ranch, moved through McGregor grain fields, and "burned almost to Lacrosse [12 miles east] before it was stopped. We fought it for hours until it burned out of the territory. One of the men was bragging about the fact that his was the only bedroll that hadn't burned up—before the fire turned and got it too. The combine—a wooden Harris—burned until it was reduced to a 'bucket of bolts.' Everything but the cookhouse burned—it was saved when the men plowed around it." [53]

The McGregors held the wheat they were able to harvest and kept portions of the lamb, wool, and hog crops while they watched regional, national, and international markets closely for signs of "bullishness." Success or failure of Columbia Plateau farming and ranching businesses was becoming less dependent on local factors—the vagaries of weather in a semiarid land, the price of wheat at Seattle or Portland—and more sensitive to international crop conditions and markets. The McGregors studied reports of wool sales in the Australian interior and wheat market conditions in China and Japan to determine when to sell their own products. By keeping a portion of the lamb crop off the Chicago market until most Western sheepmen had sold their products, the corporation was able to receive a "fairly good price": "This is the first time in three years when any of our products have given better returns than expected." But the markets were erratic and Maurice McGregor did not find the general outlook encouraging:

> This wheat market has been in a deplorable condition. There hasn't been any great decline but this continuing easing and softness is discouraging. I can see several bullish factors which might become effective the first part of this month: the poor condition of fall wheat and the reduced acreage in the Southwest, the probable reduction in estimate of spring wheat production for this year, the rapid reduction that has so far taken place in the visible supply. On the other hand the surplus still weighs heavily and the international financial situation continues very bad. This is too complicated for me to understand but I don't see any chance for any great improvement in the near future.

As economic conditions worsened, one trend could be predicted: an increasing determination on the part of bankers to reduce the amount of credit provided to the McGregor Land and Livestock Company. An August 1931 letter from Sam Kimbrough of Spokane and Eastern was typical: "From your figures as to the income from wheat and from the sale of lambs . . . we take it that you will be in a position to reduce the line which we are now carrying by $50,000 and since a part of . . . the wheat . . . is to be fed, we assume that still further reductions will be made at the time the hogs are marketed." R. L. Rutter, head of the Trust Department of Spokane and Eastern and a man who had purchased McGregor wool at Sprague in 1899, was particularly insistent upon making collections. Jennie McGregor commented: "Conditions are precarious here since we are in the hands of a real shylock, 'Mr. Rutter.' " Archie McGregor later claimed that Rutter saw the McGregor concern as "easy pickings" and recalled that Peter had decided "if he ever got even with Rutter he was going to tell him what he thought of him."[54]

Economic conditions remained dismal in 1932. Maurice McGregor noted: "If physical conditions alone are considered, conditions are excellent. Sheep, range, and wheat are in fine shape. But in combination with the prospective prices and returns, the outlook is gloomy enough." "We have a good wheat crop, a good wool crop, and a good lamb crop," creditors were informed, "but prices are so low that there is little, if any, net income." Hog prices improved markedly, and "although the picture still looks sour enough . . . it hasn't gotten any worse in the last two weeks and the hog advance shows that it isn't impossible for a commodity to swing sharply against the general trend." But the results of sheep sales were not encouraging: "We got returns on our first lot of lambs today and the telegram was poor reading matter. We got $5.75 which the wire said was top on westerns. We don't know whether to take what small comfort there may be in going at the top, or whether to feel gloomy over the prospective price of our next lot." The McGregors analyzed the availability of cheap wheat and corn in the Midwest and tried "something in the nature of an experiment": the shipment of a load of sheep to Illinois for several months of feeding prior to sale in Chicago. Maurice McGregor found "everything in connection with the feeding . . . fully up to our expectations. The price of course made the result financially unfortunate but that was something over which neither of us had any control."[55]

The corporation took further economy measures: "Wages were reduced to $50 per month for herders in the beginning of the year and further reduced in November to $40. . . . Use of trucks was somewhat restricted and teams were used when convenient resulting in some reduction in car expense." The corporation successfully urged officials of the Spokane Indian Reservation and various private parties from whom the McGregors leased summer range to lower grazing fees. The U.S. Forest Service reduced grazing charges by half and brought further savings. Similar stringent economies in other branches of the company helped bring a further reduction in expenses, from $383,498 in 1930 to $238,313 in 1931 and $197,510 in 1932. But gross sales had dropped also—from more than $335,000 in 1930 to $169,000 in 1932. The McGregor Land and Livestock Company was still losing money: "The receipts make up the sad part of this picture. The fed lambs were sold in January and February at prices about as expected. The 1932 crop of [range] lambs was sold on a very poor market, averaging a little more than $3 a head. Wool receipts were about cut in two from the previous year." Despite the horrible prices, the McGregors retained some optimism. Maurice explained: "I suppose a producer is an incurable bull and optimist on his product and after the experience of the last three years there isn't much excuse for such an attitude but nevertheless it still does look to me as if there are excellent reasons for wool and lambs to sell higher."[56]

By the winter of 1932, McGregor Land and Livestock Company was critically short of capital and badly in need of bullish markets for its wheat, sheep, and other commodities. The McGregors' neighbors on the Columbia Plateau were in similar, or worse, financial shape. The national outlook was similarly gloomy: A U.S. Department of Agriculture study concluded that the "average farmer" in 1932 had received "nothing as a return on his investment and much less than common-labor pay for his labor and management." Farmers and ranchers, traditionally opposed to government regulation of marketing and production, in desperation sought federal assistance. A few tentative attempts had already been made to assist farmers—the War Finance Corporation, for example, made loans on livestock in 1921 and the Federal Farm Board of 1929 attempted to change marketing procedures—but the programs accomplished very little. The farm programs of Roosevelt's New Deal were far more comprehensive: Credit was advanced to farmers; a "parity" system designed to give farm products a purchasing power comparable to that of the period 1910–14 was implemented; and the Agricultural Adjustment Act of 1933 sought to deal with glutted markets by paying farmers to reduce their acreage of wheat, corn, and other products either by not planting or by plowing up lands already in crop. Vernon Carstensen comments on the tragic element of this attempt to limit farm output: "There was an almost cosmic irony in this gigantic and nearly wholesale destruction of food and fiber while millions of persons nearby were ill-fed and ill-clad. This must have been the act of a very civilized people, since no primitive tribe would have served its economic institutions so well and its hungry people so badly."[57]

But the New Deal policies promised to alleviate the critical shortage of capital and oversupply of farm products. Long-time Republicans Peter, Alex, and Maurice McGregor were strongly in favor of Democratic farm programs. Maurice McGregor commented in 1933: "We are more than enthusiastic about the New Deal. It is new and experimental and many mistakes will be made, but it has meant survival for us as a business while a continuation of the conditions prevailing last winter would have brought our extinction within a short time." Peter McGregor, former Republican state senator and representative, reported: "I am still enough of a Republican to support Roosevelt's farm policy, a policy which takes steps to make the tariff effective for farm products. The Republicans have always believed in the policy of protection for our home industries but during the nineteen twenties, when the farmer was in sore need of such protection, the group in control of that party refused to take any active steps to extend the benefits to farming. Roosevelt in the AAA simply extended the tariff to the protection of agriculture." Peter expressed disagreement with the "sound money men" in control of the Republican party: "How can I, long on livestock and short of money, favor deflation and a dropping price level? I'd be a sucker to play on the creditor's side."

During the spring of 1933 the McGregors actively promoted Roosevelt's farm relief plan. The men corresponded with William Borah, Homer T. Bone, and several other western senators in an effort to secure their support for the program. Peter McGregor explained the seriousness of the issue in a letter to U.S. Senator C. C. Dill of Washington:

Everyone is aware of the present plight of the farmer but it is probably not sufficiently well realized that farm relief must come to him not in ten years nor in five years but immediately, if agriculture is to be saved from a collapse that may carry with it the rest of our economic setup.

It is obvious that deflation causes a paralysis of trade not so much because all prices fall as because prices fall with great inequality. . . . The Northwest wheat farmer, getting 25 cents for his wheat, finds most of the commodities he buys down only ten to twenty percent and that his mortgage, his interest payments, railroad rates, and taxes have not been reduced at all. It is the great virtue of this domestic allotment plan that it attempts to remedy one of the most glaring examples of price disparity.

The machinery of this plan is novel but it is conservative in purpose. It is not radical. The most radical, extreme, and hazardous course that can be pursued is to permit this situation to drift for the next twelve months.[58]

Senator Charles McNary of Oregon opposed the Roosevelt program and proposed the sale to China of fifty million bushels of wheat stockpiled by the federal government, a plan that Pacific Northwest grain traders claimed "spells ruin for commercial interests" and threatened to deprive hard-pressed farmers of a market for their wheat. Peter McGregor wrote McNary to explain his dismay with the Republican programs: "Your present obstructive tactics toward farm legislation, in such sharp contrast to your attitude of four years ago, gives some ground to the suspicion that you think of farm relief in terms of political expediency and advantage. If anything was needed to completely finish the Republican Party with the farmers, your recent performance has supplied it."

The Farm Credit Act, the Agricultural Adjustment Act, and the Commodity Credit Corporation, three New Deal programs implemented in 1933, provided immediate help to farmers and ranchers desperately short of operating capital. The Farm Credit Act provided for a series of government-sponsored regional agricultural credit agencies that provided farmers with funds in exchange for long-term crop, chattel, and real estate mortgages. By 1933, most surviving banks were reluctant to make such mortgage agreements because farmland, crops, and livestock were considered poor security risks. Nearly a million American farmers had already defaulted on debts and lost their farms since the onset of the Depression.

The Farm Credit Administration made large sums of money available on liberal terms and emerged as the major source of agricultural credit in the United States. By July 1933, McGregor Land and Livestock had acquired $54,000 in operating capital by mortgaging its lamb crop. Subsequent agreements increased the mortgage indebtedness to more than $200,000. Washington sheepmen Maurice McGregor, Thomas J. Drum-

heller, and "Jimmy" Richardson joined Oregon livestock raisers in organizing a regional credit association originally funded by the Farm
Credit Administration. Oregon cattleman Herman Oliver, a charter
member of the group, recalled that the organization became a "great
stabilizing factor for the Northwest livestock industry." Maurice Mc-
Gregor, one of the first directors of the regional credit association,
described the goals of the organization to an eastern Washington
radio audience: "It is a group of sheepmen and cattlemen of Washington, Oregon, and north Idaho. They are organized into a Production Credit Association to get the credit they need to run their outfits. It is so organized by the farmers that they can get the kind of money
they need, when they need it, and the way they need it to carry on their
operations." The association, set up with a government advance later
repaid by investors, had loan committees headed by livestock raisers. "In
other words the livestock men make their own loans. We feel that this
system is not only sound, since these men study the risks from first hand
experience, but it allows real consideration of the farmers problems by
men actually engaged in meeting the same problems themselves."[59]

The Agricultural Adjustment Administration (AAA) became involved in a wide range of activities designed to minimize farm surpluses
and raise the level of farm prices. A voluntary acreage control plan was
implemented, and cooperating farmers received payments for reducing
their acreage in crop. By cutting acreage in crop by 15 to 20 percent,
farmers became eligible for subsidy payments designed to guarantee a
parity price for their wheat crop. Farmers were told maximum and
minimum allowable acreage for their next crop and later received notices
from a "wheat allotment inspector," telling them whether it "would be
necessary to destroy" [i.e., plow under] any excess acreages in crop. The
program meant an additional income of fifteen to twenty thousand dollars annually for the McGregor farming business. Maurice McGregor, a
member of the first state board of supervisors of the AAA and a member
of the western Whitman County allotment committee, described the
response to the new program in 1933: "The farmers around here . . . are
signing up 99 percent for the allotment plan. I don't think this is to be
wondered at because the terms are so very obviously to the farmer's
advantage. But the fact that it is being entered into in such a spirit makes
me feel sure it will work and accomplish in a large measure its purpose.
I've been on the committee for the last two weeks and the farmers are
keeping us busy."

Additional funds were made available through the Commodity Credit
Corporation, an organization formed under an order by Secretary of
Agriculture Henry Wallace, which provided loans to signers of AAA

contracts. Two programs organized during the Hoover administration, the Farmers National Grain Corporation and the National Wool Marketing Corporation, played a part in price stabilization. Peter McGregor praised the former, a national cooperative grain-selling organization, declaring that "the cooperative movement has demonstrated its worth to the farmer." He noted, however, that the cooperative sales agencies were helpful primarily to the small farmers and not to large wheat merchants like the McGregors, who could make more money by handling their own grain.[60]

The outlook for the McGregor Land and Livestock Company began to improve in 1933. The turning point, the McGregors claimed, had been the election of Franklin D. Roosevelt. On the eve of Roosevelt's election, Maurice McGregor noted: "I think it is now a certainty that the wheat farmer will get some kind of subsidy on next years crop. . . . The domestic allotment plan . . . makes 60 to 80 cent wheat a probability for next

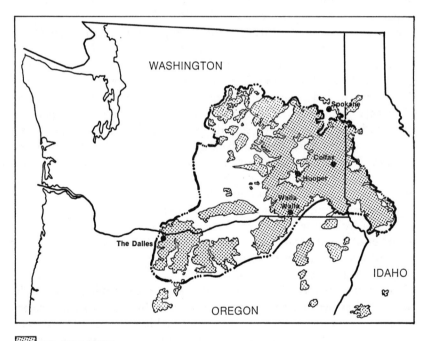

Major Wheat Districts

Columbia Plateau Boundary

The Pacific Northwest wheat region, ca. 1935 (after Orr et al., "Trends and Desirable Adjustments in Washington Agriculture," and Meinig, *Great Columbia Plain*)

season. . . . It doesn't take a very sharp pencil to figure out what this means to the entire Palouse Country. . . . The same plan applied to cotton . . . should have a sympathetic effect on the wool market and if the proposed two cents a pound is applied to hogs it should help the lamb market. . . . I think the agricultural future looks brighter than it has for four years and I can see the possibility of a very snappy agricultural comeback."

The crisis abated somewhat in 1933, and the McGregor corporation recorded a net profit of almost $38,000: "After going through three terrible years, 1933 was so much better that it looked like prosperity again. We didn't make very much money but we didn't go into the red."[61] Favorable weather helped in the production of a lamb crop with "just a little higher percent than we have ever had before." Wool was sold at "an extremely high price." "Extremely and unusually good weather" during early summer and a sharp increase in price improved prospects for the wheat business. Even on the improving market, the decision of when to sell the grain was a complex issue that required close analysis of international trends. Maurice McGregor commented:

> The general inflationary sentiment may swing wheat higher but it is not often that there is any bull market after June first without heavy spring wheat damage and my guess . . . is that . . . spring wheat will continue to improve in appearance throughout the northwest and Canada during the early summer. I see nothing in the statistical position of wheat or the growing crops to bull wheat on. There is ammunition in the London Conference, if successful, and in the working of the domestic wheat control plan. . . . But these are quite uncertain. Anyway for the first time our bullish and bearish sentiments were about in balance and when you get in that condition it is a good time to sell.

The outlook for other corporation enterprises improved: "Our store business for May is equal of the volume of 1932. This is the first time since 1929 that any months volume has been equal to the volume of the corresponding month in the preceding year." The men experimented successfully with the shearing of lambs prior to shipment to Chicago, thus departing from the western tradition of selling lambs unshorn. A thirteen-thousand-dollar payment for limiting acreage in crop helped confirm their early impression of the New Deal: "This allotment plan and the industry control bill are the goods. I think the moves made so far have been tremendous and have been carried out with astonishing competence. The future looks very bright to me." By fall the corporation was able to inform its creditors: "Our situation is entirely different from that of a year ago when we were so hard pressed."[62]

The worst of the Depression was over for the McGregors and fellow

Columbia Plateau sheep raisers and wheat growers. The McGregors bought new combines and tractors, hired additional help, raised wages, paid large dividends, and relaxed other strict economy measures. By June 1934, Maurice McGregor was able to state: "The wheat farmer is doing very well and recovery is a fact and not something to be wished for." But the crisis continued in other areas. Two former McGregor employees were rehired in 1933, one of whom said he "nearly froze to death" while riding a freight train east in search of a job. Another, Harold Magnuson, recounted similarly difficult experiences:

> *Seven years ago March 17 I started to work for you driving plow team and continued nearly three months on the old spring board. Spring will soon be here and I'd like to get out again. . . . I went to work for Rhodes Bros. I liked it—gee, it was great, long hours and long weeks but I was getting somewhere. But business, well there wasn't any—much. That called for cuts and consolidation of debts and stringent economies. But I needn't tell you about it you've been through it all. . . . I was engaged to marry a wonderful girl. A year ago tomorrow she died. The bottom dropped out of everything.*[63]

The modest profits made by Pacific Northwest wheat growers were made possible in part by the difficulties encountered by farmers from other regions. The 1937 McGregor wheat crop sold for $1.13, far above the 33¢ earned a few years before. Maurice McGregor commented: "This is a pretty good price after all, and certainly a lot better than we could have expected if drought had not ruined the Canadian crop. The Northwest is lucky again! I hope our luck holds out through several more years, but we will have to admit that we have had more than our share of the breaks." Columbia Plateau farmers found vivid evidence of the poverty of other regions in the arrival of hundreds of farm families forced out of the Great Plains by a combined tragedy—the Dust Bowl and the Great Depression. Two scientists from the Washington Agricultural Experiment Station studied the group and found that most of the families had less than five hundred dollars and that the chief economic asset for most of them was a car. The researchers commented: "The majority of the drought migrants came west with a car, usually of several years vintage, perhaps a trailer loaded with household goods, and whatever [little] money they possess."[64]

Economic conditions had begun to stabilize at Hooper by 1934. The weather continued to be cooperative: "The weather continues wonderful. This is undoubtedly the finest March weather I have ever seen. The grass is growing like it ordinarily does in April and we are able to turn the lambs out on excellent feed." Reports from the company town no longer talked of a struggle for economic survival. Maurice McGregor commented in a March letter to his uncle Archie:

> We have gone through a marvelous winter. . . . The wheat and grass is in excellent condition. Lambing has started and everything is busy around here. . . . The real excitement of the last week was the school election. The issue was whether or not to retain Cecil Milam as bus driver and whether to have dances in the Palouse Falls school house. The anti-Milam, pro-dance group won, electing Lucky Smith, Dan Barry, together with Mrs. Davidson as directors. It was an impassioned fight and the fact that it was over such irrelevant issues was the greatest possible compliment and vote of satisfaction in the main business of the school which is supposed to be teaching.

The wheat price looked "big compared with what we've had for several years," but the McGregors complained about their failure to hit a better market: "We sold our consigned wheat at the low point on the break last month. We didn't succeed in hitting the actual bottom but we came as close to it as could be expected. This is a fine performance after holding wheat through eight or nine months." The corporation increased the size of its sheep business, retaining 12,100 sheep during the winter of 1934 and the following spring. Sales of some of the lambs that had been held over resulted in "the best returns in several years." Alex C. McGregor commented: "The wool market holds in fine shape and lambs are looking like good property." [65]

The spring of 1935 was "cold, backward, but wet" and by April "the grass and crops . . . [were] making a splendid growth." Maurice McGregor found that little else had changed around the company town: "There doesn't seem to be anything new around here. Just the same yearly routine. Shearing will be finished tomorrow. The same crew and about the same number of wool sacks and the same wool buyers, looking wise and pessimistic and ready to offer two or three cents less than you think your wool is worth." The McGregors devoted a great deal of attention in 1935 to the continued process of improving the quality of an already generally efficient labor force. Wheat ranch foremen Warren Booth and Henry Lee were experienced, capable men. Maurice described Lee in 1935 as a man of "absolute honesty, energy, industry, sound common sense, and knowledge of tractors and tractor farming." Sheep foremen Jock Macrae and Emile Morod and most of the other employees won similar praise. But some problems were always encountered in maintaining a qualified crew. Maurice wrote former herder E. L. Jackson in January 1936:

> I received your letter today asking about your wages. You had $70.42 coming to you the night of December 7th, 1935. On that night you broke

out plate glass windows in the store, the repair of which has cost us $119.27. This does not include the window broken out in the bunk house, the windows in the shop nor the store window of plain glass nor the rifle you broke up hammering on the door. We have applied the $70.42 which was due to you onto the repair bill, leaving $48.85 you still owe us. However we don't want to hire you again to work this out because we are afraid you might get on another jag and break out all the glass on the place.[66]

As the McGregors relaxed their economy measures and rebuilt their businesses, they began to worry about the survival of the government loan and subsidy programs that had been so important to their corporation. The McGregors and many other Columbia Plateau farmers were convinced that "the Triple A saved us." William McGregor recalled some of the ways in which the various New Deal programs had helped the Hooper corporation:

Credit was very hard to get during the Depression. A number of the country banks around here that had farmland pledged as assets were closed by the federal inspectors because they simply wouldn't accept it as being an asset. Nobody had any money to buy wheat land or wanted to. With the banks so sour on farm mortgages, the PCA's gave us money to operate. Triple A attempted to manage grain supplies, and provided subsidies and payments for soil conservation. For awhile it was the only source of cash that wheat farmers had. Dad [Maurice] told me once that he got an $85 check from Triple A. . . . He had a stack of bills on his desk and every time he had some money he went through the stack to see which one needed paying worst. Apparently this was the day to pay the electrician in Lacrosse. The next day the banker up there showed Dad our Triple A check and it had been endorsed twelve times and had paid over a thousand dollars worth of debts.

Critics called the AAA a program of controlled scarcity. When drought in 1933 and 1934 produced blizzards of dust and scorched the wheat and corn crops of more than a dozen states, crop restrictions seemed ill-timed and inappropriate. The government agricultural programs had done little for tenants or sharecroppers, and small diversified farms, as well, were unable to gain much benefit from "set aside" payments. But for the farmers of the Columbia Plateau wheat region, the AAA had been a vital assistance. The concept of "parity" prices for farm products, incorporated into the New Deal programs from the McNary–Haugen bills, had been an idea long endorsed by the McGregors and other commercial farmers. When Secretary of Agriculture Henry Wallace came to eastern Washington in 1935, Maurice McGregor wrote: "Wallace is going to be in Walla Walla Monday. I'm going to hear him. The farm program upon which our survival as wheat growers depends is being subjected to some very heavy attacks and Henry Wallace has to be Horatius at the Bridge."

The billion and a half dollars of direct subsidies provided to American farmers by the New Deal programs had provided a margin for survival and made the McGregors and other beneficiaries enthusiastic about the Roosevelt administration. When the Supreme Court declared the original AAA unconstitutional in 1936, Congress quickly passed the Soil Conservation and Domestic Allotment Act, a bill that offered subsidies to farmers who took land out of production and planted cover crops. Maurice McGregor analyzed the new program in 1936: "My guess is that it will probably fail of its purpose to greatly reduce the surpluses of wheat or to have an adequate control over production. The farmer is encouraged to take out his least productive land which means that a 15 percent reduction in area means only a 5 to 10 percent reduction in crop. The payment for good farm practices will however be valuable and farmers can do some of the soil building they have wanted to on each farm but which the pressure for money and cash crops have prevented them from trying." [67]

Recognizing that "the wheat man in this country will be overlooking a bet unless he considers very carefully the chance this plan gives him," and convinced that "a good farmer is one who farms his land with full regard for duty to the soil," Maurice developed elaborate soil conservation programs for the McGregor ranch. He had been aware of serious erosion problems in the early 1930's: In an undated yearbook from those years, he wrote that the McGregor cropland "probably is approaching a critical stage." But plowing with the contour of the land and eliminating straw burning were about the only economically feasible changes possible in soil management during those desperate years. As economic conditions improved and government incentive payments enabled the McGregors to begin rebuilding their soils, Maurice became a leader in efforts to conserve the wheat lands of the Columbia Plateau. He served as chairman of the local soil conservation districts, became a state officer of range and cropland conservation committees, and represented the Pacific Northwest in a series of meetings with Henry Wallace. Maurice, Peter, and Alex McGregor inspected their farmland and pastures with officials of the state agricultural experiment station, followed the recommended procedures of planting crested wheatgrass as a cover crop in depleted areas, urged their neighbors to adopt similar soil rebuilding methods, and sold several varieties of grass seed needed for such programs. Their success was recognized when the Washington Agricultural Experiment Station awarded Maurice McGregor a certificate of merit "in recognition of distinguished service in the agricultural development of the Pacific Northwest."

Maurice also became one of the first Palouse country farmers to advocate the use of the "stubble mulch" (or "trashy fallow") system of soil management. The stubble mulch system, Maurice wrote, involved cultivation "so as to leave the stubble on top of the ground instead of burning it or plowing it under." A major departure from the older practice of tilling the soil into a fine, moisture-absorbing powder, stubble mulching involved pulling a blade, sweep, or rod through the soil beneath the surface while minimizing disturbance of the stubble cover. William McGregor described some of the problems encountered with the new tillage practices: "Once they started doing the trashy fallow . . . the yields dropped because the straw ties up nitrogen [as it decomposes] and the nitrogen was pretty run down anyway because there hadn't been any fertilization. So, a) it was hard to farm, b) the yields dropped because of the nitrogen tie-up, c) they immediately had cheatgrass [the practice of leaving ground cover allowed cheatgrass, an autumn-germinating annual weed, to prosper].[68]

Burning or clean fallowing offered short-run advantages but destroyed the soil structure when employed repeatedly. The McGregors continued to stubble mulch in spite of the difficulties, and they were gradually able to find ways to improve yields. Tandem discs were purchased to lessen soil pulverization and make cultivation easier. Winter and spring wheats were used in rotation to discourage weed growth. Experiments with sweet clover and alfalfa as alternate crops produced less satisfactory results on the semiarid cropland. More economically successful was the range conservation program instituted by Maurice McGregor in 1939. Soil Conservation Service range consultant John Chohlis later reported on the results of the rangeland improvements: "The McGregor Land and Livestock Company . . . was one of the first [outfits] in Washington to begin revising their [range] management system. Through fencing and water developments, they have made better and more efficient use of their range feed. By range reseeding and conversion seedings to alfalfa and grass on their wheat land they . . . have improved the condition of their grazing land and at the same time increased their per acre meat yields."

The concern about destructive methods of land use had come twenty years after agronomists first began to worry about the future of wheat production on the Columbia Plateau. Farmers had known for many years that they were losing tons of topsoil each growing season. Visible evidence of the problem was everywhere. Blowing dust and drifting soil had long been common in the Big Bend. The Palouse River and its tributaries had once supported trout and provided drinking water for Colfax and other towns. But the Palouse had since become a sluggish, dirty stream filled with runoff from the steep hills of wheat. Incentive payments encouraged Maurice McGregor and some other farmers to begin searching for ways to limit erosion. But the plateau country continued to produce good wheat crops in spite of the experts' warnings, and the pace of erosion was not slowed. In 1939, three Washington State College scientists found many farmers making no effort to conserve the soil because of "inertia, insufficient farm income, lack of appreciation of the seriousness of the situation, or an attitude of indifference . . . even though the situation is recognized." [69]

Soil conservation was challenging new work for Maurice McGregor in the late 1930's. But the McGregors had to continue to devote most of their attention to immediate matters: the quality of the wool clip, lambing percentages, and the size of the wheat crop. Inclement weather during the 1936 lambing season caused problems for McGregors and other sheepmen. Maurice commented:

> Lambing . . . is about over, and a most discouraging lambing it was. At present estimate it looks as if our percentage would be about 10 percent below last year. . . . It would seem that the increased price of wool would about make up the difference in expense this year over last year. . . . There are some wild tales running around about the terrible percentage losses of some sheep outfits, running up to 40 and 60 percent. It reminds me of the big percentages you hear about in good years except that this years rumors are in reverse.

Dry spring weather in 1937 did some damage to the wheat crop:

> The wheat is in need of moisture. The early growth this spring had an abundance of surface moisture which induced . . . a thick lower growth of foliage. The reserve moisture . . . was deficient however and when the dry spell in May was followed by a few sudden hot days the demand for moisture was greater than the supply and the lower leaves responded by burning off. This gave the fields a hell of a look for a few days. It was the old process that this country has to go through every year of cutting down a forty bushel prospect to something more in line with the actual moisture supply. The process is always painful but we go through it regularly enough to be used to it by this time. . . . The wheat crop prospect is of course the main interest now. It always is during June. The farmers get caught up with their years worrying this month and are reconciled to take what they've got by harvest time.

Prices for agricultural products fluctuated markedly and although profits continued to be made, the returns were not spectacular. Maurice McGregor said of the 1939 wool clip: "Shearing will start about the tenth. We've had no offers but something that might have been construed as a bid of 19 cents if we'd felt like doing any construing at that time. My own opinion is that something in the order of 18 or 19 cents is about what we can expect on the current market and personally I am prepared to take it and like it."[70]

The combination of government subsidies, gradually improving commodity prices, and an easing of credit restrictions enabled many Columbia Plateau farmers and ranchers to recover from the critical Depression years. Income was far less spectacular than during the boom days of World War I, but conditions had greatly improved since the early 1930's. H. Stanley Coffin provided a typical analysis of the period in a 1939 speech to the Washington Wool Growers Association: "Reviewing the past year of 1938, it has not been such a bad year for the sheepmen. A mild winter, with low priced feed, an extraordinarily good lambing, a fair price for wool, and a fair price for lambs, has put most of us out of the red." The mortgages signed during the Depression took many years to pay off—Coffin Sheep Company did not make final payment on a 1929 agreement until 1951, and McGregor Land and Livestock did not finish liquidating mortgages until after World War II. But the critical period was over well before 1940, and ranchers and farmers were able to begin the long process of recouping earlier losses. Officials of the Spokane and Eastern Trust Company congratulated the McGregors in 1935 on their ability to repay a Production Credit Association livestock mortgage: "Mighty glad to hear how you came out on your lambs . . . we are all pleased to hear the prices you got, and the fact that you are practically out of the PCA. . . . It's high time the sheepmen were having their inning." By 1935, residents of western Whitman County were so certain that Maurice, Alex, and Peter McGregor had overcome the difficulties of the Depression that a movement was begun to change the name of the town of Hooper to McGregor, Washington, "out of appreciation to the McGregors."[71]

The years 1920 to 1940 had marked a period of crisis and change for the McGregors and the thousands of other families raising wheat and livestock on the rolling hills and scabrock canyons of Washington and Oregon. The workhorses that had performed the laborious tasks of plowing, harrowing, and harvesting the wheat crops were gone, frequently to the inglorious end of becoming hog feed. The huge forces of traveling workers who had once ridden freight trains into the harvest fields of the Columbia Plateau were gone, as well. Farms and ranches were becoming larger, both in acreage and in amount of investment. Sherman Johnson, of the U.S. Department of Agriculture, described the importance of the displacement of work animals by gasoline-powered machinery: "The rapid shift from animal power to mechanical power for farm production in the interwar period constituted one of the most important changes that has ever taken place in American agriculture. It was a cornerstone in the foundation for increased production."

Several decades of intensive farming had provided evidence that the prairies and rolling hills of the Pacific Northwest did not have "inexhaustible" fertility. For the first time, some farmers became worried about the future productivity of their lands and began searching for ways to conserve their soils. Both farmers and livestock raisers found their success or failure increasingly dependent not only on local conditions, but on national and international problems as well. To market his products successfully, a Columbia Plateau sheepman or farmer had to gauge closely regional, national, and worldwide business trends. The critical years of the Depression forced the McGregors and their neighbors to turn in desperation to the federal government for assistance. So rapid had been the changes caused by the Depression, mechanization, and the increased role of the government in farming that a Washington Agricultural Experiment Station researcher concluded of the period 1930–35 alone: "It is doubtful if any previous period of equal length in the history of the State has shown such marked shifts in the State's agricultural pattern."[72]

Chapter 9

The McGregor Companies

BIOCHEMICAL AGRICULTURE ON THE
OLD SHEEP RANGES OF THE COLUMBIA PLATEAU

"If ammonia can be cheaply manufactured from atmospheric nitrogen the discovery means that a great step has been taken toward securing a material increase in the productiveness of the soil."   *The Ranch*, 1894

"The agricultural end of this business is not difficult. It is just complicated. A broad general background of business experience plus some knowledge of the sciences is about all you need. Practical experience is of some value unless such experiences should confirm you in the idea that you know all the answers. The ability to make a fresh approach is essential if you are going to keep on top in a field which is changing as rapidly as agriculture." Maurice McGregor to Sherman McGregor, 1947

"It is almost impossible to find men to take care of sheep at any price in these times. No one wants to be a sheepherder and the older men who have followed the occupation are dying off."   Emile Morod, 1951[1]

By 1940 the McGregor ranch had survived a half century in which the Columbia Plateau had changed from a region of open sheep ranges into an immensely productive land of mechanized agriculture. Peter, Alex, and Archie McGregor had survived to see their "tramp" sheep business develop into a large corporate ranch. Peter died in 1941 and Archie the following year, leaving Alex C. McGregor the only surviving member of the McGregor Brothers partnership. Although he remained company president and chairman of the board of directors until a few years before his death in 1952, Alex and his wife Jennie became less active in the McGregor enterprise. In 1945, Alex wrote to ninety-year-old Jock

Macrae, 47 years a McGregor sheepman, that the time had come for a new generation to take control:

You know you and I are getting along in years although our minds are still young. I guess we had better recognize the saying that when your mind tells you to do something that your body can't do you'd better mind what your body says. Whatever happens to us in the next few years will be softened by the realization that we have so many of our friends and dear ones on the other side that it will be worthwhile to hear them greet us with a hearty "Hello Mac" or "Hello Alex." You know Mac that House of Many Mansions was built for everybody which includes you and me. Let us not be satisfied with anything less. . . . I hope when you get to Hooper you will do as I am going to do. . . . Take it easy. We all love you and Hooper wouldn't be the same place without you so just use your rocker a little more. You have earned it.

Maurice McGregor, the forty-six-year-old son of Peter and Maude, handled the daily management of McGregor Land and Livestock Company in 1940. The leader of the family corporation since the onset of the Great Depression, Maurice would remain in charge until his death in 1956. Maurice remained an active, enthusiastic innovator. During the 1940's, for example, he raised experimental plots of garbanzo beans, dryland alfalfa, and other legumes in an unsuccessful search for alternate crops to replace summerfallow and provide added soil nutrients for wheat production. He cut the high labor costs of the irrigated lands near Hooper by tearing out the last of the apple orchards and replacing the old rill irrigation system with sprinklers. All of the irrigated lands were planted in alfalfa. His continued research in efficient soil management attracted regional attention. In 1942, soil conservation officials from throughout eastern Washington met to form a state organization and visited Hooper "to observe the soil and water conservation practices at the McGregor Land and Livestock ranch." Maurice's interests were wide-ranging—he spent several days calculating the protein and caloric content of all the groceries carried in the McGregor store to determine the most nutritious foods available for shipment to the herder's camps; he provided financial support and free meals at the Hooper Hotel every summer for Washington State College archaeologists and their students, who were excavating caves near the ranch in search of ancient Indian relics. These studies would later culminate in the discovery of the twelve-thousand-year-old "Marmes Man" skeleton near the confluence of the Palouse and Snake rivers, skeletal remains then thought to be the oldest known in the American West. Maurice also read widely and speculated about world political trends. During the late 1940's, for example, he wrote Dr. Arthur Peterson of Washington State College:

Socialism in theory is much concerned with economics but in practice it seems to be not an economic system at all but a system of political power and an amazingly effective one. Socialism everywhere seems to have a strong anti-consumer bias. The government continually proclaims new rigors and austerities for some remote and distant general good. . . . What little I know of history seems to say that men through almost all that history have lived under authoritarian regimes. The Liberalism of the 19th century both political and economic was magnificent in achievement and still bright with promise. But it may have come too soon in history and may be swamped by an upwelling from the depths of the more congenial despotisms. It would be a pity. I'm glad I don't know the answer.[2]

Writer John Gunther traveled past basalt buttes and scabrock and through "solid seas" of wheat in 1945 to spend several days visiting Maurice and Alex C. McGregor and to observe farm practices on a large corporate ranch. In his book, *Inside U.S.A.*, Gunther wrote that "everything is pretty much mechanized" on the McGregor wheat farm, with tractors, four combines with bulk grain tanks, six trucks, and a few "Cat skinners," truck drivers, and other men handling a harvest operation that had once required hundreds of workhorses and mules and numerous laborers. New strains of wheat developed by Columbia Plateau scientists were raised, including Rex, a variety "with a huge kernel like an acorn," and Orfed, "a new cross between Turkey Red and Federation." Gunther also wrote of the high labor costs required to maintain the eight thousand McGregor ewes and observed that "the trouble with sheep, I heard it said, is that they are a frontier industry, and the Northwest is no longer a frontier."

The changes Gunther described marked the beginnings of a period of transformation on the McGregor ranch and elsewhere on the Columbia Plateau. Maurice McGregor decided to seek additional management help to assist him in revising the operations of his family's ranch. His cousin Sherman McGregor, twelve years his junior and the son of Alex C. and Jennie McGregor, returned to Hooper in 1947 after ten years selling insurance and raising funds for the Community Chest in San Francisco and two years as a Red Cross field director with an all-black army unit in the Solomon Islands. A 1929 journalism graduate of Washington State College, Sherman McGregor had left Hooper in 1932 because there were "too many McGregors" and "because I felt that opportunities were not coming and I had no intention of working in the store the rest of my days." Maurice had encouraged his cousin to return to the ranch: "There are a lot of twists to our business where your experience will be of great value. I look forward with great pleasure to your arrival. Not only with pleasure Sherman but with enormous relief."[3] A year after he returned to Hooper, Sherman married Norma Gantzer, a Minnesota native he had met while she was working as a clerk in San Francisco. Sherman and Maurice were joined in the company management a few years later by William and John McGregor, the young sons of Maurice and Elgin McGregor (and the grandsons of Peter and Maude). John McGregor returned to the family farm in 1950 after receiving an economics degree at the University of California. He later married Patricia Dossee, a fellow Berkeley student and a fashion model. William McGregor, a liberal arts graduate of the University of Chicago and Stanford University, served with the infantry in Korea before returning to Hooper in 1954. He married Nancy Rohwer, a Vassar graduate and a descendant of pioneer Whitman County settlers.

The McGregor management faced the task of operating efficiently during a period described by some historians as an "agricultural revolution." Economist Harold Breimyer concluded in 1969 that the post-World War II years marked a turning point: "After countless centuries of history, production from farms is no longer so closely predestined by the mineral content of soils, the vagaries of rainfall, and the assiduousness of a labor force tied to the land." Engineers, plant breeders, animal breeders, agronomists, chemists, entomologists, and pathologists all contributed to a tremendous increase in the productivity of American agriculture. Cereal grain output per man-hour of labor more than doubled between 1949 and 1960, as farmers took advantage of improved implements and machines, better seeds, fertilizers, insecticides, and fungicides. The productivity increase was accompanied by a rapid decline in the number of Americans employed directly in agriculture. By the 1970's, less than 6 percent of the work force was on farms and ranches, a total less than half that of 1940, and far smaller than the 50 percent figure of the 1880's, when the McGregor brothers first began running sheep on the Columbia Plateau. The changes in machinery alone caused major management difficulties for American farmers: "Each change in farming that takes place as a result of the application of engineering, mechanization or technological science, results in new economic problems for the farmers. They require readjustments in farm organization and operation and present problems of management. . . . Scientific management requires budgetary methods, accounting control, and farming plans in keeping with production practices, standards of accomplishment, and future economic conditions." Advances in chemical and biological sciences during the 1930's helped lay the groundwork for further productivity increases and major changes in methods of operation.[4]

The huge demand for farm products during World War II marked an end to the Great Depression and enabled farmers to take full advantage of a backlog of improved mechanical and biochemical innovations. Prices of most farm commodities doubled during wartime. Maurice McGregor described government subsidies for wheat production and the general economic outlook in a 1946 letter to his uncle Alex:

> *I intend to take the thirty cent bonus . . . but to hold the wheat from sale . . . on the guess that price ceilings will have to be raised. . . . The general rise in prices (we are of course right now in the middle of a first class inflation) will permit the lift in parity prices by at least a dime and possibly twenty cents. So I propose to clip the government for at least thirty and possibly fifty cents before this deal is over. This price of course lifts wheat right out of the mouths of little pigs and steers that are being fattened on farms. . . .*
>
> *The weather and everything else goes well. . . . This is one of those years when we are in the chips. The government has dug up a new twist in corporation taxes. If the "accumulation" seems to be in excess of needs (the excess is determined by the judgment of the Internal Revenue Department) a further tax of 27½ percent may be added to the 38 percent now normal. Well, ho hum, this is the sort of thing we have to live with these days. Anyway you can't go broke taking profits.*

The prosperity of the postwar years enabled Columbia Plateau farmers to begin applying synthetic chemicals to their wheat fields. The most dramatic changes came as the result of the introduction of anhydrous ammonia (a foul-smelling natural gas derivative that contains more than 80 percent nitrogen and is stored as a liquid under pressure) and a series of chemically manufactured "dry" fertilizers, produced and applied in granular form.[5] For almost fifty years, a few scientists and farmers had worried that the once "inexhaustible" soils were becoming deficient in nitrogen, phosphate, and other plant foods. But the only available commercial fertilizers—blood, bone meal, tankage from packing plants, and sodium nitrate, frequently produced from Chilean guano—were expensive and of questionable economic benefit. An organic fertilizer—manure from sheep, cattle, and horses—was cheap and in ample supply. Yet manure generally contained only meager amounts of nitrogen (less than 5 percent by weight), the most important nutrient needed for Columbia Plateau wheat fields. The use of commercial plant foods became feasible only after scientists learned how to extract nitrogen from the air, a procedure made possible after German chemist Fritz Haber discovered the nitrogen-fixing process before World War I. Commercial ammonia plants that combined hydrogen from natural gas wells with atmospheric nitrogen were in operation in the thirties, and the product was used as a fertilizer for row crops in California. After World War II, concentrated synthetic fertilizers became available at a relatively inexpensive cost. Ammunition plants built by the federal government were sold to private chemical companies and converted from explosives production to fertilizer manufacturing.[6]

An additional series of commercially produced chemicals was useful for killing weeds, insects, and fungi. DDT, a chlorinated hydrocarbon developed in the 1930's by a Swiss chemist, was being sold in America by 1940 as an all-purpose insecticide. Two USDA scientists described the new product as "effective against a wider variety of agricultural pests than any other synthetic insecticide heretofore tested . . . and, wonderful to relate, its effect lasts, sometimes as long as a year." The new chemicals were accepted uncritically, for they were remarkably effective tools far superior to previous pesticides—such as bluestone, kerosene, arsenic, whale oil, and even ice water and boiling water. These early agricultural chemicals had been either completely ineffective (such as the ice water Washington State College scientists suggested as a cure for red spiders in the McGregor apple orchards) or far too toxic. McGregors used arsenic in the orchard in 1926 and, although the apples "showed too much arsenic to be reassuring," they decided "that if the sorters wipe every apple with their gloves they will get by" state inspection. Fifty-five years later the alfalfa grown on the land remains stunted in places where arsenic was used on the apple trees. The new petroleum-based chemicals were selective products that could kill a specific weed or insect without damaging the crop. In 1958, Washington State College weed scientist T. J. Muzik noted that: "The hoe and the cultivator are rapidly being replaced with sprayers to apply chemicals having remarkable selective properties for controlling specific weeds. New chemicals, new methods of application, and new formulations of chemicals are pouring out in a constant stream from commercial companies. Many of these chemicals have new and unusual properties. Very few of them have been adequately investigated."[7]

The biochemical advances offered farmers the intriguing possibility of improving the profit per acre of crop production. But a great deal of research needed to be done before the new farming techniques could be used to advantage. The McGregor management developed an avid interest in the practical use of agricultural science, sharing the belief of the nineteenth century Wisconsin farmer who did not want "science floating in the skies" and urged researchers to "bring it down and hitch it to our plows." For more than forty years, the McGregor family had paid attention to the research done at the state agricultural experiment station, since the days when Peter McGregor had been chairman of the board of overseers at that institution. The ties between farmer and scientist became closer in 1950, when veteran agricultural researcher Harley Jacquot began a career of almost twenty-five years as full-time agronomist for the McGregors. Jacquot had served for several years as superintendent of the state dryland experiment station at Lind before he received a grant to study the effects of nitrogen on soil fertility in the Palouse country. In upland areas with relatively high rainfall, the program proceeded smoothly: "In the upper country farmers had already tried to furnish nitrogen by raising peas, sweet clover, and alfalfa. But aphids ruined the clover and they lost most of the peas to the weavel. And alfalfa kept the land out of wheat production so long that they lost money. So when I started on the fertilizer the farmers in the upper country . . . were very much interested in the work I was doing and wanted it right away. I was making speeches all the way over into Idaho telling them how much to put on. Boy that was music to their ears."

But in the semiarid lowlands of the western Palouse, Umatilla, Horse Heaven, and Big Bend, areas that comprise most of the farmlands of the Columbia Plateau, both farmers and scientists were skeptical about the usefulness of chemical fertilizers. Jacquot later described the opposition in one of his annual two-hundred-page "McGregor Ranch Agronomic Reports": "When . . . [I] first proposed the use of nitrogen fertilizer in 1947 for the setting up of field testing plots in west Whitman county, the soil experts at the Washington Agricultural Experiment Station were firmly in the belief that under dry land agriculture moisture was the major factor limiting production of cereal crops and that applying nitrogen fertilizer would not increase the crop yield enough to be economically feasible." Jacquot recalled the circumstances that led him to become perhaps the first and only full-time agronomist on any Pacific Northwest wheat ranch. The professors in the soils department at Washington State College

> swore up and down that nitrogen did not have an important effect. They made things hot for me. They'd even take out a book and show me where they learned you cannot use nitrate fertilizers. Boy I really tore into them. I said "that book was written years ago. You don't have any experimental plots out and you're just teaching what you learned from the book." I didn't make very many friends. We really drew a hot battle because it was a concept they couldn't accept. But I started carrying on experiments and Maurice McGregor, who'd known my work for twenty years, came to me and said. . . . "We've been farming for over 40 years now and possibly we could benefit from a new method of farming. We have a large area and we're pretty well in debt now, about a quarter of a million dollars, and just producing wheat under the conventional method isn't helping out too much. . . . In the event that something happens and

you aren't staying with the state college I'd be very interested in your working with us. Don't let that interfere with your program because I think your program is too important to let go." When funds were diverted from my work . . . I came to McGregors and carried on experiments through Maurice's encouragement. . . . He's the one that really put this fertilizer program on the map.[8]

The McGregors were convinced that "there's a lot of technical skill and information which is just going to waste because farmers don't take advantage of it." The research was expected to return profits. John McGregor explained in 1953: "What we do in our research work is not done entirely out of scientific curiosity. It's a business proposition which must pay off in dollars and cents. We feel we've already profited handsomely in the first few years of research in our fertilizer programs." Maurice McGregor emphasized the need to exercise caution in the experimentation: "One return you can't measure very well is the negative answer, which can keep you from making some damn fool mistake that might cost you a lot of money. . . . You can play around with a lot of ideas, but none of that is going to do you any good unless you stay solvent."

If the McGregors remained careful and always attentive of their year-end financial statements, they were nevertheless able to "play around with a lot of ideas" after World War II. The annual pre-tax net earnings of McGregor Land and Livestock climbed from $30,000 annually during the early 1940's to $242,000 in 1950. The income of other farmers also increased during the years 1941–53, the most prosperous period for American agriculture since 1910. Increased farm output, demands for food and fiber during the world war and the Korean conflict, price supports, foreign aid, and a brisk export market to nations whose farmlands had been ravaged by war all spurred the new prosperity. One of the largest ranching and farming businesses on the Columbia Plateau, McGregor Land and Livestock had the financial strength to take advantage of new scientific advances. Soil Conservation Service consultant G. John Chohlis reported on the innovations of the McGregor management in a 1953 article in *Farm Management*, an agricultural trade journal: "Several of us find we have to talk to the McGregors every now and then just to keep up with what they are doing. . . . Closely-held control . . . the intimate relationship between the land and the family . . . and an adventuresome spirit. . . . Mix them together and you come up with a ranch that sets a fast pace for Northwest agriculture."[9]

Maurice McGregor told sixty-three farmers from Dayton, Waitsburg, and Pomeroy who came to visit the ranch in 1952 of his goal of increasing wheat yields to sixty-five bushels per acre. He told of a grass and alfalfa rotation designed to build soil humus and help prevent erosion. "This year," a reporter noted, he is going to try seeding "alfalfa [on land usually fallowed] with barley as a nurse crop and then this fall over-seeding the alfalfa with grass." But the farmers were most interested in learning about the McGregors' experiments with commercial fertilizers, for these appeared to offer immediate promise of higher yields. The McGregors had set up their own soil testing laboratory, where soil samples were baked in an oven to determine moisture content and run through a chemical analysis to ascertain the amount of available nitrogen. When the McGregors first fertilized a hundred acres of test plots a few years earlier, the results had been dramatic: Untreated plots yielded 33 bushels, areas fertilized with 30 pounds of nitrogen produced 46 bushels, a 60-pound rate resulted in 59 bushels, and 90 pounds of nitrogen produced almost 69 bushels of wheat from a land where 25 bushels was a long accepted average. Maurice McGregor and Harley Jacquot also questioned the traditional practice of summerfallowing the semiarid croplands. Perhaps nitrogen, not moisture, was the major factor limiting annual crop production. The yields were smaller on lands that were fertilized and cropped every year. But this experiment also showed promise. Editor Harold Rogers of the *Washington Farmer* reported in 1952 on lands put into wheat every year by McGregor Land and Livestock: "A 100-acre field on the McGregor ranch . . . has grown four grain crops in four years, averaging 27 bushels a year, under normal rainfall of 13 inches. A good average for an unfertilized summerfallow crop in the same area is 32 bushels. The difference between 27 bushels every year and 32 bushels every second year makes a noise loud enough to be heard all over what is called the intermediate rainfall area. . . . And the echoes can be distantly heard even farther out in the dry lands." Annual cropping became impractical a year later when government allotment programs and subsidies for limiting crop acreage, removed during World War II and its aftermath, were reinstituted. The results of fertilizing under the summerfallow system were often less dramatic than they had been during the first year of experimentation. But the McGregors had learned that applying chemicals to their wheat fields brought definite productivity increases. Maurice commented in a 1952 issue of *Washington Farmer*: "The most surprising thing to me . . . was not what we learned from the experiments, but the fact that we did not know already. I have lived here all my life, and I keep asking myself, 'Why didn't we find all this out a long time ago?' " [10]

The McGregor research program was expanded every year. During the 1959 crop year, for example, more than 1,100 test plots were harvested on the McGregor ranch. Jacquot explained his research work in a 1959 issue of *Western Crops and Farm Management*: "Experimental work done on . . . the McGregor Ranch in the last 12 years has involved every conceivable problem of dryland agriculture, including fertilizing, tillage, weed control, seeding methods, moisture and nitrate studies, rotation of crops and varietal testing. Each of these problems was given as much attention as time and energy would permit, with emphasis constantly shifting from one major factor to another to facilitate application of the most promising method to field operation as soon as practicable." The McGregors demonstrated the results of their experiments to visiting farmers in a series of field days, held annually during the month of June. Jacquot spoke at twenty to thirty farmer meetings per year and published numerous journal articles explaining the results of his research. Farmers from many portions of the Columbia Plateau came to inspect the Hooper farm, and a trade magazine reported that, during the 1962 field tours, "another group visited The McGregor Ranch, as hundreds of groups and individuals had before. The major difference was that the gentlemen had traveled all the way from western Australia. Through correspondence the Australian farmers had learned that their soil was similar to that in the Northwestern United States and that McGregors operations were recommended for study." The demonstrations and tours served a definite economic purpose. The McGregors had begun selling chemical fertilizers to their neighbors in 1948 as a sideline to their general merchandise business. Beginning with a crew of two—Sherman McGregor and store clerk Cliff Rollins—the corporation developed a large farm chemical business. The Australian farmers ordered McGregor-manufactured chemical application equipment for shipment to Perth, Australia. Sherman McGregor explained the benefits of the field tours in 1958:

> Most of Harley Jacquot's work has been on our own ranch and he has proven it and sold us on his theories. That has been our greatest sales tool. We can not only tell a person what we think, but we can take him to our own ranch and show him exactly what we are talking about, without attempting to sell him anything we don't actually do ourselves. Harley's work has been demonstrated to the people of southeastern Washington each year and during the month of June our company holds three field days. . . . [Farmers] visit the experimental plots, see Harley's field application . . . and spend an afternoon visiting and discussing our experimental work. We have probably averaged 150 people each season during the tour week alone.[11]

The improvement of soil fertility and productivity was a long-term process of trial and error. Government wheat acreage restrictions prompted the McGregors to experiment with safflower, alfalfa, and a series of other crops on the lands taken out of wheat production. But only barley, used for livestock feed, proved feasible—and barley commanded dismally low market prices. In higher rainfall areas further east, peas and lentils emerged as logical alternatives to wheat production. By the 1960's, the Palouse country uplands raised more than 90 percent of the dry peas and lentils grown in the United States. Unfavorable weather continued to be an adversary in grain production. A hailstorm destroyed 45,000 bushels of McGregor wheat in 1955. Jacquot reported: "As far as any old-timers can remember, this was the worst storm that ever happened on the McGregor Ranch." The 1961 crop season was particularly discouraging, with a yield of less than 30 bushels per acre from what had been potentially "a record breaking crop":

> *Within the last eleven years of experimental work on the McGregor ranch, 1961 was the most disappointing one of all. . . . The extreme favorable climate during the crop year was apparently quite optimum for high infection of diseases which the wheat crops were incapable of resisting. Weeds, particularly cheatgrass, flourished exceedingly well because of not only the natural resistance it carried against yellow stripe rust, but also its adaptibility. . . . [Excessive moisture brought] a host of diseases that ordinarily would have no significant effect on the yield of wheat. . . . The cool, wet spring . . . stimulated the development of the pathogenic organisms with sufficient magnitude to render tremendous destruction to the growing crop.*

Harley Jacquot sometimes complained that the McGregors and their employees were too slow in implementing new farming methods. In one of his annual reports, Jacquot contended that "the total loss suffered from delaying the seeding a full month . . . was a fantastic $30 per acre. Just the matter of delaying the date of seeding was a costly privilege of mismanagement." The McGregors were deliberate and cautious before committing the thousands of acres in crop to a new procedure. Ranch foreman Hans Kahler, a McGregor employee for almost forty years, and the crew of veteran "Cat skinners" were reluctant to abandon farm practices they had used successfully for many years. But if there were sometimes differences of opinion among farm owners, farmhands, and the agronomist, the methods of operation were gradually modified and wheat output increased. Jacquot, Maurice McGregor (wheat ranch manager until his death in 1956), and his successor William McGregor worked to combine soil conservation practices, maximum fertilizer use, and innovative farming techniques into an economically feasible farming system. Synthetic fertilizers had a clearly demonstrable effect on farm income: Jacquot estimated that fertilizer use on the McGregor ranch brought a return of three dollars per dollar invested. In 1972, Jacquot analyzed the response to the soil fertilization program he helped pioneer: "In 20 years, the grain farmers in eastern Washington have been convinced of the value of nitrogen fertilizer applications . . . [and] nearly 100 percent of them are now using optimum amounts of fertilizer for dryland grain production."

Stubble mulch summerfallowing, a procedure the McGregors had used for three decades, was far less popular than fertilizers and pesticides. "Clean fallow," long a standard practice in much of the Columbia Plateau wheat country, continued to cause serious erosion. Jacquot worried in 1957 about "the tendency toward destruction of all the wheat land soils of the Pacific Northwest" and wondered how much longer existing methods of farming could be continued before the land suffered irreparable damage. But plowing under or burning the stubble, in spite of the warnings of the experts, generally resulted in better weed control and slightly higher yields. Fertilizers and the vast array of available farm chemicals may have slowed the changes in cultivation practices by shielding wheat growers from economic losses caused by erosion of topsoil and destruction of cropland humus. Jacquot and the McGregors continued to save the stubble and found that herbicides used in conjunction with this system produced almost seventeen dollars per acre more profit than did clean fallowed land. Jacquot and his employers received recognition for their interest in improved methods of farming: In 1976, William McGregor was one of three farmers honored by Washington State University for outstanding support of agricultural research; in 1965, Jacquot received an award from the Philadelphia-based Soil Conservation Society of America "for outstanding work on the control of soil erosion."[12]

The development of higher yielding, disease-resistant varieties of wheat by the state agricultural experiment station was an important factor in the increasingly large yields recorded on the McGregor ranch and throughout the Columbia Plateau. Plant breeders worked to develop new varieties of wheat that would allow farmers to take advantage of improvements in fertilizer technology. The varieties of wheat available when fertilizer came into use in the late 1940's often grew long chaff, shattered easily, and did not make efficient use of the soil's increased fertility. Plant breeder Orville Vogel of the U.S. Department of Agriculture, stationed at Washington State College, explained in 1952 that he and other experiment station scientists were seeking varieties capable of increased yields, with "very short straw and low ratio of straw to grain and low tillering capacity and slow recovery in the spring to prevent excessive vegetative growth and damage from late spring frost." Attempts were also made to reduce "the losses from stinking smut, lodging, shattering, winterkilling, etc."

The scientists were engaged in a never-ending battle to develop new disease-resistant varieties of wheat faster than new fungi appeared. In the 1920's, scientists had given the Columbia Plateau the dubious honor of being "the wheat smut center of the world." Researcher E. F. Gaines won a temporary victory against the fungus in 1924 by developing Ridit, the first smut-resistant strain in the Pacific Northwest. Ridit later became susceptible to dwarf smut. New varieties were developed, and by 1941 the plant breeders had helped Pacific Northwest farmers cut the percentage of wheat graded as 'smutty" from 50 percent to 3 percent. But new varieties of smut, snow mold, bunt, foot rot, and other diseases continually appeared. By the mid-1950's, Columbia Plateau wheat farmers lost more than five million dollars a year because of smut alone. The number of known races of smut had increased from a very few to more than thirty. In 1966 B. R. Bertramson, chairman of the agronomy department at Washington State College, described some of the difficulties encountered in the struggle to develop disease-resistant wheat varieties:

> The battle of wheat breeders with diseases is well depicted by what has happened within the past 15 years. Elmar replaced Elgin which smutted badly and then in 1956, Elmar was replaced by Omar and smut declined to where it was almost an oddity. But in 1961 and 1965, Omar yield was cut 25 to 50 percent in some areas because of heavy stripe rust infestations. Gaines came into the fray. It yields in spite of stripe rust infection, but does take the disease in the seedling stage. Now, Moro has been released and it is as resistant to stripe rust as Omar was to smut![13]

The scientists had made great advances in the sixty years since W. J. Spillman initiated Columbia Plateau wheat breeding research. The most promising new wheat was Gaines, a variety developed by O. A. Vogel from the progeny of his 1949 crossbreeding of Norin 10 (a Japanese "semi-dwarf" wheat) and Brevor, a Pacific Northwest variety. Vogel had also developed Omar, Brevor, Burt, and Orfed, varieties that were widely used on the Columbia Plateau in the 1950's. Gaines was readily accepted by the McGregors and other farmers. In 1963, the first year Gaines was in commercial production, more than 40 percent of the wheat sown on the plateau was of this variety. A strain of wheat able to produce high yields through efficient fertilizer use, Gaines had short straw, resisted lodging, and was resistant to many diseases. B. R. Bertramson estimated that during 1964–74 Gaines brought Washington, Oregon, and Idaho farmers a total additional income of $770 million because of its high-yielding abilities. Vogel won the National Medal of

Science in 1975 for developing Gaines and its successor, Nugaines. Nobel-Prize-winning plant breeder Norman Borlaug noted that "it was from this genetic material that we were able to breed and develop the Mexican dwarf wheat varieties that subsequently revolutionized wheat production in Mexico, India, and Pakistan." But diseases continued to cause serious losses on Columbia Plateau farms despite improved strains of wheat and fungicidal seed treatments. In 1970, for example, fusarium root rot and "strawbreaker" foot rot caused losses in wheat output. Delayed seeding, the best measure to control "strawbreaker," contributed to soil erosion. An experiment station scientist, J. M. Cook, noted that farmers would have to decide "which is best, erosion or foot rot," when they seeded their crops. Cook did research on a new chemical fungicide that gave farmers an effective weapon against foot rot. But the price of foot rot control was high—fourteen dollars per acre annually. Several new varieties of wheat were introduced in the 1970's, including Paha, Luke, and Jacmar, a variety developed by McGregor agronomist Harley Jacquot.[14]

The improved varieties of wheat developed by Vogel and other researchers, and the more than fivefold increase in fertilizer use on Columbia Plateau wheat farms after 1950, led to major gains in output. Yields in Whitman County increased from twenty to thirty bushels in the 1940's, to nearly forty bushels in the next decade, and to fifty-three bushels during the period 1965–75. On the McGregor ranch, at the semiarid western edge of the county, yields climbed from twenty-five bushels in the 1940's to forty-five bushels in the 1960's. The McGregors had a sixty-one bushel crop in 1972 and later two crops above fifty-five bushels—exceptional averages for several thousand acres of farmland in a region with less than fourteen inches of rainfall. By 1955, the Columbia Plateau counties of Whitman, Lincoln, and Adams led the nation in wheat output, with crops generally averaging 12, 10 and 8 million bushels annually. The plateau country produced even larger crops in later years. By the early 1970's, wheat output in Whitman County had reached 25 million bushels.

Jacquot analyzed the program that had made the productivity increase possible in his last two McGregor Ranch Agronomic Reports, issued before he became a part-time consultant for the corporation in 1974: "The most prominent factor may be the effect of the fertilizer application. . . . One may consider that the agricultural improvement resulted from a chain reaction starting with the use of fertilizers which in turn necessitated the development of new varieties more adapted to higher soil fertility." Coupled with the optimum use of fertilizers and higher-yielding varieties were a "better understanding of the conservation of soil moisture by suitable soil management, effective use of herbicides for controlling the weed population, and the adoption of an earlier date of seeding by making use of better and up to date seeding equipment."[15]

The management of the farming business became increasingly difficult during a period in which agriculture was undergoing a series of major alterations. Changes in farm equipment accompanied the biochemical innovations. Seven men, equipped with three self-propelled, air-conditioned combines; a "bankout wagon" (a huge diesel-powered machine, similar in appearance to an earth mover, that travels with ease over the steep hillsides hauling wheat from the combines to trucks waiting at the edge of the fields); and three trucks by 1970 handled harvest operations that had once required a crew of 100 men aided by 310 horses and mules. The new machines required only a third of the manpower of tractors and combines in use during World War II. Even more elaborate equipment would be marketed on the plateau, including a $160,000 wheel tractor that could pull vast tonnages at amazing speed over the steep hills, and a $120,000 hillside combine said to be the "world's largest" with a 24-foot cutter bar, an unloading speed of two bushels a second, four-wheel drive, digital engine readout, and a cab so quiet and comfortable one farmer described it as "just like sitting in a rocking chair in your living room." The power, speed, comfort, and price of the elaborate farm machinery far surpassed early petroleum-powered equipment, which had sold for five thousand dollars or less. But the high cost of improved technology, escalating fuel costs (and resultant price increases in petroleum-based fertilizers and chemicals), coupled with often-sluggish wheat markets and the vagaries of weather, further heightened the risks of grain production.[16]

The huge volume of wheat produced on the Columbia Plateau made the region more dependent than ever upon export markets. Most of the starchy white wheat was sold for use in noodles, pastries, and thin bread cakes in Japan, Korea, Taiwan, India, and Iran. During his terms as president of the Washington Association of Wheat Growers and the Western Wheat Associates, William McGregor traveled to Japan, India, Singapore, and other foreign marketplaces to promote actively the sale of Columbia Plateau wheats. He spent five weeks in the Soviet Union in 1973 as a member of the exploratory trade team of the Department of Commerce and Economic Development. The huge crops grown year after year by farmers of the northwest wheat belt helped feed the multitudes of Asia, but left growers more vulnerable than ever to political instability and crop conditions in distant lands. But by 1980, the McGregor corporation had been able to record an operating profit from its farmland for forty-seven consecutive years, since the worst of the Great

Depression, while revising methods of operation and reacting to rapidly changing circumstances.[17]

The spectacular results of experiments conducted on their own farm prompted the McGregors to begin purchasing and storing large supplies of agricultural chemicals in the late 1940's. Other farmers became interested in the new products, and the McGregors began selling sacks of dry fertilizer to their neighbors. The chemicals were in short supply, and the McGregors had difficulty keeping up with the demand. Farmers from many areas of the Columbia Plateau traveled to the Hooper store to urge the McGregors to sell them new products. Sherman McGregor was able to locate only one source for nitrogen, the Spokane office of the Balfour, Guthrie Company, an international grain marketing firm. By visiting the Spokane agency every week and reminding the firm that the McGregors had sold their grain to Balfour, Guthrie for forty years, he was able to overcome the company's reluctance to part with their small supplies. As the sacked dry fertilizers became more readily available, the volume of McGregor sales began to exceed five hundred thousand dollars per year.

When anhydrous ammonia, a concentrated product containing 82 percent nitrogen, first became available on the plateau in 1952, Sherman McGregor and fellow store clerk Cliff Rollins developed makeshift techniques for handling the acrid, pressurized gas. They custom-fitted a derrick to the back of a two-ton flatbed truck, placed heavy-duty 300-gallon tanks on the vehicle and pumped them full of ammonia from a railroad car of the product, and hauled to the field where a tank was unloaded on a converted Graham-Hoeme plow that had tubes running down the plowshares to inject the gas six inches underground. Unloading the first railcar of ammonia shipped to the town of Colfax, they inadvertently jarred open the main valve and a fog of ammonia vapor began moving into an adjacent residential area. Rollins got ammonia in his eye and was rushed to the hospital. After several tries, McGregor succeeded in racing through the caustic fog to pull his gas mask from the truck, only to find it inoperable. Aided by the Red Cross, he ran from house to house to warn townspeople until a chemical engineer who happened to be in Colfax arrived and shut the valve. No one was injured and the local newspaper editor joked that McGregor had performed a service by "ammoniating" all the toothpaste in town. But the new disaster was a lesson in the dangers of mishandling commercial fertilizers.

The McGregors built fertilizer handling facilities away from residential areas and developed ammonia application equipment designed for efficiency and safety. Sherman McGregor recalled that the converted Graham-Hoeme plow equipment "was exceedingly awkward. . . . It took long hours and backbreaking work to get these machines set up and ready to apply ammonia. . . . It was considerable work getting them taken down and onto the road and moved to the next field." The Mc-Gregors built a manufacturing plant a few miles from Colfax, in the middle of the Palouse country farming district, where they built big, wide fertilizer applicators and herbicide sprayers: implements that were up to 110 feet in width, with masses of steel; a complex system of tanks, valves, and gauges; and huge airplane tires to prevent the equipment from digging up the loose soils. One serviceman could fold each machine into an eight-foot-wide unit for road travel. Cliff Rollins and shop foreman Chester Field developed a finger-like "shank" specially designed to insert ammonia from the applicator into the soil as a vapor. Much of this machinery became standard throughout the Northwest wheat belt and on the Canadian prairies. The McGregors and their competitors later built "triple shooters," even more elaborate implements that farmers could use for simultaneous application of liquid nitrogen, phosphorus, and sulfur to their wheat fields.[18]

The McGregor farm chemical business expanded rapidly during the 1950's. As the McGregors began to supply products to new areas distant from Hooper, Sherman McGregor hired young men with farm backgrounds to sell products in these districts. Farmland was expensive and opportunities limited for men who were not in a position to inherit a farm but wanted to stay in the Palouse country areas where they had been raised. By locating competent, ambitious men and giving them a great deal of control over the marketing of farm supply products in their own communities, the McGregors were able to build a sizable business. Grange supply stores and some businesses begun by other farmers competed with the Hooper firm, but the McGregors had some advantages. They had entered the trade early and had learned from their mistakes before most of their rivals had entered the business. They had on their staff an agronomist who had become widely known by farmers as one of the foremost advocates of fertilizer use. As the owners of a large corporate farm, the McGregors had the financial backing to afford the expensive new machinery required for anhydrous ammonia. By 1956, the rapidly increasing sales and steadily improving profits from farm chemicals had reached a volume sufficient to justify the incorporation of a new organization, The McGregor Company, a wholly owned subsidiary of the McGregor Land and Livestock Company. William, John, and Sherman McGregor were owners and officers of both concerns. Sherman McGregor became the president and manager of the subsidary. Sales increased from about a million dollars annually in the mid-1950's to four million in the 1960's and twenty million in the 1970's. The marketing of farm chemicals never failed to produce a profit for the McGregors.

The corporation became the major supplier of farm chemicals in the Palouse country. Warehouses, shops, offices, and fertilizer handling equipment were installed, and crews were hired to sell McGregor products in eleven Palouse country towns: Lacrosse (opened in 1952), Endicott (1952), Colfax (1953), Garfield (1958), Palouse (1959), Pullman (1962), Uniontown (1963), Thornton (1963), Oakesdale (1965), Plaza (1969), and Genesee, Idaho (1968). Further expansion to the Camas Prairie (a plant at Grangeville, Idaho, opened in 1969), the Walla Walla country (with a facility at Pomeroy), the Big Bend (served through Pasco), and eastern Oregon (with the development of facilities at Hermiston and Boardman) enabled The McGregor Company to serve farmers in most districts of the Columbia Plateau. Eighteen-thousand-dollar fertilizer applicators, improved with hydraulic devices that eliminated most of the physical labor of chemical farming, were sold by the hundreds each year to dealers in Alberta, Manitoba, and Saskatchewan and throughout much of the American West. Supply depots for applicator parts were established at Red Deer, Alberta; Melfort, Saskatchewan; and Brandon, Manitoba.

The plants at Hermiston, Boardman, and Pasco were in the middle of an area of sagebrush and sand dunes (receiving only about six inches of rainfall a year) once used for the flocks owned by Adrien Magallon, Coffin Sheep Company, Baldwin Sheep and Land Company, Rugg Brothers, Prior Land and Livestock, and other sheep businesses. Farmers using huge, automated, circular sprinkler systems (each supplying Columbia River water to 160 acres of land) and large quantities of fertilizers (a ton or more per acre) raised potatoes, sugar beets, corn, and wheat on desert topsoils composed almost entirely of sand. The desert lowlands of this district became the fastest growing portion of the Columbia Plateau after 1965. The largest irrigated farms, sometimes five to ten thousand acres or more in size, were often operated by multinational corporations or wealthy outside investors interested in participating in the rapid development of a barren land. Ramshackle sheep cabins were razed, sand dunes leveled, and water pumped several miles from the Columbia through six-foot-high steel pipes that traversed the steep river canyon. The scale of capital investment was enormous. Individual farm businesses sometimes required more than fifty thousand dollars worth of fertilizer in a day, delivered in precise mixtures of nitrogen, boron, potash, zinc, sulfur, phosphorus, and other elements, with additional amounts of herbicides, fungicides, and insecticides mixed into the desert

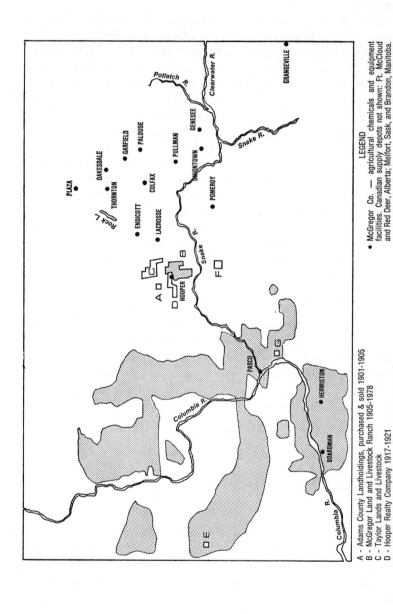

LEGEND

A - Adams County Landholdings, purchased & sold 1901-1905
B - McGregor Land and Livestock Ranch 1905-1978
C - Taylor Lands and Livestock
D - Hooper Realty Company 1917-1921
E - "California Ranch" - owned and operated in late 1920's
F - "Starbuck Ranch" - early 1920's
G - McGregor Feedlot

● McGregor Co. — agricultural chemicals and equipment
  facilities. Canadian supply depots not shown: Ft. McCloud
  and Red Deer, Alberta; Melfort, Sask, and Brandon, Manitoba.

▨ Irrigated lands. The rest of the plateau, except for scabrock,
  river canyons, and other scattered areas, produces dryland
  wheat.

Irrigated lands, ranch holdings, and McGregor plants, 1900–78 sands. Farming was as unstable in this new capital-intensive area of irrigated agriculture as it had been in the frontier days of the Palouse: Every year in the late 1960's and early 1970's as many as a third of the irrigated projects changed hands. Large corporations became discouraged with the poor return on investment and sold their holdings when potato and sugar beet prices dropped. As land values climbed, those who had been interested in irrigated farming as a speculative investment also sold their lands. Bankruptcies and foreclosures were commonplace as marginally financed operators were confronted with the huge costs of turning poor sheep pastures into productive land. The farm chemical supply business was intensely competive, and many of these businesses lost money. The McGregors sometimes sold five million dollars' worth of products in a year in this area, only to realize a very small return or take a loss.

The dryland wheat region remained the mainstay of the McGregor chemical business. Here the McGregor managers and their employees worked with the same farmers year after year and emphasized service and new fertilizer machinery as their main selling points. The McGregor farm supply enterprise was fortunate to have among the 150 fertilizer employees many capable, experienced people who remained with the company for ten, twenty, and even thirty years. In 1969, Sherman McGregor credited the "accomplishments of high quality, well-trained managerial people who, in turn, have recruited top field and service personnel" for making the farm chemical business successful. McGregor, Cliff Rollins, and Dick Walter, the three men who first sold chemicals as a part-time addition to their work in the Hooper store, each remained with the firm more than twenty-five years—Walter as a plant manager and salesman, Rollins as general manager, and McGregor as company president and director of several regional and national trade groups. The McGregor Company was able to survive as the farm chemicals business underwent a rapid period of change. By the early 1970's, most of the independent locally owned fertilizer businesses of the Columbia Plateau had been sold—often to companies owned by national oil-producing corporations. The small farmer-owned granges and farm supply stores became part of national "cooperatives," some of which sold more than a billion dollars' worth of supplies to farmers in the Midwest and Pacific Slope states every year. By expanding and developing sixteen outlets and various warehouses and storage facilities, the McGregors were able to compete successfully with their new rivals.

But the future had become filled with uncertainties for wheat farmers and farm chemical dealers of the biochemical age. The productivity of Columbia Plateau farms had become dependent on nitrogen produced from Alaskan and Canadian natural gas, phosphate from Florida and Morocco, and hundreds of herbicides and pesticides manufactured from petroleum. The Columbia Plateau had its first serious fertilizer shortage in 1974. Manufacturers in the American West ran out of oil needed to produce the synthetic chemicals. An adequate supply of anhydrous ammonia had been produced in Alaska. But the only American-made ship equipped to haul the product sank and the Jones Act, intended to protect American laborers and shippers, prohibited the use of foreign vessels for the hauling of American products between domestic ports. The Alaskan ammonia was sold to Japan and Mexico until temporary suspension of the Jones Act allowed the resumption of shipments to the Pacific Northwest. During the crisis, regional distributors affiliated with national oil companies were given allotments of the chemicals insufficient to meet customer demand. The McGregors were also short of product, although their status as independents gave them some flexibility. Seven million pounds of calcium nitrate, produced by a Norwegian company through a process requiring electric power and large amounts of limestone, were purchased in a frantic search for product. Sherman McGregor explained in a December 1973 letter to fertilizer customers:

> *This spring our first shortage will be in topdressing nitrogen products. There simply isn't enough ammonium nitrate or 32 solution available to go around. To help this situation, we are importing 3,500 tons of bulk calcium nitrate from Norway which will be unloaded from a ship at Vancouver, barged up the river to Pasco where it will be warehoused in space leased from a major producer who doesn't need it because they have no reserve product to store for spring usage.*
>
> *This has never been done before. We have already run into unforeseen problems like finding a mud bar at the entrance to the warehouse dock making us use smaller barges and then having the Norwegian government change its currency values recently making our cost $5 a ton more, but hopefully all will go well from here on. . . . We need you in the years to come and will certainly do our best to take care of your needs today.*[19]

The crisis eased in 1975 and adequate supplies of chemicals were again available for Pacific Northwest dealers and farmers. But the hazards of the use of the immensely productive chemicals and fertilizers remained: The heavy usage rates meant that a careless employee could do thousands of dollars' worth of damage to a farm crop in a single day. The fertilizers, herbicides, insecticides, fungicides, rodenticides, and other products that had enabled farmers to make spectacular increases in productivity after World War II came to be viewed as a mixed blessing. Biologist Rachel

Carson, in her 1962 book *Silent Spring*, presented a horrifying account of the detrimental effects of DDT and a host of other chemicals on birds, fishes, animals, and humans. The Swedes, who had presented Paul Muller of Switzerland with the Nobel Prize for his discovery of DDT, an effective and long-lasting tool in the war against crop destruction, banned the chemical in the early 1970's. Aldrin, dieldrin, DDT, chlordane, and other products were outlawed in the United States. Carson criticized the discoveries made by chemists and entomologists: "It is our alarming misfortune that so primitive a science has armed itself with the most modern and terrible weapons, and that in turning them against the insects it has also turned them against the earth." T. J. Muzik, a Washington State University scientist, noted in 1970: "There has been a polarizing of the American public by the fear of what our technology is doing to us. Scientists who have traditionally been admired by society are losing their position of esteem, not only because of their intimacy with technology, but also because they publicly disagree among themselves over environmental issues."

Farmers on the Columbia Plateau and elsewhere in the nation had become deeply committed to the use of the new chemical products. A Tennessee Valley Authority scientist estimated that national output of food and fiber would decline by at least a third without commercial fertilizers. Washington State University agronomists estimated in 1970 that "without herbicides, we would need at least 10 million more acres in production and about 22 million more [agricultural] workers to produce the same amount of food we are currently producing. . . . We would use approximately 100 million more gallons of gasoline annually. . . . The quality of produce would go down, but the cost would go up. . . . [Herbicides] . . . have become an integrated and essential part of American agriculture."[20]

Farmers in the fertile, steeply sloped lands of the Palouse faced a further obstacle in their struggle to maintain high levels of productivity. Rachel Carson in 1962 noted that "the 'agricultural engineers' speak blithely of 'chemical plowing' in a world that is urged to beat its plowshares into spray guns," but she did not face the damage done by the plow. Soil erosion remained a serious problem, despite forty years of conservation work. The tiny Palouse River carried more than twenty million tons of topsoil past the McGregor ranch every year, an amount sufficient to cover 160 acres of land to a depth of eighty feet. One small soil conservation district annually lost the equivalent of a 148-mile-long train of gondola cars filled with silt. "The worst erosion in the United States," a scientist noted in 1973, "is the Palouse Country." Minimum tillage, the most effective way to limit erosion and reduce diesel fuel consumption, required as a trade-off an increased dependence on petroleum-based herbicides. The productivity of the wheat fields of the interior Northwest had become closely tied to the advances in applied chemistry.[21]

The livestock businesses of the Columbia Plateau likewise underwent a period of rapid transformation. The number of cattle in the region increased rapidly after 1950. Unlike lambs, most of which became sufficiently fat for market on range feed, the cattle had an intermediate stop at feedlots on their way to the slaughterhouse. Large-scale commercial cattle feedlots, a rarity before World War II, were created to take advantage of the burgeoning demand for fat beef. William McGregor recalled that "grass fed cattle were tough, older animals and not too fat. . . . The thousand pound steer at four years old was good for you but it wasn't very good eating." Americans liked the taste and texture of grain-fed cattle and per capita beef consumption almost doubled in two decades.

McGregor Land and Livestock began feeding cattle after World War II to take advantage of a government subsidy offered to farmers who fed their grain to livestock. John McGregor remembered that two old horse barns, capable of holding 400 cattle, were used for the first containment operation. "We used a tractor and an old Bear Cat grinder and chopped hay and then ground grain into a tank inside the barn. Part of the roustabout's job was to put forkfuls of hay into the manger, weigh out wheat on a scale, and then add buckets full of grain to the troughs. He kept records on a piece of cardboard on the wall." Cattle feeding became increasingly popular in the fifties, in large part because of the wheat allotment program, which offered price supports to farmers who planted alternate crops. On much of the plateau barley was the only other crop that could be grown. The McGregors "ended up with a pile of pretty cheap barley" and built a new 500-head cattle feedlot to use the grain. George Hemmer, a veteran ranch hand and cattleman who began his fifty-seventh year with the company in 1982, served as foreman of the cattle-feeding operations.

Postwar improvements in technology and equipment offered definite advantages to the large-scale operator. John McGregor recalled:

> *We were able to concentrate large numbers of cattle without encountering health problems because of antibiotics developed during the war. Probably more important was the rise of the chain store which created demand for large regular quantities of beef that could be bought in specified USDA grades. That created a broader market all over the country. About that time the nutritionists got more scientific and came up with better feed supplements. The advent of electronic controls has changed*

the technology of milling. Computers and better and larger equipment have continued to rationalize the feeding process. The big lots have the lowest yardage costs. That's driven feedlot operators to get bigger or get out.[22]

The McGregors steadily increased the size of their feedlot operations. By 1961, more than ten thousand cattle were fattened in the lots at Hooper each year. Annual sales reached $2 million. Small feeder steers from several western states were given large quantities of feed for 130 to 150 days, until they reached proper weight for shipment to slaughterhouses west of the Cascades. Various strains of Angus and Hereford cattle were preferred, but other varieties were acquired when available for a good price. In 1962, for example, the McGregors purchased eight thousand gaunt Mexican steers (some of which had been used in the television western, "Rawhide") and shipped them by rail to Hooper, where they were quickly fattened for West Coast markets.

By 1963, the McGregors had moved their feedlot operations from their Palouse country ranch to the Columbia Basin, near Pasco, where plentiful silage was available from irrigated fields of potatoes, sugar beets, and corn that had been developed on old desert sheep ranges. The Pasco site had two main advantages—a better supply of roughage was available nearby, and the drier climate and improved drainage of the desert sands minimized the danger of foot rot, a common problem in the often soggy lots of the Palouse. The first Pasco lot had thirty-six pens, more than a mile of cement feed troughs, a mechanical mixing plant for feeds, and a capacity of 20,000 head per year. In the early 1970's, a new cattle feeding enterprise was initiated. The Atlantic Richfield Company agreed, as part of a contract with Hanford Atomic Works, to build a facility that would generate new business for the Pasco, Kennewick, and Richland areas. The corporation constructed a huge new feedlot and a packing plant south of Pasco, near the town of Wallula.

The McGregors sold their first Pasco lot and purchased the new feeding business. The Wallula lot, the largest in Washington and Oregon, surpassed $70 million in yearly sales by the late seventies. The cattle feeding business was changed from a division of McGregor Land and Livestock to become a wholly owned subsidiary, McGregor Feedlot, Inc. Almost 150,000 cattle per year were fed in the facility, with 52,000 head in the pens at any one time. Marketing was staggered so that two thousand cattle per week went to the adjacent slaughterhouse. There the cattle were processed into steaks and hamburger. Hides, horns, and even hoofs were saved and marketed, and tallow was processed in a million-dollar annex designed to produce cooking oil for french fries in fast-food restaurants. In 1979 alone the feedlot cattle gained 34 million pounds on 204,000 tons of potato silage (a soup-like mix from what John Mc-Gregor described as the "french fry patch"—discarded potatoes, peelings, misshapen fries, and a slurry recovered during potato processing), as well as 81,000 tons of barley, 32,000 tons of hay cubes, 27,000 tons of silage, 8,000 tons of beet pulp, and 12,000 tons of supplements, nutrients, antibiotics, and additives (including MGA—which stops the estrus cycle in heifers and thus promotes faster weight gain).[23]

The McGregors purchased feeder cattle in Washington, Idaho, Oregon, Nevada, Montana, Iowa, California, and Canada and their fattened beef was sold by the adjacent packing plant to supermarkets in the Northwest and California. When the packinghouse was closed in the mid-1970's, the McGregors found themselves without a ready local market for their fat stock. They purchased the controlling interest in the plant and hired a crew of more than 190 employees to dismantle the carcasses and prepare the beef for market. Three years later, the McGregors found a national packing firm interested in the location, and once again concentrated on cattle feeding alone. The McGregor Feedlot and a half dozen other big feeding facilities on the plateau were among the 422 large lots (with capacities of 30,000 head per year or more) that fattened half the beef sold in the nation. Commercial cattle feeders, operating with large amounts of working capital in low-margin enterprises and often faced with radically fluctuating beef and feed grain prices, required expert managers, accountants, computer operators, nutritionists, buyers, and veterinarians to be successful. The stakes were high: McGregor Feedlot generally had more than $20 million invested in cattle inventory alone. A single feed truck, equipped with elaborate scales that measured and recorded the precise amounts of feed dispensed at each pen, cost almost $140,000. Cattle markets were volatile and sometimes treacherous. In 1974, for example, a decline in cattle prices coupled with skyrocketing feed costs left the McGregors and other western feedlot operators with costly market-fat steers that sold for a loss and left disturbing "profit and loss" statements in their wake. But during years when feeders were cheap, grain and silage inexpensive, and markets for fat cattle rapidly advancing, large profits could be made. Both the inherent dangers and the potential rewards were far greater from cattle feeding than from range livestock operations.[24]

Farming, agricultural chemical sales, and cattle feeding all required specialized machines, commercially produced nutrients and supplements, and other capital inputs to increase productivity and displace human labor. Rapidly increasing payroll costs meant that farm businesses had to produce more and more output per hour of labor. Wheat farm employees, operating extremely versatile and expensive combines and tractors, brought far greater returns than did their prewar predecessors. Each fertilizer crewman, whether hauling truckloads of chemicals or building expensive machinery, was involved in the transfer of many thousands of dollars of goods and services. A feedlot "cowboy," running a feed mill or driving a truck that distributed rations to thousands of cattle, produced far more income for his employers than did his earlier counterparts.

Only range sheep production resisted these changes and remained labor intensive. Range sheep operations declined drastically after 1940. The number of ewes kept on Washington ranches and farms fell almost 90 percent—from 583,000 in 1940 to 62,000 in 1975. The range sheepmen, the major users of the Columbia Plateau grazing lands before World War II, were all but gone by the mid-1970's. The McGregor Land and Livestock Company was one of half a dozen range sheep businesses remaining out of the hundreds of outfits that raised sheep on the semiarid lands of Washington and northeastern Oregon after the turn of the century. Most of the sheep remaining in the region were in "farm flocks," small operations of a few hundred head or less owned by wheat farmers using year-round pastures adjacent to their farmlands. National sheep production fell rapidly, from more than 56 million sheep in 1942 to only 13 million in 1976. The 1976 total was the smallest figure registered since the USDA began tabulating livestock production in 1867, when there were more than 46 million head.[25]

The major innovations made by western sheepmen before 1940 had done nothing to decrease the extensive manpower requirements of the trade. Transhumance, the seasonal migration pattern imported from Europe in the nineteenth century, had made sheep production possible in areas poorly suited to year-round grazing. Historical geographer Daniel Gomez-Ibanez comments: "Transhumance was qualitatively different from many technical innovations during the nineteenth century in that it did not decrease the need for human labor or even increase its productivity, but instead allowed the exploitation of a previously unused 'source' of energy: mountain pasture." The two major features of transhumance—seasonal movement and large amounts of highly skilled labor—were poorly adapted to a postwar agriculture characterized by rapidly rising labor costs and scarce and expensive rangeland. A technique developed to use the extensive ranges of the nineteenth century frontier would have to be adapted to the age of agribusiness. Shed lambing, a procedure that required a large, skilled seasonal labor force to increase the productivity of range sheep operations, was also poorly suited to the new circumstances.

Sheepmen encountered further troubles in their efforts to market the lamb and wool crops. First generation immigrants, particularly those from southern and eastern Europe, traditionally had been large consumers of lamb and mutton. Their "Americanized" offspring abandoned lamb in favor of hamburger and steaks cut from grain-fed beef. Demand from other American consumers also slackened. Repeated "lamb promotion" campaigns sponsored by William McGregor and other Washington Wool Growers' Association officials (and by several woolgrowers' organizations from other states) failed to halt the decline in demand for lamb. U.S. Department of Agriculture statisticians estimated that yearly lamb consumption fell from 7 pounds per American during World War II to 1.7 pounds in 1976. Postwar American consumers responded enthusiastically to the introduction of Dacron, polyesters, and other synthetic fibers manufactured from oil, and for many years these products commanded market premiums in competition with wool. American clothing manufacturers more than doubled their use of various apparel fibers during the years 1946–71. But the production of woolen clothing fell 63 percent during the same twenty-five-year period.[26]

The onset of World War II marked the beginning of the battle for economic survival of the range sheep business. Conditions were far different than they had been during the prosperous wartime years 1914 to 1919. The federal government had long provided sheepmen with high tariffs and a degree of paternalism seldom extended to other agricultural endeavors. But a series of wartime regulations crippled the sheep business. On December 8, 1941, the day after the bombing of Pearl Harbor, the federal government placed a price freeze on wool, a commodity viewed as essential to the war effort. While huge quantities of wool were stockpiled, a federal wool conservation program restricted mills to the production of civilian clothing containing not more than 65 percent raw wool, a move that provided impetus to the development of synthetic fibers. Ceilings were placed on the price of lamb and other red meats. Oregon sheepman Herman Oliver described another troublesome regulation: "During the last war, the sheepmen were in trouble. They were issued coupons for gas, groceries, and supplies. . . . It was scientifically figured that 40 percent of the groceries were fresh things . . . but sheep herders move every day and they are far out in the mountains where there isn't any grocery store."

The costs of sheep production were anything but frozen. Expenses per head increased more than 50 percent in five years. Herders' wages jumped from $60 or $70 per month to $175 or $200 between 1940 and 1944. Sheepmen were unable to secure adequate labor even with the new wage scale. Columbia Plateau woolgrowers lost their crews to more lucrative employment in wartime industries. Any herder "who knew how to push

a broom" could earn far higher wages at the Naval Shipyards in Brem-
erton than by staying with the sheep. Many sheepmen had crews composed primarily of alcoholics hired from run-down bars on Trent Avenue
in Spokane. Donald Bell, professor of animal husbandry at the University of Idaho, recalled his difficulties securing a herder for the band
of sheep kept by an experiment station: "I remember when I was herding for a sheep outfit . . . in 1932—I would have been fired if the boss had
come around and caught me asleep during the day, but in those trying
years of '42 through '47 and '48, if I went out to the sheep herd and
found the herder asleep, I was very careful not to waken him abruptly
lest he might quit. . . . One winter I became so exasperated with the in-
cessant demands of the continuing change of herders that I went out and
herded the sheep all winter myself." The commercial range sheepmen
of the Columbia Plateau could not do all the herding themselves: Numerous men were needed to tend the flocks throughout the year, and
additional helpers were essential during lambing.[27]

A government study of conditions in the eleven western range states
concluded that sheepmen had lost an average of 12 cents per head on
lamb sales and 3 cents per pound on wool sold in 1943. The 1944 estimate was $1.22 loss per head on lamb and an 11¢ loss on each pound of
wool. Cattle production required far less labor and supervision. Profits
were greater. Only those woolgrowers who were convinced that the
sheep business would recover from its doldrums and who adopted extremely efficient management practices remained in the trade. Tom
Drumheller, Jr., was able to keep a good crew by adopting a labor-
saving method of lambing that was "a combination of lambing in the
sheds at night and then range lambing in the daytime" and by relying on
the abilities of a capable sheep foreman.

> He stayed with me for many years. During lambing I drove a truck
> which could haul a hundred ewes and their lambs. When I'd come back
> to the field he'd have all those little lambs up and counted and moth-
> ered. He had a sharp mind. When I was docking our lambs he'd have the
> percentage figured out by the time I cut the last tail off. He was the
> one I relied on. He was the one fellow in the bunk house that would
> stick up for the boss. . . . Its a wonder one of those pool hall bums didn't
> stab him. He was the only fellow that ever worked for me that I gave a
> gold watch when he left and told him that he had earned really way
> more than I was able to give him. I suppose he hocked that watch prob-
> ably two days later. But he was the only fellow with tears in his eyes
> when he left.[28]

McGregor Land and Livestock managers and foremen made a series
of modifications in their sheep operation and continued to make a profit

for forty-five consecutive years—from 1933 to 1978. The McGregors had solid economic reasons for retaining their ninety-six-year-old sheep business: They averaged 35.8 percent net return on sales in the 1940's, 24 percent in the 1950's and 1960's, and 45.2 percent in the 1970's. The corporation averaged 30.2 net return on sheep sales during the years 1909–76. Range cattle had brought them far smaller returns. But the sheep business needed major modifications during a period of rapid agricultural change. Many sheepmen decided to abandon the trade during the critical wartime years. During the years 1940–51, Washington sheep production fell 47 percent, from 589,000 head to 311,000, and Oregon output declined 68 percent, from 1,958,000 to 637,000.

The McGregors improved their varieties of sheep, reseeded rangeland, managed their labor force closely, experimented with extensive feeding programs, cross-fenced their pastures, and tried a series of other innovations designed to improve operating efficiency. All four members of the McGregor management devoted some time to the sheep business. John McGregor worked with the sheep for a few years after entering the company in 1950, until cattle feeding grew into a business that required all his attention. Sherman McGregor, likewise, spent some time managing the sheep after his return to Hooper in 1947 until the fertilizer trade became a full-time business. But Maurice and William McGregor were the two who devoted most of their efforts to sheep production. Maurice handled much of the supervisory work until his death in 1956. William then began more than twenty years as head man of the McGregor sheep business. The McGregors were fortunate to have the services of Emile Morod, a company employee since 1913 and sheep foreman from the early 1940's until 1968. Morod is remembered by veteran shearer Bill Dorman, long-time sheep ranch employees Clemente Barber and Juan Miquelez, and many of the rest of us who were once in his employ, as a dedicated, extremely hard-working person, quick to anger but equally quick to apologize, a good supervisor of large crews, and a man who had a gentle way of reproaching inexperienced personnel. Morod and the McGregor management had to acquire and keep a capable crew and make major alterations in a business characterized by high costs and fluctuating markets. Close management was essential. Veteran Washington sheepman Charles Brune comments: "The sheep business requires all the attention you can give it all the time. Always something you can do a little better. And with sheep you have some new problem every day."[29]

The labor situation was a pressing problem. Between 1940 and 1945, McGregor Land and Livestock hired 147 men for a sheep business that required a dozen year-round workers and a lambing crew of 26. The turnover was rapid: Only 25 of the 147 men returned for more than one year of service with the McGregor sheep business. Emile Morod provided a frank analysis of the capabilities of each sheep employee in his annual payroll books of the wartime period. The following comments are typical:

good	*quit—poor heart*
OK	*quit—not feeling well*
fair	*crippled*
drunkard—good for a month	*good for 2 months*
the cook—drunk—quit	*no good—can*
no good—fired	*very good*
quit—want more money	*fair*
canned—brought booze to camp	*very good*
quit—trouble with the cook	

A reliable group of herders stayed with the McGregors through the wartime period: Maurice Morod, the older brother of foreman Emile Morod, had been a McGregor herder for almost forty years; Mickey Purcell and Clyde Copple each had herded for the Hooper firm for more than a decade; and Cyril Dodson, Harry Weaver, Lee Burden, Anton Onderland, and a few others returned for many years. The combination of experienced herders and closely supervised migrant laborers provided the McGregors with an adequate work force for the wartime years. Many other sheepmen, unable to find any steady workers, had begun applying to the U.S. Immigration and Naturalization Service for a waiver of the alien contract labor law that would allow use of herders from the Basque provinces of Spain. Immigration officials, learning that the McGregors had been successful in employing American herders, wrote to the Hooper company and asked for advice about the need for new laborers. Maurice McGregor described the national origins of the McGregor laborers: Five were American-born, and individual herders were from Russia, Yugoslavia, France, Germany, Scotland, and Ireland. The McGregors, too, were worried about the future availability of herders and crews: The dedicated men who had remained with the company for many years were getting old, and few younger American men were qualified and willing to live a lonely life tending the flocks.

The western sheepmen had been short of herders before. In 1906, for example, an Oregon correspondent to the *American Sheep Breeder* claimed that "owing to the scarcity of help on the western ranges, some of the flockmasters are thinking of trying Japs as shepherds. These brave little sons of Nippon may not know much about sheep, but it will not take them long to learn quite a good deal about them." Few Japanese actually took up the trade. But French, Scotch, and Irish immigrants

and American-born sheepherders were generally hired in numbers sufficient for the successful operation of most sheep enterprises. As these
people became less interested in herding and began migrating to urban
areas, Spanish Basques emerged as the major labor force of the Columbia
Plateau sheep country. Without the Basques, an already declining range
sheep business would have become virtually extinct by the late 1950's.
Although only a few Basques had participated in the sheep business of
the region before World War II, they had been extremely successful
sheepherders and sheep owners in many other areas, particularly in
Nevada, the San Joaquin Valley of California, and the Jordan Valley of
Southern Idaho. The *Shepherd's Criterion* commented in 1907: "Many
young Spaniards are coming over to this country and going into sheep
herding. They are doing this to get a start and pretty soon they will be
sheep owners as some of them are now. Thus old friends meet again
for the original stock of the range sheep came from Spain." The Basques
were widely praised for their dependability, loyalty, and devotion to
the sheep. A sociologist who studied the Jordan Valley Basques provides
a typical observation: "As sheepherders these immigrant boys made
good. They were hard working and faithful and were able to stand the
solitude because of some inner deep-rooted qualities and attitudes acquired from their Old World culture. . . . The Basque sheepherder is
known for his willingness to do almost anything to save even a single
sheep or lamb. He takes pride in excelling in his work." [30]

The National Wool Growers' Association, assisted by those who
viewed declining wool production as a danger to national defense, in
the early 1950's began a campaign for legislation authorizing the importation of qualified Basque herders. Maurice McGregor, chairman of the
labor committee of the Washington Wool Growers' Association, and
fellow committee members Sebastian Etulain (one of the few Basque
sheep owners in the state), Simon Martinez, and John McGregor worked
to generate regional support for the Basque herder program. Senator
Patrick McCarran of Nevada, a former sheepman, won Congressional
approval in 1952 for a bill that allowed 500 Basque herders into the country and authorized sheepmen to use collective action to recruit foreign
herders. The McCarran-Walter Omnibus Immigration Bill, also ap-
proved in 1952, contained a proviso for the temporary importation of
sheepherders on contracts. The Basque herders were employed as contract laborers under a program organized by the California-based Western Range Association, a group composed primarily of sheep owners
who had been born in Spain. The association interviewed prospective
herders in Bilbao, Spain, administering qualification tests to ensure that

only experienced sheep herders were obtained. A western sheepman wishing to hire one of the herders had to provide room and board, a minimum wage ($165–$230 per month), and a deposit to cover travel expenses to and from Spain (the latter could subsequently be deducted from the herder's pay). The contracts ran for three years but could usually be renewed (sometimes the herder had to return to Spain to reapply). Many herders eventually became American citizens.

The young Basque immigrants had a strong motivation to enter the American sheep business: McGregor sheepman Clemente Barber recalled that the monthly wages compared very favorably with the 25 pesetas (80¢) daily pay for farm work in Spain. Many of the men planned to save their money and return to Spain to marry and run a business or farm. Most of the large sheep operators in Washington quickly hired contract laborers. McGregor Land and Livestock, Coffin Sheep Company, Hislop Sheep Company, Tom Drumheller, Jr., and Simon Martinez all procured a number of the foreign workers. The new employees soon verified their reputation as capable sheep tenders. H. Stanley Coffin, Jr., commented in 1952: "We find the Basque boys so much better at herding than some of the *winos* we had to hire during the war."[31]

The Basque herders provided the McGregors with a dedicated, stable, and experienced crew. Alfonso Barber, Fernando Arbea, and Felix Zozaya were the first three immigrant sheepmen to reach Hooper, arriving in November 1952. Barber and Arbea were from Ezcaroz and Oronz, two small villages a mile and a half apart in Valle de Salazar, in the rugged Pyrenees foothills of the province of Navarra. Zozaya came from Arizu, a small Navarra town in a mountain valley further west. The three Basques stayed with the Hooper firm for an average of ten years each. They urged their siblings and friends to come to Hooper. Two more Zozayas, Lorenzo and Jeronimo, and their relative Juan Miquelez left Arizu for Hooper. Lorenzo Zozaya was a McGregor herder for twenty-four years, until he retired in 1977. "Jerry" Zozaya stayed three years and Juan Miquelez tended sheep for fifteen years. Victorio and Benito Arbea followed brother Fernando to Hooper and each spent eight years with the McGregor sheep. Clemente and Modesto Barber and their cousin, Domingo Navarro, came to herd sheep a few years after the arrival of Alfonso Barber. Domingo Navarro worked with the sheep for fifteen years, Modesto Barber for four, and Clemente Barber has remained twenty-six years with the McGregor sheep enterprise, where he is now foreman. Several other men who had been acquainted with the Barbers and Arbeas came from Ezcaroz, Oronz, and the adjacent village of Jaurrieta, including the Loperana brothers, Modesto and Lorenzo, who stayed for sixteen and eighteen years, and Ignacio Recalde, who remained for ten.

For many years, the McGregors had twelve Basques in their crew of fifteen full-time sheepmen. The first eight to arrive—two Barber brothers, two Zozayas, the two Loperana brothers, Fernando Arbea, and Ignacio Recalde—averaged almost fifteen years' service with the company. The twenty-five Basques hired between 1952 and 1976, including those who had to return to Spain before becoming American citizens, worked almost nine years each for the Hooper firm. None ever had to be dismissed by Morod as "no good" or "drunk in camp." Most had worked with livestock for many years before their arrival in America. Clemente Barber, for example, had begun herding his family's cattle at age nine and at ten had been given charge of the sheep flock. At seventeen he started on his own, herding sheep on shares for a transhumant outfit that trailed from the arid lowlands to the Pyrenees summer ranges. The men were familiar with climatic conditions somewhat similar to those of the Channeled Scablands and the Pacific Northwest mountain ranges. They were used to living in small towns. The transition from Spain to a new country was eased by the presence of a closely knit group of friends and relatives in Hooper. Spanish was the accepted language of the sheep camps, and even the sheep dogs were taught to respond to commands issued in that language. Quiet pride and dignity and a willingness to work hard were common attitudes. I remember asking a Basque herder a few years ago about the health of one ewe in a band of 3,000 head. The herder looked at the ewe and said, "I remember her. Two years ago when she was a lamb I find her abandoned and get a ewe to claim her. Last year twice I pull her out of mud holes to save her."

The Basque herders have pursued widely disparate careers since their years with the McGregor Land and Livestock Company. Alfonso Barber owns an appliance repair shop in Miami. Lorenzo Loperana and Juan Miquelez are railroad workers near Hooper. "Jerry" Zozaya owns his own farm in eastern Washington. Domingo Navarro works in a meat market in Pasco. Isidro Gutierrez was a camptender on the McGregor summer range before enrolling at Washington State University in the fall of 1976. Fernando Arbea is a logger and welder in Canada. Felix Zozaya owns a restaurant and bar in Spain. Guillermo Celay returned to his homeland to purchase and operate a tavern and barber shop. Desiderio Rodrigo, Modesto Barber, Angel Haulde, Benito Arbea, Francisco Samper, and Morino Loperana are among the many others who have gone back to Spain: Rodrigo became a forest ranger; Barber, a meat market operator; Hualde, a carpenter; Arbea, a plumber; Samper works in a sausage factory; and Loperana is "taking it easy" after a long career with the McGregor sheep. Few young Basques arrived in their stead. The province of Navarra has become industrialized, and fewer young people have had experience working with sheep. The Spanish sheep business has been declining during the last decade, partly because of a critical need for laborers, who find ample opportunities available in the more lucrative industrial trades. The standard of living in Spain improved greatly in the 1970's, with farm laborers averaging more than twenty dollars per day in wages. Even higher pay could be secured by working in urban factories.[32]

A few veteran herders of other nationalities remained in the sheep business of the Columbia Plateau. McGregor herder George Cullinane, for example, is a man of Irish descent and eastern schooling who has spent many decades tending the sheep of H. Stanley Coffin, George Hislop, the McGregors, and other sheepmen of Washington, Oregon, Australia, and beyond. But the declining availability of Basque herders brought another acute labor shortage to the rangeland. In 1961, Phil Kern, the secretary of the Washington Wool Growers' Association, assessed the importance of the Basques to the sheep business in the inland region: "We fully realize that the sheep industry in this state would not be able to operate without the services of the . . . Basque herder program. There just aren't enough . . . herders in this state or in other states to supply the needs of the sheep industry. With the high costs of production we must be able to operate without high losses. It takes a great deal of skill to prevent these losses. About the only effective means of preventing them is to have skilled herders."

With a capable foreman and crew watching the band of sheep, the McGregors sought to modernize a business that was rapidly approaching obsolescence. The men invested capital in a series of ventures designed to increase productivity and minimize the expenses for the major item of a sheepman's budget—labor. An accelerated program of range reseeding, selective breeding for large fleeces and heavier lambs, construction of a series of cross-fences that would limit winter herding expenses, and better feeding programs were all viewed as possible areas for improvement. Rapidly escalating land values meant that the McGregors and other owners of range sheep and cattle businesses had to face the difficult task of finding a method for getting a return on land commensurate with its market value. The 3 or 4 percent annual return on investment commonly recorded by range operators, William McGregor explained, was less than the percentage of interest needed to cover bank loans. The high land values increased the net worth of a rancher. But the gain was generally realized only by selling out or dying, when the estate paid taxes on the valuable land. William McGregor analyzed the prospect for the range sheep industry in 1957:

> The range sheep business is an old and important one in this area but has fallen out of favor in the last ten years. . . . The range sheep business has not declined owing to any natural unsuitability to the conditions of eastern Washington. On the contrary, sheep are in some ways much better adapted than cattle to this area. Our dry grass ranges are not good summer ranges for any class of livestock and the winter feeding period on our higher ranges is very long. By moving from winter to summer ranges sheep are able to utilize both types of ranges at their peak condition. Cattle typically spend the whole year on one range area. . . . The decline is due to the familiar cost-price squeeze which is, today, a standard feature of the agricultural picture. The sheep business, being a high cash cost operation, ran into trouble from rising operating costs while the cattle business was still enjoying a pretty good spread between selling price and cost of production and at that time a good many range sheepmen went into cattle. Sheep require a pretty elaborate outfit as compared with cattle and the cost of rented pasture and moving the bands is also very high, but the big expense in any range sheep operation is the cost of manpower. Sheep require a lot of handling. We figure that we will need one man year of labor for every 440 ewes that we run. This figure may sound high but if you consider all the support jobs such as fencing, water hauling, hay chopping, etc. . . . in addition to herding you can see where labor is going. Since labor is the most expensive thing that you have to buy today this puts the sheepman right in the middle of the cost-price problem. In our own case, our cost per ewe year has gone up 63 percent in the last ten years and we expect it to rise faster in the future.
>
> Another factor which is less obvious but pretty important in the decline of the range sheep business is the difficulty of management. A sheep outfit runs on know-how and attention to detail. When you are moving sheep, renting pasture, setting up camps, taking camps down, vaccinating dogs, hauling water and building fence, all at the same time, the detail can get a little out of hand. There is a good deal of truth to the notion that to raise sheep you have to learn to live with them and pretty much like them. In view of the poor returns from the business, some sheepmen have felt that there were better ways that they could spend their time.
>
> Looking at the sheep business today, the picture is a little brighter. The business is just as much a madhouse as ever and production costs are still climbing, but the operation is making a little money and more money than the same operator could make in cattle. . . . Our operating figures for 1956 show . . . a net return per ewe of $8.00. How good is the sheep business? . . . Take a figure between $5 and $10 that you think may be reasonable average net per head. Figure that you can run eight to

ten sheep on the range that would support a cow the year 'round. . . .
Your net per head multiplied by 8 or 10 is the net per head you would
have to make in cattle to equal the return from sheep. . . .

In the long run, however, the range sheep business will have to look
to technological improvements to keep the cost of production from
squeezing it out of existence. I am fairly optimistic about this. . . . There
is a great deal of technical knowledge which is not being applied. Further, there has been relatively little technical investigation of the problems of the sheep industry. I hope that such investigations may prove as
rewarding as they have in other branches of agriculture.[33]

The McGregors placed increased emphasis on the development of a
more productive flock of sheep. Columbia rams, from a newly developed
breed raised at the U.S. Sheep Experiment Station of Dubois, Idaho,
were crossed with the Rambouillet strain of ewes that the McGregors
had been improving for many decades. Sheep that had produced smaller
than average fleeces and lambs were removed from the bands and sent
to market. The culling and cross-breeding required careful management,
as indicated by a few portions of the extensive notes William McGregor
kept on the procedures for flock improvement:

*If 2% males and 50% females become parents, 75% hereditary gain is
from males. Proportion is greater if male generation is short. . . . Relative
emphasis of any trait is equal to its economic importance X heritability.
Selection for n traits advances $\sqrt{n}$ times as fast as selection for one trait.
If several traits are selected it is more advantageous to select simulta-
neously than in series. . . . Pounds of lamb raised/ewe is most important
consideration in lamb production. . . . Ewes that twin raise approx. 40
lbs. more lamb per year than singling ewes. . . . Weaning weight is next
most important characteristic (30% in Rambouillet, 17% in Columbias).
Type and condition are less important (13% & 4% in Rambouillets, 7%
& 21% in Columbias). . . . In Rambouillet each 1 lb. increase in weaning
weight of ewe = ½ lb. increase in weight of her lambs. . . . Ewes born
as twins have 6.8% more twins than ewes born as singles. . . . Twinning
varies with the age of grand dam. . . . Staple length is important both
for clean fleece weight and for itself. Increase of ½ inch in staple increases weight ½ lb. in half-bloods and more in fine wools.*

Emile Morod, Maurice McGregor, and William McGregor successfully developed a selection process that brought heavier, longer fleeces
plus bigger and fatter lamb crops. Morod played a critical role in the
improvement process. Veteran sheep shearer Bill Dorman recalled: "It
was Emile Morod who made the McGregor sheep business work—he
took a great deal of care improving the sheep, fixing up the old corrals,
and working with the men." Tom Drumheller, Jr., was also successful

with a program of crossing Lincoln, Rambouillet, and Columbia sheep and culling out inferior lambs by checking the size, face ("open faced" sheep with only a little wool on their faces produced better lambs and wool than the "closed faces"), teeth, and udder of the ewes. The assistance of his foreman was a vital factor in the program:

> *Gregorio Zorazua, my Basque foreman, was one of the best judges of ewes. I mean he could bag [check the udder of] a ewe—that's an important job that few people know how to do. He was good at mouthing ewes—their teeth don't always break the same and sometimes we'd put yearling ewes out with the old ewes. In the fall we'd go out and the two of us could do in nothing flat what used to take me all day to do. We'd bag those ewes and anything with a good, big bag would surely have had twins the year before. We'd check the faces and the bag and the size of the ewe and all the rest of it. We raised our average ewe weight from 130 to 165 in a period of about 10 years. We raised the average of our lamb crops until we got above 152% to market. I had one band that reached 181%. . . . It was a wonderful deal.*
>
> *That foreman was on the job all the time. . . . I don't know why his wife ever stayed with him because he never went home. . . . He wouldn't even go at Christmas time. I tried to get him to go but he would never leave until all those boys were all cared for at the camps. All the years that he was with me I think I healed up my ulcers and I was beginning to live a little bit. He really was a Godsend. . . . If it hadn't been for him I'd have sold my sheep long before I did.[34]*

The McGregors also worked to increase output by reseeding depleted rangeland and experimenting with the application of fertilizer on the pastures. John McGregor explained the reasons for the program in 1955:

> *My father started experimental seedings in the 1930's. He tried almost every technique ever suggested to him and a few of his own and finally concluded that it was virtually impossible to establish grasses in our area without previous cultivation. Consequently our seedings are confined to areas having at least two feet of soil depth. . . . We have about 1650 acres of reseeded range out of a possible 5000 that may be suitable. Our most successful reseeding techniques have been . . . disc plowing in the late spring before the cheatgrass has headed, summer fallowing, discing in the fall and seeding after the soil is moist. . . . The only special equipment used is a very old and battered set of the implements of choice, since even under the best conditions we leave an interesting trail of parts around those rocky fields. Our favorite grass is crested wheatgrass. It is the best and most consistent producer. . . .*
>
> *Reseeding costs run between $7 and $9 per acre and fencing adds another $7 when small units are enclosed. How do we justify these expenses? First, in increased carrying capacity . . . from ½ to 1 sheep month per*

*acre . . . to 4 sheep months per acre. . . . Second . . . is the fact that
these pastures have a unique value to us in being ready for grazing before
the native range. . . . [Third] these fences . . . will pay for themselves in
saving a herder's wages and expenses. Fourth, lambs run on these pastures
consistently do better than those run on the open range . . . because
their level of nutrition is higher and partly, I suspect, because they are
not frustrated in their grazing by the attending of a herder who is primarily a carnivore and doesn't really know what a sheep is thinking about.
These lambs weigh more at shipping time and cut a higher percentage of
fats than the lambs run on native range.*

Fertilizer was used to further increase the forage available to sheep.
McGregor agronomist Harley Jacquot spent several years searching for
an economically feasible method of range nitrogen application. Washington State University agronomists J. K. Patterson and V. E. Young conducted additional tests on the Hooper ranch and reported their results
in the *Journal of Range Management*. But the application of fertilizer
to the cheatgrass and bunchgrass was expensive and not always economically feasible.

William McGregor participated in regional and national organizations
that sought to make other modifications in the woolgrowing trade. He
traveled to Washington, D.C., to urge the lifting of the three-year re-
striction on Basque herders and to testify on behalf of the National
Wool Act of 1954, an act that provided badly needed price support and
helped forestall the collapse of a declining industry. During his terms as
president, vice president, and research chairman of the Washington Wool
Growers' Association, he promoted new projects for agricultural researchers, traveled to New Zealand to observe production methods on the
extensive sheep ranges of that nation, and sought other methods of increasing the returns of a high-expense business.[35]

Expenses had to be cut if the transhumant sheep business was to continue. The McGregors had been able to make gradual reductions in the
labor force during and after World War II. Fencing the rangeland helped
to accelerate the reductions. William McGregor explained at the 1966
"Sheep Day" held at Washington State University:

*Running sheep under fence without a herder is one solution to the most
pressing problem of the range sheep industry: cutting the payroll. Sheep-
tight fencing has not been very popular in Washington but I believe that
it offers some real opportunities for cost cutting. . . . We got into sheep-
tight fencing some years ago when we built a few miles of woven wire
fence to control grazing on grass seedings. . . . We now have 20,000 acres
fenced into 32 pastures using 80 miles of woven wire fence. This pretty
well completes our fencing program for the present as the remaining*

*unfenced areas all present some special problem. When we first turned
lamb bands out under fence we expected to take higher death losses as
the price for eliminating the herder. This did not happen. We actually
lost fewer lambs. . . . I am now convinced that it takes a very good herder
to equal a woven wire fence for lamb production.*

*[The cost of fencing is $667 per mile.] The return on the cost of the
fence is $10 per man day times the 765 man days saved or $7,650. On 72
miles of fence this is $106.25 per mile or a return of 15.93% on the cost of
$667. This figure considerably understates the value of the fence as it
allows nothing for increased production, better use of the range . . ., and
greatly simplified management. Even as it stands, however, it is a pretty
fair return for the range sheep business.*

Emile Morod, Clemente Barber, and William McGregor combined
their almost one hundred years of experience in the sheep business to
construct a new, more efficient lambing facility to replace the fifty-year-
old lambing headquarters at Archie's Camp. The new operation brought
a further reduction in labor and eliminated most of the seasonal laborers
required at lambing time. A 500 percent increase in herders' wages between 1935 and 1955 made these cuts imperative. Significant reductions
were made after 1955: The sheep labor force worked an average of
4,597 man-days per year for the period 1964–66, almost 18 percent less
than the 5,580 man-day average of 1954–56. A further reduction of
more than 24 percent, 1,116 man-days per year, was made between 1966
and 1968. An additional 300 man-days were eliminated during the next
three years. The improvements enabled the McGregors to remain in
the sheep business. But costs of labor, summer range, and other necessities had continued to rise at a discouraging rate. During the twenty-six-
year period 1941–67, gross sales were up 230 percent. Costs were up
more than 400 percent. Income had remained at about the same dollar
level. William McGregor analyzed the outlook in 1967: "Labor costs
and scarcity continue to be the biggest problem in this operation. Have
proceeded to the point where we will have to make major changes in
the next few years. . . . The cattle alternative: a) sedentary cattle are
cheap and easy but production is relatively low. Profit is safe but represents a miserable return on the opportunity cost. b) intensive cattle get
you into the same problems you have with sheep. Therefore, we are
going to try intensive sheep."

The McGregors increased the emphasis on their range improvement
program and began "dry lotting" a portion of their lamb crop (i.e., feeding them grain in a feedlot) to eliminate the need for one of the two
costly summer pastures. Rapid advances in the costs of grain and hay
made the feedlot system economically inadvisable a few years later.

There were other problems as well. By the early 1970's coyotes outnumbered sheep in Washington by three to one. A federal ban on the use of the most effective coyote poison, "1080," brought serious losses. In 1973, the McGregors lost 400 lambs, with a market value of almost $20,000, to the predators.[36]

The value of lamb and wool increased rapidly after 1971, while cattle prices plummeted. The annual profits of the McGregor sheep business jumped more than sixfold between 1971 and 1972 and more than doubled again during the following year. But the difficulties in finding people willing and able to herd sheep, the rapidly increasing expenses, and the uncertainties of marketing combined to reduce a business that was once the most important source of income from the Columbia Plateau ranges almost to the status of a historical relic. In 1973, the McGregor sheep began sharing the rangeland with cattle. The McGregor Land and Livestock flock, for many years the largest in the state, slowly diminished in size after 1974, when the corporation began sending all replacement ewe lambs to the slaughterhouse. The remaining Columbia–Rambouillets, some of them ten years old—twice the age at which range ewes were long considered too old to survive—continued to produce large fleeces and big lamb crops for several years. Oregon sheepshearer Pete Williams, a member of the 1976 McGregor shearing crew, described the aging bands of sheep kept by the Hooper firm as superior to 90 percent of the range sheep of the Columbia Plateau: a tribute to the durability and productivity of the improved crossbreds. The McGregors had expected to be out of the sheep business by 1976, but the old ewes kept producing big lamb crops, including a 165 percent crop in 1978. The chronic labor and expense problems of sheep production remained, and after ninety-seven years of sheep raising, the McGregors sold all but a few dozen of their ewes in 1979.

Most of the old range sheep businesses of the Pacific Northwest had been gone for a decade or more—these included the Drumheller, Coffin, Jaussaud, Hislop, Prior, Lesamiz, and Richardson operations and many others. A few Peruvian herders were brought into the region by some of the surviving sheep businesses. But the severe labor shortage continued. Sheep shearers, for example, had become scarce by the mid-1970's. The Sheep Shearers' Union of North America—the only union of American shearers—had only 135 members left out of a group that once numbered more than 2,000. Bill Dorman, head of a crew that had shorn McGregor sheep since 1941, described his work as a rewarding profession filled with frustrations and joys. The pay was relatively high—a dollar for each of the 125 head or more each worker sheared in a day. But the work was dirty, hot, and backbreaking and the lack of fringe benefits, retirement pay, and unemployment benefits made few young people willing to enter the trade. Dorman's crew was busy throughout the year, shearing and traveling the long distances among the sheep operations of Washington, Oregon, Idaho, and Nevada. The pride and sense of accomplishment in the hard physical labor and the accompanying camaraderie and boisterous revelry during trips to town were not sufficient to prompt men to enter the business. The shearers, herders, and transhumant sheepmen of the Columbia Plateau did not face a bright future by 1978.[37]

By the late 1970's, the McGregors had almost a thousand Simmenthal-Brown Swiss–Angus crossbred cows on their sheep pastures. A few Columbia Plateau cattlemen moved their cattle to summer pastures. But this was expensive and labor-intensive, and the McGregors and most range cattle raisers kept their herds on lowland pastures all year long. The McGregor cattle herders were equipped with three-wheeled motor-

Veteran shearer Bill Dorman at work on the McGregor ranch in late April 1976. Dorman, a McGregor shearer for almost forty years, travels every year to shearing camps in Nevada, Montana, Washington, Oregon, and Idaho. (Drawing by Ruth Burden)

cycles instead of horses. The motorized equipment was easy to maintain and operate and proved surprisingly maneuverable on the steep scabrock rangeland. The livestock employees still herded the last band of aged sheep on foot with the assistance of well-trained dogs. But only two of the Basque immigrants who had made the sheep business a success—Modesto Samper and Clemente Barber—remained on the payroll by the fall of 1978. And they spent most of their time at other tasks—Barber superintended the cattle business, and Samper worked on the irrigated alfalfa fields and herded cattle.

Even before the McGregors began selling their young ewes, the sheep enterprise had become a minor part of a corporate agribusiness. Lamb and wool sales, generally averaging about $300,000 annually, accounted for one-half of 1 percent of the $60 million of business done by McGregor Land and Livestock and its two subsidiaries in 1976. Three years later the McGregor companies surpassed $100 million in annual sales, while the scale of the sheep enterprise declined.[38]

The business interests of the McGregor families had expanded beyond sheep raising and the company town of Hooper. All three McGregor families built or purchased homes outside the Channeled Scablands—Norma and Sherman McGregor in Pullman, Patricia and John McGregor in Walla Walla, Nancy and William McGregor in Spokane. The three families moved in part to take advantage of the good high schools available for their children in the larger towns. Sherman and John McGregor also left the company town to be closer to their main business offices—the fertilizer headquarters near Colfax, fifteen miles north of Pullman, and the cattle feedlot near Wallula, thirty-five miles west of Walla Walla. All three families continued to have homes in Hooper but only William McGregor, the manager of the wheat and range livestock operations, used Hooper as a full-time business headquarters.

The company town itself changed slowly. The writer, Alex C. McGregor, for example, received his eighth grade diploma from the chairman of the board of directors of Hooper Grade School—his father, Sherman McGregor. Sherman McGregor, forty years earlier, received his eighth grade diploma from the chairman of the board of Hooper Grade School—his father, Alex C. McGregor. The Hooper community had won a bitter fight in 1955 and 1956 against an attempt by state officials and the Whitman County School Reorganization Committee to consolidate Hooper and two other small schools into the larger Lacrosse school system. Wilbur Copp of Hooper told a crowd of more than 75 patrons of the small schools attending a reorganization committee meeting in Colfax that the state legislature was promoting "community murder" by encouraging consolidation. Pioneer Hooper rancher Jimmy Richardson told the reorganization committee that "all this crowd wants is a good 'leaving alone.'" Sherman McGregor presented a petition against consolidation, signed by 78 residents of the Hooper district, and read a statement:

> We . . . are proud of our school. . . . We view with distrust any effort by any outside group to remove our local control. . . . A community blessed with an interest in its school . . . should be encouraged, not left to sink into the all too common condition of lethargy which characterizes entirely too many schools today. . . . We have no quarrel with La-crosse . . . but we feel we have the right to continue with a system that has served us well for many years.

The Hooper store, one of the few small-town general stores left in the region, had changed little since its construction in 1915 (although patrons could no longer buy harvest equipment, lumber, automobiles, or insurance or obtain loans). After 1970, the store was operated more as a community service than as a profit-making enterprise. But the fifty-thousand-dollar inventory of groceries and hardware became increasingly hard to move, particularly after the McGregors began phasing out the sheep business and cutting their payroll. The state highway by-passed Hooper in 1975, and this led to a further decline in sales. In December 1977, after almost seventy-five years as merchants, the Mc-Gregors closed their general store. The large brick store building was then used for office space and storage. Sara Goude, a long-time clerk at the McGregor store, in 1978 rented a much smaller building from McGregor Land and Livestock and opened Sara's Country Store, to serve the grocery needs of the forty people living in Hooper and nearby rural families. After 1975 the Hooper Hotel, once known as the Glen-more and operated throughout the year, was opened only during lamb-ing, shearing, and harvest seasons. The Hooper School was closed and torn down in 1975 after its directors had fought for more than twenty years against concerted efforts by public education officials to close country schools. Hooper children were bused more than thirty miles a day to attend elementary school in Lacrosse. In the 1970's the Hooper community lost some of the long-time residents who gave the area much of its vigor and spirit with the deaths of veteran sheep foreman Emile Morod, his wife and Hooper postmaster Ruby Morod, cattleman and wheat grower Ralph Snyder, "West End" foreman Ernest Osmond, ranch foreman Hans Kahler, and veteran electrician Wilbur Copp. The quiet little community, like the sheep business, remained as a reminder of an earlier period of ranching and farming.

The area had changed greatly in the hundred years since Archie Mc-Gregor walked through the Columbia Plateau with his bedroll on his back and became a "tramp" herder with his brother Peter. Sheep, the most efficient users of the native rangeland, diminished in importance as an immensely productive style of mechanized, petrochemical agriculture was developed. Never a wholly isolated ranching and farming region, the prosperity of the Columbia Plateau became closely related to the demand for wheat in Iran, Korea, India, and Japan; the availability of nitrogen fertilizers produced with natural gas from Alaska and Canada; phosphates produced from deposits in Florida and Morocco; and herbicides, pesticides, fungicides, and cow feed additives—products that were the fruit of the agricultural colleges' and the chemical industry's research. The huge crews of harvest workers have largely been replaced by expensive machinery. Because the large labor force of herders, camptenders, night men, and shearers could not be replaced efficiently, the sheep have given way to low-labor range cattle businesses and to capital-intensive feedlots.

The very survival of the McGregor Land and Livestock Company through this period of dramatic change marks it as unusual. Philip Raup, an economist studying "Corporate Farming in the United States," concluded that "up to 1950 the record was one of almost consistent failure." The four McGregor Brothers—John, Archie, Peter, and Alex—combined luck with hard work, good business judgment, a willingness and capacity to adapt to changing circumstances, and a generally harmonious working relationship to form a large and successful farm corporation. The Northern Pacific Railroad had, in a sense, forced prosperity on the sheepherding brothers by threatening to evict them from railroad rangeland. Faced with the choice of moving to overcrowded ranges elsewhere or renting land, John McGregor leased 23,000 acres, cajoled railroad officials into accepting late payment, and later joined his brothers in the purchase of many thousands of acres of additional lands. The 1896 lease was signed at an extraordinarily fortunate time for the poorly financed sheepmen—land values multiplied rapidly in the next decade, the price of wool and mutton increased at a fast pace, and experiments soon proved the desolate hills to be excellent farmland.[39]

The McGregor brothers possessed essential qualities of excellent business judgment and a capacity to adapt and innovate in the face of new conditions. These attributes were tempered in the Scotchmen with a cautious skepticism toward changes that might jeopardize the future of their family corporation. Their business endeavors outside ranching and farming and away from the company town were often disastrous: They learned the limitations of their expertise through failures as town lot speculators, hardware merchants, gold mine investors, range cattle-men, and irrigation project operators. Working in their own town, where they knew the customers and the requirements of successful business management, the four McGregors developed an almost paternal relation-ship with their neighbors—selling them groceries, implements, clothing, lumber, automobiles, seed wheat, insurance, land, and other farming and ranching needs; providing credit, loans, and other banking services, and sometimes even keeping their books and filing their tax returns; and then purchasing the products of their ranches and farms and selling them in bulk shipments to distant buyers. If they lacked the penuriousness that John Kenneth Galbraith finds typical of the Ontario Scotch-Canadians, they nonetheless directed their energies in ways closely calculated to improve the returns of their ranching and farming busi-nesses.

The second and third generations of McGregor management—Mau-rice, Sherman, John, and William McGregor—infused new ideas into an old company and reacted creatively to a whole series of new problems—the Great Depression, mechanization, soil conservation, labor shortages, depleted rangeland, petrochemical farming, international marketing, and many others. Like their predecessors, they kept an alert watch on the research of agricultural college scientists. But some of the most successful innovations were done on their own. Guided by the work of ranch agronomist Harley Jacquot, the McGregors increased the profits from their own farm and developed a prosperous agricultural chemical business by refusing to accept a prevailing opinion of state college scien-tists. "The use of fertilizers for maintaining soil fertility," a 1948 "Prog-ress Report" issued by the Washington Agricultural Experiment Station warned farmers, "is not practical in dry-land farming. During years of abundant rainfall, the addition of a small amount of fertilizer will pro-mote more normal development of plants in the early growing period. However, the increase in grain yield has not been sufficient to cover the cost of applying the fertilizer. . . . Since moisture is the limiting factor in crop production, the yield is naturally affected very little by the ap-plication of fertilizer."[40]

Perhaps more than any other factor, the success of the McGregors in hiring and keeping a capable, hard-working, and dedicated crew of man-agers and employees was crucial to the success of the family corporation. The McGregors possessed an exceptional capacity to recognize and use talent. The two men who served as sheep foremen from 1898 to 1968, Jock Macrae and Emile Morod, each worked for the Hooper firm for more than fifty years. Their successor as sheep (and cattle) foreman, Clemente Barber, and the other men who came from the Basque provinces of Spain to herd McGregor sheep, helped the McGregors continue to make consistent profits in a business that had been collapsing, both regionally and nationally, for more than thirty years. Veteran wheat foreman Hans Kahler was typical of many of the capable employees: Even when in his seventies, he was always the first member of the harvest crew to reach the wheat fields, and the last to leave. Despite his advancing years, he would join those of us in a teenage crew specially hired to hand-pull wild rye from the wheat fields, generally walking further and faster through the fields, outdistancing his youthful employees despite the steep hills and temperatures frequently in excess of one hundred degrees. The determination and abilities of the employees made possible the transition by the three generations of McGregors from open range sheep to corporate agribusiness.

The varied experiences of the McGregor family and their employees during a century of life on the Columbia Plateau, from the opening of the region through its settlement and development, provide an unusual record of the dramatic changes that occurred in management and operation of ranching and farming on one of America's last frontiers. The McGregor Brothers partnership and its successors, the McGregor Land and Livestock Company and its subsidiaries, became involved in many of the important aspects of the region's agriculture: wheat farming, sheep production, irrigation, range cattle, feedlots, fertilizers, meatpacking plants, and other enterprises. By comparing and contrasting the experiences of this one family and the residents of its town with other pioneer ranchers and farmers—the Coffins, Drumhellers, Snyders, Coxes, Brunes, Jaussauds, Harders and many others—one can obtain an indication of the ways many sheepmen, cattlemen, and wheat raisers reacted to changes that would convert an area once viewed as curious, hostile, and forbidding into a region of capital-intensive, highly productive agriculture.

The voluminous records kept by the McGregors and evidence available from fellow flockmasters provide detailed information about the changes in sheep production since open range days. Once one of the most important professions of the western range states, sheep raising has remained a field that has attracted little historical attention. Business records of Columbia Plateau wheat raisers, likewise, have seldom been the subject of detailed historical research. The development of the McGregor wheat operation from the days of header boxes and horses through mechanization, the Great Depression, and into petrochemical agriculture suggest some of the major problems and changes encountered in the semiarid farming region. The records of the Hooper company also provide an unusual opportunity to look at what was once thought to be the most important irrigation program in Washington: a flume that would irrigate hundreds of thousands of acres of arid lands between Pasco and Hooper with Palouse River waters. The grandiose dreams of promoters from Holland, Philadelphia, New York, and Tacoma about the "miracle of irrigation," and the final failure of the miserably small ditch after its acquisition by the McGregors, suggest the meager results of some of the plans that preceded the highly successful Columbia Basin project.

The transformation of the sandy deserts of central Washington from poor sheep ranges into fertile potato, corn, and sugar beet production and the emergence of the Palouse country as the leading area in the nation in wheat output are indicative of the striking changes that have occurred in a century. The semiarid sheep pastures have been converted into a land of complex agribusiness in the one hundred years since the McGregor brothers borrowed two hundred dollars from their father, reconnoitered the region, and decided to become tramp sheepherders. By tending closely to the welfare of their flocks, the sheepmen built the framework for a diverse and highly productive style of agriculture. Emile Morod commented on the McGregor agribusiness: "It all come out of them damned sheep."[41]

Appendix 1

McGREGOR FAMILY BACKGROUND

Scotland (1793–1841)

Several MacGregor families lived in the tiny village of Ardchoirk, on the southeast corner of the Isle of Mull, in the Parish of Torosay, County of Argyll, Scotland, according to parish marriage and baptismal records and census returns of the years 1793–1841. The name "MacGregor" was proscribed by the British Crown in the eighteenth century because of the rebellious activities of the clan. Before 1815, all the MacGregor families in Ardchoirk used the pseudonym "McGhiel." From 1815 to 1827 they were referred to as "McGhiel" or "McGrigor." After 1827 "Mac-Gregor" (occasionally "McGregor") was used as a last name.

The MacGregor men were listed in census returns as "tenants." Young single women mentioned "female servant" as their occupations.

The following MacGregor families lived in Ardchoirk during these years:

Peter and Janet McGhiel and their eleven children
John and Mary McGhiel and their six children
Malcolm and Margaret McGhiel and their ten children
Alex. and Janet McGhiel and their seven children
Alex. and Anne McGhiel and their seven children
James and Sarah McGhiel and their five children

Between 1841 and 1851 all but one MacGregor family left Ardchoirk. Most probably went to Canada. Several descendants of the one family to stay in Scotland (Malcolm and Margaret McGhiel family) emigrated to Canada as well. Peter and Janet McGhiel were the ancestors of the McGregors who settled in the Pacific Northwest.

The MacGregors of Scotland and Ontario

Peter McGhiel (1776–ca. 1849) and Janet Lamont (1776–1866)
Both were born in the Parish of Torosay, Isle of Mull, and lived at Ard-choirk, where they had a tenant farm, before emigrating to the township of Sydenham, near Owen Sound, Ontario, in 1842 with their family. Peter served as deacon and elder of the Church of Scotland at Torosay and as representative to the Presbytery of Mull.

Children:
Mary (baptized 1802).
Anne (1805–82) married Hugh Livingstone of nearby Kilpatrick in 1831. They both emigrated with the rest of the family and farmed land adjacent to the lands claimed by her siblings in Ontario.
Euphemia ("Effy") (bapt. 1807). She was listed as a "female servant" in Scotland. Later married John Murray of Syndeham, Ontario.
Janet (bapt. 1809).
Catherine (bapt. 1811).
Dougald (bapt. 1813). A bachelor, he farmed land in Ontario next to his parents and siblings.
Donald (1815–96) married and farmed in Ontario near the rest of his family.
John (bapt. 1818) died as an infant.
"child" (bapt. 1820) died as an infant.
John (1822–91). A bachelor, he farmed and claimed land in Sydenham adjacent to his parents.
Peter (1824–99), Sydenham farmer (see below).

The MacGregors (McGregors) of Canada and Washington State

Peter MacGregor (1824–99) and Mary Campbell (1834–1918)
Farmed in Ontario after their marriage in 1859. She spent much of her time with her children in the West after Peter's death. Their children, particularly the boys who came to eastern Washington, usually short-ened their last name to "McGregor."

Children:
Dougald (1860–1938) m. Elizabeth Morrison. Operated the family farm in Ontario except during the years 1908–18 when they rented it and lived in Hooper. Their children were William (who owned and

operated the Ontario farm after his father's death); Jean, a high school teacher in Washington State; and Elizabeth, an Ontario teacher.

Archibald (1861–1942) m. Nellie Thomas (1876–1948). Lived in Hooper, Washington, until 1919, when they moved to southern California with their daughters, Marie, Jessie, and Genevieve.

Peter (1862–1941) m. Maude Taylor (1874–1929). Active in Hooper ranch and political affairs. Their eldest son, John M. ("Maurice") (1894–1956), married Elgin Warren and was a McGregor Land and Livestock manager from 1925 until his death.

The two children of Maurice and Elgin also were active in the family business: John (m. Patricia Dossee) ran the cattle feeding operations after 1950 and William (m. Nancy Rohwer) managed the ranch at Hooper after 1954.

The other child of Peter and Maude, Alexander Taylor ("Alex T.") McGregor (1897–1944), ran the Bar U Ranch (Taylor Land and Livestock) near Hooper.

William (1864–98). A bachelor, William came west shortly before his death and wrote extensive letters to his family that appear in the text.

John (1866–1918) m. Minnie Taylor (1877–1931). He managed the Hooper ranch until his death. Their daughter, Esther, died as a young woman. Their son, Donald, worked at the Hooper ranch for a few years before pursuing other occupations.

Alexander Campbell ("A.C.") (1869–1952) m. Jennie Sherman (1882–1965). Active in the family business at Hooper. Their eldest child, Alexander Sherman ("Sherman") (m. Norma Gantzer) became manager of the fertilizer and chemical branch of the family business after his return to Hooper in 1947. His sisters, Mary, Helen, and Marjorie, pursued other careers (as a pianist, radio announcer, and actress, respectively) before marrying and settling in Portland, Los Angeles, and New York.

The author is the grandson of A. C. and Jennie and the son of Sherman and Norma McGregor.

Sarah (b. 1871) died as an infant.

Euphemia (1871–1970), a school teacher in Spokane; she later moved to Calgary. She never married.

Jessie (1873–1959) m. Frank Skene, a contractor, in 1912. She worked as a nurse in Portland and Spokane before her marriage, then moved to Calgary.

Donald (1875–1946) m. Esther Miller (1871–1961). He was a Presbyterian minister in Ontario. She was a novelist who wrote numerous books under the pen name "Marian Keith."

SOURCES: Baptismal and marriage records and Kirk Session Minute Book, Parish of Torosay, Isle of Mull; 1841 census for Torosay; 1851–71 censuses of Sydenham Township, Grey County, Ontario (based on research done in Scotland and Canada by Mark Lemon, Annan, Ontario). Other sources include obituaries, correspondence, and biographical information in ML&L/Hooper, ML&L/WSU, and ML&L/ACM as well as family background materials gathered by Euphemia S. MacGregor (MD/Calgary) and Marie Boone and Betty Jean Peatross of Glendale, California.

Appendix 2

McGREGOR LAND AND LIVESTOCK,
CORPORATE EARNINGS, 1909–50

Key

Column 2 (total cost of sales and expenses) equals the cost of sales adjusted for increases or decreases in inventory.

Column 4 (general expenses) includes officers' salaries, taxes, and miscellaneous charges. Included in column 2 during years 1909–13.

Column 5 (other income or deductions) includes interest earnings and expenses, insurance commissions, income from post office, etc. Not listed separately, 1918–34.

During the years 1909–13, the company did not separately list beginning and ending inventories by department, except for the store. Only the merchandise department and overall corporate earnings are listed for these years.

The corporation kept detailed records for each department from 1914 to 1934. One peculiarity of these figures is that fixed assets purchased were included in operating expenses and in ending inventory for the accounting period in which they were acquired. The increase in inventory negated the expense, thus having no overall effect on that year's departmental earnings. After 1934, the accounting firm of Lemaster and Daniel prepared the annual statements. Fixed assets were removed from inventory and set up separately on the books and were put on depreciation schedules. Only marketable items were included in inventory thereafter. The changed bookkeeping methods did not have a significant impact on annual earnings figures. McGregor Land and Livestock accountant C. J. Storey helped me collect and organize statistics from the voluminous records kept by the company, its accountants, and the archivists at Washington State University. Glenn Mickelson of Lemaster and Daniels, Spokane, also provided corporate financial information.

OVERALL CORPORATE EARNINGS

Year	Sales	Total Cost of Sales & Expenses	Net Operating Income or (Loss)	General Expenses	Other Income or (Deductions)	Net Earnings (pre-tax)	% Pre-Tax Net/Sales
1909	144,812	89,077	55,735		(5,979)	49,756	34.4
1910	125,713	99,333	26,380		(25,586)[a]	18,102[a]	14.4
1911	156,850	110,661	46,189		(9,597)	36,592	23.3
1912	168,586	126,464	42,122		(8,778)	33,344	19.8
1913	146,501	121,330	25,171		(6,735)	18,437	12.6
1914	149,729[b]	115,908	33,821	(4,320)	2,278	31,779	21.2
1915	169,480	124,004	45,476	(6,025)	5,307	44,758	26.4
1916	198,442	123,904	74,538	(6,025)	6,122	74,635	37.6
1917	366,082	249,920	116,162	(9,330)	5,339	112,171	30.6
1918	304,219	251,775	52,442	(7,072)		45,370	14.9
1919	409,454	301,375	108,079	(22,624)		85,455	20.9
1909–1919	$2,339,868					$550,399	23.5
1920	387,562	335,474	52,088	(6,412)		45,676	11.8
1921	263,547	234,355	29,192	(4,829)		24,363	9.2
1922	285,583	261,935	23,648	(6,041)		17,607	6.2
1923	318,091	244,893	73,198	(8,708)		64,490	20.3
1924	392,353	368,568	23,785	(9,739)		14,046	3.6
1925	688,402	601,867	86,535	(11,761)		74,774	10.9
1926	555,917	535,997	19,920	(10,345)		9,575	1.7
1927	658,728	619,889	38,839	(9,113)		29,726	4.5
1928	398,887	339,360	59,527	(9,510)		50,017	12.5
1929	363,408	326,861	36,547	(9,203)		27,344	7.5
1920–1929	$4,312,478					$357,618	8.3

OVERALL CORPORATE EARNINGS (continued)

YEAR	SALES	TOTAL COST OF SALES & EXPENSES	NET OPERATING INCOME OR (LOSS)	GENERAL EXPENSES	OTHER INCOME OR (DEDUCTIONS)	NET EARNINGS (PRE-TAX)	% PRE-TAX NET/SALES
1930	335,185	375,022	(39,837)	(8,476)		(48,313)	LOSS
1931	224,021	231,911	(7,890)	(6,404)		(14,294)	LOSS
1932	169,194	191,863	(22,669)	(5,647)		(28,316)	LOSS
1933	229,537	183,177	46,360	(8,802)		37,558	16.4
1934	214,592	186,676	27,916	(8,997)		18,919	8.8
1935	244,843	189,405	46,438	(14,985)	(6,782)	24,671	10.1
1936	252,184	204,489	47,695	(20,064)	(4,587)	23,044	9.0
1937	234,592	183,661	50,931	(20,070)	(4,590)	26,271	11.2
1938	158,350	120,636	37,714	(21,498)	(4,179)	12,037	7.6
1939	188,003	147,181	40,822	(25,815)	(2,641)	12,366	6.6
1930– 1939	$2,250,501					$63,943	2.8
1940	222,184	157,273	64,911	(27,766)	(2,128)	35,017	15.8
1941	214,013	116,212	97,801	(28,296)	(2,351)	67,154	31.4
1942	236,472	152,360	84,112	(28,657)	(1,890)	53,565	22.7
1943	367,323	272,514	94,809	(27,128)	(4,758)	62,924	17.1
1944	358,122	256,948	101,173	(33,642)	(5,910)	61,622	17.2
1945	336,218	225,547	110,671	(44,683)	(2,037)	59,660	19.0
1946	497,842	260,752	237,090	(43,071)	(374)	193,645	38.9
1947	549,513	307,391	242,122	(55,048)	(3,220)	183,853	33.5
1948	732,044	387,602	344,442	(56,327)	(2,396)	285,720	39.0
1949	565,412	435,499	129,912	(54,871)	(2,190)	72,852	12.9
1950	767,630	469,012	298,618	(59,333)	2,919	242,204	31.6
1940– 1950	$4,846,773					$1,318,216	27.2

[a]A $17,308 "depreciation" in the value of the wheat crop was disallowed by the Internal Revenue Director.

[b]Sales figures modified to include interest payments on store bills and miscellaneous store income during the years 1914–29.

SHEEP

Year	Sales	Cost of Sales & $ Expenses	% of Costs & Expenses to Sales	Net Operating Income or (Loss)	% of Net to Sales
1914	43,602	25,203	57.8	18,399	42.2
1915	50,269	29,293	58.3	20,976	41.7
1916	51,725	26,800	51.8	24,925	48.2
1917	93,398	45,375	48.6	48,023	51.4
1918	123,239	102,643	83.3	20,596	16.7
1919	138,713	91,186	65.7	47,527	34.3
1920	108,019	75,801	70.2	32,218	29.8
1921	62,142	48,615	78.2	13,527	21.8
1922	72,033	65,327	90.7	6,706	9.3
1923	90,692	59,200	65.3	31,492	34.7
1924	69,330	64,023	92.3	5,307	7.7
1926	81,561	72,459	88.8	9,102	11.2
1925	99,997	82,265	82.3	17,732	17.7
1927	94,293	60,068	63.7	34,225	36.3
1928	104,841	70,008	66.8	34,833	33.2
1929	82,320	79,112	96.1	3,208	3.9
1930	50,609	56,166	111.0	(5,557)	LOSS
1931	54,485	55,288	101.5	(803)	LOSS
1932	42,564	44,454	104.4	(1,890)	LOSS
1933	41,371	15,516	37.5	25,855	62.5
1934	35,695	22,969	64.3	12,726	35.7
1935	91,992	76,751	83.4	15,241	16.6
1936	70,472	58,111	82.5	12,361	17.5
1937	68,198	46,885	68.7	21,313	31.3
1938	58,535	34,903	59.6	23,632	40.4
1939	64,348	61,877	96.2	2,471	3.8
1940	67,457	42,114	62.4	25,343	37.6
1941	95,576	47,963	50.2	47,613	49.8
1942	90,057	59,545	66.1	30,512	33.9
1943	119,467	72,251	60.5	47,216	39.5
1944	100,597	79,584	79.1	21,013	20.9

SHEEP (continued)

Year	Sales	Cost of Sales & $ Expenses	% of Costs & Expenses to Sales	Net Operating Income or (Loss)	% of Net to Sales
1945	103,597	76,782	74.1	26,815	25.9
1946	150,774	81,050	53.8	69,724	46.2
1947	145,979	93,948	64.4	52,031	35.6
1948	177,179	93,280	52.6	83,899	47.4
1949	148,794	115,824	77.8	32,970	22.2
1950	189,944	129,157	68.0	60,787	32.0

Aggregate

Year	Sales	Cost of Sales & $ Expenses	% of Costs & Expenses to Sales	Net Operating Income or (Loss)	% of Net to Sales
1914–50	3,333,864		70.8	972,068	29.2

WHEAT RANCH

Year	Sales	Cost of Sales & $ Expenses	% of Costs & Expenses to Sales	Net Operating Income or (Loss)	% of Net to Sales
1914	16,129	12,237	75.9	3,892	24.1
1915	19,511	4,692	24.0	14,819	76.0
1916	24,237	5,096	21.0	19,141	79.0
1917	34,210	20,833	60.9	13,377	39.1
1918	20,293	7,293	35.9	13,000	64.1
1919	24,630	5,049	20.5	19,581	79.5
1920	8,715	5,410	62.1	3,305	37.9
1921	14,066	2,516	17.9	11,550	82.1
1922	5,262	2,135	40.0	3,127	60.0
1923	3,999	(3,147)	CREDIT	7,146	179.0
1924	22,561	29,948	132.7	(7,387)	LOSS
1925	130,609	93,296	71.4	37,313	28.6
1926	94,120	76,693	81.5	17,427	18.5
1927	143,504	98,147	68.4	45,357	31.6

WHEAT RANCH (continued)

Year	Sales	Cost of Sales & $ Expenses	% of Costs & Expenses to Sales	Net Operating Income or (Loss)	% of Net to Sales
1928	114,102	96,882	84.9	17,220	15.1
1929	98,331	74,860	76.1	23,471	23.9
1930	46,097	57,218	124.1	(11,121)	LOSS
1931	42,034	46,922	111.6	(4,888)	LOSS
1932	23,467	26,940	114.8	(3,473)	LOSS
1933	71,777	48,642	67.8	23,135	32.2
1934	60,685	39,734	65.5	20,951	34.5
1935	73,964	34,396	46.5	39,568	53.5
1936	89,478	56,100	62.7	33,378	37.3
1937	94,203	56,053	59.5	38,150	40.5
1938	34,610	17,337	50.1	17,273	49.9
1939	58,018	15,670	27.0	42,348	73.0
1940	85,936	50,162	58.4	35,774	41.6
1941	46,334	(3,705)	CREDIT	50,039	108.0
1942	58,249	5,676	9.7	52,573	90.3
1943	155,100	103,438	66.7	51,662	33.3
1944	168,941	85,976	50.9	82,965	49.1
1945	142,263	59,362	41.7	82,901	58.3
1946	253,965	81,030	31.9	172,935	68.1
1947	299,036	94,016	31.4	205,020	68.6
1948	419,596	139,294	33.2	280,302	66.8
1949	249,375	121,168	48.6	128,207	51.4
1950	288,668	95,935	33.2	192,733	66.8
1914–50	$3,536,075		49.9	$1,772,780	50.1

SECTIONS (TENANT FARMS)

Year	Sales	Cost of Sales & Expenses	% of Costs & Expenses to Sales	Net Operating Income or (Loss)	% of Net to Sales
1914	9,138	2,195	24.0	6,943	76.0
1915	18,587	7,582	40.8	11,005	59.2
1916	15,566	(4,874) cr.	CREDIT	20,440	131.3
1917	52,732	32,080	60.8	20,652	39.2
1918	19,620	3,785	19.3	15,835	80.7
1919	32,995	9,973	30.2	23,022	69.8
1920	13,810	5,298	38.4	8,512	61.6
1921	13,637	3,009	22.1	10,628	77.9
1922	7,166	15,503	216.3	(8,337)	LOSS
1923	18,889	12,316	65.2	6,573	34.8
1924	15,809	26,367	166.8	(10,558)	LOSS
1925	–0–	28,555	–0–	(28,555)	LOSS
1914–25	$217,949			$ 76,160	34.9

WHEAT TRADING (listed separately 1926–34)

Year	Sales	Cost of Sales & Expenses	% of Costs & Expenses to Sales	Net Operating Income or (Loss)	% of Net to Sales
1926	212,510	129,666	61.0	82,844	39.0
1927	199,456	195,261	97.9	4,195	2.1
1928	45,478	39,847	87.6	5,631	12.4
1929	45,253	39,230	86.7	6,023	13.3
1930	121,676	137,844	113.3	(16,168)	LOSS
1931	54,600	28,336	51.9	26,264	48.1
1932	33,946	51,799	152.6	(17,853)	LOSS
1933	53,083	43,015	81.0	10,068	19.0
1934	44,943	36,714	81.7	8,229	18.3
1926–34	$810,945			$109,233	13.5

WOOD GULCH WHEAT RANCH

Year	Sales	Cost of Sales & Expenses	% of Costs & Expenses to Sales	Net Operating Income or (Loss)	% of Net to Sales
1924	1,102	11,782	...	(10,680)	...
1925	–0–	8,580	...	(8,580)	...

STARBUCK WHEAT RANCH

Year	Sales	Cost of Sales & Expenses	% of Costs & Expenses to Sales	Net Operating Income or (Loss)	% of Net to Sales
1924	43,713	42,404	97.0	1,309	3.0
1925	49,744	49,195	98.9	549	1.1
1926	28,922	32,312	111.7	(3,390)	LOSS
1927	69,522	50,317	72.4	19,205	27.6

All wheat operations 1914–50
$4,757,972 $1,956,586   41.1

CATTLE

Year	Sales	Cost of Sales & $ Expenses	% of Costs & Expenses to Sales	Net Operating Income or (Loss)	% of Net to Sales
1914	711	(184)	CREDIT	895	125.9
1915	4,319	3,677	85.1	642	14.9
1916	6,298	3,816	60.6	2,482	39.4
1917	7,021	5,632	80.2	1,389	19.8
1918	6,998	5,467	78.1	1,531	21.9
1919	13,711	15,560	113.5	(1,849)	LOSS
1920	7,305	6,085	83.3	1,220	16.7
1921	1,159	379	32.7	780	67.3
1922	7,733	11,133	144.0	(3,400)	LOSS
1923	7,364	7,435	101.0	(71)	LOSS
1924	7,872	6,800	86.4	1,072	13.6
1925	–0–	70		(70)	LOSS
		No cattle on ranch 1925–50			
1950	65,400	27,344	41.8	38,056	58.2

		Aggregate			
1914–25	70,491			4,626	6.6
Overall	135,891			42,677	31.4

REAL ESTATE

Year	Sales	Cost of Sales & $ Expenses	% of Costs & Expenses to Sales	Net Operating Income or (Loss)	% of Net to Sales
1914	19,032	18,667	98.1	365	1.9
1915	6,443	4,730	73.4	1,713	26.6
1916	5,964	4,178	70.1	1,786	29.9
1917	64,729	26,998	41.7	37,731	58.3
1918	7,586	6,899	90.9	687	9.1
1919	22,046	10,211	46.3	11,835	53.7
1920	16,025	9,673	60.4	6,352	39.6
1921	14,144	14,846	105.0	(702)	LOSS
1922	12,587	12,400	98.5	187	1.5
1923	47,750	34,657	72.6	13,093	27.4
1924	13,693	7,639	55.8	6,054	44.2
1925	10,780	6,931	64.3	3,849	35.7
1926	9,086	7,062	77.7	2,024	22.3
1927	12,202	78,876	646.4	(66,674)	LOSS
1928	8,559	7,836	91.6	723	8.4
1929	8,500	7,590	89.3	910	10.7
1930	8,061	7,889	97.9	172	2.1
1931	5,000	2,408	48.2	2,592	51.8
1932	–0–	7,015	–0–	(7,015)	LOSS
1933	188	4,520	–0–	(4,332)	LOSS
1934	10	3,991	–0–	(3,981)	LOSS

Aggregate

Year	Sales			Net Operating Income or (Loss)	% of Net to Sales
1914–34	292,385			7,369	2.5
1914–23	216,306			73,047	33.7

NOTE: Most of the income listed under "real estate" after 1923 reflects a grazing fee charged to the sheep division. Very few tracts were sold. The substantial loss in 1927 reflects the sale of the Starbuck ranch, which was sold for a low figure.

MERCHANDISE (STORE)

Year	Gross Sales	Interest Payments and Other Income	Total Proceeds	Net Departmental Income or (Loss)	% of Net to Sales
1909	96,345		96,345	11,979	12.4
1910	53,990		53,990	1,401	2.6
1911	67,453		67,453	6,451	9.6
1912	62,242		62,242	10,629	17.1
1913	58,624		58,624	7,485	12.8
1914	49,544	9,258	58,802	7,124	14.4
1915	59,051	7,868	66,919	(408)	LOSS
1916	81,129	8,174	89,303	11,990	14.8
1917	100,855	10,176	111,031	4,132	4.1
1918	100,869	8,247	109,116	3,231	3.2
1919	138,330	12,967	151,297	24,981	18.1
1920	203,964	19,830	223,794	14,663	7.2
1921	115,713	28,647	144,360	5,456	4.7
1922	116,789	41,668	158,457	26,070	22.3
1923	113,092	30,111	143,203	23,142	20.5
1924	89,255	39,490	128,745	29,685	33.3
1925	156,197	18,240	174,437	14,704	9.4
1926	103,945	10,603	114,548	4,561	4.4
1927	117,856	9,496	127,352	6,891	5.8
1928	107,081	8,212	115,293	5,095	4.8
1929	101,846	11,694	113,540	5,667	5.6
1930	91,961			(3,962)	LOSS
1931	63,754			(10,494)	LOSS
1932	52,393			(4,026)	LOSS
1933	54,106			(7,481)	LOSS
1934	63,088			(8,170)	LOSS
1935	69,414			(6,780)	LOSS
1936	81,234			4,218	5.2
1937	69,665			619	.9
1938	64,511			3,920	6.1
1939	64,348			2,471	3.8
1940	67,564			7,148	10.6
1941	69,836			4,930	7.1
1942	76,651			7,143	9.3

MERCHANDISE (STORE) (continued)

Year	Gross Sales	Interest Payments and Other Income	Total Proceeds	Net Departmental Income or (Loss)	% of Net to Sales
1943	67,845			(945)	LOSS
1944	56,094			4,451	7.9
1945	76,651			7,143	9.3
1946	72,547			4,247	5.9
1947	91,737			5,771	6.3
1948	121,299[a]			6,726	5.6
1949	161,828[a]			14,438	8.9
1950	204,879[a]			21,853	10.7

Aggregate

1909–50	$3,835,575			278,149	7.3

[a]Includes fertilizer sales.

"WEST END"

Year	Sales	Cost of Sales & $ Expenses	% of Costs & Expenses to Sales	Net Operating Income or (Loss)	% of Net to Sales
1914	1,689	4,019		(2,330)	
1915	3,392	6,226		(2,834)	
1916	5,180	11,209		(6,029)	
1917	2,958	11,768		(8,810)	
1918	17,367	19,430		(2,063)	
1919	22,042	26,395		(4,353)	
1920	9,894	24,076		(14,182)	
1921	13,349	25,077		(11,728)	
1922	6,043	9,981		(3,938)	
1923	112	8,289		(8,177)	
1924	89,528	80,545		8,983	

"WEST END" (continued)

YEAR	SALES	COST OF SALES & $ EXPENSES	% OF COSTS & EXPENSES TO SALES	NET OPERATING INCOME OR (LOSS)	% OF NET TO SALES
1925	222,835	173,242		49,593	
1926	15,170	107,818		(92,648)	
1927	12,399	16,759		(4,360)	
1928	10,614	14,589		(3,975)	
1929	15,464	18,196		(2,732)	
1930	16,781	19,982		(3,201)	
1931	4,148	24,709		(20,561)	
1932	16,824	5,236		11,588	
1933	9,012	9,897		(885)	
1934	10,171	12,010		(1,839)	
1935	9,473	11,064		(1,591)	
1936	11,000	13,262		(2,262)	
1937	2,526	11,677		(9,151)	
1938	694	7,805		(7,111)	
1939	1,289	7,757		(6,468)	
1940	1,226	4,581		(3,355)	
1941	2,266	7,049		(4,783)	
1942	11,515	17,631		(6,116)	
1943	24,911	28,035		(3,124)	
1944	32,490	39,746		(7,256)	
1945	13,707	19,895		(6,188)	
1946	20,556	30,372		(9,816)	
1947	12,760	33,460		(20,700)	
1948	13,970	40,455		(26,485)	
1949	5,414	51,117		(45,703)	
1950	18,739	33,551		(14,812)	

| | CITY LOTS | | | PALOUSE FALLS | |
| | | | (old irrigation project) | | |

Year	Sales	Net Operating Income or (Loss)	Year	Sales	Net Operating Income or (Loss)
1914	626	(1,467)	1921	690	(319)
1915	40	(437)	1922	16,302	3,233
1916	169	(197)	1923	6,082	–o–
1917	3	(332)			
1918	–o–	(375)			
1919	4,020	(12,665)			

Appendix 3

McGREGOR LAND AND LIVESTOCK SHEEP BUSINESS,
ANNUAL RETURNS ON INVESTMENT AND
OPERATING EXPENSES, 1921–27

Annual sheep inventory—average—January 1—8,474
(During summer months the inventory, including lambs,
averaged about 19,000)

Annual sheep losses

Summer	*Winter*
From shipping count on leaving home range for mountains until separating in fall	From separating time in fall to shipping count
473 . . . . 1921 184	
449 . . . . 1922 268	
615 . . . . 1923 253	
491 . . . . 1924 68	
595 . . . . 1925 784	
569 . . . . 1926 67	
396 . . . . 1927 435	
Average 512	Average 294

Sheep Operating Profit, 1921–27[a]
Gross receipts less operating expense, payroll, leases, supplies

1921......$23,027
1922...... 15,633
1923...... 41,493
1924...... 18,306
1925...... 28,152
1926...... 17,102
1927...... 42,726

Per head—costs & receipts,
1923–30
[this column was computed two
years later]

Average receipts $10.78
Expenses
  labor 2.45
  groceries .... .72
Summer range & stubble .. .61
Freight & Taxes .... .93
Grain & Hay 1.43
       Total expenses .....$ 6.78

Fixed charges, 1921–27

Average real taxes $3,500
Average income tax 3,460
Supervision 3,000
              $9,960

Average net profit—1921–1927 ....$16,645.77

Investment
23,000 acres grazing land—at tax valuation $7.50 ....$172,500
Total equipment & outfit—at less than replacement cost 25,000
8,200 sheep at $12.50 102,500
                                    $300,000

[a]The figures used here by Peter McGregor are higher than those of the company office manager, who included additional expenses before tabulating the net operating income figures for the sheep division that appear in Appendix 2.

AVERAGE RETURN ON INVESTMENT—5.55%

Peter McGregor collected the information on return on land for presentation in 1928 to the Interstate Commerce Commission, which was studying railroad requests for increases in livestock shipping charges. The data are accurate and are rather typical of the ratios between earnings and land values for other years of range sheep production. The drawback of tabulating "return on investment" is that the McGregors and many other Columbia Plateau sheepmen purchased their land for $0.75 to $2.00 per acre. Hence such tabulations show not "return on investment," but rather return on present value of the land.

Sources: Peter McGregor to Charles Mackenzie, April 20, 1928, ML&L/ACM, and McGregor Land and Livestock to S. J. Polmeteer, January 22, 1930, ML&L/Hooper. These data have been verified by an examination of the McGregor Land and Livestock books in ML&L/WSU and ML&L/Lemaster and Daniels.

Abbreviations Used in the Notes and Bibliography

AES	Bulletins from various agricultural experiment stations
BAI	Bureau of Animal Industry of U.S. Department of Agriculture
MASC/WSU	Manuscripts and Special Collections, Washington State University
MB/Glendale	Marie Boone collection, in possession of Mrs. Betty Jean Peatross, Glendale, California
ML&L/ACM	McGregor Land and Livestock records, writer's collection
ML&L/Hooper	Business records in offices of McGregor Land and Livestock Company
ML&L/Lemaster & Daniels	McGregor Land and Livestock records on file in the Spokane office of the Lemaster & Daniels accounting firm
ML&L/WSU	McGregor Land and Livestock Collection, Manuscripts and Special Collections, Washington State University
McGregor Co./Colfax	McGregor Company records, company files
McGregor Feedlot/Pasco	McGregor Feedlot records, company files
MSD/Calgary	Mary Skene Darrah collection, Calgary
NPRR/St. Paul	Northern Pacific Railroad archives, Minnesota Historical Society, St. Paul
OHQ	*Oregon Historical Quarterly*
PNQ	*Pacific Northwest Quarterly*
USDA	U.S. Department of Agriculture
WCAT/Walla Walla	Whitman College Audio Tape Series
WSC or WSU	Washington State College/Washington State University

Notes

INTRODUCTION

1. J. Russell Harper, ed., *Paul Kane's Frontier*, p. 115; Thomas W. Symons, "The Upper Columbia River and the Great Plain of the Columbia," 47th Cong., 1st sess., Sen. Exec. Doc. 186 (1882), p. 111.

2. Wheat yields: Oliver E. Baker, "Agricultural Regions of North America, Part XI" *Economic Geography* 9:2 (April 1933): 177. Ladd Haystead and Gilbert Fite in 1955 listed three Columbia Plateau counties—Whitman, Lincoln, and Adams—as the leading counties in the nation in total wheat production (see *The Agricultural Regions of the United States*, p. 253). The Washington portion of the Columbia Plateau alone accounts for almost all the wheat grown in that state, giving it ninth place among the states in acreage in crop, but ranking third, behind Kansas and North Dakota, in value of wheat crops produced (see USDA, Economic Research Service, "State Farm Income Statistics," supplement to Statistical Bulletin 576 [September 1977] p. 5). Millions of additional bushels of wheat are grown on the Oregon and Idaho portions of the plateau.

3. Donald W. Meinig, *The Great Columbia Plain*, p. 3.

CHAPTER I

Immigration to the Grasslands of the Columbia Plateau

1. Isaac Stevens, quoted in James G. Swan, *The Northwest Coast, or Three Years' Residence in Washington Territory*, p. 398; *Washington Territory: Facts Regarding Its Climate and Soil, Mineral, Agricultural, Manufacturing, and Commercial Resources, Information for Immigrants* (Washington Territory Immigrant Aid Society, 1879), pp. 10, 30.

2. For an excellent detailed description of wildlife, climate, and topography see Meinig, *The Great Columbia Plain*, pp. 3–20. Other sources used here include Bates McKee, *Cascadia*, pp. 273–74; W. A. Rockie, "The Palouse," *Yearbook of the Association of Pacific Coast Geographers* 15 (1953): 6–9; and J. E. Weaver, "A Study of the Vegetation of Southeastern Washington and Adjacent Idaho," *University of Nebraska Studies* 17:1 (January 1917): 2–109. Oscar Osborne's statement about a region "waving in bunch grass up to the horses' bellies" is typical of the comments made by pioneers; see *Told by the Pioneers*, Washington Pioneer Project, WPA Project 5841 (1938), 2:200.

3. J. Harlen Bretz, "The Channeled Scabland of Eastern Washington," *Geographical Review* 18:3 (July 1928): 446–61.

4. On Indian legends see Sam Fisher's account of the origin of the Palouse River, transcribed by J. Maurice McGregor, and other "Tales of the Rivers, Rocks, and Waterfalls," in Ella E. Clark, *Indian Legends of the Pacific Northwest*, p. 117. Also see "Sam Fisher" file in ML&L/Hooper. On Wish-poosh and Speel-yi see Gerald J. Tucker, "History of the Northern Blue Mountains" (ca. 1940; typescript made available by Virgil Bennington, Walla Walla), pp. 8–11. For geologic information see McKee, *Cascadia*, pp. 273–86; "The Channeled Scablands of Eastern Washington: The Geologic Story of the Spokane Flood," U.S. Department of the Interior, Geologic Survey (1973), p. 2.

5. T. C. Elliott, ed., "Journal of David Thompson," *OHQ* 15:2 (June 1914): 122–25; Harper, ed., *Paul Kane's Frontier*, pp. 115–21. Quote about "Sage, sand, weeds," written by Henry J. Coke, and Farnham's quote are from Meinig, *The Great Columbia Plain*, pp. 186–88. Nesmith's comments are in his "Diary of the Emigration of 1843," *OHQ* 7:4 (Dec. 1906): 355. The dry summers were in striking contrast to lands in Kansas, Nebraska, and the Dakotas through which many of the emigrants and travelers had passed—there the heaviest rainfall occurred in June, July, and August (see the rainfall maps and charts in Byron Hunter, "Farm Practice in the Columbia Basin Uplands," USDA Farmers' Bulletin 294 [1907], pp. 9–11). The view of the Columbia Plateau as a drab, monotonous region was typical of early comments about most western prairies (see James C. Malin, *The Grassland of North America*, p. 120).

6. On the impact of mining strikes on Walla Walla: A. C. McGregor, "The Economic Impact of the Mullan Road on Walla Walla," *PNQ* 65:3 (July 1974): 118–29. On the brisk demand for cattle: Walla Walla *Statesman*, September 25, 1868; also see *Statesman*, August 13, 1869; June 10, 1871; February 3, 1872. On the miners and freighters who stayed: William S. Lewis, *Early Days in the Big Bend Country*, p. 9; interview with Thomas J. Drumheller, Jr.; *Illustrated History of the Big Bend Country*, p. 895; and "Pioneers of Washington Series," 52 biographical sketches of pioneers appearing in 1953 issues of the Walla Walla *Union Bulletin*.

7. A. J. Splawn, "A Cattleman's Reminiscences," *The Ranch*, February 13,

1902; Holt quote from a July 30, 1872, letter from a collection of 33 letters written between 1854 and 1885 by a family that emigrated from a Georgia plantation to the Williamette Valley and then to "Rebel Flat" near Colfax, Washington. This collection of Holt family letters was made available by Betty Jean Peatross, Glendale, California.

8. *Statesman*, January 1, 1870, and similar comments in the October 28, 1866, and December 7, 1866, issues. Information on the miners and freighters comes from "Pioneers of Washington Series" (spring 1953 issues of the *Union Bulletin*) and from several early subscription histories of southeastern Washington. On lingering doubts about grain production, see Donald W. Meinig, "The Evolution of Understanding an Environment: Climate and Wheat Culture in the Columbia Plateau," *Yearbook of the Association of Pacific Coast Geographers* 16 (1954): 25–31.

9. "Philip Ritz," *Union Bulletin* April 19, 1953. On shipments to Liverpool: James N. Tattersall, "The Economic Development of the Pacific Northwest to 1920" (Ph.D. dissertation, University of Washington), 1960, p. 60. On marketing problems: D. W. Meinig, "Wheat Sacks Out to Sea," *PNQ* (January 1954): 13–16; "From Washington Territory," Sacramento *Daily Union*, December 2, 1871.

10. Walter Prescott Webb, *The Great Plains*, pp. 341–48.

11. On results of railroad construction: Meinig, *Great Columbia Plain*, pp. 261–64. Typically glowing reports about the Columbia Plateau: *Settler's Guide to Oregon and Washington Territory and to the Lands of the Northern Pacific Railroad on the Pacific Slope* (1872), p. 16; *Eastern Washington Territory and Oregon* (published by the Oregon Railroad and Navigation Company about 1888), p. 41. On the advance of the wheat frontier: Frank Greene, "Report on the Interior Wheat Lands of Oregon and Washington Territory," 50th Cong., 1st sess., Sen. Exec. Doc. 229 (1888), p. 16. On population increase: Lancaster Pollard, "The Pacific Northwest," in Merrill Jensen, ed., *Regionalism in America*, pp. 187–209.

12. On various homelands of the immigrants: Pollard, "The Pacific Northwest," in Jensen, ed., *Regionalism in America*, pp. 208–9; Rowland Berthoff, *An Unsettled People*, pp. 303–5. On poverty of Scots: Ian C. C. Graham, *Colonists from Scotland*, p. i. Quote is from Gordon Donaldson, *The Scots Overseas*, p. 13.

13. Information about land distribution, "hungry forties," and immigrant guidebook: Donaldson, *The Scots Overseas*, pp. 52, 85, 97, 132. On destitution on Mull and emigration plans for the poor: Helen Cowan, *British Emigration to British North America*, pp. 101, 126, 210. On "free" land in Ontario: Adam Shortt and Arthur Doughty, *Canada and Its Provinces*, vol. 18, *The Province of Ontario*, Part II, p. 565. Also see John Prebble, *The Lion in the North*, pp. 228–30, 299. The McGregor experiences are recounted in "Reminiscences of Euphemia MacGregor," MSS., MSD/Calgary. There was a certain irony when, fifty years later, the McGregors began adding to their extensive sheep ranges by buying out homesteaders.

14. Baptismal records from Ardchoirk, Parish of Torosay, Isle of Mull, Scotland; Kirk Session Minute Book, Church of Scotland; 1841 Census for Torosay; 1851–71 censuses of Sydenham Township, Grey County, Ontario (all based on research done in Canada and Scotland by Mark Lemon, Annan, Ontario). Information about Archibald Campbell comes from numerous letters and manuscripts in MSD/Calgary and from Owen Sound, Ontario *Times*, July 5, 1918. On the ocean voyage: Donaldson, *The Scots Overseas*, p. 98. Description of the vagaries of overland travel: Edwin C. Guillet, *Early Life in Upper Canada*, p. 500. On patterns of Scottish settlement: T. Arthur Davidson, *A New History of the County of Grey*, p. 289. See John Kenneth Galbraith, *Made to Last* (later title: *The Scotch*), for a pithy look at the dour Scottish-Canadians.

15. Information about land grant requirements is based on correspondence and interview by the writer with William McGregor, Annan, Ontario, present owner of the MacGregor farm. He has the original deed, which is dated April 13, 1849, and made of sheepskin with the stamp of the British Crown in one corner. The quotes are from Owen Sound *Sun Times*, June 26, 1943, and from an interview with Dougald MacGregor in the same publication on January 17, 1942. Also used here were the MSS., "Reminiscences of Euphemia MacGregor," MSD/Calgary.

16. On hauling bees and ploughing bees: Guillet, *Early Life in Upper Canada*, p. 290; also see W. L. Morton, *The Kingdom of Canada*, p. 262. Information about "logging bee" is from Dougald MacGregor interview, Owen Sound *Sun Times*, January 17, 1942.

17. Marriage Register for Grey County, Ontario, 1858–69, p. 15 (based on research done by Mark Lemon); William McGregor, Annan, Ontario, letter to writer, July 7, 1973; "Reminiscences of Euphemia MacGregor," MSD/Calgary. In his excellent study of *Early Life in Upper Canada*, pp. 194, 228–29, Guillet notes, "It was long not unusual for men and even women, to have to carry grain many miles on their backs, and return home the following day with their flour."

18. Marcus Lee Hansen, *The Mingling of the Canadian and American Peoples* 1:182–85.

19. On Dougald as railroad fireman: William McGregor, "The McGregor Farm," in Vina F. Ufland, ed., *History of Sydenham Township*, pp. 354–58. On the lure of Chicago: Hansen, *The Mingling of the Canadian and American Peoples* 1:206. On "free lunch": interview with Sherman McGregor.

20. On a million Canadians: Hansen, *The Mingling of the Canadian and American Peoples* 1:183. On Addison: "Memoirs and Reminiscences of Alex McGregor," in Lon D. Leeper, ed., "Memoirs and Reminiscences of Pioneers of Southeastern Washington," typed, 1941, MASC/WSU; interview with Euphemia MacGregor (taped by Sherman McGregor, 1967). On "a better show": Archie McGregor letter to his father, Peter MacGregor, May 14, 1883, MSD/Calgary.

21. Archie recalls promises to his mother in his letter to Nellie Thomas,

February 20, 1883. This letter and the Bible, tintype album, and autograph book are in MB/Glendale. Archie McGregor's 1918 letter to his mother is in MSD/Calgary.

22. MSS. reminiscences of Archie (MB/Glendale) and Euphemia (MSD/Calgary) McGregor. On ball and cap pistols: interview with Maurice McGregor in *Spokesman-Review*, June 25, 1950. The immigrant trains were often crowded with the optimistic and the desperate, the young and the old. William Snyder, a passenger on one of the first immigrant trains to the Columbia Plateau after the completion of the northern transcontinental line in 1883, told of a young woman who ran out of food for her seven children and tried to jump off the train. The other immigrants consoled her and "passed the hat and got them something to eat" (William Snyder in a series of taped interviews recorded by Earl Snyder, Washtucna, Washington, during the years 1948–52).

23. MSS. reminiscences of Archie (MB/Glendale) and Euphemia (MSD/Calgary) McGregor. Also see transcript of interview with William Snyder, an 1884 immigrant to the Columbia Plateau, for his description of his letter of introduction and meeting with Frank Boyer of the Baker-Boyer Bank in Walla Walla. Before following Boyer's advice that "the thing to do is to get out in the frontier," Snyder worked as a store clerk for the man who owned all the businesses in the village of Pataha. When his employer asked him to substitute for the ailing night watchman, the gullible young immigrant learned something about his preconceived ideas of the frontier:

> *I says "all right." I was a young kid. Orders was orders with me. Whatever the boss said went. . . . [He was an] old man about 70 years old. Freddy, he was the active man in the business, the son. We were all there and he gave me his gun. "Well" I says, "If I catch anybody tryin' to break in, set fire, or destroy property what do you want me to do? You want me to kill him?" The old man said "Yes." He was a great man of persuasion. "Yup, you'd better kill him." He says "I'll stay back of you. . . . You'll be in the clear." Well I was a kid. I didn't know any better. . . . I had on this high collared long overcoat. Hand in my pocket and gun in my hand. . . . So 2 o'clock Sunday morning I was following that path in the rear of the hardware business. . . . So black you couldn't see, just had to feel your way pretty near. This big fella came right towards me in the path. I stepped out of the path and was going to give it to him. And he stepped out and moved towards me. That gun went up in his face and I hollered "halt." This fella threw up both hands and said "For God's sakes, Bill, don't shoot! It's me!" "Well, what're you doing here?" Well, Fred was fussing with a girl across the creek and there was a footbridge close by. Well, he thought, I'll have some fun with Bill here the night watch.*

24. Herrell DeGraff and Ladd Haystead, *The Business of Farming*, p. 182. The instability and the optimism were typical of many areas of the western frontier (see James C. Malin, "Mobility and History," *Agricultural History*

17:4 [October 1943]: pp. 180–81; Gilbert C. Fite, "Daydreams and Night-mares," *Agricultural History* 40:4 [October 1966]: 285).

25. On some of the exotic crops, see Vernon Carstensen, "The Land of Plenty," *American Issues*, vol. 1, no. 2 (July 1975). Also see the description of sorghum production in *Rural Northwest*, March 15, 1898. Quote is from interview with William Snyder.

26. On Brune: interview with Charles Brune. On Gerling: Robert Ballou, *Early Klickitat Valley Days*, pp. 45–55. On Fries: Ulrich E. Fries, *From Copenhagen to Okanogan*, p. 45. On Cox and Harder: interviews with Arthur Cox and Jacob Harder in "Interviews Obtained from Washington Pioneers Relative to the History of Grazing in the State of Washington," WPA Historical Records Survey, 1941 MSS., MASC/WSU, pp. 21–26, 43–59. On Coffin brothers: H. Stanley Coffin, "Life, History, Experiences, Hobbies, Aspirations of Harvard Stanley Coffin," MSS. in files of Coffin Sheep Company, Yakima, Washington. On Granger, Whipple, and Mercer: *An Illustrated History of Klickitat, Yakima, and Kittitas Counties*, pp. 588, 612, 769.

27. Archie McGregor, unpublished reminiscences, MB/Glendale. On land rush in Sprague: Walter M. Yeager, "The Pioneer's Problems Of Land Acquisition Under the Public Land Laws in Southeastern Washington," master's thesis, Washington State University (1961), p. 83. On common methods of land acquisition in Washington: Roy M. Robbins, "The Federal Land System in an Embryo State," *Pacific Historical Review* 4:4 (December 1935): 362.

28. Interviews with Euphemia MacGregor; "Peter McGregor" in Lloyd Spencer and Lancaster Pollard, *A History of the State of Washington* 3:320; Fries, *Copenhagen to Okanogan*, p. 69; Alex C. McGregor in Lonnie D. Leeper, "Memoirs and Reminiscences of Pioneers of Southeastern Washington" (mss.), p. 49. Other immigrants who encouraged their families to come to the Columbia Plateau had similar difficulties. William Snyder took his parents in a wagon to a promising part of the unsettled region only to get lost; to have the wagon get stranded in the middle of two streams; to have an old road above the Tucannon River give way, leaving the wagon teetering on the edge of a five-hundred-foot precipice and forcing him "to unhook the team and carry that load of household stuff to the creek bottom again"; to have the horses bolt when crossing Willow Creek, throwing his father into the water and leaving the wagon stuck in quicksand; and to have a storm come up when they camped on a sand bar, "leaving breathing space and that was all when we woke up" (interviews with William Snyder, 1948–52, by Earl Snyder).

29. Alex C. McGregor in Leeper, "Memoirs and Reminiscences" (mss.), p. 50; Archie McGregor letter to his father, Peter MacGregor, May 14, 1883, MSD/Calgary.

30. Norwegian account: Kenneth Bjork, *West of the Great Divide*, p. 436. Other sources used here: MSS., reminiscences of Archie McGregor (MB/ Glendale) and Euphemia MacGregor (MSD/Calgary); Peter McGregor

letter to John Perrin, December 23, 1922, ML&L/WSU; interview with Sherman McGregor.

31. On "shares" system and "the very poorest men": Ezra A. Carman, H. A. Heath, and John Minto, "Special Report on the History and Present Condition of the Sheep Industry of the United States," BAI Report (1892), p. 982. R. A. Jackson and Charles Cunningham, two of the most successful Columbia Plateau sheepmen, started in similar circumstances (see *American Sheep Breeder*, May 1903, and September 15, 1904). On "severe privation": see letters in Archie McGregor file, ML&L/ACM.

CHAPTER 2

Sheep Raising on the Open Range, 1882–93

1. Carman et al., "Special Report on the Sheep Industry," p. 776. John Muir, *My First Summer in the Sierra*, p. 32.

2. Clarence W. Gordon, "Report on Cattle, Sheep, and Swine Supplementary to the Enumeration of Livestock on Farms in 1880," *Reports on Products of Agriculture as Returned by the Tenth Census*, 3:136; Wallis Nash, *Two Years in Oregon*, pp. 120, 232; Robert Ballou, *Early Klickitat Valley Days*, pp. 149–50.

3. On sheepmen expanding in the West: La Wanda F. Cox, "The American Agricultural Wage Earner, 1865–1900," *Agricultural History* 22:2 (April 1948): 104. Estimate of sheep numbers is based on census returns for the 22 Columbia Plateau counties; USDA, BAI, "Number and Value of Farm Animals, 1870–1896," Fourteenth Annual Report (1897–98), p. 301; and estimates by woolgrowers in *Rural Northwest*, March 15, 1898. On the advance of sheep raisers: Granville Stuart, "On a Montana Cattle Range," in David B. Greenberg, ed., *Land That Our Fathers Plowed*, p. 185. On the share system: Carman et al., "Special Report on the Sheep Industry," p. 725. On California sheepmen: Muir, *My First Summer in the Sierra*, p. 30.

4. J. W. McCarty, "Australia as a Region of Recent Settlement in the Nineteenth Century," "*Australian Economic History Review* 12:2 (September 1972): 150; Allan Bogue, "Farming in the Prairie Peninsula, 1830–1890," *Journal of Economic History* 23:1 (March 1963): 24. Turner's description of frontier traits: Bogue, "Social Theory and the Pioneer," *Agricultural History* 34:1 (January 1960): 22. In Kansas the shortage of capital forced farmers to raise large acreages of wheat for a minimal outlay per acre (see James C. Malin, *Winter Wheat in the Golden Belt of Kansas*, p. 106).

5. Carman et al., "Special Report on the Sheep Industry," p. 726; Frederick Coville, "Forest Growth and Sheep Grazing in the Cascade Mountains of Oregon," USDA Division of Forestry Bulletin 15 (1898), p. 12; Nash, *Two Years in Oregon*, pp. 121–22.

6. On popular impression of herding: Edward N. Wentworth, *America's*

Sheep Trails, p. 402. On unromantic trade: Judith Kenny, "Early Sheep Ranching in Eastern Oregon," *OHQ* 64:2 (June 1963): 105.

7. On original vegetation and grazing: Richard Mack, "Competitive Displacement: An Ecological Chronicle of *Bromus Tectorum*," 1980 MSS. made available by writer, pp. 4–5. Cattle fail "to lay on fat": Gordon, "Report on Cattle, Sheep, and Swine," p. 128. On changing nature of rangeland: Weaver, "Vegetation of Southeastern Washington"; Arthur Sampson, "Plant Succession in Relation to Range Management," USDA Bulletin 791 (Aug. 27, 1919), pp. 20–41; and Malin, *The Grassland of North America*, pp. 123–31. The debate about "overgrazing" and range condition is described in detail in Alex C. McGregor, "The Agricultural Development of the Columbia Plateau," Ph.D. dissertation, University of Washington, 1977, pp. 64–65.

8. Complaints of cattlemen and description of methods of operation: Gordon, "Report on Cattle, Sheep, and Swine," pp. 134–35. "Manly sport": E. V. Smalley quoted in Joseph Nimmo, "Range and Ranch Cattle Traffic," 48th Cong., 2nd sess., House Exec. Doc. 267 (1885), p. 75.

9. W. J. Davenport, "Stock Raising in Whitman County," in J. O. Oliphant, ed., "Readings in the History of Eastern Washington," 2:131, MSS. in MASC/WSU. On passing of cowman: Ballou, *Early Klickitat Valley Days*, p. 192; "The Last Big Cattle Roundup," Palouse (Washington) *Republic*, January 8, 1971. An eastern cattle buyer reported from Pataha City, W.T., in 1882: "Two years ago there was at least three times as many Cattle as there is at this time here" (quoted in Maurice Frink et al., *When Grass Was King*, p. 78).

10. On price decline: Gordon, "Report on Cattle, Sheep, and Swine," p. 137; George Stewart, "The History of Western Range Use," in *The Western Range*, 74th Cong., 2nd sess., Sen. Exec. Doc. 199 (1936), p. 123. On depression and profit in sheep: H. A. Heath, "Condition of the Sheep Industry West of the Mississippi," Sixth and Seventh Annual Reports, BAI (1889–90), pp. 247–53. On the decline of Columbia Plateau cattle production: R. Earl Zimmerman, "A History of the Development of Agriculture in Whitman County," B.A. thesis, Washington State College, 1916, p. 14. The trend in other western range areas is discussed in H. M. Taylor, "The Condition of the Cattle-Range Industry," Third Annual Report, BAI (1886), p. 105.

11. Quote is from "Report of the Public Lands Commission," 58th Cong., 3rd sess., Sen. Exec. Doc. 4 (1904–5), p. 12. Also see Will C. Barnes, *The Story of the Range*, p. 7.

12. On wool marketing: Harold Briggs, "The Early Development of Sheep Ranching in the Northwest," *Agricultural History* 11:3 (July 1937): 161. On sheep trailing: J. E. Albaugh, "History of the Settlement and Agricultural Development of Umatilla County," MSS. in Wentworth collection, University of Wyoming; Hartman Evans, "Sheep Trailing from Oregon to Wyoming" (R. H. Burns, ed.), *Mississippi Valley Historical Review* 28:4 (March 1942): 581–92. Estimate of fifteen million sheep trailed: Wentworth, *America's Sheep Trails*, p. 285. Quote is from interview with William McGregor.

13. On rapid spread of transhumance: Daniel Gomez-Ibanez, "The Origins of Transhumance in the United States," MSS. courtesy of author, pp. 11–16; Gomez-Ibanez, "The Rise and Decline of Transhumance in the United States," master's thesis, University of Wisconsin, 1967, p. 77. Veteran wheat farmer, cattleman, and conservationist Ralph Snyder discussed the condition of the range in a series of interviews with the writer. For a description of transhumance in other regions, see Langdon White, "Transhumance in the Sheep Industry of the Salt Lake Region," *Economic Geography* 2 (July 1926): 414; and Howard Critchfield, "Pastoral High-Country, South Island, New Zealand," *Yearbook of the Association of Pacific Coast Geographers*, 31 (1961): 58.

14. On grazing routes: interviews with Arthur Cox and Jacob Harder in "Interviews Obtained from Washington Pioneers Relative to the History of Grazing in the State of Washington," Works Progress Administration, Historical Records Survey, 1941 unpublished MSS., Washington State University Library (hereafter cited as "Interviews Relative to Grazing"); interviews by writer with Thomas Drumheller, Jr., and Dr. H. Stanley Coffin; information from old files of Coffin Sheep Company, Yakima.

15. On breeds of sheep: E. L. Shaw and L. L. Heller, "Domestic Breeds of Sheep in America," USDA Bulletin 94 (August 1914). On "native sheep": Gordon, "Report on Cattle, Sheep, and Swine," pp. 138–39. On sheep dogs: *Ranche and Range*, August 5, 1897, "Training a Sheep Dog"; and Wentworth, *America's Sheep Trails*, p. 407. On the difficulties faced by herders, see John M. Crowley, "Ranches in the Sky: A Geography of Livestock Ranching in the Mountain Parks of Colorado," Ph.D. dissertation, University of Minnesota, 1964, p. 286.

16. On herding for Charles Johnson: Alex C. McGregor in Leeper, "Memoirs and Reminiscences." On establishing credit: Archie McGregor, unpublished reminiscences, MB/Glendale. On purchase of sheep: Stine and McIntosh bill of sale, Whitman County Auditor's Office, old files, MASC/WSU. On "wonderful bankers": interviews with Ralph Snyder. On mortgages and credit problems: Wentworth, *America's Sheep Trails*, p. 430; Allan Bogue, *Money at Interest: The Farm Mortgage on the Middle Border*, pp. 114–24.

17. Lamb crops: Archie McGregor, unpublished reminiscences; Coville, "Forest Growth and Sheep Grazing," p. 13. Increased sheep production: L. G. Connor, "A Brief History of the Sheep Industry in the United States," American Historical Association, annual report (1918), p. 139.

18. Archie McGregor, unpublished reminiscences; interview with Phil Cox in *Spokesman-Review*, May 12, 1912; interview with Arthur Cox in "Interviews Relative to Grazing"; Gordon, "Report on Cattle, Sheep, and Swine," p. 133. On profits of sheepmen, see *Shepherd's Criterion*, October 1907, p. 14.

19. Statement about rolling hills is by pioneer cattleman in Pomeroy *East Washingtonian*, June 6, 1914. From many portions of the Columbia Plateau came reports that "the plow is turning over the bunchgrass and the fence is

forcing the cattlemen out"; "Report of the Governor of Washington Territory to the Secretary of the Interior, 1887," p. 17. On McAllister, see Ballou, *Early Klickitat Valley Days*, pp. 418–19.

20. On chaotic range conditions: Gomez-Ibanez, "The Rise and Decline of Transhumance," p. 57. On Endicott sheepmen: Archie McGregor, unpublished reminiscences; Colfax *Gazette*; April 3, May 1, May 8, 1885, and several other 1885 issues.

21. Colfax *Gazette*, June 26, November 20 and 27, 1885, and March 12 and 19, April 23, July 17, 1886; Archie McGregor, unpublished reminiscences, MB/Glendale. On stock raisers' "paradise": "Our Stock District," Colfax *Gazette*, March 9, 1878.

22. Reasons for moving to Palouse: Alex C. McGregor in Leeper, "Memoirs and Reminiscences" (MSS.). On "strong" grass: interviews with Ralph Snyder. On Pampa: Fred W. Clemens, "Remembering" (MSS. made available by writer), p. 7. Interview with Virgil Bennington by Al McVay and Vance Orchard, tape in WCAT/Walla Walla. On grazing restrictions: Colfax *Gazette*, April 23, 1886; "Keep Your Sheep Away," Colfax *Commoner*, March 2, 1888.

23. On scabies: J. E. Albaugh, "History of the Settlement and Agricultural Development of Umatilla County," MSS. in Wentworth collection, University of Wyoming. On "Scabby George": Ballou, *Early Klickitat Valley Days*, pp. 294, 418–20. For examples of some other difficulties faced by sheepmen, see Colfax *Gazette*, July 10, 1885 (poison weeds); and November 27, 1885 (leach in livers). Inspection tax: Colfax *Gazette*, January 30, 1885.

24. Colfax *Gazette*, January 30, March 27, April 3, 1885, and December 31, 1886. A good analysis of the debate about railroad rates is in Robert Higgs, *The Transformation of the American Economy, 1865–1914*, pp. 87–90. On wool buyers: Colfax *Gazette*, May 1, 1885, March 26 and December 31, 1886; Archie McGregor, unpublished reminiscences, MB/Glendale. Swindled by buyers: Carman et al., "Special Report on the Sheep Industry," p. 781.

25. William Parker describes 19th century farm financing as "a jerrybuilt structure tied together like the primitive contraptions of a farm mechanic, with bailing wire" (Parker, "The Outline of American Agricultural History, 1840–1960," 1976 MSS. p. 8). Charles Johnson mortgage is in chattel mortgage book 1, 453, Auditor's Office, Latah County courthouse, Moscow, Idaho; Archie McGregor reminiscences, MB/Glendale.

26. On hay purchases: letter from F. W. Young to Peter McGregor, July 29, 1927, ML&L/WSU; interview with Sherman McGregor; Maurice McGregor in *Spokesman-Review*, June 25, 1950. Grisly reminders of blizzards: Ray Allen Billington, *Westward Expansion: A History of the American Frontier*, p. 688. Ten percent of the sheep of Umatilla County died of starvation during the horrible winter; see USDA, Division of Statistics, Report 39 (April 1887), p. 144.

27. Colfax *Gazette*, December 20, 1889. See the comments of several Columbia Plateau livestock raisers in *Told by the Pioneers* 3:95–99. On February

weather, see W. H. Lever, *A History of Whitman County*, p. 116; also see Clel Georgetta, *Golden Fleece in Nevada*, p. 120.

28. On cattle losses: Spokane *Spokesman*, March 11, July 22, 1890. Cattle industry crushed: Todd V. Boyce, "A History of the Beef Cattle Industry in the Inland Empire," master's thesis, Washington State College, 1937, p. 45. Range piled deep: William S. Lewis, *The Story of Early Days in the Big Bend Country*, p. 15. Flocks wiped out: USDA, Division of Statistics, Report 72 (April 1890), p. 148. H. S. Coffin, "Life" (mss.), p. 27.

29. F. A. Phillips MSS. in Wentworth collection, University of Wyoming. On Hewitt, see interviews with Ralph Snyder. According to the Pioneer Edition of the Ritzville *Journal-Times* (September 15, 1949), Hewitt lost 15,000 sheep. Also see Minnie Fronek, "Pioneering in the Lower Palouse and Lacrosse Country," typescript, p. 7. The reports received by the BAI indicated that 18.4 percent of Washington sheep and 20 percent of the Oregon flocks perished (USDA, Division of Statistics, Reports 72 and 125).

30. Letter from Archie McGregor to Maurice McGregor, February 5, 1937, ML&L/WSU. On rangeland acreage: James C. Moomaw, "Some Effects of Grazing and Fire on Vegetation in the Columbia Basin Region, Washington," Ph.D. dissertation, WSC, 1956, p. 5. On country filling up: Carman et al., "Special Report on the Sheep Industry," p. 982. The Columbia Plateau was promoted as an agricultural paradise: "There is no place or country on the globe which can excel the soil of Whitman county," claimed the Colfax *Commoner* of April 20, 1888.

31. Archie McGregor, unpublished reminiscences; letter from Archie McGregor to Nellie Thomas, March 31, 1892, both from MB/Glendale. The number of sheep in eastern Montana doubled during the decade 1890–1900 (see Robert S. Fletcher, "The End of the Open Range in Eastern Montana," *Mississippi Valley Historical Review* 16:2 [September 1929]: 201).

32. On homesteaders, see interviews in *Told by the Pioneers*, 3:62–64, 116–20, 152. Quote is from interviews with Ralph Snyder.

33. Interview with Virgil Bennington. On laundry: reminiscences of Mae Carter, 1946, MSS. in ML&L/Hooper. On social activities: Archie McGregor letters, 1892–93, MB/Glendale, and "society notebook" of Nellie Thomas, 1886–93, ML&L/ACM.

34. Quotes about "loose herding" and preparation of meals: Carman et al., "Special Report on the Sheep Industry," p. 985. On "easy" work of herder: letter from William McGregor to Dougald McGregor, August 16, 1892, MSD/ Calgary.

35. On duties of camptender: Will C. Barnes, *Western Grazing Grounds and Forest Ranges*, p. 157. William McGregor to Dougald McGregor, August 16, 1892, MSD/Calgary.

36. On "soft" and "hard" fat: Coville, "Forest Growth and Sheep Grazing," p. 23. On sheep camp food: interviews with Arthur Cox and Jacob Harder in "Interviews Relative to Grazing"; Ballou, *Early Klickitat Valley Days*, p. 136; Archie McGregor letter to Nellie Thomas, March 20, 1892, MB/Glen-

dale. Also see the wry appraisal of sheep camp food in Muir, *My First Summer in the Sierra*, pp. 108–10.

37. William McGregor to Dougald McGregor, July 21 and August 16, 1892, MSD/Calgary; Archie McGregor to Nellie Thomas, August 1892, MB/Glendale; William McGregor to Dougald McGregor, August 16, 1892.

38. These letters are all from MB/Glendale and are dated in the text. These are excerpts from more than 200 pages of correspondence, all courtesy of Mrs. Marie Boone, Glendale, California.

39. Letters from Archie McGregor to Nellie Thomas, March 31, February 12, 1892, and May 14, 1893; "McGregor-Thomas marriage," undated clipping from 1893 newspaper, MB/Glendale; G. W. Kendall, *Letters from a Texas Sheep Ranch*, p. 9.

40. William McGregor to Jessie McGregor, July 21, 1892, MSD/Calgary.

CHAPTER 3

"These Hard Times": The Panic of 1893 and the Decline of the Nomadic Sheepmen, 1893–96

1. On wool prices: *Ranche and Range*, July 16, 1898. Judge Hanford: (Andrew Burleigh as Receiver for) *Northern Pacific Railroad v. Joseph Escallier, Leon Jaussaud, McGregor Bros., et al.*, District Court, Case 146, April 2–November 16, 1896. On Cascade reserve: *Ranche and Range*, April 18, 1897.

2. On "rapid growth": "Short History of Whitman County," in *Plat Book of Whitman County, Washington*. On wool and lamb crops: Barnes, *Western Grazing Grounds*, p. 206, and J. T. Jardine and Mark Anderson, "Range Management on the National Forests," USDA Bulletin 790 (August 1919), p. 28. Livestock estimates are based on census returns for the 22 counties of the Columbia Plateau. On W. W. Corbett: *The Ranch*, March 24, 1894.

3. On range cattle: *Ranche and Range*, June 24, 1897; A. J. Splawn in *The Ranch*, February 13, 1902. On the gulf between the optimism of early settlers and their actual achievements, see Fite, "Daydreams and Nightmares," *Agricultural History* 40:4 (October 1966): 285.

4. George Stewart, "History of Range Use," in *The Western Range*, p. 126; Barnes, *The Story of the Range*, p. 8; *Ranche and Range*, April 18, 1897.

5. On banks and stores: Meinig, *Great Columbia Plain*, p. 365. Graph of sheep prices: E. N. Wentworth, *Progressive Sheep Raising*, p. 23. On depressed sheep market: D. A. Spencer, M. C. Hall, et al., "The Sheep Industry," in USDA *Yearbook of Agriculture* (1923), p. 286. On local wheat raisers: W. J. Spillman, "The Hybrid Wheats," Washington AES Bulletin 89 (1909), p. 5. On colonial economy: Edwin J. Cohn, *Industry in the Pacific Northwest and the Location Theory*, p. 30.

6. Populist charges: Washington governor John R. Rogers, quoted in Harriet Crawford, *The Washington State Grange: A Romance of Democracy*, p. 63. On the infirmities of the economic foundation: Bogue, "Social Theory and the Pioneer," p. 32. Vernon Carstensen provides an overview of the agricultural unrest in *Farmer Discontent, 1865–1900*, pp. 1–15.

7. On "industrious and ingenious persons": Yeager, "The Pioneer's Problems of Land Acquisition," p. 104. On Latah: Meinig, *Great Columbia Plain*, p. 350. On land purchases: deeds from J. P. Vollmer to Archie McGregor, June 30 and July 10, 1890, Grenville Holbrook to Archie McGregor and Abraham Ensely, June 18, 1890, Abraham Ensely to Archie McGregor, December, 1890, all from deed book 8, pp. 74–77, Register of Deeds, Latah County Courthouse, Moscow. William McGregor letter to Dougald McGregor, August 16, 1892, MSD/Calgary. "Peter McGregor" in Julian Hawthorne, ed., *History of Washington, the Evergreen State* 2:599.

8. Deed from Archie McGregor to Emerson Alderman, February 12, 1916, book 72, p. 325, John McGregor to G. M. Lewis, April 16, 1915, Register of Deeds, Latah County Courthouse; Coffin, "Life" (MSS.), p. 9. Interview with Sherman McGregor. Stock sale: Archie McGregor reminiscences, MB/Glendale.

9. Archie McGregor reminiscences. Letter from Archie McGregor to Nellie Thomas, February 12, 1892, both from MB/Glendale; letter from William McGregor to Jessie McGregor, July 21, 1892, MSD/Calgary. Peter and Archie also invested $4,800 in the purchase of real property for the hardware store. Deed from R. S. Browne to Archibald and Peter McGregor, January 26, 1892; deed from F. E. Carpenter to Archie McGregor, January 20, 1892, Whitman County Courthouse, Colfax. Eugene V. Smalley, "Pullman, Palouse City, and Colfax," *Northwest*, September 10, 1892. Also see Pullman *Herald*, April 11, May 29, 1891.

10. Letters from Archie McGregor to Nellie Thomas, February 12, March 31, 1892, MB/Glendale; Archie McGregor deed to John McGregor, April 5, 1892, deed book 12, p. 43, Latah County Courthouse; Archie McGregor letters to Nellie Thomas, March 5, March 12, March 25, 1893, MB/Glendale. On "a fair competence": Hawthorne, ed., *History of Washington* 2:599.

11. A. D. Baum to John McGregor, March 8, 1892, Peter McGregor to John McGregor, June 15, 1893, John McGregor to A. D. Baum, November 8, 1892, all property deeds from Whitman County Courthouse; letter from Archie McGregor to Nellie Thomas, March 5, 1893, MB/Glendale. Wheat prices: Enoch A. Bryan, *Orient Meets Occident*, p. 198; Spillman, "The Hybrid Wheats," p. 5. Quote about harvest: J. B. West, "Memories of the Palouse," Palouse *Republic*, August 14, 1975. In addition to the problems caused by weather, an estimated 30 percent of Northwest wheat was severely damaged by smut (*The Ranch*, April 21, 1894).

12. Thomas Riddle, "Populism in the Palouse," *PNQ* 65:3 (July 1974): 100; Mrs. H. M. Jackson vs. Pullman Hardware Company, Peter McGregor, L. F. Munroe, J. F. Hill, N. C. Munroe, Whitman County Superior Court,

Case 5444, April 30, 1895; letter from Archie McGregor to Nellie Thomas, March 12, 1893, MB/Glendale.

13. Coffin, "Life" (MSS.), pp. 37, 42. Also see letter from Coffin to E. N. Wentworth, March 11, 1940, Wentworth collection.

14. Coffin, "Life" (MSS.), pp. 37–40. For examples of some of the innovative advertising programs of Coffin Brothers, see *Ranche and Range*, June 7, July 1, 1897.

15. On Republican sheepmen: Georgetta, *Golden Fleece in Nevada*, p. 309. On the tariff debate: Chester Wright, *Wool-Growing and the Tariff*, pp. 275–301. *The Ranch*, February 10, February 17, June 2, June 23, 1894. The value of Washington and Oregon sheep in 1892 was $8.2 million, an average of $1.84. Two years later the value had fallen to $4.2 million, an average of $1.09. See USDA, BAI, "Number and Value of Farm Animals, 1870–1896."

16. Ballou, *Early Klickitat Valley Days*, p. 419. Peter McGregor and F. M. Rothrock, "What Free Wool Did in Washington," *National Wool Grower*, June 1913, p. 22. Maudslay, "An Englishman Herds Sheep in Texas," in Greenberg, ed., *Land That Our Fathers Plowed*, p. 240. On unclaimed sheep: Bryan, *Orient Meets Occident*, p. 198. Phil Cox interview in *Spokesman-Review*, May 12, 1912. On wool shipment: interview with William McGregor. A similar story is in Wentworth, *America's Sheep Trails*, p. 212.

17. Alex McGregor in Leeper, ed., "Memoirs and Reminiscences" (mss.), p. 52; Archie McGregor reminiscences, MB/Glendale; Peter McGregor letter to John Perrin, December 23, 1922, ML&L/WSU; Peter McGregor and F. M. Rothrock, "What Free Wool Did in Washington," p. 22. Transportation costs: USDA, Division of Statistics, "Railway Charges for the Transportation of Wool," Miscellaneous Series Bulletin 10 (July 1896).

18. On sheep shipment: J. E. Albaugh, "History of the Settlement and Agricultural Development of Umatilla County," MSS. in Wentworth collection. On slaughter of sheep: R. H. Burns, A. S. Gillespie, W. G. Richardson, *Wyoming's Pioneer Ranches*, p. 550. *The Ranch*, February 17, March 24, June 9, 1894. On J. H. Smithson: Ellensburg *Capital*, November 30, 1893, quoted in *Illustrated History of Klickitat, Yakima, and Kittitas Counties*, p. 262.

19. On winter and spring weather: *The Ranch*, March 31, May 5, June 2, 1894. On conditions in Texas: Lehman, *Forgotten Legions*, p. 90. Also see chart of wool prices for 1890–1905 in *American Sheep Breeder*, January 15, 1907.

20. Letters from Archie McGregor to Nellie McGregor, September 30, October 14, October 30, 1894, MB/Glendale.

21. Peter McGregor and F. M. Rothrock, "What Free Wool Did in Washington," p. 22. On sheep purchase: Archie McGregor reminiscences, MB/Glendale; John and Archie McGregor mortgage to Second National Bank of Colfax, June 15, 1894, chattel mortgage book 8, p. 227, Auditor's Office, Latah County Courthouse. On Dreifus: interview with Sherman McGregor. On "character" of debtors: Wentworth, *America's Sheep Trails*, p. 430.

22. Wheat acreage estimate based on compilation of census returns for Columbia Plateau counties. On Columbia Plateau wheat production: Morton Rothstein, "New Frontiers and New Rivals" (mss.), pp. 387–95. Discussion of local climatic conditions based on "Precipitation Data for Lacrosse and Hooper, 1884–1946," typescript by U.S. Weather Bureau, ML&L/Hooper. On general climatic trends: Harold Fritts, "Tree-Ring Evidence for Climatic Changes in Western North America," *Monthly Weather Review* (July 1965), pp. 432–43. Also see Stewart, "History of Range Use," in *The Western Range*, p. 127.

23. A. J. Splawn in J. S. Cotton, "Forage Problems of Eastern and Central Washington," master's thesis, Washington Agricultural College, 1904, p. 11. On view that sheep ruin ranges for cattle: Archer Gilfillan, *Sheep: Life on the South Dakota Range*, p. 239, and H. L. Davis, *Honey in the Horn*, p. 298; E. V. Wilcox, "The Grazing Industry," Hawaii AES Bulletin, unnumbered, 1911, pp. 55–56.

24. Gomez-Ibanez, "Rise and Decline of Transhumance," p. 59. On arrests of herders: Coville, "Forest Growth and Sheep Grazing," pp. 11, 18. On quarantine law and grazing abuses: *Ranche and Range*, April 15, April 22, 1897. Also see P. C. Roberts, *Hoof Prints on Forest Ranges*, p. 3.

25. *Ranche and Range*, April 22, August 5, 1897. On cattlemen: interview with Thomas J. Drumheller, Jr. Idaho restrictions: *Ranche and Range*, January 1, 1898, and *The Ranch*, June 27, 1901. On Judge Hanford: "*Northern Pacific* v. *James Cunningham*," Circuit Court, Southern District, October 14, 1898. On Washington law: letters from Northern Pacific Land Commissioner William Phipps to Western Land Agent Thomas Cooper, June 14 and September 29, 1896, Old Leather Letterbooks, vols. 52 and 55 (accessions 5543 and 5544), both from Land Department, NPRR/St. Paul.

26. E. F. Benson to E. A. Bryan, September 16, 1926, in "Letters Concerning the Leasing of Grazing Lands by the Northern Pacific Railway Company," MASC/WSU. In same collection, see letter from Benson to Will C. Barnes, September 13, 1926, for information about impact of Northern Pacific system on federal land policies. By 1923, 17 million acres of railroad lands were leased, primarily for grazing; see L. C. Gray et al., "Farm Ownership and Tenancy," USDA *Yearbook of Agriculture* (1923), p. 525. On expansion of Northern Pacific grazing lease system to Montana: Robert S. Fletcher, "The End of the Open Range in Eastern Montana," *Mississippi Valley Historical Review* 16:2 (September 1929): 208. Northern Pacific Land Commissioner William Phipps expressed the fear that the federal leasing system proposed by Western Land Agent Thomas Cooper might adversely affect railroad indemnity land claims. But, according to Phipps, the federal leasing system would not pass Congress "if we attempt to prevent it." See letters from Phipps to Cooper, August 15, 1899, Land Department, Old Leather Letterbooks, vol. 78, NPRR/St. Paul.

27. Complaints of settlers: Cotton, "Forage Problems in Eastern and Central Washington," pp. 11–12. Sheepmen take possession: *Spokesman-Review*,

May 4, 1895. On Moore and Hewitt: interview with Ralph Snyder. The town of Hooper, near the McGregor winter range, in 1887 was nothing but a post office and a railroad sign. By 1892, an estimated 250 people lived in the vicinity. See R. L. Polk and Company, *Oregon, Washington, and Idaho Gazetteer* (1892), p. 818.

28. "To Drive Out Sheep," Colfax *Gazette*, May 8, 1896. Cattlemen told the *Gazette* correspondent that "their herds were rapidly dying off by starvation, and unless the sheep are driven off their losses will be enormous." On "family row": *Spokesman-Review*, "Not a Deadly War," June 20, 1895. On range battle: Seattle *Times*, August 1, 1896. On confrontations on Columbia Plateau ranges: R. M. Turner, "The Story of Early Livestock in This Region," *Spokesman-Review*, November 24, 1957; John Harder in *Told by the Pioneers*, 3:64. For accounts from other areas: Charles Towne and E. N. Wentworth, *Shepherd's Empire*, pp. 182–203.

29. Second National Bank of Colfax to John McGregor, May 29, 1895, Property Deeds file, grantee-grantor book 2, p. 356, Whitman County Courthouse. On loan for fencing: interview with Sherman McGregor. On "bad blood": Colfax *Gazette*, May 8, 1896. Letter from William Phipps to Thomas Cooper, February 3, 1896, Old Leather Letterbooks vol. 48, p. 332 (accession 5542), Land Department, NPRR/St. Paul.

30. Letter from William Phipps to Thomas Cooper, May 14, 1896, Old Leather Letterbooks, vol. 52 (accession 5543), Land Department, NPRR/St. Paul. Letter from G. H. Plummer, Northern Pacific General Sales Agent, to J. S. Cotton, June 13, 1903, included in appendix to Cotton, "Forage Problems of Eastern and Central Washington"; letter from E. F. Benson to E. A. Bryan, September 16, 1926, in "Letters Concerning Leasing of Grazing Lands," MASC/WSU; interview with E. F. Benson in *Spokesman-Review*, March 21, 1915. Benson claimed the railroad was "endeavoring to strengthen the livestock industry by placing the ownership in the hands of actual stockmen who will protect the ranges and conserve the grazing possibilities."

31. (Andrew Burleigh as Receiver for) *Northern Pacific Railroad v. Joseph Escallier et al.*, complaint, April 7, 1896. On "most prominent sheep owners": Frederick Coville, "Report on Systems of Leasing Large Areas of Grazing Lands," in "Report of the Public Lands Commission," p. 55. On cayuse horses: *Ranche and Range*, August 5, 1897.

32. Colfax *Gazette*, May 8, 1896; *Spokesman-Review*, May 12, 1896; demurrer, *Northern Pacific v. Escallier et al.*, Northern Pacific Land Department; stipulations of May 6 and November 5, 1896, *Northern Pacific v. Escallier et al.*, Federal Archives and Records Center; Archie McGregor reminiscences, MB/Glendale. Thomas Cooper, Western Land Agent for the railroad, comments at length on the case in "The Flocks: An Official Declaration," *Ranche and Range*, May 27, 1897. In the May 8 article, the *Gazette* claimed that more than a hundred livestock raisers were in Walla Walla to observe the case.

33. "Get Off the Grass," *Spokesman-Review*, May 14, 1896; letter from William Phipps to Thomas Cooper, June 23, 1896, Old Leather Letterbooks,

vol. 53, p. 62, Land Department, NPRR/St. Paul. Nomadic sheepmen generally ignored such edicts (see Philip Foss, *Politics and Grass: The Administration of Grazing on the Public Domain*, p. 30). On grazing lease and purchase of land: Grazing lease 1, John McGregor, "West End Grazing Leases, 1896–99"; Land contract R8690, John McGregor, Pend Oreille Division, sales book, 1890's (accession 9413), both in NPRR/St. Paul. R. M. Turner, "The Story of Early Livestock in This Region," *Spokesman-Review*, November 24, 1957, summarizes the testimony but is in error in listing Peter, rather than John, McGregor as the major participant. On Benson as land agent: Annine Harder, "The Opportunity of the Golden West," typed, n.d., pp. 25–26.

34. A complete collection of the early grazing leases is in "West End Grazing Leases, 1896–99," Land Department (accession 5719), NPRR/St. Paul. Those who signed the earliest leases received the most favorable contracts. The early leases were often for ten years; some of the later ones were only for six months. For example, see lease 29 (Hans Harder) and enclosed letter from Thomas Cooper to Harder. Also see Cooper article in *Ranche and Range*, May 27, 1897, and *Ranche and Range*, July 1, 1897, "To Lease Northern Pacific Railroad Lands." On Magallon: *Northern Pacific Railway* v. *Adrian Magallon*, Circuit Court of Washington, Ninth District, Southern Division, case 162, April-October 1897; letter from Thomas Cooper to William Phipps, August 17, 1897, enclosed with lease 139 (A. Magallon), West End Grazing Leases, NPRR/St. Paul. An additional case was necessary before full implementation of the lease plan (see *Northern Pacific* v. *James Cunningham*).

35. Letter from E. F. Benson to E. A. Bryan, September 16, 1926, "Letters Concerning the Leasing of Grazing Lands," MASC/WSU. The meeting is described in *Ranche and Range*, July 15, 1897, also see May 20 issue.

36. On leasing acreage: letter from G. H. Plummer to J. S. Cotton in "Forage Problems of Eastern and Central Washington." Information about these leases is from "West End Grazing Leases" and Seattle division, "Grazing leases, 1898–1915" (SWT 3–9449), NPRR/St. Paul. Sheepmen organize range: interview with Charles H. Brune; also useful here were interviews with Thomas Drumheller, Jr., and Ralph Snyder. E. F. Benson, the man who arranged many of the leases, commented that "the cattle and horse men were gradually eliminated, but the sheepmen became permanent tenants" (*Spokesman-Review*, March 21, 1915).

In *The Ranch*, January 23, 1902, a Yakima cattleman bitterly noted "the intelligent organization of the sheep interest" and claimed that the Foster bill, a federal leasing proposal patterned after the N.P. system, had been an attempt by sheepmen to complete "one of the most villainous steals ever perpetrated on this State." The cattleman overstated the power of the woolgrowers, but his comments illustrate the bitter feelings of cattle raisers who found their accustomed ranges already occupied.

37. Totals based on census returns for the twenty-two Columbia Plateau counties. On decline of cattlemen: *The Ranch*, April 7, 1894; *Ranche and Range*, June 7, October 7, 1897. On "lines closing in": *Rural Northwest*, July

15, 1898. The Pullman *Herald* of February 27, 1897, noted that cattlemen of
the Rock Lake district of northern Whitman County tried to use force to
remove sheep from that area. But the sheepmen "retaliated by renting, at a
small rental, large tracts of railroad lands within the disputed territory, and
warned the cattlemen that they must not allow their herds to trespass thereon.
The rented sections were enclosed with barbed wire, and this so restricted the
cattle range that the cattle owners wished they had allowed the matter to rest
undisturbed in the first place."

   38. On advantages of leasing: David Griffiths, "Forage Conditions and
Problems in Eastern Washington, Eastern Oregon, and Northwestern Nevada," USDA Bureau of Plant Industry, Bulletin 38 (July 3, 1903), p. 14. On
replacement of disorderly system: Coville, "Report on Leasing Large Areas
of Grazing Lands," in "Report of the Public Lands Commission," p. 57. On
"stockraiser with vision": Boyce, "History of the Beef Cattle Industry," p.
64. On stockmen forced out of business: J. S. Cotton, "Range Management in
the State of Washington," USDA Bureau of Plant Industry, Bulletin 75 (May
23, 1905), p. 12.

   39. The first grazing fee had been lowered to $200, according to Ralph
Snyder, because John had agreed to ship wool on the Northern Pacific (from
interviews with Ralph Snyder). On overdue bills: Contract R8690, Pend
Oreille sales book, (accession 9413), NPRR/St. Paul, Town Property Assess-
ment and Tax Roll, 1896, Auditor's Office, Whitman County Courthouse,
Colfax.

CHAPTER 4

"The Changed Times Call for Changed Methods": McGregors as Land Brokers and "The Sheep Kings of the Palouse Country"

   1. *Ranche and Range*, April 29, 1897; *American Sheep Breeder*, October
1903; *Rural Northwest*, August 15, 1898.

   2. On land values: Robert C. Nesbit and Charles M. Gates, "Agriculture in
Eastern Washington, 1890–1910," *PNQ* 37:4 (October 1946): 283; *Thirteenth
Census (1910)*, "Agriculture: Washington." On livestock raisers: Barnes, *The
Story of the Range*, p. 10, and Meinig, *Great Columbia Plain*, p. 284. Also
see *Rural Northwest*, December 1, 1897.

   3. Archie McGregor reminiscences, MB/Glendale; grazing lease #1, West
End Grazing Leases, Land Department, NPRR/St. Paul; interviews with
Ralph Snyder.

   4. Colfax *Commoner*, May 1, 1896; Phipps to Western Land Agent Thomas
Cooper May 11, 1895, and May 14, 1896, Old Leather Letterbooks, Land De-

partment, NPRR/St. Paul; West End Grazing Leases, NPRR/St. Paul; C. S. Mellen to Daniel Lamont, January 31, 1902, quoted in Ross Cotroneo, "Western Land Marketing by the Northern Pacific Railway," *Pacific Historical Review* 37:3 (August 1968): 303.

5. Interview with Ralph Snyder; William Phipps to Thomas Cooper, April 6, 1897, Letterbooks of Land Commissioner (accession 5544), vol. 59, p. 132, Contract R–8690, Pend Oreille sales book (accession 9413), NPRR/St. Paul.

6. Archie McGregor reminiscences, MB/Glendale.

7. Reports from sheep ranges: *Ranche and Range*, May 13, April 8, 1897; *Rural Northwest*, July 15, 1897; *Ranche and Range*, May 27, 1897. Two of the shearers in Mars' crew sheared 200 sheep in one day, an outstanding record considering the hand shears used at the time. Also see *Ranch and Range*, September 1, 1898, in which the Clay Smith crew estimated that it had shorn 80,000 head during the past spring. On wool sales: *Ranche and Range*, May 20, September 9, 1897; also see Donald Blinken, *Wool Tariffs and American Policy*, p. 148.

8. *Ranche and Range*, September 30, July 29, November 18, 1897; in the last issue Gray noted that he was "well satisfied with the outlook in these prosperous McKinley high tariff times." On "fat of the land": *Rural Northwest*, September 15, 1897. On "easy street": *Ranche and Range*, September 2, 1897. The Pendleton *East Oregonian* told of a man who invested $2,000 in yearling sheep in 1894, during the worst of the Panic. His investment, as the flock increased in size and prices strengthened, had reached $20,400 by 1898. Quoted in *Ranch and Range*, April 19, 1898.

9. *Ranche and Range*, August 12, 1897, and list of prices in October 20, 1898, issue. W. J. Spillman, "Farming in the Palouse Country," *Ranch and Range*, April 2, 1898. On influx of settlers: *Spokesman-Review*, June 22, 1899. On land contracts: "Payments Received—Land Contracts," Pend Oreille Division, book 4 (accession 9520), NPRR/St. Paul. On creditors: Archie McGregor reminiscences, MB/Glendale; interview with Sherman McGregor.

10. *Rural Northwest*, March 15, 1898; March 15, 1899. See *The Ranch*, February 14, 1901, for the role agricultural scientists played in a subsequent woolgrowers' meeting. On Northwest Livestock Association: Fred Clemens, *Three Hundred Years Along the Rothrock Trail*, pp. 157–60; John McGregor memo books, ML&L/ACM; *Rural Northwest*, March 1, 1898. Spillman's career is described in Roy Scott, *The Reluctant Farmer*, pp. 254–56, and "William J. Spillman," *Journal of Farm Economics*, 14:1 (January 1932): 1.

11. "The 'War' Between the Cattlemen and the Sheepmen," from unpublished reminiscences of Archie McGregor, MB/Glendale. On eastern Oregon disputes: *Rural Northwest*, October 15, 1897, February 1, 1898; May 15, June 15, August 1, 1899. For a listing of the scattered reports of shooting, poisoning, and clubbing sheep, see McGregor, "The Agricultural Development of the Columbia Plateau," p. 165. A group calling itself the "Crook County Sheepshooters Association" created a furor in 1905 by sending the Portland

Oregonian a "report of proceedings for the past year" and taking credit for killing several thousand sheep during "the last shooting season" (see Phil Brogan, *East of the Cascades,* pp. 119–20).

12. On forest reserve policies and observations of F. V. Coville: Coville, "Forest Growth and Sheep Grazing," pp. 26, 51. The description of the debate about excluding sheep and the quote from Muir's biographer are from Lawrence Rakestraw, "Sheep Grazing in the Cascade Range: John Minto vs. John Muir," *Pacific Historical Review,* 27:4 (November 1958): 371–82. The impact of the federal program is discussed in *Ranch and Range,* December 1, 1898, May 10 and October 4, 1900; *The Ranch,* March 13, 1902; and *American Sheep Breeder,* February, April, September, 1903, and January, March, 1904.

13. Archie McGregor letter of 1896 or 1897 is from MB/Glendale.

14. On wool price: *Ranche and Range,* July 16, 1898. Alex McGregor's pharmacy license and journal books are in ML&L/ACM. Other information about Alex and Jennie McGregor is from interview with Sherman McGregor.

15. Old property deeds file, ML&L/Hooper. Archie and Nellie's house remains standing and is occupied by the foreman of the McGregor wheat farm. The widow of the previous foreman lives in Peter and Maude's home. The other two houses no longer exist. On Jock Macrae: interview with Bill Dorman and letters in Macrae collection, ML&L/Hooper. Other employees are listed in Archie McGregor ledger book and Alex McGregor payroll book, ML&L/Hooper.

16. On duties of herders: *Ranche and Range,* August 19, 1897. On Vessey: *Ranch and Range,* December 1, 1898. On herders also see *Ranch and Range,* May 17, 1900, and *The Ranch,* August 22, 1901. The losses of Turner and Smithson are described in *The Ranch,* September 26, 1901, and *Ranch and Range,* August 27, 1898. Another serious loss is described in *The Ranch,* October 15, 1904.

17. Wentworth, *America's Sheep Trails,* p. 218. On the improved breeds of sheep: McGregor inventory book, 1905, ML&L/WSU, and *Ranche and Range,* June 24, July 1, 1897. On "eternal vigilance": *Ranche and Range,* September 30, 1897. On sheep diseases: *Rural Northwest,* August 15, 1897, *Ranch and Range,* April 26, May 7, 1898.

18. McGregor Brothers, "Sheep and Ranch Inventory," ML&L/WSU; 1905 inventory books, ML&L/Hooper; grazing lease #1, NPRR/St. Paul; wheat ranch inventory, 1905, ML&L/WSU. On Mangel-wurzels: David Griffiths, "Forage Conditions and Problems in Eastern Washington," p. 34. On the use of winter feed: *Ranche and Range,* April 8, 1897, and *Rural Northwest,* November 1, 1897. Archie McGregor's 1904 ledger book lists winter feed, employees, and the following sheep camp recipe:"#5 salt per pig, 3½# brown sugar, 5 cts salt peter, 5 cts black pepper. Dissolve the salt peter in hot water and mix all together and put on all sides of the meat."

19. Harder, "Opportunity of the Golden West," pp. 22–23; interview with Jacob Harder in "Interviews Relative to Grazing" (MSS.); Coffin, "Life"

(MSS.), p. 65. On winter losses: *American Sheep Breeder*, April 1904, and sheep loss records in McGregor inventory book, 1902–5, ML&L/WSU. Harder "came close to freezing to death" but "stayed with the sheep and thus saved the flock."

20. On anxieties of lambing time: Barnes, *Western Grazing Grounds*, pp. 150–54; J. T. Jardine, "The Pasturage System for Handling Range Sheep," USDA Forest Service Circular 178 (July 9, 1910), pp. 33–34; interviews with Emile Morod and William McGregor; early memo books of John McGregor, ML&L/Hooper. On shed lambing: *Ranche and Range*, August 26, 1897; *American Sheep Breeder*, August 15, 1904; *The Ranch*, April 1, 1905; and interview with George Rugg.

21. Interview with Emile Morod; interview with Harry Windus, by William McGregor. Sheepmen devised several schemes to minimize predator loss: G. E. Field, a McGregor employee, killed eleven coyotes in a day with his hounds; D. G. Goodman of North Yakima bought and killed scrub cayuse horses and poisoned the carcasses with strychnine and arsenic in an effort to kill the predators. See Colfax *Gazette*, March 15, 1901; *Ranch and Range*, November 24, 1898.

22. C. H. Shurte, "Reminiscences of the Sheep Industry," *National Wool Grower*, December 1916. *Rural Northwest*, June 1, 1897, and *Ranche and Range*, October 28, 1897, even reported that one herd of 82,000 sheep had been successfully trailed from the Columbia Plateau to Nebraska. On railroad charges: *Ranche and Range*, November 4, 1897.

23. Shurte, "Reminiscences of the Sheep Industry." On demand for young mutton: *Ranch and Range*, April 26, 1898.

24. On commission agents: *Ranche and Range*, June 7, 1897. On James Wright: Chicago *Gazette* quoted in *Ranche and Range*, July 1, 1897. On the sale of young wethers: *Ranch and Range*, September 8, 1898; John McGregor ledger books, 1900–5, ML&L/ACM. McGregor Brothers also sold "dry" (infertile) ewes. The Spokane *Daily Chronicle* of October 4, 1898, noted the sale of 1,200 McGregor dry ewes at $2.75 per hundredweight to H. A. Bender of Spokane.

25. Interview with Harry Windus; Marie Boone reminiscences, MB/Glendale; McGregor Brothers sheep inventory, 1905, ML&L/WSU; Archie McGregor, 1901–4 ledger, MB/Glendale. After haying season in 1905, Peter, who was running for the state legislature, told Windus: "Harry, you have a home to go to and these other men don't have any place to go so I will keep them for the winter. Besides, I need all the votes I can get down here and you can vote at home." Windus later visited with John Horrocks, another McGregor employee. "Horrocks said he asked Pete why he let Harry go as Harry was one of his best men." Pete said, "I know he was a good man but he talks too much." Windus says that was an accurate statement. From interview with Harry Windus.

26. See R. L. Rutter's reminiscences in letter to James Bateman, May 7, 1932, ML&L/WSU. Rutter, a buyer for Justice, Bateman and Company,

claimed that McGregors had "the best sheep in this section of the country." On shearing: interviews with Emile Morod and Harry Windus.

27. Interview with Emile Morod; Emile Morod and Jock Macrae sheep shearing records, ML&L/ACM; Colfax *Gazette*, May 11, 1900. On unionization: Cox, "The American Agricultural Wage Earner, 1865–1900," p. 105; *American Sheep Breeder*, May 1903, July 15, 1904; letter from A. A. Evans of Sheep Shearers' Union to E. N. Wentworth, December 22, 1939, Wentworth collection.

28. Old summer range leases in old vault, ML&L/Hooper. On Archie as herder: interview with Marie Boone. On bears: Colfax *Gazette*, November 29, 1901; Harder, "Opportunity of the Golden West," p. 24; interview with Emile Morod.

29. *Spokesman-Review*, May 27, 1900. *Ranch and Range* of June 7, 1900, cited reports that Columbia Plateau sheepmen "have seen their property virtually double during the last four years." Also see Coffin, "Life" (mss.), p. 51, and Colfax *Gazette*, April 13, 1900.

30. On lamb crop and condition of flocks: Colfax *Gazette*, February 22, May 10, 1901. On Archie's home: Archie McGregor to Nellie McGregor, October 30, 1894, MB/Glendale; Colfax *Gazette*, April 13, 1900. On Peter in Lacrosse: Colfax *Gazette*, May 4, 1900. On dances, literary societies, trout fishing, "Buffalo Bill's Wild West Show," and other leisure activities: McGregor, "The Agricultural Development of the Columbia Plateau," p. 171.

31. *Colfax Gazette*, April 12, 1901, May 30, 1902; *Spokesman-Review*, January 25, 1902.

32. Contract R–8690, Pend Oreille Sales Book, p. 89 (accession 9413); letterpresses of payments received on land contracts, Pend Oreille Division, Sales Books 4 and 5 (accessions 9520 and 9521); letterpresses of payments received—State of Washington (accessions 9361 and 9362), all from NPRR/St. Paul. On fencing: *Spokesman-Review*, January 25, 1902. Quote is from Phipps letter to Cooper, June 3, 1901, Old Leather Letterbooks, vol. 92 (accession 5550), Land Department, NPRR/St. Paul. On the purchase of Northern Pacific lands by other sheepmen, see interviews with Arthur Cox, Jacob Harder, and Wallace Rothrock, all in "Interviews . . . Relative to Grazing."

33. Griffiths, "Forage Conditions and Problems in Eastern Washington," pp. 15–17. Also see Coville, "Report on Leasing Large Areas of Grazing Lands," p. 9. On range crisis: *American Sheep Breeder*, February 1902, February 15, 1905. Some Washington and Montana open range sheepmen responded to the crisis by organizing a sheep business in the Aleutian Islands (see *American Sheep Breeder*, August 1903). On increased land value: *The Ranch*, March 27, 1902.

34. *American Sheep Breeder*, December 15, 1904, January 15 and April 15, 1905; "1904 sheep count" in 1904 ledger book, MB/Glendale; 1905 inventory book, ML&L/ACM.

35. Elliott to Cooper, March 31, 1910, quoted in Cotroneo, "Western Land Marketing," p. 310.

36. Jock Macrae manuscript in Marjorie McGregor file, ML&L/ACM. On the Columbia Plateau superseding California, see Morton Rothstein, "New Frontiers and New Rivals," from MSS. about American grain trade, p. 387, and Edwin Holmes, "Wheat Growing and General Agricultural Conditions in the Pacific Coast Region of the United States," USDA Division of Statistics, Miscellaneous Series Bulletin 20 (1901), p. 33.

37. Donald W. Meinig, "Environment and Settlement in the Palouse, 1869–1910," master's thesis, University of Washington, 1950, p. 48. On the increased immigration: Colfax *Gazette*, May 23, 1900, "Flocks and Droves: Immigrants are Pouring into Washington State." The *Gazette* concluded on July 22, 1904, "the Palouse Country is the garden spot of the world." National farm real estate values doubled during the decade 1900–1910 (see Marion Clawson, *Policy Directions for United States Agriculture*, p. 231). On the farmer as adversary: Meinig, *Great Columbia Plain*, p. 292. Coffin Brothers land speculation is discussed in Coffin's "Life" (MSS.), p. 50.

38. Comparison of two portions of Palouse: *Ranch and Range*, October 6, 1898. On Williamson: Colfax *Gazette*, July 19, 1901. On McKenzie: *Spokesman-Review*, August 13, 1904. On plowing: *The Ranch*, March 21, 1901. On Pampa: Colfax *Gazette*, December 20, 1901; also see August 30, 1901, issue.

39. Letter from Sadie Hunter, Escondido, California, to writer, April 8, 1976; J. M. Brown in Leeper, ed., "Memoirs and Reminiscences" (mss.); *Spokesman-Review*, May 23, 1901, and January 25, 1902.

40. Rangeland pushed back: Cotton, "Forage Problems of Eastern and Central Washington," p. 17. On Ritzville wheat shipments: Washington State, Bureau of Statistics, Agriculture and Immigration, "Biennial Report" (1903), pp. 69–70. Information about land transactions is from a series of fifteen John McGregor property deeds for the years 1895–1902 on file in Adams County Auditor's Office, Ritzville, and interview wth Sherman McGregor.

41. "Real Estate Inventory, 1902–1905," ML&L/WSU; Colfax *Gazette*, January 24, 1902; *Spokesman-Review*, January 25, 1902.

42. On weakness of land laws: John Wesley Powell, *Report on the Lands of the Arid Region of the United States*, p. 40, and the comments of Bernard DeVoto in Wallace Stegner, *Beyond the Hundredth Meridian*, pp. xix–xxi. John Clay, *My Life on the Range*, quoted in Fletcher, "The End of the Open Range in Eastern Montana," p. 200.

43. Arthur W. Page, "The Fight for a Land Conscience," *World's Work* 14:1 (November 1907): 9588–92. On the failure to provide legitimate means for acquiring adequate range: Foss, *Politics and Grass*, pp. 3 ff.

44. S. A. D. Puter, *Looters of the Public Domain*, pp. 339–56. The bribing of surveyors and General Land Office officials is also described in Marion Clawson, "Reminiscences of the Bureau of Land Management, 1947–1948," *Agricultural History* 33:1 (January 1959): 22–28. Quote is from *The Ranch*, May

15, 1904. Cunningham, the *American Sheep Breeder* claimed on September 15, 1904, had risen from "a moneyless boy" to gain "the distinction of being the largest ram raiser in the country." But circumstances had changed by 1905, and Cunningham decided to sell his flocks in what was said to be "the biggest ranch deal in the sheep history of Eastern Oregon." See *American Sheep Breeder*, November 15, 1905.

45. On "land paper": Thomas LeDuc, "State Disposal of the Agricultural College Land Scrip," *Agricultural History* 28:3 (July 1954): 103. On scrip: Colfax *Gazette*, January 27, 1882. Walter Yeager notes that "unrealistic [land] laws and inadequate administration created a favorable climate for opportunists to take advantage of the lack of safeguards and of legal technicalities and loopholes" ("The Pioneer's Problems of Land Acquisition," p. 211). Also see E. Louise Peffer, *The Closing of the Public Domain*, p. 26.

46. Alex C. McGregor in Leeper, "Memoirs and Reminiscences" (mss.), p. 50; Page, "Fight for a Land Conscience," p. 9591. On vehicle for fraud: Roy M. Robbins, *Our Landed Heritage*, p. 339. On Senate investigation: Paul W. Gates, *History of the Public Land Law Development*, p. 574.

47. "Old deeds" file, basement vault, ML&L/Hooper and deeds on file in auditor's offices of Adams and Whitman counties; "Contracts in Forest Reserve Timber Lands," 61st Cong., 2nd sess., Sen. Doc. 612 (1910), pp. 39, 54, 106, 109. On the Atlantic and Pacific land grants, also see Roberts, *Hoof Prints on Forest Ranges*, p. 25. For an indication of the methods McGregors used to acquire these lands, see Mrs. J. M. Hill to Peter McGregor, February 13, 1918, ML&L/WSU, and Santa Barbara Water Company to Alex McGregor, October 12, 1917, ML&L/ACM.

48. Phipps to Assistant Land Agent F. W. Wilsey, January 22, March 27, April 14, May 17, 1902; Phipps to Western Land Agent G. H. Plummer, February 17, February 18, 1902; Phipps to R. H. Relf, March 27, 1902; Phipps to Britton and Gray, February 27, 1902, all from Land Department, Old Leather Letterbooks, NPRR/St. Paul. On the importance of such "key tracts," see Foss, *Politics and Grass*, p. 28. Assorted information from McGregor old deeds file, ML&L/Hooper, was also useful here.

49. Information about land deals is based on extensive collection of old property deeds and related correspondence in ML&L/Hooper and ML&L/ACM. On homesteading see reminiscences of Euphemia MacGregor, MSD/Calgary.

50. Letter from G. H. Plummer to J. S. Cotton, June 13, 1903, included in Cotton, "Forage Problems of Eastern and Central Washington." On "the very strong influence" livestock raisers had in shaping state land policies: Sanford Mosk, "Land Policy and Stock Grazing in the Western United States," in Vernon Carstensen, ed., *The Public Lands*, pp. 411–29. On Peter McGregor: Washington State, *Journal of the Senate*, 1905–7; interviews with Ralph Snyder and Sherman McGregor. The McGregor leases are shown in *Plat Map of Whitman County, 1910*. McGregor Brothers took dozens of leases of state lands using the names of their wives, friends, relatives, and

business acquaintances for the transactions (see "Leased Lands–Hooper" file, ML&L/ACM). After 1899, the lessee had a preferential right to re-lease, thus assuring McGregors continued control of the rangeland (Roy Hoover, "The Public Land Policy of Washington State: The Initial Period, 1889–1912," Ph.D. dissertation, WSU, 1967, p. 85).

51. "Real Estate Inventory, 1902–1909," ML&L/WSU. Scoured wool prices, 1895–1942, Pendleton Woolen Mills, Portland, Oregon, manuscript made available by wool buyer J. H. Walters. On "grease" price of wool and value of wethers: McGregor and Rothrock, "What Free Wool Did in Washington," p. 22, and several contemporary articles in *Rural Northwest*. The *American Sheep Breeder* statement appears in the February 15, 1905, issue. Clarence Braden recalled that his parents came to Franklin County in 1900 and bought land: "That's the way they made their money." Bradens sold land purchased at $1.75 per acre a few years later for as much as $25 per acre. See Clarence Braden interview, WCAT/Walla Walla. Pierre Wibaux, an eastern Montana sheepman and cattle raiser, told of "men who made $100,000 or more" on speculation "within a few months" as a result of a similar land boom in the early twentieth century (see Fletcher, "The End of the Open Range in Eastern Montana," p. 208).

52. Lists of improvements made on the range are in "Real Estate Inventory –1915," ML&L/WSU; and John McGregor's daily business books, 1903–5, ML&L/ACM. On Hooper store: J. M. Brown and Alex McGregor interviews in Leeper, ed., "Memoirs and Reminiscences" (MSS.). Company town: Baldwin Sheep and Land Company in the early 1890's controlled the town of Hay Creek, Oregon. See the information about the Baldwin company in Wentworth collection, University of Wyoming. Coffin Brothers of North Yakima continued to be the most innovative sheepmen-merchants of the Columbia Plateau. They corralled wild horses and sold them to miners during the Alaska gold rush, shipped cattle overland and by raft to Nome, opened "the New Klondike and Farmer's Outfitting Store" in Seattle, and ran six wholesale stores in the plateau country. See Coffin, "Life" (mss.), pp. 39–40; "Yakima Grocery Company," files in Coffin Sheep Company records; and *Ranche and Range*, April 29, December 18, 1897, and March 26, 1898.

53. Interviews with Ralph Snyder and Sherman McGregor and several Columbia Plateau land ownership plat books printed between 1895 and 1910. Also see Malin, "Mobility and History," p. 182.

54. Statements by Rothrock in *Spokesman-Review*, December 29, 1918, and in Clemens, *Three Hundred Years Along the Rothrock Trail*, pp. 160–68. On Peter McGregor: Colfax *Gazette*, September 7, 1906.

55. On Bryan and Debs: Colfax *Gazette*, April 6, 1900, June 27, 1902. On railroad meeting: *Gazette*, August 8, 1902. On Peter McGregor's role in local political meetings: *Gazette*, September 2, 1904. The *Gazette*, a Republican paper, contended on May 13, 1900, that "the election of 1896—carried overwhelmingly by the Populists—seems to have brought to the surface of a dirty

pot all the scum and foul grease imaginable." The complaints about grain shipping are described in Crawford, *The Washington State Grange*, pp. 137–40.

56. Peter McGregor was one of the eighty-nine Republicans in the ninety-four-member House (see Elizabeth Leary, *Clayton's Legislative Manual of Washington, 1905*). Peter's views on direct primary are from his letter to the Colfax *Gazette*, September 14, 1906. Also see "Grange Questions," a series of questions addressed to the candidates, in the September 21 issue. On railway lobby: Colfax *Gazette*, July 15, 1904. Peter McGregor sponsored House Bill 337 "to prevent discrimination in railway freight and passenger costs," which failed to secure House approval (see Washington State Journals of the House and Senate, 1905–8).

57. Colfax *Gazette*, October 5, November 2, 1906. In his second term, Peter sponsored four bills, one dealing with freight rates, one "relative to trespass of sheepmen," another "to create office of sheep inspector," and a final one "relating to the prevention of disease in sheep" (see Washington State, Journals of the House and Senate, 1905–8). See the comments on Peter's legislative career and term as Washington State College regent in E. A. Bryan, *Historical Sketch of the State College of Washington*, p. 260.

58. *The Ranch*, January 23, 1902; *Rural Northwest*, June 1, 1899; *The Ranch*, October 17, November 14, November 20, 1900, October 31, 1901, January 23, 1902. One critic, writing in the March 15, 1903, issue of *The Ranch*, asked: "Had the expenditure lavished upon our 'State Agricultural Colleges' been subdivided and ten schools established throughout the state, where agriculture was *taught* and not *avoided*, would the Morrill and other funds not have been vastly more beneficial, and the real purposes of the grant secured?" Also see *The Ranch*, October 17 and 24, 1901.

59. Colfax *Gazette*, October 19, October 26, 1906, and the September 23, 1904, issue in which he is described as "capable in every respect and honest to a fault."

60. Interviews with Ralph Snyder. J. K. Galbraith, *Made to Last* (later edition is entitled *The Scotch*), p. 34. Coffin Brothers had the same family cohesiveness. H. Stanley Coffin remembered: "Brothers got on well together. Agreed to go on no notes and bonds. Agreed that any mistakes of one of us could not be held against him" (notes for 1914 speech delivered to Washington Wool Growers Association, Coffin Sheep Company files, Yakima).

CHAPTER 5

Boom Days in the Sheep Business, 1905–20

1. "Shepherd Boy," *Modern Sheep*, p. 165; H. L. Davis, *Team Bells Woke Me, and Other Stories*, p. 89.

2. Corporate charter, minute book 1905–13, and bill of sale from Peter, John, Archie, and Alex McGregor, July 19, 1905, all in ML&L/Hooper.

3. Reasons for incorporation: G. John Chohlis, "The McGregor Ranch: Northwest Pace-Setter," *Farm Management* 2:4 (March 1953): 15; interview with Sherman McGregor. Sheep business modified: Wallace Rothrock in "Interviews Relative to Grazing," (mss.), pp. 126–27; early Coffin Sheep Company records; and a series of articles in *American Sheep Breeder*, 1900–4.

4. On improved conditions: A. B. Genung, "Agriculture in the World War Period," in *Farmers in a Changing World*, USDA *Yearbook of Agriculture* (1940), pp. 277–78.

5. "Ya Farmer": Chohlis, "The McGregor Ranch," p. 15. Annual statements of McGregor Land and Livestock, 1909–20, ML&L/Hooper.

6. Interview with Emile Morod; Washington State, *Journal of the Senate* (1907), House Bill 187. Drumheller: *National Wool Grower*, November 1916, p. 16.

7. *National Wool Grower*, January 1918, p. 18. On herders: *American Sheep Breeder*, September 1903, p. 525; *American Shepherd's Bulletin*, December 1906, p. 92. *The Ranch* carried a tale on August 1, 1903, of one hardworking herder, "a college boy who came from the East to work on a sheep ranch" in eastern Oregon:

> He was an athlete and the champion sprinter of his school but he didn't know much about ranching. He was sent out the first day to herd the sheep. When the rancher asked him how he had got along he said all right except he had done a lot of running to keep the lambs in the flock. "I kept them there," he said, "but Lord, it made me run." "Lambs?," said the rancher in astonishment, "there are no lambs at this time of year." "Well, there are lots of them" said the new herder stubbornly, "you just come out and see." Very curious to know what it all meant, the rancher went with the herder to the pasture. As they went along two jack rabbits jumped out. "There!" shouted the herder, "there's two of 'em now, they must have got out since I went to supper."

8. On sheep crew: John McGregor memo book 1914–16, ML&L/ACM; Company payroll book, 1915, ML&L/WSU; A. C. McGregor paybook, 1906–14, ML&L/Hooper; and Alex C. McGregor in Leeper, "Memoirs and Reminiscences" (mss.), p. 53. On Macrae: William O. Douglas, *Of Men and Mountains*, p. 145. Also see Macrae collection, ML&L/Hooper.

9. On Macrae's cousin: Mrs. C. A. Isaacs to J. M. McGregor, 1945, ML&L/ACM. Macrae describes his travels in his MSS. reminiscences (typed by Helen McGregor, ca. 1940) and in "A Tribute to the Life of John Duncan Macrae," ML&L/Hooper. On whiskey sale: *U.S.A. v. John McCrea*, Yakima County Circuit Court, June 26, 1896. On application for work: interview with Sherman McGregor.

10. Open letter written by Peter McGregor, December 26, 1906, Macrae

collection, ML&L/Hooper. Macrae's comments are from his MSS. reminiscences. Also see interviews with Macrae and Alex C. McGregor in Denver *Daily Record Stockman*, February 19, 1935.

11. On Macrae's abilities: E. A. Taylor to John McGregor, December 13, 1915, ML&L/ACM. Letter from Macrae: Macrae to John McGregor, October 26, 1915, ML&L/Hooper.

12. Interviews with Emile Morod.

13. R. Kent Beattie, "Plants Used for Food by Sheep on the Mica Mountain Summer Range," Washington AES Bulletin 113 (1913), p. 6; interviews with Emile Morod. See the description of herding in rainy weather in Robert Maudslay, "An Englishman Herds Sheep in Texas," in Greenberg, ed., *Land That Our Fathers Plowed*, p. 234.

14. Interviews with Emile Morod, Willard Burden, and Marvin Burden; John McGregor to A. B. Fosseen, September 6, 1918, ML&L/WSU. On the migration of herders from sheep ranges to towns, see Michael Mathers, *Sheepherders: Men Alone*, p. 8.

15. Hooper Hotel business records, 1910–20, ML&L/Hooper; interview with Charles H. Brune. Jock Macrae claimed that his first attempt to prepare sourdough bread had been disastrous. According to William McGregor (interview):

> *Mac was out by himself with a band of sheep at a camp which had a shack and a windmill. He had a recipe for sourdough bread. He mixed it up and looked at his dough and decided it wasn't nearly enough. So he doubled the recipe. Then that didn't look like quite enough, so he put a little more in. The dough started to rise and came out of the bowl. He got a bigger bowl and then had to put it in a washtub. It was filling that up when he had to go out and tend to the windmill. As he went outside he looked across the plains and saw a cloud of dust coming. He recognized his boss in his buckboard. Mac thought he'd be in trouble for wasting food. So he quickly ran out behind the shack and dug a big hole and put the dough in it and covered it up. The boss arrived and they looked at the sheep and talked about various things. It was a cold spring day so the boss walked around on the sunny side of the shack out of the wind. As they were talking Mac swore he saw the ground starting to rise next to the shack. He tried to distract the boss, tried everything he could think of to get him to move away around to the other side of the shack. Finally the boss felt the ground rising up around him and leaped off in fear. Mac had to confess what he had done. The boss said 'Next time don't waste it. Save it. It'll keep.'*

16. Interview with Thomas J. Drumheller, Jr.

17. On herders' pay: Alex McGregor payroll books, 1906–14, ML&L/Hooper. Average farm wage: *Prices Received by Washington Farmers, 1910–1959*, Washington State and U.S. Departments of Agriculture (1960), p. 69. Archie McGregor: Lacrosse *Clipper*, October 5, 1917.

18. On winter ranges: interviews with T. J. Drumheller, Jr., Charles Brune,

H. S. Coffin III, and William McGregor. On herders' quarters: McGregor inventory books, ML&L/Hooper; interview with Emile Morod. Quote is from Archer Gilfillan, "The Sheep Herder Calls It a Day," *Atlantic Monthly* 143 (May 1929): 607.

19. On herders' supplies: Jock Macrae paybooks, 1905–20, ML&L/Hooper. Sheep dog: Gilfillan, "The Herding Day," *Atlantic Monthly* 143 (January 1929): 20.

20. On McGregor dogs: Beattie, "Plants Used for Food by Sheep," pp. 10–12. On training sheep dogs: interviews with William McGregor and Emile Morod. On McGregor herders and their dogs: undated Peter McGregor clippings and manuscripts in ML&L/Hooper and MSD/Calgary and 1928 daybook of Maurice McGregor, ML&L/WSU. See the descriptions of a dedicated sheep dog in Gilfillan, *Sheep*, p. 53.

21. H. L. Davis, *Honey in the Horn*, pp. 20–21. On diversionary tactics of coyotes: Towne and Wentworth, *Shepherd's Empire*, pp. 219–20. Also see Gilfillan, *Sheep*, p. 169. On herders and coyotes: interview with Emile Morod. Paul Sears includes a photo of 177 sheep killed in one night by a pair of dogs in "Where Is Your Dog Tonight?," *Rangeman's Journal* 3:1 (February 1976): 12–13. T. J. Drumheller, Jr., told in an interview how sheepmen of the Walla Walla Valley "went dog hunting" after losing 500 head of sheep in three days to domestic dogs.

22. *Spokesman-Review*, June 1, June 18, 1907, January 6, 1908, February 22, 1909; *National Wool Grower*, May 1916. Deep snow is the biggest danger, for sheep can stand extreme cold for prolonged periods if they can reach grass.

23. Interview with Charles Brune; hay inventories, 1914–18, ML&L/WSU; inventory books 1905–6 and memo books of John McGregor, ML&L/Hooper; letters, invoices, and memos in "Sheep–feed" file, ML&L/ACM. On alfalfa hay: *Spokesman-Review* June 10, 1916. On supplemental feeds: William Hislop, "Relative Value of Feeds for Wintering Range Sheep," *National Wool Grower*, February, 1917; interview with William McGregor.

24. Richard Mack, "Competitive Displacement: An Ecological Chronicle of *Bromus Tectorum*," 1980 MSS. made available by the author, pp. 3–9. On attempts to introduce other brome grasses: *Ranch and Range*, February 15, 1900; *Rural Northwest*, October 1, 1897, December 1, 1898.

25. On difficulties of spring and long hours: Gilfillan, *Sheep*, pp. 36, 69. On "sheep brain": Muir, *My First Summer in the Sierra*, p. 152; Jacob Harder in "Interviews Relative to Grazing" (MSS.). On lambing time: interviews with Emile Morod.

26. Gilfillan, *Sheep*, p. 67.

27. *The Shepherd's Criterion*, May 1908. H. Stanley Coffin advised members of the Washington Wool Growers' Association: "If an extra man saves a lamb a day that would have been lost, he has more than made his wages, but if it takes two men to save a lamb, you lose" (H. S. Coffin Speeches, Coffin Sheep Company, Yakima). On Shorty Ritter: interviews with Willard and Marvin Burden.

28. Arthur Cox in "Interviews Relative to Grazing" (MSS.); interviews with Emile Morod.

29. Interviews with Emile Morod and William McGregor. On problems of moving small bunches of sheep: Towne and Wentworth, *Shepherd's Empire*, p. 292; also see Jardine, "The Pasturage System for Handling Range Sheep."

30. Lambing statistics based on sheep tally books and memo books of John, Archie, and Jock Macrae ML&L/Hooper. On shed lambing: *American Shepherd's Bulletin*, May 1907. Prerequisites for successful shed operations: E. F. Rinehart in P. V. Ewing, ed., *The Golden Hoof*, p. 35. Dimensions of "big shed" provided by William McGregor.

31. Interview with Thomas J. Drumheller, Jr.; Herman Oliver, *Gold and Cattle Country*, p. 112; Wentworth, *America's Sheep Trails*, p. 218. Grafting hides on "bummers": Towne and Wentworth, *Shepherd's Empire*, p. 292. On William James: Lacrosse *Clipper*, April 19, 1912. Statistics on increased lambing percentages are from sheep tally books, ML&L/Hooper.

32. E. V. Wilcox, "Sheep Ranching in the Western States," BAI, Nineteenth Annual Report (1902), p. 81; William Hislop and C. E. Howell, "Sheep Husbandry in the Pacific Northwest," Washington AES Bulletin 134 (January 1917), p. 7. "Successful" 90 percent lamb crops: Wentworth, *Progressive Sheep Raising*, p. 119. Government investigators: Will C. Barnes and James T. Jardine, "Livestock Production in the Eleven Far Western Range States," USDA Office of the Secretary, Report 110 (1916), p. 91. On the killing of twin lambs: interview with William McGregor.

33. Sheep inventory books, 1905-20, ML&L/ACM, ML&L/WSU; *The Shepherd's Criterion*, August 1907. Peter McGregor discusses the sale of $40,000 of wool and wethers in Colfax *Commoner*, June 18, 1909.

34. Wentworth, *America's Sheep Trails*, p. 218. On decline of wethers: *National Wool Grower*, August 1914, April 1916. Comments about various breeds: Hislop and Howell, "Sheep Husbandry in the Pacific Northwest," pp. 4-7, and "Sheep Breeds" file, ML&L/Hooper. In the 1890's most Columbia Plateau sheep were "scrubs." By 1918, only 5.5 percent were "nondescript," and the rest were of a dozen specialized breeds. See Washington State, Department of Agriculture, "Fourth Biennial Report to the Governor" (1918-20), p. 51.

35. This technique of "marking" did not change until the 1960's, when a special type of rubber band was developed for use on buck lambs. On lamb-fry celebrations: interview with Sherman McGregor.

36. "Wool clip" file, ML&L/Hooper; Jock Macrae shearing paybooks, ML&L/Hooper. On Mexican shearing crews: interview with Emile Morod; *The Shepherd's Criterion*, May 1907; and Joe Lopez letter to Jock Macrae, December 26, 1918, ML&L/WSU. On shearers union: R. A. Balch to Jock Macrae, January 30, 1919, ML&L/WSU, and A. A. Evans, president of the union, to E. N. Wentworth, December 22, 1939, Wentworth collection, University of Wyoming. On "greenhorn" machine shearers: Towne and Wentworth, *Shepherd's Empire*, p. 299.

37. Complaints of sheepmen and WSC course: *Washington Farmer*, November 6, 1919. Shearer's work: Kenny, "Early Sheep Ranching in Eastern Oregon," p. 117, and Emile Morod interview.

38. *The Shepherd's Criterion*, May 1908; *National Wool Grower*, April 1916. On advantages of machines: Towne and Wentworth, *Shepherd's Empire*, p. 300. On McGregor shearing: Lacrosse *Clipper*, May 12, 1911.

39. On dangers of cold storms: *National Wool Grower*, April 1916. On McGregor losses: interview with Emile Morod; also see "Shorn Sheep Nearly Frozen," *Spokesman-Review*, June 20, 1907. In his novel *Honey in the Horn*, H. L. Davis comments (p. 254): "The reason for the low temperature was that it was sheep-shearing time."

40. *The Shepherd's Journal*, September 1913; *American Shepherd's Bulletin*, April 1906; *The Shepherd's Criterion*, September 1907. On wool buyers: correspondence files in ML&L/ACM and ML&L/Hooper. On wool prices: information in ML&L/Hooper and "Prices Received by Washington Farmers, 1910–1959," p. 34. "An unusually profitable industry": Washington State, Department of Agriculture, "Second Report to the Governor," (1914–16), p. 40. Value of McGregor clip: compiled from statements, tax returns, invoices, and other information in ML&L/Hooper. Hislop comments: *Spokesman-Review*, May 2, 1919.

41. On trailing to summer range: interviews with Charles Brune, William McGregor, and other sheepmen. Drumhellers shipped their sheep fifty miles by barge on Lake Chelan to save two weeks of trailing through rugged mountainous areas (see T. J. Drumheller, Sr., "Western Sheep Prospects," *National Wool Grower*, November 1916).

42. Interviews with Emile Morod and correspondence with herders in ML&L/ACM. Jock Macrae letter to John McGregor, October 26, 1915, is in ML&L/Hooper. Macrae's files also contain lists of expenses incurred traveling to and from the mountains, e.g., "bed 25¢, breakfast 35¢, train $1.50, fare for dog 35¢."

43. Interviews with Emile Morod; A. F. Steele to Jock Macrae, August 7, 1913. Also see Spokane Indian Agency to Macrae, July 25, 1919, both in Macrae files, ML&L/Hooper.

44. Butter Creek: *Ranch and Range*, November 1, 1900; John McGregor to A. B. Fosseen, September 6, 1918, ML&L/WSU; *The Shepherd's Journal*, June 10, 1910. Also see Arthur W. Sampson, "Poisonous Range Plants," *National Wool Grower*, December 1916.

45. Interviews with Emile Morod. Summer range lease files, ML&L/ACM, and similar material in ML&L/WSU.

46. Beattie, "Plants Used for Food by Sheep." A similar study of grazing practices on the R. A. Jackson range in the Blue Mountains is H. T. Darlington, "A Study of Grazing Conditions in the Wenaha National Forest," Washington AES Bulletin 122 (May 1915).

47. USDA, Forest Service, "Grazing Handbook: North Pacific District" (1927), p. 16; interviews with Emile Morod.

48. On forest fires: Gerald A. Tucker, "History of the Northern Blue

Mountains" (typed, 1940), pp. 136–37. On disagreements among herders: interview with Emile Morod.

49. Macrae's comments are from a series of letters he sent to the McGregors and their office manager, H. R. Rudd, ML&L/WSU, ML&L/Hooper. *Spokesman-Review*, August 12, 1918.

50. Correspondence in grazing lease files, ML&L/ACM. On dispute with Idaho officials: A. J. Humiston to L. A. Smoot, July 23, 1918; bond posted by Jock Macrae, John and Alex C. McGregor, November 28, 1918; L. A. Smoot to McGregor Land and Livestock, December 26, 1917; McGregor Land and Livestock to O. A. Decker, November 20, 1919, all in ML&L/WSU. On doubts of Indian agents: O. C. Upchurch to McGregors, September 18, 1918, ML&L/WSU. On whiskey: interview with Emile Morod. The areas included in the grazing leases remained virtually the same for more than sixty years (see 1912 and 1973 maps of Spokane Indian Reservation sheep range, ML&L/ACM). To supplement the Indian lands, state land leases were made and signed for McGregors by several Hooper residents (see "Grazing Leases-State," ML&L/ACM).

51. Wentworth, *America's Sheep Trails*, p. 505; *The Shepherd's Criterion*, February 1907; *American Shepherd's Bulletin*, February, March, and April 1907 issues and other contemporary trade journals; interview with Thomas J. Drumheller, Jr. Gerald A. Tucker, a veteran Forest Service employee, describes a ten-day meeting with sheepmen and cattlemen to organize grazing on the newly created Wenaha National Forest in 1905 in his manuscript, "History of the Northern Blue Mountains," pp. 106–8. On sales of sheep: *The Shepherd's Criterion*, May 1908; *American Shepherd's Bulletin*, November 1906; "History of the Baldwin Sheep and Land Company," MSS. in Wentworth collection, University of Wyoming. Coffin Brothers responded to the limitations by purchasing a large summer range outside the National Forests (*The Ranch*, August 1, 1905).

52. Interview with Emile Morod; *American Shepherd's Bulletin*, March 1907; *The Shepherd's Criterion*, January 1907. Also see *Washington Farmer*, September 18, 1919. On delayed McGregor shipment: Kirkland Stock Yards to McGregor Land and Livestock, December 18, 1918; C. H. Shurte to John McGregor, December 12, 1918; and four related letters written in the fall of 1918, ML&L/WSU and ML&L/ACM.

53. "Sheep—Gross Receipts," 1910–16, ML&L/ACM. Also see *Shepherd's Criterion*, May 1909, and graph of lamb prices for the years 1890–1920 in Spencer and Hall, "The Sheep Industry," p. 286. On lamb sales: *Spokesman-Review*, August 27, September 9, 1916.

54. "Very prosperous condition": *American Shepherd's Bulletin*, April 1906; see also *The Shepherd's Criterion*, January 1908. On cowmen in sheep business: *The Shepherd's Criterion*, September 1907, March 1908. On free wool: Peter McGregor and F. M. Rothrock, "What Free Wool Did in Washington," *National Wool Grower*, June 1913, p. 22. H. Stanley Coffin took a similar view: "I feel that a reduction in the tariff in any way would

practically mean the bankruptcy of the sheep industry of our state" (*National Wool Grower*, September 1911, p. 43). Drumheller: *National Wool Grower*, November 1916. On McGregor profits: ML&L/Lemaster and Daniels, ML&L/Hooper.

55. Washington State, Department of Agriculture, "Third Biennial Report to the Governor" (1916–18), pp. 5, 11; John McGregor to A. B. Fosseen, September 6, 1918, ML&L/WSU; *Spokesman-Review*, February 23, 1919. Clel Georgetta notes: "Bankers were liberal with loans and many sheepmen borrowed money to buy more sheep to make more money to buy more land to raise more sheep" (*Golden Fleece in Nevada*, p. 127). "There is no better security for a money loan than livestock," Spokane banker E. E. Flood claimed in 1919 (*Washington Farmer*, January 2, 1919).

56. Drumheller: *National Wool Grower*, November 1916. Fisk: *Spokesman-Review*, February 23, 1919.

57. *Washington Farmer*, June 19, 1919. Also see Spillman interview in March 6, 1919, issue. Peter McGregor to F. R. Marshall, July 19 and August 13, 1920, ML&L/WSU. C. L. Buel, Evans-Snider-Buel Livestock Commission Company, to John McGregor, October 2, 1918, ML&L/WSU.

58. *National Wool Grower*, January 1916; *Spokesman-Review*, June 29, 1920; Coffin, "Life" (MSS.), p. 57; Drumheller, *National Wool Grower*, November 1916. Washington sheepman R. A. Jackson in 1902 had estimated that it cost him less than a dollar a head to run sheep (*American Sheep Breeder*, October 1902).

59. "John McGregor Dies of Influenza Attack: One of Inland Empire's Most Prominent Citizens," December 1919, n.p., MB/Glendale; "John MacGregor—By a Friend," S. B. Nelson, ML&L/ACM; E. W. Downen to Archie, Alex, Peter, and Dougald McGregor, January 5, 1919, ML&L/Hooper. "Scotch love of sheep": *Spokesman-Review*, December 29, 1918; McGregor Land and Livestock, corporate resolutions, 1919, ML&L/Hooper. The dispute between Archie and Peter will be discussed in detail in Chapter 7.

CHAPTER 6

Sheepmen Take to the Plow: Wheat Raising on the Hills of the Columbia Plateau, 1905–20

1. Zane Grey, *The Desert of Wheat*, pp. 1–2; *Washington Farmer*, July 1919; *The Coast*, December 1907.

2. Henry Stewart, *The Shepherd's Manual*, p. 256. Stewart claimed that only irrigation could make the land fertile and asserted that cultivated lands "comprise but a very insignificant portion" of the vast region.

3. Greene, "Report on the Interior Wheat Lands," pp. 5–16. On early

views of climatic conditions: Meinig, "The Evolution of Understanding an Environment"; and W. McMicken, "Report of the Surveyor-General of Washington Territory," 46th Cong., 2nd Sess., House Exec. Doc. 1, part 5, p. 898.

4. On soil texture and color: Meinig, "Environment and Settlement in the Palouse," p. 48. On bankers: Fred Yoder, "Pioneer Social Adaptation in the Palouse Country of Eastern Washington, 1870–90," *Research Studies of the State College of Washington*, 6:4 (December 1938): 137–48. Railroad circulars: G. H. Atkinson, *The Northwest Coast Including Oregon, Washington and Idaho*, p. 45, and P. Donan, *Oregon, Washington, Idaho and their Resources*, p. 17. Holmes, "Wheat Growing . . . in the Pacific Coast Region."

5. William Snyder, taped interview by Earl Snyder, Washtucna, Washington. On squirrels: Ritzville *Journal-Times*, September 15, 1949; Sarah Snyder to Birney Snyder, June 14, 1889 (courtesy of Lina Buhl, Ritzville, Washington).

6. On Pacific Slope grain production: Frank Andrews, "Marketing Grain and Livestock in the Pacific Coast Region," USDA Bureau of Statistics, Bulletin 89 (1911), p. 11; Holmes "Wheat Growing . . . in the Pacific Coast Region," p. 7. On marketing and exporting: Morton Rothstein, "Around the Horn" (chap. 11 of MSS. on American grain trade), pp. 479–504; John B. Watkins, "Wheat Exporting from the Pacific Northwest," Washington AES Bulletin 201 (May 1926), p. 14.

7. William Snyder interview; Arno Dosch, "The Triumph of 'the Palouse,'" *Pacific Monthly* 13 (November 1905): 432; *Spokesman-Review*, November 28, 1903, August 13, 1904; interview with Thomas J. Drumheller, Jr.; Symons, "The Upper Columbia River and the Great Plain of the Columbia," pp. 60, 110; Andrews, "Marketing Grain in the Pacific Coast Region," p. 12.

8. Dave Carter interview, February 20, 1946, by Maurice McGregor, ML&L/Hooper; Lenora Torgeson, *Snake River Hills*, p. 9. Acreage in crop: Archie McGregor 1904 ledger book, MB/ Glendale; "1905 Ranch Inventory," ML&L/WSU; wheat ranch file, ML&L/ACM.

9. On hazards of wheat raising: interviews with William and Sherman McGregor. On Scottish tenantry system: *Spokesman-Review*, February 23, 1919. On McGregor farms: Hugh C. Todd, "Land Tenures in Whitman County," bachelor's thesis, Washington State College, 1906, pp. 25, 34.

10. William McGregor of Annan, Ontario, letter to writer, June 27, 1973; interview with Sherman McGregor; wheat ranch and tenant farm files, ML&L/ACM. Early lease agreement forms: old vault, ML&L/Hooper. Knox and Mays leases, ML&L/WSU. On improvements: ranch inventories, 1908–20, ML&L/WSU. Notice to Clemens: property deeds files, ML&L/WSU.

11. Lenora Torgeson interview. Balfour, Guthrie and three other companies bought and sold about two-thirds of the wheat raised in Washington (see Rothstein, "Around the Horn" [MSS.], p. 522). Balfour, Guthrie listed

their wide range of business dealings in a March 2, 1916, advertisement in *Commercial Review*: "Importers of grain bags, burlap, twine, and cement. Exporters of lumber, wheat, flour, and apples. Agents for Crown Flour Mills, Capital Refining Company, British and Foreign Marine Insurance Company, Ltd." Correspondence about company dealerships, wheat sales, hog sales are in "dealership file," ML&L/ACM; "wheat 1909–1920," "accounts–1907," and "ranch inventory" files ML&L/WSU; and business records in ML&L/Hooper and ML&L/Lemaster & Daniels. On food for tenants: interviews with Fred Clemens and Lenora Torgeson.

12. On Barr and McKenzie: McGregor Land and Livestock to Murphy, Favre, November 18, 1921, ML&L/ACM. On payment of tenant bills: Advance Rumely to McGregor Land and Livestock, March 28, 1921, ML&L/Hooper. On J. L. Knox: McGregor Land and Livestock to Portland Cattle Loan Company, December 4, 1920, ML&L/WSU. On John Banks: McGregor Land and Livestock to Vorhees and Canfield, November 2, 1923, and April 15, 1924, ML&L/WSU.

13. Tenant tax returns, ML&L/Hooper; D. H. Houser to Archie McGregor, August 22, 1918, ML&L/Hooper. On one day in July 1918, wheat from seventeen western Whitman farmers was hauled to the warehouse (see warehouse receipts July 26, 1918, ML&L/WSU). On threshing costs: harvest expense sheets, ML&L/WSU; 1918 harvest bills, ML&L/Hooper; McGregor Land and Livestock to Pacific Grain Company, August 19, 1920, ML&L/ACM.

14. On local meetings and demonstration trains: Colfax *Gazette*, February 9, February 16, November 23, 1900; March 29, 1901. On Campbell: R. W. Thatcher, "Nineteenth Annual Report of the State Agricultural Experiment Station," Washington AES Unnumbered Bulletin (1909), p. 14. On Spillman: Scott, *The Reluctant Farmer*, pp. 254–59. On meeting with Secretary Wilson: Pullman *Herald*, March 17, 1906. On McGregor wheat business: *Spokesman-Review*, April 19, 1911.

15. Interviews with Lenora Torgeson, Louis Banks, and Harley Jacquot; W. A. Rockie, "Man's Effect on the Palouse," *Geographical Review* 29 (January 1939): 38; Fred W. Clemens, "Remembering," pp. 13–15 (MSS. about Clemens' early days in the western Palouse, provided by Clemens). McGregor plows: ranch inventory, 1905, ML&L/WSU; also see Byron Hunter et al., "A Review of the Agriculture of the Big Bend Country," Washington AES Bulletin 192 (September 1925), p. 9. On acreage covered with various plows: M. R. Cooper *et al.*, "Progress of Farm Mechanization," USDA Misc. Publication 630 (October 1947), p. 40. On steam plowing: Washington State, Bureau of Statistics, "Biennial Report: Agriculture and Immigration" (1903), p. 71.

16. On teamsters, horses, and machinery: Thomas B. Keith, *The Horse Interlude*, pp. 37, 47, 167. On distinct regional characteristics: Holmes, "Wheat Growing . . . in the Pacific Coast Region," pp. 8, 15, 23. On labor expense: USDA, Division of Statistics, "Wages of Farm Labor in the United

States," Miscellaneous Bulletin 4 (1892); interviews with Carl Penner, Clarence Braden, Ernest McCaw, Bill Drumheller, Sr. (Vance Orchard horse era tape), all from WCAT/Walla Walla. McGregor work animals: wheat harvest file, ML&L/ACM.

17. Clemens, "Remembering" (MSS.), pp. 14–16. Interviews with Virgil Bennington and Lenora Torgeson. On shotgun seeder: interview with William Snyder; see also Hunter, "Farm Practice in the Columbia Basin Uplands," pp. 14–18.

18. On dangers of planting spring wheat: Victor Roterus, "Spring and Winter Wheat on the Columbia Plateau," *Economic Geography* 10: 4 (October 1934): 369; interviews with William McGregor and Arthur Buhl. On John McGregor: Chohlis, "The McGregor Ranch," p. 12.

19. McGregor wheats: "Wheat and Flour Investigations," Washington AES Bulletin 100 (1911). Varietal qualities: Meinig, *Great Columbia Plain*, p. 407; Hunter, "Farm Practice in the Columbia Basin Uplands," pp. 22–27; J. Allen Clark, "The Common White Wheats," USDA Farmers' Bulletin 1301 (December 1922), pp. 11, 36.

20. Spillman, "The Hybrid Wheats." On wheat for Palouse: Colfax *Gazette*, June 14, 1901. *The Ranch* on June 20, 1901, reported that Spillman had made 300 crosses of two types of spring wheat with six varieties of winter wheat in his search for a type of grain well suited to the climatic conditions of the Columbia Plateau. On success of hybrids: wheat ranch file, ML&L/ACM; *Commercial Review*, January 14, 1915. On Girard Clark: Colfax *Commoner*, February 19, 1909. On soft white wheat: C. R. Ball et al., "Wheat Production and Marketing," USDA *Yearbook of Agriculture* (1921), pp. 123–26.

21. On summerfallow: *The Ranch*, August 1, 1905; Hunter, "Farm Practice in the Columbia Basin Uplands," p. 13. On Campbell system: *The Ranch*, September 1, 1904, March 1, 1905; Colfax *Commoner*, January 8, July 23, 1909, September 9, 1910; and letter from William Phipps, Northern Pacific Land Commissioner, to Western Land Agent Thomas Cooper, January 2, 1897, Old Leather Letterbooks, vol. 57, p. 36 (accession 5544), Land Department, NPRR/St. Paul. On Campbell and dry farming: Mary W. M. Hargreaves, *Dry Farming in the Northern Great Plains, 1900–1925*. Thatcher's suggestions: Colfax *Commoner*, August 26, 1910; R. W. Thatcher, "The Nitrogen and Humus Problem in Dry Farming," Washington AES Bulletin 105 (June 1912). On dust mulch: interview with John McGregor; Rockie, "Man's Effect on the Palouse," p. 41. On McGregor packers: McGregor Land and Livestock to McCroskey Implement, March 16, 1926, ML&L/Hooper.

22. William McGregor interviews. On McGregor crews: Alex McGregor paybook, 1905–14, and interview with Ernest Osmond. On spring wheat areas: interviews with Arthur Buhl. On early weeders: Ritzville *Journal-Times*, September 15, 1949; interview with Carl Penner.

23. *Ranch and Range*, July 30, August 6, 1898; *The Ranch*, July 1, 1904.

24. "Jim Hill": "The Tumbling Mustard," June 1906 MSS. in R. Kent

Beattie Papers, 1899–1956, MASC/WSU. On state weed law: Beattie to Peter McGregor, January 25, March 3, 1907, Beattie Papers; Washington State, *Journal of the House* (1907), pp. 159–61, 692, 936. On Whitman County weed regulation: Colfax *Commoner*, June 25, 1909. For typical complaints about the invading weeds, see *Rural Northwest*, December 1, 1896, and *Ranch and Range*, February 22, 1900 (China lettuce); *Rural Northwest*, September 1, 1897 (morning glory); *Commercial Review*, June 30, 1916 (wild oats); and *Ranch and Range*, July 22, 1897 (Canada thistle).

25. "Great value" of hairy vetch: *Rural Northwest*, June 1, 1898; *Ranch and Range*, October 27, 1898. Complaints about vetch: *Ranch and Range*, November 3, 1898, January 4, 1900. On fertilizers: *Ranch and Range*, May 14, 1898, June 23, 1894; *Washington Farmer*, May 15, 1919; see also "Cost and Value of Nitrogen," *The Ranch*, January 31, 1901.

26. *Spokesman-Review*, May 6, 1909; Washington State, Department of Dry Land Demonstration, "First Annual Report," Washington AES Bulletin 119 (January 1915), pp. 4–5; Country Life Commission quoted in Theodore Salutos and John D. Hicks, *Agricultural Discontent in the Middle West, 1900–1939*, p. 20. Byron Hunter's 1907 study of the wheat country said nothing about erosion, but his 1919 revision had the following subtitles: "Summerfallowing Blow Soils," "Suggestions for Preventing the Blowing of Soils," "Suggestions for Stopping Soil Blows," and "Maintaining the Organic Matter." The changed emphasis indicated the seriousness of the problem and the increased concern of agricultural scientists about the condition of the farmland. See Hunter, "Dry Farming for Better Wheat Yields," USDA Farmers' Bulletin 1047 (July 1919).

27. "What Spillman Is Doing," *The Ranch*, April 1, 1904. On theories of soil origin, see also Hunter, "Farm Practice in the Columbia Basin Uplands," p. 11, and Meinig, *Great Columbia Plain*, pp. 419–27.

28. On erosion: interview with Carl Penner; Ernest McCaw interview, WCAT/Walla Walla; interview with Harley Jacquot. On squirrels: interview with Lenora Torgeson; Fred Clemens, "Remembering" (MSS.), p. 49. On crickets: interview with Virgil Bennington; Washington State, Department of Agriculture, "Third Biennial Report to the Governor" (1916–18), pp. 12–14. Much of the early work of experiment stations was devoted to these types of immediate problems (see Willis Peterson and Joseph Fitzharris, "The Organization and Productivity of the Federal-State Research System in the United States," Conference on Resource Allocation and Productivity in International Agricultural Research, University of Minnesota Economic Development Center, 1974).

29. On harvest methods: *Spokesman-Review*, August 30, 1909. On headers, binders, and climatic conditions: Leo Rogin, *The Introduction of Farm Machinery in Its Relation to the Production of Labor in the Agriculture of the United States During the Nineteenth Century*, p. 105. On machinery costs: Spokane General Agency, machine sales, and Northwest General Agency, Annual Statements, 3m/71L, McCormick collection, Wisconsin State His-

torical Society, Madison. On binders: *Rural Northwest*, November 15, 1898. On the importance of headers: Malin, *Winter Wheat in the Golden Belt of Kansas*, p. 62. On headers and threshers in operation: Colfax *Gazette*, August 30, 1901, July 22, 1904.

30. On combines in California: Rogin, *Introduction of Farm Machinery*, pp. 145–52. In Washington: Keith, *Horse Interlude*, pp. 67–69. Combines were in general use on the Pacific Slope well ahead of the rest of the nation. Less than 5 percent of the nation's wheat was cut by combines in 1925. See William L. Cavert, "The Technological Revolution in Agriculture, 1910–1955," *Agricultural History* 30:1 (January 1956): 19.

31. On McGregor binder: Alex C. McGregor in Leeper, "Memoirs and Reminiscences," (MSS.), pp. 56–57. On Haines-Houser: Endicott, Washington, *Index*, September 23, 1904, and Colfax *Gazette*, July 29, 1904. On McGregor combines: Conditional sales file, docket 773, Auditor's Office, Whitman County Courthouse, Colfax and harvest files, ML&L/ACM. On "bull wheeled" combines: interviews with Virgil Bennington and Arthur Buhl; Howard Burgess interview, WCAT/Walla Walla. On later models: Fireman's Fund Insurance Company to Archie McGregor, July 16, 1918, ML&L/WSU.

32. On machinery costs: Stewart H. Holbrook, *Machines of Plenty*, pp. 122–23. On rainfall in harvest: *Spokesman-Review*, October 9, October 31, 1905. *Thresherman's Review* quoted in Reynold M. Wik, *Steam Power on the American Farm*, p. 121. Even longer delays had been reported in threshing the 1897 crop: threshing work was not finished in some areas until June 1898 (*Rural Northwest*, June 4, June 11, 1898).

33. On disputes among tenants: interviews with Lenora Torgeson and daily business correspondence from harvest seasons, 1905–20, ML&L/Hooper, ML&L/WSU. On harvest crews: interview with Ernest Osmond; yearly payroll books, ML&L/Hooper, ML&L/WSU; Colfax *Gazette*, August 12, 1904; Joe Ashlock, "The Green Harvest Hand," *Washington Farmer*, July 31, 1919.

34. Alex McGregor, undated MSS., ML&L/ACM, and Lonnie D. Leeper, "Social and Economic History of Hay and Community, 1920–41," master's thesis, WSC, 1941, p. 19. Holbrook, *Machines of Plenty*, p. 125. On acreage covered per day, see Washington State, Bureau of Statistics, "Biennial Report," p. 71. A threshing hand, asked by his boss to conduct an evening prayer meeting, wryly "besought Divine assistance for each member of the crew," including "the sack-sewers, that they might so sew that the over-particular rancher would pronounce it so-so, when he came to examine it" ("The Thresherman's Prayer," *Ranch and Range*, September 22, 1898).

35. Clemens, "Remembering" (MSS.), p. 22; interviews with Lenora Torgeson and Harley Jacquot; William O. Douglas, *Go East Young Man*, p. 76. Also see Kirby Brumfield, *This Was Wheat Farming*, p. 56, and Keith, *Horse Interlude*, pp. 119–21.

36. Clemens, "Remembering" (MSS.), p. 23; Ernest McCaw interview WCAT/Walla Walla; interviews with Louis Banks and Ernest Osmond. Derrick table and forker: Brumfield, *This Was Wheat Farming*, p. 60; interview with Arthur Buhl. Illustrations of Jackson fork and other implements are in Rogin, *Introduction of Farm Machinery*, pp. 141, 143, 190.

37. Interviews with Lenora Torgeson, Dallas Hooper, Ernest Osmond; Virgil Bennington interview, WCAT/Walla Walla; H. L. Davis, *Team Bells Woke Me*, p. 216; harvest correspondence in ML&L/Hooper.

38. On size of engines: Wik, *Steam Power*, p. 108. On McGregor equipment: ML&L to J. I. Case Company, October 27, 1919, ML&L/ACM; interview with Lenora Torgeson. On firemen: Davis, *Team Bells Woke Me*, p. 223; interview with Arthur Buhl; *The Thresher's Guide*, p. 46. Engineers used the steam whistle to signal the opening, closing, or temporary stoppage of work: one short meant stop; two shorts—commence work; one long and three shorts—low on water; continuous shorts—distress (see G. F. Conner, *Science of Threshing*, p. 138).

39. Interview with Arthur Buhl. Engineer: *Thresher's Guide*, p. 8. Threshing accidents: Wik, *Steam Power*, pp. 115, 128. Separator: Clemens, "Remembering" (MSS.), pp. 24–25; interview with Lenora Torgeson. See also "Thresher Man Hurt; Is Dying," *Spokesman-Review*, August 7, 1908, which tells of a harvester who suffered a fractured skull in a drive belt accident.

40. Interviews with Ernest Osmond and Arthur Buhl; Carl Penner interview, WCAT/Walla Walla; Clemens, "Remembering" (MSS.), pp. 25–26.

41. *Washington Farmer*, July 10, 1919; Howard Burgess interview, WCAT/Walla Walla. On sack hauling: interview with Ernest Osmond. On water hauling problems: Ernest McCaw and Carl Penner interviews, WCAT/Walla Walla; wheat sales file, ML&L/WSU.

42. Interview with Lenora Torgeson. W. H. Babcock, said to be "the wheat king of Walla Walla," with 6,000 acres of wheat, had a crew of 120 men. *Ranch and Range* on August 20, 1898, reported: "To feed the large number of men employed, one fat steer each day has been killed the past month, and 13 sacks of potatoes, two sacks of cabbage, and two sacks of beets plus numerous other edibles disappear each week from the tables of this large farmer."

43. *Ranch and Range*, July 23, 1898. Harvesters leave Minneapolis: Wik, *Steam Power*, p. 114. On the lives of migrant harvesters: Patrick Renshaw, *The Wobblies*, p. 117; *Ranch and Range*, July 23, 1898; interviews with Max Torrance, Ralph Snyder, Dallas Hooper, and Howard Burgess; also see Brumfield, *Wheat Farming*, p. 109. On McGregor employees: see "Employees Hired—1919," from 1919 files, ML&L/WSU. Before 1920 Lawrence's Employment Agency of Spokane was used to secure ranch hands. After World War II, McGregors hired "occasional laborers" through Barlows, a run-down bar and employment agency in Spokane. The writer irrigated alfalfa fields, herded sheep, hauled hay, and did other jobs with some of

these men. Some were alcoholics who stayed only briefly, got drunk, and decided to leave. Others were more durable. Most had melancholy stories about losing their jobs and families and taking up seasonal labor when all else failed.

44. Interview with Arthur Buhl; Franz Wood quoted in Holbrook, *Machines of Plenty*, p. 128; interviews with Ernest Osmond. On Tom Darr: interview with Lenora Torgeson. Ernest McCaw and Howard Burgess interviews, WCAT/Walla Walla. On rattlesnakes: Douglas, *Go East, Young Man*, p. 77; see also Brumfield, *Wheat Farming*, p. 109.

45. Interviews with Lenora Torgeson and Dallas Hooper; "Wages of Farm Laborers," in *Prices Received by Washington Farmers, 1910–1959*, p. 69; Howard Burgess interview, WCAT/Walla Walla. On McGregor harvest help: Lacrosse *Clipper*, September 8–October 13, 1916.

46. On work season and pay: Archie McGregor paybook, ML&L/Hooper; McGregor harvest file, ML&L/WSU; and William Thomas memo book, ML&L/ACM. Repairing machines could be time-consuming and costly. During a two-week period in 1917, for example, Advance-Rumley of Spokane, Colfax Iron Works, Walla Walla Iron Works, and other companies were consulted for repairing drapers and feeder castings, replacing belts, and other related problems. Harvest bill on paper headed "Machine Time 33¾ days," 1917 files, ML&L/WSU.

47. On early smut problems: *The Ranch*, April 21, 1894. Later reports: Colfax *Gazette*, August 30, 1901, and similar reports in the other August issues; *The Ranch*, September 15, 1902. "Anti-Smut Club": Colfax *Commoner*, September 10, 1909. On McGregor fires: Lacrosse *Clipper*, August 13, 1915, September 22, 29, 1916. Ira Cardiff estimated that 300 Columbia Plateau separators had had fires, causing a loss in grain and machinery of more than $500,000 in the 1914 harvest season alone (Cardiff et al., "Report on Fires Occurring in Threshing Separators in Eastern Washington During the Summer of 1914," Washington AES Bulletin 117 [November 1914]). *Commercial Review* of August 25 and December 21, 1916, estimated that smut caused a loss of 5 to 15 million dollars per year for Inland Empire farmers. The 1920 crop was 70 to 80 percent infected with smut (Washington State, Department of Agriculture, "Fifth Biennial Report to the Governor" [1920–22] p. 22).

48. On Harvest Hands Union: Colfax *Gazette*, July 12, July 26, 1901; *The Ranch*, July 11, 1901. On Chief of Police Sullivan: *Spokesman-Review*, November 24, 1909. On I. W. W. efforts in harvest fields: *Spokesman-Review*, August 6, 1909; August 11, 1910; July 18, 1911; August 26, 1913.

49. Pro-German allegations: *Spokesman-Review*, February 7, 1918, "Colfax to Arm Against I.W.W." On "undesirable aliens": *Spokesman-Review*, August 17, 18, 1917. On Agricultural Workers Organization and Joe Hill song: Patrick Renshaw, *The Wobblies*, pp. 174–81; also see Nels Anderson, *The Hobo*, p. 208, and Elizabeth Gurley Flynn, *I Speak My Own Piece*, p. 189. On

Zane Grey: interviews with Earl and Ralph Snyder and Grey's novel, *The Desert of Wheat*.

50. On the general strike: Carl F. Reuss, "The Farm Labor Problem in Washington, 1917–18," *PNQ* 34:4 (October 1943): p. 345. On lack of evidence of I.W.W. violence: Keith, *Horse Interlude*, p. 121, and interviews with several farmers. On goals of bindle stiffs: interview with Max Torrance. On Joe Frost: interview with Ralph Snyder. On McGregor ranch strike: interview with Sherman McGregor. On labor-saving machinery: interview with Arthur Buhl; R. S. Washburn, "Cost of Using Horses, Tractors, and Combines on Wheat Farms in Sherman County, Oregon," USDA Bulletin 1447 (December 1926).

51. On "Golden Era": Gilbert Fite, *American Agriculture and Farm Policy Since 1900*, p. 3; Morton Rothstein, "New Frontiers and New Rivals" (from MSS. on American grain trade), p. 410. On prices: "Price of Wheat and Index of Wholesale Prices of All Commodities, 1860–1945," USDA Farm Credit Administration, undated paper, ML&L/Hooper. On Cox and farmers union: Colfax *Commoner*, February 12, March 12, June 4, 1909. More typical of convention topics were the following presentations at a December 21, 1916, meeting of growers, shippers, and millers in Pullman: "Milling Values of Different Varieties of Wheat," "Controlling Smut," "Bulk Millers and Sack Handling of Grain" (see materials on 1916 meeting in WSU Archives).

52. *The Ranch*, August 15, 1904. On inexhaustible soil: Meinig, *Great Columbia Plain*, p. 424, and interview with Harley Jacquot. Harvest reports: *Spokesman-Review*, August 2, 1906; May 25, November, 11, 1907; *The Coast*, December 1907, pp. 388, 432. See the chart of wheat prices in Crawford, *The Washington State Grange*, p. 119. Peter McGregor comments: *Spokesman-Review*, January 6, February 8, 1908.

53. *Spokesman-Review*, February 23, May 14, August 7, 1908. Yields: "Wheat and Flour Investigations," Washington AES Bulletin 100 (1911). "Highest ever": *Spokesman-Review*, February 11, 1909. Whitman County: Nesbit and Gates, "Agriculture in Eastern Washington, 1890–1910," p. 283.

54. Lacrosse *Clipper*, July 29, 1910; Colfax *Gazette*, November 18, 1910; *Spokesman-Review*, April 19, 1911; Colfax *Commoner*, July 15, 1910; Archie McGregor statement of January 6, 1911, filed with 1909 and 1910 income tax returns, ML&L/Hooper. C. J. Storey, longtime McGregor Land and Livestock accountant, was very helpful in interpreting this income tax information.

55. *Spokesman-Review*, April 17, May 22, June 11, 1911; *Commercial Review*, 1911 Annual Report; Washington State, Department of Agriculture, "Second Report to the Governor," (1914–16), p. 15. On the McGregor crops: Lacrosse *Clipper*, March 29, 1912, and correspondence and statistical information in "Wheat Crops" file, ML&L/ACM.

56. *Spokesman-Review*, October 21, 1914, March 2, 1915; Lacrosse *Clip-*

per, August 13, 1915; bank statements, tax returns, and other materials in ML&L/Lemaster and Daniels, ML&L/Hooper, ML&L/WSU.

57. On wheat export: *Commercial Review*, March 9, 1916; Colfax *Gazette*, November 30, 1900. On McGregor wheat: *Spokesman-Review*, August 15, 1916; Lacrosse *Clipper*, August 25, 1916. On George Drumheller: *Commercial Review*, April 13, 1916. Outlook for crop: *Commercial Review*, April 6, May 4, May 11, August 18, 1916. On grain hauling: Lacrosse *Clipper*, August 11, October 13, 1916.

58. *Commercial Review*, April 19, 1917; McGregor Land and Livestock annual statements, ML&L/Hooper; Lacrosse *Clipper*, May 4, 1917; *Spokesman-Review*, April 28, 1917.

59. E. E. Flood to H. R. Rudd, April 23, and November 18, 1918, ML&L/WSU. McGregor statement: E. E. Flood to H. R. Rudd, April 17, 1918, ML&L/WSU. Archie, John, and Alex: H. R. Rudd to collector of Internal Revenue, June 21, 1918, ML&L/Lemaster and Daniels.

60. Correspondence and invoices in "elevator construction" file, ML&L/ACM; ML&L to White-Dulaney Grain Company, July 14, 1920, ML&L/ACM; 1919 journal of wheat sales, ML&L/WSU. Total receipts were $112,473 for the period September 22, 1919, to July 13, 1920 (see warehouse receipts and "Detailed Account of Notes and Accounts Receivable of McGregor Land and Livestock as of December 31, 1920," ML&L/WSU). Shipmasters for many years refused to carry bulk grain, fearing that the load would shift dangerously during the 18,000-mile voyage to British markets. The steep hills of the Columbia Plateau also created difficulties for the movement of large amounts of bulked grain. See Neil Johnson and E. F. Landerholm, "Farm-Management Problems in Shifting from Sack to Bulk Handling of Grain in the Pacific Northwest," USDA Technical Bulletin 287 (February 1932); also see *Commercial Review*, April 27, 1916.

61. Journal of wheat sales, ML&L/WSU. On wartime slogan and statistics: William E. Leonard, "The Wheat Farmer of Southeastern Washington," *Journal of Land and Public Utility Economics* 2 (January 1926): pp. 27–34. On $2 wheat: *Washington Farmer*, February 6, 1919; also see Salutos and Hicks, *Agricultural Discontent*, p. 101. On tractor demonstration and bank loans: *Washington Farmer*, April 17, May 1, 1919. Quote is from Leonard, "Wheat Farmer of Southeastern Washington," pp. 28, 31. On Washington wheat: O. E. Baker, "A Graphic Summary of American Agriculture," in USDA *Yearbook of Agriculture* (1921), p. 527.

62. *Washington Farmer*, June 19, 1919; also see Spillman interview in March 6, 1919, issue. On Palouse country farmers: M. R. Cooper, "Cost of Wheat Production and Incomes from Farming in Eastern Washington and Northern Idaho for the Years 1919, 1920, and 1921," USDA Division of Cost Production and Farm Management (December 1923), p. 4. On price drop: G. F. Warren, "Prices of Farm Products in the United States," USDA bulletin 999 (August 26, 1921), p. 22. On tenants: bills of sale 1920–24, ML&L/ACM, ML&L/WSU.

CHAPTER 7

"A Remarkable Region":
Exploring New Business Opportunities
and Life in a Company Town, 1905–20

1. H. L. Davis, *Honey in the Horn*, p. 279; *The Coast* (December 1907), p. 432; *Spokesman-Review*, February 23, 1919. Davis described the wild optimism in the context of hopes for rail service. But the enthusiasm was not confined to anticipated rail connections—it also reflected the persistent belief that all the semiarid land could become immensely productive.

2. On largest cattle ranch: *The Ranch*, August 7, 1902. On the values of western pioneers: Bogue, "Social Theory and the Pioneer." On role of women: Harvey W. Starling and Fred W. Yoder, "Local Rural Leaders in Washington," Washington AES Bulletin 257 (September 1931), p. 7; Oliver E. Baker, "Agricultural Regions of North America, Part XI: The Columbia Plateau Wheat Region," *Economic Geography* 9:2 (April 1933): 194.

3. On oil wells: Colfax *Gazette*, January 11, 1901; Colfax *Commoner*, November 5, 1909. On sugar beets: *Ranche and Range*, April 22 and May 20, 1897. On businesses of Hooper: "Whitman County Directory, 1908–1909," and similar publications of the R. L. Polk Company of Seattle; weekly "Hooper Happenings" column of Lacrosse *Clipper* and Hooper columns in issues of the Colfax *Gazette*. On potential crops for irrigable lands: John C. Murphy, *The Facts Concerning the Government Palouse Project*, p. 4. The population projections are in L. N. B. Anderson, "Connell," *The Coast*, January 1911, and S. J. Chadwick, "Whitman County," *The Coast*, December 1907. Lots in Cascade City were sold at varying prices, ranging from a gift with a bottle of $2.50 patent medicine to $250 (see *Illustrated History of the Big Bend Country*, pp. 788–89, and "Cascade City" in Ritzville *Journal-Times*, September 15, 1949).

4. Land values: McGregor annual real estate inventories, ML&L/WSU, ML&L/Hooper. Information about use of scrip and purchase of "isolated tracts" based on "Old Deeds" files ML&L/Hooper, deeds on record in the Whitman and Adams County courthouses, and daily business correspondence in ML&L/Hooper and ML&L/WSU. Information about corporate decisions is from record books of McGregor Land and Livestock meetings, ML&L/Hooper.

5. On the use of land laws: letters from U.S. Land Office in 1919 and 1920 files, ML&L/WSU. Archie McGregor to H. R. Rudd, January 10, 13, 16, 1920, ML&L/WSU, ML&L/ACM. A January 6, 1920, letter to former McGregor herder Simon Polmeteer was typical: "For the past five years we have been using a State Land Lease in your name. We should like the privilege, if possible, of re-leasing the land in your name" (ML&L/WSU). All payments were made by McGregors in the name of the various lessees.

6. H. L. Davis, *Team Bells Woke Me*, p. 167; Gilfillan, *Sheep*, pp. 252–53. Also see Brogan, *East of the Cascades*, p. 94. On stock-raising homesteads: *National Wool Grower*, October 1916, March and April 1917. The magnitude of unwise homesteading is illustrated by the fact that 7,278,861 acres of Stock Raising Homesteads claimed in the Pacific Northwest, only 2,611,841 acres were patented (see Karl Landstrom, "The Land Ownership Map Situation in the Pacific Northwest States," USDA Bureau of Agricultural Economics [1934], p. 3).

7. Real estate inventories, corporate minute books, and "Record of Land Sales Contracts, 1905–23," ML&L/Hooper. Profits in land: annual statements (ML&L/Hooper) and inventory books (ML&L/WSU). Comments of correspondents: *Spokesman-Review*, April 19, 1911. Also see Lacrosse *Clipper*, April 17, 1911.

8. Minute book of meetings of the McGregor Land and Livestock Company Board of Trustees, 1905–20, ML&L/Hooper. Also see letter from McGregor Land and Livestock to David J. Williams, March 14, 1918, ML&L/Lemaster and Daniels.

9. Wallace and Wallace correspondence 1916–20, ML&L/Hooper, ML&L/WSU. On Chicago apartments: L. H. Jordan to H. R. Rudd, August 26, September 11, 1922; Peter McGregor to Jordan, October 14, 1922, ML&L/WSU.

10. "Store—General Expense and Receipts, 1915–1934," ledger 192, ML&L/WSU; Alex McGregor in Leeper, ed., "Memoirs and Reminiscences" (MSS.), p. 52. Cox store: see Whitman County directories published by R. L. Polk. Comments of Stanley Coffin and quote about Lewiston store: H. S. Coffin, "Life" (MSS.), pp. 45–46, 120. The Coffin Brothers business had become greatly diversified by 1911. The 1911 letterhead of the Yakima corporation lists the following occupations: "Coffin Brothers, Inc.—Townsites, lands, city property, sheep, wool, produce, horses, cattle, grain, loans, investments. Stores and warehouses in the states of Washington and Idaho." Coffins also operated the Yakima Grocery Company, Coffin-Runstrom Furniture Company, the Dean Clothing Company, and the Filer Townsite Company of Twin Falls, Idaho. Only the grocery company was a financial success. Based on information in files of Coffin Sheep Company.

11. Alex McGregor in Leeper, "Memoirs and Reminiscences" (MSS.), p. 52; H. R. Rudd comments in "Hooper Hotel" file, 1917, ML&L/WSU, and in "Applications for Work," file, ML&L/ACM. Hooper Hotel ad: Lacrosse *Clipper*, August 21, 1915. Correspondence, invoices, bills of lading, dealership information from ML&L/Hooper.

12. "Substantial boom": Lacrosse *Clipper*, May 12, 1911. Atkinson bill and letter: old safe, ML&L/Hooper. Excerpts from 1907 *Spokesman-Review* articles indicate some of the activities of the "boom" town:

[*May 21, 1907*]: A party of 35 French workmen from San Francisco came in yesterday on the special to do rock drilling and blasting. . . . The new railroad hospital is completed and is now being painted.

[*June 15, 1907*]: Chas. Anderson, a foreman at Johnson's and Anderson's Camp, was instantly killed and his two Austrian helpers injured yesterday by a premature explosion of powder. . . . John Ray and Peter Frazer, from Kippel, Idaho, came here to look up a location for a saloon. They decided that five saloons were enough for North Hooper and went on to Cheney.

[*June 20, 1907*]: Edstrom and Larsen have opened . . . [another] saloon.

[*Sept. 29, 1907*]: Nicholas Michaels has leased the Pioneer Restaurant, adjoining the Pioneer saloon.

[*Nov. 11, 1907*]: W. R. Pope, subcontractor on the Portland and Seattle construction work under Twohy Brothers . . . was standing directly over . . . [a] drill hole when the powder exploded and threw him 20 feet to one side and covered him with rocks and earth. . . . Pope was considerably mangled. . . . A saloon and dance hall in North Hooper . . . was closed Friday by the order of the Sheriff.

13. Washtucna *Enterprise*, February 5, 1915; McGregor Land and Livestock minute book, April, 1915, ML&L/Hooper; Lacrosse *Clipper*, November 12, 1915. The total fire loss was more than fifteen thousand dollars. Details about new structure: Lacrosse *Clipper*, May 12, June 2, 23, 1916, and *Spokesman-Review*, June 10, 1916. On red letter day for Hooper: Lacrosse *Clipper*, June 16, 1916. Also see "Store Construction" file, Sherman McGregor collection, which includes contractual agreements, labor expenses, bond and surety agreements, and assorted other materials.

14. William McGregor, Annan, Ontario, to the writer, July 8, 1973; 1915 payroll, ML&L/WSU; correspondence and store invoices from daily business records, ML&L/WSU and ML&L/ACM; interview with Ralph Snyder; interview with William McGregor of Hooper.

15. "Detailed Account of Notes and Accounts Receivable. . . . ," ML&L/WSU; "Profit and Loss" folder, ML&L/Hooper; 1917–22 accounts receivable correspondence, ML&L/Hooper. The corporation also took debtors to superior court and got garnishment of wages or was awarded lands owned by the defendants. See *McGregor Land and Livestock* v. *H. A. Brown*, case 9913, May 2, 1908; and *McGregor Land and Livestock* v. *A. R. Trogden*, case 13327, July 1918, both in Whitman County Superior Court records, Colfax, and numerous other Whitman and Adams County cases on file in the county courthouses. "Get his money": McGregor Land and Livestock to A. Barrow, 1922, McGregor Land and Livestock to H. W. Canfield, September 12, 1922, in "Profit and Loss" folder, ML&L/Hooper. On September 16, 1922, Rudd wrote a note for the folder with the comment that, with two minor exceptions, "we will not lose a dollar on accounts this year although we have had a close call on several."

16. ML&L to C. P. Blankenship, June 7, 1923, ML&L/WSU; McGregor Land and Livestock to E. E. Flood, undated 1923 letter, ML&L/ACM; annual statements, ML&L/Hooper.

17. "Notes Payable to Levi Ankeny"; land sales contract, payroll books,

and articles of incorporation for Taylor Land and Livestock, all in ML&L/ Hooper; interviews with Ralph Snyder and Mrs. W. Davis; Lacrosse *Clipper*, January 27, 1911; annual inventories, statements, and tax returns for McGregor and Taylor companies, ML&L/Hooper. A. J. Hooper estate: *In re Hooper's Estate* (*McGregor* v. *Hooper et al.*), Supreme Court of Washington, October 18, 1913. On the size of the Taylor operations after the Hooper lease: *Spokesman-Review*, January 30, 1910.

18. Alex T. "got whatever he wanted to take": *McGregor* v. *McGregor et al.* (a suit against Alex T. by his ex-wife), Supreme Court of Washington, August 1, 1946. On missing cattle: Alex T. McGregor to Whitman County Sheriff, December 13, 1919, ML&L/WSU. On death of foreman: According to State Supreme Court testimony, Alex T. invited the bootleggers into his home, drank for several hours with them, left the room with "his face and clothing covered with blood, and apparently in an intoxicated condition." Johnson, the foreman, arrived, tried to stop the trouble, and was fatally shot by the bootleggers. The court case involved an unsuccessful attempt by an insurance company to avoid paying Johnson's heirs. *McGregor* v. *New World Life Insurance Company*, Supreme Court of Washington, July 24, 1931. Also see 1930 daybook of Maurice McGregor, ML&L/ WSU. Interview with Ralph Snyder.

19. Interviews with John, William, and Sherman McGregor; interview with Ralph Snyder. On sale of sheep: interview with Emile Morod and letters in Taylor files, ML&L/Hooper. The Taylor corporation ran as many as nine thousand sheep on the winter range and leased and purchased summer grazing grounds near Priest Lake in northern Idaho.

20. Interview with Ralph Snyder; 1912 daybook of H. S. Coffin quoted in Coffin, "Life" (MSS.), p. 53; "Rosario Mines" file, Coffin Sheep Company, Yakima. Sheepman F. M. Rothrock wrote his friend, John McGregor, in 1913 about mining stock he had purchased in John's behalf: "The mining stock keeps me broke but I think it O.K. and it looks to me like a good buy at the price" (letter in ML&L/Hooper).

21. Mining stock files, ML&L/Hooper, ML&L/ACM. In particular, see letters from A. C. Cronin of Eldorado Petroleum and Refining Snydicate, Cheyenne, Wyoming, to Archie and Peter, May 1, 1918; from Tamarack and Custer Mining, Wallace, Idaho, to John, March 4, 1915; and numerous mining stock certificates from companies owned by Pickrell, Edris, and Quinlan. The letter to Peter McGregor is from Joseph Rosslow, secretary of Butte and Coeur d'Alene Mining, December 31, 1917. Alameda company: corporate minute book, deeds, and correspondence, ML&L/Hooper, ML&L/ WSU. J. L. Jackson, a Starbuck sheepman, was one of the woolgrowers who avoided the temptation to speculate in mining stock. In a 1921 interview he claimed, "Ten dollars goes into the ground for every dollar that is taken out . . . I've never invested a dollar in mining or oil stocks and I never intend to. I am a sheepman and when I make investments it is in sheep" (Walla Walla *Up-to-the Times* magazine, May 1921, p. 2881).

22. G. A. Raymer to Archie McGregor, May 25, 1918, ML&L/WSU; "material, supplies, and payroll" invoices and Alameda corporate records, ML&L/ACM; "Statement in Regard to Status of Alameda Mines Co," May 18, 1918, ML&L/WSU. Also see "Sketch Showing the Alameda, Silver King, Blue Ribbon, and Shipper Groups," MB/Glendale. On the supposed rush of miners: F. P. Maguire to Archie, January 10, January 18, 1917, ML&L/ Hooper. Archie's complaint about mining literature: Archie to Maurice McGregor, 1938, ML&L/WSU. On Peter McGregor: interview with Emile Morod. "Taking of losses": McGregor Land and Livestock to David J. Williams, collector, January 19, 1921. Williams' response was that "proof must be submitted that the mine has been permanently abandoned as worthless" (Williams to ML&L, January 23, 1921, ML&L/WSU).

23. On blessing of aridity and miracle of irrigation: William E. Smythe, *The Conquest of Arid America*, pp. 34, 41. On speculation and the Yakima project: Coulter, "The Victory of National Irrigation," p. 101. On N. G. Blalock: interview with Ralph Snyder. On a Snake River irrigation scheme for lands near Pasco: *The Ranch*, April 1, 1905.

24. Tacoma *Daily Ledger*, June 22, 1892; *The Ranch*, June 9, 1894; *Ranche and Range*, June 17, 1897, and January 8, 1898; Smythe, *Conquest of Arid America*, p. 321. See the comments about the "exceptional merit" of the Palouse plan in E. McCulloh, "The Palouse Project" in *Proceedings of the Third Annual Meeting of the Washington Irrigation Institute*. Also see the extensive Palouse Irrigation and Power Company records in ML&L/WSU and ML&L/Hooper.

25. The Adams County Index of Corporations in the Adams County Courthouse, Ritzville, lists the companies that attempted to complete the Palouse project. Also see irrigation deeds and abstracts, ML&L/WSU, ML&L/Hooper. Some of the problems encountered are described in Fronek, "Pioneering in the Lower Palouse and Lacrosse Country" (MSS.), p. 18. Information about Reclamation Service investigation: Coulter, "The Victory of National Irrigation," pp. 109–10. "Larceny" of project: Murphy, *The Facts Concerning the Government Palouse Project*, p. 14. Also see the comments of Wesley Jones in "The Victory of National Irrigation," *Washington Magazine* 1:4 (June 1906): 255.

26. Land and water contracts, Palouse Irrigation and Power, ML&L/ Hooper, ML&L/WSU. A proposal to build a dam across the two-hundred-foot-deep canyon at Palouse Falls, on the McGregor ranch, was also debated (see C. J. Oberholtzer, "Development of Palouse Falls," bachelor's thesis, WSC, 1910). On irrigation of Palouse valley: *Spokesman-Review*, June 18, 1907; *The Coast*, January 1911, p. 15; interview with Ralph Snyder. On McGregor orchards: interviews with Emile Morod and Sherman McGregor; orchard maps and correspondence and payroll books, ML&L/Hooper; Lacrosse *Clipper*, February 9, 1917; O. J. Judd to McGregor Land and Livestock, November 25, 1921, ML&L/WSU.

27. Palouse Irrigation and Power, 1908–10 cash journals and minute books,

files 256 and 274, ML&L/WSU; "Washington Exploitatie Maatschappy" (Washington Development Company), a firm organized by a lawyer, a banker, and two stockbrokers from Rotterdam, has correspondence in ML&L/Hooper. The power plant at Gildersleeve Falls, on the Palouse River, exploded, killing the night watchman (see Washtucna *Enterprise*, January 28, 1916). On Rock Lake storage problems: *Still et al.* v. *Palouse Irrigation and Power Company, et al.*, Supreme Court of Washington, August 19, 1911. On maintenance problems: Roy Zahren to Receiver John Kelleher, ten letters written between March 2 and September 4, 1913, in ML&L/WSU. Also see "Report on Operation of Canal for Season of 1912," ML&L/WSU.

28. On the decision to dig artesian wells, see minute book of the meetings of the trustees of the McGregor Land and Livestock Company, August 16, 1915. The results of the well drilling are discussed in *Spokesman-Review*, February 22, 1909; Washtucna *Enterprise*, October 2, 1914; and Lacrosse *Clipper*, June 25, 1915. Also see letter from Eugene Taylor to John McGregor, December 13, 1915, ML&L/ACM. On McGregors as customers: Kelleher to Zahren, May 31, 1912, Zahren to Kelleher, June 5, 16, 22, 1912, April 9, 1913, ML&L/WSU.

29. J. N. Pickrell to Archie McGregor, May 5, 1917, and Hooper Realty minute book, ML&L/WSU; articles of incorporation and purchase agreements, ML&L/ACM. On government hydrologists: Lacrosse *Clipper*, June 25, 1915; interview with Sherman McGregor. On well drilling problems: Hooper Realty to C. Carlson, June 27, 1917, ML&L/WSU; Lacrosse *Clipper*, August 31, 1917. Financial information: annual statements; "Report of the Chief Engineer on Investigation of Financial Records of the Hooper Realty Company," Washington State Department of Public Works, Division of Public Utilities, September 1921; and Archie McGregor to Z. E. Merriel, Engineer of Public Service Commission, July 15, 1920, all in ML&L/ACM.

30. Hooper Realty to C. Carlson, June 27, 1917, to Homer Bull, July 26, 1917, to Corporal W. C. Allan, November 19, 1919, all from ML&L/WSU. Investigation of project: see citation and "Findings of Fact and Order" of *The Public Service Commission of Washington ex. rel. G. W. Bassett et al.* v. *Hooper Realty Company*, June 15, 1920, and May 17, 1921, ML&L/Hooper. McGregor response: Hooper Realty to Public Service Commission, June 21, July 15, September 18, October 7, 1920, ML&L/ACM.

31. Hooper Realty statements in ML&L/Hooper; Archie McGregor, 1919 daybook, MB/Glendale. Quote is from Archie McGregor to Z. E. Merriel, July 15, 1920, ML&L/ACM. Archie McGregor described the sheep purchase in a letter to J. L. Lytell on February 4, 1921: "This company engaged in the sheep business 1½ years ago, but in the great depression which struck our business we went broke and now have no money and cannot get any" (ML&L/WSU). On the changing market value of lamb, see *Prices Received by Washington Farmers, 1910–1959*, p. 33.

32. Transfer of ditch to water users: Department of Public Works to

Hooper Realty, June 14, 1922, ML&L/WSU. Loans to Hooper Realty: corporate financial records, ML&L/ACM, and from interviews with Ralph Snyder, Emile Morod, and Sherman McGregor. Sale to parent company: bill of sale and several letters to McGregor lawyer H. W. Canfield, all in ML&L/Hooper. Rudd's comments: H. R. Rudd to L. H. Jordan, September 16, 1922; Rudd to Commissioner of Internal Revenue, July 30, 1922; also see Rudd to Canfield, October 22, 1925, all in ML&L/WSU.

33. Archie McGregor, personal account, 1922; Archie McGregor, correspondence 1919-25, ML&L/ACM; interview with Ralph Snyder.

34. Maurice McGregor to John A. Healy, September 2, 1935, ML&L/Hooper.

35. The major source for the materials included above is interviews with Ralph Snyder. Also based on a series of materials from interviews and various trade journals.

36. On some of the social activities of the Hooper area: Colfax *Gazette*, November 16, 1900, January 11, July 12, July 26, 1901, January 3, 1902; Colfax *Commoner*, June 25, 1909; John Harder in *Told by the Pioneers* 3:62–64. Quote is from Marie Boone, MSS, in MB/Glendale.

37. Interviews with Ralph Snyder, Sherman McGregor, Mr. and Mrs. George Thorp; Colfax *Gazette*, August 23, 1901.

38. H. S. Coffin, "Life" (MSS.), pp. 56, 86. A program from one of the Ladies Aid Socials of 1909 is in MB/Glendale. On travels of McGregors: W. P. Telford to Archie, September 7, 1919, and Jennie McGregor postcards and scrapbooks, ML&L/ACM. On activities of McGregor women: Euphemia MacGregor to Belle Bothwell, December 20, 1895, ML&L/ACM; Euphemia's reminiscences, MSD/Calgary; Colfax *Gazette*, July 21, 1905; Lacrosse *Clipper*, September 1, 1911. Archie McGregor is quoted from May 13, 1918, letter to his mother, MSD/Calgary.

39. Alex McGregor to Genevieve McGregor, March 6, 1945, MB/Glendale; church register for Hooper, 1901-26, ML&L/Hooper; Rev. J. A. Cooper to Alex McGregor, April 1, 1919, ML&L/ACM; W. P. Telford, "Appreciation of McGregor Family's Success in the West," Owen Sound, Ontario, *Sun-Times*, May 16, 1919.

40. Interviews with Marie Boone, Ralph Snyder, and Sherman McGregor; *Plat Book of Whitman County*, p. 76; *Spokesman-Review*, June 10, 1916. On stockyards: John McGregor to William Connolly, May 29, June 5, 1915, Sherman McGregor collection.

41. On Hooper school: Alex McGregor in Leeper, "Memoirs and Reminiscences" (MSS.), p. 53; old school records, ML&L/Hooper. The "Meltz Brothers Orchestra" was a typical dance band at Hooper, and featured "Spotlight dances, circular two steps, moonlight waltzes, tag dances, ladies choice, etc." (Meltz Brothers to ML&L, January 4, 1922, ML&L/WSU). Typical movies rented by McGregors for the "Hooper Theatre" were those

of June 9, 1922: "Teasing the Soil," "What's your Husband Doing?," "Valley of Giants" (invoice in ML&L/WSU). June 21, 1922, sample issue of the "Hooper Herald" is in daily business correspondence in ML&L/WSU. Comments about the company town are based on interviews with several residents and on the writer's recollections of growing up in Hooper.

42. Interviews with Mr. and Mrs. G. Thorp, Ralph Snyder, and personal correspondence of the McGregor families during the years 1911–20, ML&L/ACM. Interviews with Willard Burden and Norma McGregor, Hooper residents of later decades, were useful in describing the undercurrent of bitterness and resentment. Quote is from 1949 letter in MB/Glendale. The antagonistic feelings were sometimes expressed in small ways: the man employed to bring fresh milk to the McGregor families, instead of refilling the buckets after each stop, simply diluted the remaining milk with river water from the irrigation ditch before proceeding to the next house (interview with Sherman McGregor).

43. Marie Boone MSS., MB/Glendale. Mrs. Boone also recalled Nellie's responsibilities when her three-month-old daughter, Jessie, became sick during a smallpox epidemic: "They had to go in isolation for the prescribed time so were moved to a room that had previously been built over the cellar. Snow was on the ground and it was bitter cold. But luckily a heating stove was in the room. Food and water was taken up from the big house and left at the door. Nellie would open the door after Archie's departure—take in the provisions and quickly close the door so that the germs would not 'jump out' and infect anyone nearby. She would boil the dishes before sending them back to the house where they were again sterilized."

44. Wallace Stegner, *Wolf Willow*, p. 23. On the activities of farm wives: Inez Arnquist and Evelyn Roberts, "The Present Use of Work Time of Farm Homemakers," Washington AES Bulletin 234 (July 1929); Starling and Yoder, "Local Rural Leaders in Washington." On McGregor households: interviews with Mary McGregor Hazeltine and Norma McGregor. On Jennie McGregor: interviews with Norma and Sherman McGregor. Elgin McGregor comments are in MSS. in ML&L/Hooper. Despite some disputes on society matters, in time of crisis the family acted with unity. See letter from Jennie McGregor's brother, Cliff Sherman, to her husband Alex on the Hooper community's response to Jennie's illness with pneumonia, May 30, 1908, ML&L/ACM.

45. Lacrosse *Clipper*, September 3, 10, 17, October 8, 1915, November 16, 1917. On fundraising drives, dances, and Rally Day services: Lacrosse *Clipper*, October 5, November 16, 1917. Quote about Liberty Bond drive: H. R. Rudd to E. E. Flood, October 15, 1918, ML&L/WSU.

46. On women's clubs of the Palouse: E. A. Taylor and F. R. Yoder, "Rural Social Organization in Whitman County," Washington AES Bulletin 203 (June 1926), p. 23. Records of "Get Together Club" and the C. C. Club, 1920–65, are in ML&L/ACM. On disputes among club members: interviews with William, Sherman, and Norma McGregor. On Minnie and

Maude McGregor: interviews with Mr. and Mrs. George Thorp, Ralph Snyder, Sherman McGregor, and reminiscences of Euphemia MacGregor, MSS. in MSD/Calgary. On Jennie McGregor: interview with Norma McGregor. On Nellie McGregor: letters and notebooks in ML&L/ACM and MB/Glendale. Davis' sardonic description of small town life is in *Team Bells Woke Me*, pp. 174–75, 190. See the more impartial comments of Lewis Atherton in "The Midwestern Country Town: Myth and Reality," *Agricultural History* 26:3 (July 1952): 73–79.

47. H. R. Rudd to the collector of Internal Revenue, June 21, 1918. Peter McGregor on direct primary: Colfax *Gazette*, September 14, September 21, 1906. The controversy about judges is described in Colfax *Commoner*, July 23, 1909. Also see the March 12, July 16, August 27, and September 3, 1909, issues. The comments about "standpat" Republicans are in Colfax *Commoner*, March 2, 1909.

48. On Levi Ankeny, see the attack on his "wrecked memory and vast ignorance" and the description of him as a "Senate undesirable, who is unfit, personally and politically, to represent the state and whose main strength is his bank account," in a 1908 issue of *Collier's* in the "Northwest Biography" file, Pacific Northwest Room, University of Washington Library. Peter McGregor's votes: Journal of the Washington State Senate, 1909, and Colfax *Commoner*, April 2, 1909. Election results: Colfax *Commoner*, September 16, 1910. The impact of progressive reforms in Washington is briefly described in Keith Murray, "Issues and Personalities of Pacific Northwest Politics, 1889–1950," *PNQ* 41:3 (July 1950) 220–23. On the importance of the direct primary in western politics, see Salutos and Hicks, *Agricultural Discontent*, p. 52.

49. Peter McGregor presents "a short biographical sketch of myself" in letters to W. D. Griffin, June 25, 1937, and to John Perrin, Chairman of the Federal Reserve Board, December 23, 1922, ML&L/WSU. Also see letters from Governor Louis Hart to Peter McGregor, November 23, 1921, ML&L/WSU, and Peter McGregor to W. P. Harding, Governor of Federal Reserve Board, August 4, 1917. On Peter McGregor and the Columbia Basin survey, see *Washington Farmer*, March 27, 1919. The quote about McGregor's political career is from an interview with Ralph Snyder.

50. S. B. Nelson, the head of the Washington State College veterinary department, writes of his friendship with John McGregor and McGregor's role in the livestock industry in a eulogy in MSD/Calgary. On the breakup of the McGregor brothers partnership: "Agreement between Peter McGregor and Archibald McGregor, October 1, 1921" (sale of stock), ML&L/Hooper; Archie McGregor to Maurice McGregor, May 5, 1927, ML&L/WSU; H. R. Rudd to C. P. Schow, August 30, 1922, ML&L/Lemaster and Daniels. Also useful here were interviews with Sherman McGregor, William McGregor, and Marie Boone. Archie's later comments: Archie McGregor to Jessie McGregor Skene and Euphemia MacGregor, February 17, February 21, 1941, MSD/Calgary.

CHAPTER 8

Crisis and Change in Agriculture, 1920–40

1. H. R. Rudd to Shaw and Borden, December 22, 1921, Maurice McGregor to Al Riordan, January 30, 1931, both in ML&L/WSU; Maurice McGregor to C. V. Newman, August 3, 1932, ML&L/Hooper.

2. Lamb crop records, 1920–25, Jock Macrae to Peter McGregor, August 1920, both in ML&L/ACM. On lamb market: H. R. Rudd to Pacific Grain Company, August 19, 1920, ML&L/Hooper. E. J. Burke recalled the 1920 wool clip in his May 8, 1933, letter to Peter McGregor, ML&L/WSU. On Mel Fell: interview with William McGregor. On F. J. Hagenbarth: *National Wool Grower*, January 1921, p. 11.

3. On wheat harvest: McGregor L&L to Nelson Ross, January 17, 1921, ML&L/WSU. On apples: McGregor L&L to Burlington Railroad, December 7, 1920, ML&L/ACM. Accounts receivable: letters in "Profit and Loss" file, ML&L/Hooper. "If we ever needed money": Rudd to Great Northern Railroad, February 21, 1921, ML&L/WSU.

4. Picture and article about White House flock: "Men, Sheep, and 100 Years," *National Wool Grower* (January 1965), p. 48. On declining market prices: Reynold M. Wik, "Henry Ford and the Agricultural Depression of 1920–1923," *Agricultural History* 29:1 (January 1955): 15. On foreclosures: *The Condition of Agriculture in the United States and Measures for Its Improvement*, p. 211. Henry C. Wallace, "The Year in Agriculture," USDA *Yearbook of Agriculture* (1924), p. 17. Also see Glenn Johnson and Leroy Quance, eds., *The Overproduction Trap in U.S. Agriculture*, pp. 159–61.

5. James H. Shideler, *Farm Crisis, 1919–1923*, pp. vii, 2; Earl Heady, *A Primer on Food, Agriculture, and Public Policy*, p. 35. On soil erosion: Donald C. Blaisdell, *Government and Agriculture*, p. 13.

6. Officers: corporate minute book, ML&L/Hooper. On Rudd: interview with Sherman McGregor. On wool: wool sales 1913–26, ML&L/Hooper. On wage cut: R. A. Balch to McGregor L&L, November 22, 1920, and J. F. Sears to Peter McGregor, October 13, 1921, both in ML&L/WSU. On Jock Macrae: letters from sheep crew, ML&L/Hooper, and "Macrae and His Essex," *Spokesman-Review*, August 5, 1923. On economy measures: interview with Emile Morod and Morod and Macrae daybooks, ML&L/Hooper. Wool price: *Prices Received by Washington Farmers*, p. 34. Letter from John Hood to Maurice McGregor, August 26, 1927, ML&L/WSU. Hood never made it back to Scotland. He signed up to work on a Philippine freighter that was headed around the world for final arrival in England. But Hood wrote McGregors from the Far East, complaining that knife fights were common, a mutiny was likely at any moment, and the ship was slowly sinking. McGregors wrote several shipping companies asking about the fate of the vessel. But the ship was never seen again. See "John Hood" file, ML&L/Hooper.

7. ML&L to Babson Statistical Organization, March 29, 1921; Peter McGregor to National Wool Growers Association, July 19, August 13, 1920; ML&L to Dr. Baker, February 21, 1920; ML&L to J. H. Zimmerman, March 10, 1921, all in ML&L/WSU. "This outfit": Peter McGregor to Charles MacKenzie, April 20, 1928, ML&L/Hooper. Commission merchants: A. J. Knollin to ML&L, July 13, August 16, 1927, ML&L/WSU. Industry crippled: F. A. Clarke to McGregor L&L, March 18, 1921, ML&L/WSU. Receipts and expenses: annual inventory books, ML&L/WSU. Taxes and general expenses: see Appendix 3.

8. On tariff: R. L. Rutter to J. Bateman and Company, September 30, 1922, ML&L/Hooper; Blinken, *Wool Tariffs and American Policy*, p. 148; *National Wool Grower* (January 1965), p. 30. Quote is from woolgrowers' circular of February 24, 1922, ML&L/Hooper. Other sheep businesses ran into various difficulties during the postwar slump. Mrs. Cull White married a sheepman in the early twenties and moved from a city to his ranch. During her first winter on the Horse Heaven ranch, prolonged subzero weather caused waterholes to freeze, left a deep snow cover, and caused sheep to die or to become so emaciated they had to be shot. Charles Brune of Yakima tells of a central Washington sheepman of the twenties who got drunk at a bar in a town near his Montana summer range. When he sobered up, the sheepman found that he had promised to marry a prostitute. He hurried home to Yakima but the woman pursued him and began court proceedings. Acting on the advice of his friend, the judge, the sheepman looked as filthy as possible at the trial, with hip boots covered with sheep dung and clothes stained with blood, grime, and sheep dip. The woman dropped the court case. Interviews with Mrs. Cull White and Charles Brune.

9. W. E. Leonard, "Wheat Farmer of Southeastern Washington," pp. 29–35; *Prices Received by Washington Farmers*, p. 45. The *Commercial Review*, a journal of the grain trade, concluded on February 16, 1921: "The price collapse has stricken the whole realm of farm production." Also see M. R. Cooper, "Cost of Wheat Production," p. 11. On Mrs. Jeremiah: H. R. Rudd to Emerson Trading Company, February 2, 1921, ML&L/WSU.

10. "Hog sales" file, ML&L/ACM; hog balance sheet and related correspondence, ML&L/WSU. "Greenhorns" in grain trade: Rudd to Pacific Grain, August 19, 1920, ML&L/ACM. Local grain trade and wheat sales: consigned wheat sales file, ML&L/Hooper, correspondence with Interior Warehouse Company and White-Dulaney Company 1920–1922, ML&L/WSU, and interview with Sherman McGregor.

11. On tenants: departmental expense sheets, ML&L/WSU. On foreclosures: Leonard, "Wheat Farmer of Southeastern Washington," p. 37. Store accounts: H. L. Welty to ML&L, August 27, 1920, ML&L/WSU, and "Profit and Loss" files, ML&L/Hooper.

12. Fireman's Fund to ML&L, June 17, 1920, July 5, 1927. Earnings from miscellaneous businesses are in annual inventory books, ML&L/WSU. On Donald: "Lease Agreement between Peter McGregor and Donald Mc-

Gregor," ML&L/ACM, letter from Maurice to Archie McGregor, June 14, 1928, ML&L/Hooper, and interviews with William and Sherman McGregor. Donald McGregor was not successful in his other careers and he died while still a young man. On "red spider": Department of Horticulture, WSC, to ML&L, August 23, 1920. On aphis wooley: ML&L to Department of Horticulture, February 6, 1920, both in ML&L/WSU. On arsenic: ML&L to Harold Magnuson, September 14, 1926, ML&L/ACM. On the sale of McGregor apples in Baltimore, Chicago, Pittsburgh, Memphis, and Detroit: apple sales data in ML&L/Hooper and ML&L/WSU.

13. Rudd to Shaw and Borden, December 27, 1921; ML&L to G. H. Plummer, October 5, 1921; Plummer to ML&L, October 6, 1921, all in ML&L/ WSU. Strongest and best account: E. E. Flood to H. R. Rudd, April 17, 1918, ML&L/WSU. On Rocky Mountain oyster fry: interview with Ralph Snyder. On McGregors and bank: correspondence of Peter and Alex C. McGregor, ML&L/Hooper. On loans called in: Spencer and Hall. "The Sheep Industry," p. 246.

14. ML&L to Exchange National Bank, May 6, 1920; E. T. Coman to ML&L, January 3, 1921; Exchange bank to ML&L, January 11, January 22, 1921; ML&L to Exchange bank, March 31, 1921, all in ML&L/WSU.

15. Maurice McGregor's comments are from his letter to A. M. Laing, November 18, 1931, ML&L/WSU. On wool markets: ML&L to J. G. Kludas, February 4, 1922, ML&L/ACM, and Wood Brothers to ML&L, June 13, 1922. On shift from cattle to sheep: E. L. Potter and H. A. Lindgren, "Costs of Producing Mutton and Wool on Eastern Oregon Ranges," Oregon AES Bulletin 219 (September 1925), p. 13. On McGregor cattle herds: Boyce, "History of the Beef Cattle Industry," p. ii.

16. ML&L to Arthur M. Geary, June 23, 28, 1926; ML&L to L. Gantner and Company, June 17, 1926; O. W. Sandberg, American Farm Bureau Federation, to Charles MacKenzie and Peter McGregor, February 28, 1928, all in ML&L/ACM. Quote is from J. F. Sears to C. L. McKenzie, April 19, 1928, ML&L/Hooper. McGregor earnings: Peter McGregor to Charles MacKenzie, April 20, 1928, ML&L/ACM.

17. Interview with Emile Morod; Oliver, *Gold and Cattle Country*, p. 125; interview with T. J. Drumheller, Jr. Sheepmen have a variety of explanations for "stiff lambs" (lambs with sore joints and weak legs). Drumheller believes the problem is caused by consumption of water hemlock. McGregor sheep foreman Clemente Barber suggests infections resulting from unsanitary castration of buck lambs as a possible cause (interview with Clemente Barber).

18. Botanist F. L. Pickett to ML&L, May 14, 1926; worksheet of Dr. Baker, March 15, 1927; C. M. Hubbard to Peter McGregor, February 14, 1924, all in ML&L/Hooper; Emile Morod sheep tally books, ML&L/ACM.

19. Comments of Macrae and the herders are from numerous letters in ML&L/WSU and "herders' letters" file, ML&L/ACM.

20. On pile-up and storm: 1924 and 1925 sheep counts, ML&L/Hooper,

and interview with Emile Morod. On forest fire: Wood Brothers to Peter McGregor, August 9, 13, 1926, ML&L/WSU. On lambing: ML&L to E. E. Flood, March 21, 1927; Maurice McGregor to Archie McGregor, May 2, 1927, both in ML&L/WSU. Wool clip and lambing data: Macrae and Morod sheep tally books, ML&L/ACM, and "sheep bands—annual statistics," ML&L/ WSU.

21. On Maurice: interview with Ralph Snyder and the comments of several men and women who worked for McGregor Land and Livestock. On bucks: Frank Brown to ML&L, September 9, 1926, Glen Craig Stock Farm to ML&L, June 13, 1926, ML&L/ACM, and several letters in ML&L/WSU. Also see *Spokesman-Review*, August 22, 1924, on experiment station sheep purchased by McGregors. On mountain pastures: "Summer Range–Idaho," and "Summer Range–Washington," files, ML&L/Hooper. On suit of clothes: Maurice to W. C. Ufford, April 16, 1926, ML&L/WSU. "Entirely satisfactory tenant": Department of the Interior to Peter McGregor, May 24, 1923, ML&L/WSU. On state land leases: dozens of letters in annual business correspondence, ML&L/Hooper and ML&L/WSU. C. E. Maloy, a Seattle lawyer whose name had been used on state grazing leases since 1916, suggested to McGregor lawyer Richard Munter "that it would be perfectly appropriate if I were to cut in on the profits or benefit of such leases and re-leases to the extent of about $50," (Maloy to Munter, September 19, 1934, ML&L/ Hooper). McGregors' response to changing state lease policies is discussed in Richard Munter to Maurice McGregor, December 2, 1929, ML&L/WSU. On Idaho forest closure: typescript of comments made at Washington Wool Growers meeting, ML&L/WSU.

22. Maurice McGregor's journal of 1923 trip to Chicago and letter from John Hood to Maurice McGregor, August 26, 1927, both in ML&L/ACM. Macrae: articles and letters in Macrae collection, ML&L/Hooper. Interview with Sherman McGregor.

23. "Most intensive attention": Wood Bros. to ML&L, September 22, 1926, ML&L/WSU. Livestock Market Digest, August 13, 1926, ML&L/ Hooper. 1927 shipment: Kay Wood to Peter McGregor, August 11, 19, 1927; Ed Spain to Peter McGregor, August 17, 1927, ML&L/Hooper.

24. F. J. Sievers and H. F. Holtz, "The Silt Loam Soils of Eastern Washington and Their Management," Washington AES Bulletin 166 (January 1922), p. 32. Wheat acreage totals for 1920–30 in ML&L/ACM. On plight of tenants: Leonard, "Wheat Farmer of Southeastern Washington," p. 36. On Hendrickson: McGregor letter "to whom it may concern," October 5, 1926, ML&L/WSU, and mortgages in ML&L/Hooper. On John Banks: ML&L to Security State Bank, September 16, 1922, ML&L/WSU.

25. On tenant debts: ML&L to Vorhees and Canfield, November 2, 1923, April 18, 1924, ML&L/WSU; ML&L to J. N. Pickrell, undated letter in 1925 files, ML&L/WSU; *First State Bank of Lacrosse* v. *McGregor Land and Livestock and R. L. Jeremiah*, Supreme Court of Washington, January 6, 1927 (copy of proceedings in ML&L/WSU); several letters in ML&L/ACM.

26. On Rudd: interview with Sherman McGregor. Fourteen pertinent letters on grain trade in 1923–28 files, ML&L/WSU. The corporation successfully implemented legal action when a buyer improperly graded McGregor wheat. See letters from H. W. Canfield to ML&L, December 18, 1925, February 9, 26, 1926, ML&L/WSU. On Starbuck ranch: ML&L to Baker-Boyer National Bank, April 17, 1923, Baker-Boyer to McGregor, July 25, 1923, ML&L/WSU. On daily management problems at Starbuck: series of letters written by Maurice McGregor and Starbuck manager Art Bowman, 1925–26, ML&L/WSU. Deals with Grote: ML&L to Grote, December 29, 1922, H. W. Canfield to Rudd, January 9, 1923, ML&L/ACM, and several letters in ML&L/WSU. On low state of Grote's finances: ML&L to Vorhees and Canfield, January 27, 1923, October 19, 1925, ML&L/WSU.

27. Vorhees to Rudd, October 21, 1925; Rudd to Farm Mortgage Security Company, June 24, 1924, both in ML&L/WSU. Attempts to sell: "Grote Ranch" file, ML&L/Hooper. On Seattle property: Bruce McGregor (no relation) to ML&L, August 21, 1928; L. C. Atkinson to Maurice, August 3, 1927, both in ML&L/WSU. On Hooper Realty hangover: Maurice to H. W. Canfield, September 5, 1928, ML&L/WSU. On frost and other problems at Yakima: Maurice to Archie McGregor, May 2, 1927, ML&L/WSU, and 33 letters from W. C. Booth to Maurice, ML&L/Hooper. Buyer's scalp: Vorhees and Canfield to ML&L, January 10, 1928, ML&L/Hooper.

28. On copper carbonate: Washington Agricultural Experiment Station to ML&L, October 3, 1923, ML&L/WSU. Shearer, a veteran muleskinner, left McGregors about 1930 to set up a harness shop; his timing was poor (interview with Dallas Hooper). On bulk grain: interview with Sherman McGregor. On Hong Kong strike: Ames, Harris to ML&L, June 28, 1922, ML&L/WSU. On reuse of grain sacks: interview with William McGregor.

29. Interview with Dallas Hooper.

30. Annual wheat output: "Atlas of Washington Agriculture," 1963, p. 113; Washington State, Department of Agriculture, "Sixth Biennial Report to the Governor" (1922–24), p. 28. On 1923 crop: discussion of crop prospects in letters in ML&L/Hooper. Reports from McGregor ranch and other areas: Colfax *Gazette*, June 6, 13, 27, July 18, 1924; Alex McGregor in Leeper, "Memoirs and Reminiscences" (MSS.), p. 53. On hogs: interviews with William and Sherman McGregor; R. J. Smith, Department of Animal Husbandry, WSC, to ML&L, May 22, 1924, ML&L/WSU; hog count, 1924–25, ML&L/Hooper. Earnings figures based on annual statements (see appendix 2).

31. Acreage in crop: "1925 wheat" file, ML&L/Hooper. On "average" farms: Washington State Department of Agriculture, "Whitman County Agriculture," County Agriculture Data Series, 1956, p. 27. Harvest inventory: annual inventory books, ML&L/WSU. On fixing old machinery: interview with Dallas Hooper. Agronomists George Severance, Byron Hunter, and Paul Eke estimated that the substitution of the combine for a heading and threshing outfit saved from $491 to $835 annually ("Farming Systems for Eastern Washington and Northern Idaho," Washington AES Bulletin 244

[July 1930], p. 47). On McGregor implements: interview with Virgil Bennington and annual inventory books, ML&L/WSU.

32. An order form for a Harris Combine including specifications, illustrations, and prices is in ML&L/Hooper. Combine crew: interview with Ernest Osmond; Keith, *Horse Interlude*, p. 87. Combines in operation: interview with Arthur Buhl; Carl Penner and Virgil Bennington interviews, WCAT/Walla Walla.

33. On reasons for switching to tractors: John A. Hopkins, *Changing Technology and Employment in Agriculture*, p. 57. Number of tractors and comments of tractor-owners: E. F. Landerholm, "The Economic Relation of Tractors to Farm Organization in the Grain Farming Areas of Eastern Washington," Washington AES Bulletin 310 (April 1935), pp. 6, 40. The number of farm tractors in use nationally increased from 250,000 in 1920 to 2,500,000 in 1940 (Sherman E. Johnson, "Changes in American Farming," USDA Misc. Publication 707 [December 1949], p. 3). Clarence Braden describes his horse trading and the sale of a tractor to McGregors in WCAT interview. "Industrial revolution": *Technology on the Farm*, p. 9. Tractors at Hooper: interviews with John and William McGregor.

34. On acreage per day: M. R. Cooper *et al.*, "Progress of Farm Mechanization," p. 40. On improvement of yield: Harley D. Jacquot, "McGregor Ranch: 1966 Agronomic Report," p. 11, McGregor Co/Colfax. On failure of early tractors: Landerholm, "Economic Relation of Tractors to Farm Organization," p. 8; Wik, *Steam Power*, p. 204. On McGregors Rumely: ML&L to Kincaid Implement Company, 1925, ML&L/Hooper.

35. On Holt '75's: annual wheat ranch inventories; ML&L to Exchange National Bank, October 16, 1925; ML&L to Tractor Parts Company, Seattle, May 28, 1927, all in ML&L/WSU. On crowbars: interview with William McGregor. On Levi Sutton: Ritzville *Journal-Times* September 15, 1949. Meinig, "Environment and Settlement in the Palouse," p. 81. On wheat ranch machinery: annual inventory books, ML&L/WSU. On Holt '60's: ML&L to E. E. Flood, March 20, 1928; ML&L to Palouse Tractor Company, February 27, 1929, both in ML&L/ACM. On wheat hauling: Donald McGregor to Maurice McGregor, July 8, 1926; C. V. Huck to ML&L, June 21, 1927, both in ML&L/WSU.

36. Interview with Ralph Snyder. Population changes: "Trends in Agriculture, 1900–1930," Washington AES Bulletin 300 (1934), p. 9. Maurice McGregor, 1928 daybook, ML&L/Hooper. On the problems brought by mechanical changes in agriculture: Shideler, *Farm Crisis*, p. 79.

37. Interviews with Dallas Hooper and Arthur Buhl; Maurice McGregor to E. R. Ennis, 1928, ML&L/ACM; 1927–30 payroll books, ML&L/WSU; Ernest McCaw and Carl Penner interviews, WCAT/Walla Walla.

38. On Donahue, Swanson, Russell: McGregor letters to E. R. Ennis Insurance Company, 1927–35, ML&L/WSU. Letters similar to the following are also found in the McGregor employee files: "Can you tell me anything about where Clarence Brown has gone to? He was in your employ the 30th

of April and I answered his letter. It was returned and said he had left no address. I was surprised for he seemed to like his work very much . . . I am his mother" (May 21, 1926, ML&L/ACM). On Van Pelt and Booth: McGregor letters to Fireman's Fund, 1935–36, ML&L/Hooper. On Carmen: *Spokesman-Review*, August 13, 1930.

39. On Lee: interview with Carl Penner. On stubble burning: interview with William McGregor. E. G. Schafer to Maurice McGregor, October 9, 1934, ML&L/Hooper. In his article "Man's Effect on the Palouse," Soil Conservation Service agent W. A. Rockie included pictures of the McGregor rangeland and noted "the vegetation is luxuriant and affords an excellent ground cover" (p. 37). Studies of the poor condition of the western range helped bring about the Taylor Grazing Act of 1934, a federal leasing system for large blocks of unclaimed public domain. The Taylor act did not apply to the Columbia Plateau, where little unclaimed land remained. But it had a marked effect on livestock production in the Rocky Mountain states. See *If and When It Rains: The Stockman's View of the Range Question.*

40. Minutes of the board of directors of McGregor Land and Livestock, ML&L/Hooper; Flood to Maurice McGregor, January 31, 1928, ML&L/WSU; Kimbrough to Maurice McGregor, August 31, 1927, ML&L/ACM. On Fisher: several Department of the Interior court cases beginning with *Northern Pacific* v. *Fisher, Indian,* and continuing through the 1930's, "Sam Fisher" file, ML&L/Hooper. Fisher's Indian legends are described in letter from Maurice McGregor to Department of Anthropology, WSC, January 10, 1928, ML&L/Hooper. Also see Alex McGregor in Leeper, "Memoirs and Reminiscences" (MSS.), p. 52.

41. Dinner program in honor of Peter McGregor; collection of letters to and from Jennie, Alex, Mary, Marjorie, and Helen McGregor, all in Sherman McGregor collection, Hooper. Alex C. McGregor wrote his daughter Mary after her first performance in New York on March 5, 1931: "This is a big day in my life so I must tell you that several years ago I hope a home was made happy by the arrival of a young son who in later years became the father of Mary MacGregor, a promising young pianist from New York. His bid for fame rests a great deal in sitting in the reflected sunlight of coming events and he is very happy today in looking forward as well as backward on the finest family of kids and the finest mother that ever graced a home." Mary McGregor's career is described in: "Miss McGregor Gains Interest as Musician," Washtucna *Enterprise*, November 7, 1930.

42. On McNary-Haugen: Gilbert Fite, *American Agriculture and Farm Policy,* p. 11. W. J. Spillman of the USDA, formerly an agronomist at the experiment station in Pullman, in his 1927 book, *Balancing the Farm Output,* modified the McNary-Haugen concept and suggested an early version of the domestic allotment plan. On Peter McGregor and the Republican convention: *Spokesman-Review,* June 2, 3, 13, 1928; Colfax *Gazette,* June 8, 22, 1928. "MacGregor Staged Bolt": *Spokesman-Review,* June 15, 1928. On

Peter's reaction to article: interview with Sherman McGregor; Elgin McGregor to Maurice McGregor, 1928, ML&L/WSU.

43. Carstensen, "The Land of Plenty," *American Issues*, p. 12. Farm income: USDA, Bureau of Agricultural Economics, "Net Farm Income and Income Parity Summary, 1910–1942" (July 1942), p. 8; Pacific Northwest: R. F. Martin, *Income in Agriculture, 1929–1935*, p. 90; USDA, Bureau of Agricultural Economics, "Livestock on Farms and Ranches on January 1: Number, Value, and Classes, 1920–1939," Statistical Bulletin 88, p. 48. Corporate farms: Philip M. Raup, "Corporate Farming in the United States," *Journal of Economic History* 33:1 (March 1973), pp. 277–78. Hyde proposal: Walla Walla *Union-Bulletin*, November 28, 1930.

44. *Commercial Review*, September 1, 1931; "Formation of Whitman County Farmers Protective Association" MSS. in ML&L/WSU. Also see Walla Walla *Union-Bulletin*, August 2, 1931. McGregors in Depression: Maurice McGregor to Henry J. Davis, September 24, 1934; Maurice McGregor to Donald McGregor, September 22, 1932, both in ML&L/WSU; Alex McGregor to Mary McGregor, May 1, 1932, ML&L/ACM. The country still retained a beauty for Alex McGregor despite the desperate circumstances. In the letter to his daughter he explained: "We have had a cool pleasant spring with lots of rain which has made wonderful crop prospects. The trees are all out and many of the flowers and the range grass is wonderful. The hills have their coat of green and are beautiful. . . . Life in the wild has its advantages."

45. Maurice McGregor to A. M. Laing, November 17, 1931, ML&L/WSU. Commodity prices: *Average Prices Received by Washington Farmers, 1910–1959*, pp. 33–45; interview with William McGregor. H. Stanley Coffin in his 1929 and 1930 journals tells of additional troubles—subzero weather, blizzards, and sheep losses (Coffin Sheep Company files, Yakima). On wheat raising: Baker, "Agricultural Regions of North America," pp. 177, 188.

46. Annual departmental statements, see Appendix 2; interview with Emile Morod; correspondence with Spokane and Eastern bank, 1930–33, numerous letters in ML&L/WSU; Maurice McGregor to Chester Davis, September 30, October 5, 1938; Maurice to Alex McGregor, December 5, 1939, all in ML&L/Hooper.

47. Interview with Ralph Snyder.

48. Maurice McGregor to "Aunt Minn," March 13, 28, 1930; ML&L to H. A. Crawford, July 28, 1930; Maurice to S. A. Kimbrough, July 12, 1930, all in ML&L/WSU. Adams County: interview with Arthur Buhl. On wheat price: Maurice McGregor, 1930 daybook, ML&L/WSU. On Wood Brothers: Ed Spain to Peter McGregor August 18, 26, 1930, ML&L/WSU. On Logan and Bryan: corporate resolutions of 1930, ML&L/Hooper. By September 1929, H. S. Coffin noted in his daybook that the price of lamb was dropping 25¢ a day (daybook in Coffin Sheep Company, Yakima).

49. Maurice McGregor to S. A. Kimbrough, September 13, October 7,

November 11, 1930, ML&L/WSU; Kimbrough to Maurice, September 16, 1930, ML&L/WSU; Maurice to Wood Brothers, October 13, 1930, ML&L/Hooper; "hogs bought—1930," ML&L/WSU; hogs—prospectus, ML&L/Hooper. On Midwest hogs: A. C. Chace to ML&L, December 11, 1930; McGregor to Chace, December 13, 1930; ML&L to Hector McDonald, Extension Animal Husbandman, WSC, October 18, 1930, all from ML&L/Hooper. Interview with Ralph Snyder.

50. Interview with William McGregor; Sam Kimbrough to Maurice, November 12, December 15, December 16, 1930, ML&L/WSU; ML&L to Kimbrough, November 24, 1930, ML&L/WSU.

51. Peter McGregor to Ed Spain, January 16, 1931, August 26, 1933, ML&L/Hooper, ML&L/WSU; Ed Spain to Peter, January 20, 1931, ML&L/ACM. A complicated dispute arose between McGregors and one of the hog sellers: ML&L to R. P. Rippel, March 30, 1931; M. J. Doretal to ML&L, March 25, 1931, both in ML&L/ACM. Poor pig market: Clark Commission Company to ML&L, February 4, 5, March 12, 1931, ML&L/ACM. Treacherous market: William Hislop to Peter McGregor, May 18, 1931, ML&L/WSU.

52. "Large Scale Farming Demonstration on Ranch of McGregor Land and Livestock," June 9–12, 1931, typescript in ML&L/WSU; "1931 business prospectus," ML&L/Hooper; payroll books, 1931-2, ML&L/WSU; interview with Sherman McGregor; Maurice to Sam Kimbrough, June 2, 1931, Maurice to "Aunt Minn," June 4, 1931, both in ML&L/ACM.

53. On wheat yield: 1931 daybook of Maurice McGregor; ML&L to Fireman's Fund, July 18, 1931; Maurice to S. A. Kimbrough, August 6, 7, 1931, all ML&L/WSU; Lacrosse *Clipper*, July 31, 1931. On fires: *Union-Bulletin*, July 25, 1931; interview with Dallas Hooper; Maurice to Kimbrough, August 12, 1931, ML&L/ACM. An additional problem was the invasion of the McGregor summer range by 600 cattle. The Potlatch Forest Agency advised McGregors to " 'sheep off' the range before the cattle have destroyed it" (June 12, 1931, ML&L/WSU).

54. On international markets: National Wool Marketing Corporation to Peter McGregor, April 30, 1935, ML&L/Hooper. On lambs: S. A. Kimbrough to Maurice, August 20, 25, 1931, ML&L/WSU; Maurice to Kimbrough, September 1, 1931, ML&L/ACM. On wool: E. J. Burke to McGregor L&L, July 14, 1931, ML&L/WSU. On wheat market: Maurice to Kimbrough, December 1, 1932, ML&L/WSU. On credit: Kimbrough to Maurice, August 10, 1932. In a November 10 letter Kimbrough mentions "the possibility of revamping your financial structure somewhat." Both letters in ML&L/ACM. On Rutter: Maurice to E. F. Munley, May 22, 1934; Archie to Maurice, March, 1941, both in ML&L/WSU; Jennie McGregor to Jessie McGregor Skene, 1931, Sherman McGregor collection; and R. L. Rutter to James Bateman, May 7, 1932, ML&L/WSU.

55. Maurice to Kimbrough, June 18, 30, 1932; Maurice to F. C. Howell, July 30, 1932; E. J. Burke to Peter McGregor, May 8, 1933, all in ML&L/WSU. Lamb sales: ML&L to Kimbrough, August 22, 1932, ML&L/WSU.

Fed lambs: ML&L to Tom Marshall, Belvidere, Illinois, October 17, November 14, 1932, ML&L/ACM.

56. Business prospectus–sheep, 1932, ML&L/Hooper. Grazing fees: Deer Park Lumber Company to ML&L, March 6, 1930, ML&L/WSU; ML&L to C .V. Savage, Washington State Commissioner of Public Lands, December 23, 1932, ML&L/ACM; National Forest Service to Taylor L&L, June 19, 1933, ML&L/WSU. Business prospectus–sheep, 1932, ML&L/Hooper. "Incurable bull": Maurice to Kimbrough, August 22, 1932, ML&L/WSU.

57. McGregor finances: ML&L to G. H. Plummer, July 13, 1932, ML&L/ACM. "Average" farmer of 1932: Chester C. Davis, "The Development of Agricultural Policy Since the End of the World War," in *Farmers in a Changing World*, USDA *Yearbook of Agriculture* (1940), p. 314. Carstensen, "Land of Plenty," p. 12.

58. Maurice McGregor to Paul A. Draper, Boston woolbuyer, September 14, 1933, ML&L/WSU; Peter McGregor to Oregon sheepman Fred Falconer, June 27, 1935, ML&L/ACM. Peter McGregor to Senator C. C. Dill, January 17, 1933, ML&L/ACM. Also see Dill to Peter McGregor, January 23, March 30, 1933; Peter McGregor to Senator Borah, January 17, 1933; Senator Homer T. Bone to Peter McGregor, April 5, 1933; Peter McGregor to Senator Wesley Jones, March 22, 1930; Senator Knute Hill to Maurice McGregor, March 25, 1933, all in ML&L/WSU. Peter McGregor explained to Charles H. Frye of Seattle his opinion "that any cure for America's agricultural distress must afford some measure of relief to the corn and hog farmers of the middle west . . ." (February 20, 1933, ML&L/WSU).

59. *Commercial Review*, March 22, 1932; Peter McGregor to Charles McNary, April 17, 1933, ML&L/ACM. McGregors by January, 1933, found that "it seems almost impossible to borrow money" and hoped for "some miracle" so that additional capital would become available (ML&L to G. H. Plummer, January 25, 1933, ML&L/WSU). On Farm Credit Administration: Marion Clawson, *The Western Range Livestock Industry*, p. 283; Oliver, *Gold and Cattle Country*, pp. 227–30. Production Credit financial statements, operating budgets, and correspondence are in ML&L/Hooper. McGregor mortgage agreements are also discussed in 1933–34 corporate minute book, ML&L/Hooper. Comments are in typescript of "Across the Fence" program aired on KWSC radio, Pullman, July 3, 1941, ML&L/Hooper.

60. Description of AAA requirements based on letters, administrative rules and regulations, and other material in ML&L/Hooper. Maurice's comments are in letter to S. A. Kimbrough, September 28, 1933, ML&L/WSU. CCC: ML&L to J. D. Day, August 30, October 13, 1938, ML&L/ACM. Also see Heady, *A Primer on Food*, pp. 61–64. "Peter MacGregor Favors Grain Co-Op," Lacrosse *Clipper*, January 29, 1932.

61. Maurice to S. A. Kimbrough, November 16, 1932; ML&L to John Healy, March 14, 1934, both in ML&L/WSU. Maurice wrote Kimbrough on June 19, 1933, that the acreage reduction and domestic allotment program, "While it may have an immediately bearish effect if the farmers re-

lease old wheat more freely, is extremely bullish on the future. . . . The picture continues to improve" (ML&L/WSU). The threat of a state "road use" tax on tractors caused some worries in 1933 (Peter McGregor to state legislator Richard Ott, January 21, 1933; Al Grecol to Hill and Company, January 18, 1933, both in ML&L/WSU).

62. Wool and lamb prices: Draper and Company to ML&L, September 6, 1933; Western Wool Storage to ML&L, November 18, 1933; Maurice McGregor daybook, all in ML&L/WSU. On weather: ML&L to Fireman's Fund, July 4, 1933; ML&L to S. A. Kimbrough, March 15, 1934, both in ML&L/ACM. On wheat markets and store business: Maurice to Kimbrough, June 1, 1933, ML&L/WSU. On lamb-shearing: ML&L to F. A. Clarke, December 1, 1933, ML&L/WSU. On New Deal: ML&L to Kimbrough, June 22, 1933, ML&L/WSU. On creditors: ML&L to J. L. Day, October 24, 1933, ML&L/WSU.

63. Maurice McGregor to Gordon (no last name given), June 24, 1934, ML&L/ACM. On wages: "Suggested wage scale," in 1933 daybook of Maurice McGregor, ML&L/WSU. On new machinery: ML&L to Fireman's Fund, July 12, 1935, ML&L/WSU. Former employees: Anton Bacchus to Maurice, November 28, 1933; Harold Magnuson to Maurice, March 1933, both in ML&L/WSU.

64. Maurice McGregor to S. A. Kimbrough, July 24, 1937, ML&L/WSU; Richard Wakefield and Paul Landis, "The Drought Farmer Adjusts to the West," Washington AES Bulletin 378 (July 1939), pp. 18–19. The drought of 1934 hurt many western sheep businesses and indirectly helped Columbia Plateau sheepmen (see C. E. Fleming and C. A. Brennan, "Studies of the Range Sheep Business in Nevada," Nevada AES Bulletin 145 [August 1937], p. 6).

65. Maurice McGregor to Ruth McGregor, March 14, 1934; Maurice to "Uncle Archie," March 6, 1934. On wheat market: ML&L to Bank of California, August 20, 1934, ML&L/WSU; Maurice to Kimbrough, June 14, 1934, ML&L/ACM. On lamb and wool: ML&L to John L. Day, August 19, 1935; ML&L/WSU; Alex McGregor to Kimbrough, July 9, 1935, ML&L/ACM; Maurice to "Uncle Alex," July 31, 1934, ML&L/WSU. McGregors watched their expenses closely and when they refused to pay a $12 shipping charge on wool, Northern Pacific attorneys took them to court in an unsuccessful attempt to collect, (*Northern Pacific Railway* v. *McGregor Land and Livestock*, Whitman County Superior Court, case 19544 [1934]).

66. Maurice to Henry Lee, April 26, 1935, ML&L/ACM. In an April 17, 1935, letter to the Northwest PCA, Maurice complained that a federal attempt to control wool markets had broken down: "What is left seems to be a gentlemen's agreement. The only trouble with gentlemen's agreements is the shortage of gentlemen." But on May 28 he wrote that the government program had worked. Both letters in ML&L/ACM. On Henry Lee: Maurice to Harry Ferris, February 11, 1935, ML&L/WSU. On Jock Macrae and

Morod: Archie McGregor to Maurice, 1941, ML&L/WSU. Maurice's letter to E. L. Jackson, January 8, 1936, is in ML&L/WSU.

67. Interviews with Dallas Hooper and William McGregor; Maurice McGregor to S. A. Kimbrough, July 19, 1935, ML&L/ACM. On subsidy payments: John Schlebecker, *Whereby We Thrive: A History of American Farming, 1607–1972*, p. 241. On the soil conservation act: Maurice McGregor to J. L. Day, March 24, 1936, ML&L/ACM. McGregor records of payments received for soil conservation and for "Second AAA" of 1938 are in ML&L/ Hooper and ML&L/WSU.

68. Maurice to Kimbrough, April 10, 1936, ML&L/WSU; undated daybook, ML&L/WSU; "McGregor, Farmer-Economist, Pioneer Conservationist," Colfax *Gazette-Commoner*, April 19, 1956; "Soil conservation" file, ML&L/Hooper; Maurice to Alex McGregor, 1937, Maurice to Howard Mann, State Executive Officer, AAA, July 1, 1938; Maurice to J. M. Dillon, State Range Examiner, June 22, 1938, and other letters in ML&L/ACM. Also see "Crested Wheatgrass Is Useful on McGregor Farm," May 7, 1937; newspaper (n.p.) clipping in ML&L/Hooper; William McGregor interview.

69. Interviews with William McGregor and Harley Jacquot; Maurice to Warren Booth, September 1935, ML&L/ACM; G. John Chohlis, "Range Condition in Eastern Washington: Fifty Years Ago and Now," *Journal of Range Management*, 5:3 (May 1952): 132. Ben H. Pubols et al., "Farming Systems and Practices and Their Relationship to Soil Conservation and Farm Income in the Wheat Region of Washington," Washington AES Bulletin 374 (July 1939), p. 32.

70. Maurice McGregor to S. A. Kimbrough, April 10, 1936; Maurice to Kimbrough, June 9, 1937, both in ML&L/WSU. McGregors closely tabulated the efficiency of their power farming methods in 1937 and tabulated hours spent discing, plowing, harrowing, etc. ("Power Field Operations," 1937, ML&L/WSU). On shearing: Maurice to Kimbrough, May 6, 1939, ML&L/ACM.

71. Notes from 1939 speech by H. S. Coffin. During the early years of the Depression, Coffin urged sheepmen "to eat and talk lamb, wear and talk wool, and keep everlastingly at it" (speech file, Coffin Sheep Company). On indebtedness: McGregor ranch mortgages, ML&L/Hooper, ML&L/WSU; Coffin Sheep Company mortgage agreements, Coffin Sheep Company. On PCA: W. T. Triplett to Maurice, August 26, 1935, ML&L/ACM. On McGregor, Washington: R. S. Munter to William Theil, February 4, 1935; Petition to Postmaster General James A. Farley; Senator L. B. Schwellenbach to R. S. Munter, January 29, 1935, all in ML&L/WSU. The move apparently failed because a nearby railroad siding was named "McGregor" and Northern Pacific officials felt the change would cause confusion.

72. Sherman Johnson, "Changes in American Farming," p. 13; C. P. Heisig, "A Graphic Presentation of Changes in the Agriculture of Washington from 1930 to 1935," Washington AES Bulletin 341 (December 1936), p. 4. Wheat

farmers had become far more efficient: Martin Cooper of the USDA estimated that in 1920 farmers worked 87 hours to produce a bushel of wheat. In 1940 only 47 hours were required. See Cooper et al., "Progress of Farm Mechanization," p. 3. Indicative of the complexities of marketing is the following booklet in ML&L/Hooper 1930's file: "The Wool Trade and Wool Top Industry: Futures Markets at New York, Antwerp, and Roubaix-Tourcoing."

CHAPTER 9

The McGregor Companies:
Biochemical Agriculture on the Old Sheep Ranges of the Columbia Plateau

1. *The Ranch*, June 23, 1894; Maurice McGregor to Sherman McGregor, July 7, 1947, Sherman McGregor collection; Emile Morod comment is in Colfax *Gazette-Commoner*, April 19, 1951.

2. Alex McGregor to Jock Macrae, March 14, 1945, ML&L/ACM. "Death Summons 'Alex' McGregor, Retired Head of Large Livestock Empire," *Spokesman-Review*, March 30, 1952. On Maurice's experiments: Northrup, King to ML&L, March 23, 1948, ML&L/Hooper. On soil conservation: Oscar Camp and Paul McGrew, "History of Washington Soil and Water Conservation Districts," 1969 MSS. in "Archives" file of B. R. Bertramson, Agronomy Department, WSU. On sheep camp food: interviews with Emile Morod and several other McGregor employees. On Marmes man: based on lectures of Dr. Roderick Sprague of the University of Idaho, one of the archaeologists involved in the project. On socialism: Maurice McGregor to Dr. Arthur W. Peterson, April 19, 1947, ML&L/Hooper. Maurice was criticized by many Palouse country farmers when he was interviewed by Edward R. Murrow for a national television program, "See It Now: A Crisis in Abundance." Maurice complained that his comments had been edited selectively to make him appear as a man of great wealth. See Colfax *Gazette-Commoner*, February 2, 1956.

3. John Gunther, *Inside U.S.A.*, pp. 134–38; Sherman McGregor to Maurice McGregor, July 7, 1940, ML&L/Hooper; Maurice McGregor to Sherman McGregor, July 7, 1947, ML&L/Hooper.

4. On the agricultural revolution: Wayne Rasmussen, "A Postscript: Twenty-Five Years of Change in Farm Productivity," *Agricultural History* 49:1 (January 1975): 84. Breimyer quote: "The Three Economies of Agriculture" in Vernon Ruttan et al., eds., *Agricultural Policy in an Affluent Society*, p. 31. On increased cereal grain output: R. W. Hecht and Eugene McKibben, "Efficiency of Labor," in *Power to Produce*, USDA *Yearbook of*

Agriculture (1960), pp. 317, 322. On contributors to productivity increase: M. R. Cooper et al., "Progress of Farm Mechanization," p. 18. On farm workers: Stanley Lebergott, "Labor Force and Employment, 1800–1860," in *Output, Employment, and Productivity in the United States After 1800*, pp. 118–19. Quote on changes in farming: *Proceedings of Conference on Land Utilization*, p. 193. On advances of the thirties: Morton Rothstein, "The Big Farm: Abundance and Scale in American Agriculture," *Agricultural History* 49:4 (October 1975): 596.

5. Wayne Rasmussen, "Second Agricultural Revolution Begins with World War II," in his *Readings in the History of American Agriculture*, p. 275; Maurice McGregor to "Uncle Alex," May 8, 1946, ML&L/ACM. John Schlebecker concludes that "the use of anhydrous ammonia as a fertilizer could be considered the most significant advance [in agriculture] from 1945 to 1972" (*Whereby We Thrive*, p. 313).

6. On early fertilizer use, see the numerous references in *Ranch and Range* (e.g., "Do Fertilizers Pay Farmers?," *Ranch and Range*, October 11, 1900). McGregor agronomist Harley Jacquot tested manure on wheat crops and had very poor results; see McGregor Ranch Agronomic Reports, McGregor Co./Colfax. On nitrogen fixing: T. C. Byerly, "Systems Come, Traditions Go," in Wayne Rasmussen, ed., *Agriculture in the United States: A Documentary History*, p. 3575. On fertilizer in California: "How Green Is Our Valley," *Chemical and Engineering News*, November 1, 1948, pp. 3258–60.

7. H. L. Haller and Ruth Busbey, "The Chemistry of D.D.T.," in *Science in Farming*, USDA *Yearbook of Agriculture* (1943–47), p. 616. On early insecticides: *Ranch and Range*, April 2, 1898 (kerosene); October 6, 1898 (formaldehyde, copper sulfate, or hot water); and Prof. H. W. Wiley's article, "Insecticides and Fungicides: Chemical Composition and Effectiveness," in *The Ranch*, February 20, 1902, which lists a variety of formulations, most of them containing arsenic. On McGregor arsenic use; see chap. 8, note 12. On early weed killers: DeGraff and Haystead, *The Business of Farming*, p. 61; T. J. Muzik, "Weed Control Problems in Washington," *Agronomy and Men* (1958–59), p. 16.

8. On the Wisconsin farmer: Vernon Carstensen, "The Genesis of an Agricultural Experiment Station," *Agricultural History* 34:1 (January 1960): 13–20. Interviews with Harley Jacquot. Jacquot, "1972 Agronomic Report," p. 2, McGregor Co./Colfax.

9. The comments of John and Maurice McGregor and Chohlis are in Chohlis, "The McGregor Ranch: Northwest Pace-Setter," pp. 10–15. On corporate earnings: annual statements, ML&L/Hooper. On farm prosperity: Clawson, *Policy Directions for U.S. Agriculture*, p. 190, and interviews with William McGregor.

10. On Dayton farmers: "Group Goes on Hooper Tour," Dayton *Chronicle-Dispatch*, March 27, 1952. Results of first fertilizer tests are summarized

in Jacquot, "Agronomy Report for 1959," p. 113. Harold Rogers and Maurice's statements about the experiments: "No Idle Land," *Washington Farmer*, January 3, 1952.

11. *Western Crops and Farm Management*, vol. 9, no. 5 (May 1960). An article detailing Jacquot's work is Glenn Lorang, "How to Grow 10 bu. More Wheat Per Acre," *Farm Journal*, February 1958, pp. 35, 84–86. On Australian visitors: "McGregor—Always Looking Forward," *Selling 66*, vol. 29, no. 5 (September-October 1964). Sherman McGregor comments are from a 1958 MSS. interview by a farm journalist in McGregor Co./Colfax.

12. Jacquot, "Agronomy Report for 1955," pp. 12, 127; "Agronomic Report for 1961," pp. 1–2. Peas and lentils: 1970 Whitman County statistics MSS. in McGregor Co./Colfax; "Palouse Country," *Montsanto* Magazine 49:4 (October 1969): 1–4. Delayed seeding and comments about chemical fallow: Jacquot, "1962 Agronomy Report," pp. 44, 117–24. Also useful was Jacquot's article, "Early Seeding for Better Profits," *Western Crops and Farm Management* 9:5 (May 1960): 21–25. Farmer response to nitrogen use: Jacquot, "1972 Agronomy Report," p. 2. On conservation: "Effects of Chemical Fallow, Minimum Tillage, and Early Seeding," Jacquot paper delivered to Northwest Scientific Association and in appendix to 1963 report. William McGregor honored: *Wheat Life*, vol. 19, no. 8 (August 1976). Jacquot: "1965 Agronomic Report," 98.

13. O. A. Vogel, "Cooperative Winter Wheat Improvements," *Agronomy and Men*, 1951–52. On smut losses: Vogel, "New Wheat Varieties Can Mean More Dollars," *Agronomy and Men*, 1952–53, pp. 7–8. On wheat smut center: C. S. Holton, "The Story of Wheat Smut and What to do About it," pamphlet in ML&L/Hooper. Bertramson: "Comments from the Chairman," *Agronomy and Men*, 1965–66, p. 5.

14. Ken Migchelbrink, "Announcing the New Gaines 'Shorty' Wheat," *Agronomy and Men*, 1961–62, pp. 8–10. Bertramson estimate is in a 1974 letter to J. M. Nielson, "Archives" file of B. R. Bertramson, Agronomy Department, WSU. Borlaug's comments are in "Vogel Wins National Medal of Science," *The Agronomist*, 1976–77, p. 5. "Strawbreaker": J. M. Cook, "Root and Foot Rots of Wheat," Spillman Farm Field Day, 1971, MSS. in Bertramson "Archives" file. "Jacmar: White Club Wheat for the Northwest," *Washington Farmer-Stockman*, June 1, 1978.

15. On fertilizer use: B. R. Bertramson, "Changing Times and Faces," *Agronomy and Men*, 1967–68, p. 5. On Whitman County yields: Jacquot, "Agronomic Report for 1966," p. 11, and Colfax *Gazette*, August 14, 1975. On McGregor crops: interviews with William McGregor; Jacquot annual reports; William McGregor statement in Colfax *Gazette*, August 7, 1975. On Whitman, Lincoln, and Adams: Haystead and Fite, *The Agricultural Regions of the United States*, p. 253. Twenty-five million bushel crop: Colfax *Gazette*, August 14, 1975. By 1974, the state of Washington produced more than 122 million bushels, Oregon 51 million, and Idaho 58 million. Statistics in McGregor Company manager reports, McGregor Co./Colfax.

Jacquot's comments are in "McGregor Ranch—1972 Agronomy Report," p. 1.

16. Information about the combine and the comments of the Palouse country farmer are from a 1979 International Harvester brochure entitled "Introducing the World's Largest, Most Productive Combine: The International 1470 Axial Flow."

17. On export market problems: William McGregor, "White Wheat Price Concerns the Association," *Wheat Life*, vol. 11, no. 2 (April 1966), and his 1969 MSS., "Wheat Quality in the Export Market," ML&L/Hooper. Also useful was his 1967 statement to the House Committee on Agriculture, MSS. in ML&L/Hooper.

18. Balfour Guthrie and ammonia mishap: interview with Sherman McGregor. Graham-Hoeme adaptation: Sherman McGregor, 1958 MSS. history of farm chemical operation, McGregor Co./Colfax. *Farm Journal* and *Agrichemical West* both carried articles about McGregor equipment on September 30, 1958, and speculated that the machines were "the world's biggest anhydrous applicators." *Agrichemical West* in April 1960 noted that the coil-spring shank developed by McGregors "is in general use throughout the Northwest." An extensive collection of letters to agricultural scientists and equipment manufacturers in ML&L/Hooper details the research behind the development of suitable equipment.

19. Comments about the irrigated region are based on the writer's own observations. McGregor Company earnings are summarized in annual statements, McGregor Co./Colfax. Managerial people: "The McGregor Company," *Fertilizer Solutions*, vol. 13, no. 3 (May-June 1969). Jones Act: letters to congressmen and other materials in McGregor Co./Colfax. Calcium nitrate: Colfax *Gazette*, March 7, 1974; open letter "to McGregor customers," December 21, 1973, McGregor Co./Colfax.

20. On dangers of careless application: McGregor manager reports, 1976, McGregor Co./Colfax. Rachel Carson, *Silent Spring*, pp. 20, 29, 297. T. J. Muzik comments and estimate of herbicide value: Bob Finke, "Perspectives on Herbicides," *Agronomy and Men*, 1970–71, p. 21. TVA estimate: "Ammonia from Coal?", *Fertilizer Solutions* (July-August 1978). For a critical view of the substitution of capital for labor in agriculture, see R. G. Milk, "The New Agriculture in the United States: A Dissenter's View," *Land Economics* 48:3 (August 1972): 228–39.

21. Carson, *Silent Spring*, p. 69. Erosion estimates: C. B. Harston to B. R. Bertramson, July 25, 1973; Bertramson to Harston, August 1, 1973, both in Bertramson "Archives" files. Erosion in Palouse: R. J. Jonas, "A Bioscientist Looks at Agriculture," in "Wheat in This Changing World," O. A. Vogel Honorary Symposium, 1973, Bertramson files.

22. Interviews with William and John McGregor. Per capita beef consumption: Lyle Schertz et al., *Another Revolution in U.S. Farming?*, p. 85. The McGregor feedlot expansion is also detailed in 1950–56 correspondence in ML&L/Hooper.

23. Interview with John McGregor. Capacity of first Pasco lot: "Third Generation McGregors Retain Livestock Tradition," *The Northwest* 39:4 (July-August 1965): 8–9. Production of second lot: 1979 "feed and conversion" report, McGregor Feedlot/Pasco. The "dry weight" equivalent of the soup-like potato feed was 34,000 tons; the cattle gained one pound per 9.7 pounds of "dry weight" feed. A book of chemical additives for cattle feed mixes (in ML&L/Hooper) included Aureomycin (to promote rapid growth and feed efficiency and to prevent respiratory diseases), Oxytetracycline (for prevention of scours), stilbestrol (for rapid fattening), dimethyloplysitoxane (a bloat preventative), and numerous other compounds.

24. Trends in fed cattle: Schertz, *Another Revolution in U.S. Farming?*, pp. 86, 103. Increased demand for beef, reports of the large profits made in feedlot businesses, and tax provisions that made livestock production attractive to high-income non-farm investors all encouraged rapid expansion and helped make already unstable cattle markets even more volatile. Karl Hobson, extension marketing specialist at WSU, explains the cause of the market collapse of the early sixties in "Cattle Prices: Past, Present, and Future," 1964 MSS. in ML&L/Hooper. The 1969 issues of *Big Farmer* present typical reports of big profits in the following articles: "Plan a Feedlot That's Built to Expand"; "Take the Plunge" (i.e., build a big lot); "The Barren Waste Becomes a Beef Bonanza."

25. National sheep estimates, 1942 and 1976: "Sheep Industry Fading," *Spokesman-Review*, August 22, 1976. State estimates: "State's Sheep Population Dwindles," Seattle *Times*, April 13, 1975. Also see annual totals in USDA, *Agricultural Statistics*, 1973–80.

26. Daniel Gomez-Ibanez, "The Origins of Transhumance" (MSS.), p. 29; Gomez-Ibanez, "Rise and Decline of Transhumance," pp. 10–11. On immigrants and lamb: interviews with William McGregor. On lamb promotion: annual resolutions, Washington Wool Growers Association (WWGA old files, Ephrata, Washington). On lamb consumption: statement of Laird Noh, president of the American Lamb Feeders Association, in "Sheepmen Attempt to Revive Industry" (1975 MSS.), ML&L/Hooper; and USDA estimates in *Spokesman-Review*, August 22, 1976. On wool: apparel mill consumption statistics, made available by wool buyer J. H. Walters, Pendleton Woolen Mills, Portland, Oregon.

27. "Men, Sheep, and One Hundred Years," *National Wool Grower* 55:1 (January 1965): 54–57; Oliver, *Gold and Cattle Country*, p. 260; interview with Emile Morod; T. Donald Bell, "The Future of Sheep in the Northwest," 1957 MSS. in ML&L/Hooper.

28. "Wool Production and Prices: For Confidential Use of Directors," Federal Reserve Bank of San Francisco (Maurice McGregor was a Reserve Bank Director), June 21, 1945, MSS. in ML&L/Hooper. Interview with T. J. Drumheller, Jr.

29. Sheep earnings: based on annual statements, 1909–78, ML&L/Hooper, ML&L/Lemaster and Daniels. Declining sheep numbers: Bell, "Future of

Sheep in the Northwest" (MSS.). Interviews with Bill Dorman, Juan Miquelez, Clemente Barber, Charles Brune.

30. Payroll and sheep tally books of Emile Morod, ML&L/ACM; R. J. Norene, Immigration and Naturalization Service, to McGregor Land and Livestock, April 8, 1947, ML&L/Hooper; *American Sheep Breeder*, June 15, 1906; *Shepherd's Criterion*, October 1907. On the Basques of Jordan Valley: J. H. Gaiser, "The Basques of the Jordan Valley Area: A Study in Social Process and Social Change," Ph.D. dissertation, University of Southern California, 1944, pp. 78, 165. On the ages of Basque herders and reasons for immigration: J. A. Stafford, "Basque Ethnohistory in Kern County, California, 1872–1934," master's thesis, Sacramento State College, 1971.

31. "Men, Sheep, and One Hundred Years," *National Wool Grower* 55:1 (January 1965): 58; annual resolutions of labor committee, 1950–54, and "Western Range Association" files, Washington Wool Growers Association, Ephrata. McCarran bills: William A. Douglass and Jon Bilbao, *Amerikanuak: Basques in the New World*, pp. 311–18. "Rules and Regulations Governing the Employment of Sheepherders Under Contract to the Western Range Association," 1961 pamphlet in ML&L/Hooper. Motivation for emigration: interview with Clemente Barber. H. Stanley Coffin, Jr., to Leonard Rumpton, Chelan National Forest District Ranger, 1952, Coffin Sheep Company, Yakima.

32. Interview with Clemente Barber. Also useful were discussions with Juan Miquelez, Lorenzo Zozaya, and Isidro Gutierrez. An excellent overview of the role of the Basques on western ranges is Douglass and Bilbao, *Amerikanuak*, pp. 247–325.

33. Interview with George Cullinane; Phil Kern to J. W. Grant, February 3, 1961, Washington Wool Growers Association, Ephrata; William McGregor, "Land Use Problems of a Modern Livestock Operator," 1967 paper delivered to seminar of Washington State University Forestry and Range Management Department, ML&L/Hooper; William McGregor, "Some Aspects of Range Sheep Operation," 1957 MSS. in ML&L/Hooper. On attempts to increase output: Burch Schneider to John McGregor, December 26, 1953; John Schwendeman, USDA, to Maurice McGregor, March 21, 1947, both in ML&L/Hooper.

34. Interviews with William McGregor; William McGregor, "General Comments on Selection," MSS. in ML&L/Hooper. On Columbias: Damon Spencer, "Developments in Sheep," in *Science in Farming*, pp. 209–16. Interviews with Bill Dorman and T. J. Drumheller, Jr.

35. John McGregor, "Supplemental Pasture Development," 1955 MSS. in ML&L/Hooper. The research of Jacquot and the other two agronomists is described in McGregor Ranch Agronomic Reports, 1955–60. William McGregor told of his activities in a series of letters to the Washington Wool Growers, Washington Wool Growers Association files, Ephrata.

36. Statement of William McGregor at 1966 "Sheep Day," reprinted in Everett Davis, "Range Fencing," 1967 MSS. in Washington Wool Growers

Association files, Ephrata. On lambing camp: interview with William Mc-Gregor. On labor force: charts and data in sheep production book of William McGregor, ML&L/Hooper. Quote is from William McGregor, "Land Use Problems," 1967 MSS., ML&L/Hooper. On "dry lotting": interview with William McGregor. Coyote losses of McGregors and other sheepmen are described in Seattle *Times*, April 13, 1975. The same issue described an attempt by an Eastern Washington State College psychologist to teach coyotes not to like lamb. Baited lamb, containing a compound which made the coyote ill, was placed on the range. The program is unlikely to be feasible for range sheepmen: there are simply too many coyotes to teach.

37. On McGregor sheep business: interviews with William McGregor and Pete Williams.

38. On cattle: interview with William McGregor. Annual statements of "McGregor Land and Livestock and subsidiaries," McGregor Co./Colfax.

39. On school dispute: "Tempers Flare at Consolidation Talk," Colfax *Gazette-Commoner*, September 15, 1955. The comments about life in a company town are based on the writer's own experiences as a resident of Hooper. Marion Clawson describes the decline of small western towns: "Once it starts, the process of small-town decay is cumulative. As a town begins to go downhill, it is a less attractive place in which to live and is less likely to offer good job opportunities for its young people" (Clawson, *Policy Directions for U.S. Agriculture*, p. 62). On sheep business as major user of rangeland: Neil Johnson and Rex Willard, "Nature and Distribution of Types of Farming in Washington," Washington AES Bulletin 301 (July 1934). Corporate farming: Philip Raup, "Corporate Farming in the United States," *Journal of Economic History* 33: 1 (March 1973): 274.

40. On Scotch-Canadians: Galbraith, *Made To Last*. "Progress Report: 32nd Annual Field Day of Dryland Experiment Station" (June 18, 1948), copy in ML&L/Hooper. Morton Rothstein describes the adaptations and innovations of Pacific Slope farmers: "Many things on the Pacific slope may seem a little larger than life, but few more so than its commercial farms. Nowhere else in the nation can one find such a rich variety and heavy yield of crops, such dramatic contrasts in landscape and climate with their associated subregions, such a record of calculated shrewdness, or greed, in seizing opportunities for using machines and knowledge to bring forth ever-more-bountiful harvests" (Rothstein, "West Coast Farmers and the Tyranny of Distance," *Agricultural History* 49:1 [January 1975]: 273).

41. Interviews with Emile Morod.

Bibliography

I. BOOKS, ARTICLES, AGRICULTURAL BULLETINS AND REPORTS, GOVERNMENT DOCUMENTS, THESES AND DISSERTATIONS

Agriculture of the United States: Farms, Livestock, and Animal Products, Twelfth United States Census, 1900 (U.S. Census Office, 1902). Similar federal census reports were used for the following years: 1870, 1880, 1890, 1910, 1920, 1925, 1935, 1940. The individual citations are listed in the footnotes.

Anderson, Nels. *The Hobo: The Sociology of the Homeless Man.* Chicago: University of Chicago Press, 1923.

Andrews, Frank. "Marketing Grain and Livestock in the Pacific Coast Region." USDA Bureau of Statistics, Bulletin 89 (1911).

Arnquist, Inez, and Evelyn Roberts. "The Present Use of Work Time of Farm Homemakers." Washington AES Bulletin 234 (July 1929).

Atherton, Lewis E. "The Midwestern Country Town: Myth and Reality," *Agricultural History* 26:3 (July 1952): 73–79.

Atkinson, G. H. *The Northwest Coast Including Oregon, Washington and Idaho: A Series of Articles Upon the NPRR.* Portland: A. G. Walling, 1878.

"Atlas of Washington Agriculture." Washington State Department of Agriculture, 1963.

Bailey, Liberty H. (ed.). *Cyclopedia of American Agriculture: A Popular Survey of Agricultural Conditions, Practices, and Ideals in the United States and Canada.* New York: Macmillan, 1908.

Bainer, Roy. "Science and Technology in Western Agriculture." *Agricultural History* 49:1 (January 1975): 56–72.

Baker, Oliver E. "Agricultural Regions of North America, Part XI: The Columbia Plateau Wheat Region." *Economic Geography* 9:2 (April 1933): 167–97.

439

————. "A Graphic Summary of American Agriculture." USDA *Yearbook of Agriculture*, 1921.

Ball, C. R., C. C. Leighty, O. C. Stine, and O. E. Baker. "Wheat Production and Marketing." USDA *Yearbook of Agriculture*, 1921.

Ballou, Robert. *Early Klickitat Valley Days*. Goldendale, Wash.: Goldendale Sentinel, 1938.

Barbee, O. E. "A Comparison of Wheat Varieties in Eastern Washington." Washington AES Bulletin 289 (October 1933).

Barnes, Will C. *Western Grazing Grounds and Forest Ranges*. Chicago: Breeders Gazette, 1913.

————. *The Story of the Range*. Washington: Government Printing Office, 1926. Reprinted from hearings before the Subcommittee of the Committee on Public Lands and Surveys, U.S. Senate, 1st sess., 1922 (Sen. Res. 347).

————, and James Jardine. "Live Stock Production in the Eleven Far Western Range States." USDA, Office of the Secretary, Report 110 (1916).

Bartlett, E. S. *Sheep Shearing*. Chicago: Breeders Publications, 1938.

Beattie, R. Kent. "Plants Used for Food by Sheep on the Mica Mountain Summer Range." Washington AES Bulletin 113 (1913).

Benedict, Murray R., and Oscar Stine. *The Agricultural Commodity Programs: Two Decades of Experience*. New York: The Twentieth Century Fund, 1956.

Berthoff, Rowland. *An Unsettled People: Social Order and Disorder in American History*. New York: Harper and Row, 1971.

Billington, Ray Allen. "The Origin of the Land Speculator as a Frontier Type." *Agricultural History* 19:4 (October 1945): 204–11.

————. *Westward Expansion: A History of the American Frontier*. New York: The Macmillan Company, 1967.

Bjork, Kenneth O. *West of the Great Divide: Norwegian Migration to the Pacific Coast, 1847–1893*. Northfield, Minn.: Norwegian-American Historical Association, 1958.

Black, John D., "Agriculture." In Seymour E. Harris (ed.), *American Economic History*. New York: McGraw Hill, 1961.

Blaisdell, Donald C. *Government and Agriculture: The Growth of Federal Farm Aid*. New York: Farrar and Rinehart, 1940.

Blinken, Donald M. *Wool Tariffs and American Policy*. Washington, D.C.: Public Affairs Press, 1948.

Bogue, Allan G. *Money at Interest: The Farm Mortgage on the Middle Border*. New York: Russell and Russell, 1955.

————. "Pioneer Farmers and Innovation." *Iowa Journal of History* 56 (January 1958): 1–36.

————. "Social Theory and the Pioneer." *Agricultural History* 34:1 (January 1960): 21–34.

————. "Farming in the Prairie Peninsula, 1830–1890." *Journal of Economic History* 23:1 (March 1963): 3–29.

————. *From Prairie to Corn Belt: Farming on the Illinois and Iowa Prairies in the Nineteenth Century*. Chicago: University of Chicago Press, 1963.

Boyce, Todd V. "A History of the Beef Cattle Industry in the Inland Empire." Master's thesis, Washington State College, 1937.

Bretz, J. Harlen. "The Channeled Scabland of Eastern Washington." *Geographical Review* 18:3 (July 1928): 446–61.

———. "The Channeled Scablands of the Columbia Plateau." *Journal of Ecology* 31:8 (November–December 1923): 617–49.

Briggs, Harold E. "The Development and Decline of Open Range Ranching in the Northwest." *Mississippi Valley Historical Review* 20:4 (March 1934): 521–36.

———. "The Early Development of Sheep Ranching in the Northwest." *Agricultural History* 11:3 (July 1937): 161–80.

Brimlow, George F. *Harney County, Oregon, and Its Range Land*. Portland: Binfords and Mort, 1951.

Brisbin, James S. *The Beef Bonanza or How to Get Rich on the Plains: Being a Description of Cattle Growing, Sheep Farming, Horse Raising, and Dairying in the West*. Philadelphia: J. B. Lippincott, 1881.

Brock, A. L. "Wyoming Pioneer Experiences." *Annals of Wyoming* 2 (1924).

Brogan, Phil. *East of the Cascades* (ed. L. K. Phillips). Portland: Binfords and Mort, 1964.

Brumfield, Kirby. *This Was Wheat Farming: A Pictorial History of the Farms and Farmers of the Northwest Who Grow the Nation's Bread*. Seattle: Superior Publishing, 1967.

Bryan, Enoch A. *Historical Sketch of the State College of Washington*. Spokane: Inland American Printing, 1928.

———. *Orient Meets Occident: The Advent of the Railways to the Pacific Northwest*. Pullman, Wash.: Student Book Corporation, 1936.

Burcham, Levi T. "Cattle and Range Forage in California, 1770–1880." *Agricultural History* 35:3 (July 1961): 140–49.

Burns, R. H., A. S. Gillespie, and W. G. Richardson. *Wyoming's Pioneer Ranches*. Laramie: Top-of-the-World Press, 1955.

Calef, Wesley, "Problems of Grazing Administration in the Basins of Southern Wyoming." *Economic Geography* 28:2 (April 1952): 122–27.

Cardiff, Ira D., et al. "Report on Fires Occurring in Threshing Separators in Eastern Washington During the Summer of 1914." Washington AES Bulletin 117 (November 13, 1914).

Carman, Ezra A., H. A. Heath, and John Minto. "Special Report on the History and Present Condition of the Sheep Industry of the United States." BAI Report, 52nd Cong., 2nd Sess., House Misc. Doc. 105, 1892.

Carson, Rachel. *Silent Spring*. Boston: Houghton Mifflin, 1962.

Carstensen, Vernon. "The Genesis of an Agricultural Experiment Station." *Agricultural History* 34:1 (January 1960): 13–20.

——— (ed.). *The Public Lands: Studies in the History of the Public Domain*. Madison: University of Wisconsin Press, 1962.

———— (ed.). *Farmer Discontent, 1865–1900*. New York: John Wiley, 1974.

————. "The Land of Plenty." *American Issues* 1:2 (July 1975).

Carter, George E. "The Cattle Industry of Eastern Oregon, 1880–1890," *Oregon Historical Quarterly* 67:2 (June 1966): 139–78.

Carter, L. S., and G. R. McDole. "Stubble-Mulch Farming for Soil Defense." USDA Farmers' Bulletin 1917 (December 1942).

Cavert, William L. "The Technological Revolution in Agriculture, 1910–1955." *Agricultural History* 30:1 (January 1956): 18–27.

"The Channeled Scablands of Eastern Washington: The Geologic Story of the Spokane Flood." U.S. Department of the Interior, Geological Survey, 1973.

Chohlis, G. John. "Range Condition in Eastern Washington: Fifty Years Ago and Now," *Journal of Range Management* 5:3 (May 1952): 129–34.

————. "The McGregor Ranch: Northwest Pace-Setter." *Farm Management* 2:4 (March 1953): 10–15.

Clark, Ella E. *Indian Legends of the Pacific Northwest*. Berkeley: University of California Press, 1960.

Clark, J. Allen. "The Common White Wheats." USDA Farmers' Bulletin 1301 (December 1922).

Clawson, Marion. *The Western Range Livestock Industry*. New York: McGraw-Hill, 1950.

————. "Reminiscences of the Bureau of Land Management, 1947–1948." *Agricultural History* 33:1 (January 1959): 22–28.

————. *Policy Directions for United States Agriculture: Long-Range Choices in Farming and Rural Living*. Baltimore: Johns Hopkins University Press, 1960.

————, and Wendell Calhoun. *Longterm Outook for Western Agriculture: General Trends in Agricultural Land Use, Production, and Demand*. Berkeley: University of California Press, 1946.

Clemens, Fred W. *Three Hundred Years Along the Rothrock Trail*. Spokane: C. W. Hill, 1954.

Cohn, Edwin J. *Industry in the Pacific Northwest and the Location Theory*. New York: Kings Crown, 1954.

The Condition of Agriculture in the United States and Measures for Its Improvement: A Report by the Business Men's Commission on Agriculture. Washington, D.C.: National Industrial Conference Board, 1927.

Conner, G. F. *Science of Threshing: Treating the Operation, Management, and Care of Threshing Machinery*. St. Joseph, Mich.: Thresherman's Review, 1906.

Connor, L. G., "A Brief History of the Sheep Industry in the United States." American Historical Association, 1918 Annual Report.

"Contracts in Forest Reserve Timber Lands." 61st Cong., 2nd Sess., Sen. Doc. 612, 1910.

Cooper, J. M. "Range Sheep Production." USDA Farmers' Bulletin 1710 (August 1933).

Cooper, Martin R. "Cost of Wheat Production and Incomes from Farming in Eastern Washington and Northern Idaho for the Years 1919, 1920, and 1921." USDA Division of Cost Production and Farm Management (December 1923).

———, Glen Barton, and Albert Brodell. "Progress of Farm Mechanization." USDA Miscellaneous Publication 630 (October 1947).

Cotroneo, Ross. "Western Land Marketing by the Northern Pacific Railway." *Pacific Historical Review* 37:3 (August 1968): 299–320.

Cotton, J. S. "Forage Problems of Eastern and Central Washington." Master's thesis, Washington Agricultural College, 1904.

———. "A Report on the Range Conditions of Central Washington." Washington AES Bulletin 60 (1904).

———. "Range Management in the State of Washington." USDA Bureau of Plant Industry, Bulletin 75 (May 23, 1905).

Coulter, Calvin B. "The Victory of National Irrigation in the Yakima Valley, 1902–1906." *Pacific Northwest Quarterly* 42:2 (April 1951): 99–122.

Coville, Frederick. "Forest Growth and Sheep Raising in the Cascade Mountains of Oregon." USDA Division of Forestry Bulletin 15 (1898).

Cowan, Helen. *British Emigration to British North America: The First Hundred Years.* Toronto: University of Toronto Press, 1961.

Cox, LaWanda F. "The American Agricultural Wage Earner, 1865–1900: The Emergence of a Modern Labor Problem." *Agricultural History* 22:2 (April 1948): 95–113.

Craig, Gerald M. *Upper Canada: The Formative Years, 1784–1841.* Vancouver: McClelland and Stewart, 1963.

Crawford, Harriet. *The Washington State Grange: A Romance of Democracy.* Portland: Binfords and Mort, 1940.

Critchfield, Howard J. "Pastoral High-Country, South Island, New Zealand: The Second Century." *Yearbook of the Association of Pacific Coast Geographers* 31 (1969): 51–68.

Crowley, John M. "Ranches in the Sky: A Geography of Livestock Ranching in the Mountain Parks of Colorado." Ph.D. dissertation, University of Minnesota, 1964.

Curtiss, Charles F. "Raising Sheep for Mutton." USDA Farmers' Bulletin 96 (1899).

Danhof, Clarence H. *Change in Agriculture: The Northern United States, 1820–1870.* Cambridge: Harvard University Press, 1969.

Darlington, H. T. "A Study of Grazing Conditions in the Wenaha National Forest." Washington AES Bulletin 122 (May 1915).

Daubenmire, Rexford F. "Plant Succession Due to Overgrazing in the Agropyron Bunchgrass Prairie of Southeastern Washington." *Ecology* (January 1940): 55–65.

Davidson, T. Arthur. *A New History of the Country of Grey and the Many Communities Within Its Boundaries and the City of Owen Sound.* Owen Sound, Ontario: Richardson, Bond, and Wright, 1972.

Davis, H. L. *Honey in the Horn.* New York: William Morrow, 1935.
———. *Winds of Morning.* New York: William Morrow, 1952.
———. *Team Bells Woke Me, and Other Stories.* New York: William Morrow, 1953.
Davis, Lance, Richard Easterlin, and William Parker. *American Economic Growth: An Economist's History of the United States.* New York: Harper and Row, 1972.
Davis, Owen K. "Pollen Analysis of Wildcat Lake, Whitman County, Washington: The Introduction of Grazing." Master's thesis, Botany, Washington State University, 1975.
DeGraff, Herrell, and Ladd Haystead. *The Business of Farming.* Norman: University of Oklahoma Press, 1948.
Dingee, W., and W. F. McGregor. *Science of Successful Threshing.* Racine, Wisc.: J. I. Case, 1911.
Donaldson, Gordon. *The Scots Overseas.* London: Robert Hale, 1966.
Donan, P. *Oregon, Washington, Idaho and their Resources.* Portland: Oregon Railroad and Navigation, 1902.
Doneen, L. D. "Nitrogen in Relation to Composition, Growth, and Yield of Wheat." Washington AES Bulletin 296 (May 1934).
Dosch, Arno. "The Triumph of 'The Palouse,'" *Pacific Monthly* 14 (November 1905): 423–28.
Douglas, William O. *Of Men and Mountains.* New York: Harper and Brothers, 1950.
———. *Go East, Young Man; the Early Years: The Autobiography of William O. Douglas.* New York: Random House, 1974.
Douglass, William A., and Jon Bilbao. *Amerikanuak: Basques in the New World.* Reno: University of Nevada Press, 1975.
Drache, Hiram M. *The Day of the Bonanza: A History of Bonanza Farming in the Red River Valley of the North.* Fargo: North Dakota Institute for Regional Studies, 1964.
Drumheller, Dan. *"Uncle Dan" Drumheller Tells Thrills of Western Trails in 1854.* Spokane: Inland American Printers, 1925.
Durham, N. W. *History of the City of Spokane and Spokane Country, Washington: From Its Earliest Settlement to the Present Time.* Spokane: S. J. Clarke, 1912.
Eastern Washington Territory and Oregon: Facts Regarding the Resources, Productions, Industries, Soil, Climate, Healthfulness, Commerce, and Means of Communication. Oregon Railroad and Navigation Company, n. p., 1888.
Edelfsen, John B. "A Sociological Study of the Basques of Southwest Idaho." Ph.D. dissertation, Washington State College, 1948.
Elliott, T. C. (ed.). "Journal of David Thompson," *Oregon Historical Quarterly* 15:1 and 2 (March and June 1914): 39–63, 104–25.
Evans, Hartman K. "Sheep Trailing from Oregon to Wyoming" (ed. R. H. Burns). *Mississippi Valley Historical Review* 28:4 (March 1942): 581–92.

Ewing, P. V. (ed.). *The Golden Hoof: A Practical Sheep Book*. Chicago: Sheep Breeder, 1936.

Farmers in a Changing World. USDA *Yearbook of Agriculture*, 1940.

Fite, Gilbert C. *American Agriculture and Farm Policy Since 1900*. New York: American Historical Association, 1964.

————. "Daydreams and Nightmares: The Late Nineteenth-Century Agricultural Frontier" *Agricultural History* 40:4 (October 1966): 285–94.

————. *The Farmer's Frontier: 1865–1900*. New York: Rinehart and Winston, 1966.

Fitzgerald, Dennis A. *Livestock Under the AAA*. Washington: Brookings Institution, 1935.

Fleming, C. E. "Range Plants Poisonous to Sheep and Cattle in Nevada." Nevada AES Bulletin 95 (July 1918).

————, and C. A. Brennan. "Range Sheep Production in Northeastern Nevada: Production and Earning Power." Nevada AES Bulletin 151 (August 1940).

————. "Studies of the Range Sheep Business in Nevada: Factors, Receipts, Costs, and Earning Power Balance." Nevada AES Bulletin 145 (August 1937).

Fletcher, Robert S. "The End of the Open Range in Eastern Montana," *Mississippi Valley Historical Review* 16:2 (September 1929): 188–211.

Flynn, Elizabeth Gurley. *I Speak My Own Piece: Autobiography of the Rebel Girl*. New York: Masses and Mainstream, 1955.

Foss, Phillip O. *Politics and Grass: The Administration of Grazing on the Public Domain*. Seattle: University of Washington Press, 1960.

Freeman, Otis W. "Physiographic Divisions of the Columbia Plateau." *Yearbook of the Association of Pacific Coast Geographers* 6 (1940): 12–20.

————, and Howard Martin (eds.). *The Pacific Northwest: A Regional, Human, and Economic Survey of Resources and Development*. New York: J. Wiley, 1942.

Fries, Ulrich E. *From Copenhagen to Okanogan*. Caldwell, Idaho: Caxton Printers, 1951.

Frink, Maurice, W. Turrentine Jackson, and Agnes Spring. *When Grass Was King*. Boulder: University of Colorado, 1956.

Fritts, Harold C. "Tree-Ring Evidence for Climatic Changes in Western North America." *Monthly Weather Review* (July 1965): 421–43.

Fulmer, Elton. "Commercial Fertilizers." Washington AES Bulletin 98 (1911).

Gaines, E. F., and E. G. Schafer. "Wheat Varieties of Washington, 1929." Washington AES Bulletin 256 (July 1931).

————. "Wheat Varieties in Washington in 1939." Washington AES Bulletin 398 (April 1941).

Gaiser, Joseph H. "The Basques of the Jordan Valley Area: A Study in Social Process and Social Change." Ph.D. dissertation, Sociology, University of Southern California, 1944.

Galbraith, John Kenneth. *Made to Last.* London: Hamish Hamilton, 1964. (Later edition is retitled *The Scotch.*)

Garland, John H. "The Columbia Plateau Region of Commercial Grain Farming." *Geographical Review* 24:3 (July 1934): 371–79.

Gates, Charles M. "A Historical Sketch of the Economic Development of Washington Since Statehood," *Pacific Northwest Quarterly* 39:3 (July 1948): 214–32.

Gates, Paul W. "Cattle Kings in the Prairies." *Mississippi Valley Historical Review* 35:3 (December 1948): 379–412.

———. *History of the Public Land Law Development.* Washington: Government Printing Office, 1968.

Georgetta, Clel. *Golden Fleece in Nevada.* Reno: Venture Publishing, 1972.

Gilfillan, Archer B. "The Herding Day." *Atlantic Monthly* 143 (January 1929): 15–24.

———. "The Sheep Herder Calls It a Day." *Atlantic Monthly* 143 (May 1929): 607–15.

———. *Sheep: Life on the South Dakota Range.* (2nd. ed.), Minneapolis: University of Minnesota Press, 1957.

Gomez-Ibanez, Daniel A. "The Rise and Decline of Transhumance in the United States." Master's thesis, Geography, University of Wisconsin, Madison, 1967.

———. *The Western Pyrenees: Differential Evolution of the French and Spanish Borderland.* Oxford: Clarendon Press, 1975.

Gordon, Clarence. "Report on Cattle, Sheep, and Swine Supplementary to the Enumeration of Livestock on Farms in 1880." *Report on Products of Agriculture as Returned by the Tenth Census, 1880.*

Graham, Ian C. C. *Colonists from Scotland: Emigration to North America, 1707–1783.* Ithaca, New York: Cornell University Press, 1956.

Gray, James R. "Sheep Enterprises in Northern New Mexico." New Mexico AES Bulletin 454 (March 1961).

———. "Organization, Costs, and Incomes of Western Cattle and Sheep Ranches." New Mexico AES Bulletin 587 (October 1971).

Gray, L. C., Charles Stewart, and Howard Turner. "Farm Ownership and Tenancy." USDA *Yearbook of Agriculture*, 1923.

Greenberg, David B. (ed.). *Land That Our Fathers Plowed: The Settlement of Our Country As Told by the Pioneers Themselves and Their Contemporaries.* Norman: University of Oklahoma Press, 1969.

Greene, Frank. "Report on the Interior Wheat Lands of Oregon and Washington Territory." 50th Cong., 1st Sess., Sen. Exec. Doc. 229, 1888.

Gressley, Gene M. *Bankers and Cattlemen.* New York: Alfred A. Knopf, 1966.

Grey, Zane. *The Desert of Wheat.* New York: Grosset and Dunlap, 1919.

Griffiths, David. "Forage Conditions on the Northern Border of the Great Basin, being a Report Upon Investigations Made During July and August,

1901, in the Region Between Winemucca, Nevada and Ontario, Oregon." USDA Bureau of Plant Industry, Bulletin 15 (1902).

———. "Forage Conditions and Problems in Eastern Washington, Eastern Oregon, Northeastern California, and Northwestern Nevada." USDA Bureau of Plant Industry, Bulletin 38 (July 3, 1903).

Griliches, Zvi. "The Demand for Fertilizer: An Economic Interpretation of a Technical Change." *Journal of Farm Economics* 40 (August 1958) 591–605.

Grinnell, J. B. "Cattle Interests West of the Mississippi River." USDA Bureau of Animal Industry, First Annual Report, 1884.

Guillet, Edwin C. *Early Life in Upper Canada.* Toronto: University of Toronto Press, 1963.

Guither, Harold D. *Heritage of Plenty: A Guide to the Economic History and Development of United States Agriculture.* Danville, Ill.: Interstate Printers, 1972.

Gunther, John. *Inside U.S.A.* New York: Harper, 1947.

Hafenrichter, A. L. "Land Use and Erosion in the West." U.S. Soil Erosion Service, *The Land: Today and Tomorrow* 2:1 (January 1935).

———, and W. A. Rockie. "Ecological Aspects of Soil Erosion in the Pacific Northwest as Determined by the Reconnaissance Erosion Survey." *Northwest Science* 11:4 (November 1937).

Hansen, Marcus Lee. *The Mingling of the Canadian and American Peoples,* vol. 1. New Haven: Yale University Press, 1940.

Hargreaves, Mary W. M. *Dry Farming in the Northern Great Plains, 1900–1925.* Cambridge: Harvard University Press, 1957.

Harper, J. Russell (ed.). *Paul Kane's Frontier: Including "Wanderings of an Artist Among the Indians of North America" by Paul Kane.* Austin: University of Texas Press, 1971.

Hawthorne, Julian (ed.). *History of Washington, the Evergreen State: From Early Dawn to Daylight.* Vol. 2. New York: American Historical Publishing, 1893.

Haystead, Ladd, and Gilbert Fite. *The Agricultural Regions of the United States.* Norman: University of Oklahoma Press, 1955.

Hayter, Earl W. *The Troubled Farmer, 1850–1900: Rural Adjustment to Industrialism.* DeKalb: Northern Illinois University Press, 1968.

Heady, Earl O. *A Primer on Food, Agriculture, and Public Policy.* New York: Random House, 1967.

Heath, H. A. "Condition of the Sheep Industry West of the Mississippi River." USDA Bureau of Animal Industry, Sixth and Seventh Annual Reports (1889 and 1890), pp. 247–320.

Heisig, C. P. "A Graphic Presentation of Changes in the Agriculture of Washington, from 1930 to 1935." Washington AES Bulletin 341 (December 1936).

Higgins, F. Hal. "John M. Horner and the Development of the Combined Harvester." *Agricultural History* 32:1 (January 1958): 14–24.

Higgs, Robert. *The Transformation of the American Economy, 1865–1914: An Essay in Interpretation.* New York: John Wiley, 1971.

————. "Tractors or Horses? Some Basic Economics in the Pacific Northwest and Elsewhere." *Agricultural History* 49:1 (January 1975): 281–83.

Hill, Howard C. "The Development of Chicago as a Center of the Meat Packing Industry." *Mississippi Valley Historical Review* 10:3 (December 1923): 251–73.

Hislop, William, and C. E. Howell. "Sheep Husbandry in the Pacific Northwest." Washington AES Bulletin 134 (1917).

Historical Statistics of the United States, 1789–1945. U.S. Department of Commerce, Bureau of the Census, 1949.

History of the Yakima Valley, Washington. vol. 2, Spokane: S. J. Clarke, 1919.

Hochmuth, H. R., Earl Franklin, and Marion Clawson. "Sheep Migration in the Intermountain Region." USDA Circular 624 (January 1942).

Holbrook, Stewart H. *Machines of Plenty: Pioneering in American Agriculture.* New York: Macmillan Company, 1955.

Holden, William C. *The Espuela Land and Cattle Company: A Study of a Foreign-Owned Ranch in Texas.* Austin: Texas State Historical Association, 1970.

Holmes, Edwin S. "Wheat Growing and General Agricultural Conditions in the Pacific Coast Region of the United States." USDA Division of Statistics, Miscellaneous Bulletin 20 (1901).

Hoover, Roy O. "The Public Land Policy of Washington State: The Initial Period, 1889–1912." Ph.D. dissertation, Washington State University, 1967.

Hopkins, John A. *Changing Technology and Employment in Agriculture.* Washington: Bureau of Agricultural Economics, 1941. Reprinted in 1973 by DaCapo Press, New York.

Horner, G. M. "The Pacific Northwest Wheat Region." In *Soil*, USDA *Yearbook of Agriculture*, 1957.

Hultz, Fred S., and John A. Hill. *Range Sheep and Wool in the Seventeen Western States.* New York: John Wiley and Sons, 1931.

Humphrey, R. R. "Common Range Forage Types of the Inland Pacific Northwest," *Northwest Science* 19:1 (February 1945).

Hunter, Byron. "Farm Practice in the Columbia Basin Uplands." USDA Farmers' Bulletin 294 (1907).

————. "Dry Farming for Better Wheat Yields: The Columbia and Snake River Basins." USDA Farmers' Bulletin 1047 (July 1919).

————. "Dry Farming Methods and Practices in Wheat Growing in the Columbia and Snake River Basins." USDA Farmers' Bulletin 1545 (November 1927).

————, George Severance, and R. N. Miller. "A Review of the Agriculture of the Big Bend Country." Washington AES Bulletin 192 (September 1925).

If and When It Rains: The Stockman's View of the Range Question. Denver: American National Livestock Association, 1938.

Illustrated History of the Big Bend Country: Embracing Lincoln, Douglas, Adams, and Franklin Counties. Spokane: Western Historical Publishing, 1904.

An Illustrated History of Klickitat, Yakima, and Kittitas Counties. Spokane: Interstate Publishing, 1904.

Jackman, E. R., and R. A. Long. *The Oregon Desert.* Caldwell, Idaho: Caxton Press, 1965.

Jackson, W. Turrentine. *The Enterprising Scot: Investors in the American West After 1783.* Edinburgh: Edinburgh University Press, 1968.

Jardine, James T. "The Pasturage System for Handling Range Sheep: Investigations During 1909." USDA Forest Service Circular 178 (July 9, 1910).

Jardine, James T., and Mark Anderson. "Range Management on the National Forests." USDA Bulletin 790 (August 1919).

Jensen, Merrill (ed.). *Regionalism in America.* Madison: University of Wisconsin Press, 1951.

Johnson, Glenn L., and C. Leroy Quance, eds. *The Overproduction Trap in United States Agriculture: A Study of Resource Allocation from World War I to the Late 1960's.* Baltimore: Johns Hopkins Press, 1972.

Johnson, Neil, and E. F. Landerholm. "Farm-Management Problems in Shifting from Sack to Bulk Handling of Grain in the Pacific Northwest." USDA Technical Bulletin 287 (February 1932).

Johnson, Neil, and Rex Willard. "Trends in Agriculture in Washington, 1900 to 1930." Washington AES Bulletin 300 (June 1934).

———. "Nature and Distribution of Types of Farming in Washington." Washington AES Bulletin 301 (July 1934).

Johnson, Sherman E. "Changes in American Farming." USDA Miscellaneous Publication 707 (December 1949).

Jones, A. D., and H. R. Stucky. "Wool Producing Areas in Twelve Western States." New Mexico AES Bulletin 456 (May 1961).

Jones, Wesley, "The Victory of National Irrigation," *Washington Magazine* 1:4 (June 1906): 253–58.

Keith, Thomas B. *The Horse Interlude: A Pictorial History of Horse and Man in the Inland Northwest.* Moscow: University of Idaho, 1976.

Kendall, George W. *Letters from a Texas Sheep Ranch: Written in the Years 1860 and 1867 by George Wilkins Kendall to Henry Stephens Randall* (ed. Harry J. Brown). Urbana: University of Illinois Press, 1959.

Kennedy, P. B. "Summer Ranges of Eastern Nevada Sheep." Nevada AES Bulletin 52 (November 1903).

———, and Samuel Doten. "A Preliminary Report on the Summer Ranges of Western Nevada Sheep." Nevada AES Bulletin 51 (December 1901).

Kenny, Judith Keyes. "Early Sheep Ranching in Eastern Oregon." *Oregon Historical Quarterly* 64:2 (June 1963): 101–22.

Klemgard, J. G., and G. F. Cadisch. "Cost of Wheat Production by Power Methods of Farming, 1919–1929." Washington AES Bulletin 255 (June 1931).

Land, USDA Yearbook of Agriculture, 1958.

Landerholm, E. F. "The Economic Relation of Tractors to Farm Organization in the Grain Farming Areas of Eastern Washington." Washington AES Bulletin 310 (April 1935).

Landstrom, Karl S. "The Land Ownership Map Situation in the Pacific Northwest States." USDA Bureau of Agricultural Economics Publication, 1933–34.

Latham, H. Trans-Missouri Stock Raising: The Pasture Lands of North America—Winter Grazing, the Sources of the Future Beef and Wool Supply of the United States. Omaha: Omaha Daily Herald, 1871.

Leary, Elizabeth F. Clayton's Legislative Manual of Washington, 1905. Tacoma: Vaughn and Merrill, 1905.

Lebergott, Stanley. "Labor Force and Employment, 1800–1960." In Output, Employment, and Productivity in the United States After 1800: Studies in Income and Wealth, vol. 30, Conference on Research in Income and Wealth. New York: Columbia University, 1966.

LeDuc, Thomas. "State Disposal of the Agricultural College Land Scrip." Agricultural History 28:3 (July 1954): 99–106.

Leeper, Lonnie D. "Social and Economic History of Hay and Community." Master's thesis, Washington State College, 1941.

Lehmann, V. W. Forgotten Legions: Sheep in the Rio Grande Plain of Texas. El Paso: Texas Western Press, 1969.

Leonard, William E. "The Wheat Farmer of Southeastern Washington." Journal of Land and Public Utility Economics 2 (January 1926): 23–39.

Lever, W. H. A History of Whitman County. N.p., 1901.

Lewis, Oscar. "Bumper Crops in the Desert," Harper's Monthly 193 (1946).

Lewis, William S. The Story of Early Days in the Big Bend Country: Breaking Trails, Rush of Miners, Coming of Cattlemen, Making Homes, Pioneer Hardships in the Big Bend Country. Spokane: W. D. Allen, 1926.

Linsey, James E. "Economic History of Whitman County, Washington." Master's thesis, Washington State College, 1926.

Loomis, Ralph A., and Glen Barton. "Productivity of Agriculture: United States, 1870–1958." USDA Technical Bulletin 1238 (April 1961).

McCall, M. A., and H. F. Holtz. "Investigations in Dry Farm Tillage." Washington AES Bulletin 164 (June 1921).

McCall, M. A., and H. M. Wanser. "The Principles of Summer-Fallow Tillage." Washington AES Bulletin 183 (October 1924).

McCarty, J. W. "Australia as a Region of Recent Settlement in the Nineteenth Century." Australian Economic History Review 12:2 (September 1972).

McCulloh, E. "The Palouse Project." From Proceedings of the Third Annual Meeting of the Washington Irrigation Institute.

McGregor, Alexander C. "The Economic Impact of the Mullan Road on Walla Walla, 1860–1883," *Pacific Northwest Quarterly* 65:3 (July 1974): 118–29.

———. "The Agricultural Development of the Columbia Plateau: McGregor Land and Livestock Company, A Case History." Ph.D. dissertation, University of Washington, 1977.

McGregor, Peter, and F. M. Rothrock. "What Free Wool Did in Washington." *National Wool Grower*, June 1913.

McKee, Bates. *Cascadia: The Geologic Evolution of the Pacific Northwest.* New York: McGraw-Hill, 1972.

McKnight, Tom L. "Biotic Influences on Australian Pastoral Land Use." *Yearbook of the Association of Pacific Coast Geographers* 32 (1970): 7–22

McMicken, W. "Report of the Surveyor-General of Washington Territory." In "Report of the Secretary of the Interior," 46th Cong., 2nd Sess., House Exec. Doc. 1, part 5, 1879.

McNeilly, John T. "The Cattle Industry of Colorado, Wyoming, and Nevada and the Sheep Industry of Colorado in 1897." USDA Bureau of Animal Industry, Fifteenth Annual Report (1899).

Malin, James C. "Mobility and History: Reflections on the Agricultural Policies of the United States in Relation to a Mechanized World." *Agricultural History* 17:4 (October 1943): 177–91.

———. *Winter Wheat in the Golden Belt of Kansas: A Study in the Adaptation to Subhumid Geographical Environment.* Lawrence: University of Kansas, 1944.

———. *The Grassland of North America: Prolegomena to Its History.* Ann Harbor, Mich.: Edwards Brothers, 1947.

Manual of the Eleventh Session of the Washington State Legislature, 1909. Seattle: Pacific Press, 1909.

Martin, Robert F., *Income in Agriculture, 1929–1935.* New York: National Industrial Conference Board, 1936.

Mathers, Michael, *Sheepherders: Men Alone.* Boston: Houghton Mifflin, 1975.

Meinig, Donald W. "Environment and Settlement in the Palouse, 1868–1910." Master's thesis, Geography, University of Washington, 1950.

———. "Wheat Sacks Out to Sea: The Early Export Trade from the Walla Walla Country." *Pacific Northwest Quarterly* 45:1 (January 1954): 13–18.

———. "The Evolution of Understanding an Environment: Climate and Wheat Culture in the Columbia Plateau," *Yearbook of the Association of Pacific Coast Geographers* 16 (1954): 25–31.

———. *The Great Columbia Plain: A Historical Geography, 1805–1910.* Seattle: University of Washington Press, 1968.

Melander, A. L., and M. A. Yothers. "The Coulee Cricket." Washington AES Bulletin 137 (January 1917).

Milk, Richard G. "The New Agriculture in the United States: A Dissenter's View." *Land Economics* 48:3 (August 1972): 228–39.

Minto, John. "Sheep Husbandry in Oregon." *Oregon Historical Quarterly* 3:3 (September 1902): 219–47.

Moomaw, James C. "Some Effects of Grazing and Fire on Vegetation in the Columbia Basin Region, Washington." Ph.D. dissertation, Botany, Washington State College, 1956.

Morton, W. L. *The Kingdom of Canada: A General History from Earliest Times.* Indianapolis: Bobbs-Merrill; Toronto: McClelland and Stewart, 1963.

Mothershed, H. R. *Swan Land and Cattle, Ltd.* Norman: University of Oklahoma Press, 1971.

Muir, John. *My First Summer in the Sierra.* Boston: Houghton Mifflin, 1911.

Murphy, John C. *The Facts Concerning the Government Palouse Project: An Appeal to the People and to Congress for Rights, for Fair Play, for Irrigation, for Electric Power.* Pasco: Pasco Express, 1912.

Murray, Keith. "Issues and Personalities of Pacific Northwest Politics, 1889–1950." *Pacific Northwest Quarterly* 41:3 (July 1950): 213–33.

Nash, Wallis. *Two Years in Oregon.* New York: D. Appleton, 1882.

Nesbit, Robert C., and Charles M. Gates. "Agriculture in Eastern Washington, 1890–1910." *Pacific Northwest Quarterly* 37:4 (October 1946): 279–302.

Nesmith, James W. "Diary of the Emigration of 1843." *Oregon Historical Quarterly* 7:4 (December 1906): 329–59.

The Night the Mountain Fell, and Other Stories of North Central Washington History, n.d., n.p.

Nimmo, Joseph. "Range and Ranch Cattle Traffic." 48th Cong., 2nd sess., House Exec. Doc. 267, 1885.

North, Douglass C. *Growth and Welfare in the American Past.* 2nd ed. Englewood Cliffs, N.J.: Prentice-Hall, 1972.

Oberholtzer, C. J. "Development of Palouse Falls." Bachelor's thesis, Washington State College, 1910.

Ogle, George A. *Standard Atlas of Adams County, Washington.* Chicago: George Ogle, 1912.

Oliphant, J. Orin. "Winter Losses of Cattle in the Oregon Country, 1847–1890," *Washington Historical Quarterly* 23:1 (January 1932): 3–17.

———. "The Cattle Trade Through the Snoqualmie Pass," *Pacific Northwest Quarterly* 38:3 (July 1947): 193–214.

———. "History of the Livestock Industry in the Pacific Northwest." *Oregon Historical Quarterly* 49:1 (March 1948): 3–29.

———. *On the Cattle Ranges of the Oregon Country.* Seattle: University of Washington Press, 1968.

Oliver, Herman. *Gold and Cattle Country.* Portland: Binfords and Mort, 1962.

Olsen, Michael L. "Transplantation of Domestic Plants and Animals in the Pacific Northwest." *Journal of the West* 14:3 (July 1975): 40–50.

Oregon Almanac, 1915: Official Pamphlet Published by the State of Oregon for the Information of Homeseekers, Settlers, and Investors. Oregon State Immigration Commission (Salem, 1914).

Orr, Alden E., C. P. Heisig, and J. C. Knott. "Trends and Desirable Adjustments in Washington Agriculture." Washington AES Bulletin 335 (July 1936).

Osgood, Ernest S. *The Day of the Cattleman.* Minneapolis: University of Minnesota, 1929.

Page, Arthur W., "The Fight for a Land Conscience: The Administration's Campaign Against Timber-Frauds and Dishonest Cattlemen, Who Have Driven Out Honest Settlers," *World's Work* 14:1 (November 1907): 9588–92.

Parker, William N., and Judith Klein. "Productivity Growth in Grain Production in the United States, 1840–60 and 1900–10." In *Output, Employment, and Productivity in the United States After 1800: Studies in Income and Wealth,* vol. 30, Conference on Research and Wealth, National Bureau of Economic Research and Wealth. New York: Columbia University, 1966.

Peek, William W. "The Utilization of Range Land Resources by Beef Cattle in the Palouse." Master's thesis, Washington State College, 1941.

Peffer, E. Louise. *The Closing of the Public Domain: Disposal and Reservation Policies, 1900–50.* Stanford: Stanford University Press, 1951.

Peters, Stephen H. "The Populists and the Washington Legislature, 1893–1900." Master's thesis, University of Washington, 1967.

Pinchot, Gifford. "Grazing on the Public Lands—Extracts from the Report of the Public Lands Commission." 58th Cong., 3rd Sess., Sen. Exec. Doc. 189, 1905.

Piper, C. V. "The Russian Thistle in Washington." Washington AES Bulletin 34 (1898).

———, and H. N. Vinal. "Our Forage Resources." In USDA *Yearbook of Agriculture,* 1923.

Plant Diseases, USDA *Yearbook of Agriculture,* 1953.

Plat Book of Whitman County, Washington. Seattle: Anderson Map Company, 1910.

Polk, R. L., and Company. *Oregon, Washington, and Idaho Gazetteer,* 1892, 1901–2, 1919–20 editions.

———. *Whitman County Directory,* 1904, 1908–9 editions.

———. *Whitman and Garfield Counties Directory,* 1912–13, 1915–16, 1917–18 editions.

Potter, E. L., and H. A. Lindgren. "Cost of Producing Mutton and Wool on Eastern Oregon Ranges." Oregon AES Bulletin 219 (September 1925).

Powell, John Wesley. *Report on the Lands of the Arid Region of the United States With a More Detailed Account of the Lands of Utah.* Originally published in 1879. New edition edited by Wallace Stegner, Cambridge: Harvard University Press, 1962.

Power to Produce. USDA *Yearbook of Agriculture,* 1960.

Powers, Stephen. *The American Merino: For Wool and For Mutton.* New York: Judd and Company, 1887.

Prebble, John. *The Lion in the North: A Personal View of Scotland's History.* New York: Coward, McCann, 1971.

Pressly, Thomas J., and William Scofield. *Farm Real Estate Values in the United States by Counties, 1850–1959.* Seattle: University of Washington Press, 1965.

Prices Received by Washington Farmers, 1910–1959, Washington State and U.S. Departments of Agriculture, 1960.

Proceedings of the Convention of Producers, Shippers, and Millers: Otherwise Known as the Wheat Convention. Pullman, 1906.

Proceedings of the National Conference on Land Utilization, Chicago, 1931. Washington: Government Printing Office, 1932.

"Progress Report: 32nd Annual Field Day of Dryland Experiment Station, State of Washington" (June 18, 1948).

Prosser, W. F. *A History of the Puget Sound Country: Its Resources, Its Commerce, and Its People.* New York: Lewis Publishing Company, 1903.

Pubols, Ben H., A. E. Orr, and C. P. Heisig. "Farming Systems and Practices and Their Relationship to Soil Conservation and Farm Income in the Wheat Region of Washington." Washington AES Bulletin 374 (July 1939).

Puget Sound Business Directory and Guide to Washington Territory, 1872: Comprising a Correct History of Washington Territory. Olympia: Murphy and Harned, 1872.

Puter, S. A. D. *Looters of the Public Domain.* Portland, Oregon: Portland Printing House, 1908.

Rakestraw, Lawrence. "Sheep Grazing in the Cascade Range: John Minto vs. John Muir," *Pacific Historical Review* 27:4 (November 1958): 371–82.

Raper, Arthur F. "Graphic Presentation of Rural Trends." Bureau of Agricultural Economics (1952).

Rasmussen, Wayne D. "The Impact of Technological Change in American Agriculture, 1862–1962." *Journal of Economic History* 22:4 (December 1962): 578–91.

————, "A Postscript: Twenty-Five Years of Change in Farm Productivity." *Agricultural History* 49:1 (January 1975): 84–86.

————. (ed.) *Readings in the History of American Agriculture.* Urbana: University of Illinois Press, 1960.

————. *Agriculture in the United States: A Documentary History.* New York: Random House, 1975.

Raup, Phillip M. "Corporate Farming in the United States." *Journal of Economic History* 33:1 (March 1973): 274–90.

Renshaw, Patrick. *The Wobblies: The Story of Syndicalism in the United States.* New York: Doubleday and Company, 1967.

"Report of the Public Lands Commission." 58th Cong., 3rd sess., Sen. Exec. Doc. 4, 1904–1905.

"Reports of the Governor of Washington Territory to the Secretary of the Interior," 1887–89. Washington: Government Printing Office, 1887–89.

The Resources of the State of Oregon: A Book of Statistical Information Treating Upon Oregon as a Whole, and by Counties. Salem: W. H. Leeds, 1898.

Reuss, Carl F. "The Farm Labor Problem in Washington, 1917–18." *Pacific Northwest Quarterly* 34:4 (October 1943): 339–52.

Riddle, Thomas. "Populism in the Palouse: Old Ideals and New Realities." *Pacific Northwest Quarterly* 65:3 (July 1974): 97–109.

Robbins, Roy M. "The Federal Land System in an Embryo State," *Pacific Historical Review* 4:4 (December 1935): 356–75.

———. *Our Landed Heritage: The Public Domain, 1776–1936.* Princeton: Princeton University Press, 1942.

Robbins, W. W. "Alien Plants Growing Without Cultivation in California." California AES Bulletin 637 (1940).

Roberts, Paul C. *Hoof Prints on Forest Ranges: The Early Years of National Forest Range Administration.* San Antonio: Naylor Company, 1963.

Rockie, W. A. "Man's Effect on the Palouse." *Geographical Review* 29 (January 1939): 34–45.

———. "The Palouse." *Yearbook of the Association of Pacific Coast Geographers* 15 (1953): 6–9.

Rogin, Leo. *The Introduction of Farm Machinery in Its Relation to the Productivity of Labor in the Agriculture of the United States During the Nineteenth Century.* Berkeley: University of California, 1931.

Rollins, Philip. *The Cowboy: His Characteristics, His Equipment, and His Past in the Development of the West.* New York: Charles Scribner's Sons, 1922.

Roterus, Victor. "Spring and Winter Wheat on the Columbia Plateau." *Economic Geography* 10:4 (October 1934): 368–73.

Rothstein, Morton. "A British Investment in Bonanza Farming, 1879–1910." *Agricultural History* 33:2 (April 1959): 72–78.

———. "America in the International Rivalry for the British Wheat Market, 1860–1914." *Mississippi Valley Historical Review* 47:3 (December 1960): 401–18.

———. "The Big Farm: Abundance and Scale in American Agriculture," *Agricultural History* 49:4 (October 1975): 583–97.

———. "West Coast Farmers and the Tyranny of Distance: Agriculture on the Fringes of the World Market." *Agriculture History* 49:1 (January 1975): 272–80.

Russell, Loris. *Everyday Life in Colonial Canada.* Toronto: Copp-Clark Publishing, 1973.

Ruttan, Vernon W., Arley Waldo, and James Houck (eds.). *Agricultural Policy in an Affluent Society.* New York: Norton and Company, 1969.

Ryan's Legislative Manual, 1907. Tacoma: Commercial Bindery, 1907.

Salutos, Theodore. "Land Policy and Its Relation to Agricultural Production

and Distribution, 1862–1933," *Journal of Economic History* 22:4 (December 1962): 445–60.

————, and John D. Hicks. *Agricultural Discontent in the Middle West, 1900–1939.* Madison: University of Wisconsin Press, 1951.

Sampson, Arthur W. "Plant Succession in Relation to Range Management." USDA Bulletin 791 (August 27, 1919).

Saunderson, M. H., and Louis Vinke. "The Economics of Range Sheep Production in Montana." Montana AES Bulletin 302 (June 1935).

Sawyer, Byrd W. *Nevada Nomads: A Story of the Sheep Industry.* San Jose: Harlan-Young, 1971.

Schafer, E. G., and E. F. Gaines. "Washington Wheats." Washington AES Bulletin 121 (February 1915).

Scherz, Lyle P., et al. *Another Revolution in U.S. Farming?* USDA Agricultural Economic Report 441 (December 1979).

Schlebecker, John T. *Cattle Raising on the Plains, 1900–1961.* Lincoln: University of Nebraska Press, 1963.

————. *Whereby We Thrive: A History of American Farming, 1607–1972.* Ames: Iowa State University Press, 1975.

Science in Farming. USDA *Yearbook of Agriculture,* 1943–47.

Scott, Roy V. *The Reluctant Farmer: The Rise of Agricultural Extension to 1914.* Urbana: University of Illinois Press, 1970.

Sears, Paul B. "Where is Your Dog Tonight?" *Rangeman's Journal* 3:1 (February 1976): 12–13.

Settler's Guide to Oregon and Washington Territory and to the Lands of the Northern Pacific Railroad on the Pacific Slope. New York: Northern Pacific Railroad, 1872.

Severance, George, Byron Hunter, and Paul Eke. "Farming Systems for Eastern Washington and Northern Idaho." Washington AES Bulletin 244 (July 1930).

Shaw, E. L., and L. L. Heller. "Domestic Breeds of Sheep in America." USDA Bulletin 94 (August 17, 1914).

Shaw, R. M. "Range Sheep Industry in Kittitas County, Washington," *Pacific Northwest Quarterly* 33:2 (April 1942): 153–70.

"Sheep Ranches—Spokane Farm Credit District: Production, Income and Expense." Farm Credit Administration, Economic and Credit Research Division, May 1940.

Sheller, Roscoe. *Ben Snipes: Northwest Cattle King.* Portland: Binfords and Mort, 1966.

"Shepherd Boy." *Modern Sheep: Breeds and Management.* Chicago: American Sheep Breeder, 1907.

Shideler, James H. *Farm Crisis, 1919–1923.* Berkeley: University of California Press, 1957.

Shortt, Adam, and Arthur Doughty. *Canada and Its Provinces,* vol. 18, *The Province of Ontario, Part II.* Toronto: Glasgow, Brook and Company, 1914.

Shroyer, Peter A. "Oregon Sheep, Wool, and Woolens Industries." *Oregon Historical Quarterly* 67:2 (June 1966): 125–38.

Shurte, C. H. "Reminiscences of the Sheep Industry." *National Wool Grower*, December 1916.

Sievers, F. J., and H. F. Holtz. "The Silt Loam Soils of Eastern Washington and their Management." Washington AES Bulletin 166 (January 1922).

————. "The Fertility of Washington Soils." Washington AES Bulletin 189 (December 1924).

Smick, A. A., and Fred Yoder. "A Study of Farm Migration in Selected Communities in the State of Washington." Washington AES Bulletin 233 (June 1929).

Smout, T. C. *A History of the Scottish People, 1560–1830.* London: Collins, 1969.

Smythe, William E. *The Conquest of Arid America.* Originally published in 1899. Seattle: University of Washington Press, 1969.

Snodgrass, Milton M., and L. T. Wallace. *Agriculture, Economics, and Growth.* 2nd ed. New York: Meredith Corporation, 1970.

Soil. USDA *Yearbook of Agriculture,* 1957.

Spencer, D. A., M. C. Hall, et al. "The Sheep Industry," USDA *Yearbook of Agriculture,* 1923.

Spencer, Lloyd, and Lancaster Pollard. *A History of the State of Washington,* vol. 3. New York: American Historical Society, 1937.

Spillman, William J. "The Hybrid Wheats." Washington AES Bulletin 89 (1909).

————. *Balancing the Farm Output: A Statement of the Present Deplorable Conditions of Farming, Its Causes and Suggested Remedies.* New York: Orange Judd, 1927.

"William J. Spillman: The First President of the American Farm Management Association." *Journal of Farm Economics* 14:1 (January 1932).

Stafford, John A. "Basque Ethnohistory in Kern County, California, 1872–1934." Master's thesis, Anthropology, Sacramento State College, 1971.

Starling, Harvey W., and Fred Yoder. "Local Rural Leaders in Washington." Washington AES Bulletin 257 (September 1931).

Stegner, Wallace. *Beyond the Hundredth Meridian: John Wesley Powell and the Second Opening of the West.* Boston: Houghton Mifflin, 1954.

————. *Wolf Willow: A History, a Story, and a Memory of the Last Plains Frontier.* New York: Viking Press, 1962.

Stewart, Henry. *The Shepherd's Manual: A Practical Treatise on the Sheep, Designed Especially for American Shepherds.* New York: Orange Judd, 1882 and 1907 editions.

Strauss, Frederick, and Louis Bean. "Gross Farm Income and Indices of Farm Production and Prices in the United States, 1869–1937." USDA Technical Bulletin 703 (December 1940).

Strong, Dexter K. "Beef Cattle Industry in Oregon, 1890–1938." *Oregon Historical Quarterly* 41:3 (September 1940): 251–87.

Svobida, Lawrence. *An Empire of Dust.* Caldwell, Idaho: Caxton Printers, 1940.

Swan, James G. *The Northwest Coast, or Three Years' Residence in Washington Territory.* First published in 1857. Seattle: University of Washington Press, 1972.

Swierenga, Robert P. *Pioneers and Profits: Land Speculation on the Iowa Frontier.* Ames: Iowa State University Press, 1968.

Symons, Thomas W. "The Upper Columbia River and the Great Plain of the Columbia." 47th Cong., 1st sess., Sen. Exec. Doc. 186, 1882.

Tattersall, James N. "The Economic Development of the Pacific Northwest to 1920." Ph.D. dissertation, University of Washington, 1960.

Taylor, E. A., and F. R. Yoder. "Rural Social Organization in Whitman County." Washington AES Bulletin 203 (June 1926).

Taylor, H. M. "Condition of the Cattle-Range Industry." USDA Bureau of Animal Industry, Third Annual Report, 1886.

———. "Condition of the Cattle Interests West of the Mississippi River." USDA Bureau of Animal Industry, Fourth Annual Report, 1887.

Technology on the Farm: A Special Report by an Interbureau Committee and the Bureau of Agricultural Economics of the United States Department of Agriculture. USDA, 1940.

Terkel, Studs. *Hard Times: An Oral History of the Great Depression.* New York: Avon, 1970.

Thatcher, R. W. "Nineteenth Annual Report of the State Agricultural Experiment Station." Washington AES Unnumbered Bulletin (1909).

———. "Wheat and Flour Investigations: Crops of 1906–7." Washington AES Bulletin 91 (1910).

———. "The Nitrogen and Humus Problem in Dry Farming." Washington AES Bulletin 105 (June 1912).

Thatcher, R. W., George Olson, and W. L. Hadlock. "The Crops of 1908–09." Washington AES Bulletin 100 (1911).

The Thresher's Guide. Madison, Wisc.: The American Thresherman, 1910.

Todd, Hugh C. "Land Tenures of Whitman County." Bachelor's thesis, Washington State College, 1906.

Told by the Pioneers: Tales of Frontier Life As Told by Those Who Remember the Days of Washington Territory and Early Statehood of Washington. 3 vols. WPA Project 5841, Olympia, 1937 and 1938.

Torgeson, Lenora. *Snake River Hills.* N.p., 1976.

Tostlebe, Alvin S. "The Growth of Physical Capital in Agriculture, 1870–1950." National Bureau of Economic Research, Occasional Paper 44 (1954).

Towne, C. W., and E. N. Wentworth. *Shepherd's Empire.* Norman: University of Oklahoma Press, 1946.

———. *Cattle and Men.* Norman: University of Oklahoma Press, 1955.

Towne, Marvin W., and Wayne Rasmussen. "Farm Gross Product and Gross Investment in the Nineteenth Century," *Trends in the American*

Economy in the Nineteenth Century: Studies in Income and Wealth, vol. 24, Conference on Research in Income and Wealth, National Bureau of Economic Research, Princeton, 1960.

"Trends in Agriculture, 1900–1930," Washington AES Bulletin 300 (1934).

Ufland, Vina F. *History of Sydenham Township.* Owen Sound, Ont.: Richardson and Bond, 1967.

USDA. *Agricultural Statistics*, 1973–80. Washington: Government Printing Office.

USDA, Bureau of Agricultural Economics. "Livestock on Farms, January 1, 1867–1937, Revised Estimates, Number, Value per Head, Total Value." January 1938.

———. "Livestock on Farms and Ranches on January 1: Number, Value, and Classes, 1920–39." Statistical Bulletin 88 (1950).

———. "Net Farm Income and Income Parity Summary, 1910–42" (July 1942).

———. "Revised Estimates of Wheat Acreage, Yield, and Production, 1866–1934." 1937

USDA, BAI. "Average Price of Sheep in Chicago." Nineteenth Annual Report, 1900.

———. "Average Prices of Farm Stock, 1870–1896." Fourteenth Annual Report, 1897–98. Washington: Government Printing Office, 1898.

———. "Number and Value of Farm Animals, 1870–1986." Fourteenth Annual Report, 1897–98.

———. "Number and Value of Farm Animals, 1899." Sixteenth Annual Report, 1899.

USDA, Economic Research Service. "Costs and Returns, Commercial Wheat Farms, Pacific Northwest, Northern Plains, Southern Plains." FCR-63 (July 1969) and similar earlier studies of commercial farms: 1930–51 (Agricultural Research Service, Statistical Bulletin 197 [November 1956]); 1930–57 (Economic Research Service, Statistical Bulletin 297 [December 1961]); and 1966–67 (Economic Research Service, Agricultural Information Bulletin 230 [September 1968]).

USDA, Forest Service. "Grazing Handbook: North Pacific District." 1927.

USDA, Division of Statistics. "Report on the Area of Winter Grain, the Condition of Farm Animals, and on Freight Rates of Transportation Companies." Report 4 (April 1884). The following reports, issued under the same or similar titles, provide estimates of death losses of Columbia Plateau livestock: Bureau of Statistics Report 17 (April 1885); Report 26 (January 1886); Report 28 (April 1886); Report of the Statistician 37 (January 1887); Report 39 (April 1887); Report 48 (January 1888); Report 70 (January 1890); Report 72 (April 1890); Report 112 (January 1894); Report 114 (April 1894); Report 125 (April 1895); Division of Statistics Report 156 (April 1899).

———. "Railway Charges for the Transportation of Wool." Miscellaneous Bulletin 10 (July 1896).

————. "Wages of Farm Labor in the United States." Miscellaneous Bulletin 4 (1892).

Vogel, O. A., S. P. Swenson, Harley Jacquot, and C. S. Holton. "Marfed Wheat." Washington AES Bulletin 485 (March 1947).

Voorhis, Edwin, and W. E. Schneider. "Economic Aspects of the Sheep Industry." California AES Bulletin 473 (September 1929).

Wakefield, Richard, and Paul Landis. "The Drought Farmer Adjusts to the West." Washington AES Bulletin 378 (July 1939).

Wallace, Henry C. "The Year in Agriculture." USDA *Yearbook of Agriculture*, 1924.

Waring, Guy. *My Pioneer Past*. Boston: Bruce Humphries, 1936.

Warren, G. F. "Prices of Farm Products in the United States." USDA Bulletin 999 (August 26, 1921).

Washburn, R. S. "Cost of Using Horses, Tractors, and Combines on Wheat Farms in Sherman County, Oregon." USDA Bulletin 1447 (December 1926).

————. "Cost of Producing Winter Wheat and Incomes from Wheat Farming in Sherman County, Oregon." USDA Bulletin 1446 (January 1927).

Washington Livestock (historical and statistical trends), publication of USDA and Washington State Department of Agriculture (1967).

Washington State. *Journal of the House*. 1905 and 1907.

————. *Journal of the Senate*. 1907 and 1909.

Washington State, Bureau of Statistics, Agriculture and Immigration. "Biennial Report." 1903.

————. *State of Washington, 1901: Its Resources; Natural, Industrial and Commercial*. Olympia, 1901.

Washington State, Department of Agriculture. "Biennial Report to the Governor." Reports 2–6, issued during the years 1914–26.

————. "Adams County Agriculture." County Agricultural Data Series. 1956.

————. "Whitman County Agriculture." County Agricultural Data Series. 1956.

Washington State, Department of Dry Land Demonstration and Experiment. "First Annual Report." Washington AES Bulletin 119 (January 1915).

Washington Territory: Facts Regarding Its Climate and Soil, Mineral, Agricultural, Manufacturing, and Commercial Resources, Information for Immigrants. Washington Territory Immigrant Aid Society. Seattle: Hanford and McClaire, 1879.

Watkins, John B. "Wheat Exporting from the Pacific Northwest." Washington AES Bulletin 201 (May 1926).

Weaver, J. E. "A Study of the Vegetation of Southeastern Washington and Adjacent Idaho." *University of Nebraska Studies* 17:1 (January 1917): 2–109.

Webb, Walter Prescott. *The Great Plains*. Boston: Ginn and Company, 1931.

Wentworth, Edward N. *Progressive Sheep Raising*. Chicago: Armour's Livestock Bureau, 1929.

——. *America's Sheep Trails: History, Personalities*. Ames: Iowa State College, 1948.

The Western Range: A Great but Neglected National Resource, 74th Cong., 2nd sess., Sen. Exec. Doc. 199, 1936.

"Wheat: Acreage, Yield, Production, by States, 1886–1943." USDA Agricultural Marketing Service, Statistical Bulletin 158 (February 1955).

"Wheat and Flour Investigations." Washington AES Bulletin 100 (1911).

"The Wheat Situation—The Price and Purchasing Power of Wheat." USDA *Yearbook of Agriculture*, 1923.

White, Langdon. "Transhumance in the Sheep Industry of the Salt Lake Region." *Economic Geography* 2:3 (July 1926): 414–25.

Wik, Reynold M. *Steam Power on the American Farm*. Philadelphia: University of Pennsylvania Press, 1953.

——. "Henry Ford and the Agricultural Depression of 1920–1923." *Agricultural History* 29:1 (January 1955): 15–21.

——. "Some Interpretations of the Mechanization of Agriculture in the Far West." *Agricultural History* 49:1 (January 1975): 73–83.

Wilcox, E. V. "Sheep Ranching in the Western States." USDA Bureau of Animal Industry, Nineteenth Annual Report, 1902.

——. "The Grazing Industry." Hawaii AES Bulletin, unnumbered (1911).

Woehlike, Walter. "On the Trail of the Wheat Gamblers." *Sunset* 35 (August 1915).

Wright, Chester W. *Wool-Growing and the Tariff: A Study in the Economic History of the United States*. Boston: Houghton Mifflin, 1910.

Yeager, Walter M. "The Pioneer's Problems of Land Acquisition under the Public Land Laws in Southeastern Washington." Master's thesis, Washington State University, 1961.

Yoder, Fred R. "Pioneer Social Adaptation in the Palouse Country of Eastern Washington, 1870–90," *Research Studies of the State College of Washington* 6:4 (December 1938): 131–59.

Young, Vernon. "Changes in Vegetation and Soil of the Palouse Prairie Caused by Overgrazing." *Journal of Forestry* 41:11 (November 1943): 834–38.

Zimmerman, R. Earl. "A History of the Development of Agriculture in Whitman County." Bachelor's thesis, Washington State College, 1916.

II. MANUSCRIPTS AND UNPUBLISHED SOURCES

Ankeny, Levi. Biographical File. Pacific Northwest Biographies, Pacific Northwest Room, University of Washington Library.

Auditor's and County Clerk's Offices, Adams County Courthouse, Ritzville; Latah County Courthouse, Moscow, Idaho; Walla Walla County Courthouse, Walla Walla; Whitman County Courthouse, Colfax. Property deeds, conditional sales, corporate charters.

Beattie, R. Kent. Papers, 1899–1956. Manuscripts and Special Collections, Washington State University Library.

Bertramson, B. R. "Archives" files. Agronomy Department, Washington State University.

Boone, Marie. Collection, 1882–1941. Letters, ledgers, reminiscences, photographs, mining stock, daybooks, autograph albums, and other materials of Archie and Nellie McGregor. Betty Jean Peatross, Glendale, California.

Carstensen, Vernon. "An Overview of American Agricultural History." MSS. prepared for National Archives Conference, 1977.

Clemens, Fred W. "Remembering." MSS. about pioneering in the western Palouse, made available by the writer.

Coffin Sheep Company files, 1880–1965. "Life, History, Experiences, Hobbies, Aspirations of Howard Stanley Coffin." Business correspondence, grazing leases, mining stock and correspondence, H. S. Coffin notes for speeches, other miscellaneous documents relating to sheep production. Yakima, Washington.

Darrah, Mary Skene. Collection, 1880–1965. Letters, reminiscences, newspaper clippings, photographs, and other materials saved by Euphemia S. MacGregor, Mr. and Mrs. R. W. Darrah, Calgary, Alberta (MSD/Calgary).

District court cases, Southern District, State of Washington, 1890–1898. Summonses, court records, clerk's minute books, stipulations, other legal manuscripts. Federal Archives and Records Center, Seattle.

Fronek, Minnie Turner. "Pioneering in the Lower Palouse and Lacrosse Country." Typescript.

Gomez-Ibanez, Daniel A. "The Origins of Transhumance in the United States," made available by the writer.

Gordon Brothers. Ledger books, 1898–1901. Account books from a Pampa, Washington, general merchandise store where John McGregor purchased supplies for his sheep business. Ethel Gordon Metzger, Spokane.

Harder, Annine. "The Opportunity of the Golden West." Mimeographed. N.p., n.d.

Holt family. Letters, 1854–85. Thirty-three letters written by a family that moved from a Georgia plantation to the Willamette Valley and then to Rebel Flat, on the Columbia Plateau. Made available by Betty Jean Peatross, Glendale, California.

Hunter, Sadie. (Escondido, California). 1976 letter to the writer.

"Interviews Obtained from Washington Pioneers Relative to the History of Grazing in the State of Washington." Works Progress Administration,

Historical Records Survey, 1941. Manuscripts and Special Collections, Washington State University Library.

Jacquot, Harley D. Annual McGregor Ranch Agronomic Reports, 1953–73. Copies in McGregor Company files, Colfax, and in McGregor Land and Livestock Company files, Hooper.

Leeper, Lonnie D. "Memoirs and Reminiscences of Pioneers of Southeastern Washington," 1941. Manuscripts and Special Collections, Washington State University Library.

Lemon, Mark. Collection, 1820–1940. Records gathered from census books of Scotland and Ontario, Canada, newspaper articles, assorted other data, Owen Sound, Ontario.

"Letters Concerning the Leasing of Northern Pacific Grazing Lands." Collection of letters written by Northern Pacific officials. Manuscripts and Special Collections, Washington State University Library.

McCormick Harvesting Machine Company, 1893–1910. Letter books, sales records for Spokane and Portland agencies. McCormick collection, University of Wisconsin, Madison.

McGregor, Alexander C. 1893–1973 files. Old records of McGregor Land and Livestock and subsidiaries. Correspondence, photographs, records of sales and expenses, tax returns, Yakima Ranch, Hooper Realty, Taylor Land and Livestock, etc. In possession of the writer (ML&L/ACM).

McGregor, Sherman. Collection. Letters, reminiscences, photographs, newspaper articles, records of McGregor business operations. In possession of Sherman McGregor, Hooper, Washington.

McGregor, William. Collection, 1840–98. Personal letters and deeds, Annan, Ontario.

McGregor Company files, 1948–78. Correspondence, management reports, profit and loss records, other information from agrichemical division of the McGregor corporations. Colfax, Washington.

McGregor Feedlot files, 1972–80. Pasco, Washington.

McGregor Land and Livestock Company files, Lemaster and Daniels Company, Spokane, 1905–60. Tax returns, balance sheets, correspondence with Internal Revenue Service, other information dealing with economic conditions (ML&L/Lemaster & Daniels).

McGregor Land and Livestock Company files, McGregor Land and Livestock Company, Hooper, 1903–78. Payrolls, business correspondence, personal letters, property deeds, sheep tally books, minutes of corporate meetings, mining stock, daybooks, and other business materials (ML&L/Hooper).

McGregor Land and Livestock Company files, Manuscripts and Special Collections, Washington State University, 1901–49. One hundred and forty-seven feet of business correspondence, banking materials, records of mercantile and insurance businesses, Hooper Realty, Palouse Irrigation and

Power, Taylor Land and Livestock, and other business materials (ML&L/ WSU).

Mack, Richard. "Competitive Displacement: An Ecological Chronicle of *Bromus Tectorum*." 1980 MSS., made available by the author.

Macrae, Jock. Collection. Letters ,sheep tally books, miscellaneous business correspondence. McGregor Land and Livestock Company, Hooper, Washington.

Morod, Emile. Collection. Sheep tally books, employee records, photographs, and other business materials. In possession of the writer.

Northern Pacific Railroad Records, University of Minnesota Achives, 1890–1914. Land commissioners' correspondence, grazing leases, court cases, abstract books, letter books. St. Paul, Minnesota.

Oliphant, J. Orin. "Readings in the History of Eastern Washington." 3-volume MSS., Manuscripts and Special Collections, Washington State University Library.

Parker, William. "A History of American Agriculture." 1976 MSS., made available by Professor Morton Rothstein, Madison, Wisconsin.

Pendleton Woolen Mills, Portland, Oregon. Records of wool prices and apparel mill wool consumption, 1895–1942. Courtesy of wool buyer J. H. Walters.

Peterson, Willis, and Joseph Fitzharris. "The Organization and Productivity of the Federal-State Research System in the United States." October 1974 MSS., for Conference on Research Allocation and Productivity in International Agricultural Research, University of Minnesota Economic Development Center.

Rothstein, Morton. MSS., study of American grain trade, 1975 (Chapter 4, "King Wheat Marches Westward,"; 5, "New Frontiers and New Rivals"; 7, "The Growth of the Elevator System"; 11, "Around the Horn").

Snyder, Sarah. Correspondence, 1888–89. Lina Buhl, Ritzville, Washington.

Tucker, Gerald L. "History of the Northern Blue Mountains." Typed, 1940. Courtesy of Virgil Bennington, Walla Walla, Washington.

Warren Sheep Company files. Information about sheep production. University of Wyoming Archives, Laramie, Wyoming.

Washington Territory Census Records, 1883, 1885, 1887, 1889, MSS., from Whitman County Auditor's office, microfilm copy in Seattle Public Library.

Washington Wool Growers Association. Files, 1949–70. Annual resolutions, correspondence, Western Range Association business files, letters from William McGregor, in possession of association secretary George Rugg, Ephrata, Washington.

Wentworth, E. N. Collection. Information about sheep production. University of Wyoming Archives, Laramie, Wyoming.

Whitman County Auditor's Office. Miscellaneous files, 1883–1904. Manuscripts and Special Collections, Washington State University Library.

III. INTERVIEWS

The following people contributed recollections of their rich and varied experiences of life on the Columbia Plateau to this book. Notes, tapes, and transcripts of these interviews are in the writer's possession.

1. Interviews by the Writer
Louis Banks, Tacoma, Washington
Clemente Barber, Hooper, Washington
Virgil Bennington, Walla Walla, Washington
Marie Boone, Glendale, California
Charles H. Brune, Yakima, Washington
Arthur Buhl, Ritzville, Washington
Marvin Burden, Warden, Washington
Willard Burden, Livermore, California
Mr. and Mrs. Floyd Cameron, Washtucna, Washington
Fred Clemens, Spokane, Washington
Dr. H. Stanley Coffin, Yakima, Washington
Mr. and Mrs. Joseph Crowther, Prosser, Washington
George Cullinane, Hooper, Washington
Mrs. W. Davis, Prosser, Washington
Bill Dorman, Caldwell, Idaho
Thomas J. Drumheller, Jr., Ephrata, Washington
Isidoro Gutierrez, Hooper, Washington
Nelson and Mary MacGregor Hazeltine, Portland, Oregon
Dallas Hooper, Walla Walla, Washington
Harley Jacquot, Hooper, Washington
Grover McDougal, Colfax, Washington
John McGregor, Hooper, Washington
Norma McGregor, Hooper, Washington
Sherman McGregor, Hooper, Washington
William McGregor, Hooper, Washington
William ("Billy") McGregor, Annan, Ontario, Canada
Jessie Medby, Pasadena, California
Juan Miquelez, Hooper, Washington
Emile Morod, Hooper, Washington
Ernest Osmond, Hooper, Washington
Carl Penner, Walla Walla, Washington
George Rugg, Soap Lake, Washington
William Seigle, Spokane, Washington
Ralph Snyder, Washtucna, Washington
Mr. and Mrs. George Thorp, Hayward, California
Charles Tobin, Hooper, Washington

Lenora Torgeson, Lacrosse, Washington
Max Torrence, Colfax, Washington
Mrs. Cull White, Ephrata, Washington
Pete Williams, Monmouth, Oregon
Lorenzo Zozaya, Hooper, Washington

2. Interviews by Maurice, Sherman, and William McGregor, and Earl Snyder
Dave Carter, Hooper, Washington. Maurice McGregor interview, 1946.
Mae Carter, Hooper, Washington. Maurice McGregor interview, 1946.
Euphemia S. MacGregor, Calgary, Alberta. Sherman McGregor interview, 1967.
William Snyder, Washtucna, Washington. Earl Snyder interviews, 1948–1952.
Harry Windus, Modesto, California. William McGregor interview, 1969.

3. Interviews from Whitman College "Horse Era Tape Series," 1973 (WCAT/ Walla Walla).
Virgil Bennington
Clarence Braden
Howard Burgess
Ernest and Dwight McCaw
Vance Orchard
Carl Penner

IV. COURT CASES

First State Bank of Lacrosse v. *McGregor Land and Livestock Company and Roy Jeremiah.* Whitman County Superior Court, case 16040, January 6, 1927. Appeal to State Supreme Court: 94 *Pacific Reporter* 1085, 251 *Pacific Reporter* 865.
Sam Fisher v. *Charles Harrison.* Department of the Interior, U.S. Land Office, Spokane, Contest 4070, December 12, 1928. Copy of court case is in McGregor Land and Livestock Company files, Hooper, Washington.
Axel Holm v. *McGregor Land and Livestock Company.* Whitman County Superior Court, case 17034, May 18, 1928.
In re Hooper's Estate (Peter McGregor v. *Hooper et al.).* Supreme Court of Washington, October 18, 1913, 135 *Pacific Reporter* 813.
Mrs. H. M. Jackson v. *Pullman Hardware Company, Peter McGregor, L. F. Munroe, J. F. Hill, N. C. Munroe.* Whitman County Superior Court, case 5444, April 30, 1895.
Alex Taylor McGregor v. *New World Life Insurance Company.* Supreme Court of Washington, July 24, 1931. 163 *Washington Reporter* 677.
Gladys McGregor v. *Alex Taylor McGregor et al.* Supreme Court of Washington, August 1, 1946. 171 *Pacific Reporter* 2d 694.

Peter, Archie, and John McGregor v. *R. S. Browne*. Whitman County Superior Court, case 9061, February 1906.

McGregor Land and Livestock Company v. *Adams County*. Adams County Superior Court, case 7382, July 11, 1936.

McGregor Land and Livestock Company v. *H. A. Brown*. Whitman County Superior Court, case 9913, May 2, 1908.

McGregor Land and Livestock Company v. *C. H. Hoskins*. Whitman County Superior Court, case 11493, May 10, 1913.

McGregor Land and Livestock Company v. *E. C. Lloyd et al*. Yakima County Superior Court, case 22053, January 18, 1928.

McGregor Land and Livestock Company v. *J. S. Rustin*. Whitman County Superior Court, case 14387, September 3, 1921.

McGregor Land and Livestock Company v. *Santa Barbara Water Company*. Whitman County Superior Court, case 16730, May 19, 1927.

(Andrew F. Burleigh, as Receiver for) *Northern Pacific Railroad Company* v. *Joseph Escallier ... Leon Jassaud ... McGregor Bros., et al*. District Court Cases, Southern District, State of Washington, case 146, April 2–November 16, 1896. Complaints, demurrer, stipulations, court orders are in District Court records on file at Federal Archives and Records Center, Seattle, Washington. Summary of case and legal briefs are in "Land Department—Court Cases, West End" (W49-5945), Northern Pacific Railroad Archives, University of Minnesota, St. Paul.

Northern Pacific Railroad v. *Fisher, Indian*. Department of the Interior, U.S. Land Office, November 26, 1886. Copy in McGregor Land and Livestock Company files, Hooper.

Northern Pacific Railway v. *James Cunningham*. Circuit Court of Washington, Southern District, October 14, 1898. 89 *Federal Reporter* 594. Information on lower court proceedings is in case 175, March 30, 1898, in Federal Archives and Records Center, Seattle.

Northern Pacific Railway v. *Adrien Magallon*. Circuit Court of Washington, Ninth District, Southern Division, case 162, April-October 1897. Complaint, subpoena, restraining order, motions are in District Court cases files in Federal Archives and Records Center, Seattle.

Northern Pacific Railway v. *McGregor Land and Livestock Company*. Whitman County Superior Court, case 19544, October 1934.

Public Service Commission of Washington ex. rel. G. W. Bassett et al. v. *Hooper Realty Company*. Public Service Commission, case 5048, June 15, 1920, May 17, 1921. Copy in the writer's possession.

Still et al. v. *Palouse Irrigation and Power Company, Alex McGregor, and Archie McGregor*. Supreme Court of Washington, August 19, 1911. 117 *Pacific Reporter* 466.

United States of America v. *John McCrea*. Yakima County Circuit Court, June 26, 1896. Copy in district court records in Federal Archives and Records Center, Seattle.

V. GENERAL PUBLICATIONS: TRADE JOURNALS AND NEWSPAPERS

1. Early Trade Journals and News Magazines
American Sheep Breeder, 1902–7
American Shepherd's Bulletin, 1906–7
Breeders' Gazette, 1902–13
The Coast, 1903–15
Commercial Review, 1911–76
National Livestock Bulletin, 1907
National Wool Grower, 1911–76
Ranche and Range (Ranch and Range, The Ranch), 1894–1906
Rural Northwest (Oregon Agriculturist and Rural Northwest), 1895–99
Shepherd's Criterion, 1907–9
Shepherd's Journal, 1909–13
Up-To-The-Times monthly, Walla Walla, 1910–21
Washington Farmer, 1919–76

2. Agribusiness Publications and Trade Journals, post World War II
Agrichemical West, 1948–60
Agricultural Ammonia News, 1962–65
The Agronomist (Agronomy and Men), Agronomy Department, Washington State University, 1952–80.
Big Farmer, 1969
Farm Chemicals, 1970
Farm Journal, 1958
Farm Management (Western Crops and Farm Management), 1952–60
Fertilizer Solutions, 1965–69
Monsanto Magazine, 1969
The Northwest, 1965
Selling 66, 1958–66
Wheat Life, 1960–76

3. Newspapers
  The various names used by some of the papers are listed in parentheses.
Colfax *Commoner*, 1888–1910
Colfax *Gazette (Palouse Gazette, Gazette-Commoner)*, 1882–1976
Dayton *Chronicle-Dispatch*, 1952
Denver, Colorado, *Daily Record Stockman*, 1935
Endicott *Index*, 1904–5
Lacrosse *Clipper*, 1910–41
Moscow, Idaho, *Daily Idahonian*, 1976
Owen Sound, Ontario, *Daily Sun Times*, 1910–50

Palouse *Republic*, 1974–76
Pomeroy *East Washingtonian*, 1914
Pullman *Herald*, 1891–97
Pullman *Tribune*, 1896
Reardan *Gazette*, 1924
Ritzville *Journal-Times (Journal)*, 1949–75
Sacramento, California, *Daily Union*, 1871
Seattle *Argus*, 1975
Seattle *Times*, 1896–1976
Spokane *Daily Chronicle*, 1898
Spokane *Spokesman-Review (Spokesman)*, 1887–1956
Tacoma *Daily Ledger*, 1892
Walla Walla *Union-Bulletin*, 1931–33, 1953
Walla Walla *Washington Statesman*, 1867–80
Washtucna *Enterprise*, 1913–17
Yakima *Herald-Republic (Herald)*, 1945–73

Index